Brassey's Companion to the British Army

Also from Brassey's:

BAYNES

Far from a Donkey: The Life of General Sir Ivor Maxse

DAVID

Mutiny at Salerno: an Injustice Exposed

CONNAUGHTON

Celebration of Victory: V-E Day 1945

LAFFIN

Brassey's Battles: 3,500 Years of Conflict, Campaigns and Wars From A-Z

LAFFIN

Hitler Warned Us: The Nazis' Master Plan for a Master Race

PARKER

Winston Churchill: Studies in Statesmanship

MALCOLM

White Tigers: My Secret War in North Korea

Brassey's Companion to the British Army

Antony Makepeace-Warne

BRASSEY'S
London • Washington

Copyright © 1995 Brassey's (UK) Ltd.

First English Edition 1995

UK editorial offices: Brassey's, 33 John Street, London WC1N 2AT
UK orders: Marston Book Services, PO Box 269, Abingdon OX14 4SD

North American orders: Brassey's Inc., PO Box 960, Herndon, VA 22070, USA

Antony Makepeace-Warne has asserted his moral right to be identified as the author of this work.

Library of Congress Cataloging in Publication Data
available

British Library Cataloguing in Publication Data
A catalogue record for this book is available from the British Library

ISBN 1 85753 175 2 Hardcover

Typeset by M Rules
Printed in Great Britain by Bookcraft (Bath) Ltd.

CONTENTS

LIST OF MAPS

FOREWORD

by

Field Marshal The Lord Bramall

KG, GCB, OBE, MC

There is something about the British Army which is of enduring interest, not only to the British but also to others. It is not that it has not had its share of setbacks and even, through no fault of its own, defeats, no more so than in the first few years of World War II. But overall it has had an enviable record of success and, since World War II, has hardly put a foot wrong. Yet it is surely the diversity of the British Army's experience and the manner in which the Army's customs, dress, weapons, equipment, tactics and even its language have developed as a result of those experiences, which continues to stimulate this interest.

Unlike France and Germany, Britain has never been obsessed by martial glories. Soldiers were wisely deemed a necessary evil in times of war, and an unnecessary expense to be set aside as quickly as possible in peacetime; conscription was acceptable only in times of acute danger.

The administration of Cromwell's major-generals had produced in politicians a natural suspicion of senior officers, and the financial burdens of the Civil War had left the public with a very jaundiced view of keeping men under arms. In 1660 the Army was disbanded, with the exception of two regiments amounting to some 5,000 men, and it was in the face of considerable public reluctance that a standing army very slowly re-emerged.

Since the Restoration the monarchy has played a vital and fundamental role in many aspects of Army life and the conduct of the men and women who serve in it. Manifestations of this special relationship are evident in ceremonial, dress, titles, honours and awards. The concept of service to the Crown is deeply rooted and, together with the regimental structure, lies at the very heart of the British Army, past and present.

Two factors have influenced the expansion and contraction of Britain's Army: threats to British influence and trade overseas; and the prospect of unrest at home and in our British possessions wherever we were responsible for law and order. Increasing numbers of soldiers were needed to protect existing markets overseas and to secure new ones, ultimately leading to the need to defend an Empire, while the threat of religious or political upheaval, and particularly the republican ideas of revolutionary France, demanded that garrisons should also be maintained at home, with the means of rapidly reinforcing them in time of emergency.

The many overseas garrisons and campaigns could often only be sustained by the employment of indigenous troops and the British Army has an unparalleled record for the raising, training and command of native troops. The British soldier could not but respect the fighting qualities and loyalty to the Crown shown by these troops, often with their own long histories as warrior races, like the Gurkhas, and their histories are now firmly woven into that of the British Army.

Long tours abroad, often facing disease and extremes of climate and terrain, served to strengthen further the regimental spirit and develop the strong sense of obligation and duty within the tightly-knit military communities. Changes in the customs, dress and tactics of the British Army reflect lessons learned in these campaigns and outposts, and even today the military vocabulary is permeated by expressions which have their origin in distant parts.

Although large numbers of regular soldiers were an unwanted expense at home, it was recognised that some form of trained reserve against an emergency was prudent. Such training could clearly only be managed on a local basis, units being drawn from quite small geographical areas. The Cardwell reforms of 1868–74 created the infantry regiments in their modern form, reinforcing this territorial effect by grouping regular and reserve units by county, the existing regimental system in the regular Army having hitherto had a less defined territorial element. Cardwell formed seventy-five infantry regiments, each of two battalions – one at home and one overseas – which rapidly developed powerful and sometimes curious characters of their own.

It was the British Army which underpinned the rapid expansion of empire which took place during the reign of Queen Victoria. There was hardly a continent in which the Army was not active. This included risings in Canada; campaigns against the Chinese, Afghans, Sikhs, Sudanese, Ashanti and Zulus, the Indian Mutiny and the wars in Crimea and South Africa in which the British Army was to learn such painful lessons.

Although the war in South Africa saw all but a handful of regiments deployed to fight the Boers, it was the First world War which engaged the entire nation. Nearly every family in the country had one or more of its members in the British Army. Public interest in the operations and welfare of the local regiment could not have been deeper. However, the very regimental system which offered such comradeship, support and encouragement to the fighting man brought with it the devastating effect at home of massive casualties. In some cases the active male population of an entire urban or rural area was wiped out in one attack. Although public admiration for the courage and endurance of the British soldier remained undiminished, doubts were expressed about the competence of the military leadership because of the huge losses.

The five long years of the Second World War renewed public concern for and interest in the British Army. Most families were drawn into the war effort in some way, and they were justly proud of their contribution to the hard fought victory. Furthermore, the war not only confirmed the fighting qualities of the British soldier and his comrades in the armies of the Empire and Commonwealth, but also restored public interest and admiration for Britain's military commanders and their professional ability. After the war many former commanders returned home to take up influential positions in the political and economic life of the country and there was a wide public understanding of, and sympathy for the British Army.

The close association between the public and the British Army continued until the end of conscription in the early 1960s. But we now have a situation in which a small, all regular, all volunteer army is in danger of becoming detached from the society from which it springs. Only the Territorial Army regiments, the cadets and the regimental associations have the means and opportunity to nourish those vital local links. Few of those in public life have any experience of active service; their knowledge of the British Army is often superficial and coloured by myth and legend. The commemoration this year of the allied victory in Europe and Japan and the successful conclusion of five years of total war has done much to stimulate public interest in the recent history and achievements of the British Army; an interest which in those war years, and the years of National Service which followed, we all took for granted.

The history of the British Army has been the subject of academic attention for many years. Works of immense scholarship exist on almost every facet of army life. The Imperial War Museum and the National Army Museum house collections and archives of great national and local interest, and the regimental and corps museums contain collections of national and local interest. I am conscious that many whose interest and imagination are fired by the exploits of our Army are often deterred from further study by the use of unfamiliar terms and expressions. This book offers an excellent point of first reference on a wide variety of military matters past and present, and I commend it to all who have an interest in, and affection for, the British Army.

PREFACE

It is intended that this book should form a useful companion and point of first reference for all those with an interest in the British Army. It covers the period from the Restoration in 1660 to the present day, and is the first book to detail the changes in the organisation and structure of the Army arising from the end of the Cold War and subsequent 'Options for Change' studies.

The increasing specialisation and professionalism of military studies has produced a wealth of material, and it is now unlikely that any single reference book could hope to offer comprehensive coverage of every aspect of the British Army. The chief virtue of this book is that it can quickly, easily and clearly satisfy the most likely queries and, where appropriate, direct the reader to further sources of information. I make no apology for the inclusion of some Indian Army material; the history, customs and dress of the British Army bear witness in so many instances to the depth and breadth of the links with the Indian sub-continent.

The decision not to include entries on any living personalities may seem perverse; but it was nigh on impossible to establish any rational criteria for inclusion, and I have chosen to let history make such a selection. There is bound to be an element of arbitrariness in any selection from a host of famous men and women of the past, but I hope that I have managed to include the key figures in the history of the British Army.

In acknowledging my debts I would like to make special mention of the help given so willingly by those over-worked and dedicated officers, the Regimental Secretaries, not only in the identification of the definitive regimental histories, but also in answering a number of what may have seemed to them trivial and, I suspect, time-wasting questions. The staff of the Royal United Services Institute Library, the Prince Consort's Library, and the reading room of the National Army Museum have been both tolerant and helpful, making what could easily have been a chore a pleasure.

Salisbury   Antony Makepeace-Warne
August 1995

NOTE TO THE READER

In this book I have sought to offer definitions or descriptions of the following:

Regimental histories
British and Indian Battle Honours
Major wars and campaigns
Terms used in strategy and tactics
Key weapons, equipment and vehicles
Militia, Yeomanry, Volunteers and the Territorial Army
Dress and uniform
Gallantry and Campaign Medals
Organisations associated with the Army
Terms in general use in the Army, now or in the past

It had been my intention to include the more common words of command and drill manoeuvres, but it proved too difficult to offer definitions which reflected the changes through time.

Cavalry regiments are shown under the general headings Dragoons, Dragoon Guards, Hussars and Lancers. All Gurkha regiments are shown under the general heading of Gurkhas.

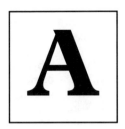

'A' The letter 'A' on arm badges in the British Army was used to indicate 'A' group tradesmen from 1944 onward. Since 30 November 1950 a yellow 'A' on a grenade with red flames has been used to indicate an ammunition technician. *See also: Ammunition Examiner and Ammunition Technical Officer.*

'A' Vehicle Generic term for all armoured vehicles. *See also: 'B' and 'C' vehicles.*

Abbot Self-propelled gun, now obsolete. A variant of the 105mm Light Gun, with a range of approximately 17km, mounted on an Armoured Fighting Vehicle 430 series chassis. The Abbot was replaced by the AS90 (qv) self-propelled gun in the early 1990s.

A Galloping 8th Hussar The regimental quick march of the King's Royal Irish Hussars, and subsequently one of the regimental quick marches of The Queen's Royal Irish Hussars.

A Galloping Queen's Hussar Regimental song of The Queen's Royal Hussars (The Queen's Own and Royal Irish).

A Hunting We Will Go An arrangement of this song forms a part of the regimental quick march of the Royal Army Veterinary Corps.

Aam Second World War battle honour marking the operations of 1-4 October 1944 when the Germans sought to destroy the Nijmegen bridgehead and includes what is known as 'the fighting on the island'. *See also: North West Europe 1944-45; Arnhem 1944 and Nederrijn.*

Aart Second World War battle honour marking the intense fighting which took place 14-20 September 1944 during the XII Corps advance from the Meuse-Escaut canal. *See also: North West Europe 1944-45; Neerpelt and Hechtel.*

Abatis or Abattis In military engineering, an obstacle to the advance of an enemy formed from a number of felled trees with the smaller branches removed, placed side by side with the butt ends toward the defenders, and secured to the ground by forked pickets.

Abercromby, Sir Ralph (1734-1801) General, born Menstrie, Clackmannanshire, educated at Rugby and studied law at Edinburgh and Leipzig. He accompanied the Duke of York on the two disastrous campaigns against the French in the Low Countries (1793 and 1799), and by his skilful administration and excellent man management, gained the affection and respect of the whole Army. In 1796 Abercromby was given command of the expeditionary force raised to suppress the uprisings of negroes and reconquer much of the West Indies, negro ambitions having been unrealistically fired by revolutionary agents and by the 'pernicious doctrines of the rights of man'. He recaptured St Lucia (1796) and Trinidad (1797). Appointed to command an expedition to drive the French out of Egypt in 1801, Abercromby was wounded during an engagement with the French at Alexandria and, though victorious, died of his wounds a week later. *See also: Aboukir; Alexandria; Sphinx superscribed Egypt and St Lucia.*

Ablution The act of washing or the place provided for washing.

Aboukir Village on Aboukir Bay, 13 miles north-east of Alexandria, Egypt, close to the site where, on 1 March 1801, Sir Ralph Abercromby (qv) defeated the French. The capitulation of the whole of the French army in Alexandria ended the war in Egypt. The French Army was allowed to return to France, but their fleet fell into English hands. *See also: Abercromby and Sphinx superscribed Egypt.*

Abraham, Plains or Heights of South-west of the city of Quebec, this was the scene of a decisive battle on 13 September 1759 in the Seven Years War (1756-63) (qv) in the Americas and West Indies. The British under General James Wolfe (qv) scaled the Heights of Abraham in a daring night operation and so achieved the fall of Quebec, defended by Montcalm and long considered an impregnable city, as a result of which the conquest of Canada was effected.

Absence A charge of absence without leave (AWOL) must demonstrate that the accused was both absent and without leave. The offence of absence exists if it is due to the deliberate intention of the accused to be absent or if it is caused by circumstances, such as drunkenness, which were within his own control, and it may fairly be said that it is his own fault that he was absent. *See also: Desertion.*

Abu Klea Battle honour marking the sharp action of 28 January 1885, during the unsuccessful expedition to relieve General Gordon, at the Sudanese village of Abu Klea, on the route from Korti to Metemma, where a British army under Major General Sir Herbert Stewart, who was mortally wounded in the battle, defeated the forces of the Mahdi (qv). *See also: Nile 1884-85; Kirbekan 1885 and Suakin 1885.*

Abutment In military engineering, the load-bearing areas which support the ends of a bridge or arch. Also used in respect of weapons or machinery to indicate the point at which resistance is obtained such as the breech of a gun.

Abyssinia Battle honour marking the campaign of 1867-68 by an expeditionary force under Sir Robert Napier. *See also: Abyssinian War 1867-68.*

Abyssinia 1940-1941 Second World War battle honour, dated either 1940 or 1941, marking operations by British, Imperial and Ethiopian patriot forces in Italian East Africa (Eritrea, Italian Somaliland and Ethiopia) and British Somaliland. Italian forces were crushed in a four month campaign based on a giant pincer movement under Generals Platt and Cunningham, with thrusts launched from the Sudan into north Ethiopia and into Eritrea, northward from Kenya into southern Ethiopia, across the Ogaden and to Harrar, while yet others penetrated west and south-west Ethiopia. Following heavy fighting at Keren, Asmara and Massawa were captured and the Italians pursued into Abyssinia where, with General Cunningham's force which had invaded Italian Somaliland in February 1941, reached Harar in March and occupied Addis Ababa on 6 April, and was now closing in from the south, the main Italian army surrendered at Amba Alagi in mid-May. After the Amba Alagi surrender remnants of the Italian army withdrew to the Gondar area and resistance finally ceased on 27 November 1941. *See also: Keren; Jebel Defeis; Jebel Shiba; Gogni; Agordat; Barentu; Karora-Marsa Taclai; Cubcub; Ad Teclesan; Mescelit Pass; Mt Engiahat; Massawa; Amb Alagi; Afodu; Gambela; El Wak; Moyale; Wal Garis; Juba; Marda Pass; Babile Gap; Bisidimo; Awash Todenyang-Namaraputh; Soroppa; Giarso; Colito; Wadara; Omo; Gondar; Fike and Lechemti.*

Abyssinian War 1867-68 An expeditionary force under the command of Sir Robert Napier, the Commander-in-Chief in Bombay, was sent to Abyssinia with the object of securing the release of a number of Britons and Europeans held prisoner by King Theodore. In spite of pessimistic predictions in the British press, such was the quality of Sir Robert Napier's organisation and logistic skill that the British/Indian force, which landed at Annesley Bay on the Red Sea south of Massawa, was able to traverse some 380 miles of roadless and

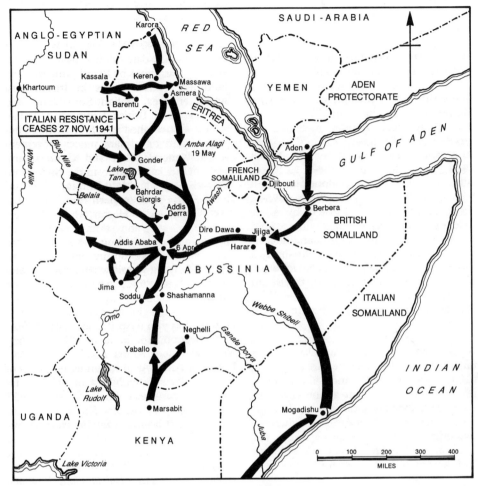

Abyssinia 1940–1941

largely unmapped country, cross mountain ranges 9,000 feet in height, storm the King's fortress and release the prisoners without the loss of a single man in action. This was the first campaign in which British troops were armed with the Snider breech-loading rifle. *See also: Abyssinia 1867-68.*

Abyssinian War Medal 1867-1868
Authorised by a General Order dated 1 March 1869.
Ribbon: White, 1" wide, with a very broad red stripe down the centre.

Acclimatisation The process whereby troops are physically prepared for differences of climate, terrain and altitude before operational commitment in a theatre where such conditions differ widely from those to which they are accustomed. Trials have been conducted by the Army Personnel Research Establishment (qv) to devise alternatives to in-theatre acclimatisation.

Accompanied Term used to describe a tour of duty, more usually overseas, undertaken by individuals, sub-units or units accompanied by their dependents. Where there is an element of risk to dependents, no suitable accommodation exists, or operations are expected to be of short duration it is usual for units and individuals to be 'unaccompanied'.

Accoutrements Equipment worn by military personnel in addition to their clothing.

Accumulated Campaign Service Medal 1994 Sanctioned in 1994 to recognize 36 or more months of aggregated service since 14 August 1969 in those theatres where the General Service Medal 1962 (qv) with clasp has been awarded. When the ribbon is worn alone clasps will be denoted by rosettes as follows: the first three clasps will be denoted by silver rosettes; four clasps by a single gold rosette; five clasps by one gold and one silver rosette; six clasps by one gold and two silver rosettes; the sequence being followed until nine clasps are denoted by three gold rosettes.
Ribbon: 1" wide, in purple and green with a vertical stripe of gold.

Acorn The acorn 'leaved and slipped' was taken into wear by The Cheshire Regiment (22nd Foot) in 1881 and said to be a reminder of an incident at the Battle of Dettingen. However, the oak sprig with acorn can be traced back to 1689 when the two original colonels of the regiment, the Duke of Norfolk and Henry Bellasis, both had this device on their coat of arms.

Acquisition The process whereby sensors, systems and reconnaissance are combined to locate, identify and monitor enemy forces and key equipments with a view to fixing, categorizing and prioritising targets for subsequent engagement.

Act of Union The amalgamation of English and Scottish military establishments begun in 1603 when James VI of Scotland became James I of England, was completed under the Act of Union of 1707.

Act of War The exercise of all force by one state or group of states against another is legally governed by the United Nations Charter whose principles have been accepted by most states. Article 51 of the Charter provides that there is an inherent right of self defence in the event of an armed attack. The term 'armed attack' necessarily contains ambiguities and it is usual for a state to declare formally that certain acts by an aggressor are, or will be, deemed to be 'Acts of War'. Should such acts then be committed, a state of war will exist in which international law has a regulatory function.

Acting Rank Unlike local rank (qv) the grant of acting rank brings with it the pay and allowances appropriate to the acting rank held. However, a Commanding Officer has the right under Queens Regulations (qv) to order the holder to revert from that rank.

Active Term applied to the situation in which equipments and sensors are operating and emitting signals. Active equipments and sensors are vulnerable to detection and attack.

Active Service Under the Army Act 1955, Section 224, the term 'active service' has a specific meaning and, once a force has been declared to be on active service special provisions apply and a more serious view is taken of offences. It is normal for the Secretary of State to declare such a state and notification to be given through General Orders.

Active Service and Peace Manoeuvres Forage Cap Described in 1883 Dress Regulations for officers as the Glengarry pattern worn by the men, but of less height. As early as the Crimean War the Foot Guards were wearing a folding cap with side flaps, also known as an 'Austrian' cap.

Ad Teclesan Second World War Abyssinian campaign battle honour awarded exclusively to 14th Foot, The West Yorkshire Regiment (The Prince of Wales's Own). *See also: Abyssinia 1940-41; Keren; Jebel Defeis; Jebel Shiba; Gogni; Agordat; Barentu; Karora-Marsa Taclai; Cubcub; Afodu; Mescelit Pass; Mt Engiahat; Massawa; Amb Alagi; Gambela; El Wak; Moyale; Wal Garis; Juba; Marda Pass; Babile Gap;*

Bisidimo; Awash Todenyang-Namaraputh; Soroppa; Giarso; Colito; Wadara; Omo; Gondar; Fike and Lechemti.

ADDER An expendable, hand-emplaced, electro-magnetic jamming device.

Aden (1839) Battle honour marking the seizing of Aden, a coaling station of growing importance, by a small expeditionary force mounted from Bombay in 1839, following the breakdown of attempts to negotiate a purchase of the territory from the local Arab ruler. Two subsequent Arab attempts to capture the town were unsuccessful.

Aden (1915) First World War battle honour commemorating the defence of the colony by British and Indian units against persistent Turkish attacks which began in mid-1915, when the Turks closed on Aden itself, and lasted almost until the end of the First World War.

Adjutant A commissioned officer, not above the rank of major, and more usually a captain, who is the personal staff officer to the officer commanding a battalion or regiment. The adjutant is responsible to the commanding officer for all personnel and disciplinary matters, the maintenance of unit records and regimental diaries, the preparation of the officers' duty roster and publication, in the commanding officer's name, of daily orders. Until the 1970s the Adjutant also undertook all the operational staff work which is now the responsibility of the Operations Officer.

Adjutant General Second Military Member of the Army Board. Responsible for all personnel services, welfare, individual training / and discipline. The appointment was created in 1685, there being in the first instance two Adjutants General: Lieutenant Colonel Robert Ramsey (Foot Forces) and Major Charles Orby (Horse Forces).

ADJUTANT GENERAL'S CORPS
Formed on 6 April 1992 and comprising four branches:

Staff and Personnel Branch Formed on 6 April 1992 by the amalgamation of The Royal Army Pay Corps (qv) and Women's Royal Army Corps (qv). The responsibilities of the Branch remained the same as those of the Royal Army Pay Corps and those members of the Women's Royal Army Corps attached to that Corps. Branch Badge: A laurel wreath surmounted by a Crown; within the wreath the Royal Crest. Beneath a scroll inscribed *'Animo et Fide'* in silver.
Branch quick march: *Imperial Echoes*.

Provost Branch Formed on 6 April 1992 from the Corps of Royal Military Police (qv) and the Military Provost Staff Corps (qv). The responsibilities of the Branch remained the same as those of the Corps of Royal Military Police and Military Provost Staff Corps.
Branch Badges: Within a laurel wreath, the royal cypher with crown above. Beneath a scroll inscribed 'ROYAL MILITARY POLICE' and the royal cypher ensigned with the crown, thereunder a scroll inscribed 'MILITARY PROVOST STAFF CORPS'.
Branch quick marches: *Watch Tower* and *The New Colonial*.

Educational and Training Services Branch Formed on 6 April 1992 from the Royal Army Educational Corps (qv). The responsibilities of the Branch remained the same as those of the Royal Army Educational Corps.
Branch Badge: A fluted flambeau of five flames, thereon a crown and below the crown a scroll inscribed 'RAEC'.
Branch quick marches: *Gaudeamus Igitur* and *The Good Comrade*.

Army Legal Services Branch Formed on 6 April 1992 from the Army Legal Corps (qv). The responsibilities of the Branch remained the same as those of the Army Legal Corps.
Branch Badge: The figure of Justice superimposed on the globe surmounted by the royal crest. Behind the globe, crossed swords with blades uppermost within a circle inscribed 'JUSTITIA IN ARMIS'. On a scroll below, 'ARMY LEGAL CORPs'.
Branch quick march: *Scales of Justice*.

The Adjutant General's Corps
Corps Badge: A laurel wreath surmounted

by a crown; within the wreath the royal crest. Beneath a scroll inscribed '*Animo et Fide*' in silver.
Motto: *Animo et Fide* (With Resolution and Fidelity).
Corps marches:
Quick march: *Pride of Lions*.
Slow march: *Greensleeves*.
Corps Headquarters: Worthy Down, Winchester, Hampshire SO21 2RG.

Adjutant General's Department The following directors, individuals and staffs fall within the Adjutant General's Department of the Ministry of Defence (Army): Director General of Army Manning and Recruiting; Director of Manning (Army); Director of Army Recruiting; Director of 'A' Information Systems (Army); Director Army Veterinary and Remount Services; Director Army Sports Control Board; Liaison Officer Brigade of Gurkhas; Director General Adjutant General's Corps; Director Staff and Personnel Support (Army); Provost Marshal (Army); Director Education and Training Services; Director of Army Legal Services; Director General of Army Medical Services; Director of Army Dental Services; Director of Army Nursing Services; Director of Security (Army); Director Discipline and Welfare (Army); Inspector of Army Music; Chaplain General; Principal Roman Catholic Chaplain (Army) and the Civil Secretary (Army).

Adrano Second World War Italian campaign battle honour marking one of the actions in Sicily following the landing of the Eighth Army and Seventh US Army on the south-east corner of Sicily on 10 July 1943 and subsequent clearance of the island which ended with the entry of the allies into Messina on 17 August 1943. *See also: Sicily 1943; Landing in Sicily; Primosole Bridge; Sferro; Regalbuto; Centuripe and Pursuit to Messina.*

Adriatic Second World War battle honour commemorating a number of raids made during 1944 to assist Yugoslav partisans, in which the Highland Light Infantry and Special Air Service Regiment featured prominently.

Advance To move towards the enemy or towards a given objective. There are three broad types of advance: an advance to contact the enemy, an advance in contact with the enemy and a pursuit.

Advance Guard A specially assembled force tasked to move ahead of the main body to identify gaps in enemy defences, clear minor opposition and prevent unexpected contact. Also used to seize objectives in depth pending the arrival of the main force and to facilitate the arrival of the main body.

Advance to Contact An advance to contact seeks to regain contact with the enemy under the most favourable conditions. In order to achieve this, forces may be employed in both protective and information seeking missions. The advance to contact is normally executed in preparation for an offensive operation.

Advance on Tripoli Second World War, North Africa campaign battle honour marking the advance into Tripolitania 15-23 January 1943 which followed the battle of El Alamein and which ended with the capture of Tripoli. *See also: North Africa 1940-43; El Alamein; Mareth and Tebaga Gap.*

Advance to Florence Second World War Italian campaign battle honour marking the advance, over the period 17 July - 10 August 1944, to close with the 'Gothic Line' - a German defensive line which stretched across Italy just north of Florence. *See also: Italy 1943-45; Incontro; Monte San Michele; Monte Domini; Monte Scalari; Monte Rotondo; Monte Gabbione; Ripa Ridge; Gabbiano and Arezzo.*

Advance to Tiber Second World War Italian campaign battle honour marking the fighting around Pantoni and between the River Moletta and the sea during the advance to and occupation of Rome 22 May - 4 June 1944. *See also: Italy 1943-45; Rome; Ficulle and Citta Della Pieve.*

Advanced Dressing Station Medical unit with surgical and treatment capacity positioned as far forward as the tactical situation allows to keep the casualty evacuation line from the forward Regimental Aid Posts as short as possible.

Adventurous Training Non-military training with an inherent mental and physical challenge which seeks to develop the individual and thus benefit the Army. Such training, which ranges from rock climbing and parachuting to major expeditions, is closely regulated and conducted in accordance with guidance given by the Army Physical Training Corps.

Advocate A command level secure speech communication system.

Aerial *See: Antenna.*

Affghanistan 1839 Battle honour awarded for services in the First Afghan War (qv) to some units in 1840 and extended to others in 1842. *See also: Ghuznee 1839; Khelat; Jellalabad; Candahar 1842; Ghuznee 1842 and Cabool 1842.*

Affiliation An association between Regiments and Corps of the British Army and ships and units of the Royal Navy and Royal Air Force. Such an association is less formal than the 'Alliance' (qv) and normally requires only the approval of the appropriate Service Boards.

AFGHAN WARS
First Afghan War (1839-42) The war was provoked by Britain's determination to replace Dost Muhammad, the ruler of Afghanistan, with Shah Sujah, a pro-British ruler, in order to create a buffer state of Afghanistan against Russian expansion into India. The campaign began with the storming of the fortress of Ghuznee on 23 July 1838, and Khelat was stormed on 13 November 1839. Continuing Afghan hostility led to a decision to evacuate the country. The withdrawing columns were under constant Afghan attack; one brigade managed to reach Jellalabad and withstood a six months' siege. A force under General Nott was tasked to release the captives in Kabul and punish the Afghans for murder-ing Sir William McNaghten, the British envoy. This was achieved, inflicting sharp defeats on the Afghans at Candahar, Ghuznee and Cabool in 1842. *See also: Affghanistan 1839; Ghuznee 1839; Khelat; Candahar 1842; Ghuznee 1842 and Cabool 1842.*

Second Afghan War (1878-80) Following the Russo-Turkish war of 1877 both Russia and Turkey sent missions to Sher Ali, Dost Muhammad's successor, to persuade him to break his treaty with the Indian government. Lord Lytton, the newly appointed (1876) Viceroy, adopted a 'Forward Policy' which envisaged the creation of a buffer state by either an exclusive alliance with a compliant Emir or the conquest and annexation of much Afghan territory. After a British ultimatum, British and Indian armies crossed into Afghanistan on 21 November 1878. The invading force captured the hill fortress at Ali Masjid and, on 2 December 1879, the Peiwar Kotal after a stubborn defence. On the death of Sher Ali in early 1879, his successor concluded a fresh treaty. However, the members of the mission in Kabul were subsequently murdered and, on 3 September, Major General Sir Frederick Roberts moved on Kabul and dispersed the Afghan army at Charasiah on 6 October. There followed a period in which the army was virtually besieged in Sherpur. A column under Sir Donald Stuart left Kandahar, and defeated a strong Afghan force near Ghuznee. After the disaster at Maiwand and an unsuccessful sortie by the besieged troops in Kandahar, Roberts' Kabul-Kandahar force, marching 310 miles in 20 days, annihilated the Afghan army at Kandahar on 1 September 1880. A long-term occupation of southern Afghanistan seemed inevitable, but for various reasons the British government decided to adopt the alternative of backing a new candidate for the Afghan throne in the person of Abdur Rahman, who pacified and greatly strengthened the country, kept the Russians at arms length and maintained friendly relations with Britain. The desired 'buffer' state was thus achieved. *See also: Ali Masjid; Peiwar Kotal; Charasiah; Kabul 1879; Ahmed Kel; Kandahar 1880 and Afghanistan 1878-9, 1878-80, 1879-80.*

Third Afghan War 1919 *See: Afghanistan 1919.*

Afghanistan 1878-79, 1878-1880, 1879-1880 Battle honours awarded in 1881 to units taking part in the Second Afghan War (qv).

Afghanistan Medal 1878-1880 Authorised on 19 March 1881 to mark service in the Second Afghan War (qv).
Ribbon: Green with crimson stripes on each edge.
Clasps: Ali Masjid; Peiwar Kotal; Charasia; Kabul; Ahmed Khel and Kandahar.

Afghanistan 1919 The Third Afghan War was not, as such, part of the First World War, but arose from political opportunism by the Afghans who, having remained neutral throughout the war, sought to be recognised as an independent nation at the Paris Peace Conference. Following rejection of their aspirations fighting broke out on 3 May 1919 when the Afghans broke through the Khyber Pass. Britain used both bombers and armoured cars in the subsequent campaign and, at the request of the Afghans, an armistice was granted on 2 June. The battle honour 'Afghanistan 1919' is not included in those awarded for the First World War and was thus emblazoned on the Regimental Colour of those regiments to which it was awarded.

Afodu Second World War Abyssinian campaign battle honour marking an action by troops operating in support of the Abyssinian insurgents in conjunction with the Sudan Defence Force. *See also: Abyssinia 1940-41; Keren; Jebel Defeis; Jebel Shiba; Gogni; Agordat; Barentu; Karora-Marsa Taclai; Cubcub; Ad Teclesan; Mescelit Pass; Mt Engiahat; Massawa; Amb Alagi; Gambela; El Wak; Moyale; Wal Garis; Juba; Marda Pass; Babile Gap; Bisidimo; Awash; Todenyang-Namaraputh; Soroppa; Giarso; Colito;Wadara; Omo; Gondar; Fike and Lechemti.*

Africa General Service Medal 1902-1956 The heads of King Edward VII, King George V and Queen Elizabeth II appear on the first, second and third issues of this medal respectively.

Ribbon: Yellow, edged with black and with two narrow green vertical stripes equidistant in the centre.
Clasps: N.Nigeria; N.Nigeria 1902; N.Nigeria 1903; N.Nigeria 1903-4; N.Nigeria 1904; N.Nigeria 1906; S.Nigeria; S.Nigeria 1902; S.Nigeria 1902-03; S.Nigeria 1903; S.Nigeria 1903-04; S.Nigeria 1904; S.Nigeria 1904-5; S.Nigeria 1905; S.Nigeria 1905-6; Uganda 1900; East Africa 1902; East Africa 1904; East Africa 1905; East Africa 1906; West Africa 1906; West Africa 1908; West Africa 1909-10; Somaliland 1901; Somaliland 1902-4; Jidballi; Somaliland 1908-10; B.C.A. 1899-1900; Jubuland; Gambia; Aro 1901-02; Lango 1901; Kissi 1905; Nandi 1905-06; Shimber Berris 1914-15; Nyasaland 1915; East Africa 1913; East Africa 1914; East Africa 1913-14; East Africa 1915; Jubuland 1917-18; East Africa 1918; Nigeria 1918 and Somaliland 1920.

Agagiya First World War Egyptian campaign battle honour marking a sharp action against the Sanussi, during which the Sanussi leader was captured, by the Dorset Yeomanry in 1915. Britain had not only to drive the Turks clear of the Suez Canal, which they did in February 1915, but also to contain a rising by the pro-Turkish Sanussi tribe near the Libyan frontier. *See also: Egypt 1915-17; Suez Canal; Rumani and Rafah.*

Agedabia Second World War North Africa campaign battle honour marking an action between the start of Rommel's first offensive in March 1941 and the British offensive Operation BATTLEAXE of 15-17 June 1941. *See also: North Africa 1940-43; Mersa el Brega; Derna Aerodrome and Halfaya 1941.*

Agent *See: Army Agent.*

Agira Second World War Sicilian campaign battle honour marking one of the actions during the capture of Sicily in July and August 1943. *See also: Sicily 1943; Landing in Sicily; Primosole Ridge; Sferro; Regalbuto and Centuripe.*

Agordat Second World War Abyssinian

campaign battle honour. *See also: Abyssinia 1940-41; Keren; Jebel Defeis; Jebel Shiba; Gogni; Barentu; Karora-Marsa Taclai; Cubcub; Ad Teclesan; Mescelit Pass; Mt Engiahat; Massawa; Amb Alagi; Afodu; Gambela; El Wak; Moyale; Wal Garis; Juba; Marda Pass; Babile Gap; Bisidimo; Awash; Todenyang-Namaraputh; Soroppa; Giarso; Colito; Wadara; Omo; Gondar; Fike and Lechemti.*

Ahmad Khel Second Afghan War (qv) battle honour. A force under the command of Sir Donald Stewart, on its way from Kandahar to Kabul, was attacked near Ghuznee on 31 March 1880 by a strong force of Afghans. At the end of an hour the situation, which had looked very threatening, was resolved and the enemy put to flight. *See also: Ali Masjid; Peiwar Kotal; Charasiah; Kabul 1879; Kandahar 1880 and Afghanistan 1878-9, 1878-80, 1879-80.*

Aide-de-Camp (ADC) Officer who acts as the personal and intimate assistant to a senior officer. Selected senior officers are appointed Aide-de-Camp to the Sovereign.

Aigrette Feather of a heron, at the base of Hussar officers' plume.

Aiguillette Arrangements of gold cords with pointed metal ends (aiglets or needles, originally used to clear the touch-hole of a pistol) now worn as a distinguishing mark. They have their origin in the needle-ended points or tags which helped affix pieces of armour to the buff undergarment in early times. When the wearing of armour was discontinued the coat continued to carry the tags or 'aiglets'. There were formerly four classes of aiguillette, but now only three exist: 1st Class, an aiguillette of gold wire cord worn on the right shoulder by a number of officers including Field Marshals, Aides-de-Camp to the Sovereign and equerries to members of the Royal family; 2nd Class, an aiguillette of gold and crimson worn on the right shoulder by military members of the Army Board and the personal staff of Governors etc. and 3rd Class, an aiguillette of gold and crimson worn on the left shoulder by military attachés and other aides-de-camps etc. All commissioned officers of the Household Cavalry wear an aiguillette (1st Class) on the right shoulder, whereas warrant officers of the Household Cavalry wear a similar aiguillette on the left shoulder. An aiguillette (2nd Class), with no coils on the ends of cords, is worn on the left shoulder by other non-commissioned officers of the Household Cavalry. A simple aiguillette, suspended from the shoulder strap, is worn by lance corporals of the Household Cavalry. Under an Army Council Instruction of March 1925 bandsmen of dragoon guards and dragoon regiments were authorised to wear aiguillettes on ceremonial occasions, at no expense to the public.

Air Term applied to all non-surface military activity.

Airborne (AB) Term used to describe parachute or glider formations and units.

Airborne Forces Britain's airborne forces were formed in 1940, reaching their maximum two division size in 1944. The 1st Airborne Division was committed to seize the bridges crossing the River Maas at Grave, the Waal at Nijmegen and the Neder Rijn at Arnhem in September 1944. The bridge at Grave was seized on 17 September and that at Nijmegen on the 20th, but the Germans moved swiftly to block the reinforcing Anglo/American force and the division was virtually destroyed. The remnants of 1st Airborne Division were evacuated on the night of 25/26 September, leaving behind some 7,000 of their number. The 6th Airborne Division was employed, with mixed results, in the North African, Normandy, Holland and Rhine campaigns. Currently the Army's airborne capability is vested in the three regular and three Territorial Army battalions of the Parachute Regiment, the three regular battalions forming the major part of 5th Airborne Brigade.

Aircraft Spotter An individual qualified in aircraft recognition. The specialisation is now obsolete, having been absorbed in the normal training requirement. A badge to be worn on the sleeve of those appropriately qualified was introduced at the end of the Second World War. The badge showed a bomber soaring upright; a wreath surrounded the bomber in the 1st Class badge.

Air Defence (AD) The protection of land operations from air attack. This is a key function and prevents the enemy using air power to break the cohesion of ground forces. Air defence artillery supports ground operations by both point and area defence.

Air Despatch The preparation and delivery by air of military personnel, stores and equipment from aircraft in flight; usually by parachute, but occasionally using other methods. This is a function in which air despatch personnel from the Royal Corps of Transport - now the Royal Logistic Corps - assist the Royal Air Force crews. A distinguishing badge showing a crowned and winged circlet within which are the letters 'AD' is worn on the sleeve by qualified air despatch personnel.

Airfield Damage Repair (ADR) The rapid repair of the runways of combat airfields following enemy attack to permit their continued use. The task is undertaken by specialised units of the Corps of Royal Engineers.

Air Force Cross Gallantry award for officers and warrant officers instituted by Royal Warrant dated 3 June 1918 for 'exceptional valour, courage or devotion to duty whilst flying though not in active operations against the enemy'.
Ribbon: Originally 1" wide of red and white alternate 1¼" horizontal stripes. From 24 July 1919 of similar stripes at a diagonal of 45°.

Air Force Medal Gallantry award for non-commissioned officers and men instituted by a Royal Warrant dated 3 June 1918 for 'an act or acts of valour, courage or devotion to duty performed whilst flying, though not in active operations against the enemy'.
Ribbon: Originally 1¼" wide of red and white alternate horizontal ¹⁄₁₆" stripes. From 24 July 1919 of similar stripes at a diagonal of 45°.

Airlanding The use of gliders or fixed- or rotary-winged aircraft to deliver forces to an area of tactical operation.

Airmobility The tactical use of helicopters to manoeuvre and position a force. Airmobile operations are much enhanced when a ground element deploys to sustain the initial effect, particularly when operating in a compatible time scale.

Air Mounting Centre (AMC) Location where personnel, vehicles and equipment destined for strategic movement by fixed-wing aircraft are held for any documentation, briefing or pre-loading checks which may be necessary before emplaning.

Airportability The use of fixed-wing aircraft for the air-landed delivery of a force to a secure airfield. Such a force is usually equipped on very light scales.

Airships The first British Army airship, Dirigible No.1, named *Nulli Secundus*, was manufactured by the Balloon Factory, Farnborough, and made her first public appearance, piloted by Colonel Capper, on 5 October 1907. She was reconstructed and reappeared in a Mark II version in July 1908. Airship development continued up to 1914 and Airships *Beta*, *Gamma* and *Delta* appeared in 1909, 1910 and 1911 respectively. *See also: Balloons.*

Airspace The atmosphere above a designated surface area of military interest over which control is exercised in support of surface operations, such as UK airspace, forward airspace etc.

Air Support Operations Air operations which are conducted in direct support of land operations. This includes tactical air reconnaissance, armed reconnaissance, close air support and battlefield air interdiction.

Air Technician The distinguishing badge of a qualified air technician in the Royal Electrical and Mechanical Engineers is a badge worn on the sleeve showing the letters 'AT' within a crowned and winged circlet bearing 'REME'.

Air to Surface Missile Missile launched from a non-surface vehicle at a target on the earth's surface.

Air Transport Aircraft, usually without offensive capability, used for the movement of personnel, vehicles and stores.

Aisne 1914 First World War battle honour marking the action of the British Expeditionary Force against German defensive positions along the River Aisne. A river crossing was carried, but only limited progress was possible and the Force dug in, consolidating its gains and initiating four years of trench warfare. *See also: France and Flanders 1914-18; Retreat from Mons; Marne 1914; La Bassée 1914; Armentières 1914 and Messines 1914.*

Aisne 1918 First World War battle honour marking the third German offensive of 1918, launched against the French in the Chemin des Dames sector, in which four British divisions which had been sent to the area for a rest, having been engaged in fierce fighting to the north, became involved. *See also: France and Flanders 1914-18; Bois des Buttes and Bligny.*

Akarit Second World War North Africa campaign battle honour marking the defeat of the Axis forces attempting to hold on the line of the Wadi Akarit on 6/7 April 1943. *See also: North Africa 1940-43; Djebel el Meida; Wadi Akarit East and Djebel Roumana.*

Alamein *See: Montgomery, 1st Viscount Montgomery of Alamein.*

Alam El Halfa Second World War North Africa campaign battle honour marking the repulse of the German attack on the El Alamein position between 30 August and 7 September 1942. The defeat of the German attack has been referred to as 'the turning point of the desert war'. *See also: North Africa 1940-43; Defence of Alamein Line; Ruweisat; Fuka Airfield; Deir El Shein; Point 93; Ruweisat Ridge and West Point 23.*

Alanbrooke, Alan Francis Brooke, 1st Viscount, (1883-1963) Educated abroad

and at the Royal Military Academy, Woolwich. Commissioned into the Royal Field Artillery in 1902, he played a significant role in the development of the artillery, especially aspects of air defence and, as Director of Military Training (1936-37), greatly improved the quality of training in the Army. His command of the 2nd Army Corps of the British Expeditionary Force (1939-40) during the withdrawal through Dunkirk was brilliant. Appointed Commander-in-Chief Home Forces in 1940, he set about preparing for the expected German invasion. He became Chief of the Imperial General Staff (qv) in December 1941 and, through his chairmanship of the Chiefs of Staff Committee and membership of the Allied Combined Chiefs of Staff, was to be a major influence on allied strategy. He became a field marshal in 1944. One of the great military intellects of his generation, he had a profound effect on the Army. Alanbrooke was Master Gunner (1946-56) and Constable of HM Tower of London (1950-57).

Albert 1916 First World War battle honour marking the opening phase of the Battle of the Somme (qv) on 1 July 1916 during which the British sustained nearly 60,000 casualties. Over the northern sector of the front there was almost no progress at all, but from Mametz southward all objectives were seized. *See also: France and Flanders 1914-18; Somme 1916; Bazentin; Delville Wood; Pozières; Guillemont; Ginchy; Flers-Courcelette; Morval; Thiepval; Le Transloy; Ancre Heights and Ancre 1916.*

Albert 1918 First World War battle honour marking the opening stage of the Second Battle of the Somme, launched in late August 1918, which successfully eliminated the salient achieved by the German March offensive. *See also: France and Flanders 1914-18; Somme 1918; Amiens; Bapaume 1918; Scarpe 1918; Drocourt-Quéant and Hindenburg Line.*

Albert Helmet Metal helmet of Prussian (or Russian) design introduced to the heavy cavalry in the 1840s by Prince Albert to replace the 'Roman' helmet. With minor alterations the helmet is of a similar design to that now worn by the Household Cavalry in full dress.

Albert Medal Gallantry award, open to all ranks and civilians, instituted by a Royal Warrant of 7 March 1866. A Royal Warrant dated 12 April 1867 added first and second class decorations. Originally awarded for gallantry displayed saving life at sea the terms were extended to include gallantry displayed saving life on land.
Ribbon:
For saving life at sea:
Gold Medal: dark blue ⅝" wide with two white stripes (until 1866); dark blue 1⅜" wide with four white stripes (from 1867).
Bronze Medal: dark blue ⅝" wide with two white stripes (until 1867); dark blue 1 3/8" wide with two white stripes (from 1904).
For saving life on land:
Gold Medal: crimson 1⅜" wide with four white stripes.
Bronze Medal: crimson ⅝" wide with two white stripes (until 1877); crimson 1⅜" wide with two white stripes (from 1904).

Albert Shako Type of cylindrical head-dress, with front and rear peaks, also known as a chaco or chakot, favoured by Prince Albert and worn by the infantry, Royal Artillery and Royal Engineers from about 1844 until 1855. *See also: Shako.*

Albuera/Albuhera Peninsula War battle honour marking the action in 1811 of part of Wellington's army under General Beresford. Beresford was besieging the frontier fortress of Badajoz when he heard that Soult was marching to relieve the siege; Beresford raised the siege and took up a position astride Soult's route at Albuhera. Severe fighting took place during which 57th Foot, later The Middlesex Regiment, earned the nickname 'Die Hards'. The day was saved by the timely arrival of the Fusilier Brigade, having made a forced march of 16 miles to reach the battle. *See also: Peninsula; Busaco; Barrosa; Fuentes d'Onor; Arroyo dos Molinos; Tarifa and Ciudad Rodrigo.*

Aldershot Garrison town in Hampshire, 35 miles from London. A military camp was first established there in 1853-54.

Sometimes known as 'The Home of the British Army'.

Alem Hamza Second World War North Africa campaign battle honour marking the unsuccessful attempt by the 4th Indian Division in late 1941 to seize the Alam Hamza feature, and thus cut off the enemy retiring to the Gazala position following their unsuccessful attack on Tobruk. *See also: North Africa 1940-43; Chor Es Sufan and Saunnu.*

Alessandra Second World War Abyssinian campaign battle honour marking one of the actions in the Battle of the Juba. *See also: Abyssinia 1940-41; Keren; Jebel Defeis; Jebel Shiba; Gogni; Barentu; Karora-Marsa Taclai; Cubcub; Ad Teclesan; Mescelit Pass; Mt Engiahat; Massawa; Amb Alagi; Afodu; Gambela; El Wak; Moyale; Wal Garis; Juba; Marda Pass; Babile Gap; Bisidimo; Awash; Todenyang-Namaraputh; Soroppa; Giarso; Colito; Wadara; Omo; Gondar; Fike and Lechemti.*

Alethangyaw Second World War battle honour, awarded to Army Commandos, marking an action which took place 8-15 April 1944 during the campaign in Burma. *See also: Burma 1942-45; North Arakan; Buthidaung; Razibil; Kaladan; Mayu Tunnels; Naungdaw; Mowdok and Point 551.*

Alexander of Tunis, Field Marshal Harold Rupert Leofric George Alexander, 1st Earl (1891-1969) Educated Harrow and Royal Military Academy Sandhurst and commissioned into the Irish Guards. He served with distinction in the First World War and was decorated and mentioned in despatches. He commanded a brigade in India and served in two campaigns on the North-West Frontier. In 1938 he was appointed to the command of 1st Division and commanded the rearguard with great skill and gallantry in the withdrawal through Dunkirk in 1940. After commanding Southern Command he was appointed to command the army in Burma, and by 1942 had contained the Japanese advance. In August 1942 he succeeded Auchinleck as Commander-in-Chief Middle East, and was to conduct a series of British and allied victories from El Alamein to the destruction of the Axis army under von Arnim in May 1943. As Supreme Commander in the Middle East he commanded the allied armies which defeated the German and Italian armies in Italy (1944-45). Appointed Field Marshal in 1944 and raised to the peerage as Viscount Alexander of Tunis in 1946 and Earl in 1952. He was Governor General and Commander-in-Chief of Canada from 1946-52.

Ali Masjid Second Afghan War (qv) battle honour marking an action by the force tasked with the invasion of Afghanistan under the command of Lieutenant General Sir Samuel Browne, which crossed the frontier at Jumrood on 21 November 1878 and advanced on Ali Masjid, the hill fortress at the Afghan entrance to the Khyber Pass. A brief skirmish took place and General Browne decided to hold the assault until his force was complete. Overnight the Afghans withdrew and the fort was occupied and the road to Kabul opened at the cost of less than 60 casualties. *See also: Peiwar Kotal; Charasiah; Kabul 1879; Ahmed Khel; Kandahar 1880 and Afghanistan 1878-9, 1878-80, 1879-80.*

Aliwal Battle honour marking the engagement at Aliwal on 28 January 1846 during the First Sikh War (1845-46) (qv) when a strong Sikh force, having crossed the River Sutlej and threatening the British line of communication at Ludhiana, was destroyed by a force under Sir Harry Smith, the latter having earlier fought a brisk and successful action at Buddiwal on 20 January. *See also: Moodkee; Ferozeshah and Sobraon.*

Alkhalak Long coat, fastening on the chest, worn by Indian cavalrymen.

All Round Defence The siting of a defensive position in such a manner that, notwithstanding the expected direction of attack, it can be defended if attacked from any direction.

All The Blue Bonnets Are Over The Border Regimental quick march (Military Band) of The Black Watch (Royal Highland Regiment), and regimental march (Pipes and Drums) of 7th Duke of Edinburgh's Own Gurkha Rifles.

Aller Second World War battle honour marking the successful crossing of the River Aller and subsequent exploitation, in spite of a number of counter-attacks, into Germany 10-17 April 1945. *See also: North West Europe 1944-45; Ibbenbüren; Leese; Brinkum and Bremen.*

Allenby, Field Marshal Sir Edmund Henry Hynman, Viscount of Meggido and of Felixstowe (1861-1936) Educated at Haileybury and Royal Military Academy Sandhurst and commissioned into the Inniskilling Dragoons (1882). Gained distinction as a column commander in the South Africa War (1899-1902). In the First World War he won a reputation as a brilliant cavalry leader, then as an army commander in France and finally as the commander-in-chief of the Egyptian Expeditionary Force. His strategy, tactics and administrative ability were of the highest order and the crushing defeat he inflicted on the Turks at Megiddo (qv) (15 September - 31 October 1918) was masterly. For his services he was given a Viscountcy and promoted Field Marshal, and parliament voted him a grant of £50,000. In 1919 he was appointed to the post of High Commissioner in Egypt returning to England in 1922 in which year Egypt, was declared an independent kingdom. The Allenby Bridge (built 1927) which carries the Jerusalem-Amman road across the Jordan is named after him.

Alliance Formal association, approved by the Crown, between individual regiments and corps of the British Army and regiments and corps of Commonwealth armies. It is usual for such alliances to be formed between regiments and corps of a similar role or with historical links. Details of all such alliances may be found in Part 1 of the Army List.

Allied Command Europe (ACE) One of the major NATO commands, covering the land area from the North Cape to

North Africa and from the Atlantic to the eastern border of Turkey. The task of ACE is to ensure the security of western Europe through the co-ordination of the allied military effort in every sphere. The Supreme Allied Commander Europe (SACEUR) has his headquarters near Mons in Belgium.

Allied Command Europe Mobile Force (Land) (AMF(L)) A multinational NATO force of about battle group size, to which Britain is a major contributor, held at a high state of readiness to deploy in a period of tension and thus demonstrate NATO solidarity.

Allied Command Europe Rapid Reaction Corps (ARRC) ARRC was formed by NATO in response to the changed circumstances brought about by the collapse of the Warsaw Pact. It is a multinational formation available for deployment to meet NATO operational objectives. The main British contribution to the ARRC is 1 (UK) Armoured Division, based in Germany. In addition 3 (UK) Division and 24 Airmobile Brigade, both based in England, could join the ARRC should the situation so demand. Britain therefore makes a major contribution to ARRC as well as providing the commander and the bulk of the headquarters staff.

Alligator An alligator badge was worn by 19th Light Dragoons at the end of the 18th century to mark the regiment having been raised in Jamaica, where the alligator formed the crest of the Jamaican coat-of-arms.

Ally Ghur Battle honour marking the storming and capture of the fortress of Ally Ghur on 3 September 1803 during the First Maratha War (1803-5) (qv) against the forces of Maharajah Scindia. *See also: Delhi 1803; Assaye; Leswarree and Deig.*

Alma Crimean War battle honour awarded in 1855 to mark the occasion in the Crimean War (1854-55) when a Franco/British force captured a Russo/Turkish position on the crest of the hills overlooking the Alma River on 20 September 1854. *See also: Balaklava; Inkerman and Sevastopol.*

Almaraz Peninsula War battle honour marking the engagement on 19 May 1811 between the French and a force under the command of General Hill, which was tasked with preventing French troops south of the river from threatening Wellington's flank by destroying the bridge over the River Tagus. *See also: Peninsula; Ciudad Rodrigo; Badajoz and Salamanca.*

Alouette The Alouette II light helicopter, manufactured by Sud Aviation, was taken into service in 1961 as a liaison, casualty evacuation, training and observation aircraft. Replaced by the Scout in the mid-1960s; a few Alouettes remained in service with Army Air Corps units in Cyprus until October 1988.

Amba Alagi Second World War Abyssinian campaign battle honour awarded uniquely to the Worcestershire Regiment (29th and 36th Foot). *See also: Abyssinia 1940-41; Keren; Jebel Defeis; Jebel Shiba; Gogni; Barentu; Karora-Marsa Taclai; Cubcub; Ad Teclesan; Mescelit Pass; Mt Engiahat; Massawa; Afodu; Gambela; El Wak; Moyale; Wal Garis; Juba; Marda Pass; Babile Gap; Bisidimo; Awash; Todenyang-Namaraputh; Soroppa; Giarso; Colito; Wadara; Omo; Gondar; Fike and Lechemti.*

Ambazzo Second World War Abyssinian campaign battle honour marking an action during operations in the Gondar area. *See also: Abyssinia 1940-41; Keren; Jebel Defeis; Jebel Shiba; Gogni; Barentu; Karora-Marsa Taclai; Cubcub; Ad Teclesan; Mescelit Pass; Mt Engiahat; Massawa; Amb Alagi; Afodu; Gambela; El Wak; Moyale; Wal Garis; Juba; Marda Pass; Babile Gap; Bisidimo; Awash; Todenyang-Namaraputh; Soroppa; Giarso; Colito; Wadara; Omo; Gondar; Fike and Lechemti.*

Amboyna Battle honour marking the capture of Amboyna from the Dutch in February 1796. However, the Treaty of Amiens (1802) restored Amboyna and the nearby islands to the Dutch, but they were reoccupied by the British in 1810. A garrison was maintained on the island until 1814 when it was once more restored to the Dutch by the Treaty of Paris. *See also: Ternate and Banda.*

Ambur Battle honour marking the successful defence of this fortress by a small garrison of British sepoys under Captain Calvert against Hyder Ali's army during the First Mysore War (qv) 1767.

Ambush An operation in which enemy forces are drawn into, or allowed to enter, an area previously selected and prepared for their destruction. Ambushes can be conducted at almost any force level and with a variety of force mixes, but surprise is the fundamental ingredient.

American War of Independence (1775-1783) The first fighting of the war was a brief and indecisive skirmish at Lexington, some 10 miles from Boston, where Royal troops engaged the colonists. However, in later fighting at Concord British losses were heavier. Following the appointment of George Washington as Commander-in-Chief of the American forces Generals Howe, Clinton and Burgoyne arrived in Boston with additional troops bringing the British force to about 10,000 men. On 17 June 1775, at the Battle of Bunker Hill (qv), a height on the peninsula which commands Boston, the British defeated the Americans, but sustained heavy losses. In March 1776 General Howe evacuated Boston because Washington had fortified Dorchester Heights and, by heavy bombardment, gained mastery of the city. Despite British successes at Long Island, White Plains and Fort Lee, and the fall of Newark, New Brunswick and Trenton, Washington defeated Lord Cornwallis at Princeton in 1777 and, in the same year, Burgoyne surrendered to General Gates at Saratoga. Late in 1777 the Americans were defeated at Brandywine and Germantown and Howe occupied Philadelphia, the capital. Clinton succeeded Howe as commander of the British forces and was ordered to evacuate Philadelphia and return to New York. Washington hung on to his flanks and, on 28 June 1778, there

was an indecisive engagement at Monmouth. By now France, Spain and Holland had joined the war on the American side, greatly inhibiting British maritime activity. Clinton occupied New York and Washington took up his position nearby at White Plains; thus the two enemies watched each other for three years while the real fighting took place in the south. In the late summer of 1781 Cornwallis found himself besieged in Yorktown by Washington and Lafayette, the French commander, and, on 19 October, he surrendered. A peace treaty, which was highly disadvantageous to Britain, was signed at Paris on 3 September 1783.

Amherst, Jeffrey, Baron (1717-97) Through the influence of the Duke of Dorset Amherst obtained an ensigncy in the Guards. In 1758 he became Commander-in-Chief of the British forces in North America. To him, perhaps more than anyone else, is due the success of British arms in North America during the Seven Years War (qv). Amherst, with Wolfe (qv) did much to further the development and tactics of the light infantry; he was raised to the peerage in 1776 and became a Field Marshal in 1776.

Amherst, William Pitt Amherst, Earl (1773-1857) A British diplomat, Amherst was sent on an embassy to China in 1816 in order to procure better terms for Anglo-Chinese trade but, through his spirited refusal to perform the 'kow-tow' to the Emperor, his embassy failed. In 1823 he was made Governor-General of India, an office he held until 1828. He conducted the First Burma War (qv) with great success and was awarded the earldom of Arakan.

Amiens First World War battle honour marking the first major British offensive of 1918, which was launched on 8 August from the Amiens area by the Fourth Army along both sides of the River Somme. Amiens is considered by many to be the most brilliant British victory on the Western Front. *See also: France and Flanders 1914-18; Albert 1918; Scarpe 1918; Drocourt-Quéant and Hindenburg Line.*

Amiens 1940 Second World War battle honour marking an action in the withdrawal of the British Expeditionary Force (qv) from the Low Countries and France. *See also: North West Europe 1940; Arras Counter-Attack; French Frontier 1940; Forêt de Nieppe; Withdrawal to Seine and Withdrawal to Cherbourg.*

Amiens 1944 Second World War battle honour marking the capture of Amiens on 31 August 1944 after a night advance by 11th Armoured Division during which three of the four bridges over the Seine were secured intact, thus dashing any hopes the Germans may have had of holding the line of the river. *See also: North West Europe 1944-45; Falaise; Dives Crossing; Lisieux and Seine.*

Ammunition Ammunition is broadly composed of two parts: the projectile, which inflicts damage on the target; and the propellant, which develops the desired velocity in the projectile. Projectiles vary widely and may achieve their effect by kinetic energy, blast, fragmentation or even through nuclear, chemical or biological fillings.

Ammunition Boots Field service boots, the prefix 'ammunition' being applied to many items from public stores issued to soldiers. *See also: Boots.*

Ammunition Examiner A badge showing the letters 'AE' within a laurel wreath was worn on the sleeve to denote those qualified as ammunition examiners. This changed to the more elaborate 'A' in the early 1950s. *See also: 'A' and Ammunition Technical Officer.*

Ammunition Technical Officer Officer, warrant officer or non-commissioned officer trained to inspect ammunition and to advise on all ammunition matters, especially safety and storage. Also trained to render safe explosive ordnance devices (qv) and, more usually, the improvised explosive ordnance devices associated with terrorism. An ammunition technical officer may only carry out these duties if licensed and continued suitability is confirmed by periodic licensing tests.

Amphibious Term related to military forces and equipment organised and designed for operations launched from the sea against objectives ashore.

Analysis Operational analysis is the use of quantitative methods to assess the probable impact of the introduction of new weapons, equipment and tactics. Nowadays, operational analysis or operational research, as it is more usually termed, is virtually a prerequisite to the allocation of funds for equipment projects of any size. The Defence Operational Analysis Centre is located at West Byfleet in Surrey.

Ancona Second World War Italian campaign battle honour marking the fall of Ancona to the Polish Corps, the 7th Hussars being under command. The city fell after fighting lasting 2-18 July 1944. *See also: Italy 1943-45; Citta di Castillo; Campriano; Poggio del Grillo; Fiesole; Montorsoli; Pian di Maggio and Citerna.*

Ancre 1916 First World War battle honour marking the final phase of the Somme offensive, known as the Battle of the Ancre. Although Beaumont Hamel was taken, success was limited and the battle effectively ended on 18 November 1916. *See also: France and Flanders 1914-18 and Somme 1916.*

Ancre Heights First World War battle honour marking the six weeks in October and November 1916 during which the Fifth Army, in spite of German counter-attacks, sought to clear the high ground dominating the Ancre valley and thus exploit the success achieved at Thiepval. *See also: France and Flanders 1914-18 and Somme.*

Ancre 1918 First World War battle honour marking the halting on 5 April 1918 of the major German offensive launched on 21 March 1918. The German advance was held astride the River Ancre, just west of Albert, by the Third Army. *See also: France and Flanders 1914-18 and Somme 1918.*

Anglesey, Henry William Paget, 1st Marquess of (1768-1854) Soldier and statesman, son of the Earl of Uxbridge. Educated at Westminster and Christ Church, Oxford. He was created Marquess of Anglesey for his bravery at Waterloo. Appointed Lord Lieutenant of Ireland in 1828, he was recalled by Wellington for supporting Catholic emancipation, though he was reappointed by Grey in 1830.

Anglesey Yeomanry A yeomanry troop from the Isle of Anglesey formed part of a squadron of the Denbighshire Hussars, recruited in Caernarvonshire in the early 1900s. The county name was subsequently incorporated in the title of 61st (Caernarvon and Denbigh Yeomanry) Medium Regiment, Royal Artillery, when it was formed in 1920, and passed to 372 (Flintshire and Denbighshire Yeomanry) Field Regiment Royal Artillery and, in 1967, to The Flintshire and Denbighshire Yeomanry Royal Artillery (Territiorials).

Angreeka Loose jacket worn by Indian infantry in the 18th century.

Anguilla An island in the West Indies in the Leeward Islands, part of the British associated state of St Kitts-Nevis-Anguilla from 1967-1980 when it reverted to British dependency status. In early 1969 there were rumours that the Mafia was planning to declare independence and turn the island into a gambling centre and, on 12 March 1969, a junior minister from the Foreign Office was chased from the island. A very small force of troops, supported by the Metropolitan Police, was sent to the island and order was restored.

Angus Yeomanry Evidence suggests yeomanry cavalry having been commissioned in December 1794, but their service is not documented. Lord Airlie sought to raise some troops in the county in 1831, but again no evidence of their activity exists. The Forfarshire Yeomanry was re-formed in 1846, but disbanded in 1862. Later in the 19th century the Forfar Light Horse was formed. *See also: Fife and Forfar Yeomanry.*

***Animo et Fide* (With Resolution and Fidelity)** Motto of the Adjutant General's Corps, and of the Staff and Personnel Support Branch of that Corps.

Ankle Boots *See: Boots.*

Anklet Broad band of leather or canvas webbing with securing straps and buckles, used to protect the lower leg just above the boot. Although trialled in 1932, anklets were not issued until 1938.

Annual Reporting Centre Point established, usually in a Territorial Army (qv) drill hall or regular unit barracks, to which selected regular reservists are required to report annually to have their equipment and documentation checked and receive a brief period of updating and training. Reservists receive a payment for reporting.

Antenna That part of a communication system by which electromagnetic waves are transmitted or received.

Anti-Aircraft Weapon systems specifically designed for the engagement and destruction of aerial vehicles.

Anti-Armour Weapons and ammunition designed primarily to penetrate the armour of armoured fighting vehicles. There are two broad methods of attack: chemical energy, based usually upon a 'shaped' or 'hollow' charge warhead, and kinetic energy. *See also: Anti-tank.*

Anti-Ballistic Missile A weapon system designed specifically for the interception and destruction of ballistic missiles in flight.

Anti-Personnel Ammunition, mines, nuclear, chemical or biological agents designed specifically to kill, wound and disable personnel.

Anti-Tank Ammunition, mines and weapons designed to disable or destroy tanks and other armoured vehicles. A badge bearing the letters AT within a wreath is worn on the sleeve of anti-tank gunners. *See also: Anti-armour.*

Anti-Tank Guided Weapon or Missile A missile with an anti-armour warhead which is guided from the launch point to the target.

Antwerp Second World War battle honour marking the entry into Antwerp of 11th Armoured Division on 4 September 1944. After stiff street fighting in parts of the city it was finally cleared by 7 September. *See also: North West Europe 1944-45; Brussels; Neerpelt; Gheel; Hechtel and Aart.*

Antwerp-Turnhout Canal Second World War battle honour marking the operations to force a crossing of the canal by the 49th Division, supported by the Polish Armoured Division, 24-29 September 1944. *See also: North West Europe 1944-45; Nederrijn; Scheldt and Aam.*

Anzac Abbreviation for the Australian and New Zealand Army Corps. Also, a First World War Gallipoli campaign battle honour marking actions in the Anzac sector. *See also: Gallipoli 1915-16; Landing at Anzac; Defence of Anzac; Suvla; Sari Bair; Landing at Suvla and Scimitar Hill.*

Anzio Second World War Italian campaign battle honour marking the landing during the Italian campaign of 1st British and 3rd American Divisions on 22 January 1944. The landing, which was unopposed, was intended to outflank the Germans and cause them to abandon the 'Gustav Line'. On landing, no attempt was made to retain the initiative and enlarge the bridgehead, or to advance to the Alban Hills and thus threaten the German position at Cassino. The Germans reacted swiftly and, when an advance was attempted, it was held short of Campoleone; thereafter the allied force was thrown onto the defensive and unable to break out until 22 May. It was only with heavy losses that the allies managed even to hold the original bridgehead in a period of violent and bloody trench warfare. *See also: Italy 1943-45, Campoleone, Aprilia and Carroceto.*

Apache Attack helicopter originally of US design and manufacture, and subsequently produced by Westland Helicopters Limited in conjunction with McDonnell Douglas. An order for 67 Apache aircraft, to be flown by the Army Air Corps in support of ground operations, was placed in July 1995. The aircraft is fitted with Longbow battlefield radar and can accept a wide variety of weapon fits including Hellfire anti-tank missiles.

Appreciation A logical, deductive analysis of the factors bearing on a problem of strategy or tactics and the possible courses of action. Such an analysis should result in a favoured course of action. Appreciations can be either lengthy written analyses, or rapid 'combat' appreciations to meet an immediate tactical problem.

Aprilia Second World War, Italian campaign battle honour, one of three battle honours marking the fighting at Anzio (qv). *See also: Italy 1943-45; Anzio; Campoleone and Carroceto.*

Apron A covering, usually of leather, animal skin or cloth worn on the chest by bass drummers, and sometimes heavy wind instrument players, and on the left leg by side drummers. Infantry pioneers and cavalry farriers also wear aprons on ceremonial occasions.

Aquino Second World War Italian campaign battle honour marking one of a number of operations in the Liri Valley (qv) which took place in the exploitation towards Rome after the capture of Cassino in May 1944. *See also: Italy 1943-45; Liri Valley; Hitler Line; Monte Piccolo; Piedemonte Hill and Melfa Crossing.*

Arabia Battle honour awarded in March 1823 to the 65th Foot (2nd Yorkshire North Riding) in recognition of their service against Arab pirates in the Persian Gulf in 1809 and 1819-20. *See also: Beni Boo Ali.*

Aradura Second World War Burma campaign battle honour marking operations by the 2nd British Division against Japanese positions astride the Imphal Road over the period 14 May - 6 June 1944. *See also: Burma 1942-45; Kohima; Defence of Kohima; Relief of Kohima; Naga Village and Mao Songsang.*

Arakan Beaches Second World War Burma campaign battle honour marking the final stages of the Arakan campaign over the period 12 January-29 April 1945. Operations were largely concentrated in the coastal area, but the battle honour also includes operations in the Kaladan valley. *See also: Burma 1942-45; Dalet; Tamandu; Taungup; Myebon; Ramree and Kangaw.*

Arc of Fire The area allocated to the fire of a specific weapon. The left and right of arc are usually defined by identifiable features in the landscape; the depth of arc being limited by the range of the weapon concerned.

Archangel 1918-19 First World War battle honour marking the engagement of British troops, originally tasked with guarding allied stores collected at Archangel and Murmansk, and later drawn into operations on the side of the White Armies in the Russian Civil War. *See also: Troitsa.*

Arcot Battle honour, unique to the Royal Dublin Fusiliers. In 1751 a small force under Captain Robert Clive from Madras entered Arcot, the capital of the Carnatic, to divert the pro-French Nawab from his siege of Trinchinopoly. Having diverted the Nawab's attention he occupied the half-ruined fort at Arcot and withstood a siege for 50 days, finally beating off a Franco/Indian attacking force on 31 August 1751. *See also: Plassey; Condore; Masulipatam and Badara.*

Ardennes Major Second World War German offensive launched in December 1944. The capture of the town of Bastogne, central to communications in the area, was a vital element in the German plan to push toward Antwerp. The 101st US Airborne Division played a fundamental part in the denial of the town to the Germans and the offensive subsequently faltered.

Area Defence The purpose of area defence is to hold ground, thus denying it to the enemy. In area defence, commanders employ most of their forces in a framework of static and mutually supporting positions with, if possible, a mobile reserve and supplemented by the ability to conduct local counter-attacks.

Area of Influence The geographical area wherein a commander is directly capable of influencing operations by manoeuvre or fire support systems normally under his command.

Area of Interest The area of concern to a commander, including the area of influence, areas adjacent thereto, and extending into enemy territory to the objectives of current or planned operations. This area also includes areas occupied by enemy forces which could affect the accomplishment of the mission.

Area of Intelligence Interest That area concerning which a commander needs intelligence of those factors and developments likely to affect his current and future operations.

Area of Intelligence Responsibility An area allocated to a commander, at any level, in which he is responsible for intelligence.

Area of Responsibility A defined area of terrain over which responsibility is specifically assigned to a commander for the development and maintenance of installations, control of movement and the conduct of tactical operations involving troops under his control, and the parallel authority to exercise these functions.

Arezzo Second World War Italian campaign battle honour marking operations in the Fifth Army sector which took place between the fall of Rome and arrival at the Gothic Line. *See also: Italy 1943-45; Monte Rotondo; Monte Gabbione; Ripa Ridge and Gabbiano.*

Argenta Gap Second World War Italian campaign battle honour marking operations between 13 and 21 April 1945 which culminated in the breaching of the German defences which had blocked the advance of Eighth Army into the Po Valley in the Italian Campaign of 1943-45. *See also: Italy 1943-45; Fossa Cambalina and San Nicolo Canal.*

Argoub El Megas Second World War North Africa campaign battle honour marking an operation which took place between the Fondouk operations of April 1943 and the end of the campaign in North Africa. *See also: North Africa 1940-43; Heidous; Banana Ridge and Djebel Djaffa Pass.*

Argoub Sellah Second World War North Africa campaign battle honour marking the capture of a hill feature during the advance of the British V Corps to occupy the line Touhabeur-Chaouach, known as the Oued Zarga operations 7-15 April 1943. *See also: North Africa 1940-43; Oued Zarga; El Kourzia and Ber Rabal.*

Argyll and Sutherland Highlanders (Princess Louise's) The 91st (Argyllshire Highlanders) Foot was raised in February 1794 by Colonel Duncan Campbell of Lochnell, initially ranked 98th but renumbered 91st in 1796. The 93rd Highlanders was raised in April 1799 by General William Wemyss of Wemyss and redesignated 93rd (Sutherland Highlanders) Foot in 1861. The 91st was renamed 91st Foot in 1809, 91st (Argyllshire) Foot in 1821, 91st (Argyllshire) Highlanders in 1864 and 91st (Princess Louise's) Argyllshire Highlanders in 1872. In May 1881, the 91st and 93rd amalgamated to form The Princess Louise's (Sutherland and Argyll) Highlanders, renamed The Princess Louise's (Argyll and Sutherland) Highlanders in July 1882. In 1920 the regiment became known as The Argyll and Sutherland Highlanders (Princess Louise's).
Headdress Badge: Within a circle inscribed 'Argyll and Sutherland', the cypher and coronet of Princess Louise. To the left a boar's head, the crest of the Argylls, and to the right a cat, the badge of the Sutherlands. All within a wreath of thistles.
Mottoes: *Ne obliviscaris* (Do not forget), and *San Peur* (Without Fear).
Regimental Marches:
Quick Marches: *Campbells are Coming* and *Hielan' Laddie* (Pipes and Drums); *The Thin Red Line* (Regimental Band).
Slow Marches: *Skye Boat Song* (Pipes and Drums) and *The Garb of Old Gaul* (Regimental Band).

Regimental Headquarters: The Castle, Stirling, Scotland, FK8 1EH.
History: *The History of the 91st Argyllshire Highlanders* by R P Dunn Pattison; *The 93rd Sutherland Highlanders* by A E J Cavendish; *History of the Argyll and Sutherland Highlanders 1st Battalion 1909-39* by R C B Anderson; and *History of the Argyll and Sutherland Highlanders 1st Battalion 1939-54* by R C B Anderson.

Arleux First World War battle honour awarded for the capture of Arleux on 28 April 1917 during the later stages of the 1917 Arras offensive. *See also: France and Flanders 1914-18; Arras 1917; Vimy 1917 and Scarpe 1917.*

Arm of Service Strip In 1940 a colour code system was evolved to indicate arm of service when in battle dress. Coloured strips, worn by officers as an underlay to the rank badges, and by soldiers as narrow strips of cloth 2" by 1/4" worn on the upper sleeve, were used. The system ceased at the end of the Second World War, although the practice continued unofficially for some time thereafter, largely on aesthetic grounds.

***Arma Pacis Fulcra* (Arms are the fulcrum of peace)** Motto of the Honourable Artillery Company.

Armentières 1914 First World War battle honour marking the push by British III Corps, after severe fighting near Meteren, which drove the Germans back and got within five miles of Lille, but was slowly forced back to a line just east of Armentières. *See also: France and Flanders 1914-18; Marne 1914; Aisne 1914; La Bassée 1914; Messines 1914 and Ypres 1914.*

Armistice A temporary suspension of hostilities between opposing belligerent powers by mutual agreement. A general armistice, as opposed to a partial or local armistice, is more usually a preliminary to peace, halting all warlike operations. It is often concluded by the opposing commanders-in-chief with the advice and authority of their governments. The famous armistice of 11 November 1918, which ended hostilities in the First World War (1914-18), was concluded by Marshal Foch and Admiral Wemyss for the allies with the civil and military representatives of Germany.

Armlet Cloth band about 3" wide, often coloured and bearing badges or initials, used to denote staff branches or other specialisation. Worn just above the elbow on the right arm by officers and traditionally on the left by other ranks.

Armour A generic term for tank formations. However, more specifically the term is applied to the protective skin, originally of steel, on some fighting vehicles. Improvements in anti-armour weapons demanded ever increasing thicknesses of steel, bringing considerable weight and thus mobility penalties. It was found that sloping armour not only increased the probability of ricochet but effectively presented a greater thickness of armour to projectiles. Modern composite armour such as 'Chobham Armour' (qv) uses special materials. Progress has be made with 'Explosive Reaction Armour' (qv) composed of explosive slabs strapped to the outside of vehicles which detonate when hit by a hollow charge projectile, thus reducing the latter's 'scabbing effect' on the internal surfaces of the armour. The production of a material known as 'Kevlar' (qv), which is relatively light and has some protective qualities, has made possible the armouring of some parts of aircraft and the production of body armour and light helmets for fighting men.

Armour Piercing Discarding Sabot (APDS) A kinetic energy anti-armour round surrounded by a sabot which enhances its velocity and accuracy and is discarded in flight.

Armoured Car Wheeled, lightly armoured fighting vehicle, proof against fragmentation weapons and small arms. Armed usually with machine guns or a light gun. Good communications, high speed on roads, desert and other firm open terrain makes them specially suitable for reconnaissance, long-distance raids, pursuit and movement control.

Armoured Delivery Regiment A unit tasked with the delivery of replacement armoured vehicles and crews to forward units to make good battle casualties. It is usual for one squadron of such a regiment to be placed in support of each division.

Armoured Fighting Vehicle (AFV) An armoured vehicle, frequently carrying a gun or missile system, more often tracked than wheeled so that it can move with tanks on the battlefield.

Armoured Personnel Carrier (APC) An armoured vehicle, tracked or wheeled, designed to transport infantry under armoured protection from small arms and fragmentation rounds, to a point where they dismount and thereafter fight on foot.

Armoured Recovery Vehicle (ARV) Tracked vehicle based upon a main battle tank chassis (currently Chieftain and Challenger) and designed specifically for the recovery and repair of large armoured vehicles as far forward as possible in the battlefield. The ARV is fitted with a dozer blade, winch and crane.

Armoured Vehicle Launched Bridge (AVLB) An extendable bridge, capable of bearing main battle tanks, carried on a tank chassis, and usually attached to armoured regiments to enhance their battlefield mobility. The current version, mounted on a Chieftain chassis, carries a bridge 24m long which can be laid in about five minutes.

Armoured Vehicle Royal Engineers (AVRE) Tracked vehicle, currently based on a Chieftain chassis, which is to replace the Centurion-based Assault Vehicle Royal Engineers (AVRE). Fitted with a mine plough and/or dozer blade and capable of carrying three fascines (qv) or rolls of trackway.

Armoury Secure place for the storage of weapons.

Arms Generic term for those elements of the Army such as armour, artillery, engineer, infantry and army aviation which actually join battle with the enemy.

Army The land force element of British defence forces. A land force formation comprising more than one corps.

Army Acts The Army Act of 1881, which required annual review by parliament, held that a standing army in time of peace was illegal without the continuing consent of parliament. It was replaced by the Army Act 1955 which, together with the Air Force Act 1955 and the Naval Discipline Act 1957, is amended and continued in force by the Armed Forces Act 1986. *See also: Military Law.*

Army Agent The appointment of agents has its origin in the 17th century. An agent was, in effect, a regiment's business manager. He was responsible for the payment of members of the regiment, the provision of clothing and the marketing of commissions. A report of 1855 defined the status of an agent as follows: 'Originally every regiment had its own agent selected by the Colonel who empowered him to ask, demand and receive all sums of money of whatsoever kind may be due to him. Though the agent is appointed by the colonel, he is recognised, in all that he does, as a servant of the public. The agent is treated as the person immediately accountable to the War Office'. Perhaps the best known agent was Richard Cox (1718-1803), the founder of Cox & Co, now Lloyds Bank (Cox's and King's Branch).

Army Air Corps The present Corps was established under Army Order 82 of 1957, although its origins can be traced back to the early days of the Second World War. In 1940 a Central Landing Establishment, consisting of No.1 Parachute Training School and No.1 Glider Training School was established. The demand for air reconnaissance and airborne artillery fire direction prompted the creation of an Air Observation Post Squadron, Royal Artillery, in 1941. Army Order 21 of 1942 established The Army Air Corps as an administrative and co-ordination centre for The Glider Pilot Regiment and The Parachute Regiment and, in 1944, the Special Air Service Regiment became the third regiment in the Corps. The Special Air Service Regiment was disbanded in 1946, reconstituted in 1947 and created as a separate corps by Army Order 66 of 1950. In 1949 The Parachute Regiment was transferred to the line infantry and, in 1950, The Army Air Corps was disbanded. In 1957 The Glider Pilot Regiment was disbanded and, in accordance with Army Order 82 of that year, The Army Air Corps was reformed to include the Air Observation Post Squadrons, Royal Artillery. The Corps has been a regular cadre since 1973.

Headdress Badge: A laurel wreath surmounted by the crown within the wreath, an eagle.

Regimental Marches:

Quick March: *Recce Flight.*

Slow March: *Thievish Magpie* and *Doges March.*

Corps Headquarters: Army Air Corps Centre, Middle Wallop, Nr Stockbridge, Hampshire, SO20 8DY.

History: *The Army in the Air* by Sir Anthony Farrar Hockley.

Army Benevolent Fund The fund was founded on 15 August 1944 under the patronage of King George VI in order to 'provide financial assistance to those organisations and benevolent funds, which already dealt with the needs of the soldier or service woman, commissioned or otherwise, whether serving or retired, and their dependents'. Up to that date individual corps and regiments had been, as they still in some measure are, responsible for the welfare of their serving and retired members, and their dependents. The heavy demands on regimental benevolence arising from the losses of the First World War placed huge strain on regimental funds and, late in the Second World War, it was realised that extra financial resources would be needed when the 4,500,000 men and women then in Army uniform returned to civilian life. Since its foundation the fund has worked in conjunction with corps and regimental benevolent institutions to help soldiers and ex-soldiers, and their families, when they are in real need and when state assistance is either inapplicable, inadequate, or unable to meet the immediate need in the appropriate time frame. The Head Office of the fund is at 41 Queen's Gate, London SW7 5HR.

Army Board Formally the Army Council (qv), the Army Board of the Defence Council was brought into effect on 1 April 1964 by Army Orders 21 and 22 of 1964. Current composition of the Army Board is: Secretary of State for Defence, Minister of State for the Armed Forces, Minister of State for Defence Procurement, Under Secretary of State for the Armed Forces, Chief of the General Staff, Second Permanent Under Secretary of State, Adjutant General, Quartermaster General, Master General of the Ordnance, Commander in Chief United Kingdom Land Forces, Commander UK Support Command (Germany) and Assistant Chief of the General Staff.

Army Cadet Force Although there is mention of James I being 'much taken with seeing little boys skirmish', and reference to a 'company of boys' in 1627, and a review of the 'Royal Juvenile Corps' by the Prince Regent in 1803, there appears to be no consecutive history. It was the formation of Volunteer Corps in 1859 which prompted the formation of cadet corps; Eton, Harrow, Rugby, Rossall and Hurstpierpoint being among the first to respond. Many Volunteer Corps also formed their own 'Cadet Companies'. Articles 279-286 of the 1863 Volunteer Regulations authorised the founding of Cadet Corps by Volunteer Battalions, the object being to provide military training for the young people. Between 1911 and 1921 there was a rapid rise in the number of cadet contingents. The Army Cadet Force became the responsibility of the War Office in April 1942 and is now well established on a county basis under a County Cadet Commandant who operates within the framework of the regional Territorial Army and Volunteer Reserve Association. Many of the contingents have strong links with regular Army regiments and corps. *See also: Combined Cadet Corps.*

Army Catering Corps Formed under Army Order 35 on 22 March 1941, the Corps provides catering services and advice to the Army. An Army School of Cookery was established at Aldershot in 1920, but until the formation of the Corps all cooks had been held on regimental establishments. In April 1993 the Corps became part of the Royal Logistic Corps (qv).
Headdress Badge: Within a circle inscribed 'Army Catering Corps' an ancient Grecian brazier, beneath a scroll bearing the motto *'We Sustain'*, the whole surmounted by a crown.
Regimental March: *Sugar and Spice.*
Headquarters: ACC Benevolence Trust, Dettingen House, The Princess Royal Barracks Blackdown, Deepcut, Camberley, Surrey GU16 6RW.
History: *The Story of the Army Catering Corps and its Predecessors* by H N Cole, published by the Army Catering Corps Association (1984) and *In Pursuit of Excellence* (50th Anniversary Edition of *Sustainer*) (1991).

Army Council The body, formed by letters patent on 10 August 1904, arising from a recommendation of the Esher (qv) Committee in 1903, for the direction of the Army. The original composition of the Army Council was: Secretary of State for War, Chief of the General Staff, Adjutant General, Quartermaster General, Master General of the Ordnance, Parliamentary Under Secretary of State, Financial Secretary of the War Office and the Secretary of the War Office. On 1 April 1964 the Army Council became the Army Board of the Defence Council, this being brought into effect by Army Orders 21 and 22 of 1964. *See also: Executive Committee of the Army Board.*

Army Department In April 1964 the War Office became the Army Department of the Ministry of Defence; the three single Service Ministries had been amalgamated to form a single Ministry of Defence under the Secretary of State for Defence, a Chief of the Defence Staff (broadly drawn from any of the Services) and a Joint Service Defence Council.

Army Field Manuals A series of manuals which form the core of tactical doctrine for the Army. *See: Doctrine.*

Army Group A land force formation consisting of two or more numbered armies.

Army Gymnastic Staff *See: Army Physical Training Corps.*

Army Kinema Corporation (AKC) Formed in March 1946, with a working capital of £435,000 provided by the Army Board from non-public funds at their disposal. The Corporation was required to: give technical advice and assistance with the production and acquisition of training films and filmstrips; maintain training and educational film libraries in all Commands; keep in repair the Army's projectors and train projectionists. During the war these functions had been performed by the Army (through the Directorate of Army Kinematography) and by the Department of National Service Entertainment (in conjunction with NAAFI). The name of the Corporation was changed to the Services Kinema Corporation (SKC) on 1 January 1969 and, on merging with the British Forces Broadcasting Service (BFBS), became The Services Sound and Vision Corporation (SSVC) on 13 May 1982. The needs of the Services and their dependents at home and abroad, and advances in technology, have significantly widened the roles and responsibilities of the Corporation: it now provides a wide range of communication services, including training and welfare services, radio and television broadcasting to the Forces and their families, the production and distribution of training films and videos for all three Services and the procurement and maintenance of training equipment.

Army of India Medal 1799–1826 Authorisation for the Honourable East India Company to issue this medal was notified in the London Gazette of 28 February 1851.
Ribbon: Light blue.
Clasps: Allighur; Battle of Delhi; Assaye; Asseerghur; Laswarree; Argaum; Gawilghur; Defence of Delhi; Battle of

Deig; Capture of Deig; Nepaul; Kirkee; Poona; Kirkee and Poona; Seetabuldee; Nagpore; Seetabuldee and Nagpore; Maheidpoor; Corygaum; Ava and Bhurtpoor.

Army Legal Corps Formed on 1 November 1978 from the Army Legal Staff. Under service law, members of the Corps provide legal advice to commanders and staff at all levels and prosecute in many cases brought for trial by Court Martial. Under civil law, the Corps also provides legal advice and assistance to members of the Army. On 6 April 1992, the Corps became the Army Legal Services Branch of the Adjutant General's Corps (qv).
Headdress Badge: The figure of Justice superimposed on the globe surmounted by the Royal Crest. Behind the Globe Crossed Swords with blades uppermost on a black background within a circle inscribed *'Justitia in Armis'.* On a scroll below 'Army Legal Corps'.
Regimental march: *Scales of Justice.*

Army Legal Services Branch Formed from the Army Legal Corps on 6 April 1992 as one of the four Branches of the Adjutant General's Corps. The duties, responsibilities, badge and regimental march of the Branch remained unchanged from those of the Army Legal Corps.
Headquarters: Directorate of Army Legal Services, Empress State Building, London SW6 1TR.

Army List The earliest printed army list of the standing army of which copies are known to exist is one of 1684 entitled 'A General and Compleat List Military of Every Commission Officer of Horse and Foot now commanding His Majesties Land-Forces in England excepting the unregimented companies'. This army list is known by the publisher's name as 'Nathan Brook's List'. The first official printed Army List was published in 1740 and, from 1754, the Army List was published annually without a break until 1878. Between 1798 and 1922 there were periods in which monthly, quarterly and half-yearly lists were published. The most famous of a number of 'unofficial' Army

Lists is that produced between 1839 and 1915 by Major H G Hart of the 49th Regiment and known as 'Hart's Army List'. The Army List is now published in three parts: Part I contains details of key appointments, headquarters and establishments, and lists by regiment and corps the officers of the British Active and Territorial Armies, regiment's insignia, battle honours, marches and mottoes being shown in full; Part II, an alphabetical list of non-effective officers in receipt of retired pay; and Part III, a biographical list, giving brief details of the service and qualifications of all serving officers.

Army Medal Office The Army Medal Office is an outstation of the Adjutant General's Department, and answerable in the first instance to the Director General Personnel Services (Army). The office is charged with all matters relating to the administration of medals for the whole of the Armed Forces, serving and discharged, and for upholding the integrity of medals and the esteem in which they are held. The formulation and publication of all policy on medals is however the responsibility of the Director Defence Personnel on the Central Staff of the Ministry of Defence. Originally based in London and known as AG4 (Medals), the branch moved to Cheltenham in June 1942, and subsequently to its present location in Droitwich in July 1943, taking its present title in April 1953. The first Officer-in-Charge of the Army Medal Office was Major H F C Lewin MBE, Royal Inniskilling Fusiliers, who as both a serving and a retired officer held the appointment for a remarkable 31 years.

Army News Services The first modern newssheets printed by and for the field army was the *Cologne Post*, first issued as a daily in March 1919. When the British Army moved to Wiesbaden the paper was re-established there as a bi-weekly and ceased publication in November 1929. In the Second World War, the earliest attempts to produce newspapers were in the western desert, where the *Eighth Army News* was published, and in Algeria where the First Army started *Union Jack*. *Circle News*, later known as *Crown News*, was produced for Commonwealth troops in the Korean theatre. Numerous publications now exist at unit, formation and garrison level but, with the wide availability of radio receivers, responsibility for the transmission of news was gradually transferred to the broadcasting services such as the British Forces Broadcasting Service.

Army Personnel Research Establishment (APRE) The establishment evolved from a number of earlier research units, the history of which dates from the early days of the Second World War. With the founding of the Directorate of Medical Research in 1942 it was redesignated the Directorate of Biological Research in December 1942, though it was still under the aegis of the Director General Army Medical Services. Between 1943 and 1965 the establishment was subject to a number of changes of title and the attachment and detachment of specialist teams to and from other organisations to meet the demands of specific studies. On 1 April 1965 APRE was formally established with its own director, responsible to the Chief Scientist (Army), through the Director of Army Operational Science and Research, with its headquarters at Farnborough, but with some physiologists, and most of the psychologists, still at West Byfleet. Although primarily concerned in its early days with purely medical problems, involvement in matters of military efficiency and tactics grew rapidly. The Establishment's current role is to advise the Army on how to make best use, in peace and war, of its most valuable resource - its men and women. This includes study of such areas as: selection and retention; protection against the environment; man-systems integration and optimising the individual's performance. On 1 April 1994 APRE merged with the Institute of Aviation Medecine and other teams and individuals from within the Ministry of Defence to form the Centre for Human Sciences (CHS), part of the Defence Research Agency, having three main departments: Aeromedecine and Neuroscience; Physiological Sciences and Psychological Sciences.

Army Physical Training Corps Formed after the Crimean War as The Army Physical Training Staff (Army Gymnastic Staff 1860-1918), the title was changed to The Army Physical Training Corps by Army Order 165 of 1940. The Corps trains all physical training instructors for the Army and provides supervision, instruction and advice for all sports, physical training and adventure (or arduous) training.

Headdress Badge: Crossed swords surmounted by a crown.

Regimental march: *Be Fit* (words from *Land and Sea Tales* by Kipling).

Corps Headquarters: The Army School of Physical Training, Queen's Avenue, Aldershot, Hampshire, GU11 2LB.

History: *History of the Army Physical Training Corps* by E A L Oldfield (1955).

Army Postal Service The origins of the Army Postal Service date back to the 17th century. In 1799 the Commander-in-Chief asked the Postmaster-General to provide an 'intelligent clerk' to accompany the Army to Europe to 'facilitate delivery and to collect letters'. Happily, such a man was found and appointed to the task. It was not until the Peninsula War (qv) that a properly organised Army postal service was established, with an office in Lisbon. In 1882 Queen Victoria authorised the raising of the Army Postal Corps, and a detachment of this Corps served with the expeditionary force in the Egyptian campaign. In 1884 a second Army Postal Corps was formed with the title 'The Royal Engineers Telegraph Reserve'; a forerunner of the Royal Corps of Signals. In 1908 the Army Postal Corps and the Telegraph Reserve amalgamated to form the Royal Engineers Postal Section, which supported the Army throughout the First and Second World Wars. The Postal and Courier Service now serves all three Services and is known as the Defence Postal and Courier Service; with the Postal and Courier Depot at Mill Hill, through which all mail for the British Forces Post Offices (BFPOs) all over the world is processed.

History: *Mailshot, A History of the Forces Postal Service* by E Wells (1987) and *History of The British Army Postal Service* (3 Vols.) by E S Proud.

Army Recruiter Originally regiments were responsible for their own recruiting, but after the First World War the task was carried out by 'Paid Pensioner Recruiters' who bore a badge with the letters PPR. In 1933 the title was changed to 'Army Recruiter', a title which was worn on the shoulder. Army Recruiters may now be identified by the wearing of two crossed Union Colours on the upper sleeve.

Army Rifle Association The Association was founded in 1893 through the amalgamation of the existing regimental rifle matches, introduced in 1874, and the Army VIII Club, which had been formed in the same year to select a Regular Army team to compete in the inter-Service National Rifle Association (qv) matches. The object was to promote interest in small arms shooting and evolve practices and standards which would lead to improved effectiveness on the battlefield. Figure targets were first used in 1908, matches were first fired on electric target ranges in 1974 and night shooting matches were introduced in 1982. The Association's main annual event is the Regular Army Skill-at-Arms Meeting, which embraces the objectives of both the inter-regimental matches of 1874 and the Army VIII Club matches. Until 4 July 1974 the Association was maintained by individual and unit subscriptions but, on 5 July 1974, through an Army Board decision, the Association became an official body, and individual and unit subscriptions ceased from 1 January 1975. The secretariat is now at the Headquarters of the Royal Logistic Corps Training Centre, Princess Royal Barracks, Blackdown, but the staff are held on the strength of the Small Arms Wing, School of Infantry.

Army Transition To War Measures Measures designed to bring the Army progressively from its peacetime strength, organisation, equipment and deployment to a full war footing.

Arnhem 1944 Second World War battle honour commemorating the attempt by 1st Airborne Division to capture the bridges over the River Nederrijn at Arnhem in the

course of Operation MARKET GAR-
DEN. A poor appreciation resulted in
British troops being dropped too far from
their objectives and facing heavier than
anticipated opposition. Part of 2nd
Parachute Battalion reached the main road
bridge and held there for 72 hours before
being overwhelmed; the remainder of the
force consolidated in the area of
Oosterbeek and held there until it was clear
that relief columns would not reach them,
and then withdrew by night across the
river. Only some 25 per cent of the
Division was recovered. *See also: North West
Europe 1944-45; Nederrijn; Nijmegen; Veghel
and Best.*

Arnhem 1945 Second World War battle
honour marking the crossing of the River
Nederrijn and capture of Arnhem by 49th
Division during the final advance into
Holland. *See also: North West Europe 1944-
45; Scheldt; Aam; Lower Maas; Meijel; Venlo
Pocket and Roer.*

Arquebus A simple matchlock gun, forerunner of the modern rifle, carrying a solid
bullet in a cylindrical barrel, and accurate
out to about 50m. Those of the earliest
construction were fired by a 'match' from
the touch hole. They were first fired from a
forked monopod rest at the height of the
chest, but the Germans invented a hooked
form of butt, and elevated the barrel. In
1486 Henry VII ordered that half the royal
guard be armed with arquebuses and, with
slight changes in lock action, calibre and
length of barrel, this simple form of
matchlock arquebus or musket endured in
the British Army until 1680. *See also:
Flintlock; Matchlock and Rifle.*

Arracan Distinction conferred in 1825 by
the Governor-General in Council on the
Bengal native regiments which took part in
the invasion of the ancient kingdom of
Arracan in the First Burma War (1824-
26).

Arras 1917 First World War battle honour
marking the British offensive at Arras
launched by General Allenby's Third Army
and the Canadian Corps of First Army on
9 April 1917 on a front extending 14 miles

southwards from Vimy Ridge. Fighting
continued until 4 May. *See also: France and
Flanders 1914-18; Vimy 1917; Scarpe 1917
and Arleux.*

Arras 1918 First World War battle honour
marking two separate battles during the
Somme offensive of 1918. The first was an
unsuccessful German attempt to extend
their offensive against the northern sector
of the Third Army. The second was the
third phase of the successful British
autumn offensives, launched on 26 August
1918 by First Army. *See also: France and
Flanders 1914-18; Somme 1918; St Quentin;
Bapaume 1918; Rosières; Avre and Ancre
1918.*

Arras Counter Attack Second World War
battle honour awarded for an action during
the campaign of 1940 in North-West
Europe. *See also: North West Europe 1940;
Amiens 1940; French Frontier 1940; Forêt de
Nieppe; Withdrawal to Seine and Withdrawal
to Cherbourg.*

Arrest A person subject to military law
found committing, alleged to have committed or reasonably suspected of having
committed an offence against the Army
Act 1955 may be arrested. Two types of
arrest exist: open arrest, where the accused
is normally free to carry out his duties; and
close arrest, where the accused is confined.
Except under exceptional circumstances an
accused may not be held in open or close
arrest for more than 72 consecutive days
without a court martial being convened.

Arroyo Dos Molinos Peninsula War battle honour awarded in 1845 for the seizure
of the town of Arroyos dos Molinos from
the French on 28 October 1811 by a force
under the command of General Hill. *See
also: Peninsula; Albuhera; Tarifa; Ciudad
Rodrigo and Badajoz.*

Arsenal An establishment where arms or
equipment are manufactured, or a reposi-
tory or magazine of arms and military
stores. An arsenal of the premier or first
class included gun and carriage factories,
laboratories, ammunition and small arms
factories, powder factory and spacious

stores. Vulnerability to attack, and the fact that weapons and equipment were increasingly produced by private companies, led to the dispersal and ultimate closure of arsenals in Britain.

***Arte Et Marte* (By Skill and by Fighting)** Motto of The Corps of Royal Electrical and Mechanical Engineers.

Articles of War Ordinances or Articles of War for the maintenance of military discipline were issued by the Sovereign, or a commander authorised by the Sovereign, at the beginning of each campaign. Such articles were usually read to all ranks at the beginning of a campaign, but bound them only for the duration of hostilities. The earliest now extant articles are those by Richard I in a charter of 1189 for the guidance and observation of those going to the Holy Land. Until the passing of the first Mutiny Act (qv) in 1789 these were the only ordinances regulating the governance of troops, and in times of peace acts such as desertion or disobedience were only liable to the civil law as breaches of contraft. The issuing of Articles of War was a Crown prerogative which was not removed by the first Mutiny Act, but was superseded in 1803 by statutory power to be found in Section 69 of the Army Act of 1881 and subsequent Army Acts. It is therefore unlikely that the power to issue Articles of War will be exercised again.

Artificer Over the years the term artificer has embraced many trades, the wheelwright and carpenter being identifiable in the mid-19th century by the wearing of a wheel badge. Ordnance artificers wore a badge of hammer and pincers as well as the wheel. In 1944 the 'A', 'B', 'C' and 'D' trade groups replaced the hammer and pincers badge except in the Royal Artillery.

Artillery A general term applied to weapons which fire explosive projectiles exceeding small arms calibre (20mm), rockets and short range ballistic missiles. The term is also used to describe those units of the Army equipped with such weapons. *See also: Royal Regiment of Artillery.*

Artists' Rifles Formed in 1859 as a volunteer corps by the eminent painter Lord Leighton PRA, the regiment's first Colonel, and other professional men. In 1881 it was attached to The Rifle Brigade, but in 1908 it was grouped with other London corps in the Territorial Army as the 28th Battalion of the County of London Regiment (Artists' Rifles), returning to The Rifle Brigade in 1937. Under Army Order 78 of 1947, it was transferred from 'P' Corps of Infantry to the Army Air Corps as 21st Battalion, Special Air Service Regiment (Artists Rifles)(TA) and subsequently became 21st Special Air Service Regiment (Artists' Rifles).
Headdress Badge: The original capbadge with the heads of Mars and Minerva in profile, symbolising the conjunction in the regiment of the Arts and War, with a scroll below inscribed 'ARTISTS', has been superseded by the Special Air Service Regiment cap badge.

Artlenberg Second World War battle honour marking one of the actions during the period between the crossing of the River Rhine and the end of the campaign in Europe. *See also: North West Europe 1944-45; Lingen; Bentheim; Dreirwalde; Uelzen and Twente Canal.*

AS90 Self-propelled gun, manufactured by Vickers Shipbuilding and Engineering Ltd, currently in service, having replaced the Abbot (qv) and M109 (qv) guns in the early 1990s. The gun is of 155mm calibre with a range of some 24km and has a crew of five. The gun is fitted with an Autonomous Navigation and Gun Laying System (AGLS), enabling it to work independently of external sighting references. A Turret Control Computer (TCC) controls the main turret functions, including gun laying, magazine control, loading systems, power distribution and testing.

Ascension Island British island, of volcanic origin, situated in the South Atlantic. The US built an airfield on the island in 1942 which is now used as a staging post by the Royal Air Force. This facility proved vital as a staging post in the operation to liberate the Falkland Islands from Argentine forces in 1982.

Ashantee 1873-74 Battle honour marking service in the expeditionary force under Sir Garnet Wolseley to end the unacceptable torture and hardship inflicted by the Ashantee monarch on the West Coast of Africa during the Ashantee War (1873-74).

Ashantee War Medal 1873-1874 Authorised on 1 June 1870.
Ribbon: 1" wide, yellow with black borders and two thin black stripes down the centre.
Clasp: Coomassie.

Ashanti 1900 Battle honour marking the expedition to relieve the Residency at Kumasi (Coomassie) during the rebellion in Ashantee in 1900.

Ashanti Medal 1900 Sanctioned in October 1901 for issue to men of the Ashanti Field Force.
Ribbon: Dark green with a vertical black stripe 4mm wide on each edge and at the centre.
Clasp: Kumassi.

Ashanti Star 1896 Issued to mark service in the 2,000-strong Ashanti expedition of December 1895 to January 1896.
Ribbon: Yellow, with a black stripe 2mm from each edge.

Ashplant A stout stick, carried by officers of The Royal Tank Regiment (qv). This custom has its origin in the early days of the tank when officers used such sticks to 'prove' the route to be taken by tanks.

Assam Battle honour marking service on the north-east frontier of India during the First Burma War (1824-26).

Assam Light Infantry, 1st Raised at Orissa as the Cuttack Legion in 1817. Became 6th Gurkha Rifles in 1903 and, since 1959 known as 6th Queen Elizabeth's Own Gurkha Rifles (qv).

Assault Boat Light craft, powered by motor or paddles, used in river crossing and amphibious operations. Assault boats should be of such a size and weight that they can be manhandled by the crew.

Assault Pioneer Infantry soldier trained to undertake field engineering tasks. It is the custom in many infantry regiments for the assault pioneer sergeant to be bearded. The specialisation is indicated by the wearing of crossed axes, or hatchets, on the sleeve.

Assault Vehicle Royal Engineers (AVRE) A tracked vehicle, based upon a tank chassis, with a gun for destroying bunkers and similar fortified positions. Capable of carrying fascines or towing a Giant Viper for minefield clearance. Usually fitted with a mine plough and/or dozer blade. The current Centurion-based AVRE is obsolescent and is to be replaced by the Armoured Vehicle Royal Engineers (AVRE), based on a Chieftain chassis.

Assaye Battle honour marking the action by Sir Arthur Wellesley (qv) in the First Maratha War (1803-5) (qv) when he defeated Scindia's finest troops on 23 September 1803. *See also: Ally Ghur; Delhi 1803; Leswarree and Deig.*

Assaye Regiment Nickname for the 74th Foot; later 2nd Battalion The Highland Light Infantry; now part of The Royal Highland Fusiliers (Princess Margaret's Own Glasgow and Ayrshire Regiment). The regiment distinguished itself at the battle of Assaye (1803) when 2,000 British and 2,500 Sepoy troops under Wellesley defeated 50,000 Mahrattas.

Assembly Area Area, usually offering some concealment, in which a command is assembled preparatory to further action.

Asten Second World War battle honour marking an action which took place between the crossing of the River Seine and the arrival on the River Rhine. *See also: North West Europe 1944-45; Heppen; Calais 1944 and Opheusden.*

Astrakhan Tightly curled black fur, usually lambskin, used for trimming officers' frock-coats.

Atbara Battle honour marking the action on 8 April 1898 by the army under Sir Herbert Kitchener, a preliminary to his advance up the River Nile and reconquest of the Sudan. Following a night approach march a frontal attack was launched on a Mahdist (qv) position on the River Atbara. The Mahdists were routed after intense hand-to-hand fighting. *See also: Hafir and Khartoum.*

Athens British troops were landed in Greece in October 1944 to prevent chaos and a communist takeover as the Germans withdrew. Civil war started with street fighting in Athens on 2 December 1944. The battle honour 'Athens' marks the actions leading to the clearing of the city and Attica of communist forces which was complete by 15 January 1945. *See also: Greece 1944-45.*

Atholl Grey Shade of grey used for the greatcoats and capes of the Foot Guards.

Atkins, Thomas (Tommy) Nickname for the British soldier; more properly 'Tommy' as in the opening poem of Rudyard Kipling's 'Barrack Room Ballads' (1892). The precise origin of the nickname is not known but the term was certainly used in correspondence from Jamaica in 1743. The name was later used in a specimen entry in an official handbook issued by the War Office (qv) after the Napoleonic Wars. There seems to be no convincing evidence that the name was that of an identifiable individual, though the theory has been advanced that a soldier of that name was mortally wounded under Wellington, then a subaltern, when serving in Holland, and that many years later the Duke, when Secretary of State, recalling the soldier's stoicism, adopted the name in an army form. The sobriquet is never associated with officers. *See also: Jock and Tom.*

Attaché An officer attached to an embassy or legation whose duties are to advise the ambassador, or minister, on Service matters, and to make himself familiar with the defence conditions of the country in which he is serving. If representing solely the army interest his title will be military attaché; if representing the interests of all three Services it will be defence attaché.

Attack There are three broad types of attack: the hasty or 'quick' attack where speed is needed to exploit an opportunity, the deliberate attack and infiltration.

Attestation Part of the enlistment procedure designed to protect the interests of both the Army and the individual seeking enlistment. The attestation procedure is set out in the First Schedule to the Army Act 1955.

Attrition A strategy or operational method whereby the enemy is defeated by the cumulative destruction of his forces rather than by manoeuvre, disruption and demoralisation.

Aubers First World War battle honour marking the launching, on 9 May 1915, of a British attack in the Neuve Chapelle sector with the object of capturing Aubers Ridge. Three separate assaults were mounted and all repulsed with heavy losses. *See also: France and Flanders 1914-18.*

Auchinleck, Sir Claude John Eyre (1884-1981) Born Ulster and educated at Wellington College. Served in Egypt 1914-15 and elsewhere in the Middle East during the First World War. Commander-in-Chief in India in the early part of the Second World War, becoming Commander-in-Chief Middle East following Wavell (qv) in July 1941. On 18 November 1941 Auchinleck launched an offensive which captured Sidi Rezegh, relieved Tobruk and recaptured Benghazi on 24 December 1941. However, the offensive failed to carry the German defensive line at El Agheila, and a German counter-offensive threw it back to Gazala and, after a few months, Rommel attacked, Tobruk fell and the British withdrew to El Alamein. Auchinleck was succeeded by Montgomery and became Commander-in-Chief India for the second time, being instrumental in the successful provision of support for the campaign in Burma. Promoted to Field Marshal on 1 June

1946, he retired shortly after Indian independence.

***Aucto Splendore Resurgo* (I rise again with renewed splendour)** Motto of 85th King's Light Infantry and later of The King's Shropshire Light Infantry. Now one of the mottoes of The Light Infantry.

Audenarde *See: Oudenarde.*

Auftragstaktik A form of decentralized command and control developed by the German army in the 18th century, in which commanders are given brief 'mission orders' which define the objective to be achieved, the resources available and the time limit. The method of execution is left to the commander.

Augusta Second World War Sicilian campaign battle honour. *See also: Sicily 1943; Landing in Sicily; Primosole Bridge; Sferro; Regalbuto and Centuripe.*

Auld Robin Gray Regimental slow march of The Duke of Edinburgh's Royal Regiment (Berkshire and Wiltshire).

Auprès De Ma Blonde A regimental quick march of the Corps of Royal Electrical and Mechanical Engineers.

Auster The Auster Mark 1 light aircraft came into service with the Army in 1939 as an Air Observation Post and liaison aircraft. Later Marks were taken into service as follows: Mark 3 (1942); Marks 4 and 5 (1944); Mark 6 (1945) and Mark 9 (1957). The Auster remained in service until 1966.

Austrian Cap A folding cap, with two large side flaps, which could be worn up or down in bad weather. The Foot Guards wore a cap of this type in the Crimean War (1854-55) and, in 1880, it was introduced as an 'active service and peace manoeuvres cap' (qv).

Austrian Knot An elaborate cord knot of Austrian origin, also known as a Tyrolean Knot', worn on the sleeves. Taken into wear by the British Army in the 19th century.

Austrian Succession, War of (1740-48) Charles VI of Austria wished to leave all his hereditary dominions to his daughter, Maria Theresa, and so he persuaded nearly all the great European powers to accept an arrangement called the 'Pragmatic Sanction' which bound them to uphold her claim. However, on the death of Charles VI, Frederick II of Prussia seized Silesia, the Elector of Bavaria claimed Austria, and both France and Spain sided with the latter. Only England and Hanover stood by the 'Pragmatic Sanction' against France, Prussia and Bavaria. George II defeated the French at Dettingen (qv) in 1744 and the English and their allies were defeated at Fontenoy in 1745. The French sought to create further difficulties for the English by supporting the Jacobite rebellion of 1745. The war ended with the Peace of Aix-la-Chapelle whereby there was a mutual restitution of conquests (except for Silesia which was retained by Prussia), Maria Theresa's husband, Francis of Lorraine, was acknowledged Emperor, France acknowledged the Protestant succession in England and the Pretender was expelled from France.

***Aut Cursu, Aut Cominus Armis* (Either in the Charge or Hand to Hand)** Motto of 16th/5th The Queen's Royal Lancers and 16th The Queen's Lancers.

Authenticate/ion Method used to ensure that the originator or recipient of a signal or instruction is in fact authorised to transmit or receive such a message.

Authorised Commander The officer empowered to authorise the firing of a reserved demolition.

Autogyro A rotary-winged aircraft which has a free-turning rotor to provide lift and a propeller for lateral movement. A number of autogyros were trialled by the Army, notably the R2 Revoplane (1930), Cierva C30 (1934) and Type WA116 (1962), but were never taken into service by the Army.

Auxiliary Territorial Service The Women's Army Auxiliary Corps (WAAC) had been formed in 1917 to perform non-combatant duties behind the lines in

France. Renamed the Queen Mary's Army Auxiliary Corps in 1918, it was disbanded the following year. In 1938 it became clear that a women's service would again be needed and the Auxiliary Territorial Service (ATS) was formed under Royal Warrant dated 9 September 1938 (Army Order 199/38), giving valuable service in most Second World War theatres. Twenty thousand ATS worked in cookhouses, 30,000 were office, mess and telephone orderlies, 14,000 were drivers, 10,000 were postal workers and some 9,000 were employed in stores and depots. Others served as butchers, bakers, ammunition inspectors, military police, gun crews and in many operational support tasks. The remaining cadre of the ATS was incorporated into the Women's Royal Army Corps (WRAC) (qv) when it formed in 1949.

History: *Britain's Own Army, The Story of the ATS* by E Bigland (1946); *Women in Uniform* by D C Wadge (1947); *No Thoughts Survive* by L Whately (1949); *Daughters of Britain* by V Douie (1949) and *The Auxiliary Territorial Service 1939-45* by J M Cowper (1949).

Ava (1825) Battle honour awarded over the period 1826-41 in recognition of service in the long and arduous First Burma War (1824-26).

Ava (1945) Second World War Burma campaign battle honour marking operations over the period 13 February to 20 March 1945 in the Battle of Mandalay which resulted in the capture of Ava by the 2nd British Division, after crossing the Irrawaddy west of Sagging. *See also: Burma 1942-45; Mandalay; Myitson; Myinmu Bridgehead; Fort Dufferin and Maymyo.*

Avre First World War battle honour marking one of the actions in the First Battle of the Somme 21 March - 3 September 1918 in which a stand was made which finally held the German advance. *See also: France and Flanders 1914-18; Somme 1918; St Quentin; Bapaume 1918; Rosières; Arras 1918 and Ancre 1918.*

Awash Second World War Abyssinian campaign battle honour. *See also: Abyssinia*

1940-41; Keren; Jebel Defeis; Jebel Shiba; Gogni; Agordat; Barentu; Karora-Marsa Taclai; Cubcub; Ad Teclesan; Mescelit Pass; Mt Engiahat; Massawa; Amb Alagi; Gambela; El Wak; Moyale; Wal Garis; Juba; Marda Pass; Babile Gap; Bisidimo; Afodu; Todenyang-Namaraputh; Soroppa; Giarso; Colito; Wadara; Omo; Gondar; Fike and Lechemti.

Axe On ceremonial occasions the farriers of cavalry regiments, especially of the Household Cavalry, carry axes. In the infantry, assault pioneers may carry felling axes on ceremonial occasions. A badge depicting crossed axes, or hatchets, is worn on the sleeve of all qualified assault pioneers.

Axis Second World War alliance between Italy, Germany and Japan, known as the Rome-Berlin-Tokio axis.

Axis of Advance A line of advance assigned for the purpose of control; often a road, a group of roads or a designated series of locations extending in the direction of the enemy.

Ayrshire Yeomanry (The Earl of Carrick's Own) Although it may well have been in existence earlier, it was not until 1798 that the Carrick Troop was accepted for service and, by 1803, there were three troops and the title Ayrshire Yeomanry Cavalry appeared. In 1817 two regiments were formed and with the Lanarkshire Yeomanry the regiments formed the 17th Company of 6th Battalion Imperial Yeomanry, for service in South Africa (1899-1902). In the First World War the regiment fought at Gallipoli (1915) and later dismounted, as 12th (Ayr and Lanark Yeomanry) Battalion of The Royal Scots Fusiliers, in Egypt, Palestine and France. The Ayrshire Yeomanry was re-formed as a cavalry regiment and in 1940 converted to artillery as 151st and 152nd (Ayrshire Yeomanry) Field Regiments Royal Artillery. In 1947 the regiment re-formed as an armoured regiment in the armoured delivery role. In 1961 two squadrons were converted to a reconnaissance role and the successor sub-unit is now 'A' (Ayrshire (Earl of Carrick's Own) Yeomanry) Squadron of The Scottish Yeomanry.

'B' The letter 'B' on arm badges in the British Army was used to indicate 'B' group tradesmen from 1944 onward.

'B' Vehicle Generic term used to describe all soft skinned vehicles. *See also: 'A' and 'C' vehicles.*

Babile Gap Second World War Abyssinian campaign battle honour marking the removal of an enemy position on the route to Harar during the period 23-25 March 1941, after the forcing of the Marda Pass. *See also: Abyssinia 1940-41; Keren; Jebel Defeis; Jebel Shiba; Gogni; Agordat; Barentu; Karora-Marsa Taclai; Cubcub; Ad Teclesan; Mescelit Pass; Mt Engiahat; Massawa; Amb Alagi; Afodu; Gambela; El Wak; Moyale; Wal Garis; Juba; Marda Pass; Bisidimo; Awash; Todenyang-Namaraputh; Omo; Soroppa; Giarso; Colito; Wadara; Gondar; Fike and Lechemti.*

Backing Black or coloured cloth sometimes worn behind headdress badges or badges of rank. This may be traditional, or for purely aesthetic reasons. A system of colour coded backing was used from 1940 until the end of the Second World War to identify arm of service. *See also: Arm of Service Strip.*

Back Loading Point Point to which damaged vehicles and equipment are brought from the forward areas and collected before subsequent transfer to repair facilities in the rear.

Badajoz Peninsula War battle honour marking the siege and assault by Wellington of Badajoz, the Spanish fortress covering the southern route into Spain. After a three week siege in April 1812, a number of unsuccessful night attacks were mounted on the two main breaches which had been mined by the defenders and caused heavy British losses. After attacks by the 3rd and 5th Divisions the town fell. *See also: Peninsula; Tarifa; Ciudad Rodrigo; Almaraz; Salamanca and Vittoria.*

Badara Battle honour awarded to the Royal Munster Fusiliers for the action on 25 November 1759 when a force under Colonel Forde defeated the Dutch near Chinsura in Bengal, thus ending any Dutch threat to the British position in India. *See also: Masulipatam and Wandewash.*

Baden-Powell, Robert Stephenson Smith, Baron Baden-Powell of Gilwell (1857-1941) Born in London, educated at Charterhouse. Commissioned into 13th Hussars (1876) with which he served in India, Afghanistan, and South Africa. Assistant Military Secretary in South Africa (1887-9) and in Malta (1890-93); commander of the native levies in Ashanti (1895); served with distinction in the Matabele campaign (1896-97); appointed to the command of 5th Dragoon Guards (1895). In the Boer War he won great popularity through his brilliant defence of Mafeking; in spite of famine and sickness, with a force of 1,200 men he held the town for 215 days until its relief on 18 May 1900. In recognition of his ability he was raised to the rank of Major General and Inspector-General of the South African Constabulary (1900); and later Inspector-General of the cavalry (1903-7). Always interested in the welfare of young people, he had written, some years before his retirement from the Army in 1910, his *Aids to Scouting*, which was widely read by young people and led to the first experimental Boy Scout camp on Brownsea Island, Poole Harbour, in 1907. This was so successful that the movement developed rapidly into an international organisation, and a parallel movement for girls, the Girl Guides, was raised in 1910. In the Boy Scout movement he was Chief Scout. He was knighted in 1909 and raised to the peerage in 1929.

Badges Distinguishing marks, produced in a variety of materials, to denote such things as regiment, corps, formation, ranks, trades appointments, proficiency, specialisation, wounds or long service.

Baghdad First World War Mesopotamia campaign battle honour marking actions which took place during the six weeks after the fall of Baghdad on 11 March 1917, when clearance operations were mounted by the British along the Tigris and Euphrates rivers. *See also: Mesopotamia 1914-1918; Basra; Shaiba; Kut Al Amara 1915; Ctesiphon; Defence of Kut Al Amara; Tigris 1916; Kut Al Amara 1917; Khan Baghdadi and Sharqat.*

Baghdad 1941 Second World War battle honour marking one of the actions against the Iraqis in May 1941 following their attack on the RAF base at Habbaniya. *See also: Iraq 1941; Defence of Habbaniya and Falluja.*

Bagpipe Badge worn on the right arm to signify a person qualified to play either the Scottish or Irish pipes, the latter having one less drone. It was not until 16 March 1949 that such badges were approved, although pipers had existed in the Army since the 17th century.

Bailey The external wall of a castle, also the outer court (the space immediately within the outer wall). When there are two courts they are distinguished as the inner and outer bailey.

Bailey Bridge A temporary bridge made

of prefabricated parts to permit rapid assembly. Named after its inventor, Sir Donald Coleman Bailey (1901-85).

Bailleul First World War battle honour marking one of the defensive actions during the German offensive of 9 April 1918, in which the Germans captured Armentières, Bailleul and the Messines and Kemmel ridges. The offensive was finally halted on 29 April, the Germans having suffered heavy casualties. *See also: France and Flanders 1914-18; Lys; Estaires; Messines 1918; Hazebrouck; Kemmel; Béthune and Scherpenberg.*

Baker Rifle Flintlock, muzzle-loader of 0.625" calibre adopted in 1800 and used by the 'Experimental Corps of Riflemen'. It was the first rifled weapon accepted for British military service. *See also: Flintlock; Matchlock; Musket and Rifle.*

Baku First World War Persian campaign battle honour marking the actions in August 1918 by a British brigade which had been sent to the Caucasus to prevent the Turks seizing the Baku oilfields. The brigade defended Baku for three weeks until, heavily outnumbered, it withdrew. *See also: Persia 1915-19 and Merv.*

Balaclava Type of knitted cap, rather like a close fitting hood over the head and neck, but open at the face. No doubt having its origin in the Crimean War, but also very popular in the First World War. A variant, with the face closed but leaving holes for the eyes and mouth, is much favoured by special forces to avoid individuals being identified during an operation.

Balaklava Crimean War battle honour marking the action against the Turks and Russians in and around the town of Balaklava on 25 October 1854 including the 'Charge of the Light Brigade', later immortalised by Tennyson. *See also: Alma; Inkerman and Sevastopol.*

Balaklava Regimental quick march of The Light Dragoons, and formerly the regimental quick march of 13th/18th Royal Hussars (Queen Mary's Own).

Baldric Broad belt worn over the shoulder to support a sword. More usually of leather, but sometimes of cloth and heavily embroidered or otherwise embellished.

Ball Buttons Spherical buttons worn by hussars, riflemen, horse artillery and some yeomanry regiments.

Ball-Tuft A ball of wool or cotton worn from 1829 on a shako. Ball-tufts were of varying colours to denote regiments, corps, companies or other special distinctions. Traditionally the colours were white and red for battalion companies, white for grenadier companies and green for light companies. *See also: Plumes and Hackles.*

Ballistic Missile Missile that follows a ballistic trajectory.

Balloons Hydrogen-filled balloons were used for military purposes by Napoleon in 1794 and rapidly became an accepted vehicle for military observation. Two Royal Engineer officers, Captains Grover and Beaumont, who had gained their experience of ballooning with civilian balloonists in the 1860s, sought between 1862 and 1873 to persuade the War Office of the military potential of balloons. Aware of the French successes, the War Office formed an establishment at Woolwich to develop military ballooning in 1878. Captains Templer and Lee were given £150 and appointed to construct a balloon to be called *Pioneer*, a task which they completed in 1880. The balloon centre was moved from Woolwich to Chatham in 1882, where it became the School of Ballooning, part of the School of Military Engineering. In 1890 the Balloon Section and Depot - the first air unit in the British Army - was formed at Chatham and moved to Aldershot in 1891-92. Balloons were deployed in Bechuanaland, the Sudan, the South Africa War (1899-1902) and, as observation balloons, in the early months of the First World War. However, it had become obvious with the success of the Zeppelin airship that the development of a power-driven aircraft was imminent. Recently there has been renewed interest in the use of balloons and airships as an inexpensive, stable and silent platform on which to mount surveillance devices in anti-terrorist operations. *See also: Airships.*

Balmoral Bonnet worn by Scottish regiments. It was usually blue in colour, but a drab variant was produced during the First World War.

Baltic Medal 1854-1855 Primarily for officers and men of the Royal Navy who had served in the Baltic from March 1854 until the blockade was lifted in August 1855; the medal was also awarded to about 100 Royal Sappers and Miners who served in HM Ships.
Ribbon: Yellow, 1" wide, with pale blue edges.

Baluchistan 1915-16 Battle honour marking actions to suppress disturbances which took place in the area to the south of the North-West Frontier, in the Kalat district of Baluchistan. *See also: Baluchistan 1918.*

Baluchistan 1918 Battle honour marking actions against the Marri and Khetran tribesmen in Baluchistan. *See also: Baluchistan 1915-16.*

Banana Ridge Second World War North Africa campaign battle honour marking an action in late April 1943 during the latter stages of the North African campaign. *See also: North Africa 1940-43; Heidous; Djebel Djaffa Pass and Argoub el Megas.*

Band The 'Band of Music' introduced into regiments and corps in the 18th century was non-combatant, unlike the drums, bugles and pipes. The band wore special dress, paid for by the colonel of the regiment or from a band fund subscribed by the officers, and usually numbered no more than eight men. Many foreigners were recruited as musicians, particularly Germans, and their dress tended to be colourful and elaborate. Early in the 18th century a custom was introduced in to the Army of employing blacks to play the drums, cymbals and similar instruments. These so-called 'Black-a-Moors' or 'Sables' were often dressed in fantastic Turkish or pseudo-oriental uniforms. At the end of the 18th century Foot Guards had special time-beating groups with drums, cymbals, tambourines and often a 'Jingling Johnny'. It is known that the 4th Dragoons had six black musicians as early as 1715. In 1830 bands were officially ordered to wear white with regimental facings and this slowly gave way to the wearing of ceremonial or levee dress of the regiment concerned. Although musicians may originally have worn a special band badge or plate on shakos, this was replaced by a badge showing crossed trumpets and a harp, which was worn on the sleeve. In due course this too was replaced by the present badge - a Greek lyre.

Banda Battle honour awarded following the capture of the Banda Islands in the Moluccas in 1796 and again in 1810.

Bandmaster In the earliest days civilians were employed as bandmasters to military bands. Although the uniform of bandmasters was more elaborate than that of the bandsmen it was not until the end of the 19th century that they wore the undress uniform of an officer, but without rank markings. By the turn of the century bandmasters were beginning to be of commissioned rank and wore officers' dress with the band badge on the lower right arm. A bandmaster may now be a warrant officer or senior non-commissioned officer in charge of a military band. He is fully responsible for all members of the band and particularly for the development of their military and musical skills. It is usual for the bandmaster to be answerable to a senior regimental officer, known as the Band President.

Bandolier/Bandoleer A belt, usually designed to be worn over the shoulder, which contains a number of small pockets or loops for cartridges or clips of ammunition.

Bangalore Torpedo An explosive device contained in long metal tubes, which can be joined together to produce any desired length, used for blowing gaps in barbed wire barriers.

Banyo First World War Cameroon campaign battle honour marking the taking of Banyo, which held a pocket of German troops, on 6 November 1915. *See also: Cameroons 1914-16; Duala and Garua.*

Bapaume 1917 First World War battle honour marking actions in March 1917 when the Germans, having withdrawn from the salient they had established just north of the Somme battlefields to new positions on the Hindenburg Line, fought a series of stout rearguard actions, particularly around Bapaume, with British troops engaged in follow-up operations. *See also: France and Flanders 1914-18; Arras 1917; Messines 1917 and Ypres 1917.*

Bapaume 1918 First World War battle honour marking two distinct battles during the Battle of the Somme in 1918. The first battle took place in the German offensive of March 1918 as a result of which Bapaume was finally lost on 24 March. The second battle took place in the British offensive, launched on 21 August, in which Bapaume was recaptured. *See also: France and Flanders 1914-18; Somme 1918; St Quentin; Rosières; Arras 1918; Avre and Ancre 1918.*

Bar Decorated metal bar attached to the ribbon of gallantry medals and used to denote the wearer has been awarded the decoration more than once, each bar representing an additional award. The decoration on the bar varies from award to award.

Barbed Wire A strong wire with sharply pointed barbs at close intervals, widely used in the creation of obstacles. *See also: Razor wire.*

Barbican A walled outwork or tower to protect the gate or drawbridge of a defensive fortification.

Bardia 1941 Second World War North Africa campaign battle honour marking an action in the first phase of the campaign. *See also: North Africa 1940-43; Capture of Tobruk; Beda Fomm; Withdrawal to Matruh and Bir Enba.*

Barentu Second World War Abyssinian campaign battle honour. *See also: Abyssinia 1940-41; Keren; Jebel Defeis; Jebel Shiba; Gogni; Agordat; Barentu; Karora-Marsa Taclai; Cubcub; Ad Teclesan; Mescelit Pass; Mt Engiahat; Massawa; Amb Alagi; Afodu; Gambela; El Wak; Moyale; Wal Garis; Juba; Marda Pass; Bisidimo; Awash; Todenyang-Namaraputh; Omo; Soroppa; Giarso; Colito; Wadara; Gondar; Fike and Lechemti.*

Barkasan Second World War battle honour marking the action against an Italian invading force in British Somaliland in August 1940. *See also: British Somaliland 1940 and Tug Argan.*

Barmine Bar-shaped anti-tank mine, 1.2m long, usually laid mechanically by a plough-type layer towed by a tracked vehicle.

Barracks A building or group of buildings specifically designed to accommodate the personnel, weapons, vehicles and equipment of an army unit or units.

Barrack-Room Lawyer Nickname for a soldier with a real or imagined knowledge of army regulations who persistently makes complaints.

Barrage A concentration of artillery and/or mortar fire, usually fired to a given timed programme, designed to reduce the capability and will of an enemy to take offensive action during the period of the barrage and for a time thereafter.

Barrel The tube through which the projectile of a firearm is discharged and which influences the projectile's direction, stability and velocity.

Barrier A co-ordinated series of obstacles designed or employed to canalise, direct, restrict, delay or stop the movement of an opposing force by imposing additional losses of personnel, equipment and time. Such barriers are formed by developing natural obstacles such as rivers, escarpments and woods with man-made obstacle belts such as minefields, route destruction and demolitions.

Barrier Treaties Three treaties (1709, 1713 and 1715) drawn up during and shortly after the War of the Spanish Succession (qv). They restored to the United Provinces the right to garrison certain tactically important towns along the southern border of the Netherlands as a line of defence against France. The first treaty also offered the Dutch generous territorial and commercial advantages, but these were much modified in the later treaties.

Barrosa Peninsula War battle honour marking a successful action by an Anglo-Portuguese force under General Graham against a numerically superior French force near Cadiz on 4 March 1811. *See also: Peninsula; Douro; Talavera; Busaco; Fuentes d'Onor; Albuhera and Bird Catchers.*

Baseplate Large metal plate, usually circular, upon which mortars and other high-elevation weapons stand, designed to prevent the recoil forces driving the weapon into the ground on firing, thus affecting accuracy.

Basha A jungle shelter. From the Urdu *Baasha* - a hut made of bamboo or leaves.

Basra First World War Mesopotamia campaign battle honour marking the capture of Basra on 22 November 1914 by a force from 6th Indian Division during the campaign in Mesopotamia 1914-18. *See also: Mesopotamia 1914-1918; Shaiba; Kut Al Amara 1915; Ctesiphon; Defence of Kut Al Amara; Tigris 1916; Kut Al Amara 1917; Baghdad; Khan Baghdadi and Sharqat.*

Bastion A projecting work in a fortification designed to permit the defender to fire to the flanks along the face of the adjacent walls. The term is now used to describe any defended location which is denied to the enemy.

BATES Abbreviation for 'Battlefield Artillery Engagement System'. An electronic system for the central command and control of artillery fire. A replacement for the obsolescent Forward Artillery Computing Equipment (FACE).

Bates Rangefinder A rangefinder in the form of an attachment to a pair of field glasses, invented by Captain C McGuire Bates of the Royal Engineers and patented by him in 1882.

Batman Formerly 'Bawman'; an individual - not necessarily a soldier paid by the government, allowed to every company on foreign service to look after the cooking utensils. Every company was allowed at government expense a 'bathorse' (pronounced 'bawhorse') to convey the cooking utensils. The word has now come to mean an officer's personal servant. On operations he is usually also a runner, radio operator and/or driver. *See also: Orderly and Soldier Servant.*

Baton Short staff presented by the Sovereign to every British field marshal on appointment as a symbol of his authority.

Baton Round Cylindrical projectile, usually of rubber or plastic material and discharged at moderate velocity. Such rounds are designed for use in riot dispersal and should not cause significant injury.

Battaglia Second World War Italian campaign battle honour marking the successful defence by units of 1st Guards Brigade of a mountain position during the period 2-12 October 1944. *See also: Italy 1943-45.*

Battalion A unit, usually infantry, composed of a number of companies and, like cavalry and artillery regiments, commanded by a Lieutenant Colonel.

Battalion Companies The basic companies of a battalion were known as the battalion companies. The extra flank companies were the grenadier and light companies. Until the shako came into use in 1800 the battalion companies wore the common hat and were known as the 'hat companies'.

Battery A unit of artillery, usually commanded by a major and broadly equivalent to a cavalry squadron or infantry company.

Battery Honour Titles The full Royal Regiment of Artillery battery honour titles are:

Royal Horse Artillery (Battery letter shown in brackets):
The King's Troop
The Chestnut Troop (A)
Sphinx (F Parachute)
Mercer's Troop (G Parachute)
Bull's Troop (I Parachute)
Sidi Rezegh (J)
Hondeghen (K)
Nery (L)
The Eagle Troop (N)
The Rocket Troop (O)
The Dragon Troop (P)
Sanna's Post (Q)
Shah Sujah's Troop (T(HQ))

Royal Artillery (Battery number shown in brackets):
Sphinx (4, 7 Commando, 11 and 73(OP))
Gibraltar 1779-83 (5, 21, 22 and 23(HQ))
Alma (8 Commando)
Plassey (9)
Assaye (10)
Minden (12 and 32)
Martinique 1809 (13)
Cole's Kop (14)
Sandham's Company (16)
Corunna (17 and 29)
Quebec 1759 (18)
Irish (24)
Strange's (27)
Roger's Company (30)
Seringapatam (34 and 38)
Arcot 1751 (36)
Alem Hamza (42)
Lloyd's Company (43)
Talavera (46)
Inkerman (49(HQ),152 and 156)
Kabul 1842 (51)
Niagara (52)
Louisburg (53)
Maharajpore (54)
The Residency (55(HQ))
Olphert's (56(HQ))
Bhurtpore (57)
Eyre's (58)
The Battle Axe Company (74)
Maude's (76)
Kirkee (79 Commando)

Arracan (88)
Le Cateau (93)
New Zealand (94)
Asten (59)
Lawson's Company (97)
Dragon (111, 127, 129)
Bengal Rocket Troop (132)
Java (137)
Tombs's Troop (143)
Maiwand (145)
Meiktila (148 Commando)
Colenso (159)
Middleton's Company (160)
Imjin (170)
The Broken Wheel (171)
Abu Klea (176)

Battipaglia Second World War Italian campaign battle honour marking one of the actions following the landing by Fifth Army at Salerno on 9 September 1943. *See also: Italy 1943-45; Salerno; St Lucia; Vietri Pass; and Salerno Hills.*

Battle An engagement between two or more forces, conducted within a limited geographic area and of limited duration.

Battle Bowler World War I soldiers slang for the issue steel helmet or 'tin hat'.

Battledress The term is particularly applied to the uniform developed just before the Second World War. In March 1938 an updated field service uniform, consisting of blouse and trousers, was introduced. Battledress became obsolescent in 1960 as it was replaced by drab olive green combat kit. *See also: Combat Kit.*

Battle Drill Standard methods of executing specific tactical operations.

Battle Group A tactical grouping, usually with armoured and infantry elements, under the command of the headquarters of an armoured regiment or infantry battalion.

Battle Honours During the last two hundred years it has been customary for the Sovereign to award battle honours to regiments of cavalry and infantry in recognition of their services in the field.

These honours are emblazoned on standards, guidons and colours and upon appointments such as drums and horse furniture; they are recorded in full by regimental title in Part 1 of the Army List (qv). Each regiment of the line carries two colours, the Queen's (or King's) Colour, which is always the Union Flag, representing the Sovereign; and the Regimental Colour representing the regiment. This system is reversed in the foot guards where the regimental colour is the Union Flag. A battle honour may record a specific battle, a campaign or, in the case of some Militia regiments, service overseas but not in a theatre of war. Battle honours are not awarded to the Royal Regiment of Artillery (although some batteries bear 'honour titles' (qv)) or the Corps of Royal Engineers. However, the Honourable Artillery Company has been awarded some battle honours because elements of the regiment seved as infantry in the First World War. In comparison with some of the continental nations Britain was comparatively late in adopting a battle honour system and the system which did emerge was, until 1882, largely illogical and often unfair. In general terms, and allowing for some exceptions, up to 1914 honours were not awarded for defeats, and it was held essential that to qualify for an honour the headquarters and at least half the regiment should be present at the action to qualify. In general terms battle honours awarded for actions in the First and Second World Wars are emblazoned on the Queen's (or King's) Colour and the earlier battle honours are carried on the Regimental Colour. The First World War posed special problems: the number of regiments involved; the duration of many of the actions and the number of brief but often bloody engagements within a particular offensive. The principle of not awarding honours for defeats had to be abandoned and, becuase of the number of battle honours, it was decided that each regiment be allowed to select ten honours to be shown on the Queen's (or King's) colour - the selected honours being shown in bold type in the Army List. A similar procedure was followed at the end of the Second World War. *See also: Commando Association.*

Battlement A form of parapet which is indented or crenellated to permit defenders to fire through the indentations (crenels or embrasures) whilst protected by the solid portions (merlons).

Battle Procedure Procedures to be followed when preparing for tactical operations.

Batu Pahat Second World War Malayan campaign battle honour marking an action during operations to hold back the Japanese from Singapore in January 1942. Attempts were made over the period 21 to 26 January to hold the Batu Pahat area on the West Coast of Johore. *See also: Malaya 1941-42; Johore and Muar.*

Bays A type of reddish-brown horse. *See also: Queen's Bays.*

Bayonet Short spear-, spike- or knife-like weapons of varying lengths affixed to the muzzles of rifles and used, particularly by the infantry, in close combat. The original weapon was thought to have been invented at Bayonne in the 17th century.

Bayonet Belt In the early 18th century both the sword and the bayonet were suspended from the infantryman's waist-belt. As the sword became obsolete for the infantryman, a fashion developed of wearing the bayonet belt over the shoulder, giving rise to the development of belt plates for infantrymen. In the 19th century the bayonet was once more suspended from the waist-belt, using a 'bayonet frog'.

Bazentin Battle honour marking the attack launched against Bazentin Ridge on 14th July 1916, part of the great British Somme offensive of 1916. *See also: Somme 1916.*

Bazooka Specifically, an obsolete US-made shoulder-fired recoilless anti-tank weapon. The term was widely used at one time to describe any weapon of similar characteristics.

Be Fit Regimental quick march of the Army Physical Training Corps; words from *Land and Sea Tales* by Kipling.

Beachhead That area of a hostile beach which is captured to permit the unloading of a force and its equipment. The rapid seizure, development and security of a beachhead is fundamental to the success of amphibious operations.

Beacon Equipment emitting an electromagnetic pulse on a selected frequency. Beacons can be activated manually, remotely or on exposure to specific physical conditions such as immersion in water. They are much used in rescue operations, navigation and target identification.

Beards The growing of beards has not been encouraged in the British Army. During the Crimean War (1854-55) beards were permitted because of the severity of the weather, and were allowed for a short period thereafter. Beards may however be worn by pipers and infantry assault pioneers. Volunteer soldiers were permitted to retain their beards.

Bearskin Tall fur cap, usually black, worn by some regiments of the British Army, most notably the Foot Guards. It may also be part of the horse furniture.

Beat Originally an order passed by drum, hence 'to beat an alarm', 'to beat a charge' and to 'beat to arms'.

Beat Retreat Originally, the drum call to summon men to camp or behind the lines when hostilities ceased at the end of the day. Also used to recall troops from the town to their quarters and for night guards to be posted. An order dated 18 June 1690 directs 'The generall to be beate att 3 clock in ye morning . . . ye retrete to beate att 9 att night, & take it from ye gards'. In 1694 an Order of William III reads; 'The Drum-Major and Drummers of the Regiment which gives a Captain to the Main-Guard, are to beat the *Retreat* through the large street, or as may be ordered. They are to be answered by all the Drummers of the other Guards, and by four Drummers of each regiment in their respective Quarters'. Over the years the time at which retreat was played has varied and it is now left to the discretion of commanding officers. The beating or sounding of retreat has developed into a formal musical entertainment including the military band and pipes, drums or bugles, as appropriate. It is usual for the national, regimental and other flags to be lowered at 'Retreat'. *See also Sound Retreat.*

Beaumont Battle honour, not conferred until 1909, marking the battle fought on 26 April 1794 to cover the siege of Landrecies during the early stages of the Revolutionary War with France.

Beaurevoir First World War battle honour marking one of the battles within the 1918 offensive against the German defences on the Hindenburg Line. Beaurevoir, a reserve position some two miles behind the main Hindenburg Line was attacked on 3 October and carried two days later. *See also: France and Flanders 1914-18; Hindenburg Line; Havrincourt; Épéhy; Canal du Nord; St Quentin Canal and Cambrai 1918.*

Beaver AL-1 Light aircraft manufactured by De Havilland and in service with the Army Air Corps for liaison and communication flights from 1961.

Beda Fomm Second World War North Africa campaign battle honour awarded for the action in February 1941 when 7th Armoured Division intercepted the Italian retreat along the coast road from Benghazi and forced the surrender of most of what remained of the Italian Tenth Army. *See also: North Africa 1940-1943; Sidi Barrani; Capture of Tobruk; Withdrawal to Matruh; Bir Enba and Bardia 1941.*

Bedfordshire Regiment (14th Foot) *See: The Prince of Wales's Own Regiment of Yorkshire (14th and 15th Foot).*

Bedfordshire Regiment (16th Foot) Raised in October 1688 by Colonel Archibald Douglas, mustered at Reading, and known as Douglas's Regiment. After James II's abdication in December 1688 Douglas was removed by William of Orange and Colonel Robert Hodges was appointed to the command. The regiment

became 16th Foot in 1751; 16th Foot (Buckinghamshire) in 1782; 16th Foot (Bedfordshire) in 1809; and subsequently, in 1881, the Bedfordshire Regiment. Redesignated the Bedfordshire and Hertfordshire Regiment (q,v.) in 1919. History: *The 16th Foot* by F Maurice (1931) and *The Hertfordshire Regiment: An Illustrated History* by J D Sainsbury (1988).

Bedfordshire Yeomanry The first troop was raised in 1797; by 1798 four troops were in being and they were formed into a regiment in 1803. A staged disbandment then took place and by 1810 the Bedfordshire Yeomanry Cavalry had ceased to exist. Re-raised in 1817, and again disbanded in 1827. In 1860 two troops of the Huntingdonshire Mounted Rifles (The Duke of Manchester's Light Horse) were raised in Bedford and Sharnbrook. The 28th (Bedfordshire) Company, Imperial Yeomanry, sometimes known as 'Compton's Horse' was raised for service in South Africa (1899-1902), and this company formed the nucleus of a new regiment, raised in 1901 as the Bedfordshire Imperial Yeomanry, which was to serve most of the First World War in France. The regiment converted to artillery in 1920 and served as such during the Second World War. Following the re-formation of the TA in 1947 a number of changes of designation took place, the regiment emerging in 1967 as 3 (Bedfordshire Yeomanry) Company, The Bedfordshire & Hertfordshire Regiment (Territorial). The successor sub-unit is 201 (Hertfordshire & Bedfordshire Yeomanry) Field Battery, 100 (Yeomanry) Field Regiment Royal Artillery (Volunteer).

Bedfordshire & Hertfordshire Regiment (16th Foot) Formed in 1919 from the Bedfordshire Regiment, the Regiment amalgamated with The Essex Regiment (44th and 56th Foot) on 2 June 1958 to form 3rd East Anglian Regiment (16th/44th Foot). On 1 September 1964 the 1st, 2nd and 3rd East Anglian Regiments and the Royal Leicestershire Regiment amalgamated to form The Royal Anglian Regiment (qv). History: *The 16th Foot* by F Maurice

(1931), *The Bedfordshire and Hertfordshire Regiment* by G W H Peters (1970) and *The Story of the Bedfordshire and Hertfordshire Regiment* (3 Vols) (1988).

Beefeater *See: Yeoman of the Guard.*

Begging In 1812 the death penalty was abolished for the crime of 'begging by soldiers without the permission of their commanding officer'.

Begone Dull Care One of the regimental quick marches of the Royal Corps of Signals.

Beehive Charge Shaped charge used for blowing holes in hard surfaces such as roads and bridges.

Behar Battle honour awarded to mark the actions of a Sikh military police battalion, later 45th (Rattray's Sikhs) Bengal Native Infantry, in the province of Bihar during the Indian Mutiny (1857). *See also: Central India and Mooltan.*

Behobeho First World War East Africa campaign battle honour marking the occasion when, in January 1917, British forces very nearly surrounded the German forces under von Lettow before they escaped across the Rufiji River. *See also: East Africa 1914-18; Kilimanjaro; Narungombe; Nyangao and Kamina.*

Beles Gugani Second World War Abyssinian campaign marking one of the actions in the Battle of the Juba. *See also: Abyssinia 1940-41; Keren; Jebel Defeis; Jebel Shiba; Gogni; Agordat; Barentu; Karora-Marsa Taclai; Cubcub; Ad Teclesan; Mescelit Pass; Mt Engiahat; Massawa; Amb Alagi; Afodu; Gambela; El Wak; Moyale; Wal Garis; Juba; Marda Pass; Bisidimo; Awash; Todenyang-Namaraputh; Omo; Soroppa; Giarso; Colito; Wadara; Gondar; Fike and Lechemti.*

Belfast Regiment Nickname given to the 35th Foot, later 1st Battalion Royal Sussex Regiment and subsequently 3rd Battalion The Queen's Regiment.

Belhamed Second World War North Africa campaign battle honour marking an action in the British offensive of 18 November 1941 in North Africa, known as Operation CRUSADER, when the southern side of the corridor into Tobruk was secured over the period 25 November to 1 December 1941. *See also: North Africa 1940-1943; Tobruk 1941; Gubi I; Sidi Rezegh 1941; Tobruk Sortie; Omars; Gabr Saleh; Taieb El Essem; Gubi II and Relief of Tobruk.*

Belize Formerly the British colony of British Honduras, renamed Belize on 1 June 1973 and granted independence on 21 September 1981. The colony had been garrisoned by the British Army since February 1948 to deter the threat of Guatemalan invasion, the size and composition of the garrison varying from time to time in response to the changing nature of the threat. In May 1993 the British government announced that, as relations between Belize and Guatemala had improved significantly, the garrison was to be reduced by 30 September 1994. After that, and at the request and with the agreement of the Belize government, the British military presence in Belize would take the form of a training operation for troops from the United Kingdom. The United Kingdom would, however, stand ready to consult with the Belize government in the event of a renewed threat to their sovereignty. *See also: British Honduras.*

Bell The piece of metal which holds the tassel on a sporran, as worn by kilted regiments.

Bell-Shape Term applied to the wide topped shako introduced after 1816. *See also: Shako.*

Belle Isle Battle honour, awarded in 1951, for an action in the spring of 1761 during the Seven Years' War (qv) when a combined naval and military force under Admiral Keppel and Major General Studholme Hodgson captured the island, which lies off the west coast of France, with a view to using it as a supply base for the fleet. *See also: Minden; Emsdorf; Warburg and Wilhelmstahl.*

Bellewaarde First World War battle honour marking one of the actions in the Second Battle of Ypres which began on 17 April 1915. *See also: France and Flanders 1914-18; Ypres 1915; Gravenstafel; St Julien and Frezenberg.*

Belted Plaid Term used to describe the early plaid which was held in place by a belt around the waist.

Belt-Plate Term applied to the metal plate fixed to waist and shoulder belts.

Bengal European Light Cavalry (HEIC), 1st Converted to 19th Hussars in 1861, became 19th (Princess of Wales's Own) Hussars in 1885 and 19th (Queen Alexandra's Own Royal) Hussars in 1905. Amalgamated with 15th The King's Hussars on 11 April 1922 to form 15th/19th Hussars. On 31 October 1932 the regiment was redesignated 15th The King's Royal Hussars, and on 31 December 1933 the regiment was redesignated 15th/19th The King's Royal Hussars. On 1 December 1992 15th/19th The King's Royal Hussars amalgamated with 13th/18th Royal Hussars (Queen Mary's Own) to form The Light Dragoons.

Bengal European Light Cavalry (HEIC), 2nd Converted to 20th Hussars in 1861 and amalgamated with 14th King's Hussars on 11 April 1922 to form 14th/20th Hussars. Redesignated 14th/20th King's in 1936. On 4 December 1992 the 14th/20th King's Hussars amalgamated with The Royal Hussars (Prince of Wales's Own) to form The King's Royal Hussars (qv).

Bengal European Light Cavalry (HEIC), 3rd Converted as 21st Hussars in 1861 and became 21st Lancers in 1897. In 1898 the regiment was redesignated 21st Lancers (Empress of India's) and it amalgamated with 17th Lancers (Duke of Cambridge's Own) on 11 April 1922 to form 17th/21st Lancers. On 26 June 1993 the 17th/21st Lancers amalgamated with 16th/5th The Queen's Royal Lancers to form The Queen's Royal Lancers (qv).

Bengal Infantry Regiment (107th) Raised in 1854 as 3rd Bengal European Infantry in the Honourable East India Company's forces, transferred to the British establishment in 1861 and amalgamated with 35th (Royal Sussex) Regiment to form The Royal Sussex Regiment in 1881.

Bengal Tigers Nickname given to 17th Foot, later the Royal Leicestershire Regiment and subsequently 4th Battalion Royal Anglian Regiment. The 17th Foot was granted the badge of a royal tiger in acknowledgement of their distinguished service in India (1804-23).

Benghazi Second World War North Africa campaign battle honour awarded for action between the British withdrawal from Agedabia and occupation of the El Alamein line in 1942. *See also: North Africa 1940-1943; Msus; Carmusa; Mersa Matruh; Point 174; Minqar Qaim and Fuka.*

Benghazi Raid Second World War North Africa campaign battle honour marking the bold but unsuccessful raid carried out by SAS forces during the period 12-14 September 1942. *See also: North Africa 1940-1943.*

Beni Boo Ali Battle honour, not awarded to any British regiment, but which marks operations in the Persian Gulf in 1809 and 1819-21 for which 65th Foot (2nd Yorkshire North Riding) was awarded 'Arabia'. *See also: Arabia.*

Bentheim Second World War battle honour marking one of a number of actions which took place between the crossing of the Rhine in March 1945 and the end of the campaign in North-West Europe. *See also: North West Europe 1944-45; Lingen; Dreirwalde; Artlenberg; Uelzen and Twente Canal.*

Ber Rabal Second World War North Africa campaign battle honour marking an action in the unsuccessful attempt to break through the German positions North of Bou Arada during the period 22-26 April 1943. *See also: North Africa 1940-1943; Oued Zarga; El Kourzia and Argoub Sellah.*

Beret During the First World War there had been some discussion about a suitable form of headdress for tank crews. In May 1918 the French 70th Chasseurs Alpins were training with the Royal Tank Corps and their beret caught the eye of General Sir Hugh Elles, Colonel of the Royal Tank Corps. However, the beret of the Chasseurs Alpins was deemed 'too sloppy' and the Basque beret of the Chars d'Assault 'too skimpy', so a compromise based on the Scottish Tam O'Shanter and black in colour was designed for the Royal Tank Corps and submitted for the approval of George V in November 1923. This approval was given in March 1924 and the beret is now found in a wide variety of colours throughout the corps and regiments of the army.

Berkeley's Dragoons Raised in 1685, later Princess Anne of Denmark's Dragoons and The Queen's Royal Irish Hussars. Also one of the regimental quick marches of The Queen's Royal Irish Hussars.

Berkshire Regiment (66th Foot) *See: The Royal Berkshire Regiment (Princess Charlotte of Wales's)*.

Berkshire Yeomanry (The Berkshire (Hungerford) Yeomanry) The first troop was raised in Abingdon in 1794 and, with three further troops, formed 1st Berkshire Cavalry in 1804, which existed until 1828. A second regiment, the East Berkshire Yeomanry Cavalry, was raised in 1805 and disbanded in 1827. In 1831 the Hungerford Troop was re-raised and formed the nucleus of the Berkshire (Hungerford) Yeomanry Cavalry, which later found 36th Company of 10th Battalion Imperial Yeomanry for service in the South Africa War (1899-1902). In the First World War the regiment served dismounted in Gallipoli, Egypt, Palestine and France. It converted to artillery in 1920, serving as such throughout the Second World War. In 1967 elements of the regiment could be found in both 'A' Company (Berkshire Yeomary) Royal Berkshire Teritorials and RHQ & 'HQ' (Berkshire and Westminster Dragoons) Squadron of the Royal Yeomanry. The successor sub-unit is now 94 (Berkshire Yeomanry) Signal Squadron, 71 (Yeomanry) Signal Regiment (Volunteers).

Berwickshire Yeomanry Two troops of Berwickshire Yeomanry Cavalry were raised in 1797 in the Duns district; further troops were raised in the Eagle district in 1801 and Coldstream in 1804. The Berwickshire Yeomanry Cavalry was disbanded in 1827, although a troop was raised in April 1848 for the East Lothian Yeomanry Cavalry. *See also: East Lothian Yeomanry Cavalry.*

Best Second World War battle honour awarded for an action in the Second Army attempt to break through to Arnhem from 17-27 September 1944. *See also: North West Europe 1944-45; Nederrijn; Nijmegen and Veghel.*

Béthune First World War battle honour marking a successful defensive action during the second large scale German offensive of 1918 when the German advance was held, in spite of a major effort by the Germans, in the important Béthune sector. *See also: France and Flanders 1914-1918; Lys; Estaires; Messines 1918; Hazebrouck; Bailleul; Kemmel and Scherpenberg.*

Bhurtpore Battle honour marking the seige and capture of the strong fortress of Bhurtpore in January 1826. The fortress had defied earlier efforts to capture it during the Second Mahratta War of 1817-18. This was the first occasion on which Gurkhas fought under the British flag.

Bicorne Hat In the early days of the Army, normal headdress was the civilian broad-brimmed hat. Passing fashion brought about the turning up of one, two (bicorne) or three (tricorne) sides of the brim, and these 'cocked' sides were often fastened with a loop, rosette or later a plume. The bicorne hat had the brim formed or 'cocked' into two points and is worn today by some officers as the 'cocked hat'. The tricorne hat is 'cocked' on three sides.

Big Bertha Nickname given to the specially constructed German naval guns which fired on Paris from the area of Coucy, a distance of some 75 miles, during the First World War. The name is an allusion to Frau Bertha von Bohlen, one of the proprietors of Krupps, the firm which made the guns.

Bingham's Dandies Nickname given to 17th Lancers, later 17th/21st Lancers and now the Queen's Royal Lancers, when the regiment was commanded by Lord Bingham - later the Earl of Lucan - from 1826 to 1837 and noted for its extravagant uniform.

Binocular Case At the end of the 19th century officers of the General Staff, Royal Artillery and Royal Engineers carried a small pair of binoculars in a case in the middle of the back.

Bir El Aslagh Second World War North Africa campaign battle honour marking the battle of Bir El Aslagh, the first real armoured clash of the German attacks on the British positions on the Gazala line, which took place 27-31 May 1942. *See also: North Africa 1940-1943; Gazala; Retma; Bir Hacheim; Cauldron; Knightsbridge; Tobruk 1942; Bir El Igela; Hagiag Er Raml; Gabr El Fachri;Via Balbia; Zt El Mrasses and Sidi Rezegh 1942.*

Bir El Igela Second World War North Africa campaign battle honour marking an action in the German attacks on the British positions on the Gazala line in 1942. *See also: North Africa 1940-1943; Gazala; Retma; Bir Hacheim; Cauldron; Knightsbridge; Tobruk 1942; Bir El Aslagh; Hagiag Er Raml; Gabr El Fachri;Via Balbia; Zt El Mrasses and Sidi Rezegh 1942.*

Bir Enba Second World War North Africa campaign battle honour marking an action during the first phase of the campaign in 1941. *See also: North Africa 1940-1943; Withdrawal to Matruh and Bardia 1941.*

Bir Hacheim Second World War North Africa campaign battle honour marking an action in the German attacks on the British positions on the Gazala line 27 May - 11 June 1942. *See also: North Africa 1940-1943; Gazala; Retma; Bir El Igela; Cauldron; Knightsbridge; Tobruk 1942; Bir El Aslagh; Hagiag Er Raml; Gabr El Fachri;Via Balbia; Zt El Mrasses and Sidi Rezegh 1942.*

BIRD CATCHERS
Nickname given to the three regiments which captured French eagle standards:

1st Dragoons, later Royal Dragoons (1st Dragoons), which merged with the Royal Horse Guards (The Blues) in 1969 to form the Blues and Royals (Royal Horse Guards and 1st Dragoons). The eagle was captured at the Battle of Waterloo (1815).

2nd Dragoons, the Royal Scots Greys, who merged with 3rd Carabiniers (Prince of Wales's Dragoon Guards) in 1971 to form The Royal Scots Dragoon Guards (Carabiniers and Greys). The eagle was captured at the Battle of Waterloo (1815).

87th Foot, later the Royal Irish Fusiliers and subsequently 3rd Battalion The Royal Irish Rangers (Disbanded 1969). The eagle was captured at the Battle of Barossa (1811).

Birdwood, Field Marshal William Riddell Birdwood, 1st Baron (1865-1951) Educated Clifton College and Royal Military College Sandhurst. Commissioned into Royal Scots Fusiliers (1883); transferred to 12th Royal Lancers (1885); captain 11th Bengal Lancers (1896). His early experience was gained in the Hazara (1891), Isazai (1892) and Tirah (1897-98) expeditions. In the South Africa War (1899-1902) he was brigade major to the Mounted Brigade in Natal and later secretary to Lord Kitchener, the Commander-in-Chief. In the First World War he served with the Mediterranean Expeditionary Force, first as General Officer Commanding Australian and New Zealand Army Corps (ANZAC) and, later, the Fifth Army in France. His skilful handling of Australian and New Zealand forces greatly enhanced his military reputation. At the close of the war he received a baronetcy and a grant of £10,000. In 1920 he was appointed General Officer

Commanding Northern Army in India and, from 1925-30, he was Commander-in-Chief of the Indian Army. Raised to the peerage in 1938 as Baron Birdwood of Anzac and Totnes. He was Master of Peterhouse College 1931-38.

Bishenpur Second World War Burma campaign battle honour marking fighting in the Bishenpur area, 15 miles south-west of Imphal, between 14 April and 22 June 1944. The 17th Indian Division and elements of 20th Indian Division were involved. *See also: Burma 1942-1945; Imphal; Tuitum; Nungshigum; Kanglatongbi; Sakawng; Tamu Road; Shenam Pass and Litan.*

Bishop to the Forces The appointment of Bishop to the Forces was created in 1944. The duties in 1961, as delegated by the then Archbishop of Canterbury, were: 'the day to day episcopal oversight of the Church of England Chaplains to the Forces'. The present incumbent and eighth to hold the appointment, The Right Reverend John Kirkham, Bishop Suffragan of Sherborne, took up the appointment on 2 September 1992 charged with: 'special responsibility for the pastoral care of the chaplains the officers and the men and women of Her Majesty's Armed Forces and the general superintendence of the work of the Church of England among them...'.

Bisidimo Second World War Abyssinia campaign battle honour. *See also: Abyssinia 1940-41; Keren; Jebel Defeis; Jebel Shiba; Gogni; Agordat; Barentu; Karora-Marsa Taclai; Cubcub; Ad Teclesan; Mescelit Pass; Mt Engiahat; Massawa; Amb Alagi; Afodu; Gambela; El Wak; Moyale; Wal Garis; Juba; Marda Pass; Bisidimo; Awash; Todenyang-Namaraputh; Omo; Soroppa; Giarso; Colito; Wadara; Gondar; Fike and Lechemti.*

Bit From the second half of the 19th century saddlers and collar-makers in the cavalry wore a badge showing a horse's bit on the right upper sleeve.

Bivouac Term originally used when troops were concentrated in the open without tents or other substantial shelter. Now used when troops are accommodated in light, one- or two-man tents or specially developed 'bivouac bags' or 'bivvy bags' which combine the functions of sleeping bag and bivouac tent.

Black Bear Regimental quick march of The Royal Gurkha Rifles.

Black-Cock Feathers Worn on the full dress Headdress of the Royal Scots, The King's Own Scottish Borderers and by pipers with Glengarries.

Black Horse Nickname given to 7th Dragoon Guards, later 4th/7th Dragoon Guards and, following amalgamation with 5th Royal Inniskilling Dragoon Guards in 1992, the Royal Dragoon Guards, because of their black facings.

Black Line Some regiments have the tradition that the black line in their lace is a sign of mourning. However, before 1830 many regiments had silver lace and the black line was used to enhance the pattern.

Black Prince (A.43) Second World War 'infantry' tank developed by Vauxhall Motors Ltd 1943-45. The Black Prince, which was never taken into service, had a crew of five, weighed 50 tons and mounted a 17pdr gun and two Besa machine guns. *See: Tank and Infantry tank.*

Blackthorn Stout stick from a thorny Eurasian rosaceous shrub *Prunus spinosa* carried by the officers of some Irish regiments.

Black Watch (Royal Highland Regiment) (42nd and 73rd Foot) The senior of the Highland regiments. Called Black Watch because of its dark tartan and the nature of its early duties when, from 1725, the six independent companies were stationed in small detachments to keep watch on the Highlands and the clans. The regiment was formed by the amalgamation of the independent companies in 1739 as 43rd Foot or Highland Regiment, being renumbered 42nd Foot in 1749 and in 1758 becoming 42nd Foot or Royal

Highland Regiment. In 1781 a second battalion of the regiment was raised and became 73rd Foot (Highland Regiment) in 1786. In 1861 the 42nd became 42nd or Royal Highland Regiment (Black Watch) and, in 1862, the old 2nd battalion became 73rd (Perthshire) Regiment. In 1881 the two regiments formed The Black Watch (Royal Highlanders) which became The Black Watch (Royal Highland Regiment) in 1920.

Headdress Badge: The star of the Order of the Thistle. Upon it, within an oval bearing the motto of the Order, the figure of St Andrew behind a cross saltire. Below, the sphinx. All ensigned with the crown.

Regimental Marches:

Quick Marches: *Hielan' Laddie* (Pipes and Drums) and *All The Blue Bonnets are Over The Border* (Regimental Band).

Slow Marches: *My Home and Highland Cradle Song* (Pipes and Drums) and *The Garb of Old Gaul* (Regimental Band).

Regimental Headquarters: Balhousie Castle, Perth, Scotland, PH1 5HR.

History: *The Black Watch* by Eric and Andro Linklater, (1977).

Bladensburg Battle honour awarded between 1826 and 1854 marking an action against the Americans at Bladensburg on 24 August 1814 during the North American war of 1812-14. *See also: Detroit; Queenstown; Miami and Niagara.*

Blanco Trade name of a powder, originally white but later in a variety of colours, which replaced whiting in 1835 and which was mixed with water and applied to equipment, especially the web equipment of the First and Second World Wars. The object was to preserve the equipment and give a smart appearance.

Blank Term used to describe ammunition which has no projectile and a very reduced propellant charge. Such ammunition is an important aid to training, being used to simulate live fire and thus prompt a response when heard during training.

Blanket Coat Not all infantrymen were issued with a greatcoat in the 18th century, although a certain number of 'watch coats'

were available for night sentries. Blankets were therefore frequently worn in the North American winters, and even in more temperate theatres.

Blanket Pin Large safety pin used to fasten the fly of the highland kilt. Also used to secure blankets to form a primitive type of sleeping bag.

Blayney's Bloodhounds The 87th Foot, the Royal Irish Fusiliers (Princess Victoria's), subsequently 3rd Battalion The Royal Irish Rangers (disbanded 1969). The regiment received the nickname in 1798 when, under the command of Lord Blayney, they were particularly effective in hunting down and capturing Irish rebels.

Blenheim Battle honour awarded in 1882 marking the British success at Blindheim, Bavaria, under Marlborough in August 1704 during the War of the Spanish Succession (1702-13) *See also: Schellenberg; Ramillies; Oudenarde and Malplaquet.*

Bleriot Experimental 2 (BE2) Biplane manufactured by the Royal Aircraft Factory in 1912 and in service with the Royal Flying Corps during the First World War.

Blighty Soldiers' slang for the United Kingdom. From the Hindi *bilayut* or *billait* – a kingdom, province or distant land. From Arabic *wilayat* (country).

Blighty Wound Soldiers' slang for a wound which is severe enough (but not too severe!) to warrant evacuation from the theatre of operations to the United Kingdom. Such a wound offers the recipient the cheering prospect of an escape from action and the opportunity to see his family.

Bligny First World War battle honour marking the heroic defence of the Mont de Bligny in the Battle of the Aisne, 1918. For this action 4th Battalion The King's Shropshire Light Infantry was awarded the Croix de Guerre. *See also: France and Flanders 1914-1918; Aisne 1918 and Bois des Buttes.*

Blimp A person, especially an officer, who is stupidly complacent and reactionary. Also referred to as Colonel Blimp and drawn from a cartoon character created by David Low.

Blind Term used to describe an explosive device, more usually a round of ammunition or grenade, which fails to explode when fired.

Blind Half-Hundred Nickname given to 50th Foot, later 1st Battalion Queen's Own Royal West Kent Regiment and subsequently 2nd Battalion Queen's Regiment, because many of the men suffered from ophthalmia during the Egyptian campaign of 1801.

Blocking Position Defensive position so sited as to deny the enemy access to a given area or prevent his advance in a given direction.

Bloodhound British surface-to-air missile which entered service in 1957 and is now obsolete. Guided by semi-active radar homing on radar signals reflected by the target.

Bloody Eleventh Nickname given to the 11th Foot, later the Devonshire Regiment and subsequently embodied in the Devonshire and Dorset Regiment, following the Battle of Salamanca (1812) when the regiment had only 71 out of over 400 men available for duty, many of those survivors being wounded.

Blowpipe A man-portable, shoulder-fired, short-range surface-to-air missile developed by Shorts from the early 1960s and in service since 1972. The weapon is fundamentally different from most systems in that it operates on a system of radio command to line of sight after infra-red gathering. Once the missile has been gathered the operator is required to guide the missile to the target using a thumb control. The missile has a high explosive warhead and a maximum range of 4km.

Blue Bonnets Are Over The Border A regimental quick march of The Royal Highland Fusiliers (Pipes and Drums) and King's Own Scottish Borderers (Pipes and Drums and Regimental Band).

Blues and Royals (Royal Horse Guards and 1st Dragoons)
Formed on 29 March 1969 through the amalgamation of the Royal Horse Guards (The Blues) and The Royal Dragoons (1st Dragoons) to form The Blues and Royals (Royal Horse Guards and 1st Dragoons). Headdress Badge: The royal cypher within a circle inscribed 'THE BLUES AND ROYALS', ensigned with a crown.
Regimental marches:
Quick Marches: *Regimental Quick March of the Blues and Royals, Grand March from Aida* and *The Royals.*
Slow March: *Slow March of The Blues and Royals.*
Headquarters Household Cavalry: Chelsea Barracks, London, SW1H 8RF.
History: *The Story of The Blues and Royals - Royal Horse Guards and 1st Dragoons 1661 - 1993* by J N P Watson.

Blue-On-Blue Term used to describe an action or engagement, in which individuals, sub-units, units, formations or weapon systems engage forces or weapon systems operating on their own side. The term is derived from the use on maps of blue to denote friendly forces, the enemy being shown in red.

Bluey Soldiers' slang for the official blue air letter form available to soldiers and their families during active service.

Blunderbuss Short musket with large bore and flared muzzle used to achieve a wide scatter of shot at short range.

Bob's Own Nickname given to the Irish Guards, Field Marshal Earl Roberts (known to the Army as 'Bobs') being the first Colonel of the Regiment.

Body Bag A heavy duty plastic bag used to cover human remains, especially those of battle casualties.

Boer Wars or South Africa War The Boer Wars occurred in two distinct phases.

The first war, between Britain and the Transvaal Boers in 1880-1, was triggered by the Boer proclamation of the Transvaal as a republic. The most notable encounters of the war were the defeat of the British at Laing's Nek and Majuba Hill in 1881. Peace was concluded thereafter, Britain recognising the independence of the Transvaal. The second war, which was on a much larger scale, took place between 1899 and 1902 with Britain on one side and the Transvaal Republic and Orange Free State on the other. The British at first suffered some very severe reverses and British troops were effectively besieged at Ladysmith from 29 October 1899 to 28 February 1900, Kimberley from 14 October 1899 to 15 February 1900 and Mafeking from 15 October 1899 to 16 May 1900. All three having been relieved, Pretoria, the capital of the Transvaal, was occupied by British troops under Lord Roberts (qv) on 5 June 1900. A Peace was signed on 31 May 1902 under which the conquered countries were given self-government, and in 1909 they were included in the Union of South Africa by the Act of Union. In the Second Boer War (1899-1902) every regiment of the regular Army was engaged with the exception of 4th Dragoon Guards, 4th Hussars, 15th Hussars and 21st Lancers. In addition, detachments of 43 Yeomanry regiments and 50 Militia battalions were present.

Bofors Gun Swedish designed 40mm cannon widely used as a light anti-aircraft weapon.

Bois Des Buttes First World War battle honour marking the gallant stand by 2nd Battalion The Devonshire Regiment in this wood, almost to the last man, during the Battle of the Aisne 1918. *See also: France and Flanders 1914-1918; Aisne 1918 and Bligny.*

Bold King's Hussars Regimental quick march of 15th/19th The King's Royal Hussars.

Bologna Second World War Italian campaign battle honour commemorating the actions over the period 14-21 April 1945 against German positions in the area of the city, part of the final offensive by the Fifth Army. *See also: Italy 1943-1945; Medecina; Gaiana Crossing; Sillaro Crossing and Idice Bridgehead.*

Bolt A sliding bar in breech-loading firearms which ejects the spent cartridge, gathers a new cartridge and guides it into the breech, holding it securely in the breech during firing.

Bomb Originally a hollow ball or 'shell' filled with explosive and projected from special types of artillery. The term has also been applied to an explosive missile or grenade thrown by hand. A badge depicting a bomb was worn on the sleeve of bomb disposal specialists during the Second World War.

Bombardier Equivalent rank of corporal in the Royal Regiment of Artillery, now distinguished by two chevrons worn on the upper sleeve. *See also: Rank.*

Bombay Bloomers Long, large and very unpopular pants, manufactured in Bombay during the Second World War and issued to the 8th Army in North Africa in 1942.

Bombay Bowler Nickname given a sun-helmet produced in India.

Bombay Light Infantry (106th) Raised in 1826 as 2nd Bombay European Regiment of Foot for service in the Honourable East India Company's forces. Transferred to the British Army in 1861 and amalgamated with 68th (Durham) Light Infantry to form The Durham Light Infantry in 1881.

Bonnie Dundee Regimental canter of the Honourable Artillery Company, and the Queen's Royal Hussars (Queen's Own and Royal Irish).

Bonnie English Rose Regimental quick march of The Green Howards (Alexandra, Princess of Wales's Own Yorkshire Regiment) (19th Foot).

Book of Remembrance It is customary for the casualties of a regiment to be recorded in a 'Book of Remembrance'; the book is normally lodged in the regimental chapel, which is itself usually within a cathedral church, minster, abbey or church associated with the regiment. It is the custom that a page of the book of remembrance be turned daily.

Boots Shoes were worn in the British Army until 1823 when half-boots were introduced. It was not until 1838 that separate lasts were produced for left and right boots - up to that point they were expected to be worn on alternate feet to give even wear on the soles. The laced boot was replaced by the 'Cossack' boot in 1838, but the ankle boot came back into use in 1873. In 1963 an ankle boot with a directly moulded sole was introduced, this was replaced in the late 1980s by the 'boot combat high'.

Booting Term given to the leather strengthening on cavalry overalls.

Border Regiment (34th And 55th Foot) Formed in 1881 by the amalgamation of 34th Foot (Cumberland), raised in February 1702 by Colonel Robert, 3rd Lord Lucas and known as Lord Lucas's Regiment, and 55th Foot (Westmorland), raised at Stirling in December 1755 by Colonel George Perry and ranked as 57th Foot, renumbered 55th in 1757. On 1 October 1959 the regiment amalgamated with the King's Own Royal Regiment (Lancaster) (4th Foot) to form the King's Own Royal Border Regiment (qv).
Headdress Badge: A cross based on that of the Order of the Bath upon a wreath, and both upon a star of the Order of the Garter. Within the cross a circle with the China Dragon and bearing the battle honour 'ARROYO DOS MOLINOS 1811'. On the arms of the cross 14 honours. All ensigned with the crown.
History: *An Historical Account of the Services of the 34th and 55th Regiments* by G Noakes (1875), *Tried and Valiant - The Story of The Border Regiment 1702-1959* by D Sutherland (1972), *The Border Regiment in The Great War* by H C Wylly (1924) and *The Story of The Border Regiment 1939-1945* by P J Shears (1948).

Borderers, The Regimental slow march (Pipes and Drums) of the King's Own Scottish Borderers.

Bordj Second World War North Africa campaign battle honour marking the defeat of a German counter-attack on 11 April 1943 as part of an Anglo/US operation to break through the Fondouk Pass towards Kairouan. *See also: North Africa 1940-1943; Fondouk; Kairouan; Pichon; Djebel El Rhorab; Fondouk Pass and Sidi Ali.*

Borneo *See: Brunei and Borneo 1962-66.*

Boss Circular cord ornament worn on Headdress. Usually as backing to a badge or similar distinguishing mark.

Bottle Soldiers' slang for courage and fighting spirit.

Bou Arada Second World War North Africa campaign battle honour marking the stand by British units during the North Africa campaign against a German offensive 18-25 January 1943. *See also: North Africa 1940-1943; Oudna; Tebourba Gap; Robaa Valley and Kasserine.*

Bou Ficha Second World War North Africa campaign battle honour marking one of the actions in the final breakthrough to the capture of Tunis in May 1943. *See also: North Africa 1940-1943; Tunis; Hammam Lif; Djebel Bou Aoukaz 1943 I; Djebel Bou Aoukaz 1943 II; Montarnaud; Ragoubet Souissi; Creteville Pass and Gromballa.*

Boulogne 1940 Second World War battle honour marking the defence of this port from 22 May until the garrison was withdrawn to England on 26 May 1940. *See also: North West Europe 1940 and Calais 1940.*

Boulogne 1944 Second World War battle honour marking the fall of this port to Canadian troops, supported by two British regiments, on 22 September 1944. *See also: North West Europe 1944-1945; Le Havre and Scheldt.*

Bound A single movement, usually from

cover to cover, made by troops, often under fire. The term is also used to describe the area between features of tactical importance, particularly on or astride the axis.

Bounty Lump sum payments sometimes made to certain members of the reserve for the satisfactory completion of specified attendance and training obligations.

Bourbon Battle honour marking the capture from the French of this island, now known as Réunion, by an expedition from India on 8 July 1810. The battle honour was awarded to 69th Foot (South Lincolnshire) in 1826 and to 86th Foot (Royal County Down) in 1823.

Bourgebus Ridge Second World War battle honour covering the offensive known as Operation GOODWOOD in 1944, designed to exploit the success at Caen (qv) and secure the Bourgebous Ridge south-east of the city. *See also: North West Europe 1944-1945; Caen; Maltot and Cagny.*

Bowles's Regiment of Dragoons
Raised in 1715, 12th Dragoons in 1751, and 12th Royal Lancers (Prince of Wales's) in 1921.

Bowman Combat radio system to replace the current Clansman system in 1998.

Boxed Epaulette Term given to an epaulette of which the bullion or fringe has been fixed instead of hanging freely.

Boxer Uprising An eight-week siege of the European embassies in Peking in 1900 by the 'Boxer' secret Society of the Righteous Harmonious Fists - Chinese opposed to Christians and to the ruling dynasty in China. The siege was raised by force of 2,000 seamen and marines from European fleets. This force had to make a stand at Tientsin, but further reinforcements relieved the embassies on 14 August. *See also: Pekin 1900.*

Boys Anti-Tank Rifle British heavy bolt action rifle of 0.55" calibre with a five-round magazine developed in the 1930s. Ostensibly for use by the infantry in the anti-tank role, it was in fact almost useless against armour and often painful to the firer. An improved tungsten-covered round was introduced in early 1940 but, apart from a brief return to popularity in 1942, the weapon was replaced by the PIAT (qv).

Bracketing Method used, particularly for artillery and mortar fire, to bring fire onto a target by systematically firing short of and beyond the target until the range is identified. by observing the rounds' fall on the target.

Braid Material taking a variety of forms and being both decorative and functional. Used to strengthen the button holes and other parts of coats and the brims of hats. Sometimes in metal wire for officers. Also called 'lace'.

Branch Staff division in a headquarters.

Breastplate Front plate of a cuirass (qv). Also, the belt plate worn on the breast.

Breastwork A temporary defensive work, usually breast high. Also called a parapet.

Breeches Trouser-like garment which finished at the knees, worn throughout the Army until replaced by trousers or overalls.

Bremen Second World War battle honour marking the operations 16-20 April 1945 which led to the capture of this city port. *See also: North West Europe 1944-1945.*

Bren Gun British light machine gun brought into Army service in the 1930s and, although now obsolete, considered by many to be one of the best light machine guns in the world. Derived from the Czech ZB26 design - hence 'Bren' from Brno/Enfield - and originally chambered for 0.303" calibre and fed from a 30 (usually 28) round curved magazine. Converted to NATO standard 7.62mm ammunition from the late 1940s. The weapon could be mounted on a tripod. Qualified Bren gunners wore a badge on the sleeve showing the letters BG within a wreath.

Bren Gun Carrier *See also: Carrier.*

Brevet Rank The practice of granting brevet rank has ceased. The term 'brevet' comes from the old French 'brievet' or letter, and was a document which authorised a commissioned officer to hold temporarily a higher military rank, but without the appropriate pay and allowances. The system was used extensively between the two Worls Wars but was suspended in 1939 when the wartime promotion code came into operation. Resumed after the Second World War, the granting of brevet rank ceased in 1952.

Bréville Second World War battle honour commemorating the repulse of German counter-attacks against the British left flank in the Bréville and Ranville areas, where the 6th Airborne Division had established itself to the east of the River Orne 10-13 June 1944. *See also: North West Europe 1944-45, Normandy Landing and Odon.*

Brickdusts Nickname given to 53rd Foot, later The King's Shropshire Light Infantry, subsequently embodied in The Light Infantry in 1968, because of their brick-red facings. The regiment was also nicknamed the 'Five and Threepennies' a pun on 53rd Foot and the old rate of an Ensign's pay.

Bridgehead An area of ground, in territory occupied or threatened by the enemy, which must be held or at least controlled to permit continuous embarkation, landing or crossing of troops and material, and provide manoeuvre space for subsequent operations.

Bridoon Rein The rein attached to the snaffle ring of a military bridle.

Brieux Bridgehead Second World War battle honour marking the defence of the bridgehead over the River Orne near Thury Harcourt by units of 59th Division in August 1944. *See also: North West Europe 1944-1945; Mont Pincon; Quarry Hill; Souleuvre; Catheolles; Le Perier Ridge; Jurques and La Varinière.*

Brigade An Army formation comprising two or more 'teeth arm' (qv) units, with supporting arms and services. Although primarily an operational formation, the term brigade has, from time to time been applied to administrative groupings of similar types of unit.

Brigadier Commissioned rank denoted by a triangle of three stars surmounted by a Crown worn on the epaulettes. A Warrant of 1705 placed Brigadiers-General below Major Generals, and an order 1860 permitted Brigadiers-General to dress as General Officers, but without badges on either collar or saddlecloth. The rank of Brigadier-General was discontinued in 1920. The rank is associated with command of a brigade or a senior staff appointment.

Brigade of Infantry An administrative grouping of infantry regiments formed under Army Order 61 of 1948. There were 15 such 'Brigades': Guards; East Anglian; Forester (Formerly the 'Midland'); Fusilier; Green Jacket; Highland; Home Counties; Lancastrian; Light Infantry; Lowland; Mercian; North Irish; Welsh; Wessex and Yorkshire. Under Army Order 34 of 1968 this 'Brigade' structure was replaced by six 'Divisions': Guards; Scottish; Queen's; King's; Prince of Wales's and Light. The Brigade of Gurkhas and the Parachute Regiment are outside the divisional structure.

Brigade of Gurkhas Formed on 1 January 1948 by transfer from the Indian Army to the British establishment of: 2nd King Edward VII's Own Gurkha Rifles (The Sirmoor Rifles); 6th Queen Elizabeth's Own Gurkha Rifles; 7th Duke of Edinburgh's Own Gurkha Rifles; 10th Princess Mary's Own Gurkha Rifles; The Queen's Gurkha Engineers (affiliated to the Corps of Royal Engineers in 1958); The Queen's Gurkha Signals (affiliated to The Royal Corps of Signals in 1958); and The Gurkha Transport Regiment (affiliated to The Royal Corps of Transport in 1965).
Headdress Badge: Two kukris upwards the blades crossed in saltire their cutting edges outwards.

Motto: *Kaphar hunnu bhanda marnu ramro* (It is better to die than live a coward). *See also: Gurkhas and Gurkha Regiments.*

Brigade Major Formerly the senior staff officer to the commander of a brigade. On assuming the NATO staff nomenclature the appointment of brigade major became known as chief of staff.

Brinkum Second World War battle honour marking the fighting around this town during the period 13-16 April 1945. *See also: North West Europe 1944-1945; Rhine; Ibbenbüren; Leese; Aller and Bremen.*

British Army of the Rhine (BAOR) The term British Army of the Rhine was first used in 1919 to describe the British Army in the Rhineland at the end of the First World War. In the Second World War, the cessation of hostilities in Europe on 5 May 1945 brought to a successful conclusion the task of 21 Army Group, and formations throughout the British Zone of Occupation set about their occupational duties, to establish the Military Government. While the machinery of the Control Commission for Germany was being established the Army was required to govern and administer an area as big as England with a population of some 20 millions. The status of 21 Army Group changed on 25 August 1945 when it was formally given the title British Army of the Rhine. On the creation of the Federal Republic of Germany on 1 September 1949 the title remained, embracing the British Army elements in Germany, fluctuating between 80,000 and 50,000 in number, and committed to NATO, the headquarters being at Rheindahlen, near Mönchengladbach. Following the reunification of Germany in 1990 the scale of the British presence in Germany was reduced to about 25,000, the major portion of which were with the Allied Command Europe Rapid Reaction Corps (qv). On 28 October 1994 the British Army of the Rhine ceased to exist, its status being changed to United Kingdom Support Command (Germany).

British East Africa 1896 Battle honour awarded in 1901 and marking the operations undertaken by 24th Baluch Light Infantry which took place in what is now Kenya in 1896.

British East Africa 1897-99 Battle honour marking operations in Kenya and, during 1898, in Uganda, by 27th Baluch Light Infantry and 4th Bombay Rifles.

British East Africa 1901 Battle honour awarded in 1905 to 116th Mahrattas for operations against the 'Mad Mullah' in British Somaliland.

British Expeditionary Force (BEF) Term applied to the British Army contingents which went to France in 1914 and 1939 in support of the left flank of the French armies. In the First World War, under the command of Field Marshal Sir John French, the BEF landed in France in August 1914, and consisted of one cavalry division and four infantry divisions, organised into two corps. Within a few weeks the force was reinforced by a further cavalry division and two more infantry divisions. In the Second World War, the British Expeditionary Force arrived in France in September 1939 under the command of General the Viscount Gort, and consisted of four infantry divisions organised into two corps. By the time of its evacuation through Dunkirk (qv) in May and June 1940 it had increased to 13 divisions. Out of a total strength of approximately 394,165, some 224,320 British personnel were recovered safely to Britain.

British Grenadiers A regimental quick march of: The Corps of Royal Engineers; Grenadier Guards; The Royal Highland Fusiliers (Military Band); The Royal Regiment of Fusiliers; The Royal Welch Fusiliers and The Honourable Artillery Company.

British Guiana 1953-64 Campaign to restore law and order following unrest arising from disaffection between the African and East Indian communities. The 1953 election, the first under conditions of universal suffrage, gave victory to the East Indian faction in the form of the better organised, and strongly leftist, People's

Progressive Party (PPP) under Dr Cheddi Jagan. Fearing a substantial shift toward communism, the British government felt obliged to suspend the constitution and, as a precautionary move, troops were moved to the colony. In 1957 a further election took place, the PPP again gaining a sweeping victory, taking 20 of the 35 seats but with only 43 per cent of the total vote. In February 1962 a general strike was called against Jagan's budget proposals and the local police, unable to contain rioting which had continued since 16 February, called on the military for help in restoring order. A further general strike was called in February 1963, accompanied by the now customary rioting. Unrest spread into the country districts accompanied by intimidation, looting and inter-factional violence. Order was largely restored by December 1963, but a garrison remained until the colony was granted independence as Guyana on 26 May 1966.

British Honduras British colony since the Anglo-Spanish treaty of 1786 and garrisoned by the Army since 1948. Both Mexico to the north and Guatemala to the West had laid claim to parts of British Honduras since the early 19th century; but never pressed those claims. In 1945, however, the Guatemalan government published a new constitution which referred to British Honduras as a province of Guatemala, and by late February 1948 there were clear indications that a Guatemalan invasion was threatened. A battalion was dispatched to the colony and no invasion took place, but it was decided to garrison the colony. This garrison was reinforced and reduced periodically in response to perceived fluctuations in the threat from Guatemala, and to help in hurricane relief work. The colony was renamed Belize on 1 June 1973 and became independent on 21 September 1981. *See also: Belize.*

British Legion *See: Royal British Legion.*

British Somaliland 1940 Second World War battle honour marking the resistance to the Italian invasion of this colony in August 1940. Eventually the small British garrison was forced to withdraw against overwhelming odds. *See also: Tug Argan and Barkasan.*

British South Africa Company's Medal 1890-1897 There are four different reverses to this medal, the first of which was sanctioned by Queen Victoria in 1896, the last by King George V in 1927. Each medal bears the words 'BRITISH SOUTH AFRICA COMPANY' with one of the following four campaigns shown above: 1. 'MATABELELAND 1893'; 2. 'RHODESIA 1896'; 3. 'MASHONALAND 1897'; and 4. (No place or date, but authorised for the Mashonaland campaign of 1890.)
Ribbon: 1.4" wide; orange-yellow with three narrow blue stripes, one in the centre and one 3mm from each edge.
Clasps: Mashonaland 1890; Matabeleland 1893; Rhodesia 1896 and Mashonaland 1897.

BRIXMIS Abbreviation used to describe the British Commander's-in-Chief Mission to the Group of Soviet Forces in Germany. Although ostensibly a liaison mission, their work was fundamentally intelligence gathering. This joint Service mission, was largely manned by British Army personnel, and supported by the British garrison in Berlin. Operating out of a Mission House in Potsdam, patrols from the mission operated throughout the Soviet zone of occupation in Germany from 16 September 1946 to 2 October 1994 in three roles: to detect preparations for war by the Soviet or East German forces; to gather information on the composition and organisation of the Soviet and East German forces; and to collect technical information. SOXMIS, a reciprocal Soviet mission based at Bünde, in the British area of occupation in West Germany, had a similar role.

Broad Arrow Symbol used to denote government property, printed or stamped on all service stores, clothing and equipment to prevent theft. The origin of the selection of this symbol is uncertain, but in 1683 one of the duties of the Lieutenant General of the Ordnance was to ensure that all ordnance property was marked with 'our mark'. This 'mark' consisted of an arrow with a 'B' for barrack on the left, and an 'O' for ordnance on the right. When such property was disposed of a further arrow, point-to-point with the existing arrow, was stamped on the item. It was certainly an offence, under an Act of 1698, to be caught in unauthorised possession of any items thus marked.

Broadsword Broad-bladed sword with enclosed hilt carried by Highlanders. Not to be confused with the Claymore (qv) which has a cross hilt.

Brodrick An undress, peak-less cap for other ranks introduced in 1902 and named after (Viscount) William Brodrick (1856-1942), Secretary of State for War in the early 1900s.

Broodeseinde First World War battle honour marking an action on 4 October 1917 in the Third Battle of Ypres. *See also: France and Flanders 1914-1918; Ypres 1917; Pilckem; Langemarck 1917; Menin Road; Polygon Wood; Poelcappelle and Passchendaele.*

Brown Bess Nickname given to a series of British flintlock (qv) muskets in use in the Army from about 1730. *See also: Matchlocks; Flintlocks; Musket and Rifle.*

Browning Machine gun named after the American designer of firearms John M Browning (1855-1926). The M2 Heavy Barrel (HB) version of this 0.5" calibre belt-fed weapon has been fitted to tanks, light armoured vehicles, light aircraft and used in a ground role mounted on a tripod.

Browning A5 Shotgun This 12-gauge five-shot smooth-bore combat shotgun entered production in 1903 and was used by British forces in the Malayan emergency in the 1950s.

Bruin Obsolescent secure communications system which linked battlefield formations with their higher headquarters. Replaced by Ptarmigan (qv).

Brunei and Borneo 1962-66 Campaign against Indonesian insurgents which began with the revolt of the North Kalimantan (Indonesian Borneo) National Army against the Sultan of Brunei on 8 December 1962; it involved jungle operations in Brunei, Sarawak, Sabah and the Malay peninsula, and ended with the signing of a peace agreement in Jakarta on 11 August 1966. British casualties in the campaign, including Gurkhas, were 118 killed and 245 wounded.

Bruneval Second World War battle honour marking the successful raid by a detachment of 2nd Parachute Regiment on the night of 27-28 February 1942, which secured and recovered to England key parts of a radio-location station on the French coast. *See also: North West Europe 1942.*

Brunswick Rifle Designed in 1837, this 0.704" calibre rifle was developed as a replacement for the Baker rifle (qv) but, due to loading difficulties caused by poorly manufactured ammunition, it was ultimately rejected.

Brussels Second World War battle honour marking the occupation of Brussels on 3 September 1944 by the Guards Armoured Division following a rapid 70 mile advance from the French frontier. *See also: North West Europe 1944-1945; Seine 1944; Amiens 1944 and Antwerp.*

Bucket Name given to the leather cup or shoe on horse furniture to hold the butt of a musket.

Buckinghamshire Regiment (14th Foot) Raised at Canterbury by Colonel Sir Edward Hales in June 1685 and numbered 14th Foot in 1751. *See also: The Prince of Wales's Own Regiment of Yorkshire.*

Buckinghamshire Regiment (16th Foot) *See: Bedfordshire and Hertfordshire Regiment.*

Buckinghamshire Volunteers (85th Foot) *See: King's Shropshire Light Infantry.*

Buckinghamshire Yeomanry (The Royal Buckinghamshire Hussars) Raised in May 1794 and first known as the

'Bucks Armed Yeomanry'. In 1802 the troops were reorganised into three regiments: 1st or Southern Regiment; 2nd or Mid-Bucks Yeomanry Cavalry and the 3rd or Northern Regiment. The 2nd Regiment remained in service without pay from 1828 to 1830 while the other two regiments disbanded. Redesignated Buckinghamshire Yeomanry Cavalry (Royal Bucks Hussars) in 1845, the regiment provided four companies for the Imperial Yeomanry between 1899 and 1902: Numbers 37 and 38 of the 10th Battalion and 56 and 57 of the 15th Battalion. In the First World War the regiment served in both mounted and dismounted roles in Gallipoli, Egypt, Palestine and, following amalgamation with the Berkshire Yeomanry, as a machine gun battalion in France. In 1920 the Bucks Yeomanry converted to artillery and served as such throughout the Second World War. On 15 September 1950 the regiment amalgamated with 387 Field Regiment Royal Artillery (Oxfordshire Yeomanry) (TA) to form 299 (Buckinghamshire and Oxfordshire Yeomanry) Field Regiment Royal Artillery (TA). In 1969 the regiment was reduced to a cadre and disbanded.

Buckler A small round shield worn on the forearm or held by a short handle. A means of protection or defence.

Buckshee Military slang for without charge, free or surplus. From the Persian *bakhshish* - to give.

Buff A soft thick flexible undyed leather used at one time for belts and other straps on soldiers' equipment.

Buffalo Second World War tracked amphibious vehicle used in the Allied landings in Normandy in June 1944. It could carry 28 men, or a four ton load, at 7mph through water. The frontal armour was just sufficient to give protection from small arms fire.

Buffs (Royal East Kent Regiment) (3rd Foot) The regiment has its origin in a body of London 'Train-Bands', distinguished by their buff facings, sent to Holland in 1572 to aid the Protestant cause. The unit was disbanded by the Dutch in 1665 when some of the officers and men returned to England to be formed by Charles II into a new 'Holland Regiment' under the command of Colonel Robert Sydney. The nickname 'Buffs' became part of the official regimental title in 1665. In 1961 the Buffs amalgamated with the other Kent regiment, the Queen's Own Royal West Kent Regiment (qv) to form the Queen's Own Buffs, The Royal Kent Regiment and, in 1966, was embodied in The Queen's Regiment. In 1992 The Queen's Regiment amalgamated with The Royal Hampshire Regiment to form The Princess of Wales's Royal Regiment (qv).

Headdress Badge: On a ground the Dragon. Below, a scroll inscribed 'THE BUFFS'.

History: *Historical Record of 3rd Regiment of Foot* and *History of The Buffs (Royal East Kent Regiment) 1572-1948 (5 Vols)*.

Bugle Horn A stringed bugle horn is the traditional insignia of light infantry and rifle regiments, and the cap badge of The Light Infantry. It is probable that the Bugle Horn reached the British Army through the Hanoverian influence following the accession of George I in 1714. There is evidence of a very similar *Halbmond* (half-moon) horn, based on the earlier *Flügelhorn*, being used by Hanoverian forces in 1758 where it was a distinguishing instrument for *Jäger* and other light troops.

Bugle Major Warrant officer or senior non-commissioned officer who commands the Bugle Platoon in light infantry and rifle regiments. The Bugle Major is responsible for the military and musical standards of the Bugle Platoon - the sub-unit in which the buglars are concentrated - and is answerable, in the first instance, to the Adjutant. The Bugle Major is also responsible for the drill of both the military band and the bugles, taking precedence over the Bandmaster on ceremonial occasions.

Bugler A soldier qualified to play the bugle. Qualified buglers in light infantry and rifle regiments wear a badge showing a stringed bugle horn on the sleeve.

Bulk Breaking Point Point at which combat supplies (qv) brought forward in bulk are broken down into unit loads for collection and movement forward.

Bull Soldiers' slang, short for bullshit. Term applied to excessive cleaning and polishing and to a particular method of polishing leather. The term is also applied to incorrect information or rumour, particularly when an element of exaggeration is involved.

Bullecourt First World War battle honour marking the attack on German positions in this village on 3 May 1917, the day before the end of the Arras offensive. There was heavy fighting for two weeks before the village was cleared. *See also: France and Flanders 1914-1918 and Arras 1917,*

Buller, General Sir Redvers Henry (1839-1908) Born near Crediton, Devon he saw service in China in 1860; in the Red River Expedition in 1870; in the Ashanti War in 1874 and in the Kaffir and Zulu campaigns of 1878-79, in which he won the Victoria Cross for rescuing three comrades. In 1881 he served in the Boer War (qv) as Chief-of-Staff to Sir Evelyn Wood; in 1882 in the Egyptian campaign as head of the intelligence branch; and in 1884-85 as Chief-of-Staff in the Sudan War. He spent ten successful years in the War Office (1887-97), first as Quartermaster General and subsequently as Adjutant General. In 1899 he became Commander-in-Chief of British forces in South Africa. Owing to several severe defeats he was superseded by Lord Roberts and, after engaging in the expulsion of the Boers from Natal, returned to England in 1900. Although regarded with genuine affection by the other ranks of the Army - for whose welfare he laboured ceaselessly - and a brave and intelligent officer, his reputation never recovered from the run of defeats in South Africa. He is wrongly identified as the epitome of the brainless, blundering blimp; a notion to which his appearance lent credence.

Bullet Solid projectile discharged from small arms of all kinds. Most modern bullets are of composite form, consisting of a cupro-nickel or coated steel jacket containing fillings which vary according to the nature of the target and ballistic qualities required.

Bullion Thick gold or silver wire or fringed cord used as a trimming on uniforms, also called bullion fringe.

Bullseye Central area of a target carrying the highest score.

Bulo Erillo Second World War Abyssinian campaign battle honour marking one of the actions in the Battle of the Juba. *See also: Abyssinia 1940-41; Keren; Jebel Defeis; Jebel Shiba; Gogni; Agordat; Barentu; Karora-Marsa Taclai; Cubcub; Ad Teclesan; Mescelit Pass; Mt Engiahat; Massawa; Amb Alagi; Afodu; Gambela; El Wak; Moyale; Wal Garis; Juba; Marda Pass; Bisidimo; Awash; Todenyang-Namaraputh; Omo; Soroppa; Giarso; Colito; Wadara; Gondar; Fike and Lechemti.*

Buq Buq Second World War North Africa campaign battle honour marking an action within the Battle of Sidi Barrani in December 1940. The 7th Armoured Division conducted an encircling movement to the coast at Buq Buq, thus cutting off many of the withdrawing Italians. *See also: North Africa 1940-1943; Egyptian Frontier 1940; Sidi Barrani and Capture of Tobruk.*

Burgoyne, John (1722-92) General. Entered the Army at a very early age and was soon obliged to sell his commission to pay his debts. He made a runaway marriage with the Earl of Derby's daughter and spent time abroad until, with the help of his father-in-law, he was restored to his rank in the Army in 1758. In 1759 he became the first commander of light infantry in the British Army and in 1761 became an MP, being promoted to Brigadier-General in 1762. At the close of the Seven Years' War (qv) he devoted himself to politics and play-writing, his first play being produced in 1775. On the outbreak of hostilities with the American colonists in 1775 he was appointed to command of a division and made a fatal atempt to attack the colonists from Canada. His force was surrounded by General Gates at Saratoga and forced to surrender with 3,500 men. He was deprived of his appointments, but these were restored to him in 1782. He retired into private life and devoted himself to his dramatic works. His most popular work, *The Heiress*, appeared in 1786 and his poetical and dramatic works were published in 1808.

Burgoyne's Light Horse Raised in 1759 by Colonel John Burgoyne as 16th Regiment of (Light) Dragoons or Burgoynes Light Horse. Redesignated 16th (or the Queen's) Regiment of Light Dragoons in 1769 and 16th (Queen's) Lancers (qv) in 1855. Amalgamated with 5th Royal Irish Lancers in 1922 to form 16th/5th Lancers (qv).

BURMA

First Burma War 1824-26 Burmese threats to invade Bengal, persistent territorial violations by Burmese troops and a series of aggressive actions in Sylhet and Cachar provoked a reluctant Britain into an invasion of Burma by four columns of British and Indian troops in 1824 and the capture of Rangoon. The subsequent campaign chiefly involved expeditions to capture stockaded positions but ended in victory near Prome in 1825. *See also: Ava; Kemmendine and Arracan.*

Second Burma War 1852-53 Continued infringements by the King of Burma of the treaty that had ended the First Burma War (qv) resulted in a second British invasion in 1852. Rangoon was captured in April 1853 and Pegu in October. *See also: Pegu.*

Third Burma War 1885-87 The absurd pretensions of the King of Burma had led to a cessation of all diplomatic links between Britain and Burma in 1879. In 1884 King Thebaw gave cause for further remonstrances by the high-handed treatment accorded to an English company trading in Burma. On 22 October 1885, a contemptuous Burmese reply to a British

ultimatum led to war. A combined British and Indian naval and military force advanced rapidly toward Mandalay, and the king then surrendered unconditionally. However, for the next two years a significant force had to be maintained in Burma to suppress dacoitry. *See also: Burma 1885-87.*

Burma 1885-87 Battle honour awarded to British units in 1890 and Indian units in 1891 to mark the Third Burma War (qv) and the actions of the expedition of 1885 under General Prendergast.

Burma 1942-45 Battle honour marking the campaign in Burma 1942-45. The Japanese invaded Burma from Thailand in January 1942 and forced the River Sittang, compelling the British to evacuate Rangoon and form a defensive line, in co-operation with Chinese forces, between Prome and Toungoo. A further Japanese offensive turned these defences and, after severe fighting around Yenangyaung, the British were forced to withdraw across the Chindwin into India; the Chinese withdrew to the north. By the end of 1942 the Japanese held virtually all Burma and the only Allied activity in 1943, apart from the first Chindit (qv) raid, was a British offensive into the Arakan, aimed at Akyab, which was repulsed by the Japanese. In January 1944 a further offensive was launched into the Arakan; this time the Japanese counter-stroke was held, allowing reinforcements to move through to the more vital sector further north. Here the main Japanese armies had launched an offensive across the Chindwin against Imphal and Kohima. There followed bitter and protracted fighting into July 1944 which ended with the complete defeat and withdrawal of the Japanese. Meanwhile, in March 1944 the much larger second Chindit expedition had been flown in to Burma with the aim of cutting the communications of the Japanese facing the Chinese forces under General Stilwell, who were pressing the Japanese in the north and with whom the British 36th Division was operating. In November 1944 General Slim led the Fourteenth Army across the Chindwin in an offensive and, continuing his advance during the monsoon, reached the Irrawaddy, which was first crossed in January 1945. However, the main thrust, forcing the river to the south, reached Meiktila at the beginning of March 1945 and this drive led to the decisive battle of the campaign. By the end of March 1945 Japanese resistance was beginning to crumble and, in early May 1945, Rangoon fell to a seaborne assault which then linked up with the main force of Fourteenth Army moving southward. Thereafter it was largely a mopping up operation to destroy the remnants of the Japanese seeking to escape through the hills of the Pegu Yomas; the campaign ended in August 1945.

Burma Gallantry Medal Gallantry award, open to Governor's commissioned officers, non-commissioned officers and other ranks of the Burma Army, the Burma Frontier Force, the Burma Military Police, the Burma Royal Naval Volunteer Reserve Force and the Burma Auxiliary Air Force, instituted on 10 May 1940, but not published in the London Gazette until 4 September 1945. To be conferred by the Governor of Burma for 'any act of conspicuous gallantry performed in connection with their duties.'
Ribbon: Dark green, 1¼" wide, with ¼"central crimson stripe.

Burma Infantry, 1st Regiment *See: Gurkhas, 10th Princess Mary's Own Gurkha Rifles.*

Burmah Battle honour awarded to the Bombay Marine Battalion for services in the First Burma War.

Burn Out The point at which the illuminated signal at the base of a tracer round expires and the trajectory of the round can no longer be easily followed.

Busaco Peninsula War battle honour awarded between 1817 and 1910 marking the action on 27 September 1810 in which Wellington inflicted a sharp defeat on Masséna, who had been tasked by Napoleon to 'drive the British into the sea', before withdrawing to the lines of Torres Vedras. *See also: Peninsula; Talavera; Barrosa and Fuentes d'Onor.*

Busby A tall fur helmet with a bag hanging from the top to the right side, particularly associated with the hussars, but also worn by the Royal Horse Artillery. The name is taken from the hatter, W Busby of the Strand in London.

Busby Bag The cloth cap worn by the original hussars had an edging of fur. When the height of the fur was increased, so was the length of the cap, which then hung out of the top falling on the right side and being known as the 'bag'.

Bushire Battle honour awarded for an action on 5 December 1856 during the Persian campaign of 1856-57. *See also: Persia 1856-7; Reshire and Koosh-Ab.*

Bush Hat Broad-brimmed hat, probably modelled on that worn by African hunters, and worn extensively during the Second World War in the Middle and Far East. Often worn with one side turned up and secured by a cap badge or formation sign.

Bush Jacket Sometimes called the bush shirt, this could be of khaki drill or drab olive green material. It was developed during the Second World War for wear in the Middle and Far East. Being a type of tunic with side pockets on the skirts, it was worn outside the shorts or trousers.

Buthidaung Second World War, Burma campaign battle honour awarded for the actions by 7th Indian Division in the area of Buthidaung between January and April 1944 during the offensive into the Arakan over the period 1 January to 12 June. *See also: Burma 1942-1945; North Arakan; Razibil; Kaladan; Mayu Tunnels; Alethangyaw; Maungdaw; Mowdok and Point 551.*

Butt The mound of earth behind the targets on a shooting range to stop projectiles, or that part of a shooting range in which the target frames are situated. Alternatively, that part of the stock of a weapon which is placed in the shoulder.

Butt Plate Plate, usually made of metal, and attached to the butt end of a gun stock.

Button Stick Small plate, originally made of brass, placed between a button and the uniform during cleaning to prevent cleaning fluid or material marking the fabric of the uniform.

Buxar Battle honour awarded to one regiment in 1829 and another in 1844 marking the action on 23 October 1764 when a British Force under Hector Munro routed the Imperial Mogul army led by the Nawab of Oudh. Before the battle Munro was faced by a mutiny among his native troops which he resolved by blowing 24 mutineers from guns. The victory at Bazaar confirmed the effects of the Battle of Plassey (qv) and led to the establishment of British garrisons as far north as Allahabad and Lucknow.

***Bydand* (Firm)** Motto of 92nd (Gordon Highlanders) Regiment of Foot; and later of The Gordon Highlanders.

'C' The letter 'C' on arm badges in the British Army was used to indicate 'C' group tradesmen from 1944 onward.

'C' Vehicles Generic term for all engineer plant such as tractors, bulldozers, fork-lift trucks and cranes. *See also: 'A' and 'B' vehicles.*

Ça Ira **(It will go on)** One of the regimental quick marches of the Prince of Wales's Own Regiment of Yorkshire (14th and 15th Foot).

Cabar Feidh **(The Deer's Horns)** Motto of 72nd (Duke of Albany's Own Highlanders) Regiment of Foot.

Cabool 1842 Battle honour marking the campaign of the so-called 'Avenging Army' following the First Afghan War (qv). The force under General Pollock relieved Jellalabad and reoccupied Kabul, arriving just ahead of General Nott's troops from Kandahar. *See also: Affghanistan 1839; Ghuznee 1839; Khelat 1839; Candahar 1842 and Ghuznee 1842.*

Cadre A group of trained men forming the basis for the training of new units or expansion. A course of military instruction.

Caen Second World War battle honour marking the clearance and capture of Caen during the period 4-18 July 1944. *See also: North West Europe 1944-1945; Normandy Landing; Hill 112; Noyers; Orne and Esquay.*

Caernarvonshire Yeomanry In the early 1900s a squadron of the Denbighshire Hussars recruited in Caernarvonshire and included a troop raised in Anglesey. The county name was incorporated in the title of 61st (Caernarvon and Denbigh Yeomanry) Medium Regiment Royal Artillery when it was formed in 1920. *See also: Denbighshire Yeomanry.*

Cage Temporary enclosure in which prisoners of war are held.

Cagny Second World War battle honour marking one of the actions during 'Operation Goodwood' which sought to exploit the success at Caen. *See also: North West Europe 1944-1945; Bourgebous Ridge; Maltot and Troarn.*

Calabritto Second World War Italian campaign battle honour marking the capture of the village of Calabritto during the battle for Monte Camino, a dominating outpost of the German 'Gustav Line' defences during November and December 1943. *See also: Italy 1943-1945; Teano and Monte Camino.*

Calais 1940 Second World War battle honour marking the heroic defence of Calais from 22-26 May 1940 which gained vital time for the British Expeditionary Force (qv) to reorganize. *See also: North West Europe 1940-1942; Defence of Arras; Boulogne 1940; St Omer-La Bassée and Dunkirk 1940.*

Calais 1944 Second World War battle honour marking one of a number of actions which took place between the crossing of the River Seine and advance to the Rhine between August 1944 and March 1945. *See also: North West Europe 1944-1945; Opheusden and Asten.*

Caldari Second World War Italian campaign battle honour marking an Eighth Army action in 1943. *See also: Italy 1943-1945; Landing at Porto San Venere; Taranto; San Salvo; Orsogna and Impossible Bridge.*

Caledonian, The Regimental slow march of the Queen's Regiment.

Caltrop Four spikes, joined in such a manner that, when placed on the ground, one spike is always pointing upward. Originally used as a device to lame enemy horses, now used to puncture vehicle tyres.

Cambes Second World War battle honour marking the capture, after bitter fighting, of the village of Cambes following the Normandy landings in June 1944. *See also: North West Europe 1944-1945; Normandy Landing; Sully; Putôt en Bessin and Bréville.*

Cambrai 1917 First World War battle honour marking the British offensive of 20 November which employed massed tanks for the first time. Though it initially met with huge success and broke through the Hindenburg Line, a German counter-offensive launched on 30 November 1917 recovered most of the ground gained. *See also: France and Flanders 1914-1918; Ypres 1917 and Somme 1918.*

Cambrai 1918 First World War battle honour marking an action during the closing phase of the Battle for the Hindenburg Line. In the face of strong German resistance the British exploited their success on the Canal du Nord in the northern sector and crossed the River Scheldt; Cambrai fell on 8 October 1918. *See also: France and Flanders 1914-1918; Hindenburg Line; Havrincourt; Épéhy; Canal du Nord; St Quentin Canal and Beaurevoir.*

Cambridge, Adolphus Frederick, 1st Duke of (1774-1850) Seventh son of George III, born Buckingham (then Queen's) Palace. He served from 1794-95 in the campaign against revolutionary France, was created Duke of Cambridge in 1801 and appointed field marshal in 1813, and was Viceroy of Hanover from 1815-36.

Cambridge, George William Frederick Charles, 2nd Duke of (1819-1904) Born Hanover, first cousin of Queen Victoria and only son of George III's seventh son Adolphus Frederick. He was made Field Marshal in 1862 and, thanks to Queen Victoria, held the position of Commander-in-Chief, an appointment for which he was unsuitable in almost every respect, from 1856 to 1895. He did much to oppose the very necessary reorganisation of the Army initiated by Edward (later Viscount) Cardwell (qv).

Cambridgeshire Regiment (30th Foot) Raised on 8 March 1689 by George Viscount Castleton and styled Lord Castleton's Regiment of Foot. Disbanded in 1698, but re-raised in 1702 as Saunderson's Regiment of Marines. The regiment amalgamated with 59th Foot (2nd Nottinghamshire Regiment) to form The East Lancashire Regiment (qv) in 1881.

Cambridgeshire Yeomanry A corps of Cambridgeshire Yeomanry Cavalry existed in November 1796, and by 1803 there were three troops. In 1831 the Whittlesey and Cambridgeshire Yeomanry was raised, and it remained in service at least until the 1850s.

Cameron Highlanders (79th Foot) *See: Queen's Own Cameron Highlanders.*

Cameronians (Scottish Rifles) (26th and 90th Foot) The 26th Foot was raised at Douglas, Lanarkshire in May 1689 as The Earl of Angus's Regiment from the amnestied survivors of the Cameronian covenanters' attempt to help William III against James II. Became 26th Foot (The Cameronians) in 1751 and 26th Cameronian Regiment in 1786. The 90th Foot was raised in May 1794 by Thomas Graham of Balgowen, later Lord Lynedoch, as 90th Perthshire Volunteers and became the Perthshire Light Infantry in 1815. In May 1881 the two regiments merged to form The Scottish Rifles (Cameronians), redesignated The Cameronians (Scottish Rifles) in July 1881. The regiment was disbanded on 14 May 1968.

Headdress Badge: The bugle horn of the 90th surmounted by a five-starred mullet (a spur-rowel from the arms of the 1st Earl of Angus) enclosed by two sprays of thistle.
Regimental marches:
Quick marches: *Kenmuir's on and awa'* and *The Gathering of the Grahams* (Pipes and Drums), and *Within a Mile of Edinboro' Town* (Regimental Band).
Slow March: *Garb of Auld Gaul* (Regimental Band).
Regimental Headquarters:
Moat Hill, Off Maar Street, Hamilton, Lanarkshire, ML3 6BY.
History: *Historical Record of The 26th or Cameronian Regiment* by T Carter (1867); *Records of The 90th Regiment Perthshire Light Infantry* by M Delavoye (1880); and *History of The Cameronians (Scottish Rifles)* Vol 1 1689-1910 by S H F Johnston (1957), Vol 2 1910-1933 by H H Story (1961) Vol 3 1933-1946 by C N Barclay (1947), Vol 4 1946-1948 by J Baynes.

Cameroons 1914-16 First World War battle honour marking the campaign waged by an Anglo-French expeditionary force which invaded the Cameroon, a German colony, in September 1914. An important radio station at Douala was destroyed and the town surrendered on 27 September. British troops were involved in fighting until November 1916, but it was the French who finally drove the remaining German forces into the Spanish territory of Rio Muni in February 1916. By April 1916 the entire territory was in Allied hands. *See also: Duala; Garua and Banyo.*

Camouflage From the French *camoufler -* to disguise. The altering or disguising of the silhouette of troops, vehicles, equipment and structures by the application of broken irregular patches of colour, thus causing them to blend with the surrounding countryside.

Camouflage Net A wide mesh net to which are affixed lengths of multicoloured scrim and foliage. The net is then suspended over vehicles and stores to break up the silhouette.

Camp A place where tents, huts or other temporary structures are erected for the use of troops.

Campaign Series of complementary military operations aimed at achieving a single objective; usually confined to one season or theatre.

Campaign Medals The first award for war service rather than gallantry, which was open to all ranks, was the medal issued by the Commonwealth to mark the defeat of Scots Royalists at the battle of Dunbar on 3 September 1650. In the early 19th century, gold crosses and medallions were awarded to senior officers and commanders for services in the Peninsula campaign, but it was not to be until the Battle of Waterloo that the issue of a campaign medal, open to all ranks, began.

Campaign Service Medal 1962 *See: General Service Medal 1962.*

Campbell, Sir Colin, Baron Clade (1792-1863) The son of a Glasgow carpenter, he fought at Walcheren and throughout the Peninsula War (qv), earning a Captaincy. He became Lieutenant Colonel in 1837 and, for outstanding service in the Second Sikh War (qv), particularly at Chillianwallah and the Punjab, was knighted and appointed to command in Peshawar. He commanded the Highland Brigade in the Crimea. In the year of the mutiny, when appointed by Palmerston to be Commander-in-Chief in India, he started from London the next day and stamped out the rebellion in a few months. Made Baron Clade and Field Marshal in 1858, he returned home in 1860.

Campbells are Coming A regimental quick march (Pipes and Drums) of the Argyll and Sutherland Highlanders (Princess Louise's), and regimental gallop of the Queen's Royal Hussars (Queen's Own and Royal Irish).

Campoleone Second World War Italian campaign battle honour marking the attempts to extend the western face of the Anzio beachhead during the period 24-31

January 1944. *See also: Italy 1943-1945; Anzio; Aprilia and Carroceto.*

Campriano Second World War Italian campaign battle honour marking the capture on 28 July 1944 of Campriano, which dominated the lateral road to Arezzo, during the advance up Italy. *See also: Italy 1943-1945; Monte Cedrone; Citta di Castillo; Poggio del Grillo and Fiesole.*

Canada General Service Medal 1866-1870 An Army Order of January 1899 authorised the Canadian Government to issue this medal to members of the Imperial forces and Canadian Militia engaged in the Fenian Raids and the Red River Expedition under Colonel Wolseley.
Ribbon: Equal vertical divisions of red, white and red.
Clasps: Fenian Raid 1866; Fenian Raid 1870 and Red River 1870.

Canal Du Nord First World War battle honour marking the crossing of the Canal du Nord and subsequent assault on the German defences north of the main Hindenburg Line along the St Quentin Canal on 27 September 1918. The success of this operation meant in effect that the Hindenburg Line had been broken. *See also: France and Flanders 1914-1918; Hindenburg Line; Havrincourt; Épéhy; Canal du Nord; Beaurevoir and Chambray 1918.*

Candahar 1842 Despite the reverses suffered by the main army during the First Afghan War (qv), Kandahar remained in British hands; the garrison repelling at least two serious Afghan attacks, the most serious in March 1842. This battle honour marks 'the actions of the garrison. *See also: Affghanistan 1839; Ghuznee 1839; Khelat; Ghuznee 1842 and Cabool 1842.*

Candahar, Ghuznee and Cabul Medals 1841-1842 First Afghan War (qv) medal authorised by a General Order in India in October 1842. There are four different strikings of this medal: 'CANDAHAR 1842'; 'CABUL 1842'; 'GHUZNEE and CABUL 1842'; and 'CANDAHAR, GHUZNEE and CABUL 1842'. However,

only one medal could be awarded to anyone individual.
Ribbon: 1" wide, rainbow pattern watered red, white, yellow, white and blue. *See also: Ghuznee Medal 1839.*

Canea Second World War Crete campaign battle honour marking the defence of the main town on the north coast and the fighting in the Maleme and Suda Bay areas from 20-27 May following the German airborne attack on Crete on 20 May 1941. *See also: Crete; Heraklion; Retimo and Withdrawal to Sphakia.*

Cannon A badge showing a cannon was used to distinguish artillerymen as early as 1821. Crossed gun or cannon barrels are also used to denote particular artillery specialisations.

Cannonade An intense and protracted artillery bombardment.

Cannoneer A soldier who served and fired a cannon; an artilleryman.

Cannon Fodder Individuals or groups committed to action without full knowledge of, or inadequately prepared for, the military situation.

Canteen A vessel to hold water or a container for cooking utensils. Also, a refreshment room provided in barracks or camp. *See also: Navy, Army and Air Force Institute.*

Canton Battle honour marking the capture and occupation of the city in December 1857 by a force from Hong Kong during the Second Chinese War of 1857-60.

Cap Term applied to Headdress of cloth, leather, metal or other material, without a brim, although often with a peak.

Cap Comforter Khaki, woollen, tube-like scarf, which could be rolled up and worn on the head either on its own or inside a steel helmet. The cap comforter was first issued during the First World War.

Cap Lines Lines or cords secured to the cap and the body to prevent the loss of the cap should it fall from the head.

CAPABILITY

Capability may be defined as the fighting power necessary to permit a force to successfully execute any military task it may be given. The components of capability, combined to a greater or lesser extent, are a product of the principles of war (qv) and doctrine (qv), and may be broadly defined as:

Command and Control Command being the authority to direct, co-ordinate and control a military force; control being the means by which command is exercised.

Deployability The ability to respond at short notice, at the appropriate level, and deploy a suitable force over long distances. The need to balance speed of deployment against force potency may emerge.

Protection Protection is necessary to conserve the potential of a force until the chosen time and place for its application is reached. The term protection embraces both active and passive protective measures.

Sustainability The ability to sustain a force will govern the tempo and duration of operations.

Information and Intelligence The ability to collect, collate and disseminate information is fundamental to the success of any military enterprise.

Precision Interdiction The ability to strike precisely and decisively throughout the theatre of conflict will reduce the cost in both human and materiel terms.

Firepower Firepower is an essential ingredient in the destruction of an enemy's will and ability to fight.

Manoeuvre The ability to move in relation to the movement of an enemy force to achieve a relative positional advantage.

Control of the Electro-Magnetic Spectrum Successful operations depend increasingly on use of the electro-magnetic spectrum.

Cape The term cape was used in the 18th century to describe the large turned-down collar of a coat. Coats with capes were used by the cavalry in the 19th and 20th centuries, and there are some examples of infantry coats with capes.

Cape of Good Hope 1806 Battle honour marking the capture in 1806 by a force under Sir David Baird of what later became Cape Colony. The area had been captured by the British in 1796, but was returned to the Dutch under the Treaty of Amiens in 1802.

Cape of Good Hope General Service Medal 1880-1897 Issued in 1900 by the Cape Government with the approval of the Crown. Although it was largely issued to colonial troops, a number of British officers and men were involved in the periodic suppression of small uprisings.
Ribbon: Equal vertical bands of dark blue, light biscuit and dark blue.
Clasps: Transkei; Basutoland and Bechuanaland.

Cappezano Second World War Italian campaign battle honour marking one of the actions in the Fifth Army advance to the Gustav Line. *See also: Italy 1943-1945; Capture of Naples; Monte Stella; Cava di Tirreni; Scafati Bridge; Cardito; Volturno Crossing; Monte Maro Roccheta e Croce and Colle Cedro.*

Captain Commissioned rank above lieutenant and below major. In February 1810 the rank of captain was indicated by the wearing of one epaulette on the right shoulder. With the introduction of the tunic rather than the coatee in 1855, epaulettes became obsolete and rank was worn on the collar, a captain having lace or braid on the top and front of the collar only, but now wearing a crown and star. In October 1880 rank badges reverted to the shoulder, but now on twisted cord, with the captain rank being indicated by two stars. In May 1902 this changed to three stars, and the rank of captain is still indicated by the wearing of three stars on each epaulette. Sometimes the term Captain is used to indicate a military commander of outstanding talent. *See also: Rank.*

Captain General Certain regiments and corps, such as the Royal Regiment of

Artillery and Royal Marines, have as titular head a Captain General rather than a Colonel-in-Chief. *See also: Rank.*

Capture of Forli Second World War Italian campaign battle honour marking one of the actions during the Italian campaign in the advance from the Gothic Line. The town fell following heavy fighting between 7 and 9 November 1944. *See also: Italy 1943-1945; Santarcangelo; Monte Chicco; Casa Fortis; Cosina Canal Crossing and Lamone Crossing.*

Capture of Halfaya Pass Second World War North Africa campaign battle honour marking an action between the occupation of the Alamein Line and the end of the North African campaign in 1943. *See also: North Africa 1940-1943; Deir El Munassib; Matmata Hills; Sebkret En Noual; Chebket En Nouiges; Djebel El Telil and Djebel Tebaga.*

Capture of Meiktila Second World War Burma campaign battle honour marking the capture of Meiktila from the Japanese during the Burma campaign in March 1945. *See also: Burma 1942-1945; Meiktila; Nyaungu Bridgehead; Defence of Meiktila and Taungtha.*

Capture of Naples Second World War Italian campaign battle honour awarded to mark an action by Fifth Army units during the advance to the Gustav Line in the Italian campaign. *See also: Italy 1943-1945; Cappezano; Monte Stella; Cava di Tirreni; Scafati Bridge; Cardito; Volturno Crossing; Monte Maro; Roccheta e Croce and Colle Cedro.*

Capture of Perugia Second World War, Italian campaign battle honour marking the operations over the period 18-20 June 1944 during which positions were secured which posed a serious threat to the German Trasimene Line defences. *See also: Italy 1943-1945; Rome; Ficulle; Citta Della Pieve; Monte Malbe and Trasimene Line.*

Capture of Ravenna Second World War Italian campaign battle honour marking the fall of the city to Eighth Army units on 4 December 1944. *See also: Italy 1943-1945; Rimini Line; Savio Bridgehead; Marradi; Monte Gamberaldi and Battaglia.*

Capture of Tobruk Second World War North Africa campaign battle honour marking the capture of Tobruk from the Italians on 24 January 1941. *See also: North Africa 1940-1943; Sidi Barrani; Buq Buq; Beda Fomm; Withdrawal to Matruh; Bir Enba and Bardia 1941.*

Carabiniers Literally, soldiers armed with carbines, but widely applied to cavalry armed with the carbine. Their function was to act as skirmishers and harass the enemy. The name was abolished in the French army in 1870, but was carried in the British Army by 3rd and 6th Dragoon Guards and now rests with The Royal Scots Dragoon Guards (Carabiniers and Greys).

Carbine Or carabine, shortened form of musket or rifle carried by mounted soldiers *(see: Carabiniers)*, usually attached to the saddle.

Cardigan, James Thomas Brudenell, 7th Earl of (1797-1868) Born in Hambledon, Hampshire, he commanded the 15th and 11th Hussars and was constantly in dispute with his officers. In the Crimean War he led the famous Charge of the Light Brigade at Balaklava in 1854. Afterwards he was appointed Inspector-General of Cavalry (1855-60) and lieutenant general in 1861.

Cardiganshire Yeomanry A squadron of yeomanry was found by the county for the Pembroke Yeomanry from 1901. *See also: Pembrokeshire Yeomanry.*

Cardito Second World War Italian campaign battle honour marking one of the actions in the Fifth Army advance to the Gustav Line. *See also: Italy 1943-1945; Cappezano; Monte Stella; Cava di Tirreni; Scafati Bridge; Volturno Crossing; Monte Maro; Roccheta e Croce and Colle Cedro.*

Cardwell, Edward, 1st Viscount (1813-86) Statesman, born in Liverpool and educated at Winchester and Balliol College, Oxford. He became a barrister in 1838 and MP for Clitheroe in 1842. Sir Robert Peel made him Secretary of the Treasury (1845-46). In Lord Aberdeen's ministry he was President of the Board of Trade (1852-55) and under Lord Palmerston became Secretary for Ireland (1859-61), Chancellor of the Duchy of Lancaster (1861), and while Secretary for the Colonies (1864-66) put an end to transportation. In Gladstone's ministry he was Secretary for War (1868-74) and introduced far-reaching reforms and reorganisation to the Army in 1871-72. In spite of bitter opposition from the Duke of Cambridge and the Army establishment he: abolished flogging in peacetime (1868); introduced a shorter enlistment term of six years' active service and six years' reserve service; subordinated the Commander-in-Chief to the War Secretary (1870) and abolished the purchase of commissions (1871). He divided the War Department into three sections, of which the newly subordinated Commander-in-Chief, the Surveyor General of the Ordnance and the Financial Secretary were to be the respective heads. The three branches were concentrated in the War Office, then in Pall Mall and greatly increased powers and responsibilities were conferred on the Commander in Chief. He was given command of all land forces of the Crown, regular and auxiliary, at home and abroad, and the right of appointing officers in the Militia was removed from the Lords Lieutenant. Cardwell decided to territorialise the regiments of the line, hitherto numbered. He divided Great Britain and Ireland into 69 regimental districts, each containing the depot of the regiment to be associated with that area. Each of these 'county' regiments was to comprise at least two regular battalions, with one, two or three battalions of Militia, and generally all the Volunteer infantry belonging to the district. Cardwell also rearmed the infantry with the more efficient Martini-Henry rifle. Cardwell's reforms fell short in two areas: the Duke of Cambridge remained Commander in Chief, and from then until his resignation in 1895 obstructed progress in the central direction of the Army as a modern fighting force. The second flaw was that Cardwell failed to form a proper General Staff, the lack of which produced the blunders and lack of co-ordination evident in the South African campaign of 1899.

Carl Gustav Swedish designed and manufactured shoulder-fired 84mm recoilless weapon. In service with the British Army since 1965, primarily as a medium anti-tank weapon firing a high explosive anti-tank projectile, but also capable of firing high explosive and illuminating rounds. The weapon is obsolescent and is being replaced by the Light Anti-Tank Weapon 1980.

Carmarthenshire Yeomanry The Carmarthenshire Corps of two troops was raised by Lord Dynevor in September 1794, but was disbanded in 1802. Re-raised in 1814, it served for some years thereafter. From 1901 a squadron was raised in the county for the Pembroke Yeomanry and served until conversion to artillery after the Great War. *See also: Pembrokeshire Yeomanry.*

Carmusa Second World War North Africa campaign battle honour awarded for an action during the British withdrawal from Agedabia and occupation of the El Alamein Line in 1942. *See also: North Africa 1940-1943; Msus; Benghazi; Mersa Matruh; Point 174; Minqar Qaim and Fuka.*

Carnatic Battle honour for services in repelling the invasion of the Carnatic by Hyder Ali, the ruler of Mysore and covering two periods: that of the Second Mysore War (1780-84), when Hyder Ali and his forces threatened Madras itself, and the Third Mysore War (1789-92). *See also: Sholinghur; Mangalore; Mysore and Nundy Droog.*

CARNATIC WARS

1751 While the French were besieging East India Company forces in Trichinopoly, Clive (qv) persuaded the Governor of Madras, one of the company's three most important stations in India, to march on Arcot, the political capital of the

Carnatic. Clive's force of 200 British and 300 Indian troops entered a half-ruined fort which dominated the city, repaired the defences, withstood a siege for 50 days and then beat off the attackers.

1759 Following the capture by the French of the British forts of Cuddalore and St David in 1758, a small British and Indian force commanded by Major Forde defeated the French near the mouth of the River Godavery and, in 1859, stormed the fortress of Masulipatam.

Carpinetta Second World War Italian campaign battle honour marking one of the actions which took place between the breaching of the Gothic Line and the final drive into the Po valley in April 1945. *See also: Italy 1943-1945; Montebello-Scorticata Ridge; Monte Reggiano; Savignano; San Martino Sogliano; Monte Farneto; Montilgallo; Monte Cavallo; Casa Bettini; Pideura; Pergola Ridge; Senio Floodbank; Cesena; Conventello-Comacchio; Monte Casalino; Monte La Pieve; Monte Pianoereno; Monte Spaduro; Orsara; Tossignano and Catarelto Ridge.*

Carriers Based on the earlier Vickers light tanks, carriers developed from the concept of giving tracked mobility to infantry, thus allowing them to operate more effectively with armour. Carriers were also used as prime movers in the artillery and engineers. The Oxford carrier, last in the line of gun carriers of the 1930s, was followed by the Loyd carrier, produced by Vivian Loyd & Co Ltd in 1940. A pilot model of a Cambridge carrier appeared in 1950 but was not taken into service. A family of carrier variants was developed during the course of the Second World War such as the bren gun carrier, scout or cavalry carriers, universal carriers, 3" mortar carriers, cable-laying carriers and the 'Ronson' and 'Wasp' flamethrower carriers.

Carroceto Second World War Italian campaign battle honour marking an action following the allied landing at Anzio on 22 January 1944. *See also: Italy 1943-1945; Anzio; Campoleone and Aprilia.*

Cartouche A cartridge. Also, the small box or pouch in which such cartridges were carried. The term is also used to describe an ornamental panel used on regimental standards and guidons to enclose a title, cypher or heraldic charge.

Cartridge Case containing the propellant charge, and sometimes the projectile as well, required to discharge a firearm. For small arms, the cartridge consists of a brass cartridge case, containing projectile, propellant and primer. Cartridges originally came into use for muzzle-loading rifles, and in these projectile and charge were wrapped together in a paper cylinder. When required for use, the end of the cartridge was torn or bitten off and the powder poured down the muzzle. The projectile and the cartridge paper were then rammed down on top with a ramrod.

Casa Bettini Second World War Italian campaign battle honour marking one of a number of actions which took place between the breaching of the Gothic Line and the final drive into the Po valley in April 1945. *See also: Italy 1943-1945; Montebello-Scorticata Ridge; Monte Reggiano; Savignano; San Martino Sogliano; Monte Farneto; Montilgallo; Monte Cavallo; Carpinetta; Pideura; Pergola Ridge; Senio Floodbank; Cesena; Conventello-Comacchio; Monte Casalino; Monte La Pieve; Monte Pianoereno; Monte Spaduro; Orsara; Tossignano and Catarelto Ridge.*

Casa Fabri Ridge Second World War Italian campaign battle honour marking the breaking by elements of Eighth Army of the German defensive line in the Rimini area between 14 and 21 September 1944. *See also: Italy 1943-1945; Rimini Line; Ceriano Ridge; Monte Colombo; Montescudo; Frisoni and San Marino.*

Casa Fortis Second World War Italian campaign battle honour marking the clearance of Forli in November 1944, involving bitter house-to-house fighting, after the town had 'officially' been captured. *See also: Italy 1943-1945; Monte Chicco; Capture of Forli; Cosina Canal and Lamone Crossing.*

Casa Sinagogga Second World War Italian campaign battle honour marking an action in the second period of fighting around Monte Cassino over the period 11-18 May 1944. *See also: Italy 1943-1945; Cassino II; Massa Vertecchi and Massa Tambourini.*

Cashier Obsolete term, from the French *casser* (to break), for the dismissal with ignominy or disgrace of a commissioned officer. Third in the scale of punishments, after death and imprisonment. An officer sentenced to imprisonment had first to be cashiered.

Cassel Second World War battle honour marking the defence, for three days from 26 May 1940, as troops from St Omer-La Bassée line withdrew to Dunkirk. *See also: North West Europe 1940; Calais 1940; St Omer-LaBassée; Wormhoudt and Dunkirk 1940.*

Cassino I Second World War Italian campaign battle honour marking the protracted and bloody fighting over the period 20 January - 25 March 1944 to capture Monte Cassino, the dominant height crowned by its monastery, which covered the Liri Valley and was the linchpin to the Gustav Line. *See also: Italy 1943-1945; Monastery Hill; Castle Hill and Hangman's Hill.*

Cassino II Second World War Italian campaign battle honour covering the fighting which took place between 11 and 18 May 1944 and resulted in the final capture of Monte Cassino. *See also: Italy 1943-1945; Massa Vertecchi; Massa Tambourini and Casa Sinagogga.*

Cassock Long outer coat worn in the 17th century by cavalry and infantry.

Castle Hill Second World War Italian campaign battle honour marking one of the fierce actions during the unsuccessful attempts to take Monte Cassino during the period 20 January to 25 March 1944. *See also: Italy 1943-1945; Cassino I; Monastery Hill and Hangman's Hill.*

Catarelto Ridge Second World War, Italian campaign battle honour marking an action which took place between the breaching of the Gothic Line and the final drive into the Po valley in April 1945. *See also: Italy 1943-1945; Montebello-Scorticata Ridge; Monte Reggiano; Savignano; San Martino Sogliano; Monte Farneto; Montilgallo; Monte Cavallo; Carpinetta; Pideura; Pergola Ridge; Senio Floodbank; Cesena; Conventello-Comacchio; Monte Casalino; Monte La Pieve; Monte Pianoereno; Monte Spaduro; Orsara; Tossignano and Casa Bettini.*

Catheolles Second World War battle honour marking the sharp fighting against German rearguards during the period 2-8 August 1944, part of the British offensive launched from the Caumont area on 20 July 1944 with the object of capturing Mont Pincon. *See also: North West Europe 1944-1945; Mont Pincon; Quarry Hill; Souleuvre; Le Perier Ridge; Brieux Bridgehead and Jurques.*

Cauldron Second World War North Africa campaign battle honour marking the British counter-attack on 5 and 6 June 1942 during the German attacks on British positions on the Gazala Line. *See also: North Africa 1940-1943 and Gazala.*

Cava Di Tirreni Second World War Italian campaign battle honour marking one of the actions in the Fifth Army advance to the Gustav Line. *See also: Italy 1943-1945; Capture of Naples; Cappezano; Monte Stella; Scafati Bridge; Volturno Crossing; Monte Maro; Roccheta e Croce and Colle Cedro.*

Cavalier Second World War Mark VII version of the cruiser tank. Only a few hundred Cavaliers were produced, and they were never used in battle as gun-tanks because the more reliable and faster Cromwells (qv) became available in quantity in 1944. The Cavalier had a crew of five, weighed 26.5 tons, and mounted a 6pdr gun and two Besa machine guns *See also: Tank and Cruiser tanks.*

Cavalry That part of the army formerly mounted on horses and now, with the exception of elements of the Household

Cavalry (qv), mounted in armoured vehicles. Only ten regiments of cavalry now exist in the regular army order of battle they are, in order of precedence: The Life Guards; The Blues and Royals (Royal Horse Guards and 1st Dragoons); 1st The Queen's Dragoon Guards; The Royal Scots Dragoon Guards (Carabiniers and Greys); The Royal Dragoon Guards; The Queen's Royal Hussars (The Queen's Own and Royal Irish); 9th/12th Royal Lancers (Prince of Wales's); The King's Royal Hussars; The Light Dragoons; and The Queen's Royal Lancers.

***Cede Nullis* (Yield to None)** Motto of 105th (Madras Light Infantry) Regiment and later of The King's Own Yorkshire Light Infantry (51st and 105th Foot). Now one of the mottoes of The Light Infantry.

***Celer Et Audax* (Swift and Bold)** Motto of The King's Royal Rifle Corps.

Centaur Second World War cruiser tank. The only Centaurs to go into action were those of the Royal Marines Armoured Support Group, which had 80 Centaurs armed with 95mm howitzers. Variants fitted with Anti-Aircraft guns or dozer blades took part in the action in North-West Europe. The Centaur had a crew of 5, weighed 27.5 tons, and mounted a 6pdr gun, 75mm or 95mm howitzer and one or two Besa machine guns. *See also: Tank and Cruiser tanks.*

Central Africa Medal 1891-1898 Marking service in a number of small campaigns in Central and East Africa between 1891 and 1894. Reissued in 1899 to mark operations between 1894 and 1898 it had on this occasion a clasp inscribed 'CENTRAL AFRICA 1894-98'.
Ribbon: Vertical equal bands of black, white and terracotta.

Central India Battle honour awarded to the regiments which, in the Indian Mutiny of 1857, advanced under Sir Hugh Rose from the Bombay Presidency through Central India, dealing with local rulers who had supported the mutineers. *See also: Behar and Mooltan 1857-58.*

Central Malaya Second World War Malayan campaign battle honour marking the British actions during the period 26 December 1941 to 10 January 1942 in the face of the Japanese advance down through Malaya between 8 December 1941 and 31 January 1942 when the last British troops withdrew to Singapore. *See also: Malaya 1941-42; Northern Malaya; Johore and Singapore Island.*

Centre-Fire A cartridge having the primer in the centre of the base. *See also: Rim-fire.*

Centre For Human Sciences *See: Army Personnel Research Establishment.*

Centurion British main battle tank produced at the Royal Ordnance Factory to meet a 1943 operational requirement for a heavy cruiser tank. Entered service in 1946, just too late for the Second World War. With a crew of four, and originally weighing 49 tons and mounting a 17pdr gun, it was later up-armoured and up-gunned to 105mm. By the time production ceased in 1962 some 4,400 tanks had been produced covering 12 different models. *See also: Tank.*

Centuripe Second World War Sicilian campaign battle honour marking the capture of this Sicilian town on 3 August 1943 following the Allied landing on the island on 10 July 1943. *See also: Sicily 1943; Landing in Sicily; Primosole Bridge; Sferro and Regalbuto.*

Centry Gown Name given to the watch coats of Charles II's reign. Only issued for night duty or foul weather.

Cerasola Second World War Italian campaign battle honour marking an action in early February 1944. *See also: Italy 1943-1945; Garigliano Crossing; Monte Ornito and Anzio.*

Ceriano Ridge Second World War Italian campaign battle honour marking the capture of the Ceriano Ridge after operations lasting from 17 to 21 September 1944, which included the crossing of the River

Ausa, in the Battle of the Rimini Line. *See also: Italy 1943-1945; Rimini Line; Monte Colombo; Casa Fabri Ridge; Montescudo; Frisoni and San Marino.*

Certa Cito (Sure and Swift) Motto inscribed of the Royal Corps of Signals and Queen's Gurkha Signals.

Cesena Second World War Italian campaign battle honour marking one of the actions which took place between the breaching of the Gothic Line and the final drive into the Po valley in April 1945. *See also: Italy 1943-1945; Montebello-Scorticata Ridge; Monte Reggiano; Savignano; San Martino Sogliano; Monte Farneto; Montilgallo; Monte Cavallo; Carpinetta; Pideura; Pergola Ridge; Senio Floodbank; Catarelto Ridge; Conventello-Comacchio; Monte Casalino; Monte La Pieve; Monte Pianoereno; Monte Spaduro; Orsara; Tossignano and Casa Bettini.*

Chaco Term used for the shako or chakot. Now more usually used to describe post-1844 patterns of this type of Headdress. *See also: Shako.*

Chalk Name given to the personnel, vehicles and freight grouped in one aircraft load. *See also: Stick.*

Challenger Second World War cruiser tank, a modification of the Cromwell (qv) design, and first drawn up in 1942. The Challenger was only used in small numbers in North-West Europe. The Challenger had a crew of five, weighed 31.5 tons, and mounted a 17pdr gun and a 0.3" Browning machine gun. *See also: Tank and Cruiser tanks.*

Challenger The current British main battle tank, derived from the Shir II (an improved design of Chieftain (qv) developed for the Shah of Iran) and taken into British service following the collapse of the Anglo-German 'Main Battle Tank 90' collaborative project in 1980. The original design has been much uprated, the present Mark III offering much improved mobility, firepower and protection. Challenger has a crew of four, weighs 62,000kg, and mounts

a 120mm gun and two 7.62mm machine guns. *See also: Tank.*

Chape Metal tip or trimming for a sword scabbard.

Chapeau-Bras Pattern of cocked hat which could be folded flat. Usually carried under the arm at levees and other formal occasions.

Chapkan An Indian coat.

Chaplains From the Restoration in 1660 until 1796 a chaplain had been held as a field officer on the establishment of every regiment and corps, their duties being spelled out in the Articles of War produced by Parliament. However, the selection of regimental chaplains was in the gift of colonels of regiments and, although the chaplain might receive pay, he did not necessarily do the work, which was more usually performed by a deputy at a stipend fixed by mutual agreement. The failure of chaplains to attend to their duties, particularly in the case of regiments serving abroad, was so widespread that it was decided to abolish regimental chaplains and by Royal Warrant of 23 September 1796 the Army Chaplains' Department came into being. In the Army today chaplains are described as Chaplains to the Forces, serve under conditions laid down by the Army Department of the Ministry of Defence and are uniformed, rank-bearing members of the Royal Army Chaplains Department. Chaplains are appointed by the Parliamentary Under-Secretary of State for the Armed Forces on the nomination of an accredited representative of the various denominations, and in their ministrations to the troops are under the oversight of the given representative. Anglican chaplains serve under the Chaplain General. *See also: Chaplain General and Royal Army Chaplains' Department.*

Chaplain-General The appointment of Chaplain-General was created by Royal Warrant dated 23 September 1796; the first Chaplain-General to be officially appointed being the Reverend John Gamble MA. This order sought to rectify the much abused existing system of regimental chaplains, which had failed to produce chaplains of the right quality, in the right quantities, in the regiments and corps, especially when serving abroad. The order stated that 'Lastly We do hereby subject all Regular Chaplains, desiring to be continued in Our Service, to the orders of the person whom We shall hereafter appoint to be Chaplain-General of Our Army, and who is to govern himself by such Instructions as We shall from time to time think fit to give him through Our Secretary at War'. *See also: Chaplains and Royal Army Chaplains' Department.*

Chapplis Sandals worn by Indian infantry in the 18th and 19th centuries.

Charasiah Battle honour marking the action at Charasiah, six miles from Kabul, on 6 October 1879, in which the Kabul Field Force under Sir Frederick Roberts, advancing to exact retribution for the massacre of the British Mission, routed the Afghan field army during the Second Afghan War. *See also: Afghanistan 1878-80; Ali Masjid; Peiwar Kotal; Kabul 1879; Ahmad Khel and Kandahar* 1880.

Charjama A thick saddlecloth used in the 19th century by Indian cavalry.

Charlemont's Regiment Raised in 1701, later 36th Foot, and in 1881 The Worcestershire Regiment.

Charger A large strong horse formerly ridden into battle. The term is now applied to any service horse.

Chaum-Ni Korean War battle honour. *See also: Korea 1950-53; Naktong Bridgehead; Pakchon; Imjin; Kowang San; The Hook 1952; The Hook 1953; Chongju; Chongchon II; Seoul; Hill 327; Kapyong-Chon; Kapyong; Maryang San and Hill 227 I.*

Cheesemongers Nickname for the 1st Life Guards (qv), stemming from 1788 when the regiment was remodelled; some commissions were refused because certain officers were the sons of merchants and hence not 'gentlemen'.

Chebket En Nouiges Second World War North Africa campaign battle honour marking an action between the occupation of the Alamein Line and the end of the campaign in 1943. *See also: North Africa 1940-1943; Deir El Munassib; Matmata Hills; Sebkret En Noual; Capture of Halfaya Pass; Djebel El Telil and Djebel Tebaga.*

Chelsea Pensioner *See: Royal Hospital.*

Chemical Warfare The use of toxic chemical agents, usually gases or aerosols, to kill or incapacitate an enemy. These agents are broadly classified by their effect on the target such as blood, choking, blister, nerve, and the less dangerous lachrymatory or 'tear' agents.

Cherry-Pickers Nickname given to the 11th Hussars when a detachment of the regiment was allegedly surprised by French cavalry while picking cherries in a Spanish orchard in 1811 and were obliged to fight a dismounted action.

Cherubims Nickname given to the 11th Hussars when they adopted crimson overalls (trousers) in 1840. *See also: Cherry-Pickers.*

Cheshire Regiment (22nd Foot) Raised at Chester in March 1689 by Colonel Henry Howard, 7th Duke of Norfolk, known as the Duke of Norfolk's Regiment of Foot and designated 22nd Regiment of Foot in 1751. The regiment became the 22nd (The Cheshire) Foot in 1782 and The Cheshire Regiment in 1881.
Headdress Badge: An acorn leaved and slipped.
Regimental marches:
Quick March: *Wha wadna fecht for Charlie.*
Slow March: *The 22nd Regiment Slow March 1772.*
Regimental Headquarters: The Castle, Chester, CH1 2DN.
History: *Historical Record of The 22nd or Cheshire Regiment of Foot* by Richard Canon (1847); *History of The 22nd (Cheshire) Regiment 1689-1849* by W Hastings Anderson (1920); *The History of The Cheshire Regiment in The Great War* by A Crookenden (1921); *The History of The*

Cheshire Regiment in The Second World War by A Crookenden (1949) and *Ever Glorious, The Story of The 22nd (Cheshire) Regiment,* Vol.1 (1689-1939), by B Rigby (1982).

Cheshire Yeomanry (The Cheshire Yeomanry (Earl of Chester's)) The first troop was raised in Macclesfield in 1797 and in 1803 a regiment, the Western Cheshire Volunteer Cavalry, The Earl of Chester's Regiment (later HRH The Prince Regent's Regiment of Cheshire Yeomanry) was formed. A further regiment was raised in 1819, the regiments being known as the 1st and 2nd Regiments, substituting the title 'King's' for 'Prince Regent's' in 1820. The 2nd Regiment disbanded in 1828. The regiment provided two companies, the 21st and 22nd, for the 2nd Battalion Imperial Yeomanry in the South Africa War (1899-1902). In the First World War the regiment served dismounted in Egypt. Amalgamated with the Shropshire Yeomanry (qv) in 1917, the regiment subsequently served in France as 10th Battalion The King's Shropshire Light Infantry. Between 1920 and 1942 the regiment retained its cavalry role and was redesignated 17th Line of Communication Signals (Cheshire Yeomanry) in 1944. In 1947 the Cheshire Yeomanry reformed as an armoured, and later a reconnaissance, regiment, becoming The Cheshire Yeomanry (Earl of Chester's Territorials) in 1967. The regiment's successors may now be found in 'C' (Cheshire Yeomanry) Squadron of The Queens Own Yeomanry; and in 80 (Cheshire Yeomanry) Signal Squadron, 33 Signal Regiment (Volunteers).

Cheux Second World War battle honour marking the opening action of the Odon offensive in Normandy shortly after the Allied landing in June 1944 which sought to capture the high ground around Cheux. *See also: North West Europe 1944-1945; Villers Bocage; Tilly Sur Seulles; Odon; Fontenay Le Pesnil; Defence of Rauray and Caen.*

Chevron V-shaped badge worn on the sleeve to denote rank, length of service or wounds. A system of using chevrons to denote the rank of non-commissioned officers was introduced in 1803. A sergeant-major and quartermaster-sergeant wore four chevrons, a sergeant three and a corporal two; an order of May 1803 directed that the chevrons be worn 'point down'. Originally worn on the upper sleeve, in 1869 the four of the sergeant-major were worn on the lower sleeve with the points toward the elbow, now only the case for drum, pipe and bugle majors. Service and wound chevrons are worn on the left sleeve.

Chief of the General Staff Appointment arising from the recommendations of the Esher Committee in 1903, accepted by the Balfour government, which led to the creation on 10 August 1904 of the Army Council (Army Board of the Defence Council from April 1964) with the Chief of the General Staff as First Military Member and professional head of the Army responsible for the fighting effectiveness, management, overall efficiency and morale of the Army. The Chief of the General Staff directs the work of the Army in accordance with policy directives and budgets for the main areas of expenditure determined under the direction of the Office of Management and Budget in conjunction with the Central Defence Staffs in the Ministry of Defence. Detailed management of the Army is the responsibility of the Executive Committee of the Army Board (qv) chaired by the Chief of the General Staff.

Chief of the Imperial General Staff Command of the Army had rested with the Commander-in-Chief (1660-1852 and 1887-1904), Commanding-in-Chief (1852-87) and Chief of the General Staff (1904-09), until 1909 when the appointment of Chief of the General Staff was retitled Chief of the Imperial General Staff, and so remained until 1964 when it reverted to the original.

Chief of Staff Senior staff officer in a headquarters whose function is to direct and co-ordinate the work of the staff in such a manner as to ensure that the commander's objectives are met.

Chieftain Obsolescent British main battle tank developed to meet a 1958 requirement for a Centurion replacement. Chieftain was developed by the Royal Ordnance Factory and entered service in 1967. Chieftain, which is being replaced by Challenger, has a crew of four, weighs 51 tons, and mounts a 120mm gun and two 7.62mm machine guns. *See also: Tank.*

Chillianwallah Battle honour marking the action at Chillianwallah on 13 January 1849 between a force under Lord Gough and the Sikh army under Shere Singh during the Second Sikh War (qv). Due to poor reconnaissance and inadequate orders, British casualties were high and included the loss of one of the 24th Foot's Colours and the Colours of two Bengal native regiments. The heavy casualties and loss of the Colours caused outrage in England and it was decided to replace Gough. *See also: Mooltan, Goojerat and Punjaub.*

Chin-Chain Strap of linked metal loops found on some patterns of Headdress. The chain would pass under or across the chin from one side of the Headdress to the other, thus securing it on the head.

Chin-Scales Term applied in the 19th century to the small metal plates or scales attached to the chin-strap (qv) of a helmet or shako and intended as some protection against cutting weapons.

Chin-Strap A strap of leather or similar durable material found in some form on most patterns of Headdress. The chin-strap would pass under or across the chin from one side of the Headdress to the other, thus securing it on the head. Except in the case of the combat helmet the chin-strap is now largely decorative and secured above the peak of a cap when not in use. The term 'to be on one's chin-strap' is used to denote a state of extreme fatigue.

CHINA
First China War (Opium War) 1839-41 This war, widely known as the 'Opium War', arose when the Chinese government, alarmed by the increase in the use of opium among the Chinese, banned its importation. However, British merchants, who had made large profits by the trade, continued to smuggle it into the country. Stocks and cargoes of the drug were destroyed by royal authority, and Captain Eliot, the British Commissioner, was imprisoned. Compensation was demanded and war declared on China in 1840. In May 1841 the Bogue Forts at the mouth of the Canton River were taken, and Canton itself on 24 May. In August Amoy was occupied and in October, Chusan. Following further vacillation by the Chinese during the winter, Ningpo was taken in March 1842 and Chapoo in May. The British force pushed up the Yangtse Kiang River in July, threatening the very heart of China. In 1842 the Treaty of Nanking was concluded by which Canton, Amoy, Foochow, Ningpo and Shanghai were opened to British trade; Hong Kong was ceded to Britain and an indemnity of $21,000,000 paid. *See also: China (with Dragon).*

Second China War 1857-60 The full terms of the treaty entered into after the First China War (qv) were not adhered to by the Chinese, and interference with British commercial shipping, notably a vessel called the *Arrow*, led to the despatch of a punitive force from England in 1857. Canton was captured in January 1858 and the Treaty of Tientsin (1858), under which additional ports were opened to British trade, British travellers were allowed to travel into the Chinese interior and a British ambassador was received in Pekin, brought hostilities to an end. However, it soon became clear that the Chinese remained unconvinced of Britain's will and ability to enforce treaty obligations and that only a demonstration of force at the centre of China would make the Chinese comply. An expeditionary force under Lieutenant General Sir Hope Grant carried the Taku Forts on 12th August 1860 and Pekin on 12th October 1860. *See also: China 1858-59; China 1860-62; Canton 1858; Taku Forts and Pekin.*

China With Dragon *See also: Dragon Superscribed China.*

China 1858-59 Battle honour marking actions during the Second China War.

China 1860-62 Battle honour marking the operations of the expeditionary force under Lieutenant General Sir Hope Grant following the Second China War. *See also: Taku Forts and Pekin 1860.*

China 1900 Battle honour awarded in 1906 to regiments, other than those awarded 'Pekin 1900', which served in the Boxer Rising (qv).

Chindits The name, that of a mythical Burmese dragon, given to members of the force raised by Brigadier Orde Wingate (qv) in 1942 to operate against the Japanese lines of communication in Burma. The first expedition, launched in January 1943, achieved little other than slightly damaging the Mandalay to Myitkyina railway. The expedition did prove that such operations could be sustained by air and that British troops were more than a match for the Japanese in the jungle. However, some 1,000 of the 3,000 strong force became casualties. A second expedition, nearly five brigades strong, was launched in February 1944, being inserted by glider and air landing at pre-prepared airstrips. Some damage was done to the railway again, and Japanese preparations for invading India were disrupted. Casualties were again heavy, and after the death of Wingate on 25 March 1944 enthusiasm declined and the force was withdrawn in July 1944. *See also: Chindits 1943 and Chindits 1944.*

Chindits 1943 Second World War Burma campaign battle honour marking the operations of the first Chindit expedition behind the Japanese lines, which lasted from January to June 1943. *See also: Burma 1942-45.*

Chindits 1944 Second World War Burma campaign battle honour marking the operations of the second Chindit expedition behind Japanese lines, which lasted from February to August 1944. *See also: Burma 1942-45.*

Chipmunk Light aircraft manufactured by De Havilland, and in service with the Army Air Corps as a training aircraft since 1954.

Chitral Battle honour marking the campaign mounted to relieve the garrison of the fort at Chitral following the rebellion of 1895 which was prompted by the murder of the Ruler. *See also: Defence of Chitral.*

Chobham Armour Composite armour developed at the Royal Ordnance laboratory at Chobham. The precise composition is classified, but it is based upon alternate layers of steel, ceramic and titanium plates laminated between layers of nylon or Kevlar (qv) mesh.

Choga Indian coat of camelhair with a portion for covering the head.

Choky Soldiers' slang for prison. From the Hindi *chauki*, which is itself evolved from the sanskrit *chatur* meaning four or four-sided - as is a cell.

Cholera Belt Flannel belts introduced in the mid-19th century and worn round the waist next to the skin, with a view to preventing cholera. Later versions were of thick wool and pulled on. The practice continued into the early 20th century.

Cholmondeley's Regiment Raised in 1740, later 48th Foot and in 1881 The Northamptonshire Regiment.

Chongchon II Korean War battle honour. *See also: Korea 1950-53; Naktong Bridgehead; Pakchon; Imjin; Kowang San; The Hook 1952; The Hook 1953; Chaum-Ni; Chongchon II; Seoul; Hill 327; Kapyong-Chon; Kapyong; Maryang San and Hill 227 I.*

Chongju Korean War battle honour. *See also: Korea 1950-53; Naktong Bridgehead; Pakchon; Imjin; Kowang San; The Hook 1952; The Hook 1953; Chaum-Ni; Chongchon II; Seoul; Hill 327; Kapyong-Chon; Kapyong; Maryang San and Hill 227 I.*

Chor Es Sufan Second World War North Africa campaign battle honour marking the attempt over the period 27-30 December 1941 to envelop the enemy position at Agedabia. *See also: North Africa 1940-1943;*

Tobruk 1941; Alem Hamza; Saunnu and Gazala.

Churchill Second World War British infantry tank originally designed for the close support of infantry and brought into service in June 1941. The Churchill was first used in the Dieppe raid of August 1942. It had a crew of five, later marks weighed 40 tons, and mounted a 75mm gun and 2 Besa machine guns. A number of specially modified Churchill tanks were used in the allied invasion of Normandy in June 1944 such as the Churchill VII Crocodile flamethrower tank, the Armoured Vehicle Royal Engineers (AVRE) mounting a 12" spigot petard mortar, an Armoured Ramp Carrier (ARK) and a 4.8 ton bridgelayer tank. *See also: Tank and Infantry tank.*

Cipher Off-Line A method of encryption which takes place before transmission and is independent of the transmission system. The resulting encrypted message can be sent by any means.

Cipher On-Line An automatic method of encryption which is part of the transmission system, whereby signals are encrypted and transmitted in one process.

Citadel Fortress situated in or near a city, to keep the inhabitants submissive, and also to form a rallying point and last place of defence when the town was attacked.

Citerna Second World War Italian campaign battle honour marking an action during the Eighth Army advance to the Gothic line during June and July 1944. *See also: Italy 1943-1945; Pian Di Maggio and Gothic Line.*

Citta Di Castillo Second World War Italian campaign battle honour marking the capture of the town as a result of heavy fighting between 16 and 22 July 1944. *See also: Italy 1943-1945; Montone; Monte Cedrone; Campriano; Poggio Del Grillo and Fiesole.*

Citta Del Pieve Second World War Italian campaign battle honour marking the

carrying of an outpost on the Trasimene Line over the period 16-19 June 1944. *See also: Italy 1943-1945; Rome; Ficulle; Capture of Perugia; Monte Malbe and Trasimene Line.*

City of London Yeomanry (The Rough Riders) *See: London Yeomanry.*

Ciudad Rodrigo Peninsula War (qv) battle honour marking the capture of this Spanish fortress, which covers the main route from Portugal to Spain, from the French in January 1812. In the capture of the fortress the whole French siege train fell into British hands. *See also: Peninsula; Albuhera; Arroyo Dos Molinos; Tarifa; Badajoz; Almaraz and Salamanca.*

Clackmannanshire Yeomanry A record dated 1818 records two troops of Clackmannan and Kinross Yeomanry Cavalry. A proposal to raise a third troop was made in 1818 but no evidence exists of this having happened.

Clansman A combat radio system due to be replaced by Bowman in 1998.

Clasp Metal bar, usually bearing the name of a particular action, worn on campaign medals.

CLASSIC Seismic and thermal intrusion alarm system.

Claymore From the Gaelic, meaning 'Great Sword'. Two-handed sword of the Scottish highlanders. The name is incorrectly given to the single-handed basket-hilted broadsword, which was frequently single-edged and which is carried by the officers of some Scottish regiments.

Claymore Mine An anti-personnel mine consisting of a crescent-shaped container, holding some 700 ball-bearings, mounted on a pair of bipod legs. The mine can be fired remotely discharging the ball-bearings over a 60° arc out to 300m.

Cleve Second World War battle honour marking the capture of the Materborn feature and town of Cleve during the advance from the River Roer to the Rhine during the period 8 February to 10 March 1945. *See also: North West Europe 1944-1945; Rhineland; Reichswald; Goch; Weeze; Schaddenhof; Hochwald; Waal Flats; Moyland; Moyland Wood and Xanten.*

Clifton's Regiment Raised in 1685, later 15th Foot, and in 1881 The East Yorkshire Regiment.

Clive, Robert, Baron (1725-74) Born in Shropshire, he obtained a clerkship at 18 with the East India Company (qv) in Madras. Rivalry between France and the British East India Company for influence in India was intense. In 1746 the French captured Madras, Clive was taken prisoner, but he escaped to Fort St David. In 1747 he was appointed to an ensign's commission in the East India Company's service and rose rapidly through the ranks after a succession of dazzling victories which greatly enhanced Britain's position in India. In 1753 Clive was invalided home, returning famous and with a fortune, which he rapidly spent, and he returned to India in 1756. From 1757 to 1760 Clive was Governor of Bengal; he then returned to England, was elected MP for Shrewsbury and created Baron (Irish peerage) Clive in 1762. In 1764 Clive returned to Bengal to set the administration on a sound footing, in the process making many enemies. He was recalled to England to face a parliamentary enquiry which found his dealings with Mir Jaffa as tainted by greed and sharp practice. The Commons unanimously accepted that Clive had 'rendered great and meritorious services to his country'. However, the censure further undermined Clives's already broken health and mental stability. He took opium, and ultimately committed suicide.

Close Air Support Air action against hostile targets which are in close proximity to friendly forces and which requires detailed integration with land force activity.

Close Observation Platoon Sub-unit, based on the infantry reconnaissance platoon, specially trained for close observation tasks, particularly in Northern Ireland.

Close Order Formation in which there is only one arm's length between the ranks, thus inhibiting any movement between the ranks. *See also: Open order.*

Close Support Action against targets or objectives which are sufficiently near the supported force to require detailed integration or co-ordination of the supporting action with the fire, movement and other actions of the supported force.

Coatee A coat or jacket which has the skirts removed in front, leaving tails at the back, or sometimes a simple back.

Cobra A three-dimensional phased array radar currently under development for the Royal Artillery.

Coburg Regimental slow march of 9th/12th Lancers; Royal Hussars; and King's Royal Hussars.

Cochin Battle honour awarded in 1840 to mark the gallant defence of the Residency at Cochin on the Malabar Coast during the 1809 rebellion in Travancore.

Cock o' the North The regimental quick march (Regimental Band and Pipes and Drums) of the Gordon Highlanders.

Cock's Feathers These curled feathers replaced the ostrich feathers worn in the cocked hats of general officers at the start of the 19th century. They were also used to ornament the Headdress of lancers, light dragoons, rifle officers and yeomanry.

Codeword A codeword is a single word, usually issued by the Ministry of Defence from an approved list of codewords, used to provide security when referring to a classified operation or similar matter. For example, CORPORATE and GRANBY were respectively the codewords for the Falklands and Gulf operations. *See also: Nickname.*

Coldstream Guards The regiment was raised in 1650 during the Commonwealth as General Monck's Regiment, also known as 'The Coldstreamers', and served in

Scotland until 1660, when it accompanied Monck on his march to London, where it played a significant part in the Restoration. The regiment's name is taken from its stay in the border village of Coldstream in the winter of 1659-60. Following the Restoration the regiment was renamed the Lord General's Regiment of Foot in 1661 and Lord General's Regiment of Foot Guards in 1662. In 1670 the regiment became The Coldstream Regiment of Foot Guards (also 2nd Foot Guards) and, in 1817, the Coldstream Guards.

Headdress Badge: star of the Order of the Garter.

Regimental marches:

Quick march: Regimental march of the Coldstream Guards *Milanello*.

Slow march: *Figaro*.

Regimental headquarters: Wellington Barracks, Birdcage Walk, London SW1E 6HQ.

History: *The Early History of the Coldstream Guards* by G Davies (1924); *A History of the Coldstream Guards 1815-1895* by Ross of Bladensburg (1896); *A History of the Coldstream Guards 1885-1914* by Hall (1929); *A History of the Coldstream Guards 1914-1918 (2 Vols)* by Ross of Bladensburg (1928); *No Dishonourable Name* (2nd and 3rd Battalions) by Quilter (1947); *A History of the Coldstream Guards 1920-1946* by H Sparrow (1951); *A Distant Drum* (5th Battalion) by Pereira (1948); and *A History of the Coldstream Guards 1946-1970* by Crichton (1972).

Colito Second World War Abyssinian campaign battle honour marking the crossing of the River Billate on 19 May 1941 during the advance towards Soddu. *See also: Abyssinia 1940-41; Keren*; *Jebel Defeis; Jebel Shiba; Gogni; Agordat; Barentu; Karora-Marsa Taclai; Cubcub; Ad Teclesan; Mescelit Pass; Mt Engiahat; Massawa; Amb Alagi; Afodu; Gambela; El Wak; Moyale; Wal Garis; Juba; Marda Pass; Bisidimo; Awash; Todenyang-Namaraputh; Omo; Soroppa; Giarso; Babile Gap; Wadara; Gondar; Fike and Lechemti.*

Colle Cedro Second World War Italian campaign battle honour marking one of the actions during the Fifth Army advance to

the Gustav Line. *See also: Italy 1943-1945; Capture of Naples; Cappezano; Monte Stella; Scafati Bridge; Volturno Crossing; Monte Maro; Roccheta e Croce and Cava di Tirreni.*

Colonel Commissioned rank above Lieutenant Colonel and below Brigadier. From February 1810 the rank of colonel was indicated by the wearing of two epaulettes, each bearing a crown and star. The introduction of the tunic instead of the coatee in 1855 continued the same marking, but on the collar, the collar being laced all round, as epaulettes were obsolete. In October 1880 the rank was again worn on the shoulder, this time on twisted cords, the rank of colonel now being indicated by two stars surmounted by a crown. The rank of colonel is now indicated by the wearing of the red, or other coloured, gorget patches of the staff and two stars surmounted by a crown on each epaulette. *See also: Rank.*

Colonel Commandant Honorary appointment equivalent to a Colonel of the Regiment.

Colonel-in-Chief The titular head of a corps or regiment, usually a member of the Royal Family. *See also: Rank.*

Colonel of the Regiment An honorary appointment, usually filled by a distinguished senior serving or retired member of the corps or regiment concerned. The colonel of a regiment speaks for the regiment or corps on all matters affecting the regiment's interests. He is responsible for regimental benevolence, funds, property and regimental orders, usually as chairman of a regimental council. It is usual for the colonel of a regiment to report periodically to the Colonel-in-Chief. *See also: Rank.*

Colours Colours, Standards and Guidons are carried by regiments of the Royal Armoured Corps and Infantry. In the past these standards acted as a rallying point in the confusion of battle, but they rapidly became an embodiment of the spirit of a regiment and the link binding the soldiers of the time with the glorious history of their regiment and the gallantry and sacrifice of the past. Colours have not been carried in battle since 26 January 1881 when the 58th Foot (later 2nd Battalion The Northamptonshire Regiment) carried them at Laing's Nek in the First Boer War. A Royal Warrant of 1743 abolished Company Colours for infantry of the line and introduced the present system of two Colours for each regiment and battalion: the King's (or Queen's) Colour and the Regimental Colour. Royal Warrants of 1747 and 1751 contained further controls on both Colours and dress. The King's (or Queen's) Colour is a Union flag, except in the case of the regiments of foot guards, and both Colours have battle honours (qv) and distinctions blazoned thereon. Both Colours measure 3' 9" by 3', the pike being about 8' 6". Rifle regiments do not have Colours. Regiments of the Royal Armoured Corps carry Standards or Guidons. *See also: Standard and Guidon.*

Colour Party Party composed of officers, warrant officers and senior non-commissioned officers charged with the carriage and close protection of the Colours.

Colour Sergeant The rank of colour sergeant was introduced in 1813 to give some reward to sergeants of good standing. The first 'colour badge' to be introduced was of a single colour, with crossed swords on the pike, to be worn on the sleeve. Certain regiments, notably the Foot Guards, produced their own variations and, in 1868, the pattern changed to two crossed union colours without swords, but with a crown above and three chevrons. In 1915 the colour-sergeants' badge disappeared leaving the crown and three chevrons. The 'colour badge' was subsequently taken into use by Army Recruiters (qv). A colour sergeant is now the highest non-commissioned rank, rating above sergeant but below warrant officer 2nd class, and equates with staff sergeant in non-infantry units and staff corporal in the Household Cavalry. *See also: Rank.*

Combat Clothing A range of camouflaged clothing designed to meet a wide spectrum of climatic and terrain conditions on the battlefield. The clothing is designed on the layer principle with additional layers being worn to match temperature reductions.

Combined Cadet Force (CCF) The Combined Cadet Force came into being on 1 April 1948 when the school contingents of the Sea Cadet Corps, Junior Training Corps (formerly the Officers Training Corps) and the Air Training Corps were merged. The aim of the force is to provide the framework of a disciplined organisation with a military flavour, within and through which young people can develop qualities of endurance, self-reliance, leadership and a sense of public service. In June 1963 the CCF was reorganised and the Army element fixed at an establishment of 40,000. Cadets are expected to take proficiency tests at various stages of training.

Combat Effectiveness The ability of any unit, weapon system, vehicle or equipment to perform assigned missions or functions. Assessments are normally expressed as a level or percentage and take into account factors such as leadership, equipment status, logistics, training and morale.

Combat Engineer Tractor Versatile tracked vehicle with a swimming capability introduced in 1977. Mounted with dozer blade for earth moving, rocket-launched anchor and winch, tow hook and crane. The combat engineer tractor has a crew of two and is fitted with a 7.62mm machine gun.

Combat Supplies Ammunition, fuel and rations.

Combined Operations Those operations in which the forces of more than one nation are operating together.

Come Lassies and Lads An arrangement of this tune forms part of the Regimental quick march of The Staffordshire Regiment.

Comet Second World War cruiser tank introduced in 1944 but not used in action until the crossing of the Rhine in early

1945. The Comet had a crew of five, weighed 32.5 tons, and mounted a 77mm gun and two Besa machine guns. *See also: Tank and Cruiser tanks.*

Command There are five broad command relationships, each offering differing levels of authority. In diminishing order of authority they are: full command, operational command, operational control, tactical command and tactical control.

Command Control Communication and Information Systems (C³I) Those systems which are concerned with the handling and transmission of command and control information.

Commandant Title given in the past to the officer in command of a besieged fortress or military station, without regard to his rank. The name is now more usually applied to the officer in charge of military colleges, academies and schools.

Commander Officer, warrant officer or non-commissioned officer appointed to the command of a theatre, force, formation, unit or sub-unit. Where no commander has been appointed it is usual for the senior rank present to assume the responsibilities and duties of commander.

Commander-in-Chief Formerly the highest appointment in the British Army. Before 1855 the office was largely independent of the Secretary of State for War, but from 1904 was subordinated to that minister. The duties devolved upon the Army Council (qv) in 1904 and the title is now bestowed on the senior officer in the theatre.

Commanding Officer The person appointed to command of a unit. Within the meaning of the Army Act 1955 the term commanding officer means 'such officer having powers of command over a person as may be determined by or under regulations of the Defence Council'.

Commando Afrikaans word meaning a small (usually mounted) battalion. The word was subsequently applied to small

bodies of British and Allied troops specially trained to carry out raids on the enemy held coasts during the Second World War. The Army Commandos, most of which were raised in 1940 and disbanded in 1946, were numbered consecutively from 1 to 12, and then 14, 30 and 60 Commandos, the latter forming the basis of the Special Air Service Regiment. In 1946 Commandos became wholly a Royal Marine concern.

Commando Association A service association of charitable status for members of the Army Commandoes of the second World War. As these commandoes were all disbanded in 1946 a unique arrangement was created when, on 16 Septmber 1957, Her Majesty Queen Elizabeth II directed that the Commando Association should be custodian of the battle honours awarded to commando units. The following battle honours were awarded only to the Commando Association: *Vaagso; Norway 1941; St Nazaire; Dieppe; Djebel Choucha and Alethangyaw.* Other Association battle honours are: *Normandy Landing; Dives Crossing; Flushing; Westkapelle; Rhine; Leese; Aller; North West Europe 1942; North West Europe 1944-1945; Litani; Syria 1941; Steamroller Farm; Sedjenane I; North Africa 1941-43; Landing in Sicily; Pursuit to Messina; Sicily 1943; Landing at Porto San Venere; Termoli; Salerno; Monte Ornito; Anzio; Valli di Comacchio; Argenta Gap; Italy 1943-45; Greece 1944-45; Crete; Madagascar; Adriatic; Middle East 1941-43, '44; Myebon; Kangaw and Burma 1943-45.*

Commendation Formal act of praise, usually by a commander-in-chief or general officer commanding, for the actions of an individual. Such commendations are also recorded on the individuals' personal records and published in unit and formation orders.

Commission The document by virtue of which an officer is authorised to perform military duty for the service of the state. The current text of a commission reads: *'Elizabeth the Second by the Grace of God of the United Kingdom of Great Britain and Northern Ireland and of Her other Realms and*

Territories Queen, Head of the Commonwealth, Defender of the Faith. To Our Trusty and well beloved . . . Greeting! We, reposing especial Trust and Confidence in your Loyalty, Courage and good Conduct, do by these Presents, Constitute and Appoint you to be an Officer in Our Land Forces, from the . . . day of . . . .You are therefore carefully and diligently to discharge your Duty as such in the Rank of...or in such other Rank as We may from time to time hereafter be pleased to promote or appoint you to, of which a notification will be made in the London Gazette, or in such other manner as may for the time being prescribed by Us in Council, and you are in such manner and on such occasions as may be prescribed by Us to exercise and well discipline in their duties such officers, men and women as may be placed under your orders from time to time and use your best endeavours to keep them in good order and discipline. And We do hereby Command them to Obey you as their superior Officer, and you to observe and follow such Orders and Directions as from time to time you shall receive from Us, or any your superior Officer; according to the Rules and Discipline of War; in pursuance of the Trust hereby reposed in you. Given at Our Court of Saint James's, the . . . day of . . . in the . . .Year of Our Reign'.

Committee of Imperial Defence Established as the 'Committee of Defence' in 1903 following an Esher Committee (qv) recommendation. Chaired by the Prime Minister, and responsible for overseeing and co-ordinating naval and military activity. Renamed the Committee of Imperial Defence in 1908.

Commonwealth War Graves Commission Originally the Imperial War Graves Commission, founded by royal charter in 1917, and responsible for the permanent marking and maintenance of the graves of members of the commonwealth who lost their lives in the two World Wars and subsequent actions and for the commemoration by name of those who have no known grave. The central monuments in cemeteries administered by the commission are the Cross of Sacrifice, designed by Sir Reginald Blomfield, and the Stone of Remembrance, by Sir Edwin Lutyens. The Cross stands in nearly all but the smallest cemeteries and bears upon its shaft a crusader's sword of bronze. The Stone of Remembrance, a great altar-like monolith which can be accepted by people of every faith, is erected in the larger cemeteries and has carved upon it 'Their Name Liveth for Evermore'.

Company Sub-unit, usually of infantry, commanded by a major and with a strength of about 120 men, and itself composed of two or more platoons. A company equates broadly with a squadron or battery.

Concentration The act of bringing together military forces.

Concentration Area An area, usually in the theatre of operations, where troops are brought together, briefed, rehearsed, administered and prepared for battle. The area must be free from enemy interference, concealed and have room for manoeuvre.

Condore Battle honour marking the action on 9 December 1758 when a British force sent from Bengal to the Northern Circars under Colonel Forde defeated the French under Conflans. *See also: Plassey; Masulipatam and Badara.*

Conductor Title given to some senior warrant officers class I in the Royal Army Ordnance Corps, now the Royal Logistic Corps, holding specific appointments. *See also: Rank.*

Confidential Report Annual report on an officer by his superiors. The term is also used more widely to describe all annual reports on individuals.

Congreve's Rocket In 1805, William Congreve produced a projectile known as the Congreve Rocket. Although he thus introduced rocket projectiles into the British Army, they had long been in use elsewhere. The Congreve Rocket could be fired from wheeled frames, portable tripods or from earthen ramps. The British Army retained the Congreve Rocket until 1860, and its successor, the stick-less Hale Rocket, was still held in ammunition stores when the First World War began.

Connaught Rangers (88th and 94th Foot) The original 88th Foot (Royal Highland Volunteers) was raised in 1760, disbanded in 1763, raised again as 88th Foot in 1779 and disbanded again in 1783. In 1793 88th (Connaught Rangers) Foot was raised in Connaught by the Hon John Thomas de Burgh. The 94th was raised and disbanded, under different names but always 94th Foot, four times between 1760 and 1818. Raised for the fifth time in 1823 as 94th Foot, the two regiments were brought together as The Connaught Rangers (88th and 94th Foot) in 1881, a product of the order of that year combining infantry battalions. The regiment was disbanded in 1922 following a 'mutiny' in India triggered by the Irish troubles of that year.

Headdress Badge: A Harp surmounted by a Crown. Below, a scroll inscribed 'CONNAUGHT RANGERS'.

History: *The Connaught Rangers* by H F N Jourdain and E Fraser (3 Vols.) (1924, 1926 and 1928).

Conqueror British post-Second World War main battle tank. Conqueror had a crew of four, weighed 65 tons, and mounted a 120mm gun. *See also: Tank.*

Conscientious Objector A person who claims to object on moral or religious grounds to military service in a fighting capacity. Special measures were taken to deal with such objectors in the Military Service Act of 1916 and, under the Representation of the People Act 1918, such objectors were disqualified from voting for five years after the First World War. Provision was made in the Military Training Act of 1939 for the exemption of objectors and employment in other roles of service to the nation. Objectors in the Second World War were released from further obligations by the National Service (Release of Conscientious Objectors) Act of 1946. Some of the medical units serving with the airborne forces were composed largely of objectors and the combatant arms had the highest regard for the courage and devotion to duty of the objectors.

Conscription Compulsory military service. Except for two brief periods, 1916-19 and 1939-60, the British Army has been manned on a voluntary basis. An Act of 1702 permitted the release of imprisoned debtors in return for their agreement to enlist for the duration - or find a suitable substitute. The same act permitted the conscription of unemployed men and paupers. This practice was revived briefly in 1756.

Conspicuous Gallantry Cross Authorised by a Royal Warrant of 7 February 1995. Ranking between the Victoria Cross and the Military Cross and awarded for, '...acts of conspicuous gallantry during active operations against the enemy to all members, of any rank, of Our Naval, Military and Air Forces...'. The award is also open to foreign and commonwealth forces operating in association with British forces.

Ribbon: 1¼" wide of white with a stripe of dark blue at each edge and one stripe of crimson, twice the width of the blue stripes, in the centre.

Conspicuous Gallantry Medal (Flying) By a Royal Warrant of 10 November 1942 the Conspicuous Gallantry Medal, hitherto confined to Royal Navy personnel, was extended to warrant officers, non-commissioned officers and men of the Army and Royal Air Force for gallantry 'whilst flying in active operations against the enemy'. The medal is identical to the Naval Conspicuous Gallantry Medal, but the ribbon differs.

Ribbon: Light blue, 1¼" wide, with a dark blue marginal stripe ⅛" wide.

Contact Battle Area The area where manoeuvre units engage each other with direct fire weapons and where indirect fire and air-to-ground weapons must be closely integrated with the manoeuvre plan.

Contemptible Little Army During September 1914 a British Expeditionary Force (qv) Routine Order was issued in which was published a copy of an order, alleged to have been issued by the German emperor, referring to the British Army as 'General French's contemptible little army'. This was seized upon by recruiters and proved a most effective piece of propaganda. To be an 'Old Contemptible' is now deemed an honour, and an association of ex-soldiers now bears that name. In 1925 the matter was referred to the ex-Kaiser at Doorn, who denied ever having used such an expression with reference to an army, the high value of which he had always appreciated.

Conventello-Comacchio Second World War Italian campaign battle honour marking one of the actions between the breaching of the Gothic Line and the final drive into the Po valley in April 1945. *See also: Italy 1943-1945; Montebello-Scorticata Ridge; Monte Reggiano; Savignano; San Martino Sogliano; Monte Farneto; Montilgallo; Monte Cavallo; Carpinetta; Pideura; Pergola Ridge; Senio Floodbank; Cesena; Catarelto Ridge; Monte Casalino; Monte La Pieve; Monte Pianoereno; Monte Spaduro; Orsara; Tossignano and Casa Bettini.*

Coote's Regiment Raised in 1702, later 39th Foot, and in 1881 The Dorsetshire Regiment.

Copenhagen Battle honour marking the action on 2 April 1801 when the Danish fleet was destroyed at Copenhagen. As a result of this action three regiments were allowed to add a Naval Crown to the dates of the fleet actions and a Naval Crown superscribed '2 April 1801' was added to Colours in 1951.

Copenhagen 1807 Battle honour marking the actions of 28 July 1807 when the reserve division under Sir Arthur Wellesley captured ten guns and 10,000 Danish prisoners and of 5 September when, after the briefest of sieges, the Danes surrendered unconditionally. Trophies included 18 line-of-battle ships, 15 frigates and the prize money accruing to the two Commanders-in-Chief (Admiral James Gambier and General Lord Cathcart) in excess of £300,000.

Cordite Strands or cords of a gelatinous compound of nitro-cellulose (gun-cotton pyroxylin) and nitroglycerine with stabiliser, widely used as a smokeless propellant.

Coriano Second World War Italian campaign battle honour marking the fighting for the Coriano Ridge over the period 3-15 September 1944 during the Battle of the Gothic Line. *See also: Italy 1943-45; Gothic Line; Tavoleto; Croce and Gemmano Ridge.*

Corinth Canal Second World War Greek campaign battle honour marking the action fought on 26 April 1941 when German airborne troops overwhelmed Allied forces, crossed the Corinth Canal and thus entered the Peloponnese. *See also: Greece 1941; Veve and Proasteion.*

Cork Helmet Lightweight cork sun helmet introduced in India in the mid-19th century as an alternative to the ordinary helmet or shako.

Corn Rigs Are Bonnie An arrangement of this tune forms part of the Regimental quick march of The King's Own Royal Border Regiment.

Cornet In the 18th century and up to 1871 cornet was the lowest commissioned rank in the cavalry, corresponding to ensign in the infantry, and expected to carry the troop's cornet (flag). Between 1855 and 1871, a cornet wore one star on the collar. In 1871 the title of cornet was abolished and replaced by that of Second Lieutenant. *See also: Rank.*

Cornwall Light Infantry (32nd Foot) *See: Duke of Cornwall's Light Infantry.*

Cornwall's Regiment (9th Foot) Raised in June 1685 as Colonel Henry Cornwall's Regiment. *See also: Royal Norfolk Regiment.*

Cornwall Yeomanry Between 1794 and 1838 some 18 troops were raised in the county, beginning with Launceston troop from which the North Cornwall Hussars was formed. The Duke of Cornwall's (Loyal Meneage) Yeomanry Cavalry was accepted for service in 1797. The West Penwith Guides, raised in 1803, was accepted as Yeomanry Cavalry in 1805 and became the third of the Cornish regiments, designated 2nd Cornwall (Penwith) Yeomanry Cavalry. All three regiments were subsequently ordered to disband and all had done so by 1838. Cornish squadrons of 1st Royal Devon Yeomanry existed from time to time, the last being in 1903.

Cornwallis, Charles, Marquess (1738-1805) On leaving college he entered the Army, and in 1761 served in the campaign in Germany. In 1762 he succeeded to the earldom and estates of his father. He was appointed Governor of the Tower in 1770. When the American War of Independence (qv) broke out he accompanied his regiment and was victorious over General Gates at Camden in 1780 and over General Greene at Guildford in 1781. However, at Yorktown, Virginia on 19 October 1781 he was forced to surrender and the English cause in America was overthrown. In 1786 he was appointed Governor-General of India and while there made many reforms. In 1791 he captured Bangalore and, having completed a treaty with Tippoo Sahib, returned to England in 1793. He was raised to the rank of marquess and, in 1798, appointed to the vice royalty of Ireland, where he subdued the rebellion of 1798 and showed integrity and wisdom in obtaining a peace. Having been replaced in Ireland in 1801 by Lord Hardwicke, he negotiated the peace of Amiens in 1802. In 1805 he was sent to India as Governor-General in the place of Lord Wellesley, but died at Ghazipur.

Coronation Blues Following the First World War, full dress uniform for soldiers was not restored. As a result there was a shortage of such uniforms for the Coronation in 1937. Blue tunics and trousers were produced, but only in sufficient numbers to equip those men actually on parade. This limited issue was given the nickname 'Coronation Blues'.

Corporal Non-commissioned rank between sergeant and lance corporal. The rank is distinguished by the wearing of two chevrons on the upper sleeve. A corporal in the Royal Regiment of Artillery bears the title Bombardier. *See also: Rank.*

Corporal of Horse A sergeant in the Household Cavalry. *See also: Rank.*

Corps In the 18th and 19th centuries the terms corps and regiment were interchangeable when referring to regiments of the line. The term is also applied to an army formation of two or more divisions, and itself forming part of an army.

Corps of Royal Electrical and Mechanical Engineers The corps was formed under Army Order 70 of 1942 to provide specialist electrical and mechanical servicing and repairs. On formation, most of the personnel were transferred from the parent corps, the Royal Army Ordnance Corps, but some specialists were also drawn from the Corps of Royal Engineers and the Royal Army Service Corps. The present title dates from Army Order 148 of 1949.
Headdress Badge: Upon a lightning flash, a horse forcene gorged with a coronet of four fleur-de-lys, a chain reflexed over its back and standing on a globe. Above, a crown upon a scroll bearing the letters 'REME'.
Motto: *Arte et Marte* (By skill and by fighting).
Regimental marches:
Quick march: *Lillibulero* and *Auprès de ma Blonde.*
Slow March: *Duchess of Kent.*
Corps Headquarters: Arborfield, Reading, RG2 9NN.
History: *'Craftsmen of the Army' - The Story of the Royal Electrical and Mechanical Engineers* by B B Kennett and J A Tatman (1970).

Corps of Royal Engineers One of the oldest corps of the British Army, tracing its origins back to the Board of Ordnance in the 15th century. In 1717 a separate officer Corps of Engineers of the Board of Ordnance was formed, taking precedence after the Royal Regiment of Artillery. However, the Artificer Companies remained civilian. The first non-officer Army unit was formed in 1772 as a Soldier Artificer Company for duty at Gibraltar. In 1787 the Corps of Engineers was granted the title 'Royal' and became the Corps of Royal Engineers, supplying officers to the Corps of Royal Military Artificers which had been formed in the same year. The Gibraltar Company was absorbed into the new Corps of Royal Military Artificers in 1797 and, in 1812, the title was changed to the Corps of Royal Sappers and Miners. On the abolition of the Board of Ordnance in 1855 the officer Corps of Royal Engineers and the Corps of Royal Sappers and Miners were transferred to the control of the Commander-in-Chief. In 1856 the Corps of Royal Sappers and Miners was absorbed into the Corps of Royal Engineers, and in 1862 the British officers and non-commissioned officers of the Presidency Corps of the East India Company Engineer Corps were transferred to the British establishment. In 1912 the Royal Flying Corps (Military Wing) was formed and remained a branch of the Corps of Royal Engineers until the formation of the Royal Air Force in 1918. In 1920 the Royal Corps of Signals was formed from the Royal Engineer Signal Service, and in 1965, on the formation of the Royal Corps of Transport, Royal Engineer Transportation and Movement Control Services were transferred to the new Corps and bomb disposal duties were shared with the Royal Army Ordnance Corps.

Headdress Badge: The royal cypher within the garter and motto, all enclosed in a laurel wreath and ensigned with the crown. Below, a scroll inscribed 'Royal Engineers'.

Mottoes: *Ubique* (Everywhere) and *Quo Fas et Gloria ducunt* (Where right and glory lead).

Regimental marches:

Quick marches: *Wings* and *The British Grenadiers*.

Corps Headquarters: Brompton Barracks, Chatham, Kent ME4 4UG.

History: *The History of the Corps of Royal Engineers*, (12 Vols).

Corps of Armourer-Sergeants Raised in 1858, later Royal Army Ordnance Corps.

Corps of Royal Military Police Although the office of Provost Marshal dates from the 15th century, it was not until 1885 that 15 cavalry non-commissioned officers were selected to act as mounted police. These mounted police proved so successful, particularly in the garrison towns, that the strength increased to about 150 within the next 20 years and led to the formation of the Military Mounted Police. In 1885 the Military Foot Police was formed, and in 1926 the two elements were amalgamated to form the Corps of Military Police; the title 'Royal' being granted under Army Order 167 of 1946. On 6 April 1992 the Corps of Royal Military Police and the Military Provost Staff Corps became the Provost Branch of the Adjutant General's Corps (qv).

Headdress Badge: Within a laurel wreath, the royal cypher with crown above. Beneath, a scroll inscribed 'Royal Military Police'.

Regimental marches:

Quick marches: *The Watchtower* and *The Metropolitan*.

Branch Headquarters: Roussillon Barracks, Chichester, West Sussex.

History: *The Corps of Royal Military Police* by S F Crozier (1951); *The Story of The Royal Military Police* by A V Lovell-Knight (1977) and *The Redcaps: A History of the Royal Military Police and its Antecedents from The Middle Ages to the Gulf War* by G D Sheffield (1994).

Corps of Waggoners Raised in 1794, later Royal Corps of Transport.

Corunna Peninsula War (qv) battle honour marking the action on 16 January 1809 by Sir John Moore's army against the French under Soult. Moore had conducted a masterly withdrawal and the perfectly timed counter-attack at Corunna, during which he was mortally wounded, permitted most of his army to embark safely. *See also: Peninsula; Roliça; Vimiera; Sahagun; Douro; Talavera and Busaco.*

Corunna Majors A toast drunk in the Queen's Own Royal West Kent Regiment (50th and 97th Foot) on the anniversary of the Battle of Corunna on 16 January 1809, in honour of the great bravery of Majors Napier and Stanhope of the 50th or West Kent Regiment of Foot. Both officers were later killed in battle.

Corygaum Battle honour marking an action on 1 January 1818 during the Second Mahratta War (qv) in which a small British force, under 1,000 strong, held out against 25,000 Mahrattas under Peishwa. The Mahrattas withdrew on the approach of a column under General Smith.

Cos Second World War battle honour marking action on the island, which had been occupied by the British in September 1943, following Italian surrender. In October the island fell to German air- and seaborne forces. *See also: Leros.*

Cosina Canal Crossing Second World War Italian campaign battle honour marking the establishment of bridgeheads over the Cosina Canal during the period 20-23 November 1944, forcing a German withdrawal to the River Lamone. *See also: Italy 1943-1945; Santarcangelo; Monte Chicco; Capture of Forli; Casa Fortis; Lamone Crossing; Lamone Bridgehead and Senio Pocket.*

Cotterell's Marines Raised in 1742, later 49th Foot, and in 1921 The Royal Berkshire Regiment (Princess Charlotte of Wales's).

Counter-Battery Fire Fire delivered for the purpose of destroying or neutralising indirect fire weapons systems.

Counter Insurgency Operations against forces waging revolutionary war against the constitutional government and seeking to persuade the population by force to do things they do not wish to do.

County of Dublin Regiment (83rd Foot) Raised in Dublin in September 1793 by Colonel William Fitch. Amalgamated with 86th (Royal County Down) Regiment of Foot in 1881 to form the Royal Irish Rifles. The regiment was retitles The Royal Ulster Rifles on the formation of the Irish Free State in 1921. *See also:Royal Irish Regiment.*

County of London Yeomanry
1st (Middlesex, Duke of Cambridge's Hussars).

2nd (Westminster Dragoons).
3rd (The Sharpshooters).
See also: London Yeomanry.

Court Martial Court usually convened for the purpose of trying offences against military discipline or administering martial law. Before 1640 ordinances were issued by the sovereign for the trial of such offences, and justice was administered under the old court of chivalry of which the earl marshal was president. There are three classes of courts martial: District, General, and Field General. A District Court Martial must be composed of at least three officers. A General Court Martial is the only court with authority to try an officer and must consist of at least five officers. The Field General Court Martial is convened on active service when it is not possible to convene an ordinary general court martial. The sentences which may be handed down by each type of court are clearly set out in the Army Act. *See also: Military law.*

Courtrai First World War battle honour marking the final advance of Second Army in mid-October 1918, leading to the capture of Menin and Courtrai, and of the capture of Lille by the Fifth Army. *See also: France and Flanders 1914-1918; Ypres 1918; Selle;Valenciennes and Sambre.*

Covenanter Second World War Mark V cruiser tank developed by the London Midland and Scottish Railway but, due to technical problems, mainly associated with the engine cooling system, it was never used in battle. Some 1,771 Covenanters were built and used for training in the United Kingdom and, in small numbers, in the Middle East. Covenanter had a crew of four, weighed 18 tons and mounted a 2pdr gun and a Besa machine gun. *See also: Tank; Crusader; Cavalier; Centaur; Cromwell; Challenger and Comet.*

Covering Force A force operating apart from the main force for the purpose of intercepting, engaging, delaying, disorganising and deceiving the enemy before he encounters the force covered. The term may also be applied to any group which provides security for a larger force by observation, reconnaissance, attack or defence.

Covert Operations Operations deliberately concealed from, and unobservable by, an enemy or potential enemy.

Crab Second World War modified US Sherman tank, armed with a 75mm gun and fitted with power-driven rollers with a rotary chain flail to clear a path through minefields.

Crete Second World War campaign honour marking the actions of British and New Zealand forces on the island following the German airborne attack launched on 20 May 1941. In spite of gallant actions by the New Zealanders the Germans were able to capture the vital airfield at Maleme and gradually build up their forces by an airlanded operation. Although the German offensive was successful their casualties were so heavy that they never again attempted a major airborne operation. *See also: Canea; Heraklion; Retimo and Withdrawal to Sphakia.*

Creteville Pass Second World War North Africa campaign battle honour marking one of the actions in mid-1943 during the final breakthrough to Tunis and following exploitation towards the Cape Bon Peninsula, which resulted in the surrender of Axis forces in North Africa. *See also: North Africa 1940-1943; Tunis; Hammam Lif; Djebel Bou Aoukaz 1943 I; Djebel Bou Aoukaz 1943 II; Montarnaud; Ragoubet Souissi; Gromballa and Bou Ficha.*

Crimean War 1853-56 The Crimean War was largely caused by the territorial ambitions of Tsar Nicholas I of Russia, who had visions of a Russian empire embracing the whole of south-east Europe, and was determined to win Constantinople. As a vehicle for invasion the Tsar used an obscure quarrel between the various Christian communities in Jerusalem, claiming the right to the guardianship of the holy places at Jerusalem and the right to protect all Christian subjects which were under Turkish rule in those countries bordering the Danube. In 1853 England, France,

Austria and Prussia held a conference at Vienna and, in what is called the 'Vienna Note' forwarded a proposal to the Sultan that he should accede to the Tsar's claims. The Sultan refused and the Tsar declared war on Turkey. France and Britain entered the war on the side of Turkey; the former because it was anxious to avenge Moscow and the latter because it feared that, if successful, Russia would threaten British eastern possessions. There were some naval engagements in the Baltic, but interest centred on Sevastopol, the Russian stronghold in the Crimea. The allied forces mustered at Varna, but in 1854 were transported to Eupatoria, having been ravaged by cholera. The victory at Alma in September 1854 cleared a way to Sevastopol. In October the Russians attacked the British headquarters at Balaklava, the Heavy Brigade inflicting a significant defeat on the Russian cavalry and the Light Brigade making its famed charge. A further Russian assault at Inkerman in November was defeated and a winter siege was laid on Sevastopol. Tempests wrecked the transports carrying ammunition, clothing and medical supplies and stores for the winter. As a result the troops had to endure a Crimean winter totally unprepared, exposed to acute suffering and deprivation, Florence Nightingale doing what she could to alleviate suffering. In 1855 the war was prosecuted vigorously, a railway was constructed from Balaklava to the camps to move stores rapidly forward and, in September 1855, after a months' incessant bombardment, two strong fortresses, the Malakof and the Redan, were taken by assault and Sevastopol fell. Peace was concluded by the Third Treaty of Paris in 1856 under which Russia agreed not to re-fortify Sevastopol or to keep a fleet in the Black Sea. *See also: Alma; Balaklava; Inkerman and Sevastopol.*

Crimean War Medal 1854-1856 The medal was authorised by Queen Victoria in December 1854 whilst the war was still in progress.
Ribbon: Light blue with yellow edges.
Clasps: Alma; Inkerman; Balaklava; Sebastopol and, for those operating with naval forces, Azoff.

Croce Second World War Italian campaign battle honour awarded for an action during the operations to breach the Gothic Line in Italy. The village of Croce, having changed five times during the period 3-15 September 1944, was finally captured with heavy casualties. *See also: Italy 1943-1945; Gothic Line; Tavoleto; Coriano and Gemmano Ridge.*

Crocodile Used in the Second World War, a modified Churchill Mark VII tank fitted with a flame gun and drawing a two-wheeled armoured trailer containing 400 gallons of flame thrower fuel and nitrogen bottles necessary to develop the pressure required to project the burning fuel over a maximum range of 100m.

Croix de Guerre Decoration instituted in France and Belgium in 1915 and awarded for acts of gallantry, devotion to duty and similar feats. Although usually awarded to individuals, it was also awarded to some British Army units.

Cromwell, Oliver, Lord Protector of England (1599-1658) Born Huntingdon, educated at Huntingdon Grammar School and Sidney Sussex College, Cambridge, and later read law at Lincoln's Inn. Joined the parliamentary army as a captain and, impressed by the superiority of the royalist horse at Edgehill (1642), he conceived the idea of meeting his opponents' enthusiasm with puritan zeal, strict discipline and training. He raised and trained a troop in his own district with such success that the whole parliamentary army was remodelled on the same lines. By the Restoration, the only regiment remaining of the highly successful New Model Army was Monk's Regiment, later the Coldstream Guards.

Cromwell Second World War heavy cruiser tank which was brought in to service from 1943. The Cromwell had a crew of five, weighed 28 tons, and, although originally fitted with a 6pdr gun, later Marks mounted a 95mm howitzer and two Besa machine guns *See also: Tank and Cruiser tanks.*

Crossbelts Nickname given to the 8th Hussars. During the Battle of Almenara

(1710), when the regiment virtually destroyed a Spanish cavalry regiment, the Hussars removed the Spaniards' crossbelts and wore them over the right shoulder.

Crown The crowns depicted on badges and horse furniture in the Army differ in pattern. The Hanoverian and Victorian crown differ by the shape of the arches which support the orb and cross. The Imperial or Tudor crown has high curved arches and is often named the 'King's Crown'.

Crows-Foot Cord or braid formed into three loops, used in the decoration of uniforms.

Cruiser Mark I Second World War cruiser tank in service until late 1941. Crew six, weight 12 tons, mounting a 2pdr gun and three Vickers machine guns. A variant mounting a 3.7" howitzer instead of the 2pdr gun was also produced. *See also: Tank and Cruiser tanks.*

Cruiser Mark II Second World War cruiser tank in limited service until late 1941. Crew four, weight 13.75 tons, mounting a 2pdr gun and a Vickers machine gun. Variants with alternative armament were also produced. *See also: Tank and Cruiser tanks.*

Cruiser Mark III Second World War cruiser tank in limited service until late 1940. Crew four, weight 14 tons, mounting a 2pdr gun and a Vickers machine gun. *See also: Tank and Cruiser Tanks.*

Cruiser Mark IV/IVA Second World War cruiser tank in service until late 1941. Crew four, weight 14.75 tons, mounting a 2pdr gun and a Vickers machine gun. Variants with different armament were also produced. *See also: Tanks and Cruiser tanks.*

Cruiser Tanks The designation 'cruiser' tank came into use in about 1938 for what had previously been described as 'medium' tanks. The pilot model of the first cruiser tank, the Mark I or A.9 as it was also known, designed by Sir John Carden of Vickers-Carden-Loyd, appeared in April

1936. A limited number were taken into service and saw action with 1st Armoured Division in France in 1940, and in the Middle East until about 1941. The Cruiser Mark II or A.10 was developed in parallel with the Mark I, but only produced in limited numbers, the last tanks being completed in September 1940. A small number of Cruiser Mark III tanks, using the American Christie suspension and produced by Nuffield Mechanisations and Aero Ltd, saw service in 1940 and early 1941. A Cruiser Mark IV, very similar to the Mark III, but with improved armour and Besa instead of Vickers machine guns, was produced in very limited numbers and also saw service in 1940 and 1941. Further Cruiser tanks, with the approximate date of introduction, were: Covenanter (1,771 produced, but never used in battle); Crusader (1940); Cavalier (1942, limited production only, used as gun-tanks); Centaur (1943, limited production only); Cromwell (1943); Challenger (1943, limited production only); and Comet (1944). In addition anti-aircraft variants were developed using the chassis of obsolescent cruiser tanks. *See also: Tank; Cruiser (Various Marks); Covenanter; Crusader; Cavalier; Centaur; Cromwell; Challenger and Comet.*

Crusader Second World War Mark VI heavy cruiser tank, first used in North Africa in June 1941. The later Crusader III had a crew of three, weighed 19 tons, and mounted a 6pdr gun and two Besa machine guns. Crusader was also produced in a variant fitted with anti-aircraft guns. *See also: Tank and Cruiser tanks.*

Crying Down Credit In 1695 a proclamation was published directing that for the future, upon arrival of any troops in a place, publication was to be made by sound of trumpet or beat of drum, that 'no officer or soldier be trusted in their quarters beyond the rates that have been or shall be prescribed by Act of Parliament.' This procedure was known as 'Crying Down Credit'.

Ctesiphon Second World War Mesopotamia campaign battle honour. A division under Major General Townshend

was sent up the River Tigris to assess the possibility of reaching Baghdad. After winning battles at Qrna and later, on 28 September 1915, at Kut-al-Amara he met a superior Turkish force at Ctesiphon and was defeated on 22 November, recovering to Kut where he was besieged. *See also: Mesopotamia 1914-18; Kut al Amara 1915; Defence of Kut al Amara; Tigris 1916 and Kut al Amara 1917.*

Cubcub Second World War Abyssinian campaign battle honour. *See also: Abyssinia 1940-41; Keren; Jebel Defeis; Jebel Shiba; Gogni; Agordat; Barentu; Karora-Marsa Taclai; Colito; Ad Teclesan; Mescelit Pass; Mt Engiahat; Massawa; Amb Alagi; Afodu; Gambela; El Wak; Moyale; Wal Garis; Juba; Marda Pass; Bisidimo; Awash; Todenyang-Namaraputh; Omo; Soroppa; Giarso; Babile Gap; Wadara; Gondar; Fike and Lechemti.*

Cuff Originally, the turned back sleeve of a military coat or jacket. Now applied to the facing sewn on the lower sleeve, often in distinctive patterns.

Cuidich'n Righ **(Help to the King)** Motto of The Highlanders (Seaforth, Gordons and Camerons), The Queen's Own Highlanders (Seaforth and Camerons), The Seaforth Highlanders (Ross-Shire Buffs, The Duke of Albany's), 78th (Highland) Regiment of Foot and the 51st Highland Volunteers.

Cuirass Armour covering the chest and back consisting of a shaped front and back plates held together by straps and shoulder 'scales' worn by the Household Cavalry.

Culloden Moor (known to Scots as Drummossie Moor) in Invernessshire and famed for the victory gained on 16 April 1746 by the Duke of Cumberland (qv) over the 'Young Pretender', Charles Stuart.

Cumberland, William Augustus, Duke of (1721-65) Third son of George II, then Prince of Wales. He entered the Army and at the age of 21 was gazetted Major General. Two years later he was appointed to command the allied forces in the Netherlands with Königsegg as his adviser;

and in 1745 the office of Captain General of the British forces at home and in the field, dormant since Marlborough's day, was revived in his favour. He took an active part against the rising of 1745, and after the battle of Culloden (qv) in 1746 treated the rebels with such severity that he was nicknamed 'Butcher'.

Cumberland Regiment (34th Foot) Raised in February 1702 by Colonel Robert, 3rd Lord Lucas, and ranked 34th Foot. Amalgamated with 55th (Westmorland) regiment in 1881 to form The Border Regiment.

Cumberland Yeomanry *See: Westmorland Yeomanry.*

Cunningham's Dragoons Raised in 1689, 7th or Queen's Own Dragoons in 1751, and in 1958 The Queen's Own Hussars.

Cunningham's Regiment of Dragoons Raised in 1693, 8th Light Dragoons in 1775, and 8th King's Royal Irish Hussars in 1921.

Curragh Mutiny The occasion in March 1914 when the commander and 56 other officers of 3rd Cavalry Brigade, stationed at the Curragh, near Dublin, opted for dismissal rather than to 'coerce' the Ulster Protestants to accept Irish Home Rule. The incident may in part explain why the government of the day was not prepared to force Ulster to accept home rule. The Secretary for War, J E B Seely (later 1st Baron Mottistone; 1868-1947), and Sir John French, the Chief of the Imperial General Staff, indicated that officers should not be required to serve against the north. The cabinet disagreed and Seely and French resigned their offices.

Cutchee Battle honour marking operations against tribesmen in the southern part of Baluchistan during the First Afghan War (qv) from 1839 to 1842.

Cuttack Legion Raised in 1817, later 6th Queen Elizabeth's Own Gurkha Rifles.

Cycle A badge showing a cycle wheel was worn on the sleeve of trained cyclists in the early 1900s. The cycle wheel also featured on the cap badges of a number of cyclist regiments in the First World War.

Cyclonite An explosive substance. *See also: Research Department Explosive (RDX).*

Cymbeline Track- or wheel-mounted mortar locating radar with a range of approximately 20km from radar to mortar, also used for the adjustment of artillery and mortar fire.

Cymru Am Byth **(Wales for ever)** Motto of the Welsh Guards.

Cypher Initials or letters in cursive fashion linked together to form a special device.

Cyprus 1954-60 Campaign against EOKA (Ethniki Organosis Kypriou Agonistou), led by self-styled General George Grivas, a retired Greek Army colonel, the military wing of the Greek-Cypriot movement for ENOSIS, or union with Greece, led by Archbishop Makarios. The island, which had been ceded to Britain by Turkey in 1878, remained a largely dormant colony until 1954 when, coincidental with the transfer from Egypt to Cyprus of Middle East Headquarters, anti-British activity began. Although largely limited to politically inspired rioting, the situation deteriorated rapidly until, on 1 April 1955 a series of bombs exploded on the island leading to the deportation of Archbishop Makarios and the declaration of a State of Emergency on the island in November 1955. There followed an increasingly bloody guerilla war conducted by EOKA and directed at both Britons and Turks. On 19 February 1959 an agreement was signed between the United Kingdom, Greece, Turkey and the Greek and Turkish Cypriots which provided that Cyprus would become an independent republic on 16 August 1960, with Britain retaining two Sovereign Base Areas, some 99 square miles in all, around Episkopi and Dhekelia. By the end of the campaign against EOKA the British Army had suffered 99 killed and 414 wounded. However, the 1960 constitution proved unworkable and there were serious inter-communal troubles which resulted in intervention by the UN and establishment of the United Nations Force in Cyprus (UNFICYP), to which Britain contributes a significant contingent, in March 1964. On 15 July 1974, mainland Greek officers of the Greek Cypriot National Guard launched a *coup d'état* against President Makarios and installed a former EOKA terrorist and convicted murderer, Nikos Sampson, as President. This action prompted the Turkish invasion of northern Cyprus, and the establishment of a Turkish Federated State of Cyprus in the northern part of the island in 1975.

'D' The letter 'D' on arm badges in the British Army was used to indicate 'D' group tradesmen from 1944 onward.

Daffadar A sergeant in the Indian cavalry. The ranks of Acting Lance Daffadar (Lance Corporal) and Lance Daffadar (Corporal) were also used.

Dah The long sound used, in combination with the short sound 'dit', in the spoken representation of Morse and other telegraphic codes.

Dalet Second World War Burma campaign battle honour marking the crossing of the Dalet Cawing and capture of the village on 4 March 1945 in the final stages of the Arakan campaign in Burma. *See also: Burma 1942-1945; Arakan Beaches; Tamandu and Taungup.*

Damascus First World War Palestine campaign battle honour marking the exploitation to Damascus, which fell on 1 October 1918, after General Allenby's victory at Megiddo. *See also: Palestine 1917-1918; Gaza; El Mughar; Nebi Samwil; Jaffa; Jerusalem; Tell Asur; Jordan; Megiddo; Sharon and Nablus.*

Damiano Second World War Italian campaign battle honour marking the capture, and holding against vigorous counterattack over the period 18-30 January 1944, of Point 114 on the Damiano Ridge. *See also: Italy 1943-1945; Garigliano Crossing; Minturno; Monte Tuga and Monte Ornito.*

Dannebrog The cross of this Danish order of Knighthood features in the badge

of the 19th Hussars, the Green Howards and the Queen Alexandra's Royal Army Nursing Corps.

DAYS
  C Day The day on which a deployment commences or is due to commence.
  D Day The day on which an operation commences or is due to commence.
  E Day The day on which a NATO exercise begins.
  G Day The day on which an order is given to deploy a unit.
  K Day The day on which a convoy system is introduced on a given route.
  M Day The day on which mobilisation commences or is due to commence.
  T Day The day of transfer of authority.

Days We Went A-Gipsying An arrangement of this tune forms part of the regimental quick march of the Staffordshire Regiment (The Prince of Wales's).

DD Tank Second World War US Sherman 'Duplex Drive' amphibious tank. The tank was fitted with a surrounding flotation canvas screen supported by air pillars and steel struts which stood above the turret and gave it the buoyancy necessary to swim. Propulsion was by two propellers at the rear driven by the tank engine. Once free of the water the screen was rapidly dismantled.

De Lisle Carbine A British silenced carbine produced in the Second World War and intended for use on special operations. It consisted of the bolt from the Lee Enfield rifle married to a 9" long silenced barrel, chambered for the Colt .45" round, and with a magazine of ten rounds.

De Normandie One of the regimental slow marches of the Royal Regiment of Fusiliers.

Dead Ground An area within the maximum range of a weapon, radar or observer which cannot be covered by fire or observation because of intervening obstacles, the nature of the ground, the characteristics or the trajectory, or even the limitations of the vertical or horizontal traverse of the weapon.

Death Or Glory Boys Nickname given to the 17th Lancers because their cap badge, chosen by the first colonel in memory of General Wolfe (q.v.), was a Death's Head with the motto 'Or Glory'.

Deception Measures designed to mislead the enemy by manipulation, distortion or falsification of evidence to induce him to react in a manner prejudicial to his interests.

Deckle Edge Ornamental edge to cloth, particularly the lining or decoration of horse furniture. Sometimes scallop-edged.

Deep Battle Area The deep battle area lies between the Fire Support Coordination Line (q.v.) and the Reconnaissance and Interdiction Planning Line (q.v.), and even beyond.

Defeat To diminish the effectiveness of the enemy to such an extent that he is unable to participate further in the battle, or at least fulfil his intention.

DEFENCE

To hold a defined area against enemy attack; to halt or repel an attack in order to defeat or destroy the enemy. There are five broad categories of defence:

Positional Defence The bulk of the defending force is disposed in selected tactical localities where the decisive battle is to be fought. Principal reliance is placed on the forces in the defended localities to maintain their positions and to control the terrain between them. A reserve is used to add depth, to block or to restore the position by counter-attack.

Mobile Defence The type of defence in which manoeuvre is combined with fire and the use of ground to defeat or destroy the enemy.

Hasty Defence A defence normally organised while in contact with the enemy or when contact is imminent and time limited. Such defence is characterised by the improvement of the natural defensive strength of the terrain by entrenchments and obstacles.

Deliberate Defence A defence normally organised when out of contact with the enemy or when contact is not imminent and time is available to organise a defence which includes an extensive fortified zone incorporating pillboxes, bunker systems, communicating trenches or tunnels and strongpoints.

Defence in Depth The siting of mutually supporting defence positions designed to prevent initial observation of the whole position absorb and progressively weaken an attack and allow the defending commander to manoeuvre his reserves.

Defence Attaché *See: Attaché.*

Defence Council Instruction Instructions, numbered consecutively by year, issued from time to time by the Defence Council and applicable to all three Services or to a particular Service ie. Defence Council Instruction (Army).

Defence of Alamein Line Second World War North Africa campaign battle honour marking the First Battle of El Alamein 1-27 July 1942, when the British under General Auchinleck (q.v.) finally halted the Axis advance into Egypt. *See* also: *North Africa 1940-1943; Ruweisat; Fuka Airfield; Deir El Shein; Point 93 and Ruweisat Ridge.*

Defence of Anzac First World War Gallipoli campaign battle honour marking operations in the Anzac sector. *See also: Gallipoli 1915-1916; Landing at Anzac; Suvla; Sari Bair; Landing at Suvla and Scimitar Hill.*

Defence of Arrah Battle honour marking an action during the Indian Mutiny 1857 when an ad hoc force of 16 Englishmen, one Moslem gentleman, and 50 men of 45th (Rattray's Sikhs) Bengal Native Infantry held out against the mutineers.

Defence of Arras Second World War battle honour marking the delaying action fought in the area of Arras, 19-25 May 1940 by 'Petreforce'. *See also: North West Europe 1940; Dyle; Withdrawal to Escaut; Defence of Escaut; Boulogne 1940; Calais 1940 and Dunkirk 1940.*

Defence of Chitral Battle honour marking the holding of Chitral by a small garrison from March 1895 until relieved in April. *See also: Chitral.*

Defence of Escaut Second World War battle honour marking the holding of the line of the River Escaut 19-22 May 1940 during the rapid German advance and efforts to reach the channel coast. *See also: North West Europe 1940; Dyle; Withdrawal to Escaut; Defence of Arras; Boulogne 1940; Calais 1940 and Dunkirk 1940.*

Defence of Habbaniya Second World War Iraq campaign battle honour marking an action during the 1941 campaign in Iraq when the RAF base at Habbanniya near Baghdad was held against an Iraqi attack. *See also: Iraq 1941; Falluja and Baghdad 1941.*

Defence of Kelat-i-Ghilzie Medal 1842 The medal was issued to mark the defence of the fort of Kelat-i-Ghilzie by some 900 men, mostly Indian, between February and May 1842.
Ribbon: 1" wide, rainbow pattern watered red, white, yellow, white and blue.

Defence of Kimberley South Africa War battle honour marking the successful defence of Kimberley during the Boer War (q.v.), which was besieged by the Boers from 14 October 1899 until 15 February 1900. *See also: South Africa 1899-1902; Defence of Ladysmith; Relief of Ladysmith; Modder River; Relief of Kimberley and Paardeburg.*

Defence of Kohima Second World War Burma campaign battle honour marking the defence of the town against attacks by Japanese 31st Division 4-18 April 1944. *See also: Burma 1942-1945; Kohima; Aradura; Relief of Kohima; Naga Village and Mao Songsang.*

Defence of Kut Al Amara First World War Mesopotamia campaign battle honour marking the defence of Kut Al Amara by the force under Major General Townshend during the campaign in Mesopotamia. After the battle of Ctesiphon (q.v.) Townshend fell back on Kut Al Amara where he was besieged by the Turks. Attempts to relieve him failed, and in April 1916 Townshend surrendered. *See also: Mesopotamia 1914-1918; Basra; Kut Al Amara 1915; Ctesiphon; Tigris 1916; Kut Al Amara 1917; Baghdad; Khan Baghdadi and Sharqat.*

Defence of Ladysmith South Africa War battle honour marking the defence of Ladysmith during the Boer War (q.v.), which was besieged by the Boers from 29 October 1899 to 28 February 1900. *See also: South Africa 1899-1902; Defence of Kimberley; Relief of Ladysmith; Modder River; Relief of Kimberley and Paardeburg.*

Defence of Lamone Bridgehead Second World War Italian campaign battle honour marking the defence of the Lamone bridgehead against heavy enemy attack on 9 December 1944 during the advance from the Gothic line. *See also: Italy 1943-1945; Lamone Crossing and Lamone Bridgehead*

Defence of Meiktila Second World War Burma campaign battle honour marking one of the actions following the capture of Meiktila in March 1945. *See also: Burma 1942-45; Meiktila; Nyaungu Bridgehead; Capture of Meiktila and Taungtha.*

Defence of Rauray Second World War battle honour marking the defeat of the German counter-attack against the right flank of the Odon offensive which followed the Allied landings in Normandy in June 1944. *See also: North West Europe 1944-*

1945; Odon; Fontenay Le Pesnil; Cheux and Caen.

Defence of Swinzweya Second World War Burma campaign battle honour marking an action in the Ngakyedauk Pass operations, and covers the defence of the Corps Maintenance Centre, generally known as the 'Battle of the Boxes' 5-29 February 1944. *See also: Burma 1942-45; North Arakan and Ngakyedauk Pass.*

Defence of the Realm Act The name applied to legislative measures enacted by the British government at different periods of the First World War. The first of the series, known as the Defence of the Realm Consolidated Act 1914, authorised the trial by court martial, or in the case of minor offences by courts of summary jurisdiction, and punishment of persons committing offences against such regulations as might be made by the King in council for securing the public safety and the defence of the realm. The Act also made it lawful for the Admiralty or Army Council to take over the whole or part of the output of any factory or workshop engaged in the manufacture of arms, ammunition or warlike stores; or indeed take over the factory itself. In May 1915 the Act gave wide powers to the state over the supply and sale of intoxicating liquors in certain areas. Though highly unpopular, the regulations under this type of legislation were revived just before the outbreak of the Second World War.

Defence of Tobruk Second World War North Africa campaign battle honour marking an action in the North African campaign 1940-43. On the British withdrawal into Egypt in April 1941 a garrison was left in Tobruk, which was successfully defended from 8 April until relieved on 10 December 1941. *See also: North Africa 1940-43; Sidi Barrani; Capture of Tobruk; Beda Fomm and Tobruk 1941.*

Defended Locality Term used in fighting in built-up areas to describe a series of buildings prepared as mutually supporting strong points so that penetration within them is virtually impossible.

Defensive Fire Fire delivered by supporting units to assist and protect a unit engaged in defensive action.

Defilade Protection from hostile observation and fire, provided by an obstacle such as a hill, ridge or bank, which permits engagement of the enemy's flank. Thus, from a defilade position enfilade (q.v.) fire is produced.

Deig Battle honour marking the storming of the fortress at Deig on 23 December 1804, following a six-week seige, during the First Mahratta War (1803-4). *See also: Ally Ghur; Delhi 1803; Assaye and Leswarree.*

Deir El Munasib Second World War North Africa campaign battle honour marking an action which took place in the period between the occupation of the Alamein line in mid-1942 and the end of the campaign in May 1943. *See also: North Africa 1940-1943; Capture of Halfaya Pass; Matmata Hills; Sebkret En Noual; Chebket En Nouiges; Djebel El Telil and Djebel Tebaga.*

Deir El Shein Second World War North Africa campaign battle honour marking one of the actions in the defence of the Alamein line 1-27 July 1942. *See also: North Africa 1940-1943; Defence of Alamein Line; Ruweisat; Fuka Airfield; Point 93 and Ruweisat Ridge.*

Deir Es Zor Second World War Syria campaign battle honour. In May 1941 German aircraft landed in Syria with the consent of the Vichy authorities. This posed a serious threat to allied interests and an invasion was launched from Palestine on 7 June 1941. After unexpectedly strong Vichy French resistance, the Vichy forces sued for an armistice on 12 July 1941. *See also: Syria 1941; Merjayun; Palmyra and Jebel Mazar.*

Delaying Action An operation in which a force under pressure trades space for time by slowing enemy momentum and inflicting maximum damage on the enemy without, in principle, becoming decisively engaged.

Delhi 1803 Battle honour marking the battle in which General Lake defeated a Mahratta army under the French General Bourquien at Delhi on 11 September 1803 during the First Mahratta War (1803-4). *See also: Ally Ghur; Assaye; Leswarree and Deig.*

Delhi 1857 Battle honour marking the actions of May to September 1857 during the early months of the Indian Mutiny, which concluded with the successful storming of the city on 6 September and six days' bitter street fighting. *See also: Lucknow; Central India; Defence of Arrah and Behar.*

Deliberate Attack An offensive action identified by pre-planned, co-ordinated employment of firepower and manoeuvre to close with and destroy or capture the enemy. *See also: Attack.*

Delville Wood First World War battle honour marking an action during the 1916 British Somme offensive. Delville Wood was fought over for six weeks, yard by yard, and it was not until the end of August that the 'Devil's Wood' was finally cleared. *See also: France and Flanders 1914-1918; Somme 1916; Albert 1916; Bazentin; Pozières; Guillemont; Ginchy; Flers-Courcelette; Morval; Thiepval; Le Transloy; Ancre Heights and Ancre 1916.*

Demolition There are two broad types of demolition: preliminary and reserved. A preliminary demolition is a target, earmarked for destruction, which can be destroyed as soon as the demolition has been prepared, provided that prior authority has been given. A reserved demolition is a target which is prepared for demolition and for which, because of its strategic or tactical importance, authority for destruction is retained at a specific level of command.

Demolition Firing Party The party which is technically responsible for the demolition.

Demolition Guard A local force positioned to ensure that a target is not captured by an enemy before the order for its demolition has been given by the appropriate level of command and before the demolition has been successfully fired. The demolition guard commander is responsible for the operational command of all troops at the demolition site, and for transmitting the order to fire the demolition to the demolition firing party.

Denbighshire Yeomanry Troops of the Denbighshire Hussars were formed at Wrexham in 1795 and Denbigh in 1799. By 1820 the regiment consisted of five troops and, in 1828 the regiment did not disband but served on without pay until 1831. In the South Africa War (1899-1902) the regiment found two companies of 9th Battalion Imperial Yeomanry. In 1916 the Denbighshire Hussars served in Egypt and Palestine, ending the First World War in France as 24th (Denbighshire Yeomanry) Battalion The Royal Welch Fusiliers. The Denbighshire Yeomanry was amalgamated with the Caernarvon Royal Garrison Artillery in 1920 and served as artillery throughout the Second World War. The Denbighshire Yeomanry was re-formed in 1947 as a medium artillery regiment, later 372nd Light and 372nd Field Regiments. Reduced to a cadre in 1969. The successor unit is 'B' (Flint and Denbighshire Yeomanry) Company of 3rd (Volunteer) Battalion The Royal Welch Fusiliers.

Denial The prevention of enemy access by blocking, disruption, dislocation and/or fire.

Denims Stout hard-wearing working dress.

Denmark One of the regimental slow marches of the 15th/19th The King's Royal Hussars.

Depth Battle Area The depth battle area lies between the Direct Fire Weapons Line (q.v.) and the Fire Support Co-ordination Line (q.v.).

Depth Fire The engagement of targets beyond the Contact Battle Area (q.v.) in order to destroy, disrupt and delay enemy forces before they are involved in the direct fire battle. This includes the engagement of enemy headquarters, artillery, follow-up forces and any bypassing or breakthrough formations which may for the moment not be directly involved in the battle.

Derbyshire Regiment (95th Foot) Raised in December 1823 by Colonel Sir Colin Halkett as 95th Regiment of Foot. In 1881 the regiment amalgamated with 45th (Nottinghamshire-Sherwood Foresters) Regiment of Foot to form The Derbyshire Regiment (Sherwood Foresters). *See: The Worcestershire and Sherwood Foresters Regiment.*

Derbyshire Yeomanry Four troops were raised in Derbyshire in 1794, and served until 1828, only the Radbourne Troop serving - without pay - until 1830. Two troops were raised in 1831 and 1843, being regimented in 1864 as The Derbyshire Yeomanry Cavalry. The regiment provided one company of 4th Battalion Imperial Yeomanry in the South Africa War (1899-1902). In the First World War the regiment served in Egypt, Gallipoli and Macedonia. After the war the regiment was reduced, but in 1938 two regiments, 1st and 2nd Derbyshire Yeomanry were raised, which served in North Africa, Italy and North West Europe. The Derbyshire Yeomanry was re-formed in 1947 and amalgamated with the Leicestershire Yeomanry in 1956 to form The Leicestershire and Derbyshire (Prince Albert's Own) Yeomanry which was subsequently disbanded. Successor sub-units may be found in 'B' (Leicestershire and Derbyshire Yeomanry) Squadron of The Royal Yeomanry; 7th (Volunteer) Battalion The Royal Anglian Regiment; and 3rd (Volunteer) Battalion The Worcestershire and Sherwood Foresters Regiment (29th/45th Foot).

Dereliction of Duty The deliberate, conscious or wilful neglect of duty.

Dering's Regiment of Foot Raised at Kent in March 1689, later ranked 24th Foot. *See also: South Wales Borderers.*

Derna Aerodrome Second World War North Africa campaign battle honour marking an action which took place in the period between Rommel's first offensive in March 1941 and the unsuccessful British Operation BATTLEAXE 15-17 June 1941. *See also: North Africa 1940-1943; Mersa El Brega; Agedabia and Halfaya 1941.*

Desant A Soviet term, taken from the French, used to describe a force of any kind placed in the enemy's rear by any means and at any level of command.

Desert Boot Ankle-high, laced, suede boot with soft sole.

Desert Rats Nickname given to the 7th Armoured Division in the Second World War, the divisional sign being a desert rat (jerboa), adopted to mark its 'scurrying and biting' tactics in the North African campaign. The title is currently borne by 7th Armoured Brigade, which featured prominently in the 1991 campaign against Iraq in the Gulf.

Desert Rose Nickname for improvised latrine much used in North Africa during the Second World War and consisting of a length of pipe with one end driven into the sand and a funnel-shaped attachment at the exposed end.

Desertion As defined by the Army Act 1955, desertion occurs when a person leaves or fails to attend his unit, ship or place of duty with the intention of remaining permanently absent from duty without lawful authority; or, having left or failed to attend at his unit, ship or place of duty, thereafter forms the like intention. Desertion also occurs when a person absents himself without leave with intent to avoid serving at any place overseas, or to avoid service or any particular service when before the enemy. *See also: Absence.*

Detail The act of assigning personnel to specific duties or tasks. The term 'daily detail' is sometimes applied to the order published daily which assigns such duties.

Detonator Small explosive charge used to initiate a larger explosion.

Detroit Battle honour marking the capture of Detroit with its garrison in August 1812 by a force under General Brock during the North American War of 1812-14. *See also: Queenstown; Miami; Niagara and Bladensburg.*

Dettingen Battle honour of the War of the Austrian Succession (1740-48) (q.v.) marking the defeat of the French at Dettingen on 27 June 1743 by an allied army under the command of King George II; this was the last occasion on which a reigning British monarch commanded his troops in action.

Device Heraldic design or figure.

Devil's Own Nickname given to two regiments, both now disbanded: The Inns of Court Rifles by George III when he discovered that the regiment consisted mainly of lawyers, and The Connaught Rangers (88th Foot) by General Picton to mark their bravery in the Peninsula War.

Devonshire Regiment (11th Foot) Raised at Bristol on 20th June 1685 as the Duke of Beaufort's Musketeers and designated 11th Foot in 1751. Redesignated 11th (North Devonshire) Foot in 1782 and The Devonshire Regiment in 1881. On 17 May 1958 the regiment amalgamated with the Dorset regiment (39th and 69th Foot) to form the Devonshire and Dorset Regiment (11th, 39th and 54th Foot) (q.v.).
Headdress Badge: Upon an eight-pointed star a circle, ensigned with the Crown. Within the circle the Castle of Exeter.
History: *Historical Record of the 11th Foot 1685-1845* by R Cannon (1845); *The Devonshire Regiment 1914-1918* by C T Atkinson (1926); *The Devons 1685-1945* by J Taylor (1951); *The Bloody Eleventh* Vol 1 1685-1815 by R Robinson (1988); Vol II 1816-1914 and Vol III 1915-1958 by W Aggett (1994).

Devonshire and Dorset Regiment (11th, 39th and 54th Foot) Formed on 17 May 1958 from the amalgamation of the Devonshire Regiment (11th Foot) (q.v.) and the Dorset Regiment (39th and 69th Foot) (q.v.).
Headdress Badge: The Castle of Exeter. Above, the motto '*Semper Fidelis*' (Ever True); below, on a tablet 'MARABOUT' and the motto '*Primus in Indis*' (First in India).
Regimental marches:
Quick march: Arrangement of *Widecombe Fair, We've Lived and Loved Together* and *The Maid of Glenconnel*.
Slow march: *Farmer's Boy*.
Regimental Headquarters: Wyvern Barracks, Exeter, EX2 6AE.

DEVONSHIRE YEOMANRY
    The Royal 1st Devon Yeomanry Raised in 1794, regimented in 1801 and granted the title 'Royal' in 1803, the regiment continued to serve - without pay - from 1828 until 1831 and was never disbanded. The regiment provided a company of 7th Battalion Imperial Yeomanry in the South Africa War (1899-1902). In the First World War the regiment served in Gallipoli and Egypt before amalgamating with the Royal North Devon Hussars in 1916 and serving the rest of the war dismounted as 16th Battalion The Devonshire Regiment. The Royal 1st Devon Yeomanry and the Royal North Devon Yeomanry were amalgamated in 1916, this amalgamation being formalised in 1920, and served as artillery units until 1967, when they became the Devonshire Territorials (Royal Devon Yeomanry/1st Rifle Volunteers). The successor sub-unit is 'D' (Royal Devon Yeomanry) Squadron of the Royal Wessex Yeomanry.

    The Royal North Devon Yeomanry (Hussars) First raised in 1798 and regimented in 1803. The regiment served - without pay - from 1828-31 and was never disbanded. The regiment provided a company for 7th Battalion Imperial Yeomanry during the South Africa War (1899-1902). In 1916 the regiment amalgamated with the Royal 1st Devon Yeomanry in Egypt and, after the war, the two regiments amalgamated again.

Dhofar 1970-76 Campaign waged by the forces of Sultan Qaboos of Oman's forces against disaffected Dhofaris of the marxist Dhofar Liberation Front, who were supported by the People's Democratic Republic of South Yemen. The Sultan's Armed Forces (SAF) were rapidly expanded from 1970 and, supported by a significant training and operational effort by the Special Air Service Regiment (SAS), a long-term plan to defeat the insurgents was initiated. Rebel defectors were reformed into anti-guerilla units known as *firqats*. The training organization and leadership of these *firqats* became the priority task of the SAS, who were also conducting 'hearts and minds' operations among the tribesmen. By the end of 1975 Dhofar was secure and the planned development programme began. British Army casualties in the campaign were 24 killed and 55 wounded.

Dicing A pattern of small squares, usually including red and white, which features in the dress of Scottish regiments.

Diehards Nickname given to 57th Foot (later The Middlesex Regiment) after the instruction given to his regiment by Colonel Inglis at the battle of Albuera (1811) to 'Die hard my men, die hard'.

Dieppe Second World War battle honour awarded to the Commandos to mark the Dieppe Raid (q.v.) on 19 August 1942. *See also: North West Europe 1942.*

Dieppe Raid The raid was one of a number of large-scale raids planned for 1942 to relieve German pressure on Russia. The raiding force comprised nearly three commandos, the major part of 2nd Canadian Division (including its armour) and was to be given naval gunfire and close air support. It was planned that the force would land at dawn on 19 August, capture the port and withdraw the same day. Only one commando reached its objective and the force suffered massive human and equipment casualties ashore, in the air and at sea. Through this tragedy important lessons were learned about amphibious operations which contributed to future landings and the success of the Allied invasion on 6 June 1944.

Dining In, Dining Out The custom of honouring those joining or leaving a regiment or unit at a formal dinner. It is usual for officers to be 'dined in' on first joining their regiment and to be 'dined out' at the end of their last tour with their regiment. In some regiments it is still the custom to designate certain evenings as 'dining in' nights and all members of the mess are expected to dine in the mess on such occasions.

Direct Fire Fire directed at a target which is visible to the aimer.

Direct Fire Weapons Line This line delineates the outer edge of the Contact Battle Area (q.v.). It is a line established by the contact battle commander to ensure the co-ordination of fire not under his control, indirect fire must not be put down within the line without prior reference to the appropriate contact battle commander.

Dirk Scottish dagger worn by highland regiments.

Dirty Shirts Nickname given to 101st Foot (later The Munster Fusiliers) who fought in their shirtsleeves at Delhi during the Indian Mutiny (1857).

Disbanding Act This act was passed in 1660 by the Convention Parliament for 'the speedy disbanding of the Army' of the Commonwealth; the feeling being that a standing army was 'inconsistent with the happiness of any Kingdom'. So successful was the act that by Christmas 1660 all that remained was General Monck's Coldstream Regiment and the independent companies manning the 28 key points or fortresses across the country. These were subsequently taken into Crown service and joined the regiments of Horse and Foot Guards which had accompanied the monarch in exile. A further Disbanding Act was passed in 1699 for 'Granting an aid to his Majesty for disbanding the Army and other necessary occasions'.

Distinguished Conduct Medal
Gallantry award arising from the need, recognised after the Crimean War, to provide a gallantry medal for other ranks of the Army. The award, originating in a Royal Warrant of 4 December 1854, is open to warrant officers, non-commissioned officers and men for 'distinguished service in the field', although interpretations of the nature of such service have varied widely over the years.
Ribbon: Crimson, 1" wide with a ⅜" central blue stripe.

Distinguished Conduct Medal (Dominion And Colonial Issues) A Royal Warrant dated 24 May 1894 made provision for the award of the Distinguished Conduct Medal to 'Warrant Officers, Non-commissioned Officers and Men of Our Indian Forces and Our Colonial Forces'.
Ribbon: As for the Imperial issue; except in the case of the King's African Rifles and West African Frontier Force when it was blue, 1" wide, with a ³⁄₁₆" central light green stripe flanked on either side with similar stripes of maroon.

Distinguished Flying Cross Gallantry award instituted by a Royal Warrant dated 3 June 1918, open to officers and warrant officers of all Services and of the Indian, Dominion or Colonial military forces for 'acts of valour, courage or devotion to duty performed whilst flying in active operations against the enemy'.
Ribbon: Originally 1¼" wide of violet and white alternate horizontal stripes ⅛" in depth. From 24 July 1919, similar stripes at a 45° diagonal from left to right.

Distinguished Flying Medal Gallantry award instituted by a Royal Warrant of 3 June 1918, open to non-commissioned officers and men of all Services and of the Indian, Dominion or Colonial military forces for 'acts of valour, courage or devotion to duty performed whilst flying in active operations against the enemy.'
Ribbon: Originally 1¼" wide of violet and white alternate horizontal stripes ¹⁄₁₆" in depth. From 24 July 1919, similar stripes at a 45° diagonal from left to right.

Distinguished (Formerly Conspicuous) Service Cross The Conspicuous Service Cross was instituted in June 1901 to recognise 'distinguished service before the enemy' on the part of warrant officers or subordinate officers of HM fleet. An Order in Council of 14 October 1914 extended eligibility to commissioned officers of HM fleet below the rank of Lieutenant Commander, and the cross was redesignated 'Distinguished Service Cross'. Between March 1915 and December 1943 eligibility for the award was extended, most notably by an Order in Council of 5 November 1942 which extended eligibility to officers and warrant officers of the Army serving in defensively-equipped merchant ships.
Ribbon: 1⅜" wide with equal stripes of dark blue, white and dark blue.

Distinguished Service Medal Gallantry award instituted in October 1914 to recognise such chief petty officers, petty officers and men of the Royal Navy and non-commissioned officers and men of the Royal Marines 'as may at any time show themselves to the fore in action, and set an example of bravery and resource under fire'. Between June 1916 and October 1947 eligibility was extended, most notably by an Order in Council of 1 July 1942 which extended eligibility to non-commissioned officers and men of the Army serving in defensively-equipped merchant ships.
Ribbon: Dark blue, 1" wide, with two white stripes, each approximately ³⁄₁₆" wide in the centre.

Distinguished Service Order Gallantry award instituted by Royal Warrant in 1886. Serving officers of all Services, Indian, Colonial naval or military forces and foreign officers associated in naval and military operations with British forces were eligible. On 5 February 1931 conditions for the award were amended in a Warrant which laid down that the order was to be given only 'for distinguished services under fire or under conditions equivalent to service in actual combat with the enemy'.
Ribbon: Red, 1" wide, with narrow blue borders.

District A military regional division of the United Kingdom. In peace, each military district is responsible for the administration and training of all the units, regular or reserve, within its geographical boundaries. In transition to war the district becomes responsible for security within its boundaries and the mobilisation and movement of reinforcements. Districts are answerable to Headquarters United Kingdom Land Forces. There are currently six districts: Northern Ireland; London; Scotland; Southern; Wales and Western; and Eastern. Districts are commanded by major generals, with the exception of Southern District, which is commanded by a lieutenant general.

District Court Martial *See: Court Martial.*

Dit The short sound used, in combination with the long sound 'dah' in the spoken representation of Morse and other telegraphic codes.

Diver A badge depicting a diver's helmet is worn on the sleeve of qualified divers. These are usually, but not exclusively, members of the Corps of Royal Engineers.

Dives Crossing Second World War battle honour marking the passage of the River Dives during the breakout from the Normandy beachhead in 1944. *See also: North West Europe 1944-1945; Mont Pincon; Falaise; Lisieux and Seine 1944.*

Division
1. A field formation comprising two or more brigades.
2. An administrative grouping of infantry regiments.
3. In the 18th century battalions were divided into eight equal parts or sub-units known as divisions, these divisions being further divided into two sub-divisions, the sub-division thus equates to the 20th century platoon.

Djebel Abiod *See: North Africa 1940-1943; Soudia; Tebourba; Djedeida; Djebel Azzag 1942; Longstop Hill 1942; Djebel Azzag 1943; Two Tree Hill and Djebel Aliliga.*

Djebel Aliliga Second World War North Africa campaign battle honour marking an action which took place during the German assault on Allied defensive positions in the hills of western Tunisia during the winter of 1942. *See also: North Africa 1940-1943; Soudia; Tebourba; Djedeida; Djebel Azzag 1942; Longstop Hill 1942; Djebel Azzag 1943; Two Tree Hill and Djebel Abiod.*

Djebel Ang Second World War North Africa campaign battle honour marking one of the actions during the advance of British V Corps to occupy the line Touhabeur-Chaouach over the period 7-15 April 1943. *See also: North Africa 1940-1943; Djebel Rmel; Mergeb Chaouach; Djebel Bel Mahdi and Djebel Bech Chekaoui.*

Djebel Azzag 1942 Second World War North Africa campaign battle honour marking an action which took place during the German assault on Allied defensive positions in the hills of western Tunisia during the winter of 1942. *See also: North Africa 1940-1943; Soudia; Tebourba; Djedeida; Djebel Azzag 1942; Longstop Hill 1942; Djebel Azzag 1943; Two Tree Hill and Djebel Aliliga.*

Djebel Azzag 1943 Second World War North Africa campaign battle honour marking an action which took place during the German assault on allied defensive positions in the hills of western Tunisia during the winter of 1942. *See also: North Africa 1940-1943; Soudia; Tebourba; Djedeida; Djebel Azzag 1942; Longstop Hill 1942; Djebel Abiod, Two Tree Hill and Djebel Aliliga.*

Djebel Bech Chekaoui Second World War North Africa campaign battle honour marking one of the actions during the advance of British V Corps to occupy the line Touhabeur-Chaouach over the period 7-15 April 1943. *See also: North Africa 1940-1943; Djebel Rmel; Mergeb Chaouach; Djebel Bel Mahdi and Djebel Ang.*

Djebel Bel Mahdi Second World War North Africa campaign battle honour marking one of the actions during the advance of British V Corps to occupy the line Touhabeur-Chaouach over the period 7-15 April 1943. *See also: North Africa 1940-1943; Djebel Rmel; Mergeb Chaouach; Djebel Bech Chekaoui and Djebel Ang.*

Djebel Bou Aoukaz 1943 I Second World War North Africa campaign battle honour marking an action in the Medjez Plain battle of V Corps 23-30 April 1943, when 1st Division made abortive attempts to capture this feature on 27 and 28 April. *See also: North Africa 1940-1943; Medjez Plain; Gueriat El Atach Ridge; Longstop Hill 1943 and Grich El Oued.*

Djebel Bou Aoukaz 1943 II Second World War North Africa campaign battle honour marking the capture of this feature in early May 1943 during the final breakthrough to the capture of Tunis, and subsequent exploitation towards the Cape Bon Peninsula. *See also: North Africa 1940-1943; Tunis; Hammam Lif; Montarnaud; Ragoubet Souissi; Creteville Pass; Gromballa and Bou Ficha.*

Djebel Choucha Second World War battle honour, awarded to the Commandos and marking an action during Anglo-American operations in North Africa aimed at checking the German thrust through the Kasserine Pass and breaking through the Fondouk Pass towards Kairouan in the period February-April 1943. *See also: North Africa 1940-1943; El Hadjeba; Djebel Djaffa; Sidi Nsir; Fort McGregor; Stuka Farm; Steamroller Farm; Montagne Farm; Kef Ouiba Pass; Djebel Guerba; Sedjenane I; Maknassy; Djebel Dahra and Kef El Debna.*

Djebel Dahra Second World War North Africa campaign battle honour marking an action during Anglo-American operations in North Africa aimed at checking the German thrust through the Kasserine Pass and breaking through the Fondouk Pass towards Kairouan in the period February-April 1943. *See also: North Africa 1940-1943; El Hadjeba; Djebel Djaffa; Sidi Nsir; Fort McGregor; Stuka Farm; Steamroller Farm; Montagne Farm; Kef Ouiba Pass; Djebel Guerba; Sedjenane I; Maknassy; Djebel Choucha and Kef El Debna.*

Djebel Djaffa Second World War North Africa campaign battle honour marking an action during Anglo-American operations in North Africa aimed at checking the German thrust through the Kasserine Pass and breaking through the Fondouk Pass towards Kairouan in the period February to April 1943. *See also: North Africa 1940-1943; El Hadjeba; Djebel Choucha; Sidi Nsir; Fort McGregor; Stuka Farm; Steamroller Farm; Montagne Farm; Kef Ouiba Pass; Djebel Guerba; Sedjenane I; Maknassy; Djebel Dahra and Kef El Debna.*

Djebel Djaffa Pass Second World War North Africa campaign battle honour marking an action which took place between the Fondouk operations in April 1943 and the end of the campaign in North Africa. *See also: North Africa 1940-1943; Heidous; Banana Ridge and Argoub El Megas.*

Djebel El Meida Second World War North Africa campaign battle honour marking an action during the Battle of Akarit 6-7 April 1943. *See also: North Africa 1940-1943; Akarit; Wadi Akarit East and Djebel Roumana.*

Djebel El Rhorab Second World War North Africa campaign battle honour marking one of the actions in the Fondouk operations of early April 1943. *See also: North Africa 1940-1943; Fondouk; Kairouan; Bordj; Pichon; Fondouk Pass and Sidi Ali.*

Djebel El Telil Second World War North Africa campaign battle honour marking an action which took place in the period between the occupation of the Alamein line in mid-1942 and the end of the campaign in May 1943. *See also: North Africa 1940-1943; Capture of Halfaya Pass; Matmata Hills; Sebkret En Noual; Chebket En Nouiges; Deir El Munassib and Djebel Tebaga.*

Djebel Garci Second World War North Africa campaign battle honour marking an action during the attempts by Eighth Army to penetrate the strong axis position around Enfidaville 19-29 April 1943. *See also: North Africa 1940-1943; Akarit; Enfidaville and Takrouna.*

Djebel Guerba Second World War North Africa campaign battle honour marking an action during Anglo-American operations aimed at checking the German thrust through the Kasserine Pass and breaking through the Fondouk Pass towards Kairouan in the period February to April 1943. *See also: North Africa 1940-1943; El Hadjeba; Djebel Djaffa; Sidi Nsir; Fort McGregor; Stuka Farm; Steamroller Farm; Montagne Farm; Kef Ouiba Pass; Djebel Choucha; Sedjenane I; Maknassy; Djebel Dahra and Kef El Debna.*

Djebel Kesskiss Second World War North Africa Campaigm battle honour marking one of the actions during the advance of British V Corps to occupy the line Touhabeur-Chaouach over the period 7-15 April 1943. *See also: North Africa 1940-1943; Oued Zarga; Djebel Bech Chekaoui; Mergeb Chaouach; Djebel Bel Mahdi; Djebel Tanngoucha and Djebel Ang.*

Djebel Kournine Second World War North Africa campaign battle honour marking the five unsuccessful attempts by elements of 6th Armoured, 1st and 46th Divisions to capture this feature during the period 25-30 April 1943. *See also: North Africa 1940-1943; Medjez Plain and Tunis.*

Djebel Rmel Second World War North Africa campaign battle honour marking one of the actions during the advance of British V Corps to occupy the line Touhabeur-Chaouach over the period 7-15 April 1943. *See also: North Africa 1940-1943, Oued Zarga, Djebel Bech Chekaoui, Mergeb Chaouach; Djebel Bel Mahdi; Djebel Tanngoucha and Djebel Ang.*

Djebel Roumana Second World War North Africa campaign battle honour marking an action during the Battle of Akarit 6-7 April 1943. *See also: North Africa 1940-1943; Akarit; Wadi Akarit East and Djebel El Meida.*

Djebel Tanngoucha Second World War North Africa campaign battle honour marking one of the actions during the advance of British V Corps to occupy the line Touhabeur-Chaouach over the period

7-15 April 1943. *See also: North Africa 1940-1943; Oued Zarga; Djebel Rmel; Djebel Bech Chekaoui; Mergeb Chaouach; Djebel Bel Mahdi; Djebel Kesskiss and Djebel Ang.*

Djebel Tebaga Second World War, North Africa campaign battle honour marking an action which took place in the period between the occupation of the Alamein line in mid-1942 and the end of the campaign in May 1943. *See also: North Africa 1940-1943; Capture of Halfaya Pass; Matmata Hills; Sebkret En Noual; Chebket En Nouiges; Deir El Munassib and Djebel El Telil.*

Djedeida Second World War North Africa campaign battle honour marking an action which took place during the North Africa campaign, when the Allies adopted defensive positions in the hills of western Tunisia during the winter of 1942. *See also: North Africa 1940-1943; Djebel Abiod; Soudia; Tebourba; Djebel Azzag 1942; Longstop Hill 1942; Djebel Azzag 1943; Two Tree Hill and Djebel Aliliga.*

DM A badge bearing the letters 'DM' within a wreath was used in the inter-war years to denote the driver mechanic specialisation.

DOCTRINE

The fundamental principles upon which the actions of the British Army are guided. Doctrine is authoritative but requires judgement in application. Doctrine operates at three broad levels in the British Army:

Military Doctrine Issued by the Chief of the General Staff (q.v.) and sets out the fundamental principles and considerations guiding the approach to warfare, in order to provide the foundation for the practical application of the doctrine.

Operational Doctrine Applies to specific theatres and will be developed by the theatre commander concerned, based upon probable operations, and passed to those in his command through instruction and exercises.

Tactical Doctrine This provides the main body of doctrinal instruction in the Army and is designed to ensure that all commanders have a common foundation upon which to base their plans.

Doges March Slow march of the Army Air Corps.

Doiran 1917 First World War Macedonian campaign, often referred to as the 'Salonika' campaign, battle honour marking British actions during the abortive attempts by the Allies to carry the enemy defences around Lake Doiran in 1917. *See also: Macedonia 1915-18, Kosturino, Struma and Doiran 1918.*

Doiran 1918 First World War Macedonian campaign, often referred to as the 'Salonika' campaign, battle honour. In 1918 the allies mounted the final offensive of the campaign during which there was very heavy fighting in the Lake Doiran sector. *See also: Macedonia 1915-18; Kosturino; Struma and Doiran 1917.*

Dominica Battle honour marking the successful defence of Dominica on 22 February 1805 against a greatly superior French force. *See also: Guadaloupe 1759; Martinique 1762; Havana; St Lucia 1778; Martinique 1794; St Lucia 1796; St Lucia 1803; Surinam; Martinique 1809 and Guadeloupe 1810.*

Donbaik Second World War Burma campaign battle honour awarded for a series of actions over the period 8 January-18 March 1943 during the unsuccessful Arakan offensive : four assaults were made on Donbaik and repelled on each occasion by the Japanese. *See also: Burma 1942-1945; Rathedaung; Htizwe and Point 201 (Arakan).*

Dormer's Regiment Of Dragoons Raised in 1717, 14th Light Dragoons in 1776 and later 14th King's Hussars.

Dorset Regiment (39th and 54th Foot) Raised in Ireland in February 1702 as Coote's Regiment of Foot and designated 39th Foot in 1751. Redesignated 39th (East Middlesex) Foot in 1782; and 39th (Dorsetshire) Foot in 1807. In parallel, the 56th Foot was raised in December 1755 by

Lieutenant Colonel John Campbell, Duke of Argyll; renumbered 54th Foot in 1757; and designated 54th (West Norfolk) Foot in 1782. In 1881 the 39th (Dorsetshire) Foot and the 54th (West Norfolk) Foot amalgamated to form the Dorsetshire Regiment; retitled Dorset Regiment in 1951. On 17 May 1958 the regiment amalgamated with the Devonshire Regiment (11th Foot) to form the Devonshire and Dorset Regiment (11th, 39th and 54th Foot) (q.v.).
Headdress Badge: Within a Laurel Wreath inscribed DORSET, the Castle and Key of Gibraltar. Above, the Sphinx upon a tablet inscribed MARABOUT. Below the motto *Primus in Indis* (First in India).
History: *Historical Record of the 39th Foot (Dorsetshire Regiment)* by R Cannon (1881); *Historical Record of the 54th Foot (West Norfolk Regiment)* (1881); *The Dorsetshire Regiment* (To 1939, 2 Vols.) by C Atkinson (1947); History of *The Dorsetshire Regiment 1914-1919* by Henry Ling Ltd; and *The Dorset Regiment* by H Popham (1970).

Dorset Yeomanry (The Queen's Own Dorset Yeomanry) First raised in 1794, the Queen's Own Dorset Yeomanry lapsed after the Treaty of Amiens (1802), but was re-raised in 1803, disbanded in 1814 and re-raised in 1830. The regiment provided a company for 7th Battalion Imperial Yeomanry in the South Africa War (1899-1902). Mobilised in 1914, the regiment served in Egypt, Gallipoli and Palestine. Amalgamated with the West Somerset Yeomanry and the Somerset Royal Horse Artillery in 1920, the regiment served throughout the Second World War as artillery until, in 1967, it was absorbed into the infantry as 1st Battalion The Wessex Regiment (Rifle Volunteers).

Dosimeter, Dosemeter An instrument used to measure the dose of radiation absorbed by matter or individuals, or the intensity of a source of radiation.

Double To run or move in 'double time', that is, 180 paces to the minute.

Doublet Short jacket having special skirts or flaps.

Dolman Term of German origin applied to the jacket worn by hussars.

Douglas's Regiment Raised in 1688, numbered 16th Foot in 1751 and later designated The Bedfordshire and Hertfordshire Regiment.

Douro Battle honour marking Wellesley's (q.v.) successful move against Soult during the second phase of the Peninsula War (1809-14). Soult believed himself to be secure in Oporto behind the River Douro. Over the period 10-12 May 1809 Wellesley's forces crossed the Douro, successfully engaged the enemy, and Soult retreated in haste from Portugal, leaving behind all his guns. *See also: Peninsula; Roliça; Sahagun; Corunna; Talavera; Busaco and Barrosa.*

DR A badge bearing the letters 'DR' within a wreath was used to denote the despatch rider specialisation.

Draft Party of men moving as a body from one unit to another, usually as reinforcements from training establishments to field units.

Dragon Superscribed China Battle honour marking participation in the First China War (1839-41) (q.v.), the so-called 'Opium War'.

DRAGOONS

Term originally applied to mounted soldiers trained to fight on foot; the name deriving from their weapons, a 'dragon' or short musket, so called from the dragon's head worked on the muzzle, which was first carried by the horsemen of Marshal Brissac in 1600. Later, medium cavalry.

1st Dragoons Raised in 1661 as The Tangier Horse, commanded by the Earl of Peterborough, and forming the cavalry element of Tangier's garrison. In 1684 the regiment returned to England, was augmented by two additional troops of dragoons, and designated The King's Own Royal Regiment of Dragoons in 1683. In 1690 the regiment became The Royal Regiment of Dragoons; and The 1st (Royal) Dragoons in 1751. In 1961 the regiment was renamed The Royal Dragoons (1st Dragoons) and amalgamated with The Royal Horse Guards (The Blues) on 29 March 1969 to form The Blues and Royals (Royal Horse Guards and 1st Dragoons) (q.v.).
Headdress Badge: An eagle upon a tablet bearing the numerals 105. The figures refer to the 105th French Infantry Regiment, whose eagle was captured by Captain Clarke at Waterloo.
Motto: *Spectemur Agendo* (Let us be judged by our deeds).
Regimental marches:
Quick march: *Regimental March of The Royal Dragoons (Blankenburg).*
Slow march: *Regimental March of The Royal Dragoons (Blankenburg).*
History: *History of the Royal Dragoons 1661-1933* by C T Atkinson; and *The Story of The Royal Dragoons 1939-43* by J A Pitt-Rivers.

2nd Dragoons Three independent troops of Scots Dragoons had been raised in 1678; in 1681, these and some additional troops were regimented to form The Royal Regiment of Scots Dragoons. In 1694 the regiment was ranked as 4th Dragoons by a board of William III, English regiments being given precedence. It is apparent that at this stage the regiment was already mounted on greys and certainly by 1702 such titles as 'Grey Dragoons' and 'Scots Regiment of White Horses' were in use. In 1707, as a result of the reorganisations of the military establishments of Scotland and England brought about by the Act of Union (q.v.) the regiment was renamed The Royal North British Dragoons, although the name 'Scots Greys' was in everyday use. In 1713 the regiment was renumbered 2nd Dragoons, it having been proven that there was but one English dragoon regiment when the regiment first crossed the border. In 1877 the regiment became 2nd Dragoons (Royal Scots Greys), the title being inverted in 1921 to The Royal Scots Greys (2nd Dragoons). On 2 July 1971 the regiment amalgamated with the 3rd Carabiniers (Prince of Wales's Dragoon Guards) to form The Royal Scots Dragoon Guards (Carabiniers and Greys) (q.v.).

Headdress Badge: The French Eagle.
Motto: *Nemo Me Impune Lacessit* (No one provokes me with impunity).
History: *The Royal Scots Greys* by M Blacklock (1971); *History of The Royal Scots Greys (2nd Dragoons) August 1914-March 1919* by R Pomeroy; W F Collins, W M Duguid-McCombie, J S Hardy, A I MacDougall and A D Gibbs (1928); and *Second To None: The Royal Scots Greys* by Lord Carver (1954).

3rd Dragoons Raised in August 1685 as a regiment of Dragoons, command being given to Charles Seymour, Duke of Somerset, and known as The Queen Consort's Own Regiment of Dragoons; became The King's Own Regiment of Dragoons in 1714, and 3rd (King's Own) Dragoons in 1751. In 1818 the regiment was redesignated 3rd (King's Own) Light Dragoons and became a hussar regiment - 3rd (King's Own) Hussars in 1861. The regiment was redesignated 3rd The King's Own Hussars (q.v.) in 1921.

4th Dragoons Raised in July 1685 by Colonel the Hon John Berkeley and known as Berkeley's Dragoons; later Princess Anne of Denmark's Dragoons and numbered 4th Dragoons in 1751; 4th or Queen's Own Dragoons in 1788; and 4th or Queen's Own Light Dragoons in 1818. In 1861 the regiment became a hussar regiment - 4th (The Queen's Own) Hussars and in 1921 was renamed 4th Queen's Own Hussars (q.v.).

5th Dragoons Raised in 1689 as The Royal Irish Dragoons; renamed The Royal Dragoons of Ireland in 1704 and 5th (Royal Irish) Dragoons in 1756. The regiment was disbanded in 1799, its number and honours - but not seniority - passing to a regiment raised in 1858 as 5th (Royal Irish) Lancers, renamed 5th Royal Irish Lancers in 1921. On 11 April 1922 the regiment amalgamated with 16th The Queen's Lancers to form 16th/5th Lancers; subsequently redesignated 16th/5th The Queen's Royal Lancers (q.v.) on 16 June 1954.

6th Dragoons In January 1690 independent troops of horse, which had been rapidly raised to defend Enniskillen against the Roman Catholic forces of ex-King James II, were regimented and ranked as 6th Dragoons under the command of Colonel Sir Albert Conyngham and known as Conyngham's Regiment of Dragoons; also known locally as 'The Black Dragoons'. Redesignated 6th (Inniskilling) Dragoons in 1751; and The Inniskillings (6th Dragoons) in 1921. On 11 April 1922 the regiment amalgamated with 5th Dragoon Guards (Princess Charlotte of Wales's) to form 5th/6th Dragoons and on 30 June 1935 was redesignated 5th Royal Inniskilling Dragoon Guards (q.v.).

7th Dragoons Raised in December 1690 from independent troops of Scottish dragoons, commanded by Colonel Richard Cunningham and known as Cunningham's Dragoons. Redesignated The Princess of Wales's Own Royal Dragoons in 1715, and The Queen's Own Dragoons in 1727. In 1751 the regiment was redesignated 7th or Queen's Own Dragoons, and 7th or Queen's Own Light Dragoons in 1783. In 1805 the regiment became a hussar regiment being redesignated 7th (Queen's Own) Hussars, and 7th Queen's Own Hussars in 1921 (q.v.).

8th Dragoons Raised in February 1693 and recruited from Irish Protestants; command was given to Lieutenant Colonel Henry Conyngham of the Inniskilling Dragoons. The regiment was known as Conyngham's (Cunningham's) Regiment of Irish Dragoons, redesignated 8th Dragoons in 1751. In 1775 the regiment became 8th Light Dragoons, and was redesignated 8th or The King's Royal Irish Light Dragoons in 1777. In 1822 the regiment became a hussar regiment, 8th (The King's Royal Irish) Hussars and 8th King's Royal Irish Hussars in 1921 (q.v.).

9th Dragoons Raised in July 1715 by Major General Owen Wynn as Wynn's Regiment of Dragoons and designated 9th Dragoons in 1751, becoming 9th Light Dragoons in 1783, and 9th Lancers in 1816. Redesignated 9th (Queen's Royal) Lancers in 1830, and 9th Queen's Royal Lancers in 1922. On 11 September 1960 the regiment amalgamated with 12th Royal Lancers (Prince of Wales's) to form 9th/12th Lancers (Prince of Wales's) (q.v.).

10th Dragoons Raised in July 1715 by Brigadier General Humphrey Gore as Gore's Regiment of Dragoons and designated 10th Dragoons in 1751, and 10th or Prince of Wales's Own Light Dragoons in 1783. In 1806 the regiment became a hussar regiment as 10th or Prince of Wales's Own Hussars, redesignated 10th or Prince of Wales's Own Royal Hussars in 1811, and 10th Royal Hussars (Prince of Wales's Own) in 1921 (q.v.).

11th Dragoons Raised in July 1715 by Brigadier General Philip Honywood as Honywood's Regiment of Dragoons; designated 11th Dragoons in 1751, and 11th Light Dragoons in 1783. In 1840 the regiment became 11th Prince Albert's Own Hussars and, in 1921, 11th Hussars (Prince Albert's Own) (q.v.).

12th Dragoons Raised in July 1715 by Colonel Phineas Bowles as Bowles's Regiment of Dragoons; designated 12th Dragoons in 1751, and 12th (The Prince of Wales's) Light Dragoons in 1768. In 1816 the regiment converted to Lancers as 12th (The Prince of Wales's) Lancers becoming 12th (The Prince of Wales's Royal) Lancers in 1817 and 12th Royal Lancers (Prince of Wales's) in 1921. On 11 September 1960 the regiment amalgamated with 9th Queen's Royal Lancers to become 9th/12th Royal Lancers (Prince of Wales's) (q.v.).

13th Dragoons Raised in July 1715 by Brigadier General Richard Munden as Munden's Regiment of Dragoons; designated 13th Dragoons in 1751; and 13th Light Dragoons in 1783. In 1861 the regiment converted to hussars as 13th Hussars (q.v.).

14th Dragoons Raised in July 1715 by Brigadier General James Dormer as Dormer's Regiment of Dragoons; designated 14th Dragoons in 1720, and 14th Light Dragoons in 1776. In 1798 the regiment became 14th or Duchess of York's Own Light Dragoons, and 14th The King's Light Dragoons in 1830. In 1861 the regiment converted to hussars as 14th (King's) Hussars, changing to 14th King's Hussars in 1921 (q.v.).

15th Dragoons Raised at London in March 1759 by Colonel George Augustus Eliott (1st Lord Heathfield) as 15th Light Dragoons or Eliott's Light Horse; designated 1st or King's Light Dragoons in 1766 and 15th or King's Light Dragoons in 1769. Converted to hussars in 1806 as 15th The King's Hussars, 15th (King's) Hussars in 1861, and 15th The King's Hussars in 1921 (q.v.).

16th Dragoons Raised in August 1759 by Colonel John Burgoyne as 16th Light Dragoons or Burgoyne's Light Horse; redesignated 16th or Queen's Light Dragoons in 1769. Converted to lancers in 1815 as 16th (The Queen's) Lancers, and 16th The Queen's Lancers in 1921. On 11 April 1922 the regiment amalgamated with 5th Royal Irish Lancers to form 16th/5th Lancers; redesignated 16th/5th The Queen's Royal Lancers (q.v.) on 16 June 1954.

17th Dragoons Raised in November 1759 by Lieutenant Colonel John Hale as 18th Light Dragoons; renumbered 17th Light Dragoons in 1763. Converted to lancers in 1822 as 17th Lancers and redesignated 17th Lancers (Duke of Cambridge's Own) in 1876. On 11 April 1922 the regiment amalgamated with 21st Lancers (Empress of India's) to form 17th/21st Lancers (q.v.). (An earlier cavalry regiment, also raised in 1759, bore the number 17 as 17th (Edinburgh) Light Dragoons, but was disbanded in 1763.)

18th Dragoons Raised in Ireland in 1759 by Charles Moor, 1st Marquess of Drogheda and popularly known as the Drogheda Light Horse, but designated 19th Light Dragoons; renumbered 18th Light Dragoons in 1763. Converted to hussars as 18th King's Irish Hussars in 1805, and disbanded in 1822. Re-raised in 1858 as 18th Hussars and redesignated 18th (Queen Mary's Own) Hussars in 1910 and 18th Royal Hussars (Queen Mary's Own)(q.v.)in 1919.

19th Dragoons Raised in 1759 as 19th Light Dragoons, renumbered 18th Light Dragoons in 1761, and disbanded in 1763. Re-raised in 1779 as 19th Light Dragoons and again disbanded in 1783. Re-raised in 1786 as 19th Light Dragoons and converted to lancers in 1817 as 19th Lancers; disbanded again in 1821. In 1858 the 1st Bengal European Cavalry (q.v.) converted to become 19th Hussars in 1861. Redesignated 19th (Alexandra, Princess of Wales's Own) Hussars in 1902, 19th

(Queen Alexandra's Own Royal) Hussars in 1908, and 19th Royal Hussars (Queen Alexandra's Own)(q.v.) in 1921.

20th Dragoons Raised in 1759 as 20th Inniskilling Light Dragoons and disbanded in 1763. Re-raised in 1778 as 20th Light Dragoons and disbanded again in 1791. Re-raised in 1791 as 20th Jamaica Light Dragoons; redesignated 20th Light Dragoons in 1802 and disbanded again in 1819. In 1858 the 2nd Bengal European Light Cavalry converted and was designated 20th Hussars (q.v.)in 1861.

21st Dragoons Raised in 1759 as 21st Light Dragoons and disbanded in 1763. Re-raised in 1779 as 21st Light Dragoons and disbanded again in 1783. Re-raised in 1794 as 21st Light Dragoons and disbanded in 1819. In 1858 3rd Bengal European Cavalry (of the East India Company) converted to the British establishment and was designated 21st Hussars in 1861, converting to Lancers as 21st Lancers in 1897. Redesignated 21st (Empress of India's) Lancers in 1899 and 21st Lancers (Empress of India's)(q.v.) in 1921.

DRAGOON GUARDS

1st King's Dragoon Guards Raised in June 1685 by Sir John Lanier as The Queen's, or 2nd, Regiment of Horse. Redesignated The King's Own Regiment of Horse in 1714, and 1st King's Dragoon Guards in 1746. On 1 January 1959 the regiment amalgamated with The Queen's Bays (2nd Dragoon Guards) to form 1st The Queen's Dragoon Guards (q.v.).
Headdress Badge: The double-headed eagle from the arms of Emperor Franz Josef I of Austria.
History: *The Regimental History of 1st The Queen's Dragoon Guards* by M Mann (1993).

The Queen's Bays (2nd Dragoon Guards) Raised in June 1685 as The Earl of Peterborough's Regiment of Horse; designated The 3rd Regiment of Horse in 1688, and The Princess of Wales's Own Regiment of Horse in 1711. Redesignated 2nd Queen's Dragoon Guards in 1746, 2nd Dragoon Guards (Queen's Bays) in 1872 and The Queen's Bays (2nd Dragoon

Guards) in 1921. On 1 January 1959 the regiment amalgamated with 1st King's Dragoon Guards to form 1st The Queen's Dragoon Guards (q.v.).
Headdress Badge: The title 'Bays' in old English lettering within a wreath of laurel, ensigned with the Crown.
History: *The Regimental History of 1st The Queen's Dragoon Guards* by M Mann (1993).

1st The Queen's Dragoon Guards Formed on 1 January 1959 through the amalgamation of 1st King's Dragoon Guards (q.v.) and The Queen's Bays (2nd Dragoon Guards)(q.v.).
Headdress Badge: The double-headed eagle from the arms of the Emperor Franz Josef I of Austria.
Motto: *Pro Rege et Patria* (For King and country).
Regimental marches:
Quick march: An arrangement of *Radetzky March* and *Rusty Buckles*.
Slow march: *Slow march of 1st Dragoon Guards and 2nd Dragoon Guards*.
Headquarters: Maindy   Barracks, Whitchurch Road, Cardiff, CF4 3YE.
History: *The Regimental History of 1st The Queen's Dragoon Guards* by M Mann (1993).

3rd Dragoon Guards (Prince Of Wales's) Raised in July 1685 by Thomas, 1st Earl of Plymouth, as The Earl of Plymouth's Regiment of Horse and designated The 4th Regiment of Horse in 1687, 3rd Regiment of Dragoon Guards in 1747, and 3rd (Prince of Wales's) Dragoon Guards in 1765. On 11 April 1922 the regiment amalgamated with The Carabiniers (6th Dragoon Guards) to form 3rd/6th Dragoon Guards which was in turn redesignated 3rd Carbiniers (Prince of Wales's Dragoon Guards)(q.v.) on 31 December 1928.
Headdress Badge: The Prince of Wales's plume with coronet and motto. Below, a scroll inscribed 3rd Dragoon Guards.

3rd Carabiniers (Prince Of Wales's Dragoon Guards) Formed on 11 April 1922 through the amalgamation of 3rd Dragoon Guards (Prince of Wales's) and The Carabiniers (6th Dragoon Guards) and initially designated 3rd/6th Dragoon Guards, being granted the title 3rd

Carabiniers (Prince of Wales's Dragoon Guards) on 31 December 1928. On 2 July 1971 the regiment amalgamated with The Royal Scots Greys (2nd Dragoons) to form The Royal Scots Dragoon Guards (Carabiniers and Greys) (q.v.).
Headdress Badge: On crossed carbines the Prince of Wales's plume, coronet and motto.
History: *I Serve: Regimental History of 3rd Carabiniers* by L B Oatts (1966).

4th Royal Irish Dragoon Guards Raised in July 1685 by James Hamilton, Earl of Arran, as The Earl of Arran's Horse (or Cuirassiers) and designated The 5th Horse in 1690. The regiment was redesignated The 1st Irish Horse, or The Blue Horse, in 1746; 4th (Royal Irish) Dragoon Guards in 1788, and 4th Royal Irish Dragoon Guards in 1921. On 11 April 1922 the regiment amalgamated with 7th Dragoon Guards (Princess Royal's) to form 4th/7th Dragoon Guards, redesignated 4th/7th Royal Dragoon Guards (q.v.) on 31 October 1936.
Headdress Badge: The Star of the Order of St Patrick ensigned with a Crown. Below, a scroll inscribed '4th Royal Irish D Guards'.
History: *4th Royal Irish Dragoon Guards in The Great War* by H Gibb.

5th Dragoon Guards (Princess Charlotte Of Wales's) Raised in July 1685 by Charles, Earl of Shrewsbury, as The Duke of Shrewsbury's Regiment of Horse and ranked 7th Horse. Re-ranked as 6th Regiment of Horse in 1698. Redesignated on the Irish establishment as 2nd or 'Green' Irish Horse in 1746. Redesignated 5th Dragoon Guards in 1788; 5th (Princess Charlotte of Wales's) Dragoon Guards in 1804, and 5th Dragoon Guards (Princess Charlotte of Wales's) in 1920. On 11 April 1922 the regiment amalgamated with The Inniskillings (6th Dragoons) to form 5th/6th Dragoons, redesignated 5th Inniskilling Dragoon Guards on 31 May 1927, and 5th Royal Inniskilling Dragoon Guards (q.v.) on 30 June 1935.

6th Dragoon Guards Raised in July 1685 by Richard, 1st Baron Lumley (later 1st Earl of Scarborough) and ranked as 9th Horse, Lord Lumley's or The Queen Dowager's Regiment of Horse. The regi-

ment became 8th Regiment of Horse in 1690 and The King's Regiment of Carabiniers in 1691. In 1713 the regiment was renumbered 7th Horse (The Carabiniers). Redesignated 3rd Irish Horse in 1747; the regiment was restyled in 1788 and numbered 6th Dragoon Guards (The Carabiniers) on the conversion of regiments of horse remaining on the Irish establishment. The regiment was redesignated The Carabiniers (6th Dragoon Guards) in 1920. On 11 April 1922 the regiment amalgamated with 3rd Dragoon Guards (Prince of Wales's) to form 3rd/6th Dragoon Guards, which was in turn redesignated 3rd Carabiniers (Prince of Wales's Dragoon Guards) (q.v.) on 31 December 1928.
Headdress Badge: On crossed carbines the initials VIDG within the garter, all ensigned with the crown. Below, a scroll inscribed Carabiniers.

7th Dragoon Guards (Princess Royal's) Raised on 31 December 1688 by William Cavendish, Earl of Devonshire, and ranked 10th Horse as The Earl of Devonshire's Regiment of Horse. In 1690 the regiment was known as Schomberg's Horse, or 8th Horse, and Ligonier's Horse in 1720. In 1746 the regiment was redesignated on the Irish establishment as 4th (or Black) Irish Horse, 7th (The Princess Royal's) Dragoon Guards in 1788, and 7th Dragoon Guards (Princess Royal's) in 1921. On 11 April 1922 the regiment amalgamated with 4th Royal Irish Dragoon Guards to form 4th/7th Dragoon Guards - redesignated 4th/7th Royal Dragoon Guards (q.v.) on 31 October 1936.
Headdress Badge: The crest of Earl Ligonier; a demi-lion issuing from a coronet. Below, a scroll inscribed 7th Dragoon Guards.
History: *Records of the 7th Dragoon Guards During The Great War* by F J Scott and *7th (Princess Royal's) Dragoon Guards The Story of the Regiment 1688-1902* by C W Thompson.

The Royal Scots Dragoon Guards (Carabiniers And Greys) Formed on 2 July 1971 through the amalgamation of 3rd Carabiniers (Prince of Wales's Dragoon Guards (q.v.) and The Royal Scots Greys (2nd Dragoons) (q.v.).

Headdress Badge: On crossed carbines the Eagle of the French 45th Infantry Regiment upon a tablet inscribed 'Waterloo'. Below, a scroll inscribed 'Royal Scots Dragoon Guards'.

Regimental marches:

Quick marches: *3DG's* (Military Band) and *Hielan' Laddie* (Pipes and Drums).

Slow marches: *The Garb of Old Gaul* (Military Band) and *My Home* (Pipes and Drums).

Home headquarters: The Castle, Edinburgh, EH1 2YX.

History: *In The Finest Tradition* by S Wood (1988).

4th/7th Royal Dragoon Guards
Formed on 11 April 1922 through the amalgamation of 4th Royal Irish Dragoon Guards and 7th Dragoon Guards (Princess Royal's). On 1 August 1992 the regiment amalgamated with 5th Royal Inniskilling Dragoon Guards to form The Royal Dragoon Guards (q.v.).

Headdress Badge: Upon the Star of the Order of St Patrick a circle inscribed with the motto *'Quis Separabit'* (Who shall separate us), and the date of the amalgamation of the two regiments, MCMXXII. Within the circle the Cross of St George and coronet of the Princess Royal.

Motto: *Quis Separabit* (Who shall separate us?).

Regimental marches:

Quick march: *St Patrick's Day.*

Slow March: Slow marches of 4th Dragoons and of 7th Dragoons.

Home headquarters: 3 Tower Street, York, YO1 1SB.

History: *History of 4th/7th Royal Dragoon Guards (1685-1980)*, a Brereton Publication.

5th Royal Inniskilling Dragoon Guards Formed on 11 April 1922 through the amalgamation of 5th Dragoon Guards (Princess Charlotte of Wales's) and The Inniskillings (6th Dragoons). On 1 August 1992 the regiment amalgamated with 4th/7th Royal Dragoon Guards to form The Royal Dragoon Guards (q.v.).

Headdress Badge: The monogram VDG interlaced and ensigned with the Crown.

Regimental marches:

Quick march: *Fare Ye Well Inniskilling.*

Slow march: *The Soldiers Chorus.*

Home headquarters: The Castle, Chester, CH1 2DN.

History: *The 5th (Princess Charlotte of Wales's) Dragoon Guards (1685-1922)* (2 Vols) by B J L Pomeroy; *Records of an Old Heavy Cavalry Regiment (1691-1908)* by E S Jackson; *With the Inniskilling Dragoons 1899-1902* by J Watkins Yardley; *The 5th Royal Inniskilling Dragoon Guards* by R Evans; and *Change and Challenge (1922-1978)* by Blacker and Woods.

The Royal Dragoon Guards Formed on 1 August 1992 through the amalgamation of 4th/7th Royal Dragoon Guards (q.v.) and 5th Royal Inniskilling Dragoon Guards (q.v).

Headdress Badge: The Star of the Order of St Patrick.

Regimental marches:

Quick march: *St Patrick's Day.*

Slow marches: Slow marches of 4th Dragoon Guards and of 7th Dragoon Guards.

Home headquarters: 3 Tower Street, York, YO1 1SB.

The Light Dragoons Formed on 1 December 1992 through the amalgamation of 13th/18th Royal Hussars (Queen Mary's Own) (q.v.) and 15th/19th The King's Royal Hussars (q.v.).

Headdress Badge: The monogram LD encircled by a wreath of laurel and surmounted by the Crest of England, all upon a Maltese Cross.

Mottoes: *Viret in Aeternum* (It shall flourish forever) and *Merebimur* (We shall be worthy).

Regimental marches:

Quick march: *Balaklava.*

Slow march: *Denmark.*

Home headquarters: Fenham Barracks, Newcastle-upon-Tyne, NE2 4NP.

History: *The Origins of a New Regiment, Light Dragoons* by A Mallinson (1993).

Dreirwald Second World War battle honour marking one of the actions which took place between the crossing of the Rhine in March 1945 and the end of the campaign. *See also: North West Europe 1944-1955; Lingen; Bentheim; Uelzen; Artlenberg and Twente Canal.*

Dress Term applied mainly to the uniform of officers and covering many orders of dress and undress such as full dress, mess dress and state dress.

Dress Regulations Army regulations giving a detailed description of all orders of dress. It is usual for such regulations to be supplemented by regimental dress regulations. It was not until 1822 that the first full copy of Army Dress Regulations appeared.

Drill Training in procedures, movements or manoeuvres as for ceremonial parades or the use of weapons. Strict and often repetitious training or exercises used as a method of teaching. Procedure for executing a military task.

Drill Jacket Tight fitting jacket of 'waistcoat' cut, but with sleeves, often known as a fatigue or stable jacket. Although largely obsolete by 1870, the white drill jacket continued in use in Foot Guards and Highland regiments until the First World War.

Drill Sergeant Senior non-commissioned officer in the Foot Guards charged with the instruction of drill.

Drink Puppy Drink An arrangement of this tune forms part of the regimental quick march of the Royal Army Veterinary Corps.

Driver A badge depicting a crossed whip, or whips, and spur was used to denote a qualified horse transport driver. This badge became obsolete when horse transport disappeared from the regular army. The mechanical transport driver specialisation was denoted between 1925 and 1950 by a badge depicting a steering wheel.

Drocourt-Quéant First World War battle honour marking the breaching on 2 September 1918 of the Drocourt-Quéant 'switch', connected with the main Hindenburg Line. *See also: France and Flanders 1914-1918; Amiens; Albert 1918; Scarpe 1918 and Hindenburg Line.*

Dropping Zone Area of ground selected for the landing of personnel, stores, vehicles and equipment delivered by parachute.

Drum Badge worn on the sleeve by those qualified to play the drum. It is usual for drummers to be able to play either the fife or bugle as well as the drum.

Drumhead Court Martial Military court convened to hear urgent charges of offences committed in action, from the use of a drumhead as a table around which the court martial was held.

Drumhead Service Church service in the field for which the drums are stacked to form an altar.

Drum Major Drum majors existed before the Restoration, but became of increased importance after 1661 when their duties included recruiting and the administration of punishment as well as the training of young drummers. They were granted a more distinctive uniform and carried a cane or walking stick which, in continental armies, was used for punishment purposes, but in the British Army developed into the mace which is carried by drum majors today. As the drum major's duties no longer involved drumming his two drumsticks were secured on his sash, thus leaving his hands free. In 1881 drum majors were known as 'sergeant-drummers' and wore four reversed chevrons on the cuff. In 1928 the title 'drum major' was restored but the same rank distinction was retained. The drum major is now usually a warrant officer or senior non-commissioned officer who commands the drums in infantry regiments of the line. The drum major is responsible for the military and, with the help of the Bandmaster, the musical standards of the drummers and is answerable, in the first instance, to the adjutant. The drum major is responsible for the drill of both the regimental band and the drums, taking precedence over the bandmaster on ceremonial occasions when both parade together.

Drummossie Moor *See: Culloden.*

Duala First World War Cameroons campaign battle honour marking the capture in September 1914 of Duala, the capital of the Cameroons. *See also: Cameroons 1914-16; Garua and Banyo.*

Duchess of Kent Regimental slow march of The Worcestershire and Sherwood Foresters Regiment (29th and 45th Foot), The Corps of Royal Electrical and Mechanical Engineers and the Yorkshire Volunteers; also the regimental walk of The Honourable Artillery Company.

Duke of Albany's Regiment *See: Seaforth Highlanders.*

Duke of Beaufort's Musketeers Raised at Bristol on 20 June 1685 by Colonel Henry Somerset, 1st Duke of Beaufort. later 11th Foot. *See also: The Devonshire Regiment.*

Duke of Cornwall's Light Infantry (32nd and 46th Foot) The 32nd was raised in February 1702 by Colonel Edward Fox as a regiment of marines known as Fox's Marines. The regiment disbanded in 1713 but was re-raised in 1715 as 32nd Regiment of Foot, redesignated 32nd (Cornwall) Regiment of Foot in 1782; and 32nd (Cornwall) Light Infantry in 1858. The 46th Foot was raised in January 1741 by Colonel John Price as 57th Foot and renumbered 47th in 1748. Redesignated 46th (South Devonshire) Regiment of Foot in 1782. In 1881 32nd (Cornwall) Light Infantry and 46th (South Devonshire) Regiment of Foot amalgamated to form The Duke of Cornwall's Light Infantry. On 6 October 1959 the regiment amalgamated with The Somerset Light Infantry (Prince Albert's) (13th Foot) to form The Somerset and Cornwall Light Infantry (13th, 32nd and 46th Foot) (q.v.).
Headdress Badge: A stringed bugle-horn with, above, a ducal coronet upon a scroll 'CORNWALL', all upon a red cloth backing.
History: *Historical Records of the 32nd (Cornwall) Light Infantry* by G C Swiney (1893); *Historical Record of the 46th or South Devonshire Regiment of Foot* by R Cannon (1851); *The Duke of Cornwall's Light Infantry 1914-1919* by E Wyrall (1932); *The Duke of Cornwall's Light Infantry 1939-1945* by E G Godfrey (1966); *The Duke of Cornwall's Light Infantry* by R F K Goldsmith (1970); and *Historical Record of*

the 46th Foot (South Devonshire Regiment) 1741-1851 by R Cannon (1851).

Duke of Edinburgh's Royal Regiment (Berkshire and Wiltshire) Formed on 9 June 1959 by the amalgamation of the Royal Berkshire Regiment (Princess Charlotte of Wales's) (49th and 66th Foot); and the Wiltshire Regiment (Duke of Edinburgh's) (62nd and 99th Foot). On 27 April 1994 the regiment amalgamated with the Gloucestershire Regiment (28th and 61st Foot) to form the Royal Gloucestershire, Berkshire and Wiltshire Regiment (q.v.).

Duke of Lancaster's Own Yeomanry Yeomanry cavalry regiment on the Territorial Army order of battle until 1 November 1992 when the regiment amalgamated with The Queen's Own Mercian Yeomanry (q.v.) to form The Royal Mercian and Lancastrian Yeomanry.
Headdress Badge: A rose within a wreath, laurel on the left, oak on the right. Below, a scroll inscribed 'DUKE OF LANCASTER'S OWN'. The whole ensigned with a ducal coronet.
Regimental quick march: *John O'Gaunt*.
See also: Lancashire Yeomanry.

Duke of Norfolk's Regiment of Foot (22nd Foot) Raised at Chester in March 1689 by Colonel Henry Howard, 7th Duke of Norfolk. *See also: The Cheshire Regiment (22nd Foot).*

Duke of Norfolk's Regiment of Foot (12th Foot) Formed from an independent company raised in 1660 as garrison for Windsor Castle, and commanded by Henry Howard, 7th Duke of Norfolk. In June 1685 the company was augmented and regimented as The Duke of Norfolk's Regiment of Foot, becoming 12th Foot in 1751. *See also: The Suffolk Regiment (12th Foot).*

Duke of Shrewsbury's Regiment of Horse Raised in 1685, 5th Dragoon Guards in 1784 and later 5th Royal Inniskilling Dragoon Guards.

Duke of Wellington's Bodyguard Nickname given to 5th Foot, The Royal

Northumberland Fusiliers. The nickname stems from the Peninsula War when the regiment was attached to headquarters for a long time.

Duke of Wellington's Regiment (West Riding) (33rd and 76th Foot) Raised in February 1702 as the Earl of Huntingdon's Foot and numbered 33rd Foot in 1751. Designated 33rd (1st York, West Riding) Foot in 1782 and redesignated 33rd (Duke of Wellington's) Foot in 1853. In parallel, 76th Foot was raised in 1756, disbanded in 1763 and re-raised as 76th (MacDonald's Highlanders) Foot in 1777, only to be disbanded again in 1784. In October 1787 the regiment was re-raised for service with the East India Company as 76th (Hindoostan) Foot and redesignated 76th Foot in 1812. In May 1881 33rd (Duke of Wellington's) Foot and 76th Foot amalgamated to form the Halifax Regiment (Duke of Wellington's), which was retitled the Duke of Wellington's (West Riding Regiment) two months later. In 1920 the regiment was redesignated the Duke of Wellington's Regiment (West Riding).
Headdress Badge: The Duke of Wellington's crest, with the motto '*Virtutis fortuna comes*' (Fortune favours the brave).
Regimental quick march: *The Wellesley*.
Regimental Headquarters: Wellesley Park, Halifax, Yorkshire HX2 0BA.
History: *The History of The Duke of Wellington's Regiment (West Riding) 1702-1992* by J M Brereton and A C S Savory (1993).

Duke of York One of the regimental slow marches of the Grenadier Guards (q.v.) and the regimental slow march of The Honourable Artillery Company.

Duke of York's Royal Military School Boarding school for the education of the sons of soldiers. Founded at Chelsea in 1801 by Frederick, Duke of York (1763-1827), it moved to Dover in 1909.

Dukhovskaya First World War battle honour marking the defeat of a Bolshevik advance on Vladivostok during the campaign in Siberia (1918-19). *See also: Siberia 1918-19.*

Dumbarton's Drums Regimental quick march (Pipes and Drums) of The Royal Scots (The Royal Regiment). The oldest regimental march in the British Army. Samuel Pepys records in his diary having heard the regiment play it at Rochester on 30 June 1667.

Dumbartonshire Yeomanry Two separate corps existed in 1803 which, by 1820 had risen to three. Little further information exists about Yeomanry activity in Dumbartonshire thereafter.

Dumfriesshire Yeomanry A corps of Yeomanry Cavalry was raised in 1798 and, by 1803, a second troop certainly existed. Ultimately five troops existed which appear to have served until the 1820s.

Dunkirk 1940 Second World War battle honour awarded to those regiments which defended the Dunkirk perimeter to cover the evacuation - as opposed to those units which passed through for embarkation. Due to the speed of the German advance in 1940 it became clear that the Allied forces in Belgium would very quickly be cut off from their bases in France. The British selected Boulogne, Calais, Dunkirk and Ostend as ports through which resupply could be maintained and, in parallel, plans were made to evacuate through Dunkirk. Boulogne and Calais were captured by the Germans on 26 May and the Allies rapidly moved a force back to cover Dunkirk. By 4 June 1940, 338,000 Allied troops were rescued, the evacuation being covered by a gallant and resolute rearguard action. *See also: North West Europe 1940; Dyle; Withdrawal to Escaut; Defence of Escaut; Defence of Arras; Boulogne 1940; Calais 1940; St Omer-La Bassée; Wormhoudt; Cassel and Ypres-Comines Canal.*

Durham Light Infantry (68th and 106th Foot) Raised in 1756 as 2nd Battalion, 23rd Royal Welch Fusiliers and designated 68th Foot in 1758. Redesignated 68th (Durham) Foot in 1782 and 68th (Durham Light Infantry) Foot in 1812. In 1881, the regiment merged with 106th Bombay Light Infantry, which had been raised in 1826 as 2nd Bombay

European Regiment (East India Company), to form the Durham Light Infantry. On 10 July 1968 the regiment amalgamated with the Somerset and Cornwall Light Infantry (13th, 32nd and 46th Foot), the King's Own Yorkshire Light Infantry (51st and 105th Foot) and the King's Shropshire Light Infantry (53rd and 85th) to form the Light Infantry (q.v.).

Headdress Badge: A bugle-horn stringed. Within the strings the initials DLI, ensigned with the crown.

History: *'Faithful'* by S G P Ward (1962); and *The Durham Light Infantry* by William Moore (1976).

Durham Yeomanry A corps of Yeomanry Cavalry was raised in North Durham in 1798, and in 1801 a further troop was raised in the city of Durham. By 1803 twelve troops existed in County Durham, but were apparently never regimented. Some troops were still serving in the 1820s.

Dyas and the Stormers Regimental toast of The King's Own Yorkshire Light Infantry (51st and 105th Foot). The toast is drunk standing and in silence in memory of Ensign Joseph Dyas of the 51st Foot who led the 'Forlorn Hope' (q.v.) at the siege of Badajoz in 1811 on two occasions.

D'ye ken John Peel Regimental quick march of The Queen's Own Yeomanry.

Dyle Second World War battle honour marking the successful holding of the line of the River Dyle 10-16 May 1940. From the line of the Dyle, defenders withdrew to the next defensive line on the River Escaut. *See also: North West Europe 1940; Dunkirk 1940; Withdrawal to Escaut; Defence of Escaut; Defence of Arras; Boulogne 1940; Calais 1940; St Omer-La Bassée; Wormhoudt; Cassel and Ypres-Comines Canal.*

'E' A capital letter 'E' was worn on the shoulder of non-British troops in the Indian Army before the Second World War to denote proficiency in English. A similar practice was employed with Malay, Chinese and African troops.

Ear Boss These posts, often decorated, on the headdress just above each ear, were used as fixing points for the chin-chain or chin-scales.

Ear Defenders In September 1940 the War Office decided to introduce ear protectors, in the form of rubber plugs, to each officer, other rank and member of the ATS in the United Kingdom to protect the ears against blast and 'screaming' bombs. The increasing shortage of rubber meant that by May 1944 cotton wool had taken the place of rubber plugs. Small rubber ear defenders are now issued to all ranks to protect the hearing against the potentially damaging effects of explosions, especially those incurred during the firing of high velocity weapons.

Earl of Angus's Regiment *See: The Cameronians (Scottish Rifles).*

Earl of Dumbarton's Regiment *See: The Royal Scots (The Royal Regiment).*

Earl of Mar's Grey Breeks Nickname given the 21st Foot, later the Royal Scots Fusiliers, now embodied in the Royal Highland Fusiliers (Princess Margaret's Own Glasgow and Ayrshire Regiment), from the colour of their breeches when the regiment was raised in 1678 by the Earl of Mar.

Early One Morning An arrangement of this tune formed part of the regimental quick march of the Women's Royal Army Corps.

East Africa 1914-18 First World War battle honour marking the campaign in German East Africa (Tanganyika). The campaign started in 1914 with an unsuccessful attempt by the British to capture the port of Tanga and, until March 1916, there was inconclusive fighting along the border with British East Africa (Kenya). In that month, reinforced by South African troops, the British launched an offensive, forcing the Germans to withdraw southwards. Thereafter the British sought to envelop the German forces, eventually pursuing them into East Africa (Mozambique) whence, in August 1918, they turned north and entered Northern Rhodesia. The German commander, von Lettow-Vorbeck, surrendered at Abercorn two weeks after the armistice had been signed in Europe. *See also: Kilimanjaro; Behobeho; Narungombe; Nyangao and Kamina.*

East and Central Africa Medal 1897-1899 Superseded the Central Africa Medal 1891-8 (qv).
Ribbon: Half yellow, half red.
Clasps: Lubwa's; Uganda 1897-98; 1898; 1899 and Uganda 1899.

East and West Africa Medal 1887-1900
Ribbon: 1" wide, yellow with black borders and two thin black stripes down the centre.
Clasps: 1887-8; Witu 1890; 1891-2; 1892; Witu August 1893; Liwondi 1893; Juba River 1893; Lake Nyassa 1893; 1893-94;

Gambia 1894; Benin River 1894; Brass River 1895; 1896-98; Niger 1897; Benin 1897; Dawkita 1897; 1897-98; 1898; Sierra Leone 1898-99; 1899 and 1900. (The M'wele campaign of 1895-96 failed to qualify for a clasp; instead it is engraved round the rim.)

East Anglian Brigade An administrative grouping in the infantry formed under Army Order 61 of 1948, comprising: The Royal Norfolk, Suffolk, Bedfordshire and Hertfordshire, Essex, Royal Lincolnshire and Northamptonshire Regiments. Absorbed into the Queen's Division (qv) in 1968.

East Anglian Regiment The regiment was the product of three amalgamations. On 2 June 1958 the Bedfordshire and Hertfordshire Regiment (16th Foot) and the Essex Regiment (44th, 56th Foot) amalgamated to form 3rd East Anglian Regiment (16th, 44th Foot). On 29 August 1959 The Royal Norfolk Regiment (9th Foot) and the Suffolk Regiment (12th Foot) amalgamated to form 1st East Anglian Regiment. The third amalgamation took place on 1 June 1960 when the Royal Lincolnshire Regiment (10th Foot) and the Northamptonshire Regiment (48th/58th Foot) amalgamated to form 2nd East Anglian Regiment. On 1 September 1964 the 1st, 2nd and 3rd East Anglian Regiments amalgamated with the Royal Leicestershire Regiment (17th Foot) to form the Royal Anglian Regiment (qv).
Headdress Badge: The castle and key of Gibraltar, above a scroll inscribed 'EAST ANGLIA' upon an eight-pointed star.

East Lancashire Regiment (30th and 59th Foot) Raised at Lincoln in 1689 as Lord Castleton's Regiment of Foot and disbanded in 1698. Re-raised as Sanderson's Regiment of Marines in 1702, and retitled Wills' Regiment of Foot in 1714. Designated 30th Foot in 1751, and 30th (Cambridgeshire) Foot in 1782. The 59th Foot was raised at Nottingham in 1755 and designated 59th (2nd Nottinghamshire) Foot in 1782. In May 1881 30th (Cambridgeshire) and 59th (2nd Nottinghamshire) Regiments of Foot

were amalgamated to form the 1st and 2nd Battalions The West Lancashire Regiment, being retitled the East Lancashire Regiment only two months thereafter. The two battalions were amalgamated in 1948. On 1 July 1958 the East Lancashire Regiment (30th, 59th Foot) and the South Lancashire Regiment (The Prince of Wales's Volunteers) (40th, 82nd Foot) amalgamated to form the Lancashire Regiment (Prince of Wales's Volunteers) (30th, 40th, 59th and 82nd Foot). On 25 March 1970 the Lancashire Regiment (Prince of Wales's Volunteers) amalgamated with the Loyal Regiment (North Lancashire) (47th, 81st Foot) to form the Queen's Lancashire Regiment (qv).
Headdress Badge: The Sphinx upon a tablet inscribed 'EGYPT' above the rose of Lancaster, within a laurel wreath, all ensigned with the crown.
History: *History of 30th Regiment 1689-1881; History of The East Lancashire Regiment in the Great War 1914-1918;* and *History of The East Lancashire Regiment in the War 1939-1945.*

East Surrey Regiment (31st and 70th Foot) Raised in February 1702 as Villier's Regiment of Marines; renamed Goring's Marines in 1711, numbered 31st Foot in 1714 and designated 31st (Huntingdonshire) Foot in 1782. A second battalion of 31st Foot was raised in 1756, re-numbered 70th Foot in 1758 and designated 70th (Surrey) Foot in 1782. In 1812 the 70th was redesignated 70th (Glasgow Lowland) Regiment and redesignated 70th (Surrey) Foot in 1825. In 1881 the 31st (Huntingdonshire) and 70th (Surrey) Regiments of Foot amalgamated to form the East Surrey Regiment. On 14 October 1959 the East Surrey Regiment (31st, 70th Foot) and the Queen's Royal Regiment (West Surrey) (2nd Foot) amalgamated to form the Queen's Royal Surrey Regiment (2nd, 31st and 70th Foot). On 31st December 1966 the Queen's Royal Surrey Regiment, the Queen's Own Buffs, The Royal West Kent Regiment, the Royal Sussex Regiment (35th and 107th Foot), and the Middlesex Regiment (Duke of Cambridge's Own) (57th and 77th Foot) amalgamated to form the Queen's

Regiment. On 9 September 1992 the Queen's Regiment and the Royal Hampshire Regiment 37th and 67th Foot) amalgamated to form the Princess of Wales's Royal Regiment (Queen's and Royal Hampshires) (qv).
Headdress Badge: Within an eight pointed star, ensigned with the crown, the arms of Guildford.
History: *A History of The East Surrey Regiment 1702-1919* (3 Vols).

East Yorkshire Regiment (The Duke of York's Own) (15th Foot) Raised at Nottingham in June 1685 as Clifton's Regiment; designated 15th Foot in 1751, 15th (York, East Riding) Foot in 1782, East Yorkshire Regiment in 1881 and East Yorkshire Regiment (The Duke of York's Own) in 1935. On 25 April 1958 the regiment amalgamated with the West Yorkshire Regiment (The Prince of Wales's Own) (14th Foot) to form the Prince of Wales's Own Regiment of Yorkshire (14th and 15th Foot) (qv).
Headdress Badge: The rose of York within a laurel wreath upon an eight-pointed star. Below, a scroll inscribed 'EAST YORK-SHIRE'.
History: *A History of the 15th (East Yorkshire) Regiment 1685-1914* by R J Jones; *The East Yorkshire Regiment in The Great War 1914-1918* by E Wyrall; *The East Yorkshire Regiment in the War 1939-1945* by P R Nightingale and *The East Yorkshire Regiment* by A J Barker.

Echelon The division of a unit or formation into parts or echelons which follow each other; the intervals between echelons being such that they need not be committed to action simultaneously. In more general usage the term echelon has come to mean the immediate administrative and supply elements of fighting units or formations.

Echelon Force A force not committed initially, but for which commitment on a mission vital to the success of the operation as a whole, is already planned.

Edinburgh Regiment (25th Foot) *See: The King's Own Scottish Borderers.*

Education and Training Branch of the Adjutant General's Corps Formed from the Royal Army Education Corps on 6 April 1992.

1800 Battle honour awarded to the King's Own Malta Regiment in 1897 to mark the assistance given to a British expedition in the reduction of the French garrison of Valetta.

Egmont-Op-Zee Battle honour marking the defeat of the French on 2 October 1799 by a British force under the Duke of York in an unsuccessful campaign which sought to wrest Holland from the French.

Egypt 1882 Battle honour marking the campaign against the military dictator, Arabi Pasha, who had seized power in Egypt. Britain intervened to restore order and protect foreign lives and property. Alexandria was occupied after naval bombardment, and an expedition under Sir Garnet Wolseley landed in the Suez canal area, defeated the Egyptians at Tel-El-Kebir (qv) and entered Cairo. Britain effectively retained control of Egypt for the next 60 years. *See also: Tel-El-Kebir.*

Egypt 1884 Battle honour marking operations against the Mahdists (qv) under Osman Digna in the eastern Sudan. The main actions were at El Teb and at Tamai, the latter being in the balance for some time.

Egypt Campaign Medal 1882-1889 Authorised for issue with two clasps in a General Order of 1882; five further clasps were later added and the medal reissued in 1884, but with a plain exergue.
Ribbon: Three bright blue and two white vertical stripes of equal width.
Clasps: Alexandria 11th July 1882; Tel-El-Kebir; El-Teb; Tamaii; El-Teb-Tamaii; Suakin 1884; The Nile 1884-85; Abu Klea; Kirbekan; Suakin 1885; Tofrek; Gemaizah and Toski.
See also: Khedive's Star.

Egypt 1915-17 First World War battle honour marking the campaign against the Turks 1915-17. Although Turkey was not in a state of war with Britain until 5 November 1914, she had long been under German influence and a treaty had existed for some years between the two countries. Early in November 1914 a Turkish force under Jemal Pasha, with the energetic and talented Colonel Kress von Kressenstein as his chief of staff, advanced through the Sinai peninsula and arrived at the Suez canal in three columns on 25 January 1915. The Turks raided Kubri, seven miles north of Suez, on 27 January, Kantara on 28 January and, on the night of 2-3 February, mounted a general attack between Serapeum and Tussum. However, all Turkish attempts to cross the canal failed. Successful British actions were fought against the Senussi, a Muslim non-conformist sect supported by the Turks and Germans, at Hazalin in December 1915 and Agadir in March 1916. When the Gallipoli peninsula was evacuated the British troops were evacuated to Egypt and the garrison was then reorganised by General Sir Archibald Murray. By the middle of July 1916 a large Turkish force under Colonel von Kressenstein was in contact with a British defensive line east of the canal, which they attacked on the night 3-4 August. The Turks were heavily counter-attacked and fell back in disorder and the British success was subsequently exploited; the Turks being driven from Egypt, the Sinai peninsula and Palestine. *See also: Suez Canal; Agagiya; Rumani and Rafah.*

Egyptian Frontier Second World War North Africa campaign battle honour marking the fighting along the frontier with Libya from the time Italy entered the war in June 1940 and the invasion of Egypt which began in early September. *See also: North Africa 1940-1943; Sidi Barrani; Buq Buq; Capture of Tobruk; Beda Fomm; Defence of Tobruk; Sidi Suleiman and Tobruk 1941.*

Eighth Army (Second World War) Formed in Egypt in November 1941 under Lieutenant General Sir Alan Cunningham, who was succeeded on 26 November by Major General N M Ritchie. On 25 June 1942 General Sir Claude Auchinleck assumed command, handing over to Lieutenant General Bernard Montgomery on 13 August 1942. Montgomery commanded the Eighth Army in North Africa, Sicily and Italy until, on 30 December 1943 Lieutenant General Sir Oliver Leese was appointed to command. Beside British troops South African, New Zealand, Canadian, Indian, Gurkha, Polish, French and Greek formations fought with the Eighth Army. On 3 November 1944 Lieutenant General Sir Richard McCreery assumed command until the end of the war. In the spring of 1945 Eighth Army launched a major offensive which carried it to Trieste and into Austria, and it was subsequently disbanded on 29 July 1945.

Eileen Allanagh Regimental slow march of the Royal Irish Rangers.

Ejector That part of a weapon mechanism which ejects spent cartridge cases after firing.

El Agheila Second World War North Africa campaign battle honour marking the fighting over the period 13-17 December 1942 when the Germans sought to make a stand at El Agheila, but were outflanked by the New Zealand Division and forced to withdraw. *See also: North Africa 1940-1943; El Alamein; Nofilia and Advance on Tripoli.*

El Alamein Second World War North Africa campaign battle honour marking the fighting which took place 23 October to 4 November 1942 and resulted in a decisive victory for the British under General Montgomery over Axis forces, who were forced to withdraw into Tunisia. *See also: North Africa 1940-1943; Defence of Alamein Line; Alam El Halfa; Benghazi Raid; El Agheila; Nofilia and Advance on Tripoli.*

El Hadjera Second World War North Africa campaign battle honour marking one of the actions which took place between the Kasserine operations of mid-February 1943 and the operations to break through the Fondouk Pass in April 1943. *See also: North Africa 1940-1943; Djebel Djaffa; Sidi Nsir; Fort McGregor; Stuka Farm; Steamroller Farm; Montagne Farm; Kef Ouiba Pass; Djebel Guerba; Sedjenane I;*

Maknassy; Djebel Dahra; Kef El Debna and Djebel Choucha.

El Hamma Second World War North Africa campaign battle honour marking one of the actions in the turning of the Mareth Line over the period 21-30 March 1943. *See also: North Africa 1940-1943; Tebaga Gap and Point 201 (Roman Wall).*

El Mughar First World War Palestine campaign battle honour marking an action on 13 November 1917, which resulted in the capture of Junction Station and the cutting of communications between Jerusalem and Jaffa. *See also: Palestine 1917-1918; Gaza; Nebi Samwil; Jaffa; Jerusalem; Jericho; Tell Asur; Jordan; Megiddo and Damascus.*

El Kourzia Second World War North Africa campaign battle honour marking one of the actions in the Oued Zarga operations, when an unsuccessful attempt was made to break through the German positions north of Bou Arada 22-26 April 1943. *See also: North Africa 1940-1943; Oued Zarga; Djebel Rmel; Djebel Tanngoucha; Djebel Kesskiss; Argoub Selah and Ber Rabal.*

El Wak Second World War Abyssinian campaign battle honour marking an action in which an Italian post on the Kenya border was captured in mid-December 1940. *See also: Abyssinia 1940-41; Keren; Jebel Defeis; Jebel Shiba; Gogni; Agordat; Barentu; Karora-Marsa Taclai; Afodu; Gambela; Moyale; Wal Garis; Juba; Marda Pass; Babile Gap; Bisidimo; Awash; Todenyang-Namaraputh; Soroppa; Giarso; Colito; Wadara; Omo; Gondar; Fike and Lechemti.*

Electronic Silence The deliberate prohibition of electro-magnetic emissions, normally applied for a stated period to specific equipments or frequency bands.

Electronic Warfare (EW) Military action involving the employment of electro-magnetic energy to determine, exploit, reduce or prevent hostile use of the electro-magnetic spectrum, and action to retain its effective use by friendly forces.

Elegant Extracts Nickname given to 85th King's Light Infantry, subsequently The King's Shropshire Light Infantry, now part of The Light Infantry (qv). In 1813 a number of officers were removed as a consequence of courts martial. New officers - the Elegant Extracts - were selected from other regiments to take their place.

Elliot's Light Horse One of the regimental slow marches of the 15th/19th The King's Royal Hussars.

Embroidery Term applied to the special needlework in silk or metal thread on officers' uniform. In the 18th century officers wore coats of similar colour to those of their men, but gold and silver embroidery on the button holes, pockets and elsewhere was an indication of rank.

Emsdorf Battle honour marking the victory at Emsdorf on 16 July 1760 during the Seven Years' War (1756-63). *See also: Minden; Warburg and Wilhelmstahl.*

Encirclement Envelopment from both flanks simultaneously. *See also: Envelopment.*

Encore Regimental trot of the Queen's Royal Hussars (The Queen's Own and Royal Irish).

Energa Grenade Belgian designed and produced anti-tank grenade with shaped charge warhead. Discharged from a rifle using a ballastite cartridge and muzzle adaptor.

Enfidaville Second World War North Africa campaign battle honour marking the attempts by Eighth Army (qv) to penetrate the Axis position about Enfidaville 19-29 April 1943. *See also: North Africa 1940-1943; Takrouna and Djebel Garci.*

Enfield Carbine Variant of the Enfield 1853 pattern rifle produced in 1856 as a cavalry carbine. *See also: Rifle.*

Enfield 1853 Pattern Rifle A 0.557" calibre weapon produced in 1854 by the government factory at Enfield. *See also: Minié Rifle and Rifle.*

Enfield Musketoon Version of the Enfield 1853 pattern rifle with a shortened barrel originally produced as a carbine for artillery troops. A later model produced in 1860 had the same improved rifling featured in the short rifle. *See also: Rifle.*

Enfield Short Rifle Shortened version of the 1853 pattern Enfield rifle, also of 0.557" calibre and first produced in 1856. *See also: Rifle.*

Enfilade Fire Fire which strikes the side of an enemy, usually from a defilade (qv) position.

Engineer-in-Chief (Army) Professional head of the Corps of Royal Engineers.

Ensign The name originally applied to the lowest commissioned rank of infantry officer in the British Army, who traditionally carried the Ensign or Colour. The title was changed in 1871 to Second Lieutenant.

Entrenchment General term applied to any earthwork which is thrown up to protect soldiers against an enemy. Entrenchments may be hastily made, as in the case of shell scrapes and slit trenches, or of a more complex and durable nature.

Envelopment An offensive manoeuvre in which the main attacking force passes around or over the enemy's principal defensive positions to secure objectives in the enemy's rear.

EOKA *See: Cyprus 1954-60.*

Epaulette Originally, a piece of chain-mail or other material worn across the shoulders for protection - from the French *épaule* (shoulder). Now the name given to the small piece of chain-mail worn on the shoulders of cavalry officers or, more widely, to the cloth or board strap worn on each shoulder upon which it is usual to display the badges of rank of commissioned officers.

Épéhy First World War battle honour marking one of the actions in the successive offensives against the Hindenburg Line 12 September - 6 October 1918. Épéhy was attacked on 18 September 1918. *See also: France and Flanders 1914-1918; Hindenburg Line; Havrincourt; Canal du Nord; St Quentin Canal; Beaurevoir and Cambrai 1918.*

Equerry An officer attendant upon the British sovereign. Formerly an officer in the royal household responsible for the horses.

Escort Party responsible for the close protection of a person or object ie. Sovereign's Escort, Escort to the Colour, Ammunition Escort and Prisoner and Escort.

Esquay Second World War battle honour marking one of the actions associated with the capture and clearance of Caen 4-18 July 1944. *See also: North West Europe 1944-1945; Caen; Hill 112; Noyers and Orne.*

Ess and Vellum Term used to distinguish the many patterns of gold and silver lace. Vellum indicates straight lines; 'ess' refers to the 'S' shaped pattern which is repeated throughout.

Essex Regiment (44th and 56th Foot) The 44th was raised in January 1741 by Colonel James Long and originally ranked 55th Foot; renumbered 44th Foot in 1748 and designated 44th (East Essex) Foot in 1782. The 56th Foot was raised by Colonel Lord Charles Manners in December 1755 and originally ranked as 58th Foot; renumbered 56th Foot in 1756 and designated 56th (West Essex) Foot in 1782. In 1881 44th (East Essex) and 56th (West Essex) Foot amalgamated to form the Essex Regiment. On 2 June 1958 the Essex Regiment amalgamated with the Bedfordshire & Hertfordshire Regiment (16th Foot) to form 3rd East Anglian Regiment (16th and 44th Foot). On 1 September 1964 the 1st, 2nd and 3rd East Anglian Regiments amalgamated with the Royal Leicestershire Regiment (17th Foot) to form the Royal Anglian Regiment (qv). Headdress Badge: Within an oak wreath the castle and key of Gibraltar, and above it the sphinx on a tablet inscribed 'EGYPT'. History: *Essex Units in the War 1914-1918* (6

Vols. including history of the Essex Regiment 1741-1929) by J W Burrow; and *The Essex Regiment 1929-1950* by T A Martin.

Essex Yeomanry Unregimented until 1813, when six previously independent troops formed the 1st Essex Yeomanry Cavalry. The regiment was disbanded in 1828 but re-formed as the West Essex Yeomanry Cavalry in 1830, serving without pay for five years from 1838 until again disbanded in 1877. However, an Essex Troop did serve for a number of years with the Loyal Suffolk Hussars. The regiment was re-raised in 1901, sent to France in 1914 and served mounted throughout the First World War on the Western Front. In April 1918 the regiment was divided, the three squadrons being attached to regular cavalry regiments for the remainder of the war. In 1920 the regiment was re-formed and trained as cavalry for two years before re-roling as an artillery unit in November 1921, serving as artillery throughout the Second World War. After the war the regiment was represented by Essex Yeomanry Royal Horse Artillery (Territorial) until 1967. After a short period as a cadre, this was converted to Royal Signals in 1969, and the regiment's successor sub-unit is now 70 (Essex Yeomanry) Signal Squadron, 38 Signal Regiment (Volunteers).

Estaires First World War battle honour marking the opening phase of the second main German offensive, launched in Flanders on 9 April 1918. *See also: France and Flanders 1914-1918; Lys; Messines 1918; Hazebrouck; Bailleul; Kemmel; Béthune and Scherpenberg.*

Establishment The approved strength, organisation, structure and equipment of a military unit.

Estry Second World War battle honour marking one of the actions between the Allied landing in Normandy in June 1944 and the crossing of the River Seine in late August. *See also: North West Europe 1944-1945; Tourmauville Bridge; St Pierre La Veille; Noireau Crossing; La Vie Crossing; La Touques Crossing; Risle Crossing and Foret de Bretonne.*

Ex Dentibus Ensis **(From the teeth a sword)** Motto of the Royal Army Dental Corps.

Executive Committee Of The Army Board (ECAB) The Executive Committee of the Army Board is responsible for the detailed management of the Army. The Committee is chaired by the Chief of the General Staff. The members are the Second Permanent Under Secretary of State, the Adjutant General, the Quartermaster General, the Master General of the Ordnance, the Commanders-in-Chief of The British Army of the Rhine and United Kingdom Land Forces and the Assistant Chief of the General Staff.

Exemplo Ducemus **(Leading by example)** Motto of the Corps of Royal Military Police.

Expeditionary Forces Institute (EFI) *See: Navy, Army and Air Force Institute.*

Experimental Corps Of Riflemen Raised in August 1800 from selected detachments of other regiments and armed with the Baker rifle (qv). Commanded by Colonel Coote Manningham and ranked 95th Foot in 1803. *See also: Rifle Brigade.*

Exploit To take full advantage of a successful attack by following-up and harassing a dislocated enemy with the aim of further disorganising him in depth. This may make possible the seizure of ground which was not part of the objective of the original attack. It is customary for a commander to lay down a 'limit of exploitation'.

Explosive Ordnance Disposal (EOD) The rendering harmless of explosive devices of all types. Usually applied to improvised explosive devices of terrorist manufacture. *See also: Ammunition Technical Officer.*

Explosive Reactive Armour (ERA) Boxes containing low sensitivity explosive sandwiched between thin steel plates and fixed to the more vulnerable surfaces of armoured vehicles as a protection against attack by shaped charge warheads. Detonating when struck, they deflect the penetrative effort of the shaped charge.

Extra Regimentally Employed (ERE) Holding an appointment on an establish-

ment (qv) other than that of the individual's parent regiment or corps.

Eyes Term applied to the small circles of decorative braid, cord or embroidery on uniform.

FACE Abbreviation for Forward Artillery Computing Equipment. An artillery command and control system, now obsolescent, and replaced by BATES (qv).

Facings In the 17th century soldier's coats were of thin cloth which needed a lining or facing, often of different colour to the coat. When the long sleeves were turned back to form a cuff, the collar turned down or skirts turned back, the colour of the facing was revealed. In due course coloured facings came to be used as regimental distinctions.

Fairbairn-Sykes Fighting Knife Manufactured from 1940 by Wilkinson-Sword to a design by William 'Dan' Fairbairn, formerly Assistant Commissioner of Shanghai Municipal Police, and his colleague Eric 'Bill' Sykes. The knife, with its 6 7/8" stiletto blade, two razor edges and sharp point, became known as the 'Commando Knife'. The first batch cost 13s/6d each - including the sheath. By the end of the war, Wilkinson Sword had produced 250,000 such knives.

Faithful Motto of 68th (Durham) Light Infantry and later The Durham Light Infantry. Now one of the mottoes of The Light Infantry.

Falaise Second World War battle honour marking the fighting which took place 7-22 August 1944 and which lead to the final decisive victory in Normandy, British and American forces closing on the Germans from north and south respectively. *See also: North West Europe 1944-1945; Mount Pincon; Falaise Road and Laison.*

Falaise Road Second World War battle honour marking an action in the early stages of the British advance towards Falaise from the Bourgebous Ridge. *See also: North West Europe 1944-1945; Mount Pincon; Falaise and Laison.*

Falkland Islands 1982 Battle honour marking the campaign to recapture the Falkland Islands. On 2 April 1982 Argentine forces seized the islands and a British task force sailed from Portsmouth on 5 April, landing virtually unopposed at San Carlos Bay in East Falkland on 21 May. British forces began to advance across the islands on 27 May, with bitter fighting taking place at Goose Green, Mount Longdon, Tumbledown Mountain and Wireless Ridge. On 14 June the Argentine defence collapsed. A major contribution to the success of the campaign was made by Special Air Service (qv) and Special Boat Section operations. *See also: Tumbledown Mountain; Goose Green; Mount Longdon and Wireless Ridge.*

Falluja Second World War Iraq campaign battle honour marking an action during operations against pro-German Iraqi forces in 1941. *See also: Iraq 1941; Defence of Habbaniya and Baghdad 1941.*

False Front The positioning of forces and/or dummy positions forward of a defensive position in order to deceive an enemy as to the true location of that defensive position.

Fanfare Flourish or short tune, usually played on trumpets or bugles, used as a signal or salute at ceremonial events.

Far o'er the Sea Regimental quick march (Pipes) of the Queen's Gurkha Engineers.

Fare Thee Well Inniskilling Regimental quick march of 5th Royal Inniskilling Dragoon Guards and the Royal Dragoon Guards.

Farman Experimental (FE2) Biplane manufactured by the Royal Aircraft Factory and in service with the Royal Flying Corps in the First World War.

Farmers Boy Regimental quick march of the Devonshire and Dorset Regiment, the Duke of Edinburgh's Royal Regiment, the Princess of Wales's Royal Regiment, Royal Yeomanry and Wessex Regiment (Rifle Volunteers).

Farrier Non-commissioned officer or trooper tasked to look after horses in a cavalry regiment and, more especially, to attend to the shoeing of the animals. The specialisation is denoted by a badge, worn on the sleeve, depicting a horseshoe, farrier sergeants wearing the badge above their chevrons. On ceremonial occasions farriers traditionally wear blue coats and carry an axe.

Fascines Originally, large brushwood bundles, now formed from plastic tubing in large bundles and weighing some 2.5 tons each. Once used for a wide variety of military engineering tasks; now more usually placed in ditches to improve battlefield mobility, particularly for tracked vehicles.

Faugh a Ballagh **(Clear the Way)** Motto of the Royal Irish Rangers, The Royal Irish Fusiliers (Princess Victoria's) and 87th (Royal Irish Fusiliers) Regiment of Foot.

Fencibles Forces raised during the American War of Independence (qv) and the French revolutionary wars in both the United Kingdom and North America. Those raised in the latter in 1775 were called 'The Royal Fencible Americans'. They were patterned on the regular Army but, like the militia, had no liability for foreign service.

Fear Naught Motto of the Royal Tank Corps and Royal Tank Regiment.

Fenian Raids At the end of the American Civil War many Irish soldiers who had been engaged in that war sought to challenge British authority in Canada, England and Ireland. A force of 'Fenians' under O'Neill invaded Canada from America, but were rapidly pushed back over the United States border, where many of them were arrested, by the Canadian Militia. A second raid into Canada by Fenians coincided with a rebellion by the self-styled 'General' Louis Reil, whose supporters occupied Fort Garry, imprisoned many residents and seized the Hudson Bay Company treasury. This raid also dissolved on the arrival of Imperial forces and Canadian Militia. Reil escaped, however, and was responsible for a second rebellion 15 years later. In Ireland the Fenians attempted a general uprising in 1867, but this was suppressed by the Irish Constabulary with little bloodshed. In England there was a Fenian plot to seize arms from Chester Castle, but this was frustrated by the treachery of one of the conspirators. There were also Fenian attacks on Manchester and Clerkenwell prisons.

Fern Leaf Symbol carried on all vehicles of the Queen's Royal Hussars (Queen's Own and Royal Irish) (qv) commemorating the association between 3rd Hussars and 2nd New Zealand Division at the Battle of El Alamein (qv). The honour was granted by General Lord Freyberg who commanded the New Zealand expeditionary forces in the Second World War.

Ferozeshah Battle honour marking the action at Ferozeshah on 21 December 1845 during the British conquest of the Punjab. The conquest of the Punjab took place in two distinct phases: the Sutlej campaign of 1845-46 and the other, better known, Punjab War of 1849. *See also: Moodkee; Aliwal; Sobraon; Chillianwallah; Mooltan; Gujerat and Punjab.*

Ferret Light wheeled armoured vehicle used primarily for reconnaissance and liaison. Developed by Daimler in response to a 1946 staff requirement, and brought into service in the early 1950s. The Mark IV Ferret has a crew of three, weighs some 4.4 tons, and mounts a 0.30" Browning machine gun or a 7.62mm general purpose machine gun. The Ferret Mark V carries four Swingfire anti-tank missiles in bins mounted on the turret.

Festoon An elaborately plaited cord across the front of shakos, particularly in cavalry regiments, which had two long cords with tassels attached to the body to prevent the headdress being lost.

Festubert 1914 First World War battle honour marking the repulse of a German attack on this village, which lies about two miles north-west of La Bassée, in late November 1914. *See also: France and Flanders 1914-1918; Givenchy 1914 and Neuve Chapelle.*

Festubert 1915 First World War battle honour marking a British attack in the Festubert sector in mid-May 1915. The battle lasted ten days with an advance of about 600m across the attack frontage. However, much of the ground gained was lost in subsequent German counter-attacks. *See also: France and Flanders 1914-1918; Ypres 1915; Aubers; Hooge 1915 and Loos.*

Feu de Joie A salute of small arms fire fired successively by each man in turn along the ranks and back again.

FH70 The FH70 gun is the result of a NATO collaborative project between Italy, Germany and Britain. Taken into service in the British Army in 1978, the gun is towed into action by the FH70 Foden 6x6 tractor and, in emergencies, can use a small Volkswagen petrol engine mounted on the gun to move short distances on the battlefield. The gun is of 155mm calibre and can fire high explosive, illuminating and smoke rounds. The FH70 has a crew of eight, and a maximum range of 24km.

Ficulle Second World War Italian campaign battle honour marking a sharp action against German rearguards on 15 June

1944 in the Italian campaign. *See also: Italy 1943-1945; Liri Valley; Rome; Citta Della Pieve and Capture of Perugia.*

Fide Et Fiducia (In faith and trust) Motto of the Royal Army Pay Corps.

Fieldcraft The movement and concealment skills employed in the field; associated with a deep understanding of terrain and vegetation.

Field Dressing Sterile wound dressing, sometimes referred to as the 'First Field Dressing'; smaller than the shell dressing (qv), it is issued to all members of the Army and always carried about the person during operations or exercises. Available as a dressing of first resort in the event of wounding. The first field dressings - a calico bandage, lint and pins - was issued in the Crimean War. The first antiseptic dressing was not issued until 1884.

Field General Court Martial *See: Court Martial.*

Field of Fire The area which a weapon or group of weapons may cover effectively with fire from a given position.

Field Marshal Highest rank attainable in the British Army. The rank is indicated by crossed batons within a wreath surmounted by a crown, worn on the shoulders. The rank had existed in the Prussian army as early as 1658, but was introduced into the British army by George II in 1736; the first British field marshals being both Scots, the Earl of Orkney and the Duke of Argyll. For a considerable period the appointment was considered of little significance and actually lapsed between 1773 and 1797. Field marshals are presented with a baton (qv) by the Sovereign as a symbol of their rank.

Field Officers In the British Army field officers are those above the rank of captain and below general officer rank. *See also: Rank.*

Fiesole Second World War Italian campaign battle honour marking a sharp action on 25 August 1944 in the hills north-east of Florence. *See also: Italy 1943-1945; Citta Di Castillo; Campriano; Poggio Del Grillo; Montorsoli; Ancona; Pian Di Maggio; Citerna and Gothic Line.*

Fife Musical instrument which, with the drum, usually formed the 'music' for a company between the 16th and 20th centuries. Only simple melodies can be executed on it and it is usual for members of the corps of drums of infantry and Foot Guards regiments to be able to play the bugle and fife in addition to the drum.

Fifeshire Yeomanry (The Fife and Forfar Yeomanry) The Kirkaldy Troop was formed in 1797 which amalgamated with the Fife Yeomanry Cavalry in 1803. The regiment was disbanded in 1828, re-raised in 1831 and again disbanded in 1838. In 1860 the Fife Volunteer Mounted Rifles was raised, later designated the Fife Light Horse and amalgamated with the Forfar Light Horse in 1901, together providing a company of 6th Battalion Imperial Yeomanry for the war in South Africa (1899-1902). In the First World War the regiment landed in Gallipoli 1915 and served there until transferred to Egypt in 1916. Redesignated 14th (Fife and Forfar Yeomanry) Battalion The Black Watch, the regiment fought in the Palestine campaign before being transferred to France in May 1918, serving there until the end of the war. Between the wars the Fife and Forfar Yeomanry served as the 20th Armoured Car Company, Royal Tank Corps, rapidly expanding in 1939 to form two divisional cavalry regiments equipped with light tanks and bren gun carriers for a reconnaissance role. The first regiment went to France in January 1940 and was recovered through Dunkirk. The second regiment landed in Normandy on 17 June 1944 and fought through Normandy to the Baltic. The Fife and Forfar Yeomanry was re-formed in 1947, amalgamated with the Scottish Horse in 1956 and the successor unit is 'C' (Fife & Forfar Yeomanry/Scottish Horse) Squadron, The Scottish Yeomanry.

Figaro Regimental slow march of the Coldstream Guards.

Fighting Fifth Nickname given to 5th Foot, the Royal Northumberland Fusiliers; now embodied in the Royal Regiment of Fusiliers. The name comes from a saying attributed to the Duke of Wellington, 'The Ever-Fighting, Never-Failing Fifth'.

Fighting Vehicle 432 (FV432) Tracked armoured personnel carrier, one of the FV430 series of vehicles. First introduced in 1962, the vehicle is now obsolescent and being replaced by the Warrior Mechanised Combat Vehicle (MCV) (qv). In the infantry variant the vehicle could carry ten fully-equipped men and mounted a 7.62mm general purpose machine gun. The FV432 was produced in four Marks, capable of fulfilling about 14 different roles, the most important being command post vehicle, mortar carrier, Wombat anti-tank gun carrier, ambulance and minelayer.

Fighting Patrol A tactical unit detached from the main body to engage in independent fighting or to protect the flanks or rear. Such patrols may be tasked to harass, ambush, attack or create a diversion, and the strength and weaponry will depend on the specific task given. *See also: Patrols.*

Fike Second World War Abyssinian campaign battle honour. *See also: Abyssinia 1940-41; Keren; Jebel Defeis; Jebel Shiba; Gogni; Agordat; Barentu; Karora-Marsa Taclai; Afodu; Gambela; Moyale; Wal Garis; Juba; Marda Pass; Babile Gap; Bisidimo; Awash; Todenyang-Namaraputh; Soroppa; Giarso; Colito; Wadara; Omo; Gondar; El Wak and Lechemti.*

Filo Second World War Italian campaign battle honour marking an action following the fall of Menate on 10 April 1945. The German rearguards were driven back in three days of fighting. *See also: Italy 1943-1945; Senio; Menate and Argenta Gap.*

Final Assault Position An area close to the objective where the assault troops, if not already so deployed, adopt their final assault formation.

Final Protective Fire (FPF) An immediately available, pre-arranged barrier of fire designed to impede enemy movement across defensive lines or areas.

Finial Term applied to the spearhead or crown on the staff or pike of a regimental Standard, Guidon or Colour.

Fire and Forget Term used for weapons which require no external guidance after launch, either because they are unguided or because they employ some form of autonomous guidance or homing.

Fire And Movement A tactical principle sometimes referred to as 'one foot on the ground'. When in contact, or likely to be in contact with an enemy, an element of the force should be static in a position from which it can provide intimate fire support to those other elements of the force which may be on the move.

Fire Support Co-ordination Line (FSCL) A line established by the appropriate ground commander, which forms the focus for the co-ordination of land/air operations, and is normally set at about the maximum reach of conventional ground weapons, including any naval gunfire support.

Fire Support Group (FSG) The group which provides intimate direct fire support onto the objective during an attack.

Fire Team One half of an infantry section, usually not less than a non-commissioned officer and three men.

Firm Motto of The Worcestershire and Sherwood Foresters Regiment, The Worcestershire Regiment and 36th (Herefordshire) Regiment of Foot.

First Aid Nursing Yeomanry (FANY) An unofficial organisation, recruited largely from volunteer ladies of gentle birth, formed in London in 1907 to provide a medical service for mounted troops and called the First Aid Nursing Yeomanry (FANY). Many volunteers served as ambulance drivers and nurses in the First World War and, in 1927, official, but unfunded, recognition was given to the corps. In 1937 the Nursing Yeomanry became part of the Women's Transport Service with units serving in India, Kenya and Britain.

First Army (Second World War) Raised in Britain in 1942 under the command of Lieutenant General K A N Anderson, it landed in French North Africa in the second week of November 1942. Of little more than divisional strength, the First Army advance on Tunis was checked by the Germans at Medjez on 6 December, and it did not enter Tunis until 7 May 1943. In July 1943 First Army was dispersed, most of its units being transferred to Eighth Army (qv).

First China War Medal 1840-1842 Awarded for service in the First China War or 'Opium War'.
Ribbon: Crimson with yellow edges. 1" wide.
See also: China - First China War.

First Light That time at the dawn of the day when there is sufficient light to make dismounted fighting possible without artificial light. The precise time of 'First Light' will vary according to capability of individual weapon systems.

First World War The origins of the First World War or 'Great War' may be found in the aggressive spirit of Germany, driven by Bismarck's creed of 'Blood and Iron', and her rivalry with Britain for maritime and commercial supremacy; the deep-rooted hostility between France and Germany and the rivalry between Austria and Prussia for influence in the Balkans. The traditional balance of power had been lost and Europe was split into two opposing camps; the Triple Alliance of Germany, Austria and Italy (although Italy broke the alliance and attacked Austria in 1915), and the Triple Entente of Russia, France and Britain. The 'Agadir Incident' of 1911 fuelled German resentment, and the murder of the Austrian Archduke Franz Ferdinand on 28 June 1914 triggered mobilisation in Europe.

On Sunday 2 August 1914 orders for mobilisation were issued in Britain and, on Tuesday 4 August 1914 a state of war came into existence between Britain and Germany. The rapid fall of Belgium exposed the French left flank and the small British Expeditionary Force (qv) under Sir John French (qv) took up position on the French left flank near to Mons on 22 August, making contact with the Germans on the following day. On 22 August the French Fifth Army had been attacked at Charleroi and fallen back in confusion. A breach was thus opened in the French line and, on the same day, the French Fourth and Third armies to the East also withdrew leaving the British isolated against a hugely superior German force. Learning of the French withdrawal Sir John French ordered the evacuation of Mons (qv) and by nightfall on 25 August the British had reached a line Mariolles, Landrecies, Le Cateau (qv) to Serainvilliers near Cambrai, re-establishing links with the French. The British lines of communication to and through the channel ports were under threat from the rapid German advance and, by 5 September, the British were firm behind the Grand Morin river due east of Paris. General Joffre launched his counter-attack, which developed into the First Battle of the Marne (qv) and by mid-September the Germans had been driven back to a line running from the Oise beyond Compiègne to the Aisne, along that river to Berry-au-Bac, and across Champagne and the Argonne to Verdun.

The Germans having been checked and the Allies unable to dislodge the Germans from the high ground along the River Aisne (qv), the lines now stabilised between Rheims and the Alps and, all the principles of war being set aside, trench warfare began. Early in October the British army was transferred to Flanders, close to its bases, to meet the German threat to the channel ports. The struggle which then followed, which had begun as attempts at out-flanking movements on both sides, developed into a 'race to the coast' to establish the final position at the most favourable possible point. On 28 September 1914 the Germans began the siege of Antwerp, which was evacuated and fell on 10 October. The Germans advanced, but with immense difficulty because the Belgians opened the sluices of

the River Yser, to Dixmude but were unable to cross the River Yser. At the same time fierce fighting was taking place around Arras and Ypres (qv). The final German attack on Ypres began on 20 October, but with the arrival on 17 November of French reinforcements, the Germans broke off their attempt to breach the line and the principles of war were set aside for a campaign of trench warfare and attrition on a line running Ostend, Armentières, Douai, Saint Quentin, Rheims, Verdun and Saint Mihiel to Lunéville.

Meanwhile, on the Eastern front the Russian advance into East Prussia, which for a time even threatened Berlin, was halted when the Russians were decisively beaten at Tannenberg on 31 August 1914 and later at the Masurian Lakes. The Germans advanced on Warsaw, but further south a Russian advance in Galicia drove back the Austrians.

Turkey, which had been drawn into the war on the German side in November 1914, was threatening British interests in the Near and Middle East. The Turks entered in Egypt in February 1915, seeking to secure the Suez Canal, but by September 1918 had been repulsed and driven back through Sinai and Palestine (qv) to be destroyed at Megiddo (qv). Britain was also obliged to engage the Turks or their agents in Mesopotamia (qv) and Persia (qv) to protect oil interests. In an attempt to defeat Turkey and protect the Russian flank a landing was made on the Gallipoli (qv) peninsula in April 1915 following unsuccessful naval attempts to pass through the Dardanelles. However the campaign in Gallipoli was unsuccessful and the force was withdrawn in December 1915. Unsuccessful Austro-Hungarian attempts to occupy Serbia and Montenegro in 1914 were followed by these countries being overrun in 1915 by the Bulgarians, who had joined the German side in October 1915.

Britain's first offensive of 1915 on the Western front was at Neuve Chapelle (qv) in March; countered by the major German offensive of the year, the second battle of Ypres (qv), which started on 27 April and was to last for a month during which the

Germans employed chlorine gas and flamethrowers. The main British offensive of 1915 was launched in September at Loos (qv) in the flat coal-mining district south of the La Bassée canal. No major advances were made by either side during 1915; certainly the gains could not compensate for the massive casualties suffered during the year. In December 1915 Sir John French was replaced as commander of the British Expeditionary Force by Sir Douglas Haig (qv).

After denouncing its partnership in the Triple Alliance, and being promised significant territorial gains, Italy entered the war on the Allied side in May 1915. Austro-Italian fighting on the Isonzo River was inconclusive until late 1917, when the Italians were routed at Caporetto *(See: Italy 1917-18)*, and Italy became a liability rather than an asset to the Allies.

Except for the conquest of most of Germany's overseas colonies *(See: East Africa 1914-18, Tsingtao, Cameroons 1914-16 and South West Africa 1914)* by the British and Japanese, 1916 opened with a dark outlook for the allies. On 1 July 1916 the great British offensive of the Somme (qv) was launched on a 15-mile front, lasting for four months with only meagre gains and huge casualties. A major German offensive had been launched in February 1916 against the French at Verdun, but by December 1916 a French counter-offensive broadly restored the situation to what it had been in January 1916. Portugal and Rumania had joined the Allies in 1916, and Greece had been drawn into the war by the Allied campaign in Salonika *(See: Macedonia 1915-18)* which began in October 1915.

In March 1917 the Germans withdrew from the large salient they had established just north of the Somme battlefields to their new defensive positions on the Hindenburg Line. British forces following up the withdrawing Germans were engaged in some brisk fighting near Bapaume (qv). A major British offensive, on a front extending for 14 miles southwards from Vimy Ridge, was launched at Arras (qv) on 9 April 1917 and fighting continued until 4 May with some useful gains being made. A further British offen-sive, officially called the 'Third Battle of Ypres', but more often referred to by its closing phase at 'Passchendaele', was launched on 31 July 1917 and lasted until 10 November. At the end of the offensive the greatest gain was about five miles, gained at the cost of some 300,000 casualties. However, the United States entered the war on 6 April 1917, opening up their almost unlimited industrial and manpower resources, which were to be decisive in winning the war. The first troops of the American Expeditionary Force arrived in France in June 1917. Before the year closed the British were to launch one final offensive at Cambrai (qv) in the Southern sector of their front, on 20 November. Although the opening phase met with considerable success, German counter-attacks had virtually restored their line by 30 November.

On 21 March 1918 the Germans mounted a major attack on the Somme (qv) against the British Fifth Army and the right flank of Third Army. When the German advance was finally halted on 5 April they had gained as much as 40 miles in some areas. The Germans launched two further offensives in 1918: at Lys (qv) on 9 April and against the French in the Chemin des Dames sector, which also involved four British divisions sent there for a rest in the battle of Aisne (qv). Much of the territory captured by the Germans in the Somme offensive of March-April was recovered and the Hindenburg Line breached during the second battle of the Somme (qv) which began at Amiens on 8 August 1918 and was the major British offensive of the year. On 4 November 1918 the final stage of the British offensives, attacking German defences astride the River Sambre (qv), was launched by First, Third and Fourth Armies. By last light the advance had covered five miles and the Germans were in full retreat.

Bulgaria capitulated on 30 September, Turkey concluded an armistice on 30 October, Austria-Hungary, in a state of dis-integration, surrendered on 4 November and Germany, her manpower and material resources exhausted, morale collapsed and a political revolution on her hands, signed the armistice on 11 November 1918. The war ended without a truly decisive battle having been fought and with Germany still in possession of territory from France to the Crimea. A precise figure has not been given, but it is believed that a conservative estimate of the total losses attributable to the war were some 10 million dead and 20 million wounded. *See also: France and Flanders 1914-1918; Egypt 1915-1917; Palestine 1917-1918; Mesopotamia 1914-1918; Persia 1915-1919; Gallipoli 1915-1916; Macedonia 1915-1918; Italy 1917-1918; Aden; Tsingtao; East Africa 1914-1918; Cameroons 1914-1916; SW Africa 1914; NW Frontier; India 1914-15 and 1916-17; Baluchistan; Archangel 1918-1919; Troitsa; Murmansk 1918-1919; Siberia 1918-1919 and Dukhovskaya.*

FIRST WORLD WAR MEDALS

1914 Star Authorised in April 1917 for those who served in France or Belgium between 5 August and midnight on 22 November 1914.
Ribbon: Red, white and blue, shaded and watered.
Clasp: 5TH AUG-22ND NOV. 1914.

1914-1915 Star Sanctioned in 1918 for issue to all who saw service in any theatre of the war, including the North-West Frontier in 1915, but not those who saw service where the Africa General Service (qv) or Sudan 1910 (qv) medal was granted.
Ribbon: Red, White and blue, shaded and watered.

British War Medal 1914-1920 Although the award is dated 1914-1918 the period was extended to 1920 to include operations in various parts of Russia.
Ribbon: A broad orange watered centre flanked on each side by vertical white, black and blue stripes.

Victory Medal 1914-1918 Awarded to all who had received either of the Stars and, with a few exceptions, the War Medal.
Ribbon: 1.55" wide; rainbow pattern with the colours merging. From the centre working out to each edge they are; red, yellow, green, blue and violet.

Territorial Force War Medal 1914-1919 Authorised in April 1920 for members of the Territorial Force, including nursing sisters, who, on or before 30 September 1914, undertook to serve abroad, did so between the outbreak of war and the armistice, and were not eligible for either the 1914 or 1914-15 Star.
Ribbon: Watered yellow with a green vertical stripe 4mm wide a similar distance from each edge.

Fishguard Battle honour awarded to the Pembroke Yeomanry (qv) in 1853 to mark the defeat of the French landing at Fishguard in 1767. It is alleged that the French mistook the red cloaks of the Welsh women on the cliffs for the red coats of British soldiers.

Fish Tail Term given to the black ribbons, sometimes cut with a V-shaped notch, on the back of Scottish Headdress. The term is also applied to garter flashes worn under the turned down tops of hose or hose tops and similarly notched.

Flail Rotating cylinder mounted on the front of a vehicle, usually tracked, and fitted with heavy duty chains which 'flail' the ground ahead of the vehicle as it advances, detonating mines and thus clearing a lane through any minefield.

Flak Jacket Armoured jacket offering some protection for the upper part of the body against small arms and fragmentation weapons.

Flame-Thrower First used by the Germans against the French in 1915. The first British flame-throwing system was devised by Captain Vincent of the Corps of Royal Engineers, but was cumbersome, dangerous to the operator and of limited range. An improved design was produced by Captain Livens and, by the Second World War, this had been developed in both a man-pack form and into Crocodile, a trailer-borne, napalm-based system towed behind a Churchill tank.

Flamers, The Nickname given the 54th Foot, later 2nd Battalion The Dorset Regiment, now embodied in the Devonshire and Dorset Regiment. In September 1781 the 54th Foot was part of a force which captured the privateer base of New London. After a fierce fight the force burnt the town and a number of ships in the harbour.

Flank Company Term derived from the old flank companies, which were sometimes grenadier or light companies, and still used by some regiments of Foot Guards to describe two (Left Flank and Right Flank) of the companies in a battalion.

Flank Guard A security force operating to the flank of moving or stationary forces to protect it from enemy ground observation, direct fire or surprise attack.

Flanker Soldiers' slang for a ploy designed to avoid an unpleasant duty: 'to work a flanker'. The term is drawn from the tactical manoeuvre used to circumvent enemy positions.

Flannelette Cotton imitation of flannel. In the Army more usually associated with the cleaning of small arms and issued in rolls 4" wide and marked off at 2" intervals by red stripes. A piece of 'Four by Two' is used to clean the barrel of a rifle.

Flap-Cuff Term applied to those turned back cuffs which had been slit and were held in place by an upright 'flap' or piece of cloth.

Flash Term given to the ends of the ribbon which kept the queue in order and the associated dressing off the uniform; retained by the Royal Welch Fusiliers.

Flash to Bang The time between seeing the flash of an explosion and hearing the same explosion, caused by the difference between the speed of light and sound. The term is also used to describe the time between an order or idea and its realisation or, in an unflattering manner, the time taken for an individual to comprehend an idea, concept or order.

Flaskcord The cord used by cavalry which passed over the shoulder and held the powder flask.

Flechette Small dart-like projectiles designed to produce maximum wounding effect on human targets. Flechettes may be fired singly from small arms, cased in a small sabot which is discarded in flight, or in clusters from shells or bombs.

Flers-Courcelette First World War battle honour marking the British drive towards the third line of German defences to the left of Delville Wood in mid-September 1916. Tanks were used for the first time, but their mechanical unreliability and inadequate numbers meant that they did not have significant impact on the action. *See also: France and Flanders 1914-1918; Somme 1916; Albert 1916; Bazentin; Delville Wood; Pozières; Guillemont; Ginchy; Morval; Thiepval; Le Transloy; Ancre Heights and Ancre 1916.*

Fleur-de-Lys This emblem from the French coat-of-arms is part of the drummers' lace in regiments of the Foot Guards.

Flight Sub-unit of the Army Air Corps, a squadron being composed of a number of flights.

Flintlock The flintlock dates from about 1640, gradually replacing the matchlock (qv), and is probably of Italian origin; the wheel-lock and the Dutch *Snaphans-lock* (Snaphaunce) being developed in parallel. While the true flintlock was in use on cavalry pistols and carbines during and after the Civil War, rearmament, so far as the standing Army was concerned, did not actually take place until the 1730s, when the old matchlocks and doglocks of the Cromwellian era were superseded by the traditional 'Brown Bess' (qv) flintlock. Although in common use in civilian life, the percussion system did not enter Army service until the formation of the 'Experimental Corps of Riflemen' (later the Rifle Brigade) in 1800, and was used by them in the Peninsula War. Total rearmament of the Army did not take place until the issue of the Enfield of 1854. *See also: Matchlock; Snaphaunce; Musket and Rifle.*

Flintshire Yeomanry Cavalry This corps was raised in 1831 by Lord George

Grosvenor and, although only in existence for seven years, found four well-recruited troops at Eaton Hall, Mold Hawarden and Holywell. The county name reappears in 1967 in association with the Denbighshire Yeomanry. *See also: Denbighshire Yeomanry.*

Flotation The movement of vehicles or equipment across a water obstacle made possible by the provision of additional buoyancy. In the case of vehicles the means for providing such buoyancy comes in the form of 'Flotation Kits'.

Flushing Second World War battle honour marking an action during operations for the clearance of the Scheldt estuary. Flushing was captured after four days' fighting on 4 November 1944. *See also: North West Europe 1944-1945; Scheldt; Walcheren Causeway; Westkapelle and South Beveland.*

Fly Plaid Plaid attached to the left shoulder and allowed to hang freely down the back.

Fondouk Second World War North Africa campaign battle honour marking Anglo-American operations aimed at breaking through the Fondouk Pass towards Kairouan in early April 1943. *See also: North Africa 1940-1943; Kairouan; Bordj; Pichon; Djebel El Rhorab; Fondouk Pass and Sidi Ali.*

Fondouk Pass Second World War North Africa campaign battle honour marking an action during Anglo-American operations aimed at breaking through the Fondouk Pass in early April 1943. *See also: North Africa 1940-1943; Kairouan; Bordj; Pichon; Djebel El Rhorab; Fondouk and Sidi Ali.*

Fontenay Le Pesnil Second World War battle honour marking the capture of Fontenay le Pesnil, necessary to cover the right flank of the British offensive across the River Odon in June 1944 following the Allied landings in Normandy in June 1944. *See also: North West Europe 1944-1945; Normandy Landing; Villers Bocage; Tilly Sur Seulles; Odon; Cheux; Defence of Rauray and Caen.*

Foot Term applied to the infantry; as opposed to 'Horse' (cavalry). It was usual for infantry regiments to be referred to as 'regiments of foot'.

Forage Cap Soldier's undress cap originally introduced for wear on foraging expeditions, now worn on undress occasions. In 1898 a broad topped peaked cap, based on the naval pattern and called a forage cap, was introduced as a trial and set the basic design of the present forage cap.

Forced March A march in which other considerations may be subordinated to the need for speed.

Foreman of Signals Foremen of Signals are selected from the Technicians Group, less the mechanics, of the Royal Corps of Signals (qv), and are the senior non-commissioned engineers of that corps. Their primary functions are: the supervision and control of the servicing, repair and specification of Royal Signals telecommunications equipment; to plan and control workshop facilities, maintenance systems, power supplies and to supervise equipment installation programmes. Foremen of Signals also plan and supervise signals projects including specifications and financial estimates, and organise 'on the job' training for tradesmen in the technicians group. The title Foreman of Signals was certainly in use by June 1921, but may have been in use before that date.

Forester Brigade An administrative grouping in the infantry formed under Army Order 61 of 1948 comprising: the Royal Warwickshire, (to Fusilier Brigade in 1963); Royal Lincolnshire (to East Anglian Brigade in 1957); Royal Leicestershire (to East Anglian Brigade in 1963); and Sherwood Foresters (to Mercian Brigade in 1962) Regiments. The Forester Brigade was retitled from the previous Midland Brigade in 1962 and dispersed in 1963. The regiments of the brigade were absorbed into the Queen's Division (qv) in 1968.

Forêt De Bretonne Second World War battle honour marking one of the actions which took place between the Allied landings in Normandy in 1944 and the crossing of the River Seine. *See also: North West Europe 1944-1945; Port-en-Bessin; Tourmauville Bridge; St Pierre la Veille; Estry; Noireau Crossing; La Vie Crossing; La Touques Crossing and Risle Crossing.*

Forêt De Nieppe Second World War battle honour marking an action in France during the campaign of 1940 which culminated in the withdrawal through Dunkirk. *See also: North West Europe 1940; Amiens 1940; Arras Counter Attack; French Frontier 1940; Withdrawal to Seine and Withdrawal to Cherbourg.*

Forgotten Army *See: Fourteenth Army.*

Forlorn Hope A small party of volunteers which formed the point or vanguard of a storming party. Successful leadership of a forlorn hope was one of the few ways in which an officer of slender means could catch the eye of the commander and thus advance his career.

Formation Formal grouping of units such as corps, divisions and brigades.

Forming Up Place (FUP) The last position held by an assaulting echelon before it crosses the line of departure (qv). Also called the 'attack position'.

Fort Dufferin Second World War Burma campaign battle honour marking actions between 9 and 20 March 1945 leading to the capture of Mandalay. *See also: Burma 1942-1945; Mandalay; Myitson; Ava; Myinmu Bridgehead and Maymyo.*

Fort McGregor Second World War North Africa campaign battle honour marking one of the actions which took place between the Kasserine and Fondouk operations, February to April 1943. *See also: North Africa 1940-1943; El Hadjeba; Djebel Djaffa; Sidi Nsir; Stuka Farm; Steamroller Farm; Montagne Farm; Kef Ouiba Pass; Djebel Guerba; Sedjenane I; Maknassy; Djebel Dahra; Kef El Debna and Djebel Choucha.*

Forth To The Battle One of the regimental slow marches of the Royal Welch Fusiliers.

Fortification The art or science of fortifying places in order to defend them against an enemy. Fortifications may be divided into three broad groups: permanent, semipermanent (when conflict seems imminent), and field fortifications which are peculiar to a specific battle or campaign.

Forward Air Controller (FAC) An officer, warrant officer or senior non-commissioned officer tasked with the direction of close air support (qv) sorties on to their selected targets and, if necessary, marking such targets during the attack. Forward air controllers may be on foot, vehicle mounted, or light aircraft- or helicopter-borne depending upon the situation.

Forward Arming And Refuelling Point An installation forward in the combat zone (qv) at which helicopters are rearmed and refuelled.

Forward Edge of the Battle Area (FEBA) Term used to describe the foremost limits of a series of areas in which ground combat units are deployed; excluding the areas in which covering or screen forces are operating. A wide and precise understanding of the location of the forward edge of the battle area is fundamental to the co-ordination of fire support and positioning of forces or manoeuvre units.

Forward Line Own Troops (FLOT) A line indicating the most forward positions of friendly forces in any kind of military operation at a specific time.

Forward Observation Officer (FOO) An officer, warrant officer or senior non-commissioned officer from a supporting fire unit, who moves with the forward elements of the force being supported in order to assist with the observation and direction of fire support. It is usual for the forward observation officer to be in communication with both the supporting fire unit and the unit being supported.

Forward Operating Base (FOB) A location in the combat zone (qv) which offers the full range of infrastructure and facilities for the planning, command and support of helicopter operations.

Forward Slope Any slope which descends towards the enemy and on which positions are therefore exposed to direct fire and observed indirect fire. *See also: Reverse Slope.*

Fossa Combalina Second World War Italian campaign battle honour marking an action during the Argenta Gap battle 13-21 April 1945. *See also: Italy 1943-1945; Argenta Gap and San Nicolo Canal.*

Fossacesia Second World War battle honour marking an action during the Battle of the Sangro 19 November - 3 December 1943. *See also: Italy 1943-1945; Sangro; Mozzagrogna and Romagnoli.*

Fourteenth Army (Second World War) Sometimes known as the 'Forgotten Army' because of the nation's apparent preoccupation with Italy and North-West Europe, Fourteenth Army was formed in 1943 from India's Eastern Army. It contained British, Indian, Gurkha, West and East African, and Burmese troops. Commanded by Lieutenant General W J Slim, it was the principal Allied fighting formation in the Burma campaign. The 'Chindits' (qv) were part of Fourteenth Army. The Fourteenth Army was commanded by General Sir Miles Dempsey from September 1945 until it disbanded in December 1946.

Fox Light four-wheeled armoured reconnaissance vehicle developed by Daimler from the smaller Ferret (qv). Brought into service in 1973 for the reconnaissance platoons of infantry battalions and UK-based armoured reconnaissance regiments. Fox has a crew of three, weighs some 6.12 tons. and mounts a 30mm Rarden cannon and a 7.62mm general purpose machine gun.

Foxhole Individual trench or scrape hastily dug to provide a level of protection against hostile fire.

Fragmentary Orders An abbreviated form of operation order issued as required, which eliminates the need to restate information contained in a basic operation order. Such orders may be issued in sections and are well-suited to fast moving situations.

France and Flanders 1914-18 First World War (qv) campaign honour awarded to 115 British and seven Indian Army regiments.

Francofonte Second World War Sicilian campaign battle honour. *See also: Sicily 1943; Landing in Sicily; Primosole Bridge; Sferro; Regalbuto; Centuripe; Solarino; Vizzini; Augusta; Lentini; Simeto Bridgehead; Gerbini; Agira; Adrano; Sferro Hills; Salso Crossing; Simeto Crossing; Monte Rivoglia; Malleto and Pursuit to Messina.*

Freedom Honour bestowed by the a civic authority on a regiment or corps expressing a special relationship between the authority and the regiment. The granting of the freedom permits a regiment to march through the city, borough or town with 'Colours flying, band playing and bayonets fixed', a right which the regiment exercises periodically.

Free Runner Term used to describe a vehicle or vehicles taking part in a planned move, but proceeding independently rather than in convoy.

French, John Denton Pinkstone, 1st Earl of Ypres (1852-1925) Born Ripple, Kent and educated at Harrow and Eastman's Naval Academy, Portsmouth. Having joined HMS *Britannia* and served in the Royal Navy for four years, he was commissioned into 8th Hussars in 1874, soon transferring to 19th Hussars; he took part in the Sudan campaign (1884-85), and was present at Abu Klea (qv), Gubut and Metammah. He fought with distinction in South Africa, and in 1900 was appointed to command of East Transvaal, and took part in the operations against the rebels in Cape Colony until the end of the war. He commanded 1st Army Corps at Aldershot from 1901 to 1907 and was made field marshal in 1913, being appointed commander-in-chief of the

British Expeditionary Force (qv) at the beginning of the First World War. His failure, at Neuve Chapelle and Loos in 1915, to pierce the German line was very costly, and he was recalled and given command of all the forces in the United Kingdom. He was created Viscount in 1916 and Earl of Ypres in 1921.

French and American Indian War (1754-60) The last of a series of American wars between France and Britain, the French being assisted by several American Indian tribes. The principle events were the capitulation of Washington and Fort Necessity in 1754, Braddock's defeat in 1755, the capture of Oswego and Fort William Henry by General Montcalm 1756-57 and the surrender of Montreal in 1760. *See also: Ticonderoga; Niagara and Quebec.*

French Frontier 1940 Second World War battle honour marking an action in France during the campaign of 1940 which culminated in the withdrawal through Dunkirk. *See also: North West Europe 1940; Amiens 1940; Arras Counter Attack; Forêt de Nieppe; Withdrawal to Seine and Withdrawal to Cherbourg.*

Frezenberg First World War battle honour marking one of the actions during the Second Battle of Ypres April-May 1915. *See also: France and Flanders 1914-1918; Ypres 1915; Gravenstafel; St Julien and Bellewaarde.*

Frisoni Second World War Italian campaign battle honour marking an action during the break-through of the Rimini Line 14-21 September 1944. *See also: Italy 1943-1945; Rimini Line; Ceriano Ridge; Monte Colombo; Casa Fabri Ridge; Montescudo and San Marino.*

Frizzen Rough surface from which the flintlock (qv) struck sparks. When the trigger was squeezed the armature holding the flint struck downward against the curved frizzen.

Frock Long skirted coat, from the French *froc*, worn by officers for undress occasions.

Subsequently it became shorter, but has remained an essentially simple garment.

Frog A loop or other attachment on the belt to hold the scabbard of a sword or bayonet. Also, a decorative fastening of looped braid or cord.

Frogging Collective term for the ornamental frogs on uniforms.

Front The total area in which opposing armies face each other. Alternatively, the lateral space in which a military unit or formation is operating i.e. to advance on a broad front, or the direction in which troops are facing when in a formed line.

Front Line That part of a force nearest the enemy.

Fuentes d'Onor Battle honour marking the battle between the forces of Wellington and Masséna which took place 3-5 May 1811 during the Peninsula War (qv). *See also: Peninsula; Douro; Talavera; Busaco; Barrosa; Albuhera; Arroyo Dos Molinos; Tarifa and Ciudad Rodrigo.*

Fuka Second World War North Africa campaign battle honour marking an action which took place in the period between the British withdrawal from Agedabia in April 1941 and subsequent occupation of the El Alamein Line. *See also: North Africa 1940-1943; Msus; Benghazi; Carmusa; Mersa Matruh; Point 174 and Minqar Qaim.*

Fuka Airfield Second World War North Africa campaign battle honour marking an action during the defence of the El Alamein Line 1-27 July 1942. *See also: North Africa 1940-1943; Defence of Alamein Line; Ruweisat; Deir El Shein; Point 93 and Ruweisat Ridge.*

Fuller, John Frederick Charles, Major General (1878-1966) British 20th century military philosopher. He achieved particular recognition for his views on the development of tanks. Fuller was commissioned into the Oxfordshire & Buckinghamshire Light Infantry and served in the South Africa War 1899-1902, in which he led an anti-guerilla force, and the First World War. It was mainly through his energetic advocacy and the part he played in the employment of tanks in the First World War that they became a success so soon after their first large-scale employment at Cambrai (qv). His work *Tanks in the Great War, 1914-18 (1920)*, reveals the grasp he had on the potential of these fighting vehicles. His other works include: *British Light Infantry in the Eighteenth Century (1925); Foundations of the Science of War (1926); The Generalship Of Ulysses Grant (1929); War and Western Civilisation 1832-1932 (1932); The Army in My Time (1935); Towards Armageddon (1937); Armaments and History (1946); The Second World War 1939-45 (1948); Decisive Battles of the Western World (1954); The Conduct of War 1789-1961(1961); and Julius Caesar (1965)*.

Funk Hole Soldiers' slang for the dugout or trench to which he withdraws in case of sudden attack.

Furniture Term originally applied to the full armour, trappings etc., for man and horse. Now more usually applied to the ceremonial harness for horses. The term is also applied to the non-metallic parts of weapons, especially small arms.

Fuse A lead of combustible material in a waterproof covering (safety fuse), or a lead containing explosive material in a waterproof covering (detonating fuse), used to fire an explosive charge.

Fusiliers Originally soldiers armed with a 'fusil', a firearm with a flintlock introduced to replace the matchlock. The term Fusilier is now used to denote a private soldier in the Royal Regiment of Fusiliers, Royal Welch Fusiliers and Royal Highland Fusiliers.

Fusilier Brigade An administrative grouping in the infantry formed in 1957 comprising The Royal Northumberland Fusiliers (from Yorkshire Brigade), Royal Fusiliers (from Home Counties Brigade), Royal Warwickshire Fusiliers (from Forester Brigade in 1963) and the Lancashire Fusiliers (from Lancastrian Brigade). The regiments of the brigade were absorbed into the Queen's Division in 1968.

Future Family of Light Armoured Vehicles (FFLAV) Generic term for the new family of light armoured vehicles, still at the design stage, due to replace the present range over the next ten years.

Gabbiano Second World War Italian campaign battle honour marking an action which took place in the Fifth Army sector between the fall of Rome and the establishment of contact with the Gothic Line positions in the period May - August 1944. *See also: Italy 1943-1945; Monte Rotondo; Monte Gabbione; Ripa Ridge and Arezzo.*

Gab Gab Gap Second World War North Africa campaign battle honour marking a subsidiary action in the battle of Medjez Plain 23-30 April 1943. *See also: North Africa 1940-1943; Medjez Plain; Gueriat El Atach Ridge; Longstop Hill 1943; Grich El Oued; Peter's Corner; Si Mediene; Si Abdallah; Sidi Ahmed and Djebel Bou Aoukaz 1943.*

Gabr El Fachri Second World War North Africa campaign battle honour marking an action during the battle of Gazala 26 May - 21 June 1942. *See also: North Africa 1940-1943; Gazala; Bir El Igela; Hagiag Er Raml; Via Balbia; Zt El Mrasses and Sidi Rezegh 1942.*

Gabr Saleh Second World War North Africa campaign battle honour marking an action in the Battle of Tobruk in November 1941. *See also: North Africa 1940-1943; Tobruk 1941; Gubi I; Sidi Rezegh 1941; Tobruk Sortie; Omars; Belhamed; Taieb El Essem; Gubi II and Relief of Tobruk.*

Gaiana Crossing Second World War Italian campaign battle honour marking an action by Fifth Army against German positions in the Bologna area over the period 14-21 April 1945. *See also: Italy 1943-1945; Bologna; Medicina; Sillaro Crossing and Idice Bridgehead.*

Gaiters Buttoned covering of leather, cloth, canvas or other material for the lower leg, worn in the 17th century to protect soldiers' hose. In 1862, short leather gaiters were introduced for the infantry, these were replaced by puttees (qv) and, just before the Second World War, by canvas gaiters or anklets.

Gaiter Trousers Early form of tight-fitting infantry trousers which finished with buttons on the lower leg.

Gallipoli 1915-16 First World War campaign honour marking the assault on the Gallipoli peninsula. The immediate purpose of the attack on the Dardanelles was to force the straits in order to inflict a defeat on the Turks on such a scale as to relieve pressure on Russia and deter Bulgaria from active adherence to the cause of the Central Powers. It was resolved to send a force to co-operate with the fleet. This force, it was hoped, would land on the European side of the peninsula, storm Gaba Tepe and Achi Baba and thereby facilitate the task of the ships in running the 40 mile gauntlet of the straits.

In the last week of April 1915 two divisions of the Australian Imperial force and troops of the 29th Division effected a landing, against intense opposition, at Helles and at Anzac Cove, some 15 miles north of Cape Helles. A French brigade landed at Kum Kale on the Adriatic Coast. Following the landings, it was decided to make a combined advance from both the south and west, the objective being the commanding height at Achi Baba. Bloody fighting, without any significant territorial gain, followed in May, June and July with additional Turkish and British reinforcements arriving in theatre.

A new plan was developed to land forces at Suvla Bay, and by a combined advance from there, and from Anzac Cove, on the heights of Sari Bair, to cut Turkish communications on the Gallipoli peninsula. The operation began on 6 August and, although the heights were reached, casualties were extremely heavy and Turkish counter-attacks managed to recover much of the key terrain. However, far more casualties occurred through dysentery, lack of water and the general disorganisation of support services than through fighting. The attempt to clear the European side of the straits was abandoned; the troops dug in and months of testing trench warfare followed until the Allies withdrew in January 1916. The campaign was a disaster and nothing of significance was achieved. The career of the British commander Hamilton was irreparably damaged; the Allies suffered some 265,000 casualties and the Turks 300,000. *See also: Helles; Landing at Helles; Krithia; Anzac; Landing at Anzac; Defence of Anzac; Suvla; Sari Bair; Landing at Suvla and Scimitar Hill.*

Gambela Second World War Abyssinian campaign battle honour awarded to units operating in support of the Abyssinian insurgents in conjunction with the Sudan Defence Force. *See also: Abyssinia 1940-41; Keren; Jebel Defeis; Jebel Shiba; Gogni; Agordat; Barentu; Karora-Marsa Taclai; Cubcub; Ad Teclesan; Mescelit Pass; Mt Engiahat; Massawa; Amb Alagi; Afodu; El Wak; Moyale; Wal Garis; Juba; Marda Pass; Babile Gap; Bisidimo; Awash; Todenyang-Namaraputh; Soroppa; Giarso; Colito; Wadara; Omo; Gondar; Fike and Lechemti.*

Garb Of Old Gaul Regimental slow march of The Scots Dragoon Guards, The Queen's Royal Hussars, Scots Guards, The Royal Scots, The Royal Highland Fusiliers, The King's Own Scottish Borderers, The Black Watch, The Queen's Own Highlanders, The Gordon Highlanders, The Highlanders (Seaforth, Gordons and Camerons), The Argyll and Sutherland Highlanders, the Scottish Yeomanry and The Royal Gurkha Rifles.

Garigliano Crossing Second World War Italian campaign battle honour marking an action during operations against the western sector of the Gustav Line 17-31 January 1944. *See also: Italy 1943-1945; Minturno; Damiano; Monte Tuga and Monte Ornito.*

Garryowen Regimental quick march of the Ulster Defence Regiment.

Garter Early gaiters (qv) needed a garter to prevent them slipping down. These were made of leather or stout cloth and buckled. Garters disappeared from about 1823 when trousers replaced breeches. Drum majors in the Foot Guards in full dress still wear white gaiters and garters.

Garter Flash Coloured tapes, sometimes with ornamental or fish-tail (qv) ends which protrude below the turned-down top of the hose. Also worn with hosetops in tropical dress.

Garua First World War Cameroons campaign battle honour marking the action when Garua, in the north-west of the country, was reached after much bush fighting on 31 May 1915 and fell ten days later. *See also: Cameroons 1914-16; Duala and Banyo.*

Gas *See: Chemical Warfare.*

Gaudeamus Igitur One of the regimental quick marches of the Royal Army Educational Corps and the Educational and Training Services Branch of the Adjutant General's Corps.

Gauntlet Leather glove with large stiff leather cuff attached. Worn originally by heavy cavalry as a protection against edged weapons. Now a feature of cavalry full dress and also worn by Army motor cyclists, infantry pioneers and some musicians.

Gauntlet-Cuff The cuff on a Scottish doublet which is open to the rear.

Gaza First World War Palestine campaign battle honour marking an action during the campaign in Palestine when British forces forced a Turkish withdrawal from their positions at Gaza in late 1918. *See also: Palestine 1917-18; El Mughar; Nebi Samwil; Jaffa; Jerusalem; Jericho; Tell Asur; Jordan; Megiddo; Sharon; Nablus and Damascus.*

Gazala Second World War North Africa campaign marking the fighting in North Africa which took place between the launching of the first German attacks on the British Gazala Line positions on 26 May 1942 until 21 June when the defeated British forces withdrew over the Egyptian border and Tobruk had fallen. *See also: North Africa 1940-1943; Retma; Bir El Aslagh; Bir Hacheim; Cauldron; Knightsbridge and Tobruk 1942.*

Gazelle Light helicopter produced by Westland Aircraft Ltd/Aerospatiale in service with the Army since 1974 for observation, training and communications. There is also provision for the fitting of anti-tank missiles, rocket pods and machine guns. Capable of carrying three passengers or about 500kg of cargo at a cruising speed of 120 knots over a range of about 469 miles.

Gazette *See: London Gazette.*

Geilenkirchen Second World War battle honour marking the capture of the town and the exploitation beyond over the period 18-23 November 1944 during the campaign in North-West Europe. *See also: North West Europe 1944-1945; Lower Maas; Meijel; Venlo Pocket; Ourthe; Roer; Zetten and Rhineland.*

Gelib Second World War Abyssinian campaign battle honour marking an action during General Cunningham's drive north from Kenya, crossing of the River Juba and seizure of Kismayu in Italian Somaliland in February 1941. *See also: Abyssinia 1940-41; Keren; Jebel Defeis; Jebel Shiba; Gogni; Agordat; Barentu; Karora-Marsa Taclai; Cubcub; Ad Teclesan; Mescelit Pass; Mt Engiahat; Massawa; Amb Alagi; Afodu; Gambela; El Wak; Moyale; Wal Garis; Juba; Bulo Erillo; Beles Gugani; Alessandra; Goluin; Marda Pass; Babile Gap; Bisidimo; Awash;* Todenyang-Namaraputh; Soroppa; Giarso; Colito; Wadara; Omo; Gondar; Fike and Lechemti.

Gemmano Ridge Second World War Italian campaign battle honour marking one of the actions between 25 August and 22 September 1944, when the German defensive system on the Gothic Line was breached. *See also: Italy 1943-1945; Gothic Line; Tavoleto; Coriano; Croce; Monte Gridolfo; Montegaudio; San Clemente; Poggio San Giovanni and Pian di Castello.*

General General officer ranking above lieutenant general and below field marshal. Rank denoted by a crossed baton and sabre surmounted by a star and a crown, worn on the shoulders. *See also: Rank.*

General Court Martial *See: Court Martial.*

General List In most cases successful candidates for commissions are appointed to a commission on the 'Active List' of their Arm or Service. Very exceptionally, some will be appointed to commissions on the 'General List'. More usually appointments to the 'General List' are confined to officers of the Hong Kong Military Service Corps, Industrial Exchange officers, University Cadets and Graduate Entry Officers awaiting sponsorship, and officers commissioned to a specific appointment not normally remunerated from Army funds. *See: Special List.*

General Officer Any officer bearing the rank of major general, lieutenant general or general. *See also: Rank.*

General Purpose Machine Gun (GPMG) British-made version of the Belgian Fabrique Nationale (FN) Mitrailleuse d'Appui Général (MAG), first produced in 1957. Currently in British Army service as the L7A1 GPMG, and widely known as the 'Gimpy'. The weapon is belt-fed, firing a 7.62mm calibre round and has a range of 800m in the light role, and 1,800m in the sustained fire (SF) role. Although the gun can be used in the light role with a detachable butt and bipod, it is now more usually used in the SF role mounted on a tripod and fitted with a dial sight The weapon may also be used in the air defence role.

General Service Corps Formed under the authority of Army Order 19 of 1942 to provide a 'holding and selection' pool for prospective officers before they were posted to the appropriate arm or service. Before the formation of the Intelligence Corps for example, officers were held on the strength of the General Service Corps or the parallel 'General List'.

General Service Medal 1918-1964 Instituted in 1923 for the Army and Royal Air Force. There are six different issues of the medal each with a different obverse.
Ribbon: Purple, with a broad vertical green stripe in the centre.
Clasps: S.Persia; Kurdistan; Iraq; N.W.Persia; Southern Desert-Iraq; Northern Kurdistan; Palestine; S.E.Asia 1945-46; Bomb and Mine Clearance 1945-49; Palestine 1945-48; Malaya; Cyprus; Near East; Arabian Peninsular and Brunei.

General Service Medal 1962 Instituted in 1964 for award to all three Services, the reverse bearing the words 'FOR CAMPAIGN SERVICE'.
Ribbon: Purple with green edges.
Clasps to date: Borneo; Radfan; South Vietnam; South Arabia; Malay Peninsula; Northern Ireland; Dhofar; Lebanon; Mine Clearance-Gulf of Suez; Gulf; Kuwait and N.Iraq & S.Turkey.

General Staff The following directors, individuals and staffs fall within the General Staff branch of the Ministry of Defence (Army): Chief of the General Staff; Assistant Chief of the General Staff; Head of the General Staff Secretariat; Director Army Staff Duties and Engineer-in-Chief (Army).

General Support Artillery That artillery which fires in support of an operation as a whole, rather than in support of a specific subordinate unit.

Geneva Conventions The original convention or treaty was adopted at a national conference held at Geneva in 1864, and was later replaced by the convention of 6 July 1906, also at Geneva. This was an international agreement, chiefly respecting the succour of the wounded in time of war, and forbade all cruel methods of warfare. International conferences promoting the same objects were also held at Paris and Berlin. The adoption of the new Geneva Convention of July 1906 resulted in a new edition being adopted at the Peace Conference of 1907. A further convention was made in 1929, to update the convention in the light of First World War experiences, and there have been further amendments since. In 1949 a new convention was signed, after preliminary talks in 1946, incorporating amendments suggested by the experiences of the Second World War.

Geneva Cross The Geneva or 'Red Cross' badge was worn on the sleeve of non-officer qualified medical personnel from the late 1860s until the beginning of the First World War.

George Boot A light pattern boot, higher sided than a shoe but not as high as an ammunition boot, introduced in 1951 for wear by officers with Nos 1 and 3 dress.

George Cross Gallantry award instituted by a Royal Warrant dated 24 September 1940 for 'acts of the greatest heroism or of the most conspicuous courage in circumstances of extreme danger'. The award was open to all servicemen and civilians of 'Our United Kingdom of Great Britain and Northern Ireland, India, Burma, Our Colonies, and of Territories under Our Suzerainty, Protection or Jurisdiction'.
Ribbon: Blue, now 1½" wide; previously 1¼" wide.

George Medal Gallantry award instituted by a Royal Warrant of 24 September 1940 for 'acts of great bravery'. The award was open to all servicemen and civilians of 'Our United Kingdom of Great Britain and Northern Ireland, India, Burma, Our Colonies, and of Territories under Our Suzerainty, Protection or Jurisdiction'.

Ribbon: Red, 1" wide, with five equidistant narrow vertical blue stripes.

Gerbini Second World War Sicilian campaign battle honour marking an action during the advance through Sicily in July and August 1943. *See also: Sicily 1943; Landing in Sicily; Primosole Bridge; Sferro; Regalbuto and Centuripe.*

Gheel Second World War battle honour marking the establishment of a bridgehead over the Albert Canal on 11 September 1944 during the campaign in North-West Europe. *See also: North West Europe 1944-1945; Brussels; Antwerp; Neerpelt; Hechtel; Aart and Le Havre.*

Gheluvelt First World War battle honour marking an action during the First Battle of Ypres in 1914 when a German offensive astride the Menin Road on 29 October was repulsed. *See also: France and Flanders 1914-1918; Ypres 1914; Langemarck 1914; Nonne Boschen and Festubert 1914.*

Ghuznee 1839 Battle honour marking the successful storming of the fortress of Ghuznee on 23 July 1839 during the First Afghan War (qv). *See also: Afghanistan 1839; Khelat; Kahun; Jellalabad; Khelat-i-Ghilzie; Candahar 1842; Ghuznee 1842; Cabool 1842 and Cutchee.*

Ghuznee 1842 Battle honour marking a successful skirmish at the fortress of Ghuznee in 1842 during the British withdrawal from Afghanistan at the end of the First Afghan War (qv). *See also: Afghanistan 1839; Khelat; Kahun; Jellalabad; Khelat-i-Ghilzie; Candahar 1842; Ghuznee 1839; Cabool 1842 and Cutchee.*

Ghuznee Medal 1839 Issued to mark the storming of the fort at Ghuznee on 23 July 1839 in the First Afghan War (qv).
Ribbon: Originally half green and half yellow; later changed to half crimson and half green. *See also: Candahar; Ghuznee and Cabul Medals.*

Giant Viper Explosive hose used for clearing lanes through minefields. The hose is launched from a trailer which is usually towed by a tracked armoured vehicle. The Giant Viper should clear a lane 7.5m wide and 180m long.

Giarso Second World War Abyssinian campaign battle honour marking the reconnaissance towards Giarso made on 9 April 1941 with a view to an advance west of Lake Marghareta. *See also: Abyssinia 1940-41; Keren; Jebel Defeis; Jebel Shiba; Gogni; Agordat; Barentu; Karora-Marsa Taclai; Cubcub; Ad Teclesan; Mescelit Pass; Mt Engiahat; Massawa; Amb Alagi; Afodu; Gambela; El Wak; Moyale; Wal Garis; Juba; Bulo Erillo; Beles Gugani; Alessandra; Goluin; Marda Pass; Babile Gap; Bisidimo; Awash; Todenyang-Namaraputh; Soroppa; Gelib; Colito; Wadara; Omo; Gondar; Fike and Lechemti.*

Gibraltar 1704-5 Battle honour marking the seizure and subsequent defence of Gibraltar against a Franco-Spanish army. A number of successful sorties were made by the garrison against the besieging force. The final assault in February 1705 penetrated the outer defences, but this was checked and repulsed at the main gate, and the siege was subsequently raised.

Gibraltar 1779-83 Battle honour marking the defence of the fortress against the French and Spanish during the American War of Independence (qv). The siege began, largely as a blockade for the first two years, in June 1779, but with the arrival of a large French force, the number and intensity of attacks increased. A major assault was launched in September 1782 with heavy losses to the attackers and, in February 1783, the siege was lifted. Originally awarded without a date, subsequently added in 1909, the battle honour together with the 'Key and Castle' badge and the motto 'Montis Insignia Calpe' was granted to the 12th, 39th, 56th and 58th Foot. In 1908 the battle honour, with the dates 1780-83 and the badge and motto, was awarded to the Highland Light Infantry.

Gibson's Regiment of Foot Raised by Colonel John Gibson in March 1694, numbered 28th Foot in 1751. *See also: The Gloucestershire Regiment.*

Gillies, Sir Harold Delf (1882-1960)
Born Dunedin, New Zealand and educated at Wanganui College, Caius College, Cambridge and St Bartholomew's Hospital. His experiences in the Royal Army Medical Corps (qv) during the First World War made him realise the urgent need for specialised treatment for facial wounds. He returned to England from France and opened a special unit at Aldershot and later (1917) at Queen's Hospital, Sidcup. By the end of the war he had treated some 11,000 wounded, and his work brought him international acclaim as a pioneer of plastic surgery. During the Second World War he was closely concerned with the medical organisation for the treatment of casualties and was director of the plastic surgery unit at Rooksdown House, Basingstoke.

Ginchy First World War battle honour marking one of the actions in the Somme offensive of 1916. The village of Ginchy, which lies some 600 yards beyond Delville Wood, was finally captured on 9 September. *See also: France and Flanders 1914-1918; Somme 1916; Albert 1916; Bazentin; Delville Wood; Pozières; Guillemont; Flers-Courcelette; Morval; Thiepval; Le Transloy; Ancre Heights and Ancre 1916.*

Givenchy 1914 First World War battle honour marking the action in late 1914 when the Germans attacked and captured the village of Givenchy, to the south of Festubert, but were driven out by robust counter-attack. *See also: France and Flanders 1914-1918; Ypres 1914; Langemarck 1914; Gheluvelt; Nonne Bosschen; Festubert 1914; Neuve Chapelle and Hill 60.*

The Glamorgan Yeomanry Raised in 1797, the regiment was heavily engaged in the Merthyr Tydfil riots of 1831, and disbanded shortly thereafter. In 1901 the Glamorganshire Imperial Yeomanry was raised and was to serve dismounted in Egypt in 1916. In 1917 the regiment was amalgamated and became 24th (Pembroke and Glamorgan) Battalion, The Welch Regiment, fighting in Palestine and from 1918 on the Western front. The Glamorganshire Yeomanry was converted

to artillery in 1920 and served as such throughout the Second World War, crossing to Normandy in June 1944 and taking part in the campaign in North-West Europe. The Glamorgan Yeomanry title was not officially included in the post-war Territorial Army, but the regiment can be identified with 'E' (Glamorgan Yeomanry) Troop, 211 (South Wales) Light Air Defence Battery, 104 Light Air Defence Regiment Royal Artillery (Volunteer) since 1967.

Glasgow Highland Regiment Of Foot (71st Foot) *See: Highland Light Infantry.*

Glasgow Lowland Regiment Of Foot (70th Foot) *See: East Surrey Regiment.*

Glengarry Scottish woollen, folded bonnet. Often with diced headband, red toorie and ribbons to the rear.

Gliders Between late 1940 and mid-1942 research and development effort culminated in the production of a number of military gliders for the operational delivery of men, vehicles and materiel. All bore names beginning with the letter 'H'. *See also: Hadrian; Hamilcar; Hengist; Horsa and Hotspur.*

Glider Pilot Regiment *See: Army Air Corps.*

Gloucestershire Regiment (28th and 61st Foot) The 28th Foot was raised in March 1694 as Gibson's Regiment of Foot, numbered 28th Foot in 1751 and designated 28th (North Gloucestershire) Foot in 1782. The 61st Foot was raised in 1756 as a second battalion of the 3rd Foot (The Buffs), reconstituted as 61st Foot in 1758 and designated 61st (South Gloucestershire) Foot in 1782. In 1881 the 28th (North Gloucestershire) and 61st (South Gloucestershire) Regiments of Foot amalgamated to form the Gloucestershire Regiment (28th and 61st).
Headdress Badge: within a laurel wreath upon a pedestal inscribed 'Egypt', a sphinx. It should be noted that, uniquely to the regiment, a miniature of this badge is also worn at the rear of headdress.

Regimental marches:
Quick march: *The Kinnegad Slashers.*
Slow march: *28th/61st.*
Regimental Headquarters: Custom House, Commercial Road, Gloucester, GL1 2HE.
History: *Cap of Honour* by D Scott Daniell (2nd Edn.1975); and *The Glosters* by C Newbould and C Beresford (1992).

Gloucestershire Yeomanry (The Royal Gloucestershire Hussars) The first troop was raised in Cheltenham in 1795 and, with other troops in the county, remained independent until disbanded in 1827. A new troop was raised in 1831 and the regiment formed in 1834, providing a company for the 1st Battalion of the Imperial Yeomanry in the Boer War. In the First World War the regiment went to Egypt, fought dismounted at Gallipoli (qv) in 1915, and then fought again as cavalry during the campaign in Palestine, finishing the war in Syria. Between the wars the regiment was reduced to squadron strength, but expanded rapidly at the outbreak of the Second World war to form two regiments. The first regiment became a training regiment of the Royal Armoured Corps and finished the war on garrison duties in Austria. The second regiment fought in the Western Desert from late 1941, sustaining very heavy casualties and, although some members of the regiment fought at El Alamein, the regiment was never reconstituted. After the war the regiment formed an armoured car regiment, but was reduced to cadre strength in 1969 and is now represented by RHQ and 'A' (Royal Gloucestershire Hussars) Squadron, and Regimental Band, of The Royal Wessex Yeomanry.

Glubb, Sir John Bagot (1897-1986) Educated at Cheltenham and the Royal Military Academy, Woolwich. After service in the First World War he became a political officer in Iraq, serving among the Arab tribes on the Saudi Arabian frontier. In 1932 he was transferred to Transjordan and put in command of the Arab Legion, where he formed the 'desert patrol' and system of forts on the Transjordan-Palestine border. During the Iraqi campaign of 1941 he was attached to the Transjordan Frontier Force and took part in the operations in the Habbaniya (qv) area, in the Syrian campaign later that year and in the operations in north-east Africa and at Palmyra. In 1956 he and other British officers in the Arab Legion were dismissed by King Hussein of Jordan. On his return to England he was knighted and promoted to Lieutenant General.

Goch Second World War battle honour marking one of the actions in the advance from the River Roer to the Rhine over the period 8 February to 10 March 1945. The town of Goch was captured after heavy fighting 12-21 February 1945. *See also: North West Europe 1944-1945; Rhineland; Reichswald; Cleve; Weeze; Schaddenhof; Hochwald; Waal Flats; Moyland; Moyland Wood and Xanten.*

God Bless The Prince Of Wales Regimental quick march of 9th/12th Lancers and regimental slow march of The Prince of Wales's Own Regiment of Yorkshire, The Staffordshire Regiment, 2nd King Edward VII's Own Gurkha Rifles and The Royal Gurkha Rifles.

Gogni Second World War Abyssinian campaign battle honour. *See also: Abyssinia 1940-41; Keren; Jebel Defeis; Jebel Shiba; Giarso; Agordat; Barentu; Karora-Marsa Taclai; Cubcub; Ad Teclesan; Mescelit Pass; Mt Engiahat; Massawa; Amb Alagi; Afodu; Gambela; El Wak; Moyale; Wal Garis; Juba; Bulo Erillo; Beles Gugani; Alessandra; Goluin; Marda Pass; Babile Gap; Bisidimo; Awash; Todenyang-Namaraputh; Soroppa; Gelib; Colito; Wadara; Omo; Gondar; Fike and Lechemti.*

Going Bald-Headed At It Saying originating from the Battle of Warburg (1760) when the Marquis of Granby, eager to remove the slur of the cavalry's inactivity at Minden (1759), led the cavalry charge himself. His hat and wig blew off in the charge exposing his bald head.

Golden Spurs Regimental slow march of the Royal Army Veterinary Corps.

Goliath Small, remote-controlled, tracked equipment for the investigation and destruction of suspicious explosive devices.

Goluin Second World War Abyssinian campaign battle honour marking an action during General Cunningham's drive north from Kenya, crossing of the River Juba and seizure of Kismayu in Italian Somaliland in February 1941. *See also: Abyssinia 1940-41; Keren; Jebel Defeis; Jebel Shiba; Giarso; Agordat; Barentu; Karora-Marsa Taclai; Cubcub; Ad Teclesan; Mescelit Pass; Mt Engiahat; Massawa; Amb Alagi; Afodu; Gambela; El Wak; Moyale; Wal Garis; Juba; Bulo Erillo; Beles Gugani; Alessandra; Gogni; Marda Pass; Babile Gap; Bisidimo; Awash; Todenyang-Namaraputh; Soroppa; Gelib; Colito; Wadara; Omo; Gondar; Fike and Lechemti.*

Gondar Second World War Abyssinian campaign battle honour marking actions during the period 15 October to 27 November 1941 which culminated in the fall of Gondar. *See also: Abyssinia 1940-41; Keren; Jebel Defeis; Jebel Shiba; Giarso; Agordat; Barentu; Karora-Marsa Taclai; Cubcub; Ad Teclesan; Mescelit Pass; Mt Engiahat; Massawa; Amb Alagi; Afodu; Gambela; El Wak; Moyale; Wal Garis; Juba; Bulo Erillo; Beles Gugani; Alessandra; Gogni; Marda Pass; Babile Gap; Bisidimo; Awash; Todenyang-Namaraputh; Soroppa; Gelib; Colito; Wadara; Omo; Goluin; Fike and Lechemti.*

Good Comrade, The One of the regimental quick marches of the Royal Army Education Corps and the Education and Training Services Branch of the Adjutant General's Corps.

Good Conduct Badges Inverted chevrons, worn just above the cuff of the left sleeve, indicating service and good conduct. Each chevron indicating a given length of service:
one chevron - two years
two chevrons - five years
three chevrons - 12 years
four chevrons - 16 years
five chevrons - 21 years

Goojerat Battle honour marking the last battle of the Second Sikh War (qv), fought on 21 February 1849, which resulted in a decisive defeat for the Sikh army. *See also: Mooltan; Chillianwallah and Punjaub.*

Goose Green One of five battle honours awarded for the Falklands Islands (qv) campaign of 1982. *See also: Falkland Islands 1982; Tumbledown Mountain; Mount Longdon and Wireless Ridge.*

Gordon, Charles George (1833-85), General The 'Hero of Khartoum'. Born at Woolwich, Gordon was present at the assault on the Redan (1855) in the Crimean war (qv). In 1860 he joined the British expedition which forced its way to Pekin (qv). When Shanghai was threatened during the Taiping rebellion, Gordon was selected by Li Hung Chang to lead the foreign-officered 'Ever Victorious Army' which, in conjunction with Imperial forces, finally defeated the rebels in 1864. In 1871 Gordon was appointed commissioner for superintending the Danube navigation, and in 1873 he was appointed Governor of the Sudan, but resigned in 1880. In 1884 he was again sent to the Sudan where a revolt had broken out under Mohammed Ahmed, who proclaimed himself the Mahdi. The British government had ordered Egypt to abandon the Sudan, and Gordon was deputed to go there and evacuate the Egyptian population. The situation was beset with difficulties, and Gordon was surrounded and besieged in Khartoum. The siege had endured for five months when a relief party was sent from England. On 28 January 1885 the advance guard reached Khartoum to find that the place had been captured by rebels two days before, and Gordon had been put to death.

Gordon Highlanders (75th and 92nd Foot) The 75th Foot was raised by Colonel Robert Abercromby at Stirling in October 1787 for service with the East India Company's forces and designated 75th (Highland) Regiment of Foot; it was retitled 75th Regiment of Foot in 1807 and redesignated 75th (Stirlingshire) Foot in 1862. The 92nd Foot was originally raised by the 4th Duke of Gordon in February 1794, command being given to his son George, Marquis of Huntly (later 5th and last Duke of Gordon); ranked as 100th (Gordon Highlanders) Foot in 1794, renumbered 92nd (Highland) Regiment in

1798 and 92nd (Gordon Highlanders) Foot in 1861. In 1881 the 75th (Stirlingshire) Foot and 92nd (Gordon Highlanders) Foot amalgamated to form The Gordon Highlanders. On 17 September 1994 the regiment amalgamated with The Queen's Own Highlanders (Seaforth and Camerons) to form The Highlanders (Seaforth, Gordons and Camerons) (72nd, 75th, 78th, 79th and 92nd Foot) (qv).

Headdress Badge: The crest of the Marquess of Huntly within a wreath of ivy, with the motto *'Bydand'* (Watchful).

Regimental marches:

Quick march: *Cock o' the North* (Drums and Pipes and Regimental Band).

Slow marches: *St Andrews Cross* (Drums and Pipes) and *The Garb of Old Gaul* (Regimental Band).

Regimental Headquarters: Viewfield Road, Aberdeen, Scotland AB1 7XH.

History: *The Life of a Regiment, Vol 1 1794-1816* and *Vol 2 1816-1898* by C Greenhill Gardyne (1929); *Vol 3 1898-1914* by A D Greenhill Gardyne (1972); *Vol 4 1914-1919* by C Falls (1958); *Vol 5 1919-1945* by W Miles (1961); *Vol 6 1945-1970* by C Sinclair-Stevenson (1974); *Vol 7 1970-1994* (in progress); and *The Gordon Highlanders* by C Sinclair-Stevenson (1968).

Gorget Crescent-shaped piece of armour used in early times to protect the throat by covering the gap between the cuirass and the helmet. Traditionally, it was the first piece of armour to be put on and the last to be removed when fitting or removing armour. Over time its size was much reduced and, often made of silver and heavily engraved, it became the mark of an officer.

Gorget-Patch Traditionally, cloth pieces on the collar where gorget ribbons had been fastened. Now decorative only and worn in scarlet or other colour by officers of colonel rank and above, and in white by officer cadets. First introduced in 1887 for wear with khaki drill uniform by general officers and extended to all staff officers in 1913. By 1921 the wearing of gorget patches had become so uncontrolled that it was restricted to colonels and above, although officer cadets continued to wear white gorget patches.

Gort, John Standish Vereker, 1st Viscount (1886-1946) Educated at Harrow and the Royal Military Academy Sandhurst; succeeded his father as 6th Viscount Gort of Limerick in 1902. Commissioned into the Grenadier Guards in 1905, Aide-de-Camp to Sir Douglas Haig in 1914. Appointed to the command of 4th Battalion Grenadier Guards, he led that battalion with great courage and ability at the opening of the Third Battle of Ypres on 31 July 1917, and took part in the Battle of Cambrai (1917). In March 1918 he commanded 1st Battalion Grenadier Guards at Arras. Conspicuous service near Hamel while in temporary command of 1st (Guards) Brigade, notably at Flesquières. Frequently wounded, was awarded the Victoria Cross for his gallantry. Commandant of the Staff College (1936), Military Secretary (qv) and Chief of the Imperial General Staff (1937). Led the British Expeditionary Force to France (1939), but was forced to withdraw and evacuate France in 1940. Governor and commander-in-chief of Gibraltar (1941) and later of Malta, he achieved in the defence of Malta one of the great successes of his career, and was promoted Field Marshal in 1943. In 1944 he became high commissioner for Palestine and Transjordan, but soon retired because of ill health.

Gothic Line Second World War Italian campaign battle honour commemorating the breaching of the German defensive line which ran from Pisa to Rimini, known as the Gothic Line, during the period 25 August to 22 September 1944. The Eighth Army having turned the German line in the east and captured Rimini, the Fifth Army broke through in the centre. *See also: Italy 1943-1945; Tavoleto; Coriano; Croce; Gemmano Ridge; Monte Gridolfo; Montegaudio; San Clemente; Poggio San Giovanni and Pian di Castello.*

Gough, Sir Hubert de la Poer (1870-1963), General Educated at Eton and The

Royal Military Academy Sandhurst. He was commissioned into 16th Lancers (1889), took part in the Tirah expedition (1897-98), and was severely wounded in the Boer War (1899-1902). As a Brigadier General in command of 3rd Cavalry Brigade at the Curragh in March 1914 he was the most senior officer who refused to be employed against any resistance from Ulster if the Home Rule Act was passed. During the early part of the First World War he commanded 2nd Cavalry Division, 7th Division (1915) and 1st Army Corps (1916). He commanded the Fifth Army from 1916-18 including the actions at Pozières, Thiepval, Beaumont-Hamel, Ancre, Langemarck and Somme 1918. He retired with the rank of General.

Granby, John Manners, Marquess of (1721-70) Entered parliament in 1741, but undertook military duties as well, taking part in the campaign in Flanders. He was appointed Colonel of the Royal Horse Guards in 1758 and was present at the battle of Minden (1759), where the cavalry failed to distinguish itself. He was eventually appointed general to the British force in Ferdinand's army, where he gained great distinction. In 1766 he was appointed commander-in-chief, but resigned his post after three years due to ill health. *See also: Going bald-headed at it.*

Grand March From Aida and The Royals One of the regimental quick marches of The Blues and Royals.

Gravel Belly Nickname for a person who spends a significant amount of time small arms firing, especially competition shooting. The name is derived from the gravel surface found on the firing point of many small arms ranges.

Gravenstafel First World War battle honour marking one of the actions in the Second Battle of Ypres in 1915. The battle began on 27 April with a German offensive which was held by British troops on the ridge by Gravenstafel. *See also: France and Flanders 1914-1918; Ypres 1915; St Julien; Frezenberg and Bellewaarde.*

Greece 1941 Second World War campaign honour marking the actions of a British, New Zealand and Australian force which arrived in Greece in late March 1941 to meet an expected German invasion. A defensive line was formed along the River Aliakmon, just north of Mount Olympus and, when the Germans did land on 6 April, they quickly turned the defensive line and, with the Greek Army disintegrating, it was decided to evacuate the country. A number of rearguard actions were fought on the routes down to the ports and beaches in the Peloponnese, where the bulk of the force embarked. *See also: Veve; Proasteion and Corinth Canal.*

Greece 1944-45 Second World War battle honour arising from the landing of British troops in Greece in October 1944 to prevent a communist takeover after the German withdrawal. Civil war did break out in December and British troops were engaged against communist rebels until mid-January. *See also: Athens.*

Green Dragoons Nickname given to the 13th Dragoons (qv) in the period 1715-1784 when they wore green facings; later the 13th Hussars, 13th/18th Royal Hussars, and now the Light Dragoons (qv).

Green Facings Regimental quick march of the Royal Army Dental Corps.

Green Howards (Alexandra, Princess of Wales's Own Yorkshire Regiment) (19th Foot) So called from the colour of their facings and Sir Charles Howard, colonel of the regiment 1738-48. Raised as independent companies by Colonel Francis Luttrell in November 1688. These companies were augmented and regimented in February 1689. Numbered 19th Foot in 1751 and designated 19th (1st Yorkshire, North Riding) Foot in 1782 and 19th (1st Yorkshire, North Riding - Princess of Wales's Own) Foot in 1875. In May 1881 the regiment was redesignated The North Yorkshire Regiment (Princess of Wales's Own) and, only two months later, The Princess of Wales's Own (Yorkshire) Regiment. In 1921 the regimental title was altered to The Green Howards (Alexandra, Princess of Wales's Own Yorkshire Regiment).

Headdress Badge: The cypher of Her Royal Highness Alexandra, Princess of Wales, interlaced with the Dannebrog enscribed with the date '1875', the roman numerals XIX below and the whole surmounted by the coronet of the Princess.

Regimental Marches:

Quick march: *Bonnie English Rose*.

Slow march: *Maria Theresa*.

Regimental headquarters: Trinity Church Square, The Market Place, Richmond, Yorkshire, DL10 4QN.

History: *History of The Green Howards, Three Hundred Years of Service* by G Powell (1992).

Green Jackets *See: Royal Green Jackets*.

Green Jackets Brigade An administrative grouping in the infantry formed under Army Order 61 of 1948 comprising: The Oxfordshire and Buckinghamshire Light Infantry (from Light Infantry Brigade as 1st Green Jackets in 1958); The King's Royal Rifle Corps (redesignated 2nd Green Jackets in 1958)\ and The Rifle Brigade (Prince Consort's Own) (redesignated 3rd Green Jackets in 1958). The regiments of the brigade were absorbed into the Light Division (qv) in 1968.

Green Linnets Nickname given, because of the colour of their facings, to 39th Foot, later 1st Battalion The Dorset Regiment, now part of the Devonshire and Dorset Regiment.

Greensleeves Regimental slow march of the Women's Royal Army Corps and of the Adjutant General's Corps.

Grenade Type of small bomb, from *Granade* a pomegranate, thrown by hand or projected from a launcher, usually with a timed fuse of four seconds to ensure that the grenade is clear of the thrower before detonating. Grenades may be of a variety of types including: fragmentation, smoke, phosphorous and the 'stun' grenades used by special forces, which produce a bright flash and loud detonation, but which are largely harmless. Normally, hand-thrown grenades are referred to as defensive; launched grenades, having a greater range, are offensive.

Grenadier Originally a soldier trained to throw grenades, a role for which height and strength were deemed an advantage. Subsequently the name was applied to a member of the grenadier company.

Grenadier Guards The regiment has its origins in a regiment of royalist refugees raised for Charles II in Flanders in 1656 and brought back to England at the Restoration to become The King's Royal Regiment of Guards in 1660. In 1685 the regiment was retitled The First Regiment of Foot Guards. Following their defeat of the Grenadiers of the Imperial Guard at Waterloo, the regiment assumed the title 1st or Grenadier Regiment of Foot Guards.

Headdress Badge: A grenade fired proper.

Regimental marches:

Quick marches: *The British Grenadiers* and *The Grenadiers March*.

Slow marches: *March from Scipio* and *The Duke of York*.

Regimental headquarters: Wellington Barracks, Birdcage Walk, London, SW1E 6HQ.

History: *History of the Grenadier Guards 1656-1870* by Hamilton; *History of the Grenadier Guards 1656-1949* by Bart; *The Grenadier Guards in the Great War* by Ponsonby; *The Grenadier Guards in the Second World War* by Forbes and Nicholson; and *History of the Grenadier Guards 1945-1995* by O J M Lindsay (1995).

See also: Nijmegen Company.

Grenadiers March One of the regimental quick marches of the Grenadier Guards.

Greys Nickname given to the Royal Scots Greys (2nd Dragoons), now the Royal Scots Dragoon Guards (Carabiniers and Greys). It is unclear now whether the name comes from the colour of their mounts or their uniform; but more probably the former.

Grey and Scarlet Regimental quick march of Queen Alexandra's Royal Army Nursing Corps.

Grich El Oued Second World War North Africa campaign battle honour marking one of the actions in the Medjez Plain battle 23-30 April 1943. *See also: North Africa 1940-1943; Medjez Plain; Gueriat El Atach Ridge; Longstop Hill 1943; Djebel Bou Aoukaz 1943; Peter's Corner; Si Mediene; Si Abdallah; Gab Gab Gap and Sidi Ahmed.*

Grik Road Second World War Malayan campaign battle honour marking one of the actions in the campaign against the Japanese in Malaya in December 1941. *See also: Malaya 1941-1942; Northern Malaya; Jitra; Central Malaya; Slim River; Ipoh; Johore; Batu Pahat; Muar and Singapore Island.*

Gromballa Second World War North Africa campaign battle honour marking the final breakthrough to capture Tunis and subsequent exploitation towards the Cape Bon peninsula resulted in the final surrender of the Axis forces in North Africa. *See also: North Africa 1940-1943; Tunis; Hammam Lif; Djebel Bou Aoukaz 1943 II; Djebel Bou Aoukaz 1943 I; Montarnaud; Ragoubet Souissi; Creteville Pass and Bou Ficha.*

Groundsheet Waterproof sheet used as protection from rain or laid upon the ground in a bivouac or tent. Also, soldier's slang for a woman of easy virtue.

Ground Zero Point on the earth's surface at which a nuclear weapon is detonated or, in the case of the more usual air burst, the point on the earth's surface vertically below such a detonation.

Guadaloupe 1759 Battle honour marking the landing of a British force on the island of Guadaloupe in January 1759 during the Seven Years' War (1756-1763). After three months of fighting the French garrison surrendered, but the British force lost a third of its strength through disease.

Guadaloupe 1810 Battle honour marking the capture of the island of Guadaloupe from the French during the Napoleonic Wars.

Guards Brigade An administrative grouping in the infantry formed under Army Order 61 of 1948 comprising the Grenadier, Coldstream, Scots, Irish and Welsh Guards. The regiments of the brigade were absorbed into the Guards Division in 1968.

Guards Division An administrative grouping in the infantry, created under Army Order 34 of 1968, comprising the Grenadier, Coldstream, Scots, Irish and Welsh Guards. *See also: Guards Brigade.*

Guardsman The title, authorised by King George V on 22 November 1918, given to a private soldier in the regiments of Foot Guards.

Gubi I Second World War North Africa campaign battle honour marking one of the actions in the 1941 Battle of Tobruk. *See also: North Africa 1940-1943; Tobruk 1941; Sidi Rezegh 1941; Tobruk Sortie; Omars; Belhamed; Gabr Saleh; Taieb El Essem; Gubi II and Relief of Tobruk.*

Gubi II Second World War North Africa campaign battle honour marking one of the actions in the 1941 Battle of Tobruk. *See also: North Africa 1940-1943; Tobruk 1941; Sidi Rezegh 1941; Tobruk Sortie; Omars; Belhamed; Gabr Saleh; Taieb El Essem; Gubi I and Relief of Tobruk.*

Gueriat El Atach Ridge Second World War North Africa campaign battle honour marking one of the actions in the Medjez Plain battle 23-30 April 1943. *See also: North Africa 1940-1943, Medjez Plain, Grich El Oued, Longstop Hill 1943, Djebel Bou Aoukaz 1943, Peter's Corner, Si Mediene, Si Abdallah, Gab Gab Gap and Sidi Ahmed.*

Guided Missile An unmanned, expendable, self-propelled flying vehicle equipped with some form of guidance. Such missiles are usually described or categorised by task, flight profile and launch mode.

Guidon The equivalent of infantry colours in a dragoon, hussar or lancer regiment and consisting of a small, heavily decorated flag on a lance stave, the fly-end being divided into two points. The term 'guidon' is thought to come from the French 'guide homme' - a guide. *See also: Colours and Standards.*

Guillemont First World War battle honour marking one of the actions in the Somme offensive of 1916. On 3 September 1916 the village of Guillemont, to the right of Delville Wood, was finally stormed. There followed three days of heavy German counter-attacks which were repulsed. See also: *France and Flanders 1914-1918; Somme 1916; Albert 1916; Bazentin; Delville Wood; Pozières; Ginchy; Flers-Courcelette; Morval; Thiepval; Le Transloy; Ancre Heights and Ancre 1916.*

Gulf 1991 Battle honour marking British participation in the allied coalition which in Operation DESERT STORM defeated Iraq and liberated Kuwait between 24 and 28 February 1991. The British Army contribution to the coalition forces was based upon 1st Armoured Division, consisting of 4th and 7th Armoured Brigades, brought up to war establishment by drawing heavily on the rest of the Army. The Commander British Forces Middle East for this operation was General Sir Peter de la Billière. *See also: Wadi Al Batin and Western Iraq.*

Gulf Medal 1990-1991 Awarded for service in the Gulf War for the liberation of Kuwait from Iraq. The complex terms for qualification fall into three broad groupings:
1. Thirty days continuous service between 2 August 1990 and 7 March 1991 in Saudi Arabia, Oman, United Arab Emirates, Qatar, Jordan, Bahrain, Kuwait, Iraq, Republic of Yemen and adjacent waters.
2. Seven days continuous service between 16 January and 28 February 1991 in Saudi Arabia, Bahrain, Kuwait, Iraq, United Arab Emirates, Oman, Qatar and adjacent waters.
3. Service in the Kuwait Liaison Team on 2 August 1990.
Ribbon: Pale buff central vertical stripe 1¼" wide, flanked on each side by vertical stripes ⅛" wide of light blue, red and dark blue.

Gun Name applied generally to a weapon from which a projectile is discharged by means of an explosion. The word nowadays is applied almost exclusively to artillery and sporting weapons. The lighter, smaller bore military weapons, such as muskets, rifles and pistols are referred to as small arms.

Gun Barrels A badge depicting crossed gun or cannon barrels is worn by Assistant Instructors of Gunnery in the Royal Artillery.

Gun Carriage Carriage on which a gun is mounted and from which it fires. Formerly drawn by horses, and later towed by tracked or wheeled vehicles. If the gun carriage is designed as a tracked vehicle moving under its own power the whole assembly constitutes a 'self-propelled gun'.

Gun Cotton Nitro-cellulose or cellulose nitrate, with a high degree of nitration. Cotton lint or cotton waste which has been cleaned in hot caustic soda solution, washed and dried, is added to a mixture of sulphuric and nitric acid at ordinary temperatures. Gun cotton has had a variety of uses as a propellant and, in a wet condition, as a demolition explosive. Although highly sensitive and inflammable when dry, when wet it is insensitive to mechanical shock, safe to handle and may be detonated by a charge of dry gun cotton or other explosive. Gun cotton has now largely been superseded by more modern explosives.

Gunfire Nickname for the rum-enhanced tea served to soldiers, usually by their officers and non-commissioned officers, on special occasions such as regimental days.

Gun Metal Copper based alloy containing up to 10 per cent zinc, and up to 5 per cent lead. It is a tough reddish metal, much used for making castings and formerly used for making artillery.

Gunner Title given to private soldiers in the Royal Regiment of Artillery.

GURKHAS

Members of the martial clans of Nepal, a hill people of Mongolian descent who came from the north through the Himalayan passes in prehistoric times. They unified Nepal in the 18th century under a king descended from Rajputs who fled to Nepal from the Moslem invaders of India in the 15th Century. Gurkha expansion brought them into conflict with the British East India Company and the inconclusive Anglo-Nepal War of 1814-16. After the Treaty of Friendship which concluded the war it was agreed that Gurkhas be allowed to enlist voluntarily in the armies of the Honourable East India Company. The Gurkha regiments were absorbed into the (British) Indian Army in the transfer of government from the company to the Crown in 1858 and, with the granting of independence to India in 1947, six of the ten Gurkha regiments became part of the new Indian Army; the other four Gurkha regiments were incorporated in the British Army. They are:

2nd King Edward VII's Own Gurkha Rifles (The Sirmoor Rifles) Raised at Nahan in Sirmoor in 1815 and titled 8th (or Sirmoor) Local Battalion in 1823, renumbered 6th (or Sirmoor) Local Battalion in 1826 and retitled The Sirmoor Battalion in 1850. In 1858 the regiment became The Sirmoor Rifle Regiment and was retitled 17th Regiment of Bengal Native Infantry in 1861. In 1864 the regiment was designated 2nd Goorkha (The Sirmoor Rifles), redesignated 2nd (Prince of Wales's Own) Goorkha Regiment (The Sirmoor Rifles) in 1876, changing ten years later to 2nd (The Prince of Wales's Own) Gurkha Rifles Regiment (The Sirmoor Rifles). In 1901 the regiment was redesignated 2nd (The Prince of Wales's Own) Gurkha Rifles (The Sirmoor Rifles), becoming 2nd King Edward's Own Gurkha Rifles (The Sirmoor Rifles) in 1906 and was taken on the British Army establishment in 1948 as 2nd King Edward VII's Own Gurkha Rifles (The Sirmoor Rifles). On 1 July 1994 the 2nd King Edward VII's Own Gurkha Rifles (The Sirmoor Rifles), 6th Queen Elizabeth's Own Gurkha Rifles, 7th Duke of Edinburgh's Own Gurkha Rifles and 10th

Princess Mary's Own Gurkha Rifles amalgamated to form The Royal Gurkha Rifles (qv).

Headdress Badge: The plume of the Prince of Wales. The royal and imperial cypher of King Edward VII.

Regimental marches:

Quick marches: *Lutzow's Wild Hunt* and *What's A'the Steer Kimmer?*

Slow march: *God Bless The Prince of Wales.*

History: *History of The 2nd King Edward's Own Goorkhas, The Sirmoor Rifles* (3 Vols.) by L W Shakespear (1912 and 1924) and by G R Stevens (1952) and *A Pride of Goorkhas The 2nd King Edward VII's Own Goorkhas (The Sirmoor Rifles) 1948-71* by H James and D Sheil-Small (1975).

6th Queen Elizabeth's Own Gurkha Rifles Raised at Orissa in 1817 as the Cuttack Legion. Retitled The Rangpur Light Infantry Battalion in 1823, the 8th (or Rangpur) Local Light Infantry Battalion in 1826, the 8th (or Assam) Local Light Infantry Battalion in 1828, the 1st Assam Light Infantry in 1844, the 46th Regiment of Bengal Light Infantry in 1861, the 42nd (Assam) Regiment of Bengal (Native) Light Infantry in 1864, 42nd Regiment Goorkha Light Infantry in 1886, the 42nd Gurkha (Rifle) Regiment of Bengal Light Infantry in 1891, the 42nd Gurkha Rifles in 1901 and 6th Gurkha Rifles in 1903. The regiment joined the British Army establishment in 1948 and was designated 6th Queen Elizabeth's Own Gurkha Rifles in 1959. On 1 July 1994 the 2nd King Edward VII's Own Gurkha Rifles (The Sirmoor Rifles), 6th Queen Elizabeth's Own Gurkha Rifles, 7th Duke of Edinburgh's Own Gurkha Rifles and 10th Princess Mary's Own Gurkha Rifles amalgamated to form The Royal Gurkha Rifles (qv).

Headdress Badge: Two kukris in saltire, thereunder the numeral '6', the whole ensigned with the crown.

Regimental marches:

Quick marches: *Queen Elizabeth's Own* (Pipes) and *Young May Moon* (Regimental Band).

History: *Historical Records of The 6th Gurkha Rifles 1817-1919* by D G J Ryan, G C Strachan and J K Jones (1925); *Historical Record of The 6th Gurkha Rifles 1919-48* by

H K R Gibbs (1955); *The Happy Warriors - The Gurkha Soldier in Malaya 1948-58* by A E C Bredin (1961) and *The Steadfast Gurkha - Historical Records of The 6th Queen Elizabeth's Own Gurkha Rifles 1948-82* by C Messenger (1985).

7th Duke of Edinburgh's Own Gurkha Rifles Raised at Thayetmyo, Burma, in 1902 as 8th Gurkha Rifles. Retitled 2nd Battalion 10th Gurkha Rifles in 1903 and 7th Gurkha Rifles in 1907. The regiment transferred to the British Army establishment in 1948 and was designated 7th Duke of Edinburgh's Own Gurkha Rifles in 1950. On 1 July 1994 the 2nd King Edward VII's Own Gurkha Rifles (The Sirmoor Rifles), 6th Queen Elizabeth's Own Gurkha Rifles, 7th Duke of Edinburgh's Own Gurkha Rifles and 10th Princess Mary's Own Gurkha Rifles amalgamated to form The Royal Gurkha Rifles (qv).

Headdress Badge: Two kukris points upwards, the handles crossed in saltire, the cutting edges of the blades inwards, between the blades the numeral '7' and ensigned with the cypher of His Royal Highness The Duke of Edinburgh.

Regimental marches:
Quick marches: *Old Monmouthshire* (Military Band) and *All the Blue Bonnets are Over the Border* (Pipes and Drums).
History: *The Seventh Gurkha Rifles* author unknown (1954); *History of The 7th Duke of Edinburgh's Own Gurkha Rifles* by J N Mackay (1962) and *East of Katmandu* by E D Smith (1976).

10th Princess Mary's Own Gurkha Rifles Raised in the Kubo Valley, Burma, in 1887 as the Kubo Valley Police Battalion and designated 10th (Burma) Regiment Madras Infantry in 1890, redesignated 10th Regiment (1st Burma Rifles) Madras Infantry in 1892 and 10th Regiment (1st Burma Gurkha Rifles) Madras Infantry in 1896. The regiment was retitled 10th Gurkha Rifles in 1901, transferred to the British Army establishment in 1948 and designated 10th Princess Mary's Own Gurkha Rifles in 1949. On 1 July 1994 the 2nd King Edward VII's Own Gurkha Rifles (The Sirmoor Rifles), 6th Queen Elizabeth's Own Gurkha Rifles, 7th Duke of Edinburgh's Own Gurkha Rifles and 10th Princess Mary's Own Gurkha Rifles; amalgamated to form The Royal Gurkha Rifles (qv).

Headdress Badge: A bugle horn stringed interlaced with a kukri fessewise, the blade to the sinister, above the kukri the cypher of Her Royal Highness the Princess Mary (The Princess Royal) and below it the numeral '10'.

Regimental march:
Quick march: *Hundred Pipers.*
History: *History of The 10th Gurkha Rifles - The First Battalion 1890-1921* by B R Mullaly (1924) and *Bugle and Kukri - The Story of The 10th Princess Mary's Own Gurkha Rifles* by B R Mullaly (1957).

The Royal Gurkha Rifles Formed on 1 July 1994 through the amalgamation of the four original Gurkha infantry regiments, each of two battalions, which transferred to the British Army in 1948 following Indian independence: 2nd King Edward VII's Own Gurkha Rifles (The Sirmoor Rifles), 6th Queen Elizabeth's Own Gurkha Rifles, 7th Duke of Edinburgh's Own Gurkha Rifles and 10th Princess Mary's Own Gurkha Rifles.

Headdress Badge: Two crossed kukris, points up, cutting edges outward surmounted by a crown.

Regimental marches:
Quick march: *The Black Bear.*
Slow marches: *God Bless The Prince of Wales* (Regimental Band) and *The Garb of Old Gaul* (Pipes and Drums).
Double march: *The Keel Row.*
Regimental headquarters: Headquarters The Brigade of Gurkhas, Queen Elizabeth Barracks, Church Crookham, Aldershot, Hampshire.

The Queen's Gurkha Engineers Raised at Kluang, Malaya in October 1948 as 67 Field Squadron Royal Engineers, consisting of Gurkha infantrymen attached to the Royal Engineers. In August 1950 a further squadron, 68 Field Squadron, was raised at Kluang. On 28 September 1955 the Gurkha Engineers, part of the Brigade of Gurkhas, was formed by Royal Warrant. On 1 April 1960, 70 Gurkha Field Park Squadron was raised at Sungei Besi, Malaya ; it disbanded in Singapore on 31 July 1971. 69 Gurkha Field Squadron was raised at Sungei Besi on 1 April 1961 and disbanded in Hong Kong on 17 August 1968. Redesignated The Queen's Gurkha Engineers on 21 April 1977, the Corps was reduced to one squadron, 69 Field Squadron, in 1995. Affiliated to the Corps of Royal Engineers in 1958.

Headdress Badge: Two kukris points upwards, the blades crossed in saltire, their cutting edge outwards, surmounted by the Royal Engineers' grenade, over the handles a scroll with the motto 'Ubique'. The whole surrounded by a wreath of laurel surmounted by a Queen's crown thereon issuant from the wreath a scroll: 'The Queen's Gurkha Engineers'.

Regimental marches:

Quick marches: *Far o'er The Sea* (Pipes) and *Wings* (Military Band)

Regimental headquarters: Headquarters The Brigade of Gurkhas, Queen Elizabeth Barracks, Church Crookham, Aldershot, Hampshire.

History: *Gurkha Sapper - The Story of The Gurkha Engineers 1948-70* by L E C M Perowne (1973).

Queen's Gurkha Signals Raised at Kuala Lumpur, Malaya in 1948 by Major A C Cox, Royal Signals, from Gurkha soldiers drawn from the brigade. These men, together with re-enlisted ex-servicemen of the Indian Army, British officers and soldiers of the Royal Corps of Signals, formed the Gurkha Signals Training and Holding Wing in early 1949. The first elements were designated Royal Signals Gurkha and redesignated Gurkha Royal Signals in 1952, Gurkha Signals in 1955 and, by Royal Warrant on 21 April 1977, the Queen's Gurkha Signals. The Corps was reduced to one squadron, 250 Squadron Queen's Gurkha Signals, in 1995. Affiliated to the Royal Corps of Signals in 1958.

Headdress Badge: The front of the figure of Mercury, holding a caduceus in the left hand, on a globe, all in silver, supported in his dexter hand, the Crown in gold, two kukris in saltire, the blades upwards and inwards also in silver, thereunder a scroll inscribed 'Certa Cito' (Swift and Sure) and below nine laurel leaves.

Regimental march:

Quick march: *Scotland the Brave.*

Regimental headquarters: Headquarters The Brigade of Gurkhas, Queen Elizabeth Barracks, Church Crookham, Aldershot, Hampshire.

The Queen's Own Gurkha Transport Regiment Formed in July 1958 as 28 Company Gurkha Army Service Corps, affiliated to the Royal Corps of Transport in 1965 and redesignated Gurkha Transport Regiment in that year. Redesignated The Queen's Own Gurkha Transport Regiment on 30 August 1992. Reduced to one squadron, 28 Squadron The Gurkha Transport Regiment in 1995.

Headdress Badge: On the eight-pointed star in silver a scroll inscribed 'Gurkha Transport Regiment'. Issuant therefrom a wreath of laurel all in gold, over all two kukris in saltire, also in silver, handled gold ensigned with the royal cypher also in gold.

Regimental march:

Quick march: *On Parade.*

Regimental headquarters: Headquarters The Brigade of Gurkhas, Queen Elizabeth Barracks, Church Crookham, Aldershot, Hampshire.

History: *The Story of The Royal Army Service Corps and Royal Corps of Transport 1945-82* by D J Sutton.

Gurkha Military Police Disbanded in 1965.

Headdress Badge: The Royal Cypher between two kukris in saltire, the blades upwards, all within a wreath of laurel, thereunder a scroll inscribed 'GURKHA MILITARY POLICE'.

Guzerat First Mahratta War (qv) battle honour. In 1778, a Bengal Army force was sent to the help of the Bombay presidency, crossing India from east to west. Under the command of Brigadier General Goddard, the army was constantly engaged, but with reinforcements from Madras the provinces of Guzerat and the Concan were finally reduced. This battle honour also marks the campaign fought in Guzerat during 1780 which led to the capture of Bassein and Ahmedabad. *See also: Carnatic.*

Gwalior Campaign Stars 1843 These stars mark two battles, Punniar and Maharajpoor, fought on the same day, 29

December 1843 against the Mahratta state of Gwalior.

Ribbon: Rainbow pattern watered red, white, yellow, white and blue, 1" wide.

Gwell Angau Na Chywilydd **(Better death than dishonour)** Motto of the Royal Regiment of Wales, The Welch Regiment and 41st (The Welsh) Regiment.

Habergeon A light sleeveless coat of mail worn in the 14th century under the plated hauberk.

Hackbut An alternative word for arquebus (qv).

Hackle Feathered ornament worn in the Headdress of Fusilier and some Highland regiments consisting of short feathers attached to a stem and cut or 'hacked' into shape.

Hadrian Military glider, with a crew of two and a lift of 15 passengers. Produced by the WACO Aircraft Company USA, and brought into service in 1942.

Hafir Battle honour marking an action during the first phase of the reconquest of the Sudan in 1896. Kitchener, with a force consisting largely of Egyptian Army units and supported by gunboats, advanced up the Nile to occupy the province of Dongola, the main action being fought at Hafir. *See also: Atbara and Khartoum.*

Haganah *See: Palestine 1945-48.*

Hagiag Er Raml Second World War North Africa campaign battle honour marking an action during the Battle of Gazala 26 May-21 June 1942. *See also: North Africa 1940-1943; Gazala; Retma; Bir El Aslagh; Bir Hacheim; Cauldron; Knightsbridge; Tobruk 1942; Bir El Igela; Gabr El Fachri; Via Balbia; Zt El Mrasses and Sidi Rezegh 1942.*

Haig, Douglas 1st Earl (1861-1928) Viscount Dawick and 29th Laird of Bemersyde Educated at Clifton College, Brasenose College, Oxford and the Royal Military Academy. Commissioned into 7th Hussars in 1885, he joined the Egyptian Army following attendance at the Staff College. He served in the Sudan in 1898, being at both Atbara and Khartoum. He held a number of important posts during the South Africa War (1899-1902), commanded 17th Lancers for a very short period and was sent to India as inspector general of cavalry (1903-06). After serving as director of military training at Army Headquarters (1906-07) and director of staff duties (1907-09), he returned to India as chief of staff (1909-12) and, in 1912, became general officer commanding in chief, Aldershot command. When the British Expeditionary Force (qv) went to France at the outbreak of the First World War he was in command of the 1st Army Corps, and in December 1915 succeeded Sir John French as commander-in-chief. His tour of command covered a protracted period of trench warfare and included the Battle of Passchendaele. His successful attack on the Hindenburg Line, undertaken in spite of the opposition of Marshal Foch and the war cabinet, did much to restore his reputation. For his services in the war he received the thanks of Parliament, a grant of £100,000 and was raised to the peerage. After the war he devoted himself to the interests of ex-servicemen, and the Royal British Legion (qv) remains a monument to his concern for those that had served under him.

Hair Trigger Trigger of a firearm that has been adjusted to respond to the slightest pressure.

Halberd Weapon having a wooden shaft five to six feet long with a metal head having a broad cutting edge on one side and a hook on the other. The weapon was much used from 15th to 17th centuries, and carried by infantry sergeants until 1790.

Haldane of Cloan, Richard Burdon Haldane, 1st Viscount (1856-1928) Educated at Edinburgh Academy, Edinburgh and Göttingen universities. Called to the bar in 1879 he became a QC in 1890 and entered Parliament in 1885 as Liberal member for Haddington, a seat he held until 1911. He was secretary of state for war (1905-12) and a strong supporter of Cardwell's (qv) reforms. He was instrumental in the creation of an expeditionary force, the substitution of the territorial force, later the Territorial Army, for the old volunteers and militia, and the formation of a general staff on the lines recommended by the Esher Committee (qv); reforms which not only terminated a period of drift and indecision, but reorganised and modernised the military forces so that they were in reasonable shape to meet the First World War. On the formation of the first coalition government in 1915, the conservatives demanded his exclusion from office because of a remark that, as a philosopher, he regarded Germany as his 'spiritual home'.

Halfaya 1941 Second World War North Africa campaign battle honour marking an action which took place between the start of Rommel's offensive in March 1941 and the unsuccessful British offensive Operation BATTLEAXE 15-17 June 1941. *See also: North Africa 1940-1943; Agedabia; Mersa El Brega and Derna Aerodrome.*

Half-Cock On a single action firearm, a halfway position in which the hammer can be set for safety; in such a position the trigger is cocked by the hammer, which cannot reach the primer to fire the weapon.

Half-Life The time taken for half the atoms in a radioactive material to undergo decay. The time required for half of a quantity of radioactive material absorbed by living tissue or organism to be naturally eliminated.

Half-Track A vehicle, usually armoured, on which the motive power is delivered to tracks. Steering and other load carrying is wheeled.

Hamilcar Military glider, with a crew of two and a lift of some 40 passengers or a light tank. Produced in early 1942 by the General Aircraft Company Limited.

Hammam Lif Second World War North Africa campaign battle honour marking an action on 8-9 May 1943, following the fall of Tunis, British forces drove into the Cape Bon peninsula, outflanking German units by advancing along the beach. *See also: North Africa 1940-1943; Tunis; Djebel Bou Aoukaz 1943 I; Djebel Bou Aoukaz 1943 II; Nontarnaud; Ragoubet Souissi; Creteville Pass; Gromballa and Bou Ficha.*

Hammer Part of a weapon lock which rotates about a fulcrum to strike the primer or percussion cap, either directly or through a firing pin.

Hampshire, The Regimental quick march of The Royal Hampshire Regiment (37th and 67th Foot).

Hampshire Yeomanry (The Hampshire Carabiniers) In 1794 the North Hampshire Yeomanry Cavalry was accepted for service, but was disbanded in 1828 and re-raised in 1830 as The Hampshire Yeomanry Cavalry. In 1884 the title 'Carabiniers' was adopted and the regiment provided a company for both 4th and 17th Battalions of the Imperial Yeomanry during the South Africa War (1899-1902). Remaining in England until 1916, the squadrons were sent separately to France, but the regiment was reunited in 1917 and converted to infantry as 15th (Hampshire Yeomanry) Battalion The Hampshire Regiment at the end of that year. The regiment converted to artillery in 1920 on amalgamation with the Hampshire Royal Horse Artillery and served as artillery throughout the Second World War. In 1947 the regiment re-formed as an artillery unit, 295th (Hampshire Carabiniers) Heavy Anti-Aircraft Regiment Royal Artillery, and the title was finally lost in 1967. The successor sub-unit is 227 (Hampshire Yeomanry) Amphibious Engineer Squadron of 78 (Fortress) Engineer Regiment, Royal Engineers.

Hand Grenade Small metal, plastic or similar container, designed to fragment on detonation, containing high explosive material activated by a short time fuse and used in close combat.

Handgun Firearm, such as a pistol, which can be carried and fired with one hand.

Hand-Over Line A control line marked on battle maps, which should usually follow easily identified terrain features, indicating the point at which responsibility for the conduct of combat operations is passed from one force to another.

Handset Radio or telephone mouthpiece and earpiece so mounted that they can be held simultaneously to the ear and mouth.

Hands-Off Weapon or equipment which functions wholly or in part without need of manual operation.

Hangman's Hill Second World War Italian campaign battle honour marking one of the actions in the battle for Cassino. *See also: Italy 1943-1945; Monastery Hill; Castle Hill; Cassino I; Cassino II; Massa Vertecchi; Massa Tambourini and Casa Sinagogga.*

Harding of Petherton, John, 1st Baron (1896-1989) Educated at Ilminster Grammar School, he worked for the General Post Office and was commissioned into the Post Office Rifles in 1914. At the outbreak of the Second World War he was commanding 1st Battalion The Somerset Light Infantry in India. He was posted to the Middle East and rose to major general commanding the 'Desert Rats', the 7th Armoured Division, at Alamein. Returning to England he was appointed to command 8 Corps, but events led to his transfer to Italy to command 13 Corps in 1945. After the war he had the arduous and unpleasant task of maintaining order in Trieste. A number of senior appointments followed: command of Southern Command (1947), commander-in-chief Far East Land Forces (1949), commander-in-chief British Army of the Rhine (1951) and Chief of the Imperial General Staff (1952). He was promoted to Field Marshal in 1953 and served as governor and commander-in-chief of Cyprus (1955-57), during the EOKA campaign.

Harassing Fire Fire designed to disturb the rest of enemy troops, to curtail movement and, by threat of losses, to lower morale. Harassing fire programmes are usually fired at night.

Harbour Area An area, well out of contact with the enemy, in which although protection and concealment are important, administrative convenience is the major consideration.

Harness Term used to describe the collection of straps and buckles used for securing items of equipment such as parachutes or radio headsets, and securing loads to carrying frames and animals.

Harry Hopkins Second World War light tank based upon the Tetrarch (qv) designed by Vickers Armstrong and manufactured by the Metropolitan Cammell Carriage and Wagon Co. The Harry Hopkins was the final wartime development of the British light tank, but was never used in action. The Harry Hopkins had a crew of three, weighed 8 tons, and mounted a 2pdr gun and Besa machine gun. *See also: Tank and Light tank.*

Hatchet *See: Axe.*

Hautbois This musical instrument, later developed as the oboe, was the first non-signalling instrument (trumpet, drum and bugle) to be used by the English cavalry.

Havannah Battle honour marking the actions of a British expedition on the Spanish island of Cuba, having landed in June 1762. The force, in spite of heavy casualties from dysentery and malaria, invested the capital Havana, which surrendered after a siege of about 50 days on 13 August.

Haversack Bag, traditionally of canvas, for provisions or equipment, carried on the back or shoulder. From the German *Hafer* (oats) and *Sack* (bag).

Havildar A non-commissioned officer in the Indian infantry, equivalent in rank to a sergeant.

Havrincourt First World War battle honour marking one of the actions in the battle of the Hindenburg Line. The village of Havrincourt was carried on 12 September 1918. *See also: France and Flanders 1914-1918; Hindenburg Line; Épéhy; Canal du Nord; St Quentin Canal; Beaurevoir and Cambrai 1918.*

Haybox Originally an airtight box lined with hay or other insulating material and used to keep food warm. The term is now more generally applied to any container designed to keep food warm or cold.

Hazebrouck First World War battle honour marking one of the actions during the battle for Lys, the second main German assault in April 1918. Hazebrouck, an important rail junction, was the immediate objective of the thrust from Estaires. After intense fighting the British line held about five miles from the town. *See also: France and Flanders 1914-1918; Lys; Estaires; Messines 1918; Bailleul; Kemmel; Béthune and Scherpenberg.*

Headphones Two earphones held in position by a flexible strap passing over the head. *See also: Headset and Handset.*

Headquarters (HQ) The commander, his staff and supporting communications and echelons of a military formation or unit. The building from which military operations are directed.

Headset A pair of headphones, usually with microphone attached.

Heavies Nickname given to the heavy cavalry, especially the dragoon guards, which

traditionally consisted of men of heavier build and height than those of the lancers and hussars. The term has also been applied to the larger guns manned by the Royal Artillery and one of its predecessors, the Royal Garrison Artillery.

Heavy Assault Tank A.33 Although the policy of having only two classes of tank, infantry and cruiser, still held, it was decided in 1942 to try and standardise components for both classes. The A.33, built by the English Electric Co., never went into production but had a crew of five, weighed 45 tons and mounted a 75mm gun and a Besa machine gun.

Heavy Assault Tank A.39 (Tortoise) The ultimate expression of the British taste for armour rather than mobility. Design of the A.39 began in 1942, but only six prototypes were built, and those not completed until 1947. The Tortoise had a crew of seven, weighed 78 tons and mounted a 32pdr gun and three Besa machine guns.

Heavy Tank T.O.G. Experimental tank developed in the early part of the Second World War, but never brought into service. The initials T.O.G. standing for 'The Old Gang', because Sir Albert Stern, who had played a leading part in tank production in the First World War, was invited to assemble some of his old associates to form an independent design team. The Heavy Tank T.O.G. II had a crew of six, weighed 80 tons and mounted a 17pdr gun and a Besa machine gun.

Heavy Machine Gun Term generally applied to any fully automatic weapon of larger than 7.62mm calibre, but smaller than 20mm. The most common heavy machine gun in service in the British Army is the Browning M2 0.50" (12.7mm).

Hébron Le Régiment d' *See: The Royal Scots (The Royal Regiment).*

Hechtel Second World War battle honour marking the capture of Hechtel and the seizure of a further bridgehead on the Meuse-Escaut Canal after intense fighting on 12 and 13 September 1944. *See also:*

North West Europe 1944-1945; Antwerp; Neerpelt; Gheel and Aart.

Heidous Second World War North Africa campaign battle honour marking one of the actions which took place between the Fondouk operation of April 1943 and the end of the campaign. *See also: North Africa 1940-1943; Banana Ridge; Djebel Djaffa Pass and Argoub El Megas.*

Helicopter Aircraft capable of hovering, vertical and horizontal flight drawing lift and propulsion from overhead rotating blades.

Helicopter Gunship Heavily armed helicopter used for ground attack.

Heliograph A signalling system invented by Sir Henry Mance (1840-1926). Two mirrors reflecting sunlight in any required direction, their reflection being switched on and off by a key-operated shutter, were used to send messages in morse code. First used in 1878 in the Second Afghan War (qv).

Helles First World War Gallipoli campaign battle honour marking the operations based on Cape Helles in April, May and June 1915 during the Gallipoli campaign. *See also: Gallipoli 1915-16; Landing at Helles and Krithia.*

Helmet Protective or defensive armoured headwear.

Hengist Military glider, with a lift of 15 men, produced by the General Aircraft Company Limited.

Heppen Second World War battle honour marking one of the actions fought between the crossing of the Seine in August 1944 and the arrival at the Rhine in March 1945. *See also: North West Europe 1944-1945; Calais 1944; Opheusden and Asten.*

Her Bright Smile Haunts Me Still Regimental slow march of the Royal Army Medical Corps.

Her Majesty's Body Guard of the Honourable Corps of Gentlemen at Arms Descended from the Royal Body Guard, mounted and drawn largely from the gentry, founded by Henry VIII in 1509. Originally known as 'The King's Speres', by 1540 the corps was named the 'Band of Gentlemen Pensioners' in imitation of those serving the French king and known as the *'Gentilhommes de l'Hotel du Royou Pensionnaires'*. In William IV's reign the name was changed to 'Gentlemen-at-Arms' and has since been known by every sovereign as 'Our Nearest Guard and Principal Military Corps of Our Household'. The Corps was established as a military body in 1862 and consists of senior retired officers of the British Army with distinguished records. The Corps consists of about 35 members, of whom five, The Captain, The Lieutenant, The Standard Bearer, The Clerk of the Cheque and Adjutant and the Harbinger are office holders. The Corps officiates as the personal bodyguard to the Sovereign on major state occasions.

Her Royal Highness The Princess Royal Regimental slow march of the Royal Corps of Signals.

Heraklion Second World War battle honour marking the fighting on the island of Crete in May and June 1941. *See also: Crete; Canea; Retimo and Withdrawal to Sphakia.*

Herefordshire Light Infantry In April 1860 the 1st-8th Herefordshire and 1st and 2nd Radnorshire Rifle Volunteer Corps were raised; merging in February 1861 to form 1st Administrative Battalion Herefordshire and Radnorshire Rifle Volunteers. In May 1880 the Corps were consolidated and the regiment was redesignated 1st Herefordshire Rifle Volunteer Corps (Hereford and Radnor), becoming part of the Corps of the King's Shropshire Light Infantry in July 1881. On the formation of the Territorial Army in 1908 the regiment transferred on 1 April as The Herefordshire Battalion, The King's Shropshire Light Infantry, and remained part of the Corps of that regiment when redesignated 1st Battalion The Herefordshire Regiment in March 1909.

During the First World War there were three battalions of the regiment, but only one battalion survived the inter-war years. A second battalion was raised in 1939 and the two battalions fought throughout the Second World War. In January 1947 the two battalions amalgamated and a month later the regiment was redesignated 1st Battalion The Herefordshire Light Infantry. In 1966 the Territorial Army was disbanded and replaced by the Territorial Army and Volunteer Reserve, and the regiment continued to exist within the Light Infantry Volunteers. The successor unit is now found within the companies of 5th Battalion The (Shropshire and Herefordshire) Light Infantry (Volunteers).

History: *Historical Records of The Herefordshire Light Infantry and its Predecessors* by G Archer Parfitt.

Herefordshire Regiment (36th Foot) Raised in Ireland in June 1701 by Colonel William Caulfield, Viscount Charlemont, and designated 36th Foot in 1751. *See also: The Worcestershire Regiment.*

Herefordshire Yeomanry From the available records it appears that a Corps of Yeomanry Cavalry was raised in Herefordshire in 1803 and was apparently still serving in the 1820s.

Here's A Health Unto His Majesty Regimental quick march of the Royal Army Medical Corps.

Hertfordshire Regiment (49th Foot) Raised in Jamaica by Colonel Edward Trelawny, the Governor, in December 1743. *See also: Duke of Edinburgh's Royal Regiment.*

Hertfordshire Yeomanry Five independent troops of Yeomanry Cavalry were raised in Hertfordshire in June 1794, being disbanded over the period 1807-1824. In late 1830 and early 1831 seven troops were raised, four grouped as the South Hertfordshire Corps. Of the three independent troops, only the North Hertfordshire troop survived, being amalgamated with the South Hertfordshire Corps to form the Hertfordshire Yeomanry Cavalry in 1871.

The regiment found a company of 12th Battalion Imperial Yeomanry during the South Africa War (1899-1902). During the First World War the regiment served in both the mounted and dismounted role in Egypt, Gallipoli, Mesopotamia and Palestine. On amalgamation with the two Hertfordshire batteries of the Royal Field Artillery in 1920, the regiment converted to artillery, elements of the regiment serving in that role during the Second World War in Malaya, Singapore and North-West Europe. After the war two regiments were formed, both artillery and designated 'Herts Yeomanry'. In 1967 this had reduced to battery size as 201 (Hertfordshire & Bedfordshire Yeomanry) Battery, 100 (Eastern) Medium Regiment Royal Artillery (Volunteer). The successor sub-unit is now 201 (Hertfordshire & Bedfordshire Yeomanry) Battery, 100 (Yeomanry) Field Regiment Royal Artillery (Volunteer).

Hessian Boots An elegant and light boot which finished below the knee with a 'V' notch to the front. Of Hessian derivation, the boot was popular with light cavalrymen at the beginning of the 19th century, and continued in use by some into the 20th century.

Hexamine Abbreviation of hexamethylenetetramine. Type of fuel produced in small solid blocks or tablets for use in small field cookers.

High Velocity Missile *See: Starstreak.*

Highland Brigade An administrative grouping in the infantry formed under Army Order 61 of 1948 comprising The Seaforth Highlanders; Queen's Own Cameron Highlanders, Black Watch, Highland Light Infantry (to Lowland Brigade in 1959), Gordon Highlanders and Argyll and Sutherland Highlanders. The regiments of the brigade were absorbed in to the Scottish Division in 1968.

Highland Cradle Song One of the regimental slow marches (Pipes and Drums) of the Black Watch.

Highland Dress Introduced into the British Army in the companies of the Black Watch which were regimented in 1739.

Highland Light Infantry (City Of Glasgow Regiment) (71st and 74th Foot) The 71st Foot was raised by Colonel John Mackenzie, Lord MacLeod, in December 1777 and ranked as 1st Battalion 73rd (Highland) Foot; re-ranked 71st (Highland) Foot in 1786, 71st (Glasgow Highland) Foot in 1808, 71st (Glasgow Highland Light Infantry) Regiment in 1809 and 71st (Highland) Light Infantry in 1810. The 74th was raised by Major General Sir Archibald Campbell as 74th (Highland) Regiment of Foot in October 1787; also known as The Assaye Regiment, in 1803. Redesignated 74th Foot in 1816 and 74th (Highlanders) Foot in 1845. In 1881 71st (Highland) Light Infantry and 74th (Highlanders) Foot were amalgamated to form The Highland Light Infantry (City of Glasgow Regiment). On 20 January 1959 the regiment amalgamated with The Royal Scots Fusiliers (21st Foot) to form The Royal Highland Fusiliers (Princess Margaret's Own City of Glasgow and Ayrshire Regiment) (21st, 71st and 74th Foot) (qv). Headdress Badge: On the star of the Order of the Thistle a bugle-horn bearing the monogram HLI above the elephant superscribed 'Assaye', all ensigned with the crown.
History: *Proud Heritage, The Story of the Highland Light Infantry,* Vol I (1952) *71st 1777-1881;* Vol II (1959) *74th 1777-1882;* Vol III (1961) *The Highland Light Infantry 1881-1918;* Vol IV (1963) *The Highland Light Infantry 1919-1959* all by L B Oatts and *The Highland Light Infantry* by L B Oatts (1969).

Highland Yeomanry *See: Perthshire Yeomanry - The Scottish Horse.*

Highlanders The (Seaforth, Gordons And Camerons) (72nd, 75th, 78th, 79th and 92nd Foot) Formed on 17 September 1994 by the amalgamation of The Queen's Own Highlanders (Seaforth and Camerons) (72nd, 78th and 79th Foot) and The

Gordon Highlanders (75th and 92nd Foot). Headdress Badge: A stag's head caboshed, between the attires the thistle ensigned with the crown. Below, a scroll inscribed *'Cuidich'n Righ'* (Help to the King).
Motto: *Cuidich'n Righ* (Help to the King).
Regimental marches:
Quick march: *The Wee Highland Laddie* (Pipes and Drums, and Military Band).
Slow march: *The Highlanders Slow March* (Pipes and Drums) and *The Garb of Old Gaul* (Military Band).
Regimental headquarters: Cameron Barracks, Inverness, IV2 3XD and Viewfield Road, Aberdeen AB1 7XH.

Highlanders Slow March Regimental slow march (Pipes and Drums) of The Highlanders (Seaforth, Gordons and Camerons).

High Sheriff County or city officer vested with wide judicial and executive authority. His duties are defined in the Sheriffs Act 1887. *See also: Sheriff.*

Hide An area in which a force conceals itself before operations, or before moving into battle positions or from which patrols are launched.

Hielan' Laddie Regimental quick march (Pipes and Drums) of The Royal Scots Dragoon Guards, Scots Guards, Royal Highland Fusiliers, Black Watch and The Argyll and Sutherland Highlanders.

Hill 60 First World War battle honour marking the capture of this hill, at the edge of the Ypres salient and covering the approaches to the city from the south, on 17 April 1915. In spite of vigorous German counter-attacks the position was held and was to be the scene of almost constant fighting over the next three years. *See also: France and Flanders 1914-1918; Neuve-Chapelle and Ypres 1915.*

Hill 70 First World War battle honour marking the capture by the Canadians of this hill, in the Lens sector north of Vimy Ridge, on 7 June 1917. *See also: France and Flanders 1914-1918; Arras 1917; Bullecourt; Oppy Wood and Messines 1917.*

Hill 112 Second World War battle honour marking one of the actions in the Battle of Caen 4-18 July 1944. Several attempts were made to seize the hill and the neighbouring village of Maltot, lying between the Rivers Odon and Orne. The hill was captured but could not be held when counter-attacked by German armour. *See also: North West Europe 1944-1945; Caen; Noyers; Orne and Esquay.*

Hill 227 I Korean War (1950-53) battle honour marking an action which took place on this feature. *See also: Korea 1950-53; Naktong Bridgehead; Pakchon; Imjin; Kowang-San; The Hook 1952; The Hook 1953; Chongju; Chongchon II; Seoul; Chaum-Ni; Hill 327; Kapyomg-Chon; Kapyong and Maryang San.*

Hill 327 Korean War (1950-53) battle honour marking an action which took place on this feature. *See also: Korea 1950-53; Naktong Bridgehead; Pakchon; Imjin; Kowang-San; The Hook 1952; The Hook 1953; Chongju; Chongchon II; Seoul; Chaum-Ni; Hill 227 I; Kapyomg-Chon; Kapyong and Maryang San.*

Hindenburg Line First World War battle honour marking the destruction of the strong German defensive positions on the Hindenburg Line between 12 September and 6 October 1918. *See also: France and Flanders 1914-1918; Havrincourt; Épéhy; Canal du Nord; St Quentin Canal; Beaurevoir and Cambrai 1918.*

Hindoostan Battle honour awarded for actions on various dates between 1780 and 1823. In some instances the 'Elephant and Howdah' (qv) and 'Royal Tiger' (qv) were awarded with the battle honour.

Hindustan Regiment Nickname given to 76th Foot, now The Duke of Wellington's Regiment (West Riding) because the regiment distinguished itself in the Hindustan campaign of 1803-05. *See also: Hindoostan.*

Hitler Line Second World War Italian campaign battle honour marking the break through of the German defensive line between Pontecorvo and Aquino - the

so-called Hitler Line - during operations in the Liri Valley. *See also: Italy 1943-1945; Liri Valley; Monte Piccolo; Piedemonte Hill; Aquino and Melfa Crossing.*

Hochwald Second World War battle honour marking one of the actions which took place during the advance from the River Roer to the River Rhine 8 February to 10 March 1945. *See also: North West Europe 1944-1945; Rhineland; Reichswald; Cleve; Goch; Weeze; Schaddenhof; Waal Flats; Moyland; Moyland Wood and Xanten.*

Hold To be in physical possession of a given piece of terrain and to retain it against attack. The term is also applied to the situation in which sufficient pressure is applied on an enemy to prevent him moving or repositioning the force which is 'held'.

Holdfast Radio appointment title for Royal Engineer staff or units.

Holland Regiment In 1572 a number of London 'Train-Bands' were sent to Holland to assist the Protestant cause. The unit was disbanded by the Dutch in 1665, but members were formed into a new 'Holland Regiment' by Charles II on their return to England. *See also: The Buffs (3rd Foot).*

Holster Originally a container, part of horse furniture, to hold a pistol. Later adapted more widely to denote any pistol holder.

Holy Boys Nickname given to 9th Foot, later The Royal Norfolk Regiment and now the Royal Anglian Regiment. During the Peninsula War the Spaniards thought that the regimental badge, Britannia seated, was the Virgin Mary.

Home Counties Brigade An administrative grouping in the infantry formed under Army Order 61 of 1948 comprising the Queen's Royal Regiment (West Surrey), East Surrey Regiment, The Buffs (Royal East Kent Regiment), Queen's Own Royal West Kent Regiment, Royal Fusiliers (to Fusilier Brigade in 1957), Royal Sussex

Regiment and the Middlesex Regiment (Duke of Cambridge's Own). The regiments of the brigade were absorbed into the Queen's Division (qv) in 1968.

Home Service Force (HSF) In March 1982 the Secretary of State for Defence announced the introduction of a Home Service Force. This force was to be composed of older men with service experience, but who were unable to meet the Territorial Army training liability in full. The Home Service Force was to be used for the guarding of Key Points (qv) as part of the home defence plan. A pilot scheme, consisting of four companies, was set up in the autumn of that year. The force was subsequently expanded until most home defence Territorial Army battalions had at least one Home Service Force platoon. The Home Service Force was disbanded in 1992. *See also: Territorial Army.*

Home Service Helmet A blue cloth helmet introduced in 1877, similar in design to the white 'overseas' helmet being worn in some overseas stations.

Homing The capability of a missile or weapon to guide itself to its target by sensing radiations emitted from the target and adjusting its course.

Hong Kong Second World War battle honour marking the defence of the colony against numerically superior Japanese forces from 8-25 December 1941. *See also: Malaya 1941-1942 and Burma 1942-1945.*

***Honi Soit Qui Mal y Pense* (Evil to him who evil thinks)** Motto of the Order of the Garter; also used by The Life Guards, The Blues and Royals (Royal Horse Guards and 1st Dragoons), The Royal Horse Guards (The Blues), Grenadier Guards, The Royal Regiment of Fusiliers, The Royal Warwickshire Fusiliers and The Royal Fusiliers (City of London Regiment).

Honourable Artillery Company On 25 August 1537, Henry VIII issued Letters Patent to the Overseers of the Fraternity or Guild of Saint George authorising them to

begin, found and establish a certain perpetual corporation for the better increase of the defence of the Realm, with the name of Fraternity or Guild of Artillery of Longbows, Crossbows and Handguns. At that time the term Artillery included any kind of projectile-launching weapon or weapon of volley. For over a century, this body was known by many different names, which usually incorporated the word Artillery, but was not referred to as the Artillery Company until 1656. The prefix Honourable, first used in 1685, was officially confirmed by Queen Victoria in 1860. The officers of the London Trained Bands were trained by the Artillery Company from its incorporation until 1780. Contingents from the regiment served in the South Africa War (1899-1902), and it raised three infantry battalions and seven batteries of artillery in the First World War. In the Second World War the 12th (HAC) Regiment, Royal Horse Artillery served in North-West Europe, North Africa, Sicily and Italy. Now a unit of the Territorial Army and second only in precedence to the Royal Monmouthshire Royal Engineers (Militia).
Headdress Badges:
Artillery: An old-fashioned cannon with a scroll above inscribed 'HAC' and a scroll below inscribed *'Arma Pacis Fulcra'* (Arms are the fulcrum of peace), the whole surmounted by St Edward's crown.
Infantry: A grenade with monogram 'HAC' on the ball.
Regimental marches:
Quick march: *British Grenadiers.*
Slow march: *Duke of York.*
Canter: *Bonnie Dundee.*
Trot: *The Keel Row.*
Walk: *Duchess of Kent.*
Regimental headquarters: Armoury House, City Road, London, EC1Y 2BQ.
History: *The History of the Honourable Artillery Company of the City of London* by A Highmore (1804); *The History of the Honourable Artillery Company* by G A Raikes (1879); *The Honourable Artillery Company in the Great War 1914-18* by G Goold Walker (1930); *Regimental Fire! The Honourable Artillery Company in World War II* by R F Johnson (1958); *The Honourable Artillery Company 1537-1987* by Goold

Walker (1986); *The Sparks Fly Upwards* by Armstrong (1991) and *Action Front* by Colquhoun (1992).

Hooge 1915 First World War battle honour marking the fighting around the village of Hooge, which lies on the Menin road in the Ypres salient, in late July and August 1915. The Germans used flame-throwers (qv) here for the first time against the British; although they had been used earlier against the French. *See also: France and Flanders 1914-1918; Ypres 1915; Gravenstafel; St Julien; Ferzenberg; Bellewaarde; Aubers and Festubert 1915.*

Horsa Military glider, with a crew of two and a lift of 25 passengers. Manufactured from 1941 by Airspeeds Limited. A total of some 5,000 of these aircraft were produced.

Horse Originally the term used for regiments of heavy cavalry who wore armour. By the mid-18th century they had ceased to exist except for the Household Cavalry.

Hotspur Military glider produced by the General Aircraft Company Limited from 1940. Two versions of the glider were produced, both with a crew of two; one with a lift of eight passengers, and one with a lift of 29 passengers. Some 1,000 of the 29-passenger version were produced.

HOURS

G Hour The time on which an order is given to deploy a unit.

H Hour The specific time at which hostilities or a given operation begin, the line of departure is crossed by the leading elements of an attack or, in the case of amphibious operations, the time at which the first waterborne assault elements arrive on the beach.

K Hour The time at which a convoy system is to be introduced on a given route.

L Hour The time at which the first heliborne assault wave touches down at the landing zone in amphibious or airmobile operations

N Hour The specific time for the explosion of the first of a series of tactical

nuclear weapons, as part of a specific ground force operation, or in the case of a single strike, the time planned for that explosion.

P Hour The time of the dropping of the first stick in parachute operations.

T Hour The time at which authority is to be transferred.

Y Hour In airmobile operations, the time at which the first helicopter of the first wave leaves the pick-up point.

Horse Marines Nickname given the 17th Lancers, now The Queen's Royal Lancers. In 1795, two troops of the regiment served in the frigate HMS *Hermione* on the West Indies Station.

Hose Tops Footless stockings, now obsolescent, usually in regimental or corps colour, worn with short puttees and ankle boots when wearing shorts.

Hotchkiss Mark I British-built version of the French Hotchkiss machine gun used to supplement the Vickers (qv) and Lewis (qv) machine guns in the First World War, and still in limited service in the Second World War.

Household Cavalry The Life Guards and The Blues and Royals (Royal Horse Guards and 1st Dragoons) now form the Household Cavalry.

Household Cavalry Regiment The Household Cavalry Regiment is a field service regiment formed from a union of the Life Guards and The Blues and Royals (Royal Horse Guards and 1st Dragoons).

Household Cavalry Mounted Regiment The Household Cavalry Mounted Regiment is formed from elements of the Life Guards and The Blues and Royals (Royal Horse Guards and 1st Dragoons) for ceremonial duties in peace.

Housewife Name given to the small sewing kit issued to army personnel.

Htizwe Second World War Burma campaign battle honour marking an action during the Arakan offensive of 8 January to

18 March 1943 in the campaign in Burma. *See also: Burma 1942-1945; Donbaik; Rathedaung and Point 201 (Arakan).*

Hull Down The positioning of a tank or other armoured vehicle so that, from an enemy's viewpoint, only the turret and gun are visible, the hull being protected by a natural or man-made earth embankment.

Humber 1 Ton Four-wheel-drive armoured vehicle capable of carrying an infantry section. Introduced in the mid-1950s the vehicle was in the process of being phased out, indeed many had already been sold to overseas buyers, when the emergency arose in Northern Ireland. The so-called 'pig' was brought back into service and subsequently became the workhorse for operations in Northern Ireland.

Hundred Pipers Regimental quick march of 10th Princess Mary's Own Gurkha Rifles.

Huntingdonshire Regiment (31st Foot) Raised by Colonel George Villiers in February 1702 as a regiment of marines. *See also: East Surrey Regiment.*

Huntingdonshire Yeomanry A Corps of Yeomanry Cavalry was commissioned for the county in April 1794. Three troops are recorded in 1803 and appear to have served until the 1820s. In 1860 The Huntingdonshire Mounted Rifles (The Duke of Manchester's Light Horse) was raised, with two troops in Bedfordshire. It was disbanded in 1882.

Hunt's Gap Second World War North Africa campaign battle honour marking the repulse, with heavy losses, of an attempted German advance in North Africa over the period 27-28 February 1942. *See also: North Africa 1940-1943.*

Huntsman's Chorus An arrangement of the Huntsman's Chorus forms part of the regimental quick march of The Royal Green Jackets.

Hussar Originally the name of the Hungarian cavalry raised by Mathias I in

1458. The name is derived from the old Hungarian word for 20, as every twentieth household was required to furnish a man for the corps. The term was later applied to light cavalry used largely in reconnaissance or operations where speed was of the essence. The success of these light cavalry regiments brought about the conversion of a number of British Army light dragoon regiments to hussars or lancers in the early years of the 19th Century. In 1922 there were 12 regiments of hussars in the British Army: 3rd, 4th, 7th, 8th, 10th, 11th, 13th, 14th, 15th, 18th, 19th and 20th but, with reductions in the cavalry establishment over the years, there are now only two regiments of hussars: The King's Royal Hussars, and The Queen's Royal Hussars (The Queen's Own and Royal Irish).

HUSSAR REGIMENTS

3rd The King's Own Hussars Raised as a regiment of dragoons *(See: 3rd Dragoons)* in August 1685 as The Queen Consort's Own Regiment of Dragoons, command being given to Charles Seymour, Duke of Somerset. Retitled The King's Own Regiment of Dragoons in 1714, 3rd (King's Own) Dragoons in 1751, 3rd (King's Own) Light Dragoons in 1818, 3rd (King's Own) Hussars in 1861 and 3rd The King's Own Hussars in 1921. On 3 November 1958 the regiment amalgamated with 7th Queen's Own Hussars to form The Queen's Own Hussars (qv). Headdress Badge: On a ground the White Horse of Hanover over a scroll inscribed '3rd The King's Own Hussars'. History: *The Galloping Third* by H Bolitho (1963) and *The 3rd (King's Own) Hussars 1914-1919* by H T Willcox (1925).

4th Queen's Own Hussars Raised as a regiment of dragoons *(See: 4th Dragoons)* by Colonel The Hon John Berkeley in July 1685 as Berkeley's Dragoons, later Princess Anne of Denmark's Dragoons, and numbered 4th Dragoons in 1751. Redesignated 4th or Queen's Own Dragoons in 1788, 4th or Queen's Own Light Dragoons in 1818, 4th (The Queen's Own) Hussars in 1861 and 4th Queen's Own Hussars in 1921. On 24 October 1958 the regiment amalgamated with 8th King's Royal Irish

Hussars to form The Queen's Royal Irish Hussars (qv).

Headdress Badge: Within a circle inscribed 'Queen's Own Hussars' the Roman numerals IV with, beneath, a scroll inscribed 'Mente et Manu' (With heart and hand), all ensigned with the crown.

History: *The Story of The 4th Queen's Own Hussars 1685-1958* by D Scott Daniell (1959) and *4th (Queen's Own) Hussars in The Great War* by H N D Evans (1959).

7th Queen's Own Hussars Raised as a regiment of dragoons *(See: 7th Dragoons)* in December 1690 as Cunningham's Dragoons. Redesignated The Princess of Wales's Own Royal Dragoons in 1715 and The Queen's Own Dragoons in 1727. The regiment was redesignated 7th or Queen's Own Dragoons in 1751, 7th or Queen's Own Light Dragoons in 1783, 7th (Queen's Own) Hussars in 1805 and 7th Queen's Own Hussars in 1921. On 3 November 1958 the regiment amalgamated with 3rd The King's Own Hussars to form The Queen's Own Hussars (qv).

Headdress Badge: Within a circle inscribed '7th Queen's Own Hussars', the monogram 'Q.O.' reversed and interlaced and ensigned with the crown.

History: *The 7th Queen's Own Hussars* by J M Brereton (1975); *The 7th (Queen's Own) Hussars* (2 Vols) by C R B Barrett (1914); *The Years Between: 7th Hussars 1911-1937* by R Evans (1965) and *The Seventh and Three Enemies* by G Davy (1952).

8th King's Royal Irish Hussars Raised as a regiment of dragoons *(See: 8th Dragoons)* from Irish Protestants in February 1693 as Conyngham's (Cunningham's) Regiment of Dragoons and redesignated 8th Dragoons (qv) in 1751. The regiment was redesignated 8th Light Dragoons in 1775, 8th or The King's Royal Irish Light Dragoons in 1777, 8th (The King's Royal Irish) Hussars in 1822 and 8th King's Royal Irish Hussars in 1921. On 24 October 1958 the regiment amalgamated with 4th Queen's Own Hussars to form The Queen's Royal Irish Hussars (qv).

Headdress Badge: The angel harp ensigned with the crown. Beneath, a scroll inscribed '8th King's Royal Irish Hussars'.

History: *The History of VIII King's Royal Irish Hussars 1693-1927* (2 Vols) by R H Murray (1928) and *Men of Valour, The Third Volume of The History of VIII King's Royal Irish Hussars 1927-1958* by O Fitzroy (1961).

Queen's Own Hussars Formed on 3 November 1958 through the amalgamation of 3rd The King's Own Hussars and 7th Queen's Own Hussars. In September 1993 the regiment amalgamated with The Queen's Royal Irish Hussars to form The Queen's Royal Hussars (The Queen's Own and Royal Irish) (qv).

Headdress Badge: 'Q.O.' above the White Horse of Hanover, within the arter.

Motto: *Nec Aspera Terrent* (Nor do difficulties deter).

Regimental marches:

Quick march: *Light Cavalry*.

Slow marches: *The 3rd Hussars Slow March* and *The Garb of Old Gaul*.

History: *The Queen's Own Hussars, Tercentenary Edition 1685-1985.*

Queen's Royal Irish Hussars Formed on 24 October 1958 through the amalgamation of 4th Queen's Own Hussars and 8th King's Royal Irish Hussars. In September 1993 the regiment amalgamated with The Queen's Own Hussars to form The Queen's Royal Hussars (The Queen's Own and Royal Irish) (qv).

Headdress Badge: Within a circle inscribed 'Queen's Royal Irish Hussars' the Irish harp surmounted by the royal crest. Below, a scroll inscribed 'Mente et Manu'.

Mottoes: *Mente et Manu* (With heart and hand) and *Pristinae Virtutis Memores* (The memory of former valour).

Regimental marches:

Quick march: An arrangement of *St Patrick's Day, Berkeley's Dragoons* and *A Galloping 8th Hussar*.

Slow marches: *Loretto* and *March of the Scottish Archers*.

History: *Irish Hussar, A Short History of The Queen's Royal Irish Hussars* by J Strawson, T Pierson and R Rhoderick Jones.

10th Royal Hussars (Prince Of Wales's Own) Raised as a regiment of dragoons *(See: 10th Dragoons)* by Brigadier General Humphrey Gore in July 1715 as Gore's Regiment of Dragoons and designated 10th Dragoons in 1751.

Redesignated 10th or Prince of Wales's Own Light Dragoons in 1783, 10th or Prince of Wales's Own Hussars in 1806, 10th The Prince of Wales's Own Royal Hussars in 1811 and 10th Royal Hussars (Prince of Wales's Own) in 1921. On 25 October 1969 the regiment amalgamated with 11th Hussars (Prince Albert's Own) to form The Royal Hussars (Prince of Wales's Own) (qv).

Headdress Badge: The plume, coronet and motto of the Prince of Wales. Below, a scroll inscribed '10th Royal Hussars'.

History: *Memoirs of the 10th Royal Hussars (PWO) 1715-1890* by R S Loddell (1891); *The 10th Royal Hussars and Essex Yeomanry during the First World War* by F D H C Whitmore (1920); *10th Royal Hussars in the Second World War 1939-1945* (1948) and *The 10th Royal Hussars 1715-1969* by M Brander.

11th Hussars (Prince Albert's Own) Raised as a regiment of dragoons *(See: 11th Dragoons)* by Brigadier General Phillip Honeywood in July 1715 as Honeywood's Regiment of Dragoons and designated 11th Dragoons) in 1751. The regiment was redesignated 11th Light Dragoons in 1783, 11th Prince Albert's Own Hussars in 1840, and 11th Hussars (Prince Albert's Own) in 1921. On 25 October 1969 the regiment amalgamated with 10th Royal Hussars (Prince of Wales's Own) to form The Royal Hussars (Prince of Wales's Own) (qv).

Headdress Badge: The crest of Prince Albert with below, a scroll inscribed with his motto, *'Treu und Fest'* (True and Trusty).

History: *The Historical Records of the 11th Hussars 1715-1908* by G T Williams (1908); *The Eleventh Hussars (PAO) 1908-1934* by L R Lumley (1936); *The Eleventh at War 1935-1945* by Dudley Clarke (1952) and *The 11th Hussars 1715-1969* by R Brett-Smith.

Royal Hussars (Prince Of Wales's Own) Formed on 25 October 1969 through the amalgamation of 10th Royal Hussars (Prince of Wales's Own) and 11th Hussars (Prince Albert's Own). On 4 December 1992 the regiment amalgamated with 14th/20th King's Hussars to form The King's Royal Hussars (qv).

Headdress Badge: The plume, coronet and motto of the Prince of Wales. Below, a scroll inscribed 'The Royal Hussars'.

Motto: *Ich Dien* (I serve).

Regimental Marches:

Quick march: *The Merry Month of May*.

Slow march: *Coburg*.

History: *Remember With Advantages* by H Keown-Boyd (1994).

13th Hussars Raised as a regiment of dragoons *(See: 13th Dragoons)* by Brigadier General Richard Munden in July 1715 as Munden's Regiment of Dragoons, designated 13th Dragoons in 1751 and 13th Light Dragoons in 1783. In 1861 the regiment converted to hussars as 13th Hussars and, on 11 April 1922, the regiment amalgamated with 18th Royal Hussars (Queen Mary's Own) to form 13th/18th Hussars. The regiment was redesignated 13th/18th Royal Hussars (Queen Mary's Own) on 31 December 1935.

Headdress Badge: Within a circle bearing the motto *'Viret in Aeternum'* (It flourishes for ever) the Roman numerals XIII, all within a laurel wreath and ensigned with the crown.

History: *History of XIII Hussars* (2 Vols.) by C R B Barrett and *XIII Hussars in the Great War* by H Mortimer Durand.

13th/18th Royal Hussars (Queen Mary's Own) Formed on 11 April 1922 through the amalgamation of 13th Hussars and 18th Royal Hussars (Queen Mary's Own). On 1 December 1992 the regiment amalgamated with 15th/19th The King's Royal Hussars to form The Light Dragoons (qv).

Headdress Badge: A 'Z' scroll inscribed 'XIII/XVIII Royal Hussars' superimposed on the monogram 'Q.M.O.' interlaced, all ensigned with the crown.

Mottoes: *Viret in Aeternum* (It shall flourish forever) and *Pro Rege, Pro Lege, Pro Patria conamur* (We strive for our King, our law and our country).

Regimental Marches:

Quick march: *Balaklava*.

Slow marches: *13th Hussars slow march* and *18th Hussars slow march*.

History: *History of 13th/18th Royal Hussars 1922-1947* by C H Miller.

14th King's Hussars Raised as a regiment of dragoons *(See: 14th Dragoons)* by Brigadier General James Dormer in July

1715 as Dormer's Regiment of Dragoons, designated 14th Dragoons in 1720 and 14th Light Dragoons in 1776. In 1798 the regiment became 14th or Duchess of York's Own Light Dragoons and 14th King's Light Dragoons in 1830. In 1861 the regiment converted to hussars as 14th (King's) Hussars, changed to 14th King's Hussars in 1921 and amalgamated with 20th Hussars on 11 April 1922 to form 14th/20th Hussars. On 31 December 1936 the regiment was redesignated 14th/20th King's Hussars (qv).

Headdress Badge: The Prussian Eagle. This was granted in 1798 in honour of the Princess Royal of Prussia, wife of the Duke of York.

History: *Historical Record of 14th Light Dragoons* by R Cannon; *14th (King's) Hussars Historical Record* by H B Hamilton (1901) and *14th (King's) Hussars Historical Record (Vol. 2)* by J Gilbert-Browne (1932).

14th/20th King's Hussars Formed on 11 April 1922 through the amalgamation of 14th King's Hussars and 20th Hussars. On 4 December 1992 the regiment amalgamated with The Royal Hussars (Prince of Wales's Own) to form The King's Royal Hussars (qv).

Headdress Badge: The Prussian Eagle.

Regimental marches:

Quick march: *Royal Sussex.*

Slow march: *The Eagle.*

History: *Emperor's Chambermaids (The Story of the 14th/20th King's Hussars)* by L B Oatts (1973); and *The Hawks Short History 14th/20th King's Hussars* by Perrett (1984).

15th The King's Hussars Raised as a regiment of light dragoons *(See: 15th Dragoons)* by Colonel George Augustus Eliott (1st Lord Heathfield) at London in March 1759 as 15th Light Dragoons, designated 1st or King's Light Dragoons in 1766 and 15th or King's Light Dragoons in 1769. Converted to hussars in 1806 as 15th The King's Hussars; retitled 15th (King's) Hussars in 1861 and 15th The King's Hussars in 1921. On 11 April 1922 the regiment amalgamated with 19th Royal Hussars (Queen Alexandra's Own) to form 15th/19th Hussars. Redesignated 15th The King's Royal Hussars on 31 October 1932 and 15th/19th The King's Royal Hussars on 31 December 1933 (qv).

Headdress Badge: Within the garter the royal crest upon the short title 'XVKH'. Below, a scroll inscribed *'Merebimur'* (We shall be worthy).

History: *XVth (The King's) Hussars 1759-1913* by H C Wylly (1914) and *History of 15th The King's Hussars 1914-1922* by Lord Carnock (1932).

15th/19th The King's Royal Hussars Formed on 11 April 1922 through the amalgamation of 15th The King's Hussars and 19th Royal Hussars (Queen Alexandra's Own). On 1 December 1992 the regiment amalgamated with 13th/18th Royal Hussars (Queen Mary's Own) to form The Light Dragoons (qv).

Headdress Badge: Within the garter the Royal Crest upon the numerals 'XV.XIX' and the motto *'Merebimur'*.

Motto: *Merebimur* (We shall be worthy).

Regimental marches:

Quick march: *The Bold King's Hussars.*

Slow marches: *Eliott's Light Horse* (15th Hussars) and *Denmark* (19th Hussars).

History: *The History of 15th/19th The King's Royal Hussars 1939-1945* by G Courage (1949); *The History of 15th/19th The King's Royal Hussars 1945-1980* by J Bastin (1981) and *15th/19th The King's Royal Hussars - A Pictorial History 1922-1989* by R Thompson (1989).

18th Hussars Raised in Ireland as a regiment of light dragoons *(See: 18th Dragoons)* in 1759 as 19th Light Dragoons, renumbered 18th Light Dragoons in 1763. In 1805 the regiment converted to Hussars and disbanded in 1822. Re-raised in 1858 as 18th Hussars; redesignated 18th (Queen Mary's Own) Hussars in 1910 and 18th Royal Hussars (Queen Mary's Own) in 1919. On 11 April 1922 the regiment amalgamated with 13th Hussars to form 13th/18th Hussars, redesignated 13th/18th Royal Hussars (Queen Mary's Own) (qv) on 31 December 1935.

Headdress Badge: Within a circle inscribed 'Queen Mary's Own', the Roman numerals 'XVIII', upon a laurel spray and ensigned with the crown.

History: *Memoirs of the XVIII Hussars 1759-1906* by H Malet and *Memoirs of the 18th (Queen Mary's Own) Royal Hussars 1906-1922* by C Burnett.

19th Hussars Raised in 1759 as 19th

Light Dragoons *(See: 19th Dragoons)*, renumbered 18th Light Dragoons in 1761 and disbanded in 1763. Re-raised in 1779 as 19th Light Dragoons and again disbanded in 1783. Re-raised in 1786 as 19th Light Dragoons and converted to 19th Lancers in 1817. Disbanded in 1821. In 1858 the 1st Bengal European Cavalry (qv) converted to become 19th Hussars in 1861. The regiment was designated 19th (Alexandra, Princess of Wales's Own) Hussars in 1902, 19th (Queen Alexandra's Own Royal) Hussars in 1908 and 19th Royal Hussars (Queen Alexandra's Own) in 1921. On 11 April 1922 the regiment amalgamated with 15th The King's Hussars to form 15th/19th Hussars, redesignated 15th The King's Royal Hussars on 31 October 1932 and 15th/19th The King's Royal Hussars (qv) on 31 December 1935.

Headdress Badge: The monogram of Queen Alexandra interlaced with the cross of the Danish Order of the Dannebrog, bearing the date '1855'.

History: *The Nineteenth and their Times 1759-1899* by J Murray (1899).

20th Hussars Raised in 1759 as 20th Inniskilling Light Dragoons *(See: 20th Dragoons)* and disbanded in 1763. Re-raised in 1778 as 20th Light Dragoons and disbanded again in 1791. Re-raised in 1791 as 20th Jamaica Light Dragoons, redesignated 20th Light Dragoons in 1802 and disbanded in 1819. In 1858 the 2nd Bengal European Light Cavalry converted and was designated 20th Hussars in 1861. On 11 April 1922 the regiment amalgamated with 14th King's Hussars to form 14th/20th Hussars which was redesignated 14th/20th King's Hussars (qv) on 31 December 1936.

Headdress Badge: The letter 'H' flanked by the Roman numerals 'XX' and ensigned with the Crown.

History: *20th Hussars in the Great War* by Darling.

The King's Royal Hussars Formed on 4 December 1992 through the amalgamation of The Royal Hussars (Prince of Wales's Own) and 14th/20th King's Hussars.

Headdress Badge: A Prussian Eagle.

Regimental marches:

Quick march: *The King's Royal Hussars*.

Slow march: *Coburg*.

Home headquarters:

North: Fulwood Barracks, Fulwood, Preston, PR2 4AA.

South: Peninsula Barracks, Romsey Road, Winchester, SO23 8TS.

The Queen's Royal Hussars (The Queen's Own and Royal Irish) Formed in September 1993 through the amalgamation of The Queen's Own Hussars and The Queen's Royal Irish Hussars.

Headdress Badge: The Angel Harp superimposed on the monogram 'Q.O.H' interlaced, the whole ensigned by a crown. Below, a scroll inscribed 'The Queen's Royal Hussars'.

Motto: *Mente et Manu* (With heart and hand).

Regimental marches:

Quick march: An arrangement of *Light Cavalry* (Queen's Own Hussars) and *St Patrick's Day* (Queen's Royal Irish Hussars).

Slow Marches: *3rd Hussars, Loretto, Garb of Old Gaul* and *March of the Scottish Archers*.

Gallop: *The Campbells are Coming*.

Canter: *Bonnie Dundee*.

Trot: *Encore*.

Home headquarters:

London: Regents Park Barracks, Albany Street, London NW1 4AL.

Midlands: 28 Jury Street, Warwick, CV34 4EW.

23rd Hussars Raised in 1940 and disbanded in 1948.

26th Hussars Raised in 1941 and disbanded in 1948.

Hyderabad Battle honour marking the action during the conquest of Scinde in 1843, in which Napier made a forced march in intense heat with 22nd Foot mounted on camels, and defeated the Baluch enemy outside Hyderabad and relieved the British residency. *See also: Scinde; Meanee; Maharajpore and Punniar.*

Hythe Seaside town on the Kent coast four miles west of Folkestone. For many years the home of the Army School of Musketry, later the Small Arms School and School of Infantry Small Arms Wing and Signals Wing. The extensive firing ranges at Hythe, coupled with those at Lydd, now form the major part of the Cinque Ports Training Area.

Ibbenbüren Second World War battle honour marking the fighting of 1-6 April 1945 to secure the crest of the Teutoburger Ridge. *See also: North West Europe 1944-1945; Leese; Aller and Brinkum.*

***Ich Dien* (I serve)** Motto of the Princes of Wales, carried by many regiments bearing the name 'Prince of Wales's' or 'Princess of Wales's'. Motto of 3rd Carabiniers (Prince of Wales's Dragoon Guards), 3rd Dragoon Guards (Prince of Wales's), 12th Royal Lancers (Prince of Wales's), The Royal Hussars (Prince of Wales's Own), 10th Royal Hussars (Prince of Wales's Own), The Middlesex Regiment (Duke of Cambridge's Own), The South Lancashire Regiment (The Prince of Wales's Volunteers) and 82nd Regiment of Foot (Prince of Wales's Volunteers).

Identity Discs In the South Africa War (1899-1902) the first steps were taken to ensure that casualties could be identified, and soldiers carried in their pocket a strip of tape bearing their name. The first metal discs were issued in 1902.

Idice Bridgehead Second World War Italian campaign battle honour marking an action during the breakthrough at Bologna in April 1945. See also: *Italy 1943-1945; Bologna; Medecina; Gaiana Crossing and Sillaro Crossing.*

Igniter Fuse to fire an explosive charge.

Ilkley Moor Regimental quick march of the Yorkshire Volunteers.

Image Intensifier A night viewing device which concentrates ambient light.

Imjin Korean War battle honour marking the 29th Brigade resistance to the Chinese offensive across the River Imjin 22-25 April 1951. *See also Korea 1950-53; Naktong Bridgehead; Pakchon; Kowang-San; The Hook 1952; The Hook 1953; Chongju; Chongchon II; Seoul; Chaum-Ni; Hill 327; Kapyong-Chon; Kapyong; Maryang San and Hill 227 I.*

Immortals Nickname given 76th Foot, now the Duke of Wellington's Regiment (West Riding). During the Mahratta War, almost every man had one or more wounds.

Imperial Defence College The college, now the Royal College of Defence Studies (qv), owes its origin to the recommendation of a cabinet committee in 1922 presided over by Winston Churchill, then Secretary of State for the Colonies. It was founded in 1927 its objective being 'the training of a body of officers and civilian officials in the broadest aspects of imperial strategy and the occasional examination of concrete problems of imperial defence referred to them by the Chiefs of Staff Committee'. The experience of the Second World War underlined the need for such an institution for training at the highest level and, although closed during the war, it re-opened in 1946. The current course lasts one year and is held at Seaford House, Belgrave Square, London. *See: Royal College of Defence Studies.*

Imperial Echoes Regimental quick march of the Royal Army Pay Corps and of the Staff and Personnel Branch of the Adjutant General's Corps.

Imperial War Museum Founded by the War Cabinet in March 1917 to be a record and memorial of the effort and sacrifice of the British peoples in the First World War. It records and illustrates all aspects of both World Wars and the other operations in which the forces of the British Commonwealth have been engaged since 1914. Exhibits include the armed and civil defence forces and the home front, and an extensive film and photographic library.

Imperial Yeomanry It had never been intended that the Yeomanry (qv) should serve abroad; indeed, it was specifically prevented from doing so by statute. However, the defeats inflicted on the British by the Boers in the closing months of 1899 made a raising of the force levels imperative. On 18 December 1899 the British government appealed for volunteers and special legislation was passed to allow volunteers to serve outside Britain in specially formed units. Companies of Imperial Yeomanry were formed and these were regimented into battalions of Imperial Yeomanry. The Yeomanry fought with immense distinction in the war in South Africa, and the experience of employing volunteers in campaigns abroad was to be an important factor in the formation of the Territorial Army (qv) by Lord Haldane (qv) in 1908.

Imphal Second World War Burma campaign battle honour marking the operations which resulted in the destruction of the Japanese offensive in the area of Imphal in March 1944. *See also: Burma 1942-1945; Tuitum; Nungshigum; Bishenpur; Kanglatongbi; Sakawng; Tamu Road; Shenam Pass and Litan.*

Implode To collapse or cause to collapse inward by the application of external pressure, usually by an explosive charge.

Impossible Bridge Second World War Italian campaign battle honour marking one of the actions on the Eighth Army front during 1943. *See also: Italy 1943-1945; Landing at Porto San Venere; Taranto; San Salvo; Orsogna and Caldari.*

Impressment Authorised by an Act of 1702 under which imprisoned debtors were released in return for agreeing to enlist 'for the duration', or find a suitable substitute. The same Act permitted the 'conscription' of unemployed men and paupers. This practice was revived briefly in 1756.

Improvised Explosive Device (IED) Explosive devices, usually those attributable to terrorists.

In and Out Nickname for the Naval and Military Club in Picaddilly, London. The nickname is derived from the prominent signs on the pillars at the entrance and exit.

***In Arduis Fidelis* (Faithful in adversity)** Motto of the Royal Army Medical Corps.

In This Sign Conquer Motto of the Royal Army Chaplains' Department.

***In Veritate Religionis Confido* (I trust in the truth of my faith)** Motto of The King's Own Scottish Borderers.

Incontro Second World War Italian campaign battle honour marking the fighting 5-8 August 1944 which led to the capture of Incontro during the advance to Florence. *See also: Italy 1943-1945; Advance to Florence; Monte San Michele; Monte Domini and Monte Scalari.*

India Battle honour awarded to eight British regiments in recognition of their service, over assorted periods, between 1791 and 1823.

India Medal 1895-1902 Queen Victoria died before the issue of the seventh clasp and the medal was re-struck with the bust of King Edward VII.
Ribbon: three vertical bands of crimson and two of dark green, all of equal width.
Clasps: Defence of Chitral 1895; Relief of Chitral 1895; Punjab Frontier 1897-98; Malakand 1897; Samana 1897; Tirah 1897-98 and Waziristan 1901-2.

Indian Distinguished Service Medal Gallantry award instituted by a Royal

Warrant of 26 June 1907 to reward 'the distinguished services of the Indian commissioned and non-commissioned officers and men of Our Indian Regular Forces, including the Reserve of the Indian Army, Border Militia and Levies, and Military Police and Imperial Service Troops when employed under the orders of Our Government of India...'.

Ribbon: Dark blue (as for the Indian Order of Merit), 1¼" wide, with a crimson stripe (as for the Order of British India), ½" wide.

India General Service Medal 1854-1895 The medal, to which there are 23 clasps, covers a period of 41 years.

Ribbon: Three crimson and two blue stripes of equal width.

Clasps: Pegu; Persia; North West Frontier; Umbeyla; Bhootan; Looshai; Perak; Jowaki 1887-8; Naga 1879-80; Burma 1885-7; Sikkim 1888; Hazara 1888; Burma 1887-89; Chin-Lushai 1889-90; Samana 1891; Hazara 1891; N.E.Frontier 1891; Hunza 1891; Burma 1889-92; Lushai 1889-92; Chin Hills 1892-93; Kachin Hills 1892-93 and Waziristan 1894-95.

India General Service Medal 1908-1935 This new General Service Medal was issued in December 1908 for the North-West Frontier campaign of that year.

Ribbon: Green with a dark blue vertical stripe 15mm wide at the centre.

Clasps: North West Frontier 1908; Abor 1911-12; Afghanistan N.W.F. 1919; Waziristan 1919-21; Mahsud 1919-20; Malabar 1921-22; Waziristan 1921-24; Waziristan 1925; North West Frontier 1930-31; Burma 1930-32; Mohmand 1933 and North West Frontier 1935.

India General Service Medal 1936-1939 Instituted in 1938 to replace the 1908 award (qv).

Ribbon: Stone coloured centre flanked on each side by a thin vertical red stripe and green edges 6mm wide.

Clasps: North West Frontier 1936-37; and North West Frontier 1937-1939.

India Mutiny The India mutiny may be traced to many causes: the annexation of Oudh in 1856 caused much unrest among the natives; there was a widely held belief that the British intended to introduce Christianity by force, compelling the natives to forsake their religion and the Sepoys believed that the cartridges with which they had been issued had been greased with cow's fat and hog's lard, and that they could not therefore bite the cartridges before loading without defilement and loss of caste. Furthermore, the campaign in Afghanistan and the late Crimean War (1854-55) had shaken Sepoy faith in British power. The mutiny broke out on 10 May 1857 at Meerut and spread to Delhi. Within three weeks the whole Ganges basin was in uproar and the representative of the royal line at Delhi was again proclaimed Emperor of India. There were less than 40,000 British soldiers to hold in check a population close to 100,000,000. Cawnpore and Lucknow were besieged, but the Punjab was held in check. A small British force marched against Delhi, Cawnpore was relieved and Lucknow held out against the siege. In September the tide turned: Delhi was stormed and Lucknow was relieved in November, although the city was not finally taken until the following year. Although the Central Provinces were not pacified until 1859, the mutiny may be said to have ended in 1858. The chief result of the mutiny was that the rule of the East India Company came to an end, the Government of India Act of 1858 transferring the government of India to the Crown. In 1877 Queen Victoria was proclaimed Empress of India and the Governor-General became known as the Viceroy.

India Mutiny Medal 1857-1858 Granted by the Indian Government to all armed forces of the Crown and the Honourable East India Company in 1858 and extended in 1860 to all who had borne arms in the suppression of the mutiny.

Ribbon: Three white and two red stripes of equal width.

Clasps: Delhi; Defence of Lucknow; Relief of Lucknow; Lucknow and Central India.

Indian Order of Merit (Military and Civil Divisions) The Military Division of

the Indian Order of Merit was instituted in 1837 by the Honourable East India Company, the forces of which were transferred to the Crown in 1860. The original intention had been that two military orders should be instituted for the native portion of the Company's Army, one as a reward to commissioned officers for 'long, faithful and honourable service' to be known as the Order of British India, the other, to all ranks for 'conspicuous gallantry in the field', and called the Order of Merit. The rules and regulations for these two orders were published in the General Order by the Governor-General of India, Number 94 of 1 May 1837. The Civil Division of the Order was published in the Gazette of India dated 3 May 1902. In 1903 the designation of both divisions was altered from the 'Order of Merit' to the 'Indian Order of Merit' to distinguish it from the Imperial Order of Merit. By a Royal Warrant of 25 August 1939 the Crown made provision for both divisions of the order and reduced the Civil Division to a single class; a Royal Warrant of 20 December 1944 addressed the Military Division similarly.
Ribbon: Military Division: Dark blue, $1\frac{1}{2}$" wide, with red edges. Civil Division: Dark red with blue edges, originally $1\frac{3}{8}$" wide, changing to 1" in 1939.

Indirect Fire Fire delivered at a target which cannot be seen by the firer.

Infantry Over the years the British infantry has developed an unparalleled international reputation for courage, discipline, endurance and tenacity. There are few areas of the world in which the British infantry has not at some time been deployed.

The number of infantry regiments on establishment has increased and reduced in line with the national perception of the threat. Since the second half of the 18th century there has been a constant and bewildering process of raising, merging, renumbering, amalgamating, disbanding, re-raising and placing in 'suspended animation' of regiments the complexity of which has been compounded by the transfer of regiments from the East India Company, Scottish and Irish establish-

ments. This process of adjustment continues. Until 1751 the 'marching regiments of foot' were known either by their royal or distinctive title, or by the name of their colonel. In 1751 a system of numbering was introduced to the infantry of the line and, from the summer of 1782, the identification of regiments with specific territorial areas began.

In 1872 Cardwell (qv) produced his 'localisation' scheme, which had considerable impact on the organisation of the infantry. The country was divided into 66 brigade districts, based on the county boundaries and allocated according to the population centres. Within each district regular and volunteer units were organised around a regimental depot which acted as the administrative and basic training centre for recruits. Infantry regiments from 26th Foot to 109th Foot (the 60th and 79th Foot were excepted) were linked in pairs (though at this stage still retaining their existing numbers and titles), and were brigaded with two Militia (qv) battalions and local Volunteer groups. Of the two regular battalions it was planned that one should serve overseas while the other would act as recruiter and trainer to make good casualties and wastage in both battalions. The Militia would act as a trained reserve in the event of an emergency. In spite of bitter opposition within the Army, Cardwell's restructuring plan became effective on 1 July 1881, setting the framework for the modern infantry.

Between 1918 and 1923 a number of changes took place in the infantry: line regiments were given the choice, and most chose to do so, of changing their title to reflect 'territorial' affiliation rather than their 'honour' designation and, in 1922 with the establishment of the Irish Free State, the five Irish regiments - The Royal Irish (18th Foot), The Connaught Rangers (88th and 94th Foot), The Leinster Regiment (100th and 109th Foot), The Royal Munster Fusiliers (101st and 104th Foot) and The Royal Dublin Fusiliers (102nd and 103rd Foot) - were disbanded.

In 1946 (Special Army Order 165) the foot guards and infantry were reorganised into 15 administrative corps, grouped regionally, or in the case of guards, light infantry and rifle regiments, by specialisation. These corps were lettered, with some imagination, consecutively from A to P. Under Army Order 61 of 1948 the system was four brigades based on historical origin: Guards, Fusilier, Light Infantry and Green Jacket; and 11 'regional' brigades: East Anglian, Forester, Highland, Home Counties, Lancastrian, Lowland, Mercian, Midland, North Irish, Welsh and Wessex. Meanwhile the Army Council initiated two studies: one under General Sir Lashmer Whistler in 1957 and a second, under General Sir Roger Bower in 1962, seeking to identify a more rational structure for the infantry. Both studies recommended a phased transfer to a large regiment structure with fewer regiments, but each regiment having a number of consecutively numbered battalions. Although the Army Council accepted the principle of large regiments, in the event they had no appetite for the dissent and discord an imposed solution would bring, so a 'voluntary' movement toward a large regiment structure was encouraged and a number of regiments elected to form large regiments rather than disband named battalions.

In 1968 (Army Order 61) the 'brigade' structure of the infantry was abandoned in favour of a 'divisional' structure of six divisions, each with a colonel commandant to reflect the views of the colonels of the regiments in the division, they are Guards, Scottish, Queens, King's, Prince of Wales's and Light; the Parachute Regiment and Brigade of Gurkhas did not fall within the divisional structure. The professional head of the infantry is the director of infantry. There are now five regiments of foot guards and 27 line regiments including the Royal Gurkha Rifles and the Parachute Regiment, producing a total of 40 regular infantry battalions. The infantry order of precedence is: Grenadier Guards; Coldstream Guards; Scots Guards; Irish Guards; Welsh Guards; Royal Scots; Princess of Wales's Royal Regiment; King's Own Royal Border Regiment; Royal Regiment of Fusiliers; King's Regiment; Royal Anglian Regiment; Devonshire and Dorset Regiment; The Light Infantry; Prince of Wales's Own Regiment of Yorkshire; Green Howards; Royal

Highland Fusiliers; Cheshire Regiment; Royal Welch Fusiliers; Royal Regiment of Wales; King's Own Scottish Borderers; Royal Irish Regiment; Royal Gloucestershire Berkshire and Wiltshire Regiment; Worcestershire and Sherwood Foresters Regiment; Queen's Lancashire Regiment; Duke of Wellington's Regiment; Staffordshire Regiment; Black Watch; The Highlanders (Seaforth, Gordons and Camerons); Argyll and Sutherland Highlanders; Parachute Regiment; Royal Gurkha Rifles and Royal Green Jackets.

Infantry Demonstration Battalion It had been the practice for many years to nominate a line battalion, on a two year tour, to provide support for the instructional courses at the School of Infantry. In February 1978 the secretary of state for defence announced that, in order to increase the availability of line battalions, and provide an element of continuity at the School of Infantry, an 'Infantry Demonstration Battalion' was to be formed, with an establishment tailored precisely to the needs of the School of Infantry, and manned by personnel drawn from all the infantry battalions of the Army. Once formed, the infantry demonstration battalion functioned well and offered many soldiers the opportunity of a reasonably stable period of duty. However, in August 1982 the concept was abandoned and the duty passed again to a selected line battalion on a roulement basis.

Infantry Tank The infantry or 'I' tanks were designed from the outset specifically for the close support of infantry. A contract for the Infantry Tank Mark I, designed by Sir John Carden of Vickers, was placed in April 1937 so that by 1940 they formed the greater proportion of the equipment of 1st Army Tank Brigade in France. These tanks, of which only 139 were produced, were abandoned in the evacuation of the British Expeditionary Force. Production of the Infantry Mark II, the Matilda, started in 1939. In the event nearly 3,000 Matildas of all marks were produced and had their greatest impact in the early battles in the Western Desert, that is until they came up against the German 88mm gun. The Infantry Tank Mark IV, the Valentine, was produced as a private initiative by Vickers and submitted to the War Office on St Valentine's Day 1938. A contract for the first 275 tanks was placed in July 1939 and, when manufacture ceased in early 1944, some 8,275 had been produced. Although designed as an infantry tank, a shortage of cruiser tanks in 1940-41 meant that it was used to equip the newly raised armoured divisions, despite being much too slow for this role. The Infantry Tank Mark IV, the Churchill, was introduced from 1941, and first used in the Dieppe raid of August 1942. Their heavy armour proved useful, but they were heavily out-gunned by the German tanks. By the end of the war some 5,640 Churchills had been produced. Two further Infantry Tanks, the Valiant (A.38), and the Black Prince (A.43), were developed in the latter stages of the war, but never brought into production. *See also: Tank; Matilda; Valentine; Churchill;Valiant and Black Prince.*

Infiltration The covert or clandestine penetration of enemy held territory. The use of stealth or speed to pass round, between or through an enemy force.

Inkerman Crimean War battle honour marking the Russian attack on the right, British-manned, flank of the allied army besieging Sevastopol on 5 November 1854. *See also: Alma; Balaklava; Sevastopol and Mediterranean.*

Inner The circle on a target closest to the bullseye. *See also: Bullseye, Magpie and Outer.*

Inniskilling Regiment of Foot (27th Foot) *See: Royal Inniskilling Fusiliers.*

Inns of Court and City Yeomanry *See: London Yeomanry.*

Inspector General Doctrine and Training The appointment of Inspector General Doctrine and Training was created in 1992. His responsibilities include the development, dissemination and proving of army doctrine, and the development and

testing of training facilities and standards designed to meet that requirement.

Inspectorate General Doctrine and Training The following directors, individuals and staffs fall within the Doctrine and Training Directorate: Director General Land Warfare; Director Land Warfare; Director General Army Training and Commander Initial Training Group.

Intelligence Corps Formed in July 1940 by Army Order 165 of 1940.
Headdress Badge: A union rose within two branches of laurel surmounted by a crown; below the laurel a scroll inscribed 'Intelligence Corps'.
Motto: *Manui Det Cognitio Vires* (Knowledge gives strength to the arm).
Regimental marches:
Quick march: *The Rose and the Laurel.*
Slow march: *Trumpet Tune (and Ayre).*
Corps headquarters: Templer Barracks, Ashford, Kent TN23 3HH.
History: *Forearmed, A History of the Intelligence Corps* by A Clayton (1993).

Interdiction Operations in depth to neutralise, destroy or delay an enemy force before it can bear effectively against friendly forces.

Interlocking Arcs of Fire The overlapping of individual arcs of fire (qv).

Internal Security (IS) Operations in support of the constitutional government and the forces of law and order employed under its direction.

Intimate Support Term used to describe those weapons or equipments, usually tanks, which accompany assaulting infantry to assist them in the fight through an objective.

Inverness Flap When the Scottish doublet was introduced in 1856 it was not given the normal skirts, but four 'flaps', to correspond with the ancient 'four-tailed' doublet or coat.

Invernessshire Yeomanry (The Lovat Scouts) Lord Lovat raised two companies of 'Scouts', one mounted and one dismounted, for service in the South Africa War (1899-1902). In 1901 the second contingent of Lovat Scouts was designated Imperial Yeomanry and formed the 99th and 100th Companies. Two regiments of Lovat Scouts were authorised as Yeomanry in 1903, both serving dismounted in Gallipoli and subsequently in Egypt. In September 1916 they became known as 10th (Lovat Scouts) Battalion, The Queen's Own Cameron Highlanders, and fought in Macedonia. Some detachments also served as observers in France from late 1916. Between the wars the regiment served in a specialist reconnaissance role, retaining a number of horses. In 1940 the Scouts moved as infantry to the Faroe Islands in anticipation of a German invasion. Subsequently the Scouts became a mountain reconnaissance regiment and served in Italy. In 1947 the regiment was reduced in strength and transferred to the Royal Armoured Corps as 'C' Squadron of the Scottish Horse. Shortly thereafter the Scouts converted to mountain artillery, serving in the artillery role until 1967, when the Lovat Scouts found two subunits: 'A' (Lovat Scouts) Company, The Queen's Own Highlanders (Seaforth & Cameron) and Orkney & Shetland (Lovat Scouts) Battery, The Highland Regiment Royal Artillery (Territorial). The successor sub-units are now in 2nd Battalion Highland Volunteers.

***Invicta* (Undefeated)** Motto of a number of regiments raised in Kent.

Ipoh Second World War Malayan campaign battle honour marking one of the actions during the Japanese advance 26 December 1941 - 10 January 1942. Ipoh was lost on 29 December. *See also: Malaya 1941-42; Northern Malaya; Central Malaya; Slim River; Johore; Batu Pahat; Muar and Singapore Island.*

Iraq 1941 Second World War battle honour marking the attack by Iraqi's forces in May 1941 on the Royal Air Force base at Habbaniya. A reinforcing infantry battalion was sent from India and, in conjunction with a mobile column from Palestine, the Iraqi forces were dispersed. *See also: Defence of Habbaniya; Falluja and Baghdad 1941.*

Irgun *See: Palestine 1945-48.*

Iris Infra-red intruder alarm system.

Irish Guards Raised by Queen Victoria under Army Order 77 of 1900 'to commemorate the bravery shown by the Irish regiments in the recent operations in South Africa'.
Headdress Badge: The star of the Order of St Patrick.
Regimental marches:
Quick march: *St Patrick's Day.*
Slow march: *Let Erin Remember.*
Regimental headquarters: Wellington Barracks, Birdcage Walk, London, SW1E 6HQ.
History: *The Irish Guards in the Great War* (2 Vols) by R Kipling; *History of the Irish Guards in the Second World War* by D J L Fitzgerald and *The Micks* by P Verney (1970).

Irish Regiment *See: Royal Northumberland Fusiliers (5th Foot).*

Irish Republican Army (IRA) *See: Northern Ireland.*

IRISH YEOMANRY

The Irish corps of Yeomanry were raised under different legislation from the Yeomanry Cavalry in England, Scotland and Wales. Ireland made a significant contribution to the Imperial Yeomanry during the South Africa War (1899-1902), including a number of companies and one complete Battalion - the 29th. At the end of the South Africa War two new regiments of Imperial Yeomanry, The North of Ireland and The South of Ireland were formed. The legislation creating the Territorial Force in 1908 did not extend to Ireland, so the two regiments were transferred to the Special Reserve and redesignated The North Irish Horse and The South Irish Horse.
The North Irish Horse In the early part of the First World War the regiment

served in France as divisional cavalry squadrons, the squadrons being re-grouped in 1916 to form two regiments, both serving as cavalry until mid-1917 when 2nd North Irish Horse converted to infantry as 9th Battalion, The Royal Irish Fusiliers. In March 1918 1st North Irish Horse became a cyclist battalion. Between the wars the regiment was held as a Special Reserve regiment until, in May 1939, it was re-raised as an armoured car regiment. Converting to tanks in 1940, the regiment served in Egypt and Italy. In 1947 the Territorial Army was extended to Northern Ireland and in 1967 the regiment was represented in 'D' (North Irish Horse) Squadron, Royal Yeomanry North Irish Horse (Territorial). The successor sub-units are 69 (North Irish Horse) Signal Squadron, 32 (Scottish) Signal Regiment (Volunteers) and North Irish Horse (Independent Squadron).

The South Irish Horse In the First World War the regiment moved to France and later formed two corps cavalry regiments, the 1st and 2nd South Irish Horse. These two regiments were converted to infantry in 1917 as 7th (South Irish Horse) Battalion, The Royal Irish Regiment, and served as such for the remainder of the war. In common with the other regiments recruited primarily in southern Ireland, the regiment was disbanded on partition in 1922.

Irrawaddy Second World War Burma campaign battle honour marking the operations over the period 29 March - 30 May astride the River Irrawaddy with a view to destroying the Japanese Twenty-Eighth Army. *See also: Burma 1942-1945; Mt Popa; Yenangyaung 1945; Magwe and Kama.*

Islander Light fixed-wing aircraft used by the Army for photo-reconnaissance and liaison. Payload of 700kgs or eight troops and a cruising speed of 150kts.

Isle of Man Yeomanry An unofficial body of mounted troops was formed in 1793 as the Manx Constitutional Dragoons, but the first Yeomanry corps was accepted in 1796 as the Manx Yeomanry Cavalry. The force was largely used by the Excise and in support of the civil authority, and by 1825 only one troop apparently remained.

Italian Campaign 1943-45 The Allied campaign in Sicily and Italy was preceded by the surrender, following air and naval bombardment, of Pantelleria, Lampedusa and other small Italian islands in June 1943. Anglo-American forces under Alexander (qv) as deputy commander-in-chief and Montgomery (qv) as commander of the British forces landed on the south-east corner of Sicily on 10 July 1943. There was significant resistance by the Germans, particularly in the area north of the River Simeto and in the vicinity of Mount Etna. However the rapid American advance along the north coast disrupted the German defence plan and the allies entered Messina on 17 August 1943. On 3 September 1943 elements of Eighth Army (qv) landed on the toe of Italy and fought their way northward along the west coast. On 9 September 1943 the American Fifth Army, with the British X Corps under command, landed at Salerno (qv) on the west coast in the face of stiff resistance, and struck in land and northwards up the west coast; the British Eighth Army swinging across to the east coast and capturing Foggia on 28 September.

Naples fell on 1 October 1943 and, by 5 October, the Allies were held on the German 'Gustav Line' (qv) of defences, which lay along the Rivers Garigliano and Rapido with Monte Cassino (qv) being its strong point. Bitter fighting, in very difficult terrain, followed and, in an attempt to break the deadlock an Allied force landed at Anzio (qv) to the south of Rome in January 1944, but was contained by the Germans until 25 May. Cassino fell on 18 May and, the advance having been resumed, contact was made with the force at Anzio on 25 May which led to the fall of Rome on 4 June. The Germans conducted a classic fighting withdrawal to new defensive positions on the 'Gothic Line' (qv), which stretched across Italy just north of Florence. The Allies reached the 'Gothic Line' in August 1944 and had breached it by the end of September, pushing the Germans slowly northward during the winter to a line south of Bologna. A pause followed until the advance was resumed in April 1945, initially on the Eighth Army front, and the Allies thrust forward to the Po valley. The German army in Italy surrendered on 29 April 1945. *See also: Sicily 1943 and Italy 1943-45.*

Italian Song An arrangement of this melody forms part of the regimental quick march of The Royal Green Jackets.

Italy 1917-18 First World War battle honour marking the commitment of British forces to the campaign in Italy. When the Austro-German offensive broke through at Caporetto in October 1917, a number of French and British divisions were rushed to Italy, but the defence was stabilised on the River Piave before they were extensively committed. The front remained stable until June 1918, when the Austrians launched a further offensive, which was successfully contained. The Allies took the offensive in October, the Austrian Army broke and hostilities ceased on 4 November 1918. *See also: Piave and Vittorio Veneto.*

Italy 1943-45 Second World War battle honour marking the Italian campaign from the initial landing on the toe of Italy on 3 September 1943 to the end of hostilities in April 1945.

Jackboots A term used to describe the stout cavalry boots which had been 'jacked' - or given a hard polished surface with wax and tar.

Jacket From 'jack', a small coat with short skirts worn by light cavalry and by light infantry.

Jacob, Sir Claud William (1863-1948) Educated at Sherborne School and Royal Military College Sandhurst and commissioned into the Worcestershire Regiment (29th and 36th Foot) in 1882, transferring to the Indian Army in 1884. At the outbreak of the First World War he went to France with the Meerut Division, and was the only Indian Army officer of the corps to rise to high command there. In 1915 he led the Dehra Dun Brigade at Neuve Chapelle and at Aubers Ridge. He commanded II Corps for the rest of the war, during the Somme battles 1916, when he took Thiepval by a well-planned assault, at the Ancre operations and the pursuit of the Germans to the Hindenburg Line in 1917, at the Third Battle of Ypres and at Flanders in the final Allied advance to victory in 1918. In 1920 he returned to India on appointment as chief of the general staff. In 1924 he was given Northern Command in India and promoted Field Marshal in 1926. From 1926 to 1930 he was military secretary at the India Office.

Jacob's Rifle Double-barrelled percussion rifle of 0.524" calibre. Designed by General John Jacob and issued to two regiments of the Indian Army in 1858. *See also: Rifle.*

Jaffa First World War Palestinian campaign battle honour marking the successful attack during the 1917-18 campaign in Palestine launched by the British on 21 December 1917 from Jaffa across the River Auja with the object of securing their left flank. *See also: Palestine 1917-1918; Gaza; El Mughar; Nebi Samwil; Jerusalem; Jericho; Tell Asur; Jordan; Megiddo and Damascus.*

Jaguar A secure, 'frequency hopping' combat net radio system produced by Racal Tacticom.

Jamming The obstruction, suppression or interruption of enemy electro-magnetic transmissions.

Jam-Pot Cuff A simple round cuff without decoration, worn on soldiers' tunics from 1882-1902.

Jangees Short drawers worn by Indian infantry in the 18th and 19th centuries.

Jankers Soldiers' slang, origin unknown, for the punishment awarded to defaulters.

Java Battle honour marking the short and successful campaign of an expedition mounted from India under the command of General Sir Samuel Auchmuty in 1811. The decisive event in the capture of this Dutch possession was the storming of the Lines of Cornelis against French and Dutch forces. The expedition was accompanied by Lord Minto, the Governor-General of India, who subsequently arranged for the civil administration of the Dutch islands.

Javelin Close air defence weapon with high explosive, proximity fused, warhead. Successor to the Blowpipe (qv), fitted with a more sophisticated guidance system. The firer no longer steers the missile, but simply holds the aiming mark on the target. Maximum range about 5,500m, maximum altitude 2,000m.

Jebel Defeis Second World War Abyssinian campaign battle honour. *See also: Abyssinia 1940-41; Keren; Gondar; Jebel Shiba; Giarso; Agordat; Barentu; Karora-Marsa Taclai; Cubcub; Ad Teclesan; Mescelit Pass; Mt Engiahat; Massawa; Amb Alagi; Afodu; Gambela; El Wak; Moyale; Wal Garis; Juba; Bulo Erillo; Beles Gugani; Alessandra; Gogni; Marda Pass; Babile Gap; Bisidimo; Awash; Todenyang-Namaraputh; Soroppa; Gelib; Colito; Wadara; Omo; Goluin; Fike and Lechemti.*

Jebel Mazar Second World War battle honour marking an operation during the 1941 campaign in Syria. An operation was mounted on 10 July 1941 to seize the Jebel Mazar ridge and secure Rayak airfield. *See also: Syria 1941; Merjayun; Palmyra and Deir es Zor.*

Jebel Shiba Second World War Abyssinian campaign battle honour. *See also: Abyssinia 1940-41; Keren; Gondar; Jebel Defeis; Giarso; Agordat; Barentu; Karora-Marsa Taclai; Cubcub; Ad Teclesan; Mescelit Pass; Mt Engiahat; Massawa; Amb Alagi; Afodu; Gambela; El Wak; Moyale; Wal Garis; Juba; Bulo Erillo; Beles Gugani; Alessandra; Gogni; Marda Pass; Babile Gap; Bisidimo; Awash; Todenyang-Namaraputh; Soroppa; Gelib; Colito; Wadara; Omo; Goluin; Fike and Lechemti.*

Jellalabad First Afghan War (qv) battle honour marking the defence of Jellalabad, which lies on the direct route from Kabul to India, from January to April 1842. *See also: Affghanistan 1839; Ghuznee 1839; Khelat; Candahar 1842; Ghuznee 1842 and Cabool 1842.*

Jellalabad Medals 1841-42 These medals commemorate the defence of Jellalabad during the First Afghan War (qv). The first medal, known as the 'Mural Crown' was authorised in a General Order from Allahabad dated 30 April 1842. The second medal, issued in March 1845 and known as the 'Flying Victory' was produced because there were apparently insufficient of the first medal minted and the Governor-General of India was dissatisfied with the rather crude design of the first medal.
Ribbon: Common to both medals; 1" wide, rainbow pattern watered red, yellow, white and blue.

Jerboa *See: Desert Rats.*

Jericho First World War Palestinian campaign battle honour marking the capture of Jericho on 21 February 1918. *See also: Palestine 1917-1918; Gaza; El Mughar; Nebi Samwil; Jerusalem; Jaffa; Tell Asur; Jordan; Megiddo and Damascus.*

Jerrycan Flat sided can with a capacity of about five gallons used for storing or transporting liquids, such as water and motor fuel. Originally of German design - hence 'Jerry' - and adopted by the British Army during the Second World War.

Jersey Battle honour marking the defence of the island by the Royal Jersey Militia in 1781 against French attack during the American War of Independence.

Jerusalem First World War Palestinian campaign battle honour marking the defence of Jerusalem. The Turks launched an attack on the city from the north in late December 1917 and were defeated after five days of heavy fighting. *See also: Palestine 1917-1918; Gaza; El Mughar; Nebi Samwil; Jericho; Jaffa; Tell Asur; Jordan; Megiddo and Damascus.*

Jitra Second World War Malayan campaign battle honour marking the defence of Jitra against the Japanese advance from Thailand during the early part of the campaign 8-23 December 1941. *See also: Malaya 1941-42; Northern Malaya; Grik Road; Central Malaya; Johore and Singapore Island.*

Jock Term commonly used to describe a Scot in the army; but more particularly the private soldiers in Scottish infantry regiments.

Jodhpur Indian cavalry breeches; tight in the leg but loose elsewhere.

John Peel An arrangement of this melody forms part of the regimental quick march of the King's Own Royal Border Regiment.

Johore Second World War Malayan campaign battle honour marking the attempts to hold back the Japanese from Singapore 14-31 January 1942 during the later part of the campaign. *See also: Malaya 1941-42, Northern Malaya, Central Malaya, Slim River, Ipoh, Batu Pahat, Muar and Singapore Island.*

Joint Term applied to operations, staffs or establishments involving two or more of the three Services.

Joint Air Attack Team A co-ordinated attack involving a combination of army aviation and close air support, normally supported by artillery or naval gunfire.

Joint Service Defence College (JSDC) Originally founded at Latimer in Buckinghamshire in 1947 at the direction of the Chiefs of Staff as the Joint Services Staff College (JSSC); 'a centre to nourish and to disseminate amongst the higher commanders of all Services and their staffs that mutual understanding and inter-Service comradeship-in-arms which, in war, were the very basis of our success and without which we should be in poor shape to face a future war'. In August 1971 the JSSC was renamed the National Defence College (NDC), and the aims slightly adjusted. The courses became more academic and only UK students were accepted. In 1982 it was decided to move the course to the Royal Naval College Greenwich where it became the Joint Service Defence College. As a result of recent savings exercises the future location and content of the course is now under discussion.

Jordan First World War Palestine campaign battle honour marking the establishment of a bridgehead across the River Jordan at Ghoraniye in March 1918, from which an abortive attempt was made to reach Amman and cut the Hedjaz railway. *See also: Palestine 1917-1918; Gaza; El Mughar; Nebi Samwil; Jerusalem; Jaffa; Tell Asur; Jericho; Megiddo and Damascus.*

Juba Second World War Abyssinian campaign battle honour marking the opening battle of General Cunningham's drive north from Kenya, involving crossing of the River Juba and the capture of Kismayu in Italian Somaliland during February 1941. *See also: Abyssinia 1940-41; Keren; Gondar; Jebel Defeis; Giarso; Agordat; Barentu; Karora-Marsa Taclai; Cubcub; Ad Teclesan; Mescelit Pass; Mt Engiahat; Massawa; Amb Alagi; Afodu; Gambela; El Wak; Moyale; Wal Garis; Jebel Shiba; Bulo Erillo; Beles Gugani; Alessandra; Gogni; Marda Pass; Babile Gap; Bisidimo; Awash; Todenyang-Namaraputh; Soroppa; Gelib; Colito; Wadara; Omo; Goluin; Fike and Lechemti.*

Judge Advocate General of the Forces Judicial officer, normally a barrister of not less than ten years standing, appointed by the sovereign on the recommendation of the Lord Chancellor. The office of the Judge Advocate General of the forces is part of the Lord Chancellor's Department and exercises judicial functions on a joint service basis in relation to Army and Royal Air Force courts martial. He also acts as legal adviser in matters of military and air force law to the Secretary of State for Defence. The responsibility for acting or not acting on his advice remains however with the Secretary of State. The office of Judge Advocate General as a continuous appointment dates back to the 17th century, though existing earlier intermittently. For a long time the holder of the office also acted as secretary of the Board of General Officers. After this board was abolished in 1793 he functioned as legal adviser to the commander-in-chief and his mouthpiece in the House of Commons. During the 19th century the office was held by a privy councillor, who was also a member of the government, but from 1893, while the extinction of the office was being considered, the duties were temporarily discharged, without emoluments, by a High Court judge. In 1905 the duties were assigned to a barrister on the basis of a permanent appointment. The present status and responsibilities of the office are the result of the recommendations of the Lewis Committee of 1948 (endorsing similar recommendations by the Oliver Committee of 1938) and take statutory authority from the Court Martial (Appeal) Act 1951. *See also: Court Martial.*

Jungle Boot Light canvas 'high' boot with stout rubber sole and lace-up front. Introduced in June 1944 as part of a range of jungle clothing for use in the Far East.

Jungle Green Sometimes known as 'Olive Green' or 'OG'. Dark green cloth introduced to replace the unsuitable light khaki drill cloth or 'KD' first used in the Far East.

Jungle Hat A 'deerstalker' type hat with a floppy brim, made of light jungle green cloth. Introduced in June 1944 as part of a range of jungle clothing for use in the Far East. Sometimes embellished with twisted cords or tapes or regimental patches.

Junior Entry There have been boy soldiers serving with the Army since mediaeval times. During the 18th and, more particularly the 19th, centuries a number of schools, colleges and foundations were established at which teenagers could receive an education, with a strong military bias, with a view to ultimately joining the Army. More recently the junior entry fell into three broad groups: Apprentices, Junior Leaders and Junior Soldiers or Tradesmen. The raising of the school leaving age and cutbacks in recruiting have brought about the cessation of the Junior Leader and Junior Soldier entry, leaving only the Apprentices. The Apprentices are high quality, specially selected young men who are given a mixed military and technical training at an Army Apprentice Colleges at either Chepstow (Royal Engineers), Harrogate (Royal Signals) and Bordon (Royal Electrical and Mechanical Engineers) to take technical appointments. The Junior Leaders were young men of high ability who were given a mixture of education and special-to-arm military training in special to arm regiments with a view to preparing them to become the future warrant officers and non-commissioned officers of their respective regiments or corps. Junior Soldiers were men too young for adult service, who were given a mixture of education and military training before attending the standard recruit training for their corps or regiment. History: *Sons of the Brave - The Story of Boy Soldiers* by A W Cockerill (1984).

Jurques Second World War battle honour marking one of the actions during the British Mont Pincon offensive launched south-westwards from the Caumont area on 30 July 1944. *See also: France and Flanders 1914-1918; Mont Pincon; Quarry Hill; Souleuvre; Catheolles; Le Perier Ridge and Brieux Bridgehead.*

***Justitia In Armis* (Justice in arms)** Motto of the Army Legal Corps and the Army Legal Services Branch of the Adjutant General's Corps.

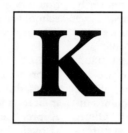

Kabul 1879 Battle honour marking an action during the Second Afghan War (qv). In December 1879 there was a general uprising of the Afghan tribes and General Roberts, who was commanding at Kabul, concentrated his troops in the Sherpur cantonment outside Kabul. After some three weeks of fighting a final Afghan assault was beaten off on 23 December and a cavalry pursuit turned this action into a decisive victory for the British. *See also: Afghanistan 1878-80; Ali Masjid; Peiwar Kotal; Charasiah; Ahmad Khel and Kandahar 1880.*

Kabul to Kandahar Star 1880 Awarded to all who had taken part in General Robert's famous march to relieve Kandahar 9-31 August 1880.
Ribbon: Rainbow pattern watered red, white yellow, white and blue.

Kaffir Wars Sometimes known as the Cape Frontier Wars. The title covers almost 100 years (1779-1879) of intermittent warfare between the Cape colonists and the Xhosa tribes of the Eastern cape in South Africa. The wars ended with the annexation of their territory and incorporation of the Xhosa people. The Kaffir wars were: 1779 (1st war); 1793 (2nd war); 1799-1801 (3rd war); 1811 (4th war); 1818-19 (5th war); 1835 (6th war); 1846-47 (7th war); 1851-53 (8th war) and 1877-79 (9th war). See also: *South Africa 1835; South Africa 1851-52-53. and South Africa 1877-78-79.*

Kahun First Afghan War (qv) battle honour marking the defence of the fort at Kahun against attacks by Baluchi tribesmen from May to September 1840. *See also: Affghanistan 1839; Ghuznee 1839; Khelat; Jellalabad and Candahar 1842.*

Kairouan Second World War North Africa campaign battle honour marking one of the actions during Anglo-American operations aimed at breaking through the Fondouk Pass towards Kairouan in early April 1943. *See also: North Africa 1940-1943; Fondouk; Bordj; Pichon; Djebel El Rhorab; Fondouk Pass and Sidi Ali.*

Kaladan Second World War Burma campaign battle honour marking an action during the operations in north Arakan 1 January to 12 June 1944. *See also: Burma 1942-1945; North Arakan; Buthidaung; Razibil; Mayu Tunnels; Alethangyaw; Maungdaw; Mowdok and Point 551.*

Kalewa Second World War Burma campaign battle honour marking an action in which the river port of Kalewa was captured and a bridgehead established across the Chindwin 13 November-16 December 1944. *See also: Burma 1942-1945; Mawlaik; Pinwe; Shwebo and Ukhrul.*

Kama Second World War Burma campaign battle honour marking an action during operations astride the River Irrawaddy 29 March-30 May 1945. *See also: Burma 1942-1945; Irrawaddy; Mt Popa;Yenangyaung 1945 and Magwe.*

Kamina First World War East Africa campaign battle honour. Kamina, an important radio station, was the objective of an Anglo-French expedition which invaded Togoland in August 1914. The expedition concluded with the surrender of Kamina on 26th August. *See also: East Africa 1914-1918; Kilimanjaro; Behobeho; Narungombe and Nyangao.*

Kampar Second World War Malayan campaign battle honour marking an action during the fighting in central Malaya 26 December 1941-10 January 1942. *See also: Malaya 1941-1942; Northern Malaya; Central Malaya; Slim River; Ipoh; Johore; Batu Pahat; Muar and Singapore Island.*

Kandahar 1880 Second Afghan War (qv) battle honour marking the decisive defeat of the Afghans under Ayub Khan outside Kandahar on 1 September 1880. *See also: Afghanistan 1878-80; Ali Masjid; Peiwar Kotal; Garasiah; Kabul 1879 and Ahmad Khel.*

Kangaroo Second World War Canadian tank from which the turret had been removed to provide space for a section of infantry. Although protected by armour on all sides there was no overhead protection and, without the main armament, the vehicle had little offensive capability. The vehicle was used as an armoured personnel carrier.

Kangaw Second World War Burma campaign battle honour marking one of the actions during the final stages of the Arakan campaign 12 January-29 April 1945. *See also: Burma 1942-1945; Arakan Beaches; Dalet; Tamandu;Taungup; Myebon and Ramree.*

Kanglantongbi Second World War Burma campaign battle honour marking an action in which the Kohima-Imphal road was reopened during the operations which took place around Imphal between March and June 1944. *See also: Burma 1942-1945; Imphal; Tuitum; Nungshigum; Sakawng; Bishenpur; Tamu Road; Shenam Pass and Litan.*

Kaphar Hunnu Bhanda Marnu Ramro (It is better to die than live a coward) Motto of the Brigade of Gurkhas.

Kapyong Korean War (qv) battle honour.

See also: Korea 1950-1953; Naktong Bridgehead; Pakchon; Imjin; Kowang-San; The Hook 1952; The Hook 1953; Chongju; Chongchon II; Seoul; Chaum-Ni; Hill 327; Kapyong Chon; Maryang San and Hill 227 I.

Kapyong-Chon Korean War battle honour. *See also: Korea 1950-1953; Naktong Bridgehead; Pakchon; Imjin; Kowang-San; The Hook 1952; The Hook 1953; Chongju; Chongchon II; Seoul; Chaum-Ni; Hill 327; Kapyong; Maryang San and Hill 227 I.*

Karora-Marsa Taclai Second World War Abyssinian campaign battle honour. *See also: Abyssinia 1940-41; Keren; Gondar; Jebel Defeis; Giarso; Agordat; Barentu; Jebel Shiba; Cubcub; Ad Teclesan; Mescelit Pass; Mt Engiahat; Massawa; Amb Alagi; Afodu; Gambela; El Wak; Moyale; Wal Garis; Juba; Bulo Erillo; Beles Gugani; Alessandra; Gogni; Marda Pass; Babile Gap; Bisidimo; Awash; Todenyang-Namaraputh; Soroppa; Gelib; Colito;Wadara; Omo; Goluin; Fike and Lechemti.*

Kasserine Second World War North Africa campaign battle honour marking the action by 6th Armoured Division which checked the German thrust through the Kasserine Pass in mid-February 1943. *See also: North Africa 1940-1943;Thala and Sbiba.*

Keel Row Regimental double march of the Light Infantry and The Royal Gurkha Rifles, and regimental trot of the Honourable Artillery Company.

Keep The main tower within the walls of a medieval fortress. Term also applied to the main, usually headquarter, building in a Cardwell barracks.

Kef El Debna Second World War North Africa campaign battle honour marking one of the actions which took place between the Kasserine operation in mid-February 1943 and the Fondouk operations in April 1943. *See also: North Africa 1940-1943; El Hadjeba; Djebel Djaffa; Sidi Nsir; Fort McGregor; Stuka Farm; Steamroller Farm; Montagne Farm and Kef Ouiba Pass.*

Kef Ouiba Pass Second World War North Africa campaign battle honour marking one of the actions which took place between the Kasserine operation in mid-February 1943 and the Fondouk operations in April 1943. *See also: North Africa 1940-1943; El Hadjeba; Djebel Djaffa; Sidi Nsir; Fort McGregor; Stuka Farm; Steamroller Farm; Montagne Farm and Kef El Debna.*

Kemmel First World War battle honour marking the successful defence of Kemmel Ridge against a series of German assaults 17-19 April 1918 during the Battle of the Lys. *See also: France and Flanders 1914-1918; Lys; Estaires; Messines 1918; Hazebrouck; Bailleul; Béthune and Scherpenberg.*

Kemmendine First Burma War (qv) battle honour marking the defence of this post, a short way up-river from Rangoon, in December 1824. *See also: Ava; Arracan; Assam and Burmah.*

Kennedy Peak Second World War Burma campaign battle honour marking the capture of a Japanese position on this 8,000ft mountain near Tiddim on 7 November 1944. *See also: Burma 1942-1945; Tengnoupal; Mawlaik; Pinwe; Kalewa; Shwebo; Ukhrul; Shweli and Kyaukmyaung.*

KENT YEOMANRY

The Royal East Kent Mounted Rifles (Duke of Connaught's Own) Independent troops of yeomanry were commissioned in 1794 and fully regimented in 1813. The regiment was disbanded in 1828, but re-raised in 1830. Designated 'Mounted Rifles' in 1853, subsequently the Duke of Connaught's Own Royal East Kent Mounted Rifles. The regiment found a company for 11th Battalion Imperial Yeomanry in the South Africa War (1899-1902). In the First World War the regiment served at Gallipoli (qv), Egypt and Palestine. Redesignated 10th Battalion The Buffs, the regiment served as infantry for the last six months of the war. In 1920 the regiment amalgamated with The Queen's Own West Kent Yeomanry and the

new regiment converted to artillery, serving as such in the Second World War in North-West Europe, Iraq and North Africa. In 1947 the regiment was reconstituted, still in the artillery role. The regiment's successors may be found in the Territorial Army in 'C' (Kent & Sharpshooters Yeomanry) Squadron of The Royal Yeomanry.

The Queen's Own West Kent Yeomanry Raised in 1797 from independent troops which had existed since the inception of Yeomanry Cavalry in 1794. The regiment was disbanded in 1827 and re-raised in 1830, and found a company for 11th Battalion Imperial Yeomanry during the South Africa War (1899-1902). In the First World War the regiment served at Gallipoli (qv), Egypt and Palestine. In 1920 the regiment amalgamated with The Royal East Kent Mounted Rifles (Duke of Connaught's Own) (qv). The regiment's successor sub-unit is HQ and 265 (Kent and County of London Yeomanry) Signal Squadron, (The Sharpshooters), 71 (Yeomanry) Signal Regiment (Volunteers).

Kenya 1952-56 Campaign against the Mau Mau rebel movement, which recruited largely from the Kikuyu, Embu and Meru tribes of Kenya. The conflict arose from disputed European ownership of land in the Kikuyu tribal territory. The campaign was successfully concluded by December 1956 and, although the British Army remained in Kenya until 1965, troops were deployed once more on offensive operations to suppress the short-lived mutiny of the Kenyan Army in 1964. British Army casualties in the campaign were 12 killed and 69 wounded.

Keren Second World War Abyssinian campaign battle honour marking the decisive battle, fought over the period 3 February-31 March 1941, of the Northern advance into Abyssinia. *See also: Abyssinia 1940-41; Karora-Marsa Taclai; Gondar; Jebel Defeis; Giarso; Agordat; Barentu; Jebel Shiba; Cubcub; Ad Teclesan; Mescelit Pass; Mt Engiahat; Massawa; Amb Alagi; Afodu; Gambela; El Wak; Moyale; Wal Garis; Juba; Bulo Erillo; Beles Gugani; Alessandra; Gogni; Marda Pass; Babile Gap; Bisidimo; Awash;*

Todenyang-Namaraputh; Soroppa; Gelib; Colito; Wadara; Omo; Goluin; Fike and Lechemti.

Kerr Rifle Based upon the Enfield 1853 pattern rifle, this 0.557" calibre weapon was issued when government arms production could not meet the demands of the newly-raised volunteer militia regiments. *See also: Rifle.*

Kevlar A synthetic fibre of very high tensile strength which can be woven into a fabric suitable for making protective garnets. With an epoxy resin Kevlar can be moulded into solid sheets or plates of lightweight armour.

Key A badge depicting a key was worn by some regiments to indicate they had been present at the great siege of Gibraltar (1779-1783).

Key Point A concentrated site or installation, the loss or destruction of which would seriously affect the war effort or the success of operations.

Key Terrain Any locality, or area, the seizure or retention of which affords a marked advantage to either combatant.

Khaki A dull yellowish-brown colour adopted by the Army for field service uniform. From the Persian and Urdu for 'dust' or 'dusty' and originating from India where local cotton garments were dyed or stained in the mid-19th century into a hue which offered an early form of camouflage. It was the Corps of Guides raised in India in 1846 who are said to have first died their uniforms with river mud, and the colour was certainly used by 74th Foot in Africa in 1851-53 and by the 93rd Highlanders at Lucknow in 1857, and widely used in the South Africa War 1899-1902. Now a colour generally associated with the Army and used for non-ceremonial uniform, but replaced by disrupted pattern combat kit for field service. *See also: Uniform.*

Khan Baghdadi First World War Mesopotamian campaign battle honour. In early 1918 the Turks advanced down the River Euphrates toward Baghdad. The attack was defeated and in the follow-up the British defeated them decisively at Khan Baghdadi. *See also: Mesopotamia 1914-1918; Basra; Shaiba; Kut Al Amara 1915; Ctesiphon; Defence of Kut Al Amara; Tigris 1916; Kut Al Amara 1917 and Baghdad.*

Khartoum Battle honour awarded for the final defeat of the Mahdists at Omdurman, close to Khartoum where the Mahdi (qv) had established his capital. The new Maxim machine guns employed by the British caused heavy losses among the Mahdists and prevented them closing with the British. *See also: Hafir and Atbara.*

Khedive's Star These five-pointed bronze stars were awarded by the Khedive to all recipients of the Egypt 1882-1889 campaign medal.

Khedive's Sudan Medal 1896-1908 Instituted in 1897 and awarded until 1908 to those who served in the reconquest of the Sudan.
Ribbon: 1" wide, yellow with a vertical broad blue stripe at the centre.
Clasps: The Atbara; Khartoum; Firket; Hafir; Abu Hamed; Sudan 1897; Gedaref; Gedid; Sudan 1899; Bahr-El-Ghazal 1900-02; Jerok; Nyam-Nyam; Talodi; Katfia and Nyima.

Khelat First Afghan War (qv) battle honour marking the capture of the fortress at Khelat, stronghold of the Baluchi Chief Mehrab Khan on 13 November 1839. *See also: Affghanistan 1839; Ghuznee 1839; Kahun; Jellalabad and Khelat-i-Ghilzai.*

Khelat-I-Ghilzai First Afghan War (qv) battle honour marking the successful defence of this fortress on the road from Kabul to Kandahar for a period of six months. *See also: Affghanistan 1839; Ghuznee 1839; Kahun; Jellalabad and Khelat.*

Khoger Native saddlery used in India.

Kiddies Nickname given to the Scots Guards when, in 1686, James II formed a large camp on Hounslow Heath as a precaution against disturbances in London. The (then) three regiments of foot guards were all present and the Scots Guards, being the junior, were called 'the Kiddies'.

Kilimanjaro First World War East Africa campaign battle honour marking the British offensive launched in the Mount Kilimanjaro area in March 1916. *See also: East Africa 1914-18; Behobeho; Narungombe; Nyangao and Kamina.*

Killaloe Regimental quick march of the Royal Irish Rangers and the Royal Irish Regiment.

Killing Area An area in which a commander plans to force the enemy to concentrate, so as to destroy him with conventional or nuclear weapons.

Kilmarnock Scottish town in which bonnets were made for the British Army. The name was given to a simple bonnet worn by Scottish regiments which could be stiffened and made into various shapes. A full dress version was subsequently produced.

Kinetic Energy Weapon A weapon which depends for its destructive effect upon the rapid transfer of energy from an object in motion to the target.

King Edward's Horse (The King's Overseas Dominions Regiment) *See: London Yeomanry.*

King's (Later Queen's) Commendation For Brave Conduct In the First World War some civilians had been commended for 'good service' and, by 1939 commendations, roughly corresponding to a 'mention in despatches' for civilians were regularly being made. It was soon found that occasions arose where Servicemen performed acts of gallantry for which a mention in despatches or other award was inappropriate, and the commendation lost its purely civilian aspect.

King's Division An administrative grouping in the infantry created under Army Order 34 of 1968, comprising The King's

Own Royal Border Regiment, The King's Regiment, The Prince of Wales's Own Regiment of Yorkshire, The Green Howards, The Queen's Lancashire Regiment and The Duke of Wellington's Regiment (West Riding).

Kingsman Title given to a private soldier in the King's Regiment (8th, 63rd and 96th Foot), and the regimental quick march of that regiment.

King's (Later Queen's) Medal For Bravery (South Africa) Gallantry medal, sometimes known as the 'Woltemade Medal', instituted in 1881, originally as a reward for acts of gallantry performed by military or civilian personnel within the Union of South Africa or territories under the control of the Union. Qualification for the medal was 'Gallantry performed in the face of imminent and obvious peril by those who endanger their own lives in saving or endeavouring to save the lives of others.'
Ribbon: Dark blue, 1" wide, with narrow orange borders.

King's Own Royal Border Regiment (4th, 34th and 55th Foot) Formed on 1 October 1959 through the amalgamation of The King's Own Royal Regiment (Lancaster) (4th Foot) and The Border Regiment (34th and 55th Foot).
Headdress Badge: The lion of England within a laurel wreath, ensigned with the crown.
Regimental marches:
Quick march: An arrangement of *John Peel* and *Corn Rigs are Bonnie.*
Slow march: *Trelawny.*
Regimental headquarters: The Castle, Carlisle, Cumbria, CA3 8UR.
History: *A History of The King's Own Royal Border Regiment* by R K May (1984).

King's Own Royal Regiment (Lancaster) (4th Foot) Raised by Colonel Charles Fitzcharles, 1st Earl of Plymouth, for the garrison in Tangier in July 1680 as the Tangier Regiment and ranked 4th Foot. Retitled The Duchess of York and Albany's Regiment in 1684, The Queen's Regiment in 1685, The Queen

Consort's Regiment in 1688, the Queen's Marines in 1702 and The King's Own Regiment in 1715. Designated The 4th or King's Own Regiment in 1751 and redesignated The 4th (The King's Own Royal) Regiment in 1687. In May 1881 the regiment was redesignated The Royal Lancaster Regiment (King's Own), and this was changed in July of that year to The King's Own Royal Regiment (Lancaster). On 1 October 1959 the regiment amalgamated with The Border Regiment (34th and 55th Foot) to form The King's Own Royal Border Regiment (4th, 34th and 55th Foot) (qv).

Headdress Badge: The lion of England upon the title 'THE KING'S OWN'.

History: *The King's Own - The Story of a Royal Regiment* (Vols 1 & 2) by L I Cowper (1939); (Vol 3) by J M Cowper (1957) and *Lions Of England - A Pictorial History of The King's Own Royal Regiment (Lancaster) 1680-1980* by S Eastwood (1991).

King's Own Scottish Borderers (25th Foot) Raised by Act of the Scottish Parliament on 18 March 1689, with David Melville, 3rd Earl of Leven as Colonel, and tasked with the defence of Edinburgh Castle against the forces of ex-King James II under the command of the Earl of Claverhouse. Brought onto the regular establishment by King William III in April 1689 and initially known as The Edinburgh Regiment of Foot. Designated 25th (Edinburgh) Foot in 1751. The regiment was redesignated 25th (Sussex) Foot in 1782 and 25th (The King's Own Borderers) Foot in 1805. In May 1881 the regiment was redesignated The York Regiment (King's Own Borderers; this was changed in July of that year to The King's Own Borderers. The regiment was redesignated The King's Own Scottish Borderers in 1887.

Headdress Badge: Upon a saltire, the Castle of Edinburgh with mottoes *'In veritate religionis confido'* (I believe in the truth of my faith) and *'Nisi dominus frustra'* (In vain without the Lord), all ensigned with the royal crest.

Regimental marches:

Quick march: *Blue Bonnets are over the Border* (Pipes and Drums and Regimental Band).

Slow marches: *The Borderers* (Pipes and Drums) and *The Garb of Old Gaul* (Regimental Band).

Regimental Headquarters: The Barracks, Berwick-on-Tweed, Northumberland, TD15 1DG.

History: *The Records of The King's Own Borderers (1689-1872)* by R T Higgins (1873); *The KOSB In The Great War* by S Gillon (1930); *Borderers in Battle, The War Story of The King's Own Scottish Borderers (1939-1945)* by H Gunning (1947); *A Short History of 1st Battalion The King's Own Scottish Borderers in North West Europe (6 June 1944-8 May 1945)* privately published (1945); *The Borderers in Korea* by J F M MacDonald (1953) and *All The Blue Bonnets* by R Woollcombe (1980).

King's Own Yorkshire Light Infantry (51st and 105th Foot) The 51st Foot was raised at Leeds in December 1755 as 53rd Foot, commanded by Colonel Robert Napier and renumbered 51st Foot (or Brudenell's) in 1757. The regiment was designated 51st (2nd Yorkshire, West Riding) Foot in 1782, 51st (2nd Yorkshire, West Riding, Light Infantry) Regiment in 1809 and 51st (2nd Yorkshire, West Riding, The King's Own Light Infantry) Regiment in 1821. The 2nd Madras (European Light Infantry) Regiment, a regiment of the East India Company, was raised in 1839, redesignated 2nd Madras (Light Infantry) Regiment in 1858; and 105th (Madras Light Infantry) Regiment in 1861. In May 1881 the 51st (2nd Yorkshire, West Riding, The King's Own Light Infantry) Regiment and 105th (Madras Light Infantry) Regiment amalgamated to form The South Yorkshire Regiment (King's Own Light Infantry) and in July of that year the regiment was redesignated The King's Own Yorkshire Light Infantry (51st and 105th Foot). On 10th July 1968 the regiment amalgamated with The Somerset and Cornwall Light Infantry (13th, 32nd and 46th Foot), The King's Shropshire Light Infantry (53rd and 85th Foot) and The Durham Light Infantry (68th and 106th Foot) to form The Light Infantry (qv).

Headdress Badge: A French horn, in the twist, the rose of York.

History: *History of the King's Own Yorkshire*

Light Infantry 1755-1914 (Vols I and II) by H C Wylly (1925); *History of the King's Own Yorkshire Light Infantry -The Great War 1914-1918* (Vol III) by R C Bond (1929); *Register of Officers 1755-1945* (Vol IV) by C P Deedes (1946); *Never Give Up 1919-1942* (Vol V) by W Hingston; *History of the King's Own Yorkshire Light Infantry 1939-1948* (Vol VI) by G F Ellenberger and *The King's Own Yorkshire Light Infantry* by L Cooper (1970).

King's Regiment (8th, 63rd and 96th Foot) Formed on 1 September 1958 through the amalgamation of The King's Regiment (Liverpool) (8th Foot) and The Manchester Regiment (63rd and 96th Foot); first designated The King's Regiment (Manchester and Liverpool). The regiment was redesignated The King's Regiment on 13 December 1968.
Headdress The White Horse of Hanover. Below, the title 'KING'S' in Old English lettering.
Regimental marches:
Quick march: *The Kingsman.*
Slow march: *Lord Ferrers March.*
Regimental Headquarters:
Liverpool: TA Centre, Graeme House, Derby Square, Liverpool, L2 7SD.
Manchester: TA Centre, Ardwick Green, Manchester, M12 6HD.

King's Regiment (Liverpool) (8th Foot) Raised by Colonel Robert Shirley, 1st Earl Ferrers, in June 1685 as Princess Anne of Denmark's Regiment. Redesignated The Queen's Regiment in 1702, The King's Regiment in 1716 and 8th (The King's Regiment) in 1751. In May 1881 the regiment was retitled The Liverpool Regiment (The King's) the title being reversed two months later to The King's (Liverpool) Regiment and changed again in 1921 to The King's Regiment (Liverpool). On 1 September 1958 the regiment amalgamated with The Manchester Regiment (63rd and 96th Foot) to form The King's Regiment (Manchester and Liverpool), the regiment being redesignated The King's Regiment (8th, 63rd and 96th Foot) (qv) on 13 December 1968.
Headdress Badge: The White Horse of

Hanover upon a ground. Below, the title 'KING'S' in Old English lettering.
History: *The History of The King's Regiment (Liverpool) 1914-16* (3 Vols) by E Little (1927); *The History of The King's Regiment 1914-1918* by Burke-Gaffney and *A Short History of The King's Regiment* by R P MacDonald.

King's Royal Rifle Corps (60th Foot) Raised in Pennsylvania, Virginia and Maryland in December 1755, by John Campbell, Earl of Loudon, styled 62nd (Royal American) Foot; and renumbered 60th (Royal American) Foot in 1756. The regiment was redesignated 60th (The Duke of York's Rifle Corps) in 1824, 60th or The King's Royal Rifle Corps in 1830 and the King's Royal Rifle Corps (four battalions) in 1881. On 7 November 1958 the regiment was redesignated 2nd Green Jackets (The King's Royal Rifle Corps) and on 1 January 1966 the regiment amalgamated with 1st Green Jackets (43rd and 52nd) and 3rd Green Jackets (The Rifle Brigade) to form The Royal Green Jackets (qv).
Headdress Badge: A Maltese Cross bearing a circle enclosing a stringed bugle-horn, all within a laurel wreath. On the arms of the cross 16 battle honours from 'QUEBEC' to 'PEGASUS BRIDGE'. Below, a naval crown superscribed 'COPENHAGEN, 2 APRIL, 1801'. Above, 'PENINSULA' upon a tablet, ensigned with the crown.
History: *Annals of The KRRC* (7 Vols) by Lewis Butler (Vols 1-3), Sir Stewart Hare (Vols 4&5), G H Mills and R F Nixon (Vols 6&7); *A Regimental Chronicle - 60th Royal Rifles* by N W Wallace (1879); *'Swift and Bold' -The Story of the KRRC in World War II* by Sir Hereward Wake and W F Deedes (1949); *Brief History of the KRRC* by Sir Hereward Wake (1948) and *The King's Royal Rifle Corps* by H F Wood (1967).

King's Royal Hussars *See: Hussars.*

King's (Queen's) Shilling To 'take the King's Shilling' means to enlist in the Army. Since 1694 a soldier has been required to be attested before some civil authority, both to protect him against impressment and to ensure that he understood what he was committing himself to. The giving of a shilling, and its acceptance by the soldier, was treated as an agreement by the man to enlist, and either complete his enlistment by attestation before a justice or, in default, to pay 'smart money'. The practice was abandoned in 1879.

King's Shropshire Light Infantry (53rd and 85th Foot) The 53rd Foot was raised in December 1755 as 55th Foot, renumbered 53rd Foot in 1757 and designated 53rd (Shropshire) Foot in 1782. The 85th was raised in March 1793 by Colonel Sir George Nugent from employees on the Marquis (later Duke) of Buckingham's estates, and designated 85th Regiment of Foot (Buckinghamshire Volunteers). Redesignated 85th (Bucks Volunteers) (Light Infantry) Regiment in 1808, 85th (Bucks Volunteers) (Duke of York's Own Light Infantry) Regiment in 1815 and 85th (Bucks Volunteers) (The King's Light Infantry) Regiment in 1821. In May 1881 53rd (Shropshire) Foot and 85th (Bucks Volunteers) (The King's Light Infantry) Regiment amalgamated to form The Shropshire Regiment (King's Light Infantry) and in July of that year were redesignated The King's Shropshire Light Infantry. On 10 July 1968 the regiment amalgamated with The Somerset and Cornwall Light Infantry (13th, 32nd and 46th Foot), The King's Own Yorkshire Light Infantry (51st and 105th Foot) and The Durham Light Infantry (68th and 106th Foot) to form The Light Infantry (qv).
Headdress Badge: A bugle-horn stringed, between the strings the initials 'KSLI'.
History: *The History of the Corps of The King's Shropshire Light Infantry (4 Vols)* by W Rogerson, R R Gubbins, J Moulsdale and G Archer Parfitt; *First into Antwerp (4 KSLI)* by U Thornburn (1987); *The 4th KSLI in Normandy* by U Thornburn (1990) and *After Antwerp - The Long Haul to Victory (4 KSLI)* by U Thornburn (1993).

King's South Africa Medal 1901-1902 King Edward VII authorised this medal, Queen Victoria having died on 22 January 1901, for issue to all those serving in South Africa on or after 1 January 1902 and who would complete 18 months' service before 1 June 1902.
Ribbon: Three equal vertical stripes of green, white and yellow.
Clasps: South Africa 1901 and South Africa 1902.

Kinnegad Slashers Regimental quick march of the Gloucestershire Regiment (28th and 61st Foot).

Kinross Yeomanry *See: Clackmannan Yeomanry.*

Kirbekan Battle honour marking the action on 10 February 1885 during the Sudan campaign by the force known as the 'River Column' in the advance up the River Nile for the relief of General Gordon. Mahdist forces had taken up a defensive position to bar the columns progress. Although British casualties were light the column commander, General Earle, was killed. *See also: Egypt 1884; Nile 1884-85; Abu Klea; Suakin 1885 and Tofrek.*

Kirkcudbrightshire Yeomanry Three troops of Yeomanry Cavalry were raised in the county in 1803 and served until 1826. In 1831 a corps was re-raised but soon disbanded.

Kirkee Battle honour marking an action in the Third Mahratta War (qv). On 5 November 1817 a British force under Colonel Burr defeated the Peishwa's army just outside Poona. *See also: Seetabuldee; Nagpore; Maheidpore and Corygaum.*

Kirke's Lambs Nickname given 2nd Foot, later the Queen's Royal Regiment (West Surrey) (qv) and now the Princess of Wales's Royal Regiment (Queens and Royal Hampshires). After the battle of Sedgemoor in 1685 the regiment, commanded by Colonel Percy Kirke, were feared for their cruelty in Somerset and the surrounding area when hunting down rebels. The regiment was already using the Paschal Lamb as its cap badge; hence the ironic nickname.

Kit Clothing and other personal effects.

Kitbag Long canvas bag to hold a serviceman's kit.

Kitchener, Horatio Herbert, Earl, of Khartoum and of Broome in Kent (1850-1916) After studying at Woolwich he was commissioned into the Royal Engineers in 1871. He was engaged in the Palestine survey (1874-78), and then in that of Cyprus (1878-82), after which he entered the Egyptian cavalry and took part in the Sudan campaign of 1883-85 for the relief of General Gordon. He became governor of Suakin in 1886, and Sirdar (commander-in-chief) of the Egyptian Army in 1892. In that capacity he recovered Dongola in 1896, for which he was promoted to major general. In April 1898 he defeated the Dervishes at Atbara, and in the following September won a decisive victory at Omdurman, which was followed by immediate pacification and most skilful handling of the situation in Fashoda. For these services he was raised to the peerage. When the South Africa War broke out Kitchener became chief of staff (December 1899) to Lord Roberts and in 1900 assumed supreme command in the rank of lieutenant general, bringing the war to a successful conclusion and peace in 1902. He was made a viscount and parliament voted him £50,000.

In 1902 he went to India, remaining there until 1909 when he became commander-in-chief in the Mediterranean and was made field marshal. He went to Australia and replanned the reconstitution of the commonwealth forces, was appointed agent and consul-general in Cairo and was at home on leave from Cairo when the First World War broke out

With almost universal approbation he was appointed war minister. There followed his greatest achievement, the raising of the new service battalions of volunteers which sustained the British army until conscription was able to replace the heavy losses. The magic of Kitchener's name is alleged to have added 1,700,000 men to the ranks by May 1915. After the failure at the Dardanelles the cabinet grew hostile toward him. He went to the Mediterranean in late 1915, and while there, was invited to take control in Egypt - a hint to resign the seals of office. This he did, after sending Horne to take command in Egypt in his stead. Asquith refused the resignation and Kitchener remained in office, though Sir William Robertson returned from France to become Chief of the Imperial General Staff. Kitchener was lost on 5 June 1916 when the cruiser HMS *Hampshire*, in which he was travelling to Russia, hit foul weather and sank off the Orkney Islands with the loss of all hands on 5 June 1916.

Kittle A coat worn by sergeant-drummers in the time of William III.

Knapsack The bag or sack in which the items needed by a soldier in the field were carried.

Knee-Apron Apron of leather or other material worn on the left leg by side-drummers.

Knee Boots A boot coming to just below the knee. A pattern introduced for mounted men in April 1896 had five pairs of eyelets to be laced at the instep, but other variants existed earlier.

Knickerbockers A type of loose breeches in use in India in the late 19th century. Made of serge or khaki, although a dress version of black with scarlet stripe also existed. The bottom of the legs reached to the ankles and were worn with gaiters or puttees.

Knightsbridge Second World War North Africa campaign battle honour marking the defence of the 'Knightsbridge Box' 6-7 and 12-13 June 1942. *See also: North Africa 1940-1943; Gazala; Retma; Bir El Aslagh; Bir Hacheim; Cauldron; Tobruk 1942; Bir El Igela; Hagiag Er Raml; Gabr El Fachri; Via Balbia; Zt El Mrasses and Sidi Rezegh.*

Knot Decorative shape made of cord, braid, lace or thick twisted cord found on the jackets of uniforms. The design could be simple like an Austrian Knot (qv) or more ornate.

Kohima Second World War Burma campaign battle honour marking the operations around Imphal March-June 1944 during which successive Japanese offensives were defeated. *See also: Burma 1942-1945; Tuitum; Nungshigum; Bishenpur; Kanglatongbi; Sakawng; Tamu Road; Shenam Pass and Litan.*

Koosh-Ab Battle honour marking an action on 8 February 1857 at Koosh-Ab which proved to be the decisive action of the Anglo-Persian War of 1856-57. *See also: Persia and Reshire.*

Korah Battle honour marking the defeat of Mahrub Khan, a disaffected officer in the service of Britain's ally the Nawab of Oudh, at Korah, some 25 miles from Cawnpore in 1777.

Korea Battle honour awarded to units which fought in the Korean War. Units served only short tours during the war and no unit was therefore present throughout the whole campaign to win the battle honour 'KOREA 1950-53'. However, the Royal Tank Regiment earned the honour dated '1951-52' and 17 regiments were awarded it for shorter periods. *See also: Naktong Bridgehead; Pakchon; Imjin; Kowang-San; The Hook 1952 and The Hook 1953.*

Korea Medal Sanctioned in 1951 for award to members of the British Commonwealth forces who fought under the United Nations for one or more days in the period 2 July 1950-10 June 1953.
Ribbon: Five equal vertical stripes of yellow, blue, yellow, blue and yellow.
Note: Anyone awarded the Korea Medal would also have received the United Nations medal with clasp KOREA. The ribbon of this medal has 17 alternate vertical stripes of blue and white.

Korean War 1950-53 The North Koreans invaded South Korea on 25 June 1950. The United Nations Security Council, in the absence of the Soviet representative, condemned this act of aggression and called on member nations to support South Korea. It was the United States which committed the major part of the force, but a number of member nations

offered small contingents, the first of which to arrive was the British 27th Brigade from Hong Kong, less one battalion which had been replaced by a New Zealand battalion. A New Zealand field artillery regiment and an Indian field ambulance also joined the brigade. The 29th Brigade Group arrived from the United Kingdom and 27th Brigade, 29th Brigade and a Canadian brigade group together formed a British Commonwealth division - but not until July 1951. The North Koreans launched a major offensive, which captured Seoul, the capital of South Korea, and drove the South Korean and American forces, the latter brought in from Japan, back to the south-east corner of South Korea, where by early August 1950 the Allies were on a line varying from 50 to 100 miles from Pusan.

In early September 1950, following a successful American landing at Inchon near Seoul, the United Nations force, including 27th Brigade launched a major counter-offensive which drove the North Koreans back into North Korea and which, by November 1950, was approaching the Yalu River, the frontier with the People's Republic of China. On 25 November 1950 Chinese forces crossed the Yalu River in massive strength, driving the United Nations forces back into South Korea where, by the beginning of January 1951, the line had stabilised some 50 miles south of Seoul. At the end of January 1951 the United Nations forces returned to the offensive, Seoul was recaptured in March and, following a determined Chinese counter-offensive in April, United Nations forces had closed up to the River Imjin by late May 1951. From August to November 1951 there was a series of limited actions to clear the Chinese from a number of positions beyond the Imjin River, in an area which became known as the 'Iron Triangle'.

Peace talks opened in November 1951 and dragged on throughout 1952 and much of 1953, with several sharp but localised actions being fought in the meantime. The Chinese launched a major offensive, which was contained in June 1953, and an armistice was signed the following month. Since the Korean War the

United States has maintained a strong military presence in South Korea and both North and South Korean armed forces are still held at a high state of readiness.

Kosturino First World War Macedonian campaign battle honour. In October 1915 sharp fighting took place near Kosturino between the Bulgars and a British force which was acting as flank protection to a French thrust northwards. *See also: Macedonia 1915-18; Struma; Doiran 1917 and Doiran 1918.*

Kowang-San Korean War battle honour marking the successful attack across the Imjin River by the British Commonwealth Division 3-12 October 1951. *See also: Korea 1950-1953; Naktong Bridgehead; Pakchon; Imjin; The Hook 1952; The Hook 1953; Chongju; Chongchon II; Seoul; Chaum-Ni; Hill 327; Kapyong-Chon; Kapyong; Maryang-San and Hill 227 I.*

K Ration Emergency combat rations used by US and Allied forces in the Second World War. Named after Ancel Keys, the US physiologist who developed the ration.

Krithia First World War Gallipoli campaign battle honour. Following the landings on 25 April 1915 attempts were made to extend the beachhead and secure the village of Krithia. Although Krithia was entered on several occasions it could not be held. *See also: Gallipoli 1915-16; Helles and Landing at Helles.*

Kukri Knife used in Nepal and particularly associated with Gurkha troops. The blade is keen, single-edged and doubly curved. Kukris vary in size and weight, those carried by Gurkha troops being about 14" long.

Kulkaber Second World War Abyssinian campaign battle honour marking an action during the campaign in East Africa. Following operations lasting from 15 October-27 November 1941 Gondar fell and the campaign was successfully concluded. *See also: Abyssinia 1940-1941; Keren; Karora-Marsa Taclai; Gondar;*

Ambazzo; Jebel Defeis; Giarso; Agordat; Barentu; Jebel Shiba; Cubcub; Ad Teclesan; Mescelit Pass; Mt Engiahat; Massawa; Amb Alagi; Afodu; Gambela; El Wak; Moyale; Wal Garis; Juba; Bulo Erillo; Beles Gugani; Alessandra; Gogni; Marda Pass; Babile Gap; Bisidimo; Awash; Todenyang-Namaraputh; Soroppa; Gelib; Colito; Wadara; Omo; Goluin; Fike and Lechemti.

Kullah Small close-fitting Indian cap generally pointed and usually worn as the base for a turban.

Kurtah Loose frock or blouse worn in India, reaching to the knees, with neck open to the waist.

Kut Al Amara 1915 First World War Mesopotamian campaign. A British force under General Towhshend defeated the Turks in late September 1915, following which the Turks withdrew up the River Tigris. *See also: Mesopotamia 1914-1918; Basra; Shaiba; Ctesiphon; Defence of Kut Al Amara; Kut Al Amara 1917; Tigris 1916; Baghdad; Khan Baghdadi and Sharqat.*

Kut Al Amara 1917 First World War Mesopotamia campaign battle honour. During January and February 1917 the British cleared the right bank of the River Tigris to beyond Kut and then crossed the river to a position at the rear of the Turkish main defence position. The Turks retreated and the way was open to Baghdad. *See also: Mesopotamia 1914-1918; Basra; Shaiba; Kut Al Amara 1915; Ctesiphon; Defence of Kut Al Amara; Tigris 1916; Baghdad; Khan Baghdadi and Sharqat.*

Kuwait 1961 The deployment of British forces to Kuwait in July 1961 at the request of the Emir of Kuwait. The government of General Abdul Karim Qassim of Iraq was pledged to overthrow all western-oriented régimes in the region, especially that of Kuwait where Iraq had a long standing territorial claim. British Army and Royal Marine units deployed rapidly, siting Malkara anti-tank guided missiles on the key terrain of the Mutla Ridge. The role was taken over from the British in September by an Arab League force, but prompt British action undoubtedly served to deter an Iraqi invasion.

Kvam Second World War battle honour marking one of the actions during the brief campaign in Norway (qv) in 1940. *See also: North West Europe 1940; Norway 1940; Stien; Pothus; Vist and Otta.*

Kyaumyaung Bridgehead Second World War Burma campaign battle honour marking the establishment of a bridgehead over the River Irrawaddy, and its defence against Japanese counter-attacks, over the period 9 January - 12 February 1945. *See also: Burma 1942-45; Shweli and Sagaing.*

Kyaukse 1942 Second World War Burma campaign battle honour marking the covering action fought during the British withdrawal across the River Irrawaddy 28-29 April 1942. *See also: Burma 1942-45; Pegu 1942; Taukyan; Paungde; Yenangyaung 1942 and Monywa 1942.*

Kyaukse 1945 Second World War Burma campaign battle honour marking an action during the advance to the River Irrawaddy in early 1945 in the latter stages of the campaign. *See also: Burma 1942-45; Letse and Seikpyu.*

La Bassée 1914 First World War battle honour marking an action during the so-called 'Race to the Sea' which followed the Battle of the Aisne, as the British moved to take up their place on the Allied left. The first serious clashes took place in the mining area of La Bassée. *See also: France and Flanders 1914-1918; Retreat from Mons; Marne 1914; Aisne 1914; Armentières 1914 and Messines 1914.*

Labor Omnia Vincit **(Labour conquers all)** Motto of The Royal Pioneer Corps.

Lace Term used in the Army to describe the braids of gold or silver worn by officers or coloured thread worn by other ranks. Officers' lace is made of various patterns such as oak leaves, shamrock and laurel leaves, occasionally with an added silk stripe or line. Other ranks' lace was usually white with stripes of varying patterns and colours for regimental distinction. These laces were also used on horse furniture. *See also: Ess and Vellum.*

Lacedæmonians Nickname given to 46th Foot, later The Duke of Cornwall's Light Infantry. In 1777 during the American War of Independence (qv), their Colonel is supposed to have made a long speech under heavy fire on Spartan discipline and the Lacedæmonians.

Laison Second World War battle honour marking one of the actions during the fighting around Falaise 7-22 August 1944 leading to the final decisive victory in Normandy. *See also: North West Europe 1944-1945; Falaise; Falaise Road; and Dives Crossing.*

Lambskin Lambskin was used for horse furniture, the lining (astrakhan) of cavalry patrol jackets and for the busby of officers in the 60th Rifles from 1873 until the helmet replaced it in 1881.

Lamone Bridgehead Second World War Italian campaign battle honour marking the defence of the Lamone bridgehead against heavy enemy attack on 9 December 1944. *See also: Italy 1943-45; Lamone Crossing and Rimini Line.*

Lamone Crossing Second World War, Italian campaign battle honour marking the establishment of bridgeheads over the River Lamone over the period 2-13 December 1944. *See also: Italy 1943-45; Lamone Bridgehead and Rimini Line.*

L'Attaque Regimental quick march of The Queen's Lancashire Regiment.

Lanarkshire Regiment (99th Foot) Raised in March 1824 under the colonelcy of Major General Gage John Hall as 99th (Lanarkshire) Regiment of Foot. Redesignated 99th (Duke of Edinburgh's) Regiment of Foot in 1874. Amalgamated with the 62nd (Wiltshire) Regiment in 1881 to form The Duke of Edinburgh's (Wiltshire Regiment). *See also: The Wiltshire Regiment.*

LANARKSHIRE YEOMANRY
The Lanarkshire Yeomanry Three troops of Yeomanry were raised in the Upper Ward of Lanarkshire in 1819 and this had risen to six troops by 1867. The regiment was frequently used in aid of the

civil power, being engaged on such duties for six weeks continuously in 1856. The regiment raised a company of 6th Battalion Imperial Yeomanry during the South Africa War (1899-1902). In 1915 the regiment was sent dismounted to Gallipoli and then moved to Egypt. In 1917 it amalgamated to form 12th (Ayr and Lanark Yeomanry) Battalion, The Royal Scots Fusiliers and, after service in Palestine, moved to France for the last five months of the First World War. After the war the regiment was re-formed as a cavalry regiment, retaining that role until 1940 when it converted to artillery, elements of the regiment serving as such in India, Malaya, Burma, Persia, Syria, Egypt, Palestine, Sicily and Italy. Re-formed in 1947 as an armoured regiment, the Lanarkshire Yeomanry later amalgamated with the other Lowland regiments to form the Queen's Own Lowland Yeomanry, which ceased to exist as a regiment in 1969. The successor unit may now be found in 'B' (Lanarkshire & Queen's Own Royal Glasgow Yeomanry) Squadron of the Scottish Yeomanry.

The Queen's Own Royal Glasgow Yeomanry Troops of Yeomanry Cavalry were raised at various times from 1797 in the Glasgow area and there is evidence of a connection with the Royal Glasgow Light Horse (1796) and the Glasgow Sharpshooters. The regiment was disbanded in 1802, although various corps were re-raised, only to be disbanded in 1814 and 1828. It is claimed that the Glasgow Troop never in fact disbanded. In 1848 a regiment was raised and designated The Queen's Own Royal Glasgow and Lower Ward of Lanarkshire Yeomanry, the regiment finding a company for 6th Battalion Imperial Yeomanry during the South Africa War (1899-1902). In the First World War the regiment sent squadrons to various formations in France and Flanders, was reunited as a regiment in 1916 and finished the war as 18th (Royal Glasgow Yeomanry) Battalion, The Highland Light Infantry. The regiment converted to artillery in 1920 serving in France, the Far East, the Western Desert, Sicily and Italy during the Second World War. The successor unit may now be found in 'B' (Lanarkshire & Queen's Own Royal

Glasgow Yeomanry) Squadron of the Scottish Yeomanry.

Lancashire Fusiliers (20th Foot) Raised as independent companies of Foot at Exeter in November 1688 by Sir Robert Peyton, for service with the newly landed Prince William of Orange. Regimented and taken on the English establishment as Peyton's Regiment of Foot in February 1689. Redesignated 20th Foot in 1751, 20th (East Devonshire) Foot in 1782, and The Lancashire Fusiliers in1881. On 23 April 1968 the regiment amalgamated with The Royal Northumberland Fusiliers, The Royal Warwickshire Fusiliers and The Royal Fusiliers (City of London Regiment) to form The Royal Regiment of Fusiliers (qv). Headdress Badge: A grenade with, on the base, the Sphinx upon a tablet inscribed EGYPT, within a laurel wreath. Below a scroll inscribed 'THE LANCASHIRE FUSILIERS'.
History: *The History of The Lancashire Fusiliers 1688-1821 and 1822-1903* (2 Vols) by Smythe (1903); *History of The Lancashire Fusiliers 1914-1918* by J C Latter (1949); *Regiments of the Line, The Story of The Lancashire Fusiliers* by S Ray (1963); *Lancashire Fusiliers The 20th Foot* by S Ray (1971); *Historical Record of 20th Regiment 1848* by R Cannon (1848); *A Short History XXth The Lancashire Fusiliers* by G Surtees (1955) and *The History of The Lancashire Fusiliers 1939-1945* by J McQ Hallam (1993).

Lancashire Regiment of Foot (47th Foot) *See: The Loyal Regiment (North Lancashire).*

Lancashire Regiment (Prince of Wales's Volunteers) (30th, 40th, 59th and 82nd Foot) The 30th Foot was raised on 8 March 1689 by George, Viscount Castleton and styled Lord Castleton's Regiment of Foot. The regiment was disbanded as Colonel Thomas Saunderson's Regiment of Foot in 1698, but re-raised in 1702 as Colonel Sanderson's Regiment of Marines and designated 30th Regiment of Foot in 1751 and 30th Foot (1st Cambridgeshire Regiment)in 1782. The 40th Foot was raised in Nova Scotia by Colonel Richard Phillips on 25

August 1717 as Colonel Phillip's Regiment of Foot. Numbered 40th Foot in 1751 and designated 40th (2nd Somersetshire) Regiment of Foot in 1782. The 59th Foot was raised in December 1755 by Colonel Sir Charles Montagu as 61st Regiment of Foot and renumbered 59th Foot in 1757. The regiment was redesignated 59th (2nd Nottinghamshire) Regiment of Foot in 1782. The 82nd Foot was raised by Sir Charles Leigh on 27 September 1793 and styled 82nd Regiment of Foot (Prince of Wales's Volunteers). In 1881 30th (1st Cambridgeshire) Regiment of Foot amalgamated with 59th (2nd Nottinghamshire) Regiment of Foot to form The West Lancashire Regiment. In the same year 40th (2nd Somersetshire) Regiment of Foot amalgamated with 82nd Regiment of Foot (Prince of Wales's Volunteers) to form The Prince of Wales's Volunteers (South Lancashire); the title being changed to The South Lancashire Regiment (The Prince of Wales's Volunteers) in 1938. On 1 July 1958 The East Lancashire Regiment (30th and 59th Foot) amalgamated with The South Lancashire Regiment (The Prince of Wales's Volunteers) (40th and 82nd Foot) to form The Lancashire Regiment (Prince of Wales's Volunteers). On 25 March 1970 The Lancashire Regiment (Prince of Wales's Volunteers) (30th, 40th, 59th and 82nd Foot) amalgamated with The Loyal Regiment (North Lancashire) (47th and 81st) to form The Queen's Lancashire Regiment (30th, 40th, 47th, 59th, 81st and 82nd Foot) (qv).

Headdress Badge: The plume, coronet and motto of the Prince of Wales.

History: *History of the 30th Regiment 1689-1881* (author unknown); *History of the East Lancashire Regiment in the Great War 1914-18* (author unknown); *History of The East Lancashire Regiment in The War 1939-45* (author unknown); *The South Lancashire Regiment, The Prince of Wales's Volunteers* by B R Mullaly and *'Ich Dien' The Prince of Wales's Volunteers (South Lancashire) 1914-1934* by H Whalley-Kelly.

LANCASHIRE YEOMANRY

The Duke of Lancaster's Own Yeomanry The first troop, raised at Bolton in April 1798, was joined by the Furness troop and Wigan troop in 1828 to form the Lancashire Regiment of Yeomanry Cavalry, redesignated the Duke of Lancaster's Own Yeomanry Cavalry, after their Colonel in Chief, in 1834. The regiment found a company of 8th Battalion Imperial Yeomanry for service in the South Africa War (1899-1902). In the First World War, the regiment was split with one squadron serving in the Middle East and the balance of the regiment serving initially as divisional cavalry, then regimented as a corps cavalry regiment, ending the war as an infantry battalion - 12th (DLOY) Battalion, The Manchester Regiment. Between the wars the regiment retained its horses and was mobilised as a mounted regiment in 1939. In August 1940 the regiment converted to artillery and served as such throughout the Second World War. The regiment re-formed in 1947 becoming the Duke of Lancaster's Own Yeomanry (Royal Tank Regiment) (Territorial) in 1967. The regiment was reduced to cadre strength in 1969. In 1971 the regiment was re-formed as an infantry regiment and on 1 November 1992 amalgamated with The Queen's Own Mercian Yeomanry to form The Royal Mercian and Lancastrian Yeomanry. The regiment's successor sub-unit is 'D' (Duke of Lancaster's Own Yeomanry) Squadron of the Royal Mercian and Lancastrian Yeomanry.

The Lancashire Hussars The Ashton Yeomanry Cavalry was commissioned in 1798 and served until 1823. In 1848 a new regiment was formed, largely composed of Roman Catholics, from those who were serving with the Duke of Lancaster's Own Yeomanry (qv). The regiment sent volunteers to 2nd and 8th Battalions of The Imperial Yeomanry during the South Africa War (1899-1902). The regiment was split during the First World War with elements serving in the Middle East and France both as cavalry and as 18th (Lancashire Hussars) Battalion The King's Liverpool Regiment. After the war the regiment converted to artillery, serving as such throughout the Second World War. Its successors have been absorbed in the Royal Mercian and Lancastrian Yeomanry.

Lancastrian Brigade An administrative grouping in the infantry formed by Army Order 61 of 1948 comprising: The King's Own Royal Regiment (Lancaster), The Border Regiment, King's Own Royal Border Regiment (from 1959), The King's Regiment (Liverpool), The Manchester Regiment, The King's Regiment (Manchester and Liverpool) (from 1958), The Lancashire Fusiliers (until 1957); The East Lancashire Regiment, The South Lancashire Regiment (PWV), The Lancashire Regiment (PWV) (from 1958) and The Loyal Regiment (North Lancashire). The regiments of the brigade were absorbed into the King's Division (qv) in 1968.

Lance Obsolete nuclear-capable missile launcher.

Lance Bombardier Lowest non-commissioned officer rank in the Royal Artillery. Denoted by one chevron, worn on the upper sleeve.

Lance Cap The cap with the four-sided top worn by Polish lancers and subsequently adopted for wear by British lancers, was variously known as the *czapka*, *schapka*, *schapska* and *tschapka*, but as the lance cap in official British Army publications.

Lance Corporal Lowest non-commissioned officer rank in the British Army. Denoted by one chevron, worn on the upper arm. *See also: Rank.*

Lance Sergeant A corporal in the Foot Guards or a corporal acting as a sergeant, usually on a temporary basis and without pay. *See also: Rank.*

Lancers Cavalry regiments so named from their principal arm being, or having been, the lance. Although in use since the days of chivalry, the lance declined in importance with the introduction of a serviceable firearm. Frederick the Great included a lancer troop in each hussar regiment. During the Napoleonic period the lance was seen on many battlefields in the hands of Poles, Cossacks and Arabs. After

Wagram lancers began to appear in the French ranks and a regiment of Polish lancers in the French service was raised in 1907, and in 1811 Napoleon converted nine dragoon regiments to lancers. The French lancers were prominent in the Peninsula War, particularly at Albuera, and again at Waterloo they sorely tried the British dragoons and hussars. Shortly after Waterloo a few British dragoon regiments were converted to lancers. The lance played a prominent part in many of the battles in India, South Africa and in Allenby's campaign in Palestine. Only two regiments of Lancers, 9th/12th Royal Lancers (Prince of Wales's) and The Queen's Royal Lancers, remain in the regular army order of battle.

LANCER REGIMENTS

5th Royal Irish Lancers Raised in 1689 as Wynne's Regiment of Enniskillen Dragoons, the regiment inherited the number honours - but not the seniority of - 5th (Royal Irish) Dragoons which was disbanded in 1799. Redesignated The Royal Dragoons of Ireland in 1704 and 5th (Royal Irish) Dragoons in 1756. The regiment was disbanded in 1799, re-formed in 1858 as 5th (Royal Irish) Lancers and redesignated 5th Royal Irish Lancers in 1921. On 11 April 1922 the regiment amalgamated with 16th The Queen's Lancers to form 16th/5th The Queen's Royal Lancers (qv).
Headdress Badge: Upon two lances crossed in saltire a circle bearing the motto of the Order of St Patrick '*Quis Separabit*' (Who shall separate us), within the circle the numeral 5.
History: *Historical Records of The 5th (Royal Irish) Lancers 1689-1906* by W T Willcox (1908) and *History of the 5th (Royal Irish) Regiment of Dragoons 1689-1799 and 5th Royal Irish Lancers 1858-1921* by J R Harvey (1923).

9th Queen's Royal Lancers Raised in July 1715 by Major General Owen Wynn as Wynn's Regiment of Dragoons and designated 9th Dragoons (qv) in 1751; converted to Light Dragoons as 9th Light Dragoons in 1783 and converted to Lancers as 9th Lancers in 1816. Redesignated 9th (Queen's Royal) Lancers in 1830 and 9th Queen's Royal Lancers in 1921. On 11 September 1960 the regiment amalgamated with 12th Royal Lancers (Prince of Wales's) to form 9th/12th Royal Lancers (Prince of Wales's) (qv).

Headdress Badge: Upon two lances crossed in saltire the numeral 9, below which a scroll inscribed 'LANCERS', the whole ensigned with the crown.

History: *The Ninth Queen's Royal Lancers 1715-1936* by E W Sheppard; *The Ninth Queen's Royal Lancers 1936-1945* by J Bright; and *Historical Record of the 9th Queen's Royal Lancers 1945-1960* by Thomson-Glover.

12th Royal Lancers (Prince of Wales's) Raised in July 1715 by Colonel Phineas Bowles as Bowles's Regiment of Dragoons and designated 12th Dragoons (qv) in 1751. Converted to Light Dragoons as 12th (The Prince of Wales's) Light Dragoons in 1768 and converted to Lancers as 12th (The Prince of Wales's) Lancers in 1816. Redesignated 12th (The Prince of Wales's Royal) Lancers in 1817 and 12th Royal Lancers (Prince of Wales's) in 1921. On 11 September 1960 the regiment amalgamated with 9th Queen's Royal Lancers to form 9th/12th Royal Lancers (Prince of Wales's) (qv).

Headdress Badge: Upon two lances crossed in saltire the plume and coronet of the Prince of Wales above the roman numerals XII, all ensigned with the crown.

History: *The History of XII Royal Lancers (Prince of Wales's) 1715-1945* by P F Stewart.

16th The Queen's Lancers Raised in August 1759 *(See: 16th Dragoons)* by Colonel John Burgoyne as 16th Light Dragoons (also known as Burgoyne's Light Horse) and redesignated 16th or Queen's Light Dragoons in 1769. Converted to Lancers as 16th (The Queen's) Lancers in 1815 and redesignated 16th The Queen's Lancers in 1921. On 11 April 1922 the regiment amalgamated with 5th Royal Irish Lancers to form 16th/5th The Queen's Royal Lancers (qv).

Headdress Badge: Upon two lances crossed in saltire the numerals 16, beneath a scroll inscribed 'THE QUEEN'S LANCERS', all ensigned with the crown.

History: *History of 16th The Queen's Light Dragoons (Lancers) 1759-1912* by H Graham (1912) and *History of the 16th The Queen's Light Dragoons (Lancers) 1912-1925* by H Graham (1926).

17th Lancers (Duke of Cambridge's Own) Raised by Lieutenant Colonel John Hale in November 1759 as 18th Light Dragoons; renumbered 17th Light Dragoons (See: 17th Dragoons) in 1763; and converted to Lancers as 17th Lancers in 1822. Redesignated 17th Lancers (Duke of Cambridge's Own) in 1876. On 11 April 1922 the regiment amalgamated with 21st Lancers (Empress of India's) to form 17th/21st Lancers (qv).

Headdress Badge: A death's head above the motto 'OR GLORY' inscribed on a scroll.

History: *Historical Record of the 17th Lancers 1759-1841* by R Cannon (1841); *A History of The 17th Lancers (DCO) 1759-1892* by J W Fortescue (1895); *Death or Glory Boys* (2nd Edn.) by D H Parry (1931); and *A History of The 17th Lancers (DCO) 1895-1924* by G Nicholls (1931).

21st Lancers (Empress of India's) Raised by the Marquis of Granby *(See: 21st Dragoons)* in 1760 as 21st (Granby's) Light Dragoons, or Royal Foresters, and disbanded in 1763. Re-raised in 1779 as 21st Light Dragoons and disbanded in 1783. Re-raised in 1794 as 21st Light Dragoons and disbanded in 1819. In 1858 3rd Bengal European Cavalry of the East India Company (qv) converted to the British establishment and was designated 21st Light Dragoons; redesignated 21st Hussars in 1863. The regiment converted to lancers as 21st Lancers in 1897 and was redesignated 21st (Empress of India's) Lancers in 1899. In 1921 the regiment was redesignated 21st Lancers (Empress of India's) and on 11 April 1922, amalgamated with 17th Lancers (Duke of Cambridge's Own) to form 17th/21st Lancers (qv).

Headdress Badge: Upon two lances crossed in saltire ensigned with the crown the royal cypher VRI of Queen Victoria as Empress of India, above the roman numerals XXI.

9th/12th Royal Lancers (Prince of Wales's) Formed on 11 September 1960 through the amalgamation of 9th Queen's

Royal Lancers and 12th Royal Lancers (Prince of Wales's).

Headdress Badge: Upon two lances crossed in saltire the plume of the Prince of Wales, below a scroll with the roman numerals IX-XII inscribed.

Regimental marches:

Quick March: *God Bless The Prince of Wales.*

Slow marches: *Men of Harlech* (slow march of 9th Lancers) and *Coburg* (slow march of 12th Lancers).

Home headquarters: TA Centre, Saffron Road, Wigston, Leicester, LE8 2TU.

History: *A Short History of the 9th/12th Lancers (Prince of Wales's) 1960-1985* by R Brockbank.

16th/5th The Queen's Royal Lancers Formed on 11 April 1922 through the amalgamation of 16th The Queen's Lancers and 5th Royal Irish Lancers. On 26 June 1993 the regiment amalgamated with 17th/21st Lancers to form The Queen's Royal Lancers (qv).

Headdress Badge: Upon two lances crossed in saltire the numerals 16, below a scroll inscribed 'THE QUEEN'S LANCERS', all ensigned with the crown.

Motto: *Aut cursu, aut cominus armis* (Either in the charge or hand-to-hand).

Regimental Marches:

Quick march: *Scarlet and Green.*

Slow march: *The Queen Charlotte.*

History: *History of The 16th/5th The Queen's Royal Lancers 1925-1961* by C N Barclay (1963); *A Short History of The 16th/5th The Queen's Royal Lancers* by J Lunt (1973) and *The Scarlet Lancers, A History of The 16th/5th The Queen's Royal Lancers 1689-1992* by J Lunt (1993).

17th/21st Lancers Formed on 11 April 1922 through the amalgamation of 17th Lancers (Duke of Cambridge's Own) and 21st Lancers (Empress of India's). On 26 June 1993 the regiment amalgamated with 16th/5th The Queen's Royal Lancers to form The Queen's Royal Lancers (qv).

Headdress Badge: A death's head above the motto 'OR GLORY' inscribed on a scroll.

Regimental marches:

Quick march: *The White Lancer.*

Slow march: *Rienzi.*

History: *A History of The 17th/21st Lancers 1922-1959* by R L V ffrench Blake (1962);

The 17th/21st Lancers 1959-1968 by R L V ffrench Blake (1968); *A Short History of The 17th/21st Lancers 1759-1959* by R L C Tamplin (1959); and *The 17th/21st Lancers 1759-1993* by R L V ffrench Blake (1993).

Queen's Royal Lancers Formed on 26 June 1993 through the amalgamation of 16th/5th The Queen's Royal Lancers and 17th/21st Lancers.

Headdress Badge: Upon two lances crossed in saltire a death's head and motto 'OR GLORY'.

Regimental marches:

Quick march: *Stable Jacket.*

Slow march: *Omdurman.*

Home headquarters: Coldharbour House, Prince William of Gloucester Barracks, Grantham, Lincolnshire NG31 7TJ.

Lanchester British made sub-machine gun produced in 1940 to meet an urgent operational requirement and based upon the German Bergmann MP28 with a few modifications. The weapon fired from a side-mounted magazine containing 50 9mm rounds. In the event the Lanchester was very quickly superseded by the Sten Gun (qv). *See also: Sub-machine gun.*

Landing at Anzac First World War Gallipoli campaign battle honour marking the landing by Australians and New Zealanders at 'Anzac' in April 1915. *See also: Gallipoli 1915-16; Helles; Landing at Helles; Krithia; Anzac; Defence of Anzac and Suvla.*

Landing at Helles First World War Gallipoli campaign battle honour marking the landing of United Kingdom troops at Helles in April 1915. *See also: Gallipoli 1915-16; Helles; Landing at Anzac; Anzac; Defence of Anzac; Krithia and Suvla.*

Landing at Porto San Venere Second World War Italian campaign battle honour marking one of the actions on the Eighth Army front during 1943. *See also: Italy 1943-1945; Taranto; San Salvo; Orsogna; Impossible Bridge; and Caldari.*

Landing at Sicily Second World War Sicilian campaign battle honour marking the landing at Sicily by sea and glider-borne air-landed battalions on 9 and 10

July 1943 at the start of the Allied campaign. *See also: Sicily 1943; Primosole Bridge; Sferro; Regalbuto and Centuripe.*

Landing at Suvla First World War, Gallipoli campaign battle honour marking the landing at Suvla Bay on 6 and 7 August 1915 in an attempt to seize the Sari Bair Ridge. *See also: Gallipoli 1915-16; Landing at Helles; Helles; Landing at Anzac; Anzac; Defence of Anzac; Krithia and Suvla.*

Landing Craft Family of vessels designed for the landing of troops and equipment on beaches in amphibious operations which include: landing craft logistic (LCL); landing ship tank (LST); landing craft mechanised/medium (LCM); landing craft tank (LCT) and landing craft vehicles and personnel (LCVP).

Langemarck 1914 First World War battle honour marking one of the actions in the First Battle of Ypres. Langemarck lies some four miles north-east of Ypres. *See also: France and Flanders 1914-1918; Ypres 1914; Gheluvelt and Nonne Bosschen.*

Langemarck 1917 First World War battle honour marking an action during the British offensive known as the Third Battle of Ypres which started on 31 July and finished on 10 November. *See also: France and Flanders 1914-1918; Ypres 1917; Pilckem; Menin Road; Polygon Wood; Broodseinde; Poelcappelle and Passchendaele.*

Lanyard Cord used to secure a hand gun to the person, or by an artilleryman to fire a gun. The name is now applied to the decorative cords worn around the arm and under the epaulette, except in the Light Infantry where the term 'whistle cord' is used.

Lapel The turned-back fronts of military coats which revealed the inner coloured 'facing'.

Lass of Richmond Hill Regimental quick march of The Women's Royal Army Corps.

Last Post Bugle call sounded at the close of day and at military funerals.

Late Entry Commission More properly the Regular Commission (Late Entry) Cadre. Commission offering a full pensionable career to 55 to those with service in the ranks.

La Toques Crossing Second World War battle honour marking one of the actions which took place between the Normandy landing in June 1944 and the crossing of the River Seine in late August. *See also: North West Europe 1944-1945; Tourmauville Bridge; St Pierre La Veille; Estry; Noireau Crossing; La Vie Crossing; Risle Crossing and Foret de Bretonne.*

Latrine The lavatory in a barracks or camp.

La Variniere Second World War battle honour marking one of the actions in the offensive launched south-westwards from the Caumont area on 30 July 1944 which culminated in the capture of Mont Pincon. *See also: North West Europe 1944-1945; Mont Pincon; Quarry Hill; Souleuvre; Catheolles; Le Perier Ridge; Brieux Bridgehead and Jurques.*

La Vie Crossing Second World War battle honour marking one of the actions which took place between the Normandy landing in June 1944 and the crossing of the River Seine in late August. *See also: North West Europe 1944-1945; Tourmauville Bridge; St Pierre La Veille; Estry; Noireau Crossing; La Touques Crossing; Risle Crossing and Foret de Bretonne.*

Lawrence, Thomas Edward (1888-1935) Sometimes referred to as 'Lawrence of Arabia'. On leaving Oxford he was employed on the excavations at Carchemish and travelled in Syria. When Turkey entered the First World War, he was sent to Cairo to help in the Arab Bureau. In October 1916 he went to Arabia where he became the moving spirit in the Arab revolt which protected the right flank of the British advance into Syria. At the peace conference Lawrence backed the Hashemite family, especially Feisal, and after the conference had failed to achieve what he had hoped for, Lawrence changed his name first to Ross and later to Shaw and tried to hide in the Royal Air Force. As he had become a legend at home and abroad, he was a problem to the authorities and to himself, but was at last allowed to remain in the Royal Air Force, working on fast motor boats for air-sea rescue. He died in a motorcycle accident.

Layer Artillery specialisation. One qualified to 'lay' the gun. A qualified layer wears a badge depicting the letter 'L' within a wreath on the sleeve.

Leading Staff Stick with an ornamental head, often of silver and decorated with tassels. Carried by officers leading men. Such a staff was in use in the Honourable Artillery Company as late as the first quarter of the 18th century.

Leaguer A defended formation, sometimes concealed, adopted by an armoured squadron or squadron group. Leaguers may be 'close' with vehicles near one another, or 'open' with vehicles well spaced out.

Le Cateau First World War battle honour marking an action during the retreat from Mons when II Corps made a stand at Le Cateau, which the rearmost troops had only reached by dawn on 26 August 1914. German frontal attacks were repulsed but, having been outflanked, the corps was obliged to continue the withdrawal having suffered very heavy losses. *See also: France and Flanders 1914-1918; Mons; Retreat from Mons; Marne 1914; Aisne 1914 and La Bassée 1914.*

Lechemti Second World War Abyssinian campaign battle honour. *See also: Abyssinia 1940-41; Keren; Karora-Marsa Taclai; Gondar; Jebel Defeis; Giarso; Agordat; Barentu; Jebel Shiba; Cubcub; Ad Teclesan; Mescelit Pass; Mt Engiahat; Massawa; Amb Alagi; Afodu; Gambela; El Wak; Moyale; Wal Garis; Juba; Bulo Erillo; Beles Gugani; Alessandra; Gogni; Marda Pass; Babile Gap; Bisidimo; Awash; Todenyang-Namaraputh; Soroppa; Gelib; Colito; Wadara; Omo; Goluin and Fike.*

Lee Enfield Number 4 Rifle This 0.303" calibre weapon fed by a 10-round magazine was first developed in 1920 as a replacement for the Short Magazine Lee Enfield (qv). However, it did not enter production until 1941, but remained in service with the British Army throughout the Second World War until 1957 replaced by the Self-Loading Rifle (qv). *See also: Rifle.*

Lee Enfield Number 5 Rifle Modified Lee Enfield Number 4 rifle (qv) with the barrel reduced by 5". Produced during the Second World War as a short carbine for use in densely forested and jungle areas. Withdrawn from service in 1947. *See also: Rifle.*

Lee-Metford Rifle The Martini-Henry rifle (qv) had a 0.45" calibre which made both weapon and ammunition very heavy, and trials were put in hand to develop a lighter weapon. The Swiss Rubin rifle had a 0.303" calibre, but the barrel and bolt were unsatisfactory for British Army service. The outcome was a hybrid affair known as the Lee-Metford, with a ten round magazine, which was adopted for service in 1888. *See also: Rifle.*

Leese Second World War battle honour marking the establishment of a bridgehead over the River Weser 5-8 April 1945. *See also: North West Europe 1944-1945; Rhine; Ibbenbüren; Aller; Brinkum; Bremen and Arnhem 1945.*

Leg A section or part of a route. More particularly the compass course between any two reference points on the ground.

Lehi *See: Palestine 1945-48.*

Le Havre Second World War battle honour marking the fighting which took place 10-12 September 1944 leading to the capture of the port. *See also: North West Europe 1944-1945; Brussels; Antwerp; Neerpelt; Gheel; Hechtel; Aart and Boulogne 1944.*

Leicestershire Regiment (17th Foot) *See: Royal Leicestershire Regiment.*

The Leicestershire Yeomanry (Prince Albert's Own) The Leicestershire Light Horse was raised in 1794 and disbanded in

1802. Re-raised in 1803, the regiment provided companies for 11th and 17th Battalions of The Imperial Yeomanry during the South Africa War (1899-1902). In the First World War it served as a mounted regiment in France and Flanders from November 1914 until, for a brief period in early 1918, it trained with the North Somerset Yeomanry as a machine gun battalion. Having remained a mounted regiment between the wars the regiment was mobilised as such in 1939, but converted to artillery in August 1940, serving as such in North-West Europe, Palestine, North Africa, Syria and Italy. The regiment was subsequently disbanded and its successors may now be found in 'B' (Leicestershire & Derbyshire Yeomanry) Squadron of The Royal Yeomanry; 7th (Volunteer) Battalion, The Royal Anglian Regiment and 'B' Company 3rd (Volunteer) Battalion The Worcestershire and Sherwood Foresters Regiment.

Leinster Regiment (100th and 109th Foot) *See: Prince of Wales's Leinster Regiment (Royal Canadians).*

Lentini Second World War Sicilian campaign battle honour. *See also: Sicily 1943; Primosole Bridge; Sferro; Regalbuto and Centuripe.*

Le Perier Ridge Second World War battle honour marking one of the actions in the offensive launched south-westwards from the Caumont area on 30 July 1944 which culminated in the capture of Mont Pincon. *See also: North West Europe 1944-1945; Mont Pincon; Quarry Hill; Souleuvre; Catheolles; La Varnière; Brieux Bridgehead and Jurques.*

Leros Second World War battle honour marking the occupation of the island, one of the Dodecanese, following the Italian surrender in September 1943. In November the island was subjected to a German air-and seaborne attack in overwhelming strength and compelled to surrender after four days of fierce fighting. *See also: Cos.*

Leswaree First Mahratta War (qv) battle honour marking the decisive victory over the northern armies of the Mahratta Confederacy on 1 November 1803 which resulted in Scindia formally ceding the territory between the Rivers Ganges and Jumna. *See also: Ally Ghur; Delhi 1803; Assaye and Deig.*

Let Erin Remember Regimental slow march of the Irish Guards.

Le Transloy First World War battle honour marking one of the actions during the Battle of the Somme in 1916 which was launched on 1 July and ground to a halt in foul weather in November. The battle honour covers 18 days' fighting in October as the British sought to push forward onto Le Transloy Ridge. *See also: France and Flanders 1914-1918; Somme 1916; Albert 1916; Bazentin; Delville Wood; Pozières; Guillemont; Ginchy; Flers-Courcelette; Morval; Thiepval; Ancre Heights and Ancre 1916.*

Letse Second World War Burma campaign battle honour marking one of the actions which took place after the advance to the River Irrawaddy in 1945. *See also: Burma 1942-45; Irrawaddy; Rangoon Road; Seikpyu and Kyaukse 1945.*

Levée Traditionally a public court reception held in the afternoon or evening at which a special and elaborate order of dress, Levée dress, was required. The term Levée is also used in some regiments for the routine parade at which a commanding officer hears disciplinary cases and conducts interviews. *See also: Orderly Room; Orders and Memorandum.*

Lewis Gun Light machine gun developed by the American Samuel McLean and improved by Colonel Isaac Lewis in 1910. The 'Lewis gun', which fired a 0.303" round fed from a 47 round drum, was introduced into the British Army in 1915.

Liaison Officer An officer appointed to a formation or unit to assist with the passage of information and improve co-ordination between respective commanders.

Lieutenant and Second Lieutenant The lowest commissioned ranks in the British

Army, next in rank below captain and denoted respectively by two or one stars worn on the shoulder. The name stems from the French *lieu-tenant* and Latin *Locum tenens* (holding the place of another). Collectively known as subaltern officers. The name lieutenant was applied to such officers because they 'understudy' the squadron, battery or company commander whilst themselves commanding troops or platoons. Second lieutenants were formerly called cornets or ensigns, except in Fusilier regiments where they were called second lieutenants. An alteration was made in 1871: those appointed before 26 August 1871, or from the Sandhurst 'A List', were made lieutenants as from 1 November 1871 and those appointed after 26 August 1871 were sub-lieutenants. The latter rank was altered in 1877 to second lieutenant, a rank which, although abolished from 1881 to January 1887, is still in use. In most units the duties of lieutenants and second lieutenants are the same. In February 1810 the rank of lieutenant was indicated by the wearing of one epaulette on the right shoulder, but with a thinner fringe than that carried by a captain. With the replacement of the coatee by the tunic in 1855, epaulettes became obsolete and rank was indicated on the collar by a crown, the ensign (later second lieutenant) wearing one star. Both the lieutenant and the ensign had lace or braid only on the top or front of the collar. In October 1880 rank badges reverted to the shoulder, but now on twisted cord, the lieutenant having one star and the second or sub-lieutenant having no rank badge. In May 1902 rank badges for non-field officers were changed to the system which still exists; the captain wearing three stars, the lieutenant two stars and the second lieutenant one star on each shoulder.

Lieutenant Colonel Commissioned rank below colonel and above major. In February 1810 the rank of lieutenant colonel was indicated by the wearing of two epaulettes, each bearing a crown. With the introduction of the tunic instead of the coatee in 1855 epaulettes became obsolete and rank was worn on the collar, a lieutenant colonel having his collar laced all round. In October 1880 rank badges reverted to the shoulder, but now on twisted cord, lieutenant colonel rank being indicated by a star surmounted by a crown. The rank of lieutenant colonel is still indicated by a star surmounted by a crown worn on each shoulder. It is at the rank of lieutenant colonel that command of cavalry and artillery regiments and infantry battalions lies. *See also: Rank.*

Lieutenant General General officer ranking below general and above major general. The rank is denoted by a crossed baton and sabre surmounted by a crown, worn on the epaulettes. *See also: Rank.*

Life Guards Premier regiment of the British Army, taking precedence over all others. The regiment has its origin in the royalist nobility who fled with Charles II to the continent and accompanied him during his exile. At the Restoration in 1660 they returned with the King, escorted him to London and, in January 1661 were established in the new standing army as three separate troops: His Majesties Own Troope of Guards, His Highness Royall The Duke of Yorke his Troope of Guards and his Grace the Duke of Albermarle his Troope of Guards. On the death of General Monck the latter became The Queen's Troope. There were a number of changes of title and composition between 1661 and 1788 when the separate troops were finally regimented. The 1st Troop of Horse Guards and 1st Troop of Horse Grenadier Guards formed as 1st Regiment of Life Guards, and the 2nd Troop of Horse Guards and 2nd Troop of Horse Grenadier Guards formed as 2nd Regiment of Life Guards. In April 1922 the two regiments amalgamated to form The Life Guards (1st and 2nd) redesignated The Life Guards in June 1928.

Headdress Badge: The royal cypher within a circle inscribed 'THE LIFE GUARDS', ensigned with a crown.

Regimental marches:

Quick marches: *Milanollo and Men of Harlech.*

Slow marches: *The Life Guards Slow March* and *Men of Harlech.*

Headquarters Household Cavalry: Chelsea Barracks, London, SW1H 8RF.

History: *The Story of the Household Cavalry 1651-1919* (3 Vols.) by G Arthur; *The First Household Cavalry Regiment 1939-45* by H Wyndham; *The Second Household Cavalry Regiment 1939-45* by R Orde and *Challengers and Chargers, A History of The Life Guards 1945-92* by W Lloyd.

Light Anti-Tank Weapon 1980 (LAW 80) The LAW 80, a 94mm calibre man-portable light recoilless anti-tank weapon developed by Hunting Engineering, replacing the 84mm Carl Gustav (qv) and US 66mm light anti-tank weapons in the infantry, down to section level. Improved accuracy has been achieved by the use of a built-in, semi-automatic spotting rifle. The weapon has an effective range of 500m.

Light Division An administrative grouping in the infantry, created under Army Order 34 of 1968, comprising: The Light Infantry and The Royal Green Jackets.

Light Dragoons, The *See: Dragoons.*

Light Gun A light towed gun of 105mm calibre, currently in service with parachute and commando field artillery regiments and capable of firing high explosive, high explosive anti-tank, white phosphorous, smoke and illuminating rounds. The light gun was taken into service in 1975, has a crew of six, and a maximum range of 17,000m.

Light Infantry Although there had been 'light troops' in the British Army in the 1740s, it was the North American Wars of the 1750s which saw the development of light infantry. The heavy equipment, conspicuous red and white uniforms and close formation fighting of the British Army proved' wholly unsuitable when operating in close country against Indians and French colonists with highly developed fieldcraft and marksmanship skills. Prompted by these experiences, General James Wolfe (1727-59) and Lord Amherst (1717-97) realised that a new approach was necessary. A small corps of 'Light Troops' recruited from loyal settlers was

formed in 1755. It consisted of men carefully selected for their toughness and intelligence, able to scout and skirmish, concentrating for an operation and dispersing thereafter with stealth and speed. So effective were these light troops that steps were taken to increase the number available. Regiments formed 'Light Companies' of soldiers selected for their military skills, and ability to act on their own initiative within a broad tactical plan. The bugle horn, which subsequently became the emblem of Light Infantry, replaced the drum as the means of communication between the groups of often widely dispersed light infantrymen. By the end of the 18th century it was not unusual for commanders to group the various light companies together for specific operations. Napoleon's invasion of Spain in 1802 stimulated a rapid development of the light infantry concept under the direction of the brilliant young general, Sir John Moore (qv), and it became the practice to grant, as an honour, the much coveted title of 'Light Infantry' to regiments which particularly distinguished themselves in action.

Light Infantry Regimental quick march of The Light Infantry.

Light Infantry (13th, 32nd, 46th, 51st, 53rd, 68th, 85th, 105th and 106th Foot) Formed on 10 July 1968 through the amalgamation of The Somerset and Cornwall Light Infantry, The King's Own Yorkshire Light Infantry, The King's Shropshire Light Infantry and The Durham Light Infantry.

Headdress Badge: A bugle horn stringed in silver with red cloth backing.

Mottoes: *Cede Nullis* (Yield to none), *Aucto Splendore Resurgo* (I rise again with renewed splendour) and *Faithful*.

Regimental marches:

Quick march: *Light Infantry.*

Double march: *The Keel Row.*

Regimental headquarters: Peninsula Barracks, Romsey Road, Winchester, Hampshire, SO23 8TS.

History: *'Exceedingly Lucky' A History of The Light Infantry 1968-1993* by A Makepeace-Warne (1993).

Light Infantry Brigade An administrative grouping in the infantry formed by Army Order 61 of 1948 comprising The Somerset Light Infantry (until 1959); The Duke of Cornwall's Light Infantry (until 1959), The Somerset and Cornwall Light Infantry (from 1959), The Oxfordshire and Buckinghamshire Light Infantry (until 1958), The King's Own Yorkshire Light Infantry, The King's Shropshire Light Infantry and The Durham Light Infantry. The regiments of the brigade were absorbed into the Light Division (qv) in 1968.

Light Mortar Light mortar of 51mm calibre which can be carried and fired by one man. The mortar, which has replaced the 2" mortar of the 1940s, has a range of 750m and can fire high explosive, smoke or illuminating rounds.

Light of Foot Regimental quick march of The Queen's Own Mercian Yeomanry and The Queen's Own Mercian and Lancastrian Yeomanry.

Lights Out Bugle call directing that lights be switched out to permit sleep.

Light Support Weapon (LSW) Section level light machine gun introduced to replace the General Purpose Machine Gun (GPMG) in the light role in the British Army. The weapon, a version of the L85A1 assault rifle and known as L86A1, is fitted with a bipod and standard optical sight, fires a 5.56mm round fed from a 30 round magazine, and has a range of 1,000m.

Light Tanks The light tanks of the inter-war years were derived from the series of Carden-Loyd one-man tanks, tankettes and carriers (qv) produced from 1926 onwards. The Carden-Loyd firm was taken over by Vickers Armstrong in 1928. Most of the early light tanks were used for training at the outset of the Second World War, although a few did see service in the opening stages of the North Africa campaign. The Mark VI light tank and its A, B and C models came into service in 1936, the Mark VIB being the most widely used

British light tank in the Second World War. The light tank Mark VII 'Tetrarch' (qv) entered limited service in 1940, some being landed by glider on the eve of D-Day in June 1944. The light tank Mark VIII or Harry Hopkins (qv), a development of Tetrarch, was completed in 1944 but never taken into service. Anti-aircraft variants of the light tank were in use throughout the war. *See also: Tank; Tetrarch and Harry Hopkins.*

Lillibulero Regimental quick march of The Royal Electrical and Mechanical Engineers.

Lilywhites Nickname given 13th Hussars, now The Light Dragoons. When the regiment was converted from light dragoons to hussars in 1861 buff facings were adopted, but for some reason they were pipeclayed white.

Limber Part of a gun carriage, consisting of an axle, pole and two wheels forming an ammunition container, to which horses or a prime mover are attached.

Lincelles Battle honour marking the action which took place on 18 August 1793 near Lille in France during the French Revolutionary War. A brigade of Guards under Lord Lake, after marching six miles in just on the hour, defeated a much larger French force. *See also: Nieuport; Villers-en-Couches; Beaumont; Wilems; Tournay and Egmont-op-Zee.*

Lincolnshire Regiment (10th Foot) *See: Royal Lincolnshire Regiment.*

Lincolnshire Yeomanry Independent troops of yeomanry cavalry were raised in Lincolnshire from 1794, serving until 1828. The Lincoln Light Horse comprised four troops, but a further ten existed in the county. Re-raised in 1831, the North Lincoln Regiment of Yeomanry Cavalry served until disbanded in 1846. Re-raised in May 1901 as The Lincolnshire Yeomanry, the regiment moved to Egypt in 1915, taking part in the campaign in Palestine. In 1918 the regiment joined 1/1st East Riding Yeomanry to form D

Battalion, The Machine Gun Corps, for service in France during the last five months of the war. The regiment was disbanded in 1920.

Line Term used to describe the cable which carries signal traffic.

Line of Departure A line designated to co-ordinate the departure of attack elements. Usually the line of departure is the forward edge of the 'forming up place' (qv). If there is no forming up place, the assembly area (qv) or the next significant feature forward thereof. The line must be secure and ideally at right angles to the objective.

Lingen Second World War battle honour marking one of the actions which took place between the crossing of the Rhine on 23 March 1945 and the end of the campaign in North-West Europe. *See also: North West Europe 1944-1945; Rhine; Ibbenbüren; Leese; Aller; Brinkum; Bremen; Bentheim; Dreirwalde; Uelzen; Artlenberg and Twente Canal.*

Link Term used for ammunition in which the cartridges are joined together in long belts by small metal clips or links which are dispersed on firing.

Liri Valley Second World War Italian campaign battle honour marking the actions which took place during the exploitation towards Rome following the fall of Cassino in mid-May 1944. *See also: Italy 1943-45; Hitler Line; Monte Piccolo; Piedemonte Hill; Aquino and Melfa Crossing.*

Lisieux Second World War battle honour marking the clearing of Lisieux during the breakout from the Normandy bridgehead in June 1944. *See also: North West Europe 1944-1945; Falaise; Falaise Road; Laison; Dives Crossing and Seine 1944.*

Listening Patrol A patrol sent out from the main position with the purpose of gathering information by listening for enemy activity.

Listening Post Sentries, usually deployed during the hours of darkness, sited tactically on the perimeter of a defensive position to give early warning by listening and the use of surveillance devices. The term is also employed in conjunction with mortar locating radars.

Litan Second World War Burma campaign battle honour marking one of the actions during operations around Imphal in March 1944. *See also: Burma 1942-45; Imphal; Tuitum; Nungshigum; Bishenpur; Kanglatongbi; Sakawng; Tamu Road and Shenam Pass.*

Local Rank Unpaid temporary rank usually granted for the execution of a specific short-term task in a specific location or theatre. In the event of disciplinary action a soldier will be tried in his acting (qv) or substantive (qv) rank .

Logistics The science of the movement, supplying, and maintenance of military forces in the field.

London Gazette Official organ of the British government. It first appeared on 16 November 1665 as the 'Oxford Gazette', when the court of Charles II was at Oxford to avoid the Great Plague, and became the 'London Gazette' with issue 24 on 5 February 1666. Now published by Her Majesty's Stationery Office, it has failed to appear only once, in September 1666, when the Great Fire destroyed every press in the City of London. Early issues ran to 2-4 pages of proclamations, official announcements and a few news items drawn from contemporary continental news-sheets. Nowadays each issue comprises anything up to 100 or so pages of official announcements and legal advertisements. There are regular supplements in which Army occurrences such as commissionings, promotions, retirements etc., are 'Gazetted'.

London Irish Rifles *See: London Regiment.*

London Regiment The London Regiment embraced all the infantry territorial army regiments entitled City of London and London Regiment. Each regiment within the London Regiment corresponded in all respects to a battalion of other regiments. In 1859, stimulated by Napoleon III's hostile attitude to Britain, there was an upsurge in volunteers and public pressure virtually compelled the government of the day to authorise the raising of volunteer rifle corps. An Act was passed in 1804 and many such corps were formed in the city and county of London and adjacent counties. These corps bore titles indicating their place of origin. Each separate regiment was numbered in seniority throughout the regiment. The 9th London Regiment (Queen Victoria's Rifles) claimed descent from a unit raised at the beginning of the 19th century because, when the volunteers of that period were disbanded, the corps maintained its existence as a rifle club, and was officially recognised and placed in the Army List in September 1853 as The Middlesex (The Victoria) Volunteer Rifle Corps. Of the territorial battalions of the London regiment the 5th was the London Rifle Brigade, the 13th The Kensingtons, the 14th the London Scottish, the 16th the Queen's Westminsters, the 18th the London Irish Rifles and the 28th the Artists' Rifles. The 8th City of London Battalion (Post Office Rifles) has the distinction of bearing honours for the earliest campaign in which volunteers participated, 'Egypt 1882'. During the South Africa War (1899-1902) the volunteers of London and its environs were permitted to participate either by providing service companies for regular regiments, or by joining the City Imperial Volunteers. In the First World War each regiment raised from two to six battalions which served with great distinction in every theatre. The London Regiment ceased to exist in 1937, the units which composed it being linked with line regiments or converted to artillery or signals.

London Rifle Brigade *See: London Regiment.*

London Scottish Regiment *See: London Regiment.*

LONDON YEOMANRY
The City of London Yeomanry (The Rough Riders) The regiment claims descent from the Loyal Islington Troop of 1798, which was disbanded in 1802 and re-raised in 1803 as the Loyal London Volunteer Cavalry, only to be disbanded in 1814. In December 1899 a battalion of 'Rough Riders' was raised for service in South Africa as 20th Battalion The Imperial Yeomanry. Returning members of the regiment formed the 1st County of London Imperial Yeomanry (Rough Riders), subsequently redesignated City of London, in 1901. In the First World War the regiment served mounted in Egypt, Salonika and Palestine, and dismounted at Gallipoli (qv) and, as E Battalion The Machine Gun Corps, in France. In 1920 the regiment converted to artillery and served as such throughout the Second World War. In 1947 the Rough Riders reformed as an armoured regiment and in 1961 amalgamated with the Inns of Court Regiment (qv) to form The Inns of Court and City Yeomanry, which was subsequently disbanded. The regiment's successor sub-unit is 68 (Inns of Court and City Yeomanry) Signal Squadron, 71st (Yeomanry) Signal Regiment (Volunteers) and the Band of The Royal Yeomanry .

The Inns of Court Regiment The Inns of Court first raised a volunteer corps in 1584 and descent to modern times has been continuous. Prior to the formation of the Territorial Force in 1908, the regiment was designated 14th Middlesex (Inns of Court) Rifle Volunteers and, given an officer training role as the Inns of Court Officers' Training Corps, served as such throughout the First World War. Redesignated the Inns of Court Regiment in 1932, it continued to train officers for the cavalry and infantry. In 1937 the regiment became a Territorial Army cavalry unit, with one cavalry and two tank squadrons, serving in North-West Europe as an armoured car regiment of the Royal Armoured Corps throughout the Second World War. After the war the regiment remained in that role, joined for a time in 1956 by a squadron of the Northamptonshire Yeomanry (qv). In 1961 the regiment amalgamated with the City of

London Yeomanry (qv) to form The Inns of Court and City Yeomanry, which was subsequently disbanded. The regiment's successors are 68 (Inns of Court and City Yeomanry) Signal Squadron, 71st (Yeomanry) Signal Regiment (Volunteers) and the Band of The Royal Yeomanry.

1st County of London Yeomanry (Middlesex, Duke of Cambridge's Hussars) An Uxbridge troop was raised in 1797, disbanded in 1802 and re-raised in 1830 to become the Middlesex Yeomanry Cavalry in 1830. The regiment provided companies for 11th and 14th Battalions of The Imperial Yeomanry during the war in South Africa (1899-1902). The regiment was redesignated 1st County of London Yeomanry (Middlesex Yeomanry Hussars) in 1908 - the title of 1st County of London Yeomanry having formerly been held by the Rough Riders. The regiment served mounted and dismounted in the First World War, seeing action in Egypt, Gallipoli, Macedonia, Palestine and Syria. In 1920 the regiment converted to signals, serving in that role throughout the Second World War. The regiment's successor sub-unit is 47 (Middlesex Yeomanry) Signal Squadron, 31 Signal Regiment (Volunteers).

2nd County of London Yeomanry (Westminster Dragoons) Raised in 1797 as the Westminster Volunteer Cavalry (no direct connection with The London and Westminster Light Horse Volunteers) and served until disbanded in 1802. In 1901 the 2nd County of London Imperial Yeomanry (Westminster Dragoons) was formed with a nucleus of South Africa War veterans. In 1915 the regiment, then in Egypt, was sent in the dismounted role to Gallipoli, regaining its horses following the withdrawal from Gallipoli, and serving in Egypt and Palestine. In 1918 the regiment was transferred to the Machine Gun Corps (qv), first as F Battalion and subsequently 104th Battalion, and served in France from August 1918 until the end of the war. In 1927 the regiment transferred to the Tank Corps as 22nd (London) Armoured Car Company (Westminster Dragoons) and became the principal officer-producing source for the Royal Tank Corps (Territorial Army). Expanded in 1938 to become 22nd Battalion Royal Tank Corps (Westminster Dragoons), it became 102nd Officer Cadet Training Unit at the outbreak of the Second World War. In November 1940 the regiment converted to an armoured regiment of the Royal Armoured Corps, regaining its full title. The regiment landed in Normandy on D-Day and fought in North-West Europe until the end of the war. In 1947 the regiment re-formed as an armoured regiment, amalgamating with the Berkshire Yeomanry (qv) in 1961 and converting to armoured cars. In 1967 the regiment was reduced and its successor sub-units are 'HQ' (Westminster Dragoons) Squadron and Regimental Band (Inns of Court & City Yeomanry) of The Royal Yeomanry (qv).

3rd County of London Yeomanry (The Sharpshooters) Three battalions of Sharpshooters were raised in early 1900 and formed 18th, 21st and 23rd Battalions, The Imperial Yeomanry during the South Africa War (1899-1902). Members of the regiment were most carefully selected from a large number of volunteers for their equestrian and marksmanship skills. In 1901 a regiment, designated 3rd County of London (Sharpshooters) Imperial Yeomanry, was formed and served during the First World War in Egypt, Gallipoli, Palestine and Macedonia. In 1918, with the Rough Riders (qv) it formed 103rd Battalion The Machine Gun Corps and served in France from June 1918 until the end of the war. In 1920 the regiment was reduced to an armoured car company as 23rd (London) Armoured Car Company (Sharpshooters). In 1938 the regiment expanded and converted to an armoured regiment, resumed their title and formed a second regiment, 4th County of London Yeomanry (Sharpshooters). Both regiments fought in the Western Desert, Sicily, Italy and, having suffered heavy casualties in Normandy in 1944, were amalgamated in August 1944. Remaining as an armoured regiment after the war 3rd/4th County of London Yeomanry (Sharpshooters) amalgamated with the Kent Yeomanry (qv) in 1961. The regiment successor sub-unit is 'C' (Kent & Sharpshooters Yeomanry) Squadron of The Royal Yeomanry (qv).

King Edward's Horse (The King's Overseas Dominions Regiment) Raised in 1901 as 4th County of London Yeomanry (The King's Colonials), originally comprising expatriates from the dominions and colonies, with squadrons affiliated to the dominions by name. In 1910 the regiment was redesignated King Edward's Horse (The King's Overseas Dominions Regiment). In 1913 it was judged that the Territorial Force terms and conditions of service were not appropriate to the regiment and it was transferred to the Special Reserve thus losing its yeomanry status. On mobilisation two regiments were formed almost immediately, and from April 1915 to June 1916 individual squadrons of 1st King Edward's Horse served in France as divisional cavalry. The regiment served in Italy from December 1917 to March 1918, after which it returned to France and the squadrons were, once again, split until the end of the war. From May 1915 to May 1916 2nd King Edward's Horse served in France, but not always as a complete unit. In June 1916 it was reinforced by a section of 21st Lancers (qv), regrouped as a corps cavalry unit and served as such until August 1917. The regiment was then broken up and the personnel largely absorbed into the Tank Corps. The regiment was finally disbanded in 1924.

Long Live Elizabeth Regimental slow march of The Queen's Lancashire Regiment.

Long Range Desert Group Unit, formed from volunteers, established in Libya in June 1940 during the Second World War. Its area of operations initially ranged over some 600 miles inland from the Mediterranean coast and about 1,700 miles westwards from the Nile. Originally tasked only with reconnaissance, it rapidly became clear that its mobility, training and knowledge of the desert suited it for more aggressive operations. Successful operations were carried out against enemy outposts in the Fezzan in the autumn of 1940, and against the garrisons of Benghazi, Barce and Tobruk in September 1942. The unit also surveyed the routes used by the Eighth Army in their outflanking movements against the El Agheila and Mareth positions. The basic unit was the patrol, which consisted normally of five unarmoured vehicles and 20 men. Each patrol was commanded by an officer and contained an expert navigator, vehicle fitter, radio operator and medical orderly. For most of the campaign in North Africa the group was based at the oases of Siwa or Kufra. At the conclusion of the campaign in 1943 the group returned to the delta and later to the Lebanon. It was reorganised to operate in Italy and the Balkans on foot, on skis and with animal transport and to reach its targets by parachute or sea. In September 1943 the unit was sent to the Dodecanese where it became involved in the ill-fated operations on the islands of Cos and Leros. In early 1944 the unit was moved to Italy to operate under Field Marshal Alexander and patrols thereafter operated in Italy, Greece, Albania and Yugoslavia.

Long Service and Good Conduct Medal Award instituted in the British Army by William IV in 1830. The medal is awarded to warrant officers, non-commissioned officers and other ranks after 18 years' service during which character and conduct have been irreproachable.
Ribbon: Crimson with white edges.

Long Service Stripes *See: Good Conduct Badges.*

Longstop Hill 1942 Second World War North Africa campaign battle honour marking an action which took place in the period immediately prior to the Kasserine operations of February 1942. *See also: North Africa 1940-1943; Djebel Abiod; Soudia; Tebourba; Djedeida and Djebel Azzag 1942.*

Longstop Hill 1943 Second World War North Africa campaign battle honour marking one of the actions during the Battle of Medjez Plain 23-30 April 1943 which was a preliminary to the final thrust to Tunis. *See also: North Africa 1940-1943; Medjez Plain; Gueriat El Atach Ridge; Djebel Bou Aoukaz 1943; Grich El Oued; Peter's*

Corner; Si Mediene; Si Abdallah; Gab Gab Gap and Sidi Ahmed.

Loos First World War battle honour marking the main British offensive of 1915 launched in September in the flat coal-mining district South of the La Bassée Canal. *See also: France and Flanders 1914-1918; Aubers; Festubert 1915 and Hooge 1915.*

Lord Ferrers March Regimental slow march of The King's Regiment.

Lord Lieutenant The Lord-Lieutenant of a county is nominated by the sovereign by patent under the Great Seal. He stands as the permanent local representative of the Crown and, as such, takes precedence throughout the county regardless of the internal local government organisation. The title was first created in the reign of Henry VIII, and entailed many responsibilities. The Lord Lieutenant had to maintain the efficiency of the militia of the county, and had the right of appointing his own officers. These military responsibilities were largely withdrawn in 1871 and vested in the Crown. The chief duties of the Lord Lieutenant at present consist of the recommendation for the appointment of magistrates for the county bench, the appointment of Deputy Lieutenants and the raising, if such be the need, of the militia in times of riot or invasion. He is head of the Commission of the Peace for the county and of the Territorial Army.

Loretto Regimental slow march of The Queen's Royal Irish Hussars and The Queen's Royal Hussars (Queen's Own and Royal Irish).

Lothian Yeomanry (The Lothian and Border Horse) The regiment is the product of the East Lothian Yeomanry, the first troops of which were raised in 1797, the Berwickshire Yeomanry Cavalry, the first troops of which were raised in 1797, the West Lothian Yeomanry, the first troops of which were raised in 1803 and the Royal Midlothian Yeomanry Cavalry, the first troops of which were raised in 1800. In 1808 the Berwickshire Yeomanry Cavalry

troop and the East Lothian Yeomanry were amalgamated, and joined by the Midlothian in 1888 and West Lothian in 1892 to form the Lothians and Berwickshire Yeomanry. In 1908 the regiment was redesignated the Lothians and Border Horse. The regiment found a company of 6th Battalion, The Imperial Yeomanry during the South Africa War (1899-1902). During the First World War the regiment was divided, elements serving mounted or dismounted in France and Salonika. Following the war 19th (Lothians and Border Horse) Armoured Car Company was formed - expanding rapidly to two regiments in 1939. The first regiment went as a tank regiment with the British Expeditionary Force (qv) to France, was recovered through Dunkirk, re-formed and landed in Normandy in 1944, fighting in North-West Europe until the end of the war. The 2nd Lothians and Border Horse landed in Algeria in December 1942 and fought in the Western Desert and Italy. The two regiments re-formed as one armoured car regiment in 1947. In 1956 the regiment amalgamated with the Lanarkshire and Glasgow Yeomanry Regiments (qv) to form the Queen's Own Lowland Yeomanry, serving as an armoured car regiment until disbanded in 1969. The regiment's successor sub-unit is 'HQ' (Lothians & Border Horse) Squadron of the Scottish Yeomanry.

Louisbourg Battle honour marking the action on 25 July 1758 when a British expedition under General Amherst captured the French fortress on Cape Breton Island after a siege of seven weeks. *See also: Quebec 1759; Montevideo; Detroit; Miami; Niagara and Bladensburg.*

Low Light Television A passive electro-optical night vision device. A standard video camera is linked to a signal processor which amplifies ambient light by several orders of magnitude, thus producing a visual image without artificial illumination.

Lower Maas Second World War battle honour marking operations to clear the lower reaches of the River Maas between

20 October and 7 November 1944. *See also: North West Europe 1944-1945; Aam; Venraij; Meijel and Venlo Pocket.*

Lowland Brigade An administrative grouping in the infantry formed under Army Order 61 of 1948 comprising The Royal Scots, The Royal Scots Fusiliers (until 1959), The Highland Light Infantry (1959), The Royal Highland Fusiliers (from 1959), The King's Own Scottish Borderers and The Cameronians (Scottish Rifles) (until 1968). The regiments of the brigade were absorbed into the Scottish Division (qv) in 1968.

Loyal Lincoln Volunteers Regiment of Foot (81st Foot) Raised in September 1793 by Major General Albermarle Bertie as 83rd (Loyal Lincolnshire Volunteer) regiment of Foot. Renumbered 81st in 1794. Amalgamated with 47th (Lancashire) Regiment of Foot in 1881 to form The Loyal North Lancashire Regiment. *See also: The Loyal Regiment (North Lancashire).*

Loyal Regiment (North Lancashire) (47th and 81st Foot) The 47th was raised in Scotland as Mordaunt's Regiment of Foot in January 1741 and ranked as 58th Regiment of Foot. Renumbered 47th in 1748 and designated 47th Regiment of Foot in 1751. The regiment was redesignated 47th (Lancashire) Foot in 1782. The 81st was raised at Lincoln on 23 September 1793 by Major General Albermarle Bertie as the 83rd (Loyal Lincolnshire Volunteer) Regiment of Foot, renumbered 81st to take the place of 81st (Invalids) Regiment 1759-1763, and 81st (Aberdeen Highlanders) Foot 1778-1783, in 1794; and redesignated 81st Regiment of Foot. In 1832 the regiment was redesignated 81st (Loyal Lincolnshire Volunteers) Foot. In May 1881 the 47th (Lancashire) Foot and 81st (Loyal Lincolnshire Volunteers) Foot amalgamated to form The North Lancashire Regiment redesignated The Loyal North Lancashire Regiment two months later and again in 1921 as The Loyal Regiment (North Lancashire). On 25 March 1970 the regiment amalgamated with The Lancashire Regiment (Prince of Wales's Volunteers) to form The Queen's Lancashire Regiment (qv).

Headdress Badge: The rose of Lancaster ensigned with the royal crest. Below, a scroll inscribed 'THE LOYAL REGIMENT'.

History: *The Loyal North Lancashire Regiment 1741-1918* (2 Vols) by H C Wylly; *The Loyal Regiment (North Lancashire) 1919-1953* by C G T Dean and *The Loyal Regiment* by M Langley.

Loyal Toast The customs associated with the drinking of the Loyal Toast vary widely in the Army. More usually the monarch's health is drunk while standing, but there are regiments in which the toast is drunk while seated and others in which the loyal toast is never honoured.

Loyauté M'oblige **(Loyalty binds me)** Motto of The Loyal Regiment (North Lancashire).

Lucknow Battle honour marking the gallant defence of the Residency at Lucknow which was besieged at the end of June 1857. The first relief in September by Havelock and Outram served only to reinforce the garrison; the second relief attempt by Sir Colin Campbell took place in November when the residency was evacuated. It was finally captured by Sir Colin Campbell in March 1858.

Lüneburg Heath It was at Field Marshal Montgomery's headquarters on Lüneburg Heath that the Germans surrendered all their forces in Holland, north-west Germany and Denmark in May 1945.

Lutzow's Wild Hunt One of the regimental quick marches of 2nd King Edward VII's Own Gurkha Rifles (The Sirmoor Rifles).

Lynx Utility helicopter produced by Westland Aircraft Ltd, in service with the Army since 1971 in the reconnaissance, training and anti-tank roles. Provision exists for the fitting of 7.62mm machine guns or 20mm cannon in the cabin or eight TOW anti-tank missiles on pylons (with eight re-load rounds in the cabin). Capable of carrying nine fully equipped troops or 1,360kg of freight at a cruise speed of 120kts over a range of 360 miles.

Lyre A badge depicting a lyre is worn on the sleeve of qualified musicians.

Lys First World War battle honour marking the fighting associated with the second main German offensive of 1918, launched in Flanders on 9 April. The Germans captured Armentières, Bailleul, Messines and Kemmel Ridges before they were halted on 29 April. *See also: France and Flanders 1914-1918; Estaires; Messines 1918; Hazebrouck; Bailleul; Kemmel; Béthune and Scherpenberg.*

'M' A badge bearing the letter 'M' within a wreath is worn on the sleeve of qualified mortar specialists.

M2/3 Bridge Wheeled engineer vehicle which entered service in 1972. The vehicle has flotation bags and can be driven into a river and used as a ferry, or bolted to other similar vehicles to form a bridge. The vehicle has a crew of four and is 11.3m long.

M109 A1 A United States designed tracked, self-propelled 155mm gun brought into service in the British Army in the early 1960s. The gun has a crew of six, and fires high explosive, canister, chemical or nuclear ammunition to a maximum range of 18,000m.

Macbean's Slow March One of the regimental slow marches of the Royal Regiment of Fusiliers, inherited from The Royal Warwickshire Fusiliers.

Mace Trade name for a liquid, produced in the United States, which causes acute irritation of the eyes and nausea and is used as a spray in riot control.

Macedonia 1915–18 First World War battle honour marking the campaign which started with the landing of an Allied expeditionary force under Sarrail at Salonika on 5 October 1915, and which is sometimes referred to as the Salonika campaign, the objective being to dominate the near east and assist the Serbs. The entry of Bulgaria into the war nullified the original aim, and the Allies established a defensive line on a broad front north of Salonika, the left flank resting on the Serbian frontier to the south of Monastir, the centre occupying the valley of the Vardar to Doiran, and the right flank resting on the River Struma. The immediate purpose of the offensive launched by Sarrail in August 1916 was to force the Bulgarians to defend their gains in Serbia rather than march against Rumania and, at the same time, to induce Rumania to enter the war on the side of the Allies. The Rumanians were soon advancing into Bukovina, only to be routed shortly thereafter, largely because of Sarrail's failure to press the offensive in Macedonia. Sarrail had allowed himself to be driven back from Florina, and the Bulgarians captured Koritza and Kastoria, the railway through Demir Hissar and, later, the Greek port of Kavala. In 1917 Sarrail was superseded by Guillaumat; but decisive operations did not begin until the following year when Franchet d'Esperey succeeded Guillaumat. The two decisive allied victories were those of the Vardar, 15–25 September, and Doiran, 18–19 September. British and Greek troops operated on the right flank in the region of Lake Doiran, Franco-Serb troops in the centre along the Vardar and Italian troops on the left flank in Albania. There followed the capture of Prilep, the Babuna Pass, Ishtip and finally the Bulgarian town of Strumnitza. Bulgaria then sought an armistice, which was signed on 30th September 1918. *See also: Kosturino; Struma; Doiran 1917 and Doiran 1918.*

Machete Broad bladed heavy knife used for cutting trees and vegetation, particularly in jungle operations.

Machine Gun Weapon capable of providing rapid and sustained fire. Attempts to make such a weapon began in the 16th century, but it was not until 1884 that Sir Hiram Stevens Maxim demonstrated the first such successful weapon. The 'Maxim Gun' was used by the British in the war in South Africa (1899-1902), but had been succeeded by the 'Vickers' by the outbreak of the First World War. During the First World War machine guns developed into two broad groups: 'heavy', mainly used by the Germans, and 'light', usually air-cooled, such as the British 'Lewis' gun. Between the wars machine guns were developed to fire cartridges larger than those used by service rifles; these were then classified as 'heavy' and the old 'heavies' reclassified as 'medium'. The Second World War saw little alteration in the basic concept, although the more mobile nature of operations resulted in changes in detail. In the British Army the more efficient Bren gun succeeded the Lewis gun, the Vickers medium machine gun being concentrated in specialist units. A development of the machine gun, the sub-machine gun (qv), a hand-held quick-firing weapon, also made its appearance during the Second World War. A wide variety of machine guns now exists, those of the larger calibre being generally referred to as cannon and more usually vehicle-mounted. *See also: Maxim; Vickers; Browning; Lewis gun; Hotchkiss Mark 1; Vickers-Berthier; Bren gun; General Purpose Machine Gun and Light Support Weapon.*

Machine Gun Corps At the time of the British Expeditionary Force's (qv) movement to France in 1914, the establishment of cavalry regiments and infantry battalions included a section of two machine guns. There was an acute shortage of these weapons so a 'Motor Machine Gun Service' was created in November which provided one 'battery' for each division, volunteers for the new arm being transferred to the Royal Artillery. The 'Service' was reconstituted as the Machine Gun Corps by Army Order 414 of 22 October 1915 and divided into three branches: Cavalry of the Line, Infantry of the Line and Motor Machine Gun Service. In July 1916 a 'Heavy Branch' - a cover name for the new tank arm - was formed. On the

formation of the Tank Corps on 27 July 1917 the 'Heavy Branch' ceased to exist. On 8 May 1918, a Guards Machine Gun Regiment was formed. The entire Corps was disbanded in 1922. A badge depicting crossed machine gun barrels was authorised for the Corps in 1915.

Machine Gunners A number of badges have been authorised for wear on the sleeve of qualified machine gunners; these include the letters 'LG' for Lewis Gunners, 'HG' for Hotchkiss Gunners, 'LMG' for Light Machine Gunners and 'SMG' for Sub-Machine Gunners, all within a wreath.

Madagascar Second World War battle honour. A British brigade landed in Madagascar on 5 May 1942 to ensure that the Vichy French did not co-operate with the Japanese. The main thrust against Antsirane, which dominates Diego Suarez Bay, broke through the French defences and Diego Suarez surrendered shortly afterwards. French resistance continued on a localised basis until November 1942.

Madras Light Infantry Regiment (105th) Raised in 1839 as 2nd Madras European Regiment (Light Infantry) of the Honourable East India Company's forces and redesignated 2nd Madras (Light Infantry) Regiment in 1858. The regiment transferred to the British Army in 1861 as 105th (Madras Light Infantry) Regiment. In 1881 the regiment was amalgamated with 51st (2nd Yorkshire West Riding) The King's Own Light Infantry Regiment, bringing with it the motto *Cede Nullis* (Yield to None), to form The King's Own Light Infantry (South Yorkshire Regiment). The new regiment was redesignated The King's Own (Yorkshire Light Infantry) in 1887, the brackets being discarded in 1921.

Madras Regiment of Foot (108th) Raised in India in 1854 as the 3rd Madras European Regiment of the Honourable East India Company's forces; retitled 3rd (Madras) regiment in 1858 and transferred to the British Army in 1861 as 108th (Madras Infantry) Regiment. In 1881 the regiment was amalgamated with 27th

(Inniskilling) Regiment of Foot to form The Royal Inniskilling Fusiliers. The regiment subsequently became The Royal Irish Rangers (qv).

Magazine A metal case, usually with a spring-loaded platform, containing a number of cartridges which are fed to the firing mechanism of a weapon. Alternatively building or bunker for storing weapons and ammunition.

Magersfontein Scene of a British defeat by Boer forces in 1899. In the third week of November Lord Methuen set out to relieve the beleaguered town of Kimberley. After some initial success, and when within 20 miles of his objective, he encountered a strong force of Boers near Magersfontein. He attempted to capture their position by a night march and dawn attack, but this failed with heavy losses and the advance was, for the time being, halted. *See also: South Africa 1899-1902.*

Magpie The outermost ring but one on a target.

Magwe Second World War Burma campaign battle honour marking one of the actions during operations astride the River Irrawaddy over the period March-May 1945. *See also: Burma 1942-45; Irrawaddy; Mt Popa;Yenangyaung 1945 and Kama.*

Maharajpore Battle honour marking the defeat of the Mahratta army of Scindia by a force under Sir Hugh Gough on 29 December 1843 during the Gwalior campaign. *See also: Scinde; Meeanee; Hyderabad and Punniar.*

Mahdi The title assumed by Mohammed Ahmed (1843?-85), Sudanese military leader, who led a revolt against Egypt and captured Khartoum in 1885. Title also given to Muslim messiahs seeking to forcibly convert all mankind to Islam. *See also: Nile 1884-85; Abu Klea; Kirbekan; Suakin 1885; Tofrek; Hafir; Atbara and Khartoum.*

Maheidpoor Battle honour marking the action on 23 December 1817 in which a British force under Sir Thomas Hislop routed the Mahratta army of Holkar of Indore in the Second Mahratta War (qv). *See also: Kirkee; Seetabuldee; Nagpore and Corygaum.*

MAHRATTA WARS
   First Mahratta War 1803-5 The campaign against the forces of the Maharajah Scindia was led by Lord Lake the commander-in-chief in India. His main army seized the fortress of Ally Ghur on 3 September 1803, and then fought an action at Delhi on 11 September. Twelve days later, the division commanded by Sir Arthur Wellesley (qv) took part in the hard-fought battle of Assaye, followed by Lord Lake's decisive victory at Leswaree on 1 November. The concluding action, the capture of Holkar's city of Deig, took place on 23 December. *See: Ally Ghur; Delhi 1803; Assaye; Leswaree and Deig.*
   Second Mahratta and Pindari War 1816-18 The first battle in this campaign involved a detachment of British and Indian troops commanded by Colonel Burr which was attacked at Kirkee on 5 November 1817 by the army of the Peishwa, chief of the Mahratta Confederacy, the result being a serious setback to the ambitions of the Peishwa. Following actions at Poona and Seetabuldee, the Mahratta forces were defeated at Nagpore on 16 December. The only action of the Marquess of Hastings' main army was at Maheidpoor, where Holkar's forces were routed on 22 December. *See: Kirkee; Nagpore and Maheidpoor.*

Maid of Glenconnel Regimental quick march of The Devonshire and Dorset Regiment.

Maid of Warsaw Distinctive scarlet and silver crest of the City of Warsaw worn on the left sleeve of all members of The Queen's Own Hussars and now worn by all members of The Queen's Royal Hussars (Queen's Own and Royal Irish). The honour was awarded to 7th Hussars by the commander of the 2nd Polish Corps in recognition of their valour in support of the

Polish forces during the Italian campaign in the Second World War.

Maida Battle honour marking the actions of a small British force under General Sir John Stuart sent from Sicily to Italy in mid-1806 in the hope of expelling the French from Naples, the kingdom of Britain's ally, the King of Naples. Maida was awarded for a small but well-conducted action on the shores of the Straits of Messina.

Maidan In Pakistan and India, an open space used for parades, meetings and sports. *See also: Padang.*

Main Effort The concentration of forces or means at a particular area where a commander seeks to bring about the decision. The activity which the commander considers crucial to the success of his mission at that time.

Major Commissioned officer of field rank, ranking above captain but below lieutenant colonel. In February 1810 the rank of major was indicated by the wearing of two epaulettes, each bearing a star. With the replacement of the coatee by the tunic in 1855, epaulettes became obsolete, and the rank of major was indicated by a collar with lace all round bearing a star. In October 1880 rank badges reverted to the shoulder, but this time on twisted cord, and the rank badge for a major was changed from a star to the present crown worn on each shoulder. *See also: Rank.*

Major General General officer ranking above brigadier and below lieutenant general. Rank denoted by a crossed baton and sabre surmounted by a star worn on the epaulettes. *See also: Rank.*

Maknassy Second World War North Africa campaign battle honour marking one of a number of actions which took place between the Kasserine and Fondouk operations in 1943. *See also: North Africa 1940-1943; Kasserine; El Hadjeba; Djebel Djaffa; Sidi Nsir; Fort McGregor; Stuka Farm; Steamroller Farm; Montagne Farm; Kef Ouiba Pass; Djebel Guerba; Sedjenane I; Djebel Dahra; Kef El Debna and Djebel Cuoucha.*

Malakand Battle honour marking the gallant defence of the Malakand Pass, one of the actions which took place during the campaigns on the North-West Frontier of India 1895-97 at the start of the great rising of the tribes in 1897. *See also: Defence of Chitral; Chitral; Samana; Punjab Frontier and Tirah.*

Malaya 1941-42 Second World War battle honour marking the actions fought during the Japanese invasion of Malaya. A Japanese landing on the east coast near Kota Bharu on 8 December 1941, coupled with an advance through Thailand, opened the campaign and the Japanese moved rapidly southward using jungle trails and travelling on relatively light scales, their prime objective being the capture of the British naval base on Singapore Island. The overall commander of British and Commonwealth forces in the Far East was Air Chief Marshal Sir Robert Brooke-Popham. The land forces in Malaya and Singapore were under the command of Lieutenant General A E Percival and consisted of III Corps (9th and 11th Indian Divisions), located in north and central Malaya, and the 8th Australian Division in the south. An attempt to block Japanese access to Singapore by holding on the line of the Muar River in Johore in late January 1942 failed. British troops withdrew across the causeway from Johore Bahru to Singapore Island and, after two days' heavy bombardment, the Japanese launched themselves across the narrow dividing channel on the night 8/9 February. The British defences were overrun and on 12 February the MacRitchie Reservoir, Singapore's main source of water, was captured by the Japanese - a decisive factor in the subsequent British surrender on 15 February 1942. Singapore had fallen in 70 days, the allies sustaining losses of 138,000 of whom more than 130,000 were prisoners of war, many of whom were to suffer savage treatment in Japanese hands. *See also: Northern Malaya; Central Malaya; Johore Bahru and Singapore Island.*

Malaya 1948-60 Campaign against Communist Chinese guerillas, largely remnants of those equipped and trained by the British between 1942 and 1945 for

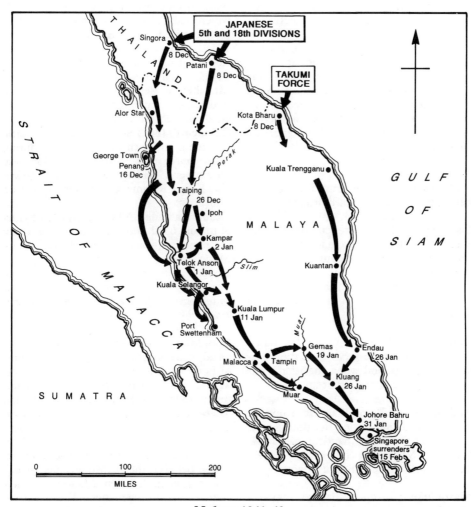

Malaya 1941-42

operations against the Japanese, and known as the Malayan People's Anti-British Army (MPABA). When the Malayan Communist Party was proscribed in July 1948 the leader, Chin Peng, took to the jungle to conduct a classical communist war of liberation. The uniformed MPABA strike force was supported, in accordance with communist doctrine, by the civilianised Min Yuen or Masses Movement. Following the murders of Europeans a State of Emergency was declared for the whole of Malaya on 18 June 1948. In an attempt to widen the appeal of the movement MPABA was renamed the Malayan Races' Liberation Army. The British Army

conducted what was to prove a classic anti-guerilla war, gaining vital experience which was to prove invaluable in the coming years. On 31 July 1960, when the State of Emergency was ended, British Army casualties, including Gurkhas, totalled 668 killed and 1,229 wounded.

Malingerer Term used to describe an individual deliberately feigning or exaggerating illness or disability to evade duty or claim a benefit.

Malkara Obsolete anti-tank guided weapon. Malkara had a wire link guidance system, a high explosive squash head warhead, and minimum and maximum ranges of 450m and 3,200m respectively.

Malleto Second World War Sicilian campaign battle honour marking one of a number of actions which took place during the Allied advance in 1943. *See also: Sicily 1943; Solarino;Vizzini;Augusta; Francofonte; Lentini; Simeto Bridgehead; Gerbini; Agira; Adrano; Sferro Hills; Salso Crossing; Simeto Crossing; Monte Rivoglia and Pursuit to Messina.*

Malplaquet Battle honour marking the battle, the fourth of Marlborough's great victories, which took place on 11 September 1709. A French force under Villars was attempting to relieve Mons and took a stance in wooded country. Although eventually driven from their position, the French suffered only half the casualties of the allies. *See also: Blenheim; Ramillies and Oudenarde.*

Malta 1940-42 Second World War battle honour marking the services of the garrison during a period when the island was under almost continuous air attack.

Maltot Second World War battle honour marking an action during the Bourgebous Ridge offensive in Normandy in July 1944. *See also: North West Europe 1944-1945; Bourgebous Ridge; Cagny and Troarn.*

Mameluke A distinctive sword originally used by Turkish troops which had cross quillons and an ivory or bone handled hilt. The sword was adopted by British cavalry fighting in Egypt in the early 19th century. Such swords are now worn only by general officers.

Manchester Regiment (63rd and 96th Foot) The 63rd Foot was raised in 1756 as 2nd Battalion, 8th (The King's) Regiment of Foot and became a regiment in its own right under the command of Colonel Robert Armiger as 63rd Foot in 1758; it was redesignated 63rd (West Suffolk) Foot in 1782. The 9th Foot was raised in January 1824 under the Colonelcy of Sir John Fuller, and inherited the traditions and honours of a previous

96th (or Queen's Own) Regiment of Foot which had been several times disbanded and re-raised, being finally disbanded in 1818. In 1881 the 63rd (West Suffolk) Regiment of Foot and 96th Regiment of Foot amalgamated to form The Manchester Regiment (63rd and 96th Foot). On 1 September 1958 the regiment amalgamated with The King's Regiment (Liverpool) (8th Foot) to form The King's Regiment (Manchester and Liverpool) (8th, 63rd and 96th Foot). On 13 December 1968 the regiment was retitled The King's Regiment (8th, 63rd and 96th Foot) (qv).
Headdress Badge: A fleur-de-lys, the badge of the old 63rd Foot. The former badge of the regiment was the arms of the City of Manchester.
History: *The History of The Manchester Regiment* (2 Vols) by Wylly and *The Manchester Regiment - Regular Battalions 1922-1948* by A C Bell.

Mandalay Second World War Burma campaign battle honour marking the operations of Fourteenth Army from 12 February to 21 March 1945 which resulted in the capture of Mandalay. *See also: Burma 1942-45; Myitson; Ava; Myinmu Bridgehead; Fort Dufferin and Maymyo.*

Mandora Battle honour marking an action between the British advance guard and a French force at Mandora on 13 March 1801 during General Abercromby's (qv) march to Alexandria following the landing at Aboukir Bay (qv). *See also: The Sphinx and Marabout.*

Mangalore Battle honour marking the capture of the port of Mangalore on the west coast of India, then the main outlet to the sea for the state of Mysore, by a small force under Major John Campbell in March 1783 during the Second Mysore War (qv). Campbell's force were subsequently obliged to defend the place against great odds from May 1783 to February 1784 when he was forced by starvation to surrender. *See also: Sholinghur.*

Mangonel An ancient war engine for hurling stones.

Manui Dat Cognitio Vires **(Knowledge gives strength to the arm)**, motto of The Intelligence Corps.

Manx Yeomanry *See: Isle of Man Yeomanry.*

Mantlet Reinforced embankment protecting those employed in the butts of a shooting range. Also a portable bulletproof screen or shelter.

Mao Songsang Second World War Burma campaign battle honour marking one of the actions during the battle of Kohima 27 March-22 June 1944. *See also: Burma 1942-45; Kohima; Defence of Kohima; Aradura; Relief of Kohima and Naga Village.*

Maori Wars The three Maori Wars: 1846-47, 1860-61 and 1863-66 were characterised by the tenacious defence by the Maoris of a number of well fortified stockades or 'pahs', from which they could only be dislodged with great difficulty. A number of Maoris co-operated with the British and, to some extent, the wars were civil wars. The Militia, Volunteers and Armed Constabulary of New Zealand were involved in the suppression of the Maoris for a period greater than that embraced by the wars. *See also: New Zealand and New Zealand Cross.*

Marabout Battle honour marking an action on 17 August 1801 during the campaign under Sir Ralph Abercromby (qv). After landing at Aboukir Bay (qv) Abercromby stormed the fort at Marabout, based on the tomb of a Muslim saint, which dominated part of the French defences at Alexandria. *See also: The Sphinx and Mandora.*

March From Scipio A regimental slow march of the Grenadier Guards; Royal Regiment of Wales; and The Royal Mercian and Lancastrian Yeomanry.

March of the Bowmen Regimental quick march of the Small Arms School Corps.

March of the Scottish Archers One of the four regimental slow marches of The

Queen's Royal Hussars (The Queen's Own and Royal Irish). The march is inherited from 8th Hussars.

Marching Orders Military orders, especially to infantry, giving instructions about a march such as destination, halts, order of march etc.

Marda Pass Second World War Abyssinian campaign battle honour marking the forcing of this pass. *See also: Abyssinia 1940-41; Keren; Jebel Defeis; Jebel Shiba; Gogni; Agordat; Barentu; Karora-Marsa Taclai; Ad Teclesan; Mescelit Pass; Mt Engiahat; Massawa; Amb Alagi; Afodu; Gambela; El Wak; Moyale; Wal Garis; Juba; Bulo Erillo; Beles Gugani; Gelib; Alessandra; Goluin; Babile Gap; Bisidimo; Awash; Todenyang-Namaraputh; Soroppa; Giarso; Colito; Wadara; Omo; Gondar; Ambazzo; Kulkaber; Fike and Lechemti.*

Mareth Second World War North Africa campaign battle honour marking the breaching of the Mareth Line 16-23 March 1943. Although the British frontal attacks were repulsed, the British turning movement through the Tebaga Gap outflanked the Mareth Line and forced its evacuation. *See also: North Africa 1940-1943; Wadi Zeuss East; Wadi Zigzau; Tebaga Gap; El Hamma and Point 201 (Roman Wall).*

Maria Theresa Regimental slow march of The Green Howards.

Marine A soldier who served at sea on ships and was part of the Army until 1748. Rank in the Corps of Royal Marines which equates to that of private soldier in the Army.

Marker An individual pre-positioned, particularly on a parade ground, to indicate the point on which a formed body should assemble. It is more usual for a marker to be a 'right' marker - with the unit forming up on his left. *See also: Pointsman.*

Marksman Designation given those who demonstrate the highest shooting skills in the periodic classification tests. Over the years a number of different badges have been authorised to denote shooting proficiency. Volunteers, Territorials and Cadets have also had their own distinctions.

Marlborough, John Churchill, 1st Duke of (1650-1722). Educated at St Paul's School, he entered the army as an ensign in the foot guards in 1667 and, after serving at Tangiers, was promoted Captain in 1672. In 1674 he became a colonel and, four years later married Sarah Jennings, maid of honour to Princess Anne, over whom she had considerable influence. Created Baron Churchill in 1682, he took an active part three years later in the suppression of Monmouth's insurrection, a service for which he was made a major general. He vowed fidelity to James II whilst at the same time assuring William of Orange of his support. When William landed, Churchill joined him, was given an earldom and, after serving in Flanders, was appointed commander-in-chief in 1701. On the accession of Anne he was made Captain General of the Forces and Master General of the Ordnance. On the declaration of war against France he commanded the forces in Holland. After the successful campaign of 1702 he was created duke. One of Britain's great commanders, a brilliant exponent of the use of fire-power and mobility, he won spectacular victories (qv) at Blenheim in 1704, Ramillies in 1706, Oudenarde in 1708 and Malplaquet in 1709. In the meantime his influence at home, and widespread resentment at his wife's imperious behaviour toward the Queen, caused his influence at home to wane. After the accession of George I he was again made Captain General and Master of the Ordnance, which offices he held until his health gave way in 1716. Although by no means a scrupulous statesman, Marlborough was, without doubt, a brilliant field commander.

Marne 1914 First World War battle honour marking the stand and counter-attack by Allied forces following the retreat from Mons. One of the decisive battles of the war, and very largely a French effort, the counter-offensive drove the Germans back from the River Marne. The British Expeditionary Force (qv) played an important part by penetrating between the German First and Second Armies. *See also: France and Flanders 1914-1918; Mons; Le Cateau; Retreat from Mons; Aisne 1914; La Bassée; Armentières 1914; Messines 1914 and Ypres 1914.*

Marne 1918 First World War battle honour marking the first of the Allied counter-offensives launched on 18 July 1918 against the German salient created by their final advance astride the River Marne. *See also: France and Flanders 1914-1918; Tardenois; Soissonnais-Ourcq and Amiens.*

Marradi Second World War Italian campaign battle honour marking the advance from the Gothic Line during the period 21-24 September 1944. *See also: Italy 1943-45; Gothic Line and Monte Gamberaldi.*

Martello Tower Circular tower constructed for coastal defence. So named after Cape Mortella in Sicily where the Royal Navy captured a tower of this type in 1794.

Martial Of, relating to, or characteristic of soldiers or the military life.

Martial Law The rule of law established and maintained by the military in the absence of civil law.

Martini-Henry Rifle This 0.45" calibre rifle became the official British service rifle in 1871, remaining in service until replaced by the Short Magazine Lee Enfield (qv) from 1907. *See also: Rifle.*

Martinique 1762 Battle honour marking the first capture of this French island by a British expedition after a months' fighting in February 1762. The capture of the islands of Dominica, Martinique and St Lucia had been a long term British objective, much delayed by the need to deploy troops in Europe and Canada. The fall of Louisburg and Quebec made available the troops needed for the task.

Martinique 1794 Battle honour commemorating the second capture of this island, one of a number of French sugar-producing islands, during the French Revolutionary War. A military force commanded by General Sir Charles Grey, greatly assisted by the guns of the fleet, landed on 6 February. The French commander surrendered on 23 March.

Martinique 1809 Battle honour marking the third capture of this French island, which had been restored to France under the terms of the Treaty of Amiens; the recapture of the island having been made necessary by the Napoleonic Wars. The force landed at St Luce Bay on 30 January and the French surrendered on 4 February.

Maryang-San Korean War battle honour. *See also: Korea 1951-1953; Naktong Bridgehead; Pakchon; Imjin; Kowang-San; The Hook 1952; The Hook 1953; Chongju; Chongchon II; Seoul; Chaum-Ni; Hill 327; Kapyong-Chon; Kapyong and Hill 227 I.*

Mascot Only nine mascots are officially authorised: A Drum Horse for The Royal Scots Dragoon Guards (Carabiniers and Greys); a Drum Horse for The Queen's Own Hussars (now The Queen's Royal Hussars (The Queen's Own and Royal Irish)); an Indian Black Buck for The Royal Regiment of Fusiliers; a Goat for The Royal Welch Fusiliers; a Goat for The Royal Regiment of Wales; a Ram for the Worcestershire and Sherwood Foresters Regiment; a Shetland Pony for the Argyll and Sutherland Highlanders and a Shetland Pony for The Parachute Regiment.

Massa Tambourini Second World War Italian campaign battle honour marking one of the actions during the fighting which took place at Cassino 11-18 May 1944. *See also: Italy 1943-45; Cassino II; Massa Vertecchi and Casa Sinagogga.*

Massa Vertecchi Second World War, Italian campaign battle honour marking one of the actions during the fighting which took place at Cassino 11-18 May 1944. *See also: Italy 1943-45; Cassino II; Massa Tambourini and Casa Sinagogga.*

Massawa Second World War Abyssinian campaign battle honour marking the occupation by British forces of this fortified seaport on 12 April 1941. *See also: Abyssinia 1940-41; Keren; Jebel Defeis; Jebel Shiba; Gogni; Agordat; Barentu; Karora-Marsa Taclai; Ad Teclesan; Mescelit Pass; Mt Engiahat; Marda Pass; Amb Alagi; Afodu; Gambela; El Wak; Moyale; Wal Garis; Juba; Bulo Erillo; Beles Gugani; Gelib; Alessandra; Goluin; Babile Gap; Bisidimo; Awash; Todenyang-Namaraputh; Soroppa; Giarso; Colito; Wadara; Omo; Gondar; Ambazzo; Kulkaber; Fike and Lechemti.*

Master General of the Ordnance Fourth Military Member of the Army Board. Responsible for the identification of the future weapon systems needed by the Army and the direction of action to meet those needs. Originally entitled Masters of the Ordnance (1414-1597) and Great Master of the Ordnance (1597-1600), the present title was brought into use in 1603. Over the years there were attempts to 'rationalise' the duties: a Director General of Artillery was created in 1855 and the post abolished in the same year; a Director General of Ordnance existed from 1861 until that post too was abolished in 1870 and the appointment of Surveyor General of the Ordnance was created in 1870 and abolished in 1888.

Master General of the Ordnance Controllerate The following directors, individuals and staffs fall within the Master General of the Ordnance Controllerate: Director General Policy and Special Projects; Director General Land Fighting Systems; Director General Guided Weapons and Electronic Systems; Head of the MGO Secretariat and the Principal Director of Contracts (Ordnance).

Master Gunner at St James's Park The title Master Gunner at St James's Park is held by the officer fulfilling duties, effectively equating to those of the Colonel of a Regiment, for the Royal Regiment of Artillery. He answers to Her Majesty The Queen, the Captain-General, and effectively the Colonel-in-Chief, for all matters

pertaining to Her Regiment. The title has varied over the years as follows:
1678-1741 Master Gunner of Whitehall and St James's Park.
1742 to date, Master Gunner of St James's Park.

Master Gunner of England The master gunner was originally a civilian craftsman who made the guns of his time; no soldier but a master tradesman pure and simple. However, as the intricacies of medieval cannon were far beyond the ability of the ordinary fighting man of the 14th and 15th centuries, the men who made the pieces were usually hired as canoniers to man them in action. Gunners and master gunners were therefore found in the field soon after the introduction of artillery. Prior to 1539, when Henry VIII began the construction of the coast defences of England with their gunner-manned forts stretching from Berwick to Milford Haven, there could have been no Master Gunner of England. The title would have been meaningless as there was no organized body of artillerymen stationed in the provinces for him to command. The senior master gunner up till then had charge of the only fee'd gunners, those at the Tower. The expression 'in the Tower and elsewhere' appears in patents soon after the completion of the coastal defences. The title, which lapsed in 1731, has changed as follows:
1484-1506 Chief Gunner.
1506-1509 Master of the Gunners of the Ordnance.
1509-1537 Chief Gunner in the Tower.
1537-1566 Master of the King's Gunners in the Tower and England.
1562-1565 Master of the Gunners in the Tower of England and Elsewhere (jointly).
1566-1571 Master of the Gunners in the Tower and Elsewhere.
1571-1707 Master Gunner of England.
1708-1731 Master Gunner of Great Britain.

Masulipatam Battle honour marking the action, during the establishment of the East India Company in India 1751-1764, which took place on 8 April 1759 when this town, at the mouth of the River Kistna, was stormed at night by a British force.

This led to the establishment of British rather than French influence in the Deccan. *See also: Arcot; Plassey; Condore; Badara; Wandewash; Pondicherry and Buxar.*

Match Slow-burning twisted cord or 'slow match' which was kept burning when a 'matchlock' musketeer was in action.

Match Case A perforated container of tin or brass, worn on the shoulder belt, particularly by grenadiers, inside which the burning end of the match could be kept alight. By the middle of the 18th century it was obsolete and was officially abolished in 1784.

Matchlock Old gunlock in which ignition was achieved by a slow-burning cord or 'match' (qv) applied to the powder in the priming pan. Firearms of this type appeared in the British service in 1486 when Henry VII ordered that half the royal guard be armed with arquebuses (qv). With slight changes in lock action, calibre and length of barrel, this simple form of matchlock arquebus or musket endured in the British service until at least 1680, and was the standard military infantry weapon for practically all European powers. Despite its simple action there were significant difficulties with the matchlock: the smoke of the matches would frequently disclose an ambush, night attacks were entirely out of the question, and efficient functioning in wet weather could not be guaranteed. The matchlock was replaced by the flintlock in the 1680s. *See also: Flintlock; Snaphance; Muskets and Rifles.*

Materiel The materials and equipment of a military force.

Matilda Second World War Infantry Mark II tank designed and produced by Vulcan Foundry Ltd. Production began in 1939 and a total of 3,000 Matildas were produced. The Matilda made a great impact on the early actions in the Western Desert but eventually became obsolete when it came up against the German 88mm gun. Matilda had a crew of four, weighed 26 tons, and mounted a 2pdr gun and Besa machine gun. Later Marks had alternative armaments. *See also: Tank and Infantry tank.*

Matmata Hills Second World War North Africa campaign battle honour marking one of the actions which took place between the occupation of the Alamein Line in 1942 and the end of the campaign. *See also: North Africa 1940-43; Deir El Munassib; Capture of Halfaya Pass; Sebket En Noual; Chebket En Nouiges; Djebel El Telil and Djebel Tebaga.*

Matross Obsolete term for an artillery-man ranking lower than a gunner.

Mau Mau *See: Kenya 1952-56.*

Maud The Maud was a grey striped plaid worn by highland and border shepherds. In 1771 it was stated that the Maud (or Maude) would be a proper covering for light infantry in place of the blanket. Some evidence exists that the Maud was taken into limited use.

Maungdaw Second World War Burma campaign battle honour marking a period of protracted operations in the North Arakan between January and March 1944 which led to the capture of Maungdaw. *See also: Burma 1942-45; North Arakan; Buthidaung; Razibil; Kaladan; Mayu Tunnels; Alethangyaw; Mowdok and Point 551.*

Mawlaik Second World War Burma campaign battle honour marking the fighting which took place 13 November and 16 December 1944 which led to capture of the river port of Kalewa and establishment of a bridgehead across the River Chindwin. *See also: Burma 1942-45; Kennedy Peak; Pinwe and Kalewa.*

Maxim Gun (Model 1884) Machine gun, invented by the American inventor Hiram Maxim (1840-1916) in 1884. The first Maxim to be used was allegedly an 1884 model purchased by a British Army officer, although the gun was not taken into service until 1889. Chambered for the 0.45" rifle round, the Maxim was fed by a canvas belt. Most British Maxims were built by Vickers,

and were either mounted on large wheeled carriages or tripods. *See also: Machine Gun.*

Maymyo Second World War Burma campaign battle honour marking an action, one of a number which took place between 12 February and 21 March 1945 and led to the capture of Mandalay. *See also: Burma 1942-45; Mandalay; Myitson; Ava; Myinmu Bridgehead and Fort Dufferin.*

Mayu Tunnels Second World War Burma campaign battle honour marking a period of protracted operations in the North Arakan between January and March 1944 which led to the capture of these tunnels and penetration of the Mayu range of hills. *See also: Burma 1942-45; North Arakan; Buthidaung; Razibil; Kaladan; Maungdaw; Alethangyaw; Mowdok and Point 551.*

McCreery, General Sir Richard Loudon (1898-1967) Educated at Eton and the Royal Military Academy Sandhurst, McCreery was commissioned into the 12th Lancers in 1915, serving in France during the First World War. In the Second World War he served in France, the Middle East and Tunisia before leading the Eighth Army under Alexander against Kesselring's German armies, launching the offensive of May 1944 which resulted in the storming of Cassino, the destruction of the Gustav Line and the subsequent fall of Rome on 4 June 1944 and Florence on 25 August 1944. In the campaign of 1945 in Italy his army, in conjunction with the US Fifth Army, brought about the destruction of the Gothic Line and ultimate surrender of the German armies in April 1945. He became General Officer Commanding-in-Chief, British Forces of Occupation in Austria, and British representative on the allied commission for Austria 1945-46. From 1946-48 he was General Officer Commanding-in-Chief the British Army of the Rhine and, from 1948-49, British Army representative, military staff committee.

Medecina Second World War Italian campaign battle honour marking one of the actions in the breakthrough of the German positions in the Bologna area 14-21 April 1945. *See also: Italy 1943-45; Bologna; Gaiana Crossing; Sillaro Crossing and Idice Bridgehead.*

Medinine Second World War North Africa campaign battle honour marking the repulse of the German attack on 6 March 1943 as the Eighth Army was preparing to assault the Mareth Line. *See also: North Africa 1940-43; Zemlet El Lebene and Tadjira Khir.*

Mediterranian Battle honour awarded to militia regiments to mark their services during the Crimean War (1854-55) when they undertook garrison duties in order to free line regiments for service at the front. *See also: St Helena.*

Medjez El Bab Second World War Italian campaign battle honour marking the capture of, and exploitation beyond, the town of Medjez El Bab 25/26 November 1942. *See also: North Africa 1940-43; Oudna; Tebourba Gap and Bou Arada.*

Medjez Plain Second World War North Africa campaign battle honour marking the battle fought by V Corps over the period 23-30 April 1943 as a preliminary to the final thrust to Tunis. *See also: North Africa 1940-43; Gueriat El Atach Ridge; Longstop Hill 1943; Djebel Bou Aoukaz 1943; Grich El Oued; Peter's Corner; Si Mediene; Si Abdallah; Gab Gab Gap and Sidi Ahmed.*

Meeanee Battle honour marking the defeat of the numerically superior Amirs of Scinde by a force under Sir Charles Napier on 17 February 1843. Hostilities with the Amirs of Scinde were the direct but inevitable result of the First Afghan War (qv). *See also: Scinde; Hyderabad; Maharajpore and Punniar.*

Megiddo First World War Palestinian campaign battle honour marking General Allenby's decisive victory over the Turkish armies in Palestine. Megiddo is an ancient town strategically located on a route linking Egypt and Mesopotamia. Allenby's offensive was launched on 18 September 1918 along the coastal plain against the

main Turkish concentration. The infantry achieved an impressive breaching of the Turkish line and the following cavalry had covered 18 miles by noon. *See also: Palestine 1917-18; Gaza; El Mughar; Nebi Samwil; Jaffa; Jerusalem; Jericho; Tell Asur; Jordan; Sharon; Nablus and Damascus.*

Meijel Second World War battle honour marking the fighting around Meijel and Asten 27 October - 8 November 1944. *See also: North West Europe 1944-1945; Aam; Venraij; Lower Maas; Venlo Pocket; Geilenkirchen and Ourthe.*

Meiktila Second World War Burma campaign battle honour marking the advance down the Myittka Valley, the passage of the River Irrawaddy at Nyaungu and the drive for Meiktila in March 1945. *See also: Burma 1942-45; Nyaungu Bridgehead; Capture of Meiktila; Defence of Meiktila and Taungtha.*

Melfa Crossing Second World War Italian campaign battle honour marking one of the actions in the Liri Valley operations of May 1944. *See also: Italy 1943-45; Liri Valley; Hitler Line; Monte Piccolo; Piedemonte Hill and Aquino.*

Memorandum Term used in some regiments to describe the routine parade at which commanding officers hear disciplinary cases and conduct interviews. *See also: Levée and Orders.*

Men Of Harlech Regimental quick and slow march of The Life Guards, slow march of 9th/12th Lancers and Welsh Guards and quick march of the Royal Regiment of Wales.

Menate Second World War Italian campaign battle honour marking an operation in which amphibious vehicles were used to cross a flooded area to seize the town of Menate on 10 April 1945. *See also: Italy 1943-45.*

Menin Road First World War battle honour marking the advance made on the southern part of the Ypres front, which resulted in the clearance of the Menin

Ridge, in mid-September 1917 during the Third Battle of Ypres. *See also: France and Flanders 1914-1918; Ypres 1917; Pilckem; Langemarck 1917; Polygon Wood; Broodseinde; Poelcappelle and Passchendaele.*

Mente Et Manu (With heart and hand), motto of The Queen's Royal Hussars (Queen's Own and Royal Irish), formally used by 4th Queen's Own Hussars and The Queen's Royal Irish Hussars.

Mentions in Despatches The practice of mentioning subordinates in despatches from commanders in the field is of long standing. In 1920 it was decided that a multiple-leaved bronze oak leaf should be worn on the Victory Medal, by those entitled to wear that medal, to denote a First World War mention. In August 1943 King George VI approved a single-leaved bronze oak leaf of a pattern different from that previously authorised, being awarded to members of the Services who had been mentioned in despatches. A mention in despatches is now normally awarded only for gallantry or distinguished service in operations against an enemy.

MENTOR The United Kingdom-wide secure speech system extended beyond the United Kingdom over strategic communication links. *See also: Patron.*

Mercian Brigade An administrative grouping in the infantry formed by Army Order 61 of 1948 comprising The Cheshire Regiment, The Worcestershire Regiment (until 1970), The Sherwood Foresters (from the Forester Brigade 1962, until 1970), The Worcestershire and Sherwood Foresters Regiment (from 1970), The South Staffordshire Regiment (until 1959), The North Staffordshire Regiment (The Prince of Wales's) (until 1959) and The Staffordshire Regiment (The Prince of Wales's) (from 1959). The regiments of the brigade were absorbed into the Prince of Wales's Division (qv) in 1968.

Nerebimur (We shall be worthy) motto of The Light Dragoons, formerly the motto of 15th The King's Hussars and 15th/19th The King's Royal Hussars.

Mergeb Chaouach Second World War North Africa campaign battle honour marking one of the actions during the advance of V Corps to occupy the line Touhabeur-Chaouach over the period 7-15 April 1943. *See also: North Africa 1940-43; Oued Zarga; Djebel Rmel; Djebel Bel Mahdi; Djebel Bech Chekaoui; Djebel Ang; Djebel Tanngoucha; Djebel Kesskiss and El Kourzia.*

Merjayun Second World War Syrian campaign battle honour marking an action which took place between 9-27 June in which the town was taken, lost and retaken, during the 1941 campaign in Syria. *See also: Syria 1941; Palmyra; Jebel Mazar and Deir Es Zor.*

Merry Month Of May Regimental quick march of The Royal Hussars (Prince of Wales's Own and 10th Royal Hussars (Prince of Wales's Own). The successor to both regiments is The King's Royal Hussars.

Mersa El Brega Second World War North Africa campaign battle honour marking one of the actions which took place in North Africa between the start of Rommel's first offensive in March 1941 and the unsuccessful British offensive, Operation BATTLEAXE, of mid-June 1941. *See also: North Africa 1940-43; Agedabia; Derna Aerodrome; Halfaya 1941 and Sidi Suleiman.*

Mersa Matruh Second World War North Africa campaign battle honour marking one of the actions which took place in the period between the British withdrawal from Agedabia in March 1941 and the occupation of the El Alamein line in late June. *See also: North Africa 1940-43; Msus; Benghazi; Carmusa; Point 174; Minqar Qaim and Fuka.*

Merv First World War Persian campaign battle honour marking the occupation of Merv in Russia by British troops from Eastern Persia at the end of 1918 during the 1915-19 campaign. *See also: Persia 1915-19 and Baku.*

Merville Battery Second World War battle honour marking the capture, in the early hours of 6 June 1944, of the German coastal battery at Merville by 9th Battalion The Parachute Regiment, some of whom were landed by glider. *See also: North West Europe 1944-45; Normandy Landing and Pegasus Bridge.*

Mescelit Pass Second World War Abyssinian campaign battle honour. *See also: Abyssinia 1940-41; Keren; Jebel Defeis; Jebel Shiba; Gogni; Agordat; Barentu; Karora-Marsa Taclai; Ad Teclesan; Massawa; Mt Engiahat; Marda Pass; Amb Alagi; Afodu; Gambela; El Wak; Moyale; Wal Garis; Juba; Bulo Erillo; Beles Gugani; Gelib; Alessandra; Goluin; Babile Gap; Bisidimo; Awash; Todenyang-Namaraputh; Soroppa; Giarso; Colito; Wadara; Omo; Gondar; Ambazzo; Kulkaber; Fike and Lechemti.*

Mesopotamia 1914-18 First World War battle honour marking the operations of British troops seeking to ensure the protection of the oilfields in the Persian Gulf area following Turkish entry into the war. Basra on the Shatt-El-Arab was captured in November 1914 and, in early 1915, operations were launched to extend the defended area, which ended in an abortive attempt to reach Baghdad. A period of stalemate followed until a successful drive to capture Baghdad was launched in February 1917. *See also: Mesopotamia 1914-1918; Basra; Shaiba; Kut Al Amara 1915; Ctesiphon; Defence of Kut Al Amara; Tigris 1916; Kut Al Amara 1917; Baghdad; Khan Baghdadi and Sharqat.*

Mess Place where servicemen eat and take recreation. It is usual for separate messes to be provided for officers, warrant officers and sergeants, non-commissioned officers and soldiers.

Mess Dress Sometimes called 'mess kit', the introduction and development of mess dress was a protracted business, and arose from the wish to have an order of dress which was both uniform and comfortable in which to dine. At the beginning of the 19th century at least one cavalry regiment wore an open jacket with the sash and belt beneath. In 1828 the 'shell' or undress jacket was worn in the Indian messes, and

the fashion gradually spread to the United Kingdom. The open mess jacket allowed scope for a decorative regimental waistcoat and, at first, this was closed to the neck, often with a stand collar. Later, a white shirt and appropriate black or white tie was worn with a low cut waistcoat. The mess jacket also took other forms, sometimes with a roll collar and big revers. Mess dress subsequently became subject to regulation not only for officers, but also for warrant officers and non-commissioned officers.

Mess Tins Containers used for the preparation and consumption of food.

Messines 1914 First World War battle honour marking operations during the opening stages of the war as British troops sought to close the gap between troops in the Armentières sector and those already near Ypres to the north. British troops were forced back to the Messines Ridge where, although heavily outnumbered, they held for two weeks before withdrawing to a new line to the West. *See also: France and Flanders 1914-18; Retreat from Mons; Marne 1914; Aisne 1914; La Bassée 1914; Armentières and Ypres 1914.*

Messines 1917 First World War battle honour marking the capture of Messines Ridge on 7 June as a preliminary step to the projected offensive at Ypres. *See also: France and Flanders 1914-1918 and Ypres 1917.*

Messines 1918 First World War battle honour marking the fierce fighting which took place on Messines Ridge on 10/11 April during the Battle of Lys. *See also: France and Flanders 1914-1918; Lys; Estaires; Kemmel; Hazebrouck; Bailleul; Béthune and Scherpenberg.*

Methuen, Paul Sanford, Field Marshal, 3rd Baron (1845-1932). Educated at Eton and commissioned into the Scots Guards in 1864. He took part in the Ashanti War of 1874 and in the Egyptian War of 1882. He commanded 'Methuen's Horse' in the Bechuanaland expedition of 1884-85. During the South Africa War (1899-1902) he commanded the 1st Division of the First Army Corps.

After defeating the Boers at Belmont, Enslin and the Modder River, he was taken prisoner by Delarey in 1902, but released. He was appointed commander-in-chief of the Eastern command in 1905 and was general officer commanding-in-chief South Africa 1908-12. From 1909-1915 he was governor of Nataland, from 1915-19, governor of Malta. He was appointed field marshal in 1911.

Metropolitan Formerly a regimental quick march of the Military Provost Staff Corps and, since 6 April 1992, one of the regimental quick marches of Provost Branch of The Adjutant General's Corps.

Miami Battle honour marking operations carried out along the Miami River, and in particular the repulse of the attacks by an American force based on Fort Meiggs on 5 May 1813 during the campaign of 1812-14 in North America. *See also: Detroit; Queenstown; Niagara and Bladensburg.*

Middle East 1942-44 Second World War battle honour recognising the operations undertaken in the Middle East between 1941 and 1944. The area includes: Crete, the Dodecanese, Madagascar and the Adriatic.

Middlesex Regiment (Duke of Cambridge's Own) (57th and 77th Foot) The 57th Foot was raised in 1741, renumbered 46th Foot in 1748, 59th Foot (under Colonel John Arabin) in 1755, 57th Foot in 1757; and redesignated 57th (West Middlesex) Foot in 1782. The original 77th Foot was raised as 77th (Montgomery Highlanders) Regiment in 1756, disbanded in 1763, re-raised in 1775, disbanded again in 1783, and finally re-raised in October 1787 under Colonel James Marsh as 77th Foot. The regiment was redesignated 77th (The East Middlesex) Regiment of Foot in 1807; and 77th (East Middlesex) (Duke of Cambridge's Own) Foot in 1876. In 1881 the 57th (West Middlesex) Regiment and 77th (East Middlesex) Regiment (Duke of Cambridge's Own) amalgamated to form The Middlesex Regiment (Duke of Cambridge's Own) (57th and 77th Foot).

On 31 December 1966 the regiment amalgamated with The Queen's Royal Surrey Regiment, The Queen's Own Buffs, The Royal Kent Regiment and The Royal Sussex Regiment to form The Queen's Regiment (2nd, 3rd, 35th, 50th, 57th, 70th, 77th, 97th and 107th Foot). On 9 September 1992 the Queen's Regiment amalgamated with The Royal Hampshire Regiment to form, The Princess of Wales's Royal Regiment (Queen's and Royal Hampshires).

Headdress Badge: Within a laurel wreath the plume, coronet and motto of the Prince of Wales, and coronet and cypher of the Duke of Cambridge. Below, the battle honour 'ALBUHERA'.

History: *History of 57th (West Middlesex) 1755-1881* (author unknown); *The Story of The Middlesex Regiment 1755-1916* by C L Kingsford; *Records of 77th Regiment 1787-1903* by W H Woollright; *The Dear Old Regiment 77th 1879* by N Tailefer; *Diehards in The Great War* (2 Vols.) by E Wyrall; *2nd Battalion The Middlesex Regiment Campaign in Europe 6 June 1944-7 May 1945* by R B Moberley and *The Diehards in Korea* by J N Shipster.

Middlesex Yeomanry *See: London Yeomanry.*

Midge A drone or battlefield reconnaissance, remotely piloted vehicle (RPV) currently in service with the Royal Artillery, but obsolescent and due to be replaced by Phoenix (qv). Midge is launched from a specially converted four-ton vehicle, and flies a pre-programmed flight path taking both conventional and infra-red photographs. When the Midge returns to the launch site the engine cuts and it descends by parachute. The film is then processed in the field. Midge has a range of approximately 150km, an operational altitude of 300-1,200m, and a speed of 740kph.

Midland Brigade An administrative grouping in the infantry formed by Army Order 61 of 1948, and subsequently renamed The Forester Brigade in 1962, comprising The Royal Warwickshire Regiment (to the Fusilier Brigade 1963),

The Royal Lincolnshire Regiment (to the East Anglian Brigade 1957), The Royal Leicestershire Regiment (to the East Anglian Brigade 1963) and The Sherwood Foresters (to the Mercian Brigade 1962). The regiments of the brigade were absorbed into the Queen's Division (qv) in 1968, with the exception of The Sherwood Foresters which amalgamated with The Worcestershire Regiment and joined the Prince of Wales's Division (qv).

Milan A second-generation medium range anti-tank guided weapon with a shaped charge warhead. The guidance system is semi-automatic command to line of sight by wire. Milan, which is currently in service, has a maximum range of just under 2,000m and a minimum range of 25m. It is expected that Milan will be replaced by third-generation weapon TRIGAT MR.

Milanollo Regimental quick march of the Life Guards and the Coldstream Guards.

MILITARY AID TO THE CIVIL AUTHORITY (MACA)

This term embraces three broad types of employment for military personnel and equipment:

Military Assistance to Civil Ministries (MACM), which is the use of military forces for non-military tasks, including assistance to maintain essential services or to undertake work of national importance.

Military Aid to the Civil Community (MACC), which is the provision of military personnel and equipment to assist the community at large and includes life-saving activities in an emergency and the provision of instructors to volunteer non-profit-making organisations.

Military Aid to the Civil Power (MACP), which is the provision of military personnel and equipment in support of the civil authority in the restoration and maintenance of law and order.

Military Attaché *See: Attaché.*

Military Cross Gallantry award instituted by a Royal Warrant dated 28 December 1914 in recognition of distinguished, gallant and meritorious services. Open to commissioned officers of the rank of captain and below, and warrant officers of 'Our Army, Our Indian or Colonial Military Forces' and 'Foreign Officers of equivalent rank to those above mentioned, who have ben associated in military operations with Our Army'. The Military Cross may now be awarded to members of the other Services when employed with the Army.
Ribbon: White, 1⅜" wide, with a ½" central purple stripe.

Military Doctrine *See: Doctrine.*

Military General Service Medal 1793-1814 Instituted in 1847 and sometimes referred to as the 'Dead Man's Medal' because it was not issued until 55 years after the first date on the medal and then only to survivors. Given the period covered there are some surprising omissions in the clasps.
Ribbon: Crimson 1¼" wide, with ⅛" wide dark blue borders.
Clasps: Egypt; Maida; Roleia; Vimiera; Sahagun; Benevente; Sahagun and Benevente; Corunna; Martinique; Talavera; Guadaloupe; Busaco; Barrosa; Fuentes D'Onor; Albuhera; Java; Ciudad Rodrigo; Badajoz; Salamanca; Fort Detroit; Vittoria; Pyrenees; St Sebastian; Chateauguay; Nivelle; Chrystlers Farm; Nive; Orthes and Toulouse.

Military Honours Ceremonial associated with royal visits, military funerals etc.

Military Knights of Windsor Body of retired officers who support the Knights of the Order of the Garter. They were formerly known as Poor Knights or Alms Knights, ranking below the ordinary knights. The institution originated in 1348, when it consisted of 26 veterans. Members are now appointed by the Sovereign from officers who have rendered meritorious service. They are granted a small stipend together with quarters in Windsor Castle, hence their designation. Until 1906 the institution was under the command of the Dean and Canons of Windsor but was then transferred to the Governor and Constable of Windsor Castle. Stipends are derived from the college revenues, and every Knight of the Garter on appointment to that order contributes a sum for apportionment among the knights. The uniform was assigned by William IV and is that of an officer on the unattached list of 1830 and worn to this day. William IV also decreed that the title should be changed from the 'Poor Knights' to the Military Knights of Windsor. The number of knights was fixed at 13 under the will of Henry VIII.

Military Law Military Law is laid down in the Manual of Military Law, issued by command of the Army Council, as being 'the law which governs the soldier in peace and in war, at home and abroad'. Military law is contained in the Army Act (qv), the Acts relating to the Reserve and Auxiliary Forces, and certain other Acts applied to the Army, supplemented by the Queen's Regulations for the Army and the Reserve Forces, Royal Warrant, Defence Council and Army Council Instructions and Army Orders. The Army Act is an act of Parliament dealing with discipline, courts martial, enlistment and allied subjects, and has in itself no permanent operation, for it continues in force only so long as parliament from time to time decides. It is annually brought into operation by the Army and Air Force Act, which must become law by 30 April, and it is by this system of annual Acts that Parliament retains control over the land forces of the Crown. The Army Act is part of the statute law of England, and though that part of it which relates to discipline is administered by army tribunals and not by civil courts, it is construed in the same manner, and carried into effect under the same conditions as to evidence and otherwise, as the ordinary criminal law of the country. There is not in England, as in many other countries, a special law defining the relationship between military and civil powers in cases of riot and insurrection or the intermediate stage known as *état de siège*. Troops when called upon to assist the civil power in Great Britain are under military law as soldiers, but they are also subject to the civil law as citizens - their military character is superimposed on their civil character and does not obliterate it. Military law must not be confused with martial law, the latter meaning the suspension of the ordinary law and government of the country or parts of it by tribunals of its own army.

Military Medal Gallantry award instituted by Royal Warrant dated 25 March 1916 for 'Bravery in the Field' by non-commissioned officers and men of the Army. Subsequent warrants made the Military Medal available to other ranks in 'Any of Our Military Forces'; to equivalent ranks of allied, or 'associated' armies, and to women.
Ribbon: Dark blue, 1¼" wide, with three white and two crimson stripes, each ⅛" wide, down the centre.

Military Pace The standard military pace is 30 inches. Quick time is 120 paces to the minute or, in the case of light infantry and rifle regiments, 140 paces to the minute.

Military Provost Staff Corps Formed under Army Order 241 of 1901 as the Military Prison Staff Corps and redesignated Military Provost Staff Corps in 1906. On 6 April 1992 the corps amalgamated with the Corps of Royal Military Police to form Provost Branch of The Adjutant General's Corps.
Headdress Badge: The royal cypher ensigned with the crown thereunder a scroll inscribed MILITARY PROVOST STAFF CORPS.

Military Secretary The post of Military Secretary was created in 1791 and became the channel for all business relating to the appointment and promotion of officers. The transfer of these duties did much to diminish the power of the Secretary of War who, up to that point, had been responsible for those functions. The Military Secretary is responsible, through a series of selection boards, for the selection of suitable officers for all staff and command appointments, officers' annual confidential reports and honours and awards.

Militia The militia, oldest of the non-regular military organisations, and therefore senior historically to both volunteers and yeomanry, has always been an essentially local force, organised by counties and cities, to provide a home defence force and a balance to the standing army. Traditionally the Militia answered to the Crown through the county High Sheriff and Lord Lieutenant, Militia officers being bound to the region by the property qualification.

Among the Anglo-Saxons, no special organisation existing, even a minimal level of efficiency was seldom reached. The nation paid for this lack of organisation and training when the Danes overran much of the country during Alfred's reign. To prevent a recurrence Alfred reorganised the Militia, or *fyrd*, dividing it into two parts to ensure continuity of service, making land the basis of numbers, but the family system that of discipline. Each shire had to furnish not only its quota in time of war, but also provide arms, keep them in repair and undertake so many days' training every year. When the Crown began to contend with the Norman barons it found an effective weapon in the revival of the Saxon Militia. The shire contingent was commanded in pre-conquest times by the *ealdorman*, later by the Sheriff and subsequently by the Lord Lieutenant until 1871.

By the Elizabethan period the defence of England was in the hands of the 'Trained (or 'Train') Bands'. The early stages of the civil war saw a series of local struggles to secure the allegiance of the local Militia and seize their magazines. An Act of 1662 reorganised the Militia, and this formed the basis of the Militia law until 1908. Monmouth's infantry in 1685 was largely composed of the Militia of the Western counties. The Militia was largely neglected until 1757 when the Seven Years' War (qv) when, most of the regular army being abroad, it was necessary to form a home defence force. Several Militia Acts were passed, notably those of 1761, 1768 and 1802.

The Militia was largely manned by voluntary recruits, but where voluntary recruitment failed, a levy by ballot could be made upon all the inhabitants of the of the locality between the ages of 18 and 50. The power of making the ballot had always

existed, and would by law have to be enforced, but for the Militia Ballot Suspension Act which, when the measure was unnecessary, was passed from year to year. Many classes were exempt from the ballot: peers, soldiers, volunteers, yeomanry, resident members of universities, clergymen, parish schoolmasters, articled clerks, apprentices, seafarers, Crown employees, free watermen of the Thames etc. The effect of this legislation was to transform the Militia from a local police and national defence force into a reserve for the regular army. Those early military functions were now fulfilled by the Volunteers (qv). Between 1808 and 1812 a series of local Militia Acts was passed to create a new compulsory home service force of men between 18 and 30. Like the general Militia, this force was recruited by Militia authorities; officers were required to be men of landed property, not necessarily an efficient method of selection. To enable the maximum number of line regiments to proceed to the Crimean War and Indian Mutiny, practically every Militia regiment was embodied for home defence.

In 1908 under the Territorial and Reserve Forces Act, a special reserve was formed into which the Militia was absorbed. The Militia in Bermuda, the Channel Islands and Malta were not affected by this legislation. In 1921 the Special Reserve was renamed the Militia, but all the units comprised in it, with one exception, were allowed to go into suspended animation. The exception, The Royal Monmouthshire Royal Engineers (qv), was continued as a Supplementary Reserve unit and became part of the Territorial Army in 1953, but was allowed to retain the word Militia in its title. The rest of the Militia, which for many years had only a nominal existence, was formally disbanded in 1953. The term 'Militia' was quite inappropriately applied to men called up under the Military Training Act of 1939. *See also: Volunteers; Yeomanry and Territorial Army.*

Milling Term used in the Parachute Regiment for a period of free boxing which takes place during the qualifying 'P' course.

Mills Bomb Obsolete high-explosive hand grenade named after Sir William Mills (1856-1932). *See: Grenade.*

Minden Battle honour marking the victory of an allied army under Prince Ferdinand of Brunswick over a French force under Marshal Contades which was seeking to invade Hanover during the Seven Years' War (qv). On 1 August 1759 six British regiments, supported by three Hanoverian, broke through three lines of French cavalry and 'tumbled them to ruin'. The battle would have been decisive if Lord George Sackville had not refused to lead his cavalry against the already disorganised French. The six British regiments - 12th, 20th, 23rd, 25th, 37th and 51st - are alleged to have plucked roses to put in their hats during their advance, and their descendants still wear roses on 'Minden Day'.

Minden Rose Regimental slow march of The Princess of Wales's Royal Regiment (Queen's and Royal Hampshires).

Mine De Sedjenane Second World War North Africa campaign battle honour marking the capture of the German position at Mine de Sedjenane in North Africa on 31 March 1943 after two days of fierce fighting. *See also: North Africa 1940-43; Kasserine; Hunt's Gap; Tamera and Fondouk.*

Mine Military mining belongs to the oldest application of engineering to the art of war. At least four centuries before the Christian era such warfare was known. Long before gunpowder was used places were captured by gaining access through mine galleries. Gunpowder was first used in mine warfare in 1487, after which mining became more common. At the siege of Sevastopol in the Crimean war over five miles of galleries were driven by the opposing armies. The First World War produced conditions similar to those of siege war, and specialist troops were trained for this. The Germans were the first to use mines, in Flanders in December 1914. The great mining feat of the war was the blowing up by the British of the Messines Ridge (*see: Messines 1917*) on 7 June 1917 using 1,000,000 lbs of explosive over a ten mile front. Improvements in the range and effectiveness of artillery and the advent of aerial bombing did much to reduce the use of mining. The generally more fluid nature of the Second World War meant that mining in the traditional sense was little practised and the term 'mine' came to mean containers of explosives or 'bombs', placed on the ground or just beneath the surface, which exploded under pressure, or were occasionally controlled by electricity, radio or other means. Two broad families of mines developed - the anti-tank and anti-personnel - with a gradual move to non-metallic casing so that they were harder to detect. A wide variety of mines and fuses now exists, and mines may be delivered by aircraft or artillery, or laid in a more traditional manner on the surface or just below by mechanical minelayer or by hand.

Mine Detector Traditionally, mine detectors took the form of metal detectors operating through the transmission and receipt of electrical signals. The advent of non-metal-cased mines has added to the problem of detection, and new means of detection have been evolved.

Minefield An area of ground containing mines, which may be anti-tank, anti-personnel or more usually a mixture, laid with or without a pattern. There are four broad types of minefield. First, the tactical minefield is part of a formation obstacle plan laid to delay, channel or disrupt an enemy advance. Second, the protective minefield is used to provide local close-in protection for a defended area. Third, the nuisance minefield is laid to delay and disorganise the enemy and hinder his use of an area or route. Fourth, the phoney minefield is an area free of live mines but marked exactly as a real minefield and designed to deceive and delay the enemy.

Minié Rifle Developed by Captain Minié, a French officer, this 0.758" calibre weapon was adopted by the British in 1831. *See also: Baker Rifle and Rifle.*

Minqar Qaim Second World War North Africa campaign battle honour marking one of the actions which took place in the period between the British withdrawal from Agedabia in March 1941 and the occupation of the El Alamein line in late June. *See also: North Africa 1940-1943; Msus; Benghazi; Carmusa; Point 174; Mersa Matruh and Fuka.*

Minturno Second World War Italian campaign battle honour marking the crossing of the river, establishment of a bridgehead and subsequent capture of the town of Minturno on the Garigliano River 17-25 January 1944 during the campaign in Italy. *See also: Italy 1943-45; Garigliano Crossing; Damiano and Monte Tuga.*

Mirliton Tall cap made of felt and modelled on an oriental design and worn by the French cavalry. Taken briefly into use by the British light cavalry, largely for undress occasions.

Misfire The failure of a weapon or ammunition to function as expected or planned.

Modder River Battle honour marking a successful action against the Boers along the Modder River on 22 November 1899 during the South Africa War 1899-1902. *See also: South Africa 1899-1902; Defence of Ladysmith; Relief of Ladysmith; Defence of Kimberley; Relief of Kimberley and Paardeburg.*

Model 1839 Musket Early British percussion musket converted from a flintlock weapon and issued to some of the armed forces. *See also: Musket and Brown Bess.*

Monastery Hill Second World War Italian campaign battle honour marking one of the actions during the early attempts to capture Monte Cassino, linchpin of the Gustav line, during the period 20 January to 25 March 1944. *See also: Italy 1943-1945; Cassino I; Castle Hill and Hangman's Hill.*

Monck, George, 1st Duke of Albermarle (1608-70). General and Admiral. Monck fought at Cadiz (1625) and Rhé (1627) and was a colonel under Charles I in the Scottish war of 1639. In 1644 he was taken prisoner by Fairfax at

Nantwich and imprisoned in the Tower of London 1644-46. He became lieutenant general of the ordnance under Cromwell, and fought with distinction at Dunbar (1650). In 1654 he became commander-in-chief Scotland. In 1659 he supported the recalled 'rump' parliament when it came into conflict with the army leaders. In 1660 the 'rump' made him captain-general and commander-in-chief. Convinced that the only solution to the existing state of political confusion was the recall of the Stuarts, he took a leading part in the restoration of Charles II. He continued to command the Army until his death. As admiral of the fleet in 1666 he won a decisive victory over the Dutch.

Monck's Regiment Of Foot *See: Coldstream Guards.*

Monmouthshire Light Infantry (43rd Foot) *See: Oxfordshire and Buckinghamshire Light Infantry (43rd and 52nd Foot).*

Monmouthshire Yeomanry The two troops of Yeomanry Cavalry in Monmouthshire were closely associated with those in Gloucestershire. In 1798 the Chepstow Troop of Gentlemen and Yeomanry Cavalry and the Loyal Monmouthshire Troop were formed, the latter in the county town. They were accepted for service again in 1803 and served at least until 1827.

Monro, Sir Charles Carmichael, General, (1860-1929). Commissioned into 2nd Foot. He succeeded Sir Ian Hamilton as commander-in-chief Gallipoli and conducted the evacuation with great skill. From 1916-20 he commanded the Indian Army, being made General in 1917. He became a baronet in 1921 and was governor of Gibraltar from 1923-28.

Mons First World War battle honour marking the first encounter on 23 August 1914 between the British Expeditionary Force (qv), manning a hastily prepared defensive position on the line of a canal, and the advancing Germans. Two British divisions successfully repulsed an attack by six German divisions, due largely to the effect of British small arms fire on the massed German infantry. *See also: France and Flanders 1914-1918; Le Cateau and Retreat from Mons.*

Montagne Farm Second World War North Africa campaign battle honour marking one of a number of actions which took place between the Kasserine and Fondouk operations in 1943. *See also: North Africa 1940-1943; Kasserine; El Hadjeba; Djebel Djaffa; Sidi Nsir; Fort McGregor; Stuka Farm; Steamroller Farm; Maknassy; Kef Ouiba Pass; Djebel Guerba; Sedjenane I; Djebel Dahra; Kef El Debna and Djebel Cuoucha.*

Montarnaud Second World War North Africa campaign battle honour marking one of the actions during the final breakthrough to the capture of Tunis and subsequent exploitation towards the Cape Bon Peninsula in April and May 1943 at the end of the campaign. *See also: North Africa 1940-1943; Tunis; Hammam Lif; Djebel Bou Aoukaz 1943 II; Djebel Bou Aoukaz 1943 I; Ragoubet Souissi; Creteville Pass; Gromballa and Bou Ficha.*

Montemello-Scorticato Ridge Second World War Italian campaign battle honour marking one of the actions which took place during the breaching of the Gothic Line in September 1944 and the launching of the final push into the Po Valley in April 1945. *See also: Italy 1943-1945; Monte Reggiano; Savignano; San Martino Sogliano; Monte Farneto; Montilgallo; Carpineta; Monte Cavallo; Casa Bettini; Pideura; Pergola Ridge; Senio Floodbank; Cesena; Conventello-Comacchio; Monte Casalino; Monte La Pieve; Monte Pianoereno; Monte Spaduro; Orsara; Tossignano and Catarelto Ridge.*

Monte Camino Second World War Italian campaign battle honour marking the action to secure this mountain feature, an outpost of the Gothic Line, which took place between 5 November and 9 December 1943 in atrocious weather. *See also: Italy 1943-1945; Teano and Calabritto*

Monte Casalino Second World War Italian campaign battle honour marking one of the actions which took place during the breaching of the Gothic Line in September 1944 and the launching of the final push into the Po Valley in April 1945. *See also: Italy 1943-45; Montemello-Scorticato Ridge; Monte Reggiano; Savignano; San Martino Sogliano; Monte Farneto; Montilgallo; Carpineta; Monte Cavallo; Casa Bettini; Pideura; Pergola Ridge; Senio Floodbank; Cesena; Conventello-Comacchio; Monte La Pieve; Monte Pianoereno; Monte Spaduro; Orsara; Tossignano and Catarelto Ridge.*

Monte Cavallo Second World War Italian campaign battle honour marking one of the actions which took place during the breaching of the Gothic Line in September 1944 and the launching of the final push into the Po Valley in April 1945. *See also: Italy 1943-1945; Montemello-Scorticato Ridge; Monte Reggiano; Savignano; San Martino Sogliano; Monte Farneto; Montilgallo; Carpineta; Monte Casalino; Casa Bettini; Pideura; Pergola Ridge; Senio Floodbank; Cesena; Conventello-Comacchio; Monte La Pieve; Monte Pianoereno; Monte Spaduro; Orsara; Tossignano and Catarelto Ridge.*

Monte Ceco Second World War, Italian campaign battle honour marking the capture and subsequent defence of this feature 3-17 October 1944. *See also: Italy 1943-1945; Marradi; Monte Gamberaldi and Battaglia.*

Monte Cedrone Second World War Italian campaign battle honour marking the capture of this feature, which dominated Citta di Castello in Northern Umbria, in July 1944. *See also: Italy 1943-1945; Citta di Castello and Campriano.*

Monte Chicco Second World War Italian campaign battle honour marking the capture of Monte Chicco after heavy fighting on 13/14 October 1944. *See also: Italy 1943-1945; Santarcangelo and Capture of Forli.*

Monte Colombo Second World War Italian campaign battle honour marking one of the actions in the Battle of the

Rimini Line in September 1944. *See also: Italy 1943-1945; Rimini Line; Ceriano Ridge; Casa Fabri Ridge; Montescudo; Frisoni and San Marino.*

Monte Domini Second World War Italian campaign battle honour marking one of the actions during the advance to Florence 17 July-10 August 1944. *See also: Italy 1943-1945; Advance to Florence; Incontro; Monte San Michele; and Monte Scalari.*

Monte Farneto Second World War Italian campaign battle honour marking one of the actions which took place during the breaching of the Gothic Line in September 1944 and the launching of the final push into the Po Valley in April 1945. *See also: Italy 1943-1945; Montemello-Scorticato Ridge; Monte Reggiano; Savignano; San Martino Sogliano; Monte Casalino; Montilgallo; Carpineta; Monte Cavallo; Casa Bettini; Pideura; Pergola Ridge; Senio Floodbank; Cesena; Conventello-Comacchio; Monte La Pieve; Monte Pianoereno; Monte Spaduro; Orsara; Tossignano and Catarelto Ridge.*

Monte Gabbione Second World War Italian campaign battlehonour marking one of the actions which took place in the period between the fall of Rome in June 1944 and the establishment of contact with the Gothic Line in July 1944. *See also: Italy 1943-1945; Monte Rotondo; Ripa Ridge; Gabbiano and Arezzo.*

Monte Gamberaldi Second World War Italian campaign battle honour marking the capture of this mountain feature on 29 September 1944 after unsuccessful attacks on 25 and 26 September. *See also: Italy 1943-1945; Marradi; Battaglia; Monte Ceco and Monte Grande.*

Montegaudio Second World War Italian campaign battle honour marking one of the actions in the battle of the Gothic Line 25 August to 22 September 1944. *See also: Italy 1943-1945; Gothic Line; Tavoleto; Coriano; Croce; Gemmano Ridge; Monte Gridolfo; San Clemente; Poggio San Giovanni and Pian di Castello.*

Monte Grande Second World War Italian campaign battle honour marking the successful defence of this feature against repeated German attacks over the period 1 November-12 December 1944. *See also: Italy 1943-1945; Marradi; Monte Gamberaldi; Battaglia and Monte Ceco.*

Monte Gridolfo Second World War Italian campaign battle honour marking one of the actions in the battle of the Gothic Line 25 August to 22 September 1944. *See also: Italy 1943-1945; Gothic Line; Tavoleto; Coriano; Croce; Gemmano Ridge; Montegaudio; San Clemente; Poggio San Giovanni and Pian di Castello.*

Monte La Pieve Second World War Italian campaign battle honour marking one of the actions which took place during the breaching of the Gothic Line in September 1944 and the launching of the final push into the Po Valley in April 1945. *See also: Italy 1943-1945; Montemello-Scorticato Ridge; Monte Reggiano; Savignano; San Martino Sogliano; Monte Casalino; Montilgallo; Carpineta; Monte Cavallo; Casa Bettini; Pideura; Pergola Ridge; Senio Floodbank; Cesena; Conventello-Comacchio; Monte Farneto; Monte Pianoereno; Monte Spaduro; Orsara; Tossignano and Catarelto Ridge.*

Monte Malbe Second World War Italian campaign battle honour marking the capture of this important feature forward of the Trasimene Line on the night of 19-20 June 1944. *See also: Italy 1943-1945; Trasimene Line and Sanfatucchio.*

Monte Maro Second World War Italian campaign battle honour marking one of the actions during the advance to the Gustav Line in late 1943. *See also : Italy 1943-1945; Capture of Naples; Cappezano; Monte Stella; Cava di Tirreni; Scafati Bridge; Cardito; Volturno Crossing; Roccheta E Croce and Colle Cedro.*

Monte Ornito Second World War Italian campaign battle honour marking the capture and subsequent successful defence of this feature 2-20 February 1944. *See also: Italy 1943-1945; Garigliano Crossing and Cerasola.*

Monte Pianoerino Second World War Italian campaign battle honour marking one of the actions which took place during the breaching of the Gothic Line in September 1944 and the launching of the final push into the Po Valley in April 1945. *See also: Italy 1943-1945; Montemello-Scorticato Ridge; Monte Reggiano; Savignano; San Martino Sogliano; Monte Casalino; Montilgallo; Carpineta; Monte Cavallo; Casa Bettini; Pideura; Pergola Ridge; Senio Floodbank; Cesena; Conventello-Comacchio; Monte La Pieve; Monte Farneto; Monte Spaduro; Orsara; Tossignano and Catarelto Ridge.*

Monte Piccolo Second World War Italian campaign battle honour marking the capture and subsequent defence, during operations in the Liri Valley of Italy, of this important feature 26-28 May 1944. *See also: Italy 1943-1945; Liri Valley; Hitler Line; Piedemonte Hill; Aquino and Melfa crossing.*

Monte Reggiano Second World War Italian campaign battle honour marking one of the actions which took place during the breaching of the Gothic Line in September 1944 and the launching of the final push into the Po Valley in April 1945. *See also: Italy 1943-1945; Montemello-Scorticato Ridge; Monte La Pieve; Savignano; San Martino Sogliano; Monte Casalino; Montilgallo; Carpineta; Monte Cavallo; Casa Bettini; Pideura; Pergola Ridge; Senio Floodbank; Cesena; Conventello-Comacchio; Monte Farneto; Monte Pianoereno; Monte Spaduro; Orsara; Tossignano and Catarelto Ridge.*

Monte Rivoglia Second World War Sicilian campaign battle honour marking one of a number of actions which took place during the allied advance in 1943. *See also: Sicily 1943; Solarino; Vizzini; Augusta; Francofonte; Lentini; Simeto Bridgehead; Gerbini; Agira; Adrano; Sferro Hills; Salso Crossing; Simeto Crossing; Malleto and Pursuit to Messina.*

Monte Rotondo Second World War Italian campaign battle honour marking one of the actions which took place during the period between the fall of Rome in June 1944 and

the establishment of contact with the Gothic Line in July 1944. *See also: Italy 1943-1945; Monte Gabbione; Ripa Ridge; Gabbiano and Arezzo.*

Monte San Michele Second World War Italian campaign battle honour marking one of the actions during the advance to Florence 17 July-10 August 1944. *See also: Italy 1943-1945; Advance to Florence; Incontro; Monte Domini; and Monte Scalari.*

Monte Scalari Second World War Italian campaign battle honour marking one of the actions during the advance to Florence 17 July-10 August 1944. *See also: Italy 1943-1945; Advance to Florence; Incontro; Monte Domini; and Monte San Michele.*

Montescudo Second World War Italian campaign battle honour marking one of the actions in the Battle of the Rimini Line in September 1944. *See also: Italy 1943-1945; Rimini Line; Ceriano Ridge; Casa Fabri Ridge; Monte Colombo; Frisoni and San Marino.*

Monte Spaduro Second World War Italian campaign battle honour marking one of the actions which took place during the breaching of the Gothic Line in September 1944 and the launching of the final push into the Po Valley in April 1945. *See also: Italy 1943-1945; Montemello-Scorticato Ridge; Monte La Pieve; Savignano; San Martino Sogliano; Monte Casalino; Montilgallo; Carpineta; Monte Cavallo; Casa Bettini; Pideura; Pergola Ridge; Senio Floodbank; Cesena; Conventello-Comacchio; Monte Farneto; Monte Pianoereno; Monte Reggiano; Orsara; Tossignano and Catarelto Ridge.*

Monte Stella Second World War Italian campaign battle honour marking one of the actions during the advance to the Gustav Line in late 1943. *See also: Italy 1943-1945; Capture of Naples; Cappezano; Monte Maro; Cava di Tirreni; Scafati Bridge; Cardito; Volturno Crossing; Roccheta E Croce and Colle Cedro.*

Monte Tuga Second World War Italian campaign battle honour marking one of the actions during operations against the western sector of the Gustav Line across the River Garigliano 17-31 January 1944. *See also: Italy 1943-1945; Garigliano Crossing; Minturno and Damiano.*

Monte Video Battle honour marking the capture of the city by a night assault on 9 February 1807. The action was part of a wider campaign against French and Spanish colonies in the Americas. *See also: Louisburg; Quebec; Detroit; Miami; Niagara and Bladensburg.*

Montgomery of Alamein, 1st Viscount of Hindhead, Field Marshal Bernard Law Montgomery (1887-1976). Educated at St Paul's School, he entered the Army in 1908, was mentioned in despatches in the First World War and promoted to lieutenant colonel in 1931. He commanded 1st Battalion The Royal Warwickshire Regiment 1931-34; was promoted to colonel in 1934, serving on the Directing Staff of the Staff College at Quetta 1934-37. He commanded 9th Infantry Brigade at Portsmouth 1937-38 and 3rd Division 1938-39, taking part in the Dunkirk evacuation. Having commanded a Corps 1940-41 he was promoted to lieutenant general and succeeded General Ritchie as commander of the British Eighth Army in August 1942 under General Sir Harold Alexander, commander-in-chief, Middle East.

Under Montgomery's command the Eighth Army won a great victory when, between 23 October and 7 November 1942, having endured the assaults of Rommel's Axis forces at El Alamein, he turned to the offensive and completely routed the Germans. Montgomery was knighted in November 1942. In March 1943 he again defeated Rommel's reinforced army at the Battle of the Mareth line and followed this with another victory at Akarit and the capture of the Tunisian ports of Gabes, Sfax and Sousse. In the winter of 1943, after a brilliant pursuit of Rommel's army across Libya and Tripolitania, he entered Tripoli and thereby completed the conquest of all Italy's African empire.

In the summer of 1944 he led the Allied armies in the great victory of the Battle of Normandy, commanding 21 Army Group from 'Normandy to the Baltic'. After the war he was appointed Chief of the Imperial General Staff, created a Knight of the Garter and raised to the peerage in 1946. In 1948 he became chairman of the commanders-in-chief of the Western Alliance, formed for the defence of Western Europe, and subsequently Deputy Supreme Commander Allied Powers Europe 1951-58.

Montgomeryshire Yeomanry The Montgomeryshire corps was raised in 1803, disbanded in 1828 and re-raised in 1831. In the South Africa War (1899-1902) the regiment found four companies for The Imperial Yeomanry. The regiment served in England until March 1916 when it moved to Egypt to serve dismounted in the Western Frontier Force. The regiment later served in Palestine, forming 25th (Montgomeryshire and Welsh Horse Yeomanry) Battalion, Royal Welch Fusiliers in 1917. The regiment moved to France in May 1918 and served there until the end of the war. In 1920 the Montgomeryshire Yeomanry was absorbed into the Royal Welch Fusiliers as the 7th (Montgomeryshire) Battalion, and the yeomanry title was never revived.

Montilgallo Second World War Italian campaign battle honour marking one of the actions which took place during the breaching of the Gothic Line in September 1944 and the launching of the final push into the Po Valley in April 1945. *See also: Italy 1943-1945, Montemello-Scorticato Ridge; Monte La Pieve; Savignano; San Martino Sogliano; Monte Casalino; Monte Reggiano; Carpineta; Monte Cavallo; Casa Bettini; Pideura; Pergola Ridge; Senio Floodbank; Cesena; Conventello-Comacchio; Monte Farneto; Monte Pianoereno; Monte Spaduro; Orsara; Tossignano and Catarelto Ridge.*

***Montis Insignia Calpe* (Sign of the rock of Gibraltar)**, motto of The Suffolk Regiment, The Essex Regiment, 56th (West Essex) Regiment of Foot, The Northamptonshire Regiment, 58th

(Rutlandshire) Regiment of Foot, The Royal Highland Fusiliers, The Royal Anglian Regiment and the Devonshire and Dorset Regiment.

Montone Second World War Italian campaign battle honour marking the seizure of the strong position at Montone in the Tiber Valley 5-7 July 1944. *See also: Italy 1943-1945; Advance to Florence; Monte Cedrone and Citta di Castillo.*

Montorsoli Second World War Italian campaign battle honour marking the fighting which took place to the North East of Florence 1-3 September 1944. *See also: Italy 1943-1945 and Fiesole.*

Mont Pincon Second World War battle honour marking the British offensive launched south westwards from the Caumont area on 30 July 1944 to support the US breakout near St Lô, and culminating in the capture of the important terrain at Mont Pincon on 6 August. *See also: North West Europe 1944-1945; Quarry Hill; Souleuvre; Catheolles; Le Perrier Ridge; Brieux Bridgehead; Jurques and La Varinière.*

Monywa 1942 Second World War Burma campaign battle honour marking an action during the withdrawal from Burma. *See also: Burma 1942-1945 and Shwegyin.*

Monywa 1945 Second World War Burma campaign battle honour marking an action during the advance to the River Irrawaddy in late 1944. *See also: Burma 1942-45 and Ukhrul.*

Moodkee Battle honour marking the opening action of the First Sikh War (qv) on 18 December 1845 when a British force under Sir Hugh Gough quite unexpectedly encountered the Sikhs, who had crossed the River Sutlej to invade British India. *See also: Ferozeshah; Aliwal; Sobraon; Chillianwallah; Mooltan; Goojerat and Punjab.*

Mooltan Battle honour marking the action in January 1849 which gave rise to the Second Sikh War (qv). Mulraj, the Governor of Mooltan, was in rebellion against the authorities in Lahore. Mooltan was besieged and finally stormed in February 1849. *See also: Moodkee; Ferozeshah; Aliwal; Sobraon; Chillianwallah; Goojerat and Punjab.*

Mooltan 1857-58 Battle honour marking the success in maintaining order in the Mooltan district during the Indian Mutiny (qv). *See also: Delhi 1857; Lucknow; Behar and Central India.*

Moro Battle honour marking the capture by storm after a months' siege of the Fort of El Moro, key to the defences of Havana, on 30 July 1762. *See also: Havannah.*

Mortar Muzzle-loading weapon with a short barrel and relatively wide bore which fires low velocity bombs in high trajectories.

Morval First World War battle honour marking one of the actions during the British Somme offensive launched on 1 July 1916. *See also: France and Flanders 1914-1918; Somme 1916; Albert 1916; Bazentin; Delville Wood; Pozières; Guillemont; Ginchy; Flers-Courcelette; Thiepval; Le Transloy; Ancre Heights and Ancre 1916.*

Mount Longdon Falklands campaign battle honour marking the attack on Mount Longdon by 3rd Battalion The Parachute Regiment. *See also: Falkland Islands 1982; Tumbledown Mountain; Goose Green and Wireless Ridge.*

Mount Sorrel First World War battle honour marking the heavy fighting which took place in the Menin Road sector of the Ypres salient in July 1916. *See also: France and Flanders 1914-1918; Loos and Somme 1916.*

Mounted Infantry Perhaps the earliest mounted infantry were in effect the dragoons, who were essentially infantrymen mounted on poor horses, mainly for conveyance to a point where they could dismount and fight on foot. In the American War of Independence (qv) forces of mounted infantry like Colonel Banastre Tarleton's 'Legion' and Simcoe's 'Rangers' were employed with considerable success. During the South Africa War (1899-1902) it became apparent that the British Army was severely disadvantaged by its lack of mounted infantry and, in January 1900, significant efforts were made to rectify the position by re-roling both cavalry and infantry regiments into a mounted infantry role. However, the most effective mounted infantry were unquestionably the colonial volunteers.

Mourning Lace *See: Black line in lace.*

Mousehole Charge Explosive charges, often fixed on a crude frame so that they can be held in position against a wall. Used in fighting in built up areas for blowing a 'mousehole' through which access can be obtained to a building, thus avoiding the more obvious points of entry.

Mowdok Second World War Burma campaign battle honour marking an action during which Mowdok was successfully defended during May and June 1944. *See also: Burma 1942-1945; North Arakan; Buthidaung; Razibil; Kaladan; Mayu Tunnels; Alethangyaw; Maungdaw and Point 551.*

***Mox Surgere Victor* (Soon to arise as victor),** motto of 81st (Loyal Lincoln Volunteers) Regiment of Foot.

Moyale Second World War Abyssinian campaign battle honour. *See also: Abyssinia 1940-41; Keren; Jebel Defeis; Jebel Shiba; Gogni; Agordat; Barentu; Karora-Marsa Taclai; Ad Teclesan; Massawa; Mt Engiahat; Marda Pass; Amb Alagi; Afodu; Gambela; El Wak; Mescelit Pass; Wal Garis; Juba; Bulo Erillo; Beles Gugani; Gelib; Alessandra; Goluin; Babile Gap; Bisidimo; Awash; Todenyang-Namaraputh; Soroppa; Giarso; Colito; Wadara; Omo; Gondar; Ambazzo; Kulkaber; Fike and Lechemti.*

Moyland Second World War battle honour marking one of the actions in the campaign in north-west Europe in the advance from the River Roer to the River Rhine 8 February to 10 March 1945. *See also: North West Europe 1944-1945; Rhineland;*

Reichswald; Cleve; Goch; Weeze; Schaddenhof; Hochwald; Waal Flats; Xanten and Moyland Wood.

Moyland Wood Second World War battle honour marking one of the actions in the campaign in north-west Europe in the advance from the River Roer to the River Rhine 8 February to 10 March 1945. *See also: North West Europe 1944-1945; Rhineland; Reichswald; Cleve; Goch; Weeze; Schaddenhof; Hochwald; Waal Flats; Xanten and Moyland.*

Mozzagrogna Second World War Italian campaign battle honour marking the fighting around the town of Mozzagrogna between 27 and 29 November 1943 during which the town was captured, lost and recaptured by British troops. *See also: Italy 1943-1945; Sangro; Fossacesia and Romagnoli.*

MSTAR A lightweight Pulse Doppler J Band all-weather radar currently replacing ZB 298 (qv) for the detection of helicopters, vehicles and infantry.

Msus Second World War North Africa campaign battle honour marking one of the actions which took place in the period between the British withdrawal from Agedabia in March 1941 and the occupation of the El Alamein line in late June. *See also: North Africa 1940-1943; Minqar Qaim; Benghazi; Carmusa; Point 174; Mersa Matruh and Fuka.*

Mt Engiahat Second World War Abyssinian campaign battle honour. *See also: Abyssinia 1940-41; Keren; Jebel Defeis; Jebel Shiba; Gogni; Agordat; Barentu; Karora-Marsa Taclai; Ad Teclesan; Massawa; Moyale; Marda Pass; Amb Alagi; Afodu; Gambela; El Wak; Mescelit Pass; Wal Garis; Juba; Bulo Erillo; Beles Gugani; Gelib; Alessandra; Goluin; Babile Gap; Bisidimo; Awash; Todenyang-Namaraputh; Soroppa; Giarso; Colito; Wadara; Omo; Gondar; Ambazzo; Kulkaber; Fike and Lechemti.*

Mt Popa Second World War Burma campaign battle honour marking an action during operations astride the River Irrawaddy 29 March - 30 May 1945 aimed at destroying the Japanese Twenty-Eighth Army and prevent the escape of enemy forces which remained to the West and in the Arakan. *See also: Burma 1942-45; Irrawaddy;Yenagyaung 1945; Magwe and Kama.*

Muar Second World War Malayan campaign battle honour marking one of the actions during the Japanese advance through Malaya when British troops sought to block Japanese access to Singapore 14-31 January 1942. *See also: Malaya 1941-42; Northern Malaya; Central Malaya; Johore; Batu Pahat and Singapore Island.*

Mufti Term used by those who customarily wear uniform to describe civilian dress. From the Urdu word meaning 'free', the term originally applied to civilian dress of a fixed pattern issued free to the soldier for walking out or private use.

Mulberry Harbour One of two prefabricated floating harbours towed across the English Channel to the French coast to support the Allied invasion of Normandy in June 1944.

Multi-Launch Rocket System (MLRS) Tracked vehicle, based on the United States M2 Bradley chassis, mounting two pallets each containing six 227mm rockets. The rocket warheads contain a large number of high explosive sub-munitions. MLRS has a range of 32,000m and is supported by a Heavy Expanded Mobility Tactical Truck (HEMTT) and trailer carrying further ammunition pallets.

Multinational A force consisting of contingents from two or more nations within a common command structure.

Multinational Airmobile Division (MNAD) NATO airmobile formation to which the British Army contribution is 24 Airmobile Brigade.

Murmansk 1918-19 First World War battle honour marking the actions of British troops at Murmansk, positioned to face a threat from German forces in Finland. The threat reduced and British forces became involved with the Bolsheviks in 1919, advancing some 800 miles to the Lake Onega area before they were withdrawn. *See also: Archangel 1918-19; Troitsa; Siberia 1918-19 and Dukhovskaya.*

Muscat and Oman 1957-59 Campaign, largely spearheaded by the Special Air Service Regiment, in support of the Sultan of Muscat against rebel forces under Imam Ghalib Bin Ali of Oman, his brother Talib Bin Ali and Suleiman Bin Hamyar, sheikh of the Beni Riyam tribe which inhabited the Jebel Akhdar region - a limestone massif with peaks reaching nearly 10,000ft, long believed impregnable. The campaign culminated in the spectacular and successful assault on the Jebel Akhdar. British casualties in the campaign amounted to six killed and six wounded.

Musket A smooth bore, long barrelled, muzzle loading, shoulder gun. Having developed from the earlier snaphaunce (qv), the perfected flintlock (qv) mechanism appeared in about 1630 and was to remain in service until the percussion lock ousted it in the 1840s. The only significant improvement was the rifling of barrels to improve accuracy. *See also: Matchlock; Flintlock; Snaphaunce; Brown Bess and Model 1839 Musket.*

Musketeer Soldier armed with a musket.

Musketry Term applied to the technique of using small arms.

Mustard Gas An oily liquid vesicant (blistering) compound used in chemical warfare. Its vapour causes blindness and burns.

Muster An assembly or parade of military personnel for duty, briefing inspection etc.

Mutiny Within the meaning of the Army Act 1955 'mutiny' is interpreted as being a combination between two or more persons subject to service law, or between persons at least two of whom are subject to service law to: 1. Overthrow or resist lawful authority in Her Majesty's forces or any forces co-operating therewith or in any part of said forces. 2. Disobey such authority in such circumstance as to make the disobedience subversive of discipline, or with the object of avoiding any duty or service against, or in connection with operations against, the enemy. 3. Impede the performance of any duty or service in Her Majesty's forces or in any forces co-operating therewith or in any part of the said forces.

Mutiny Act 1689 This act was introduced, in the absence of any other form of control, for 'punishing officers or soldiers who shall mutiny or desert their Majesties' service'.

Mutton Lancers Nickname given to 2nd Foot, later The Queen's Royal Regiment (West Surrey), and now The Princess of Wales's Royal Regiment (Queen's and Royal Hampshires). The nickname derives from the badge of the regiment when raised in 1661 - the Paschal lamb bearing a flag.

Mutual Support A condition which exists when positions are able to support each other by direct fire, thus preventing the enemy from mounting an attack against any one position without being subjected to direct fire from one or more adjacent positions.

Muzzle The end of a gun barrel farthest from the breach.

Muzzle Loader Firearm receiving the charge and projectile through the muzzle.

Muzzle Velocity The speed at which a projectile leaves the muzzle when a weapon is fired.

My Boy Willie Regimental quick march of The Royal Tank Regiment.

Myebon Second World War, Burma campaign battle honour marking one of the actions in the final stages of the Arakan campaign 12 January - 29 April 1945. Although these operations were largely confined to the coastal area, there were significant actions in the Kaladan Valley. *See also: Burma 1942-1945; Arakan Beaches; Dalet; Tamandu; Taungup; Ramree and Kangaw.*

My Home Regimental slow march (Pipes and Drums) of The Royal Scots Dragoon Guards The Royal Highland Fusiliers, and The Black Watch.

Myinmu Bridgehead Second World War Burma campaign battle honour marking one of the actions in the Battle of Mandalay 12 February - 21 March 1945. *See also: Burma 1942-1945; Mandalay; Myitson; Ava; Fort Dufferin and Maymyo.*

Myitson Second World War Burma campaign battle honour marking one of the actions in the Battle of Mandalay 12 February - 21 March 1945. *See also: Burma 1942-1945; Mandalay; Ava; Fort Dufferin and Maymyo.*

Myohaung Second World War Burma campaign battle honour marking the advance to and capture of Myohaung after ten days' fighting on 25 January 1945. *See also: Burma 1942-1945 and Arakan Beaches.*

Mysore Battle honour marking the Third Mysore War (qv), which included the capture of Bangalore and the first siege of Seringapatam. *See also: Nundy Droog and Seringapatam.*

MYSORE WARS

First Mysore War 1767 British actions against the army of Hyder Ali. Ambur, a fortress in the Carnatic, was successfully defended by a small force of British sepoys under the command of Captain Calvert. *See also: Ambur.*

Second Mysore War 1780-84 On 27 September 1781, Sir Eyre Coote's forces heavily defeated Hyder Ali's army at Sholinghur, even though outnumbered 7:1. Following a disaster to a column led by General Matthews, the commander-in-chief in Bombay, a force of about 1,800 men was besieged in the port of Mangalore by nearly 69,000 troops of Tippoo Sultan, the son of Hyder Ali, from 9 May 1783. Although news of the peace between France and England had arrived on 27 July, the siege continued until 30 January 1784, when the garrison had to surrender. *See also: Sholinghur and Mangalore.*

Third Mysore War 1789-92 The siege of Nundy Droog, a fortress north of Bangalore that had been considered impregnable, began in September 1791 and was carried in an assault by forces under Lord Cornwallis. The fall of Tippoo Sultan's stronghold of Seringapatam on 7 February ended the war that had begun with Tippoo's invasion of Travancore. *See also: Nundy Droog; Seringapatam and Mysore.*

Fourth Mysore War 1799 A further campaign against Tippoo Sultan in 1799 began with a success at Seedaseer for a Bombay column of three brigades commanded by Major General Stuart. Then, after three weeks' siege, the fortress of Seringapatam was captured on 4 May. *See also: Seringapatam.*

N

Nablus First World War Palestinian campaign battle honour marking the action resulting in the capture of the town during Allenby's (qv) decisive offensive launched on 18 September 1918 against the Turkish armies in Palestine. *See also: Palestine 1917-18; Gaza; El Mughar; Nebi Samwil; Jaffa; Jerusalem; Jericho; Tell Asur; Jordan; Megiddo; Sharon and Damascus.*

Naga village Second World War Burma campaign battle honour marking one of the actions in the Battle of Kohima 27 March to 22 June 1944. *See also: Burma 1942-45; Kohima; Defence of Kohima; Aradura; Relief of Kohima and Mao Songsang.*

Nagpore Battle honour marking an action on 16 December 1817 during the Second Mahratta War (qv) in which a force under Brigadier Doveton, intended for the support of the victors of Seetabuldee (qv) defeated Bhonsla's Mahratta army. *See also: Kirkee; Maheidpore; Corygaum; Nowah; Bhurtpore; Hindoostan and India.*

NAIAD Abbreviation for 'Nerve Agent Immobilized Enzyme Alarm System'. A device used to detect the presence of nerve agents and alert troops in the area to the hazard.

Naik An infantry Corporal in the Indian Army. The rank of Lance Naik (Lance Corporal) also existed.

Naktong Bridgehead Korean War battle honour marking the thrust by 27th Brigade from the defensive line covering Pusan, across the River Naktong and on to Songjo 15-25 September 1950. *See also: Korea 1950-53; Pakchon; Imjin; Kowang-San; The Hook 1952; The Hook 1953; Chongju; Chongchon II; Seoul; Chaum-Ni; Hill 327; Kapyong-Chon; Kapyong; Maryang-San and Hill 227 I.*

Namur 1695 Battle honour marking the capture from the French after a two month siege, of the fortress town of Namur by allied troops under King William III. The battle honour was not in fact awarded until February 1910, and is the earliest British European battle honour. However, the 18th Foot was granted the title 'Royal Regiment of Ireland' with the motto *Virtutis Namurcensis Proemium* for the action.

Nanny Goats or Royal Goats Nickname for 23rd Foot, now the Royal Welch Fusiliers, which has a goat, supplied from the Royal herd, as a mascot.

Napalm Petrol gelled by the addition of an aluminium soap of napthalmic and coconut palm fatty acids, forming a sticky flammable substance. Invented in US in 1942 and used in flame-throwers or as a filling for bombs or shells. On ignition the burning napalm clings to objects causing considerable physical and material damage.

Napier, Sir William Francis Patrick (1785-1860) Soldier and historian. Born near Dublin, he joined an Irish regiment in 1800 and subsequently fought in Denmark (1807) and in the Peninsula (1808). Noted for his *History of the War in the Peninsula* (six Vols).

Napier of Magdala, Robert Cornelis Napier, 1st Baron (1810-90) Born at Colombo, Ceylon, he served with distinction through the two Sikh Wars (qv), was present at the relief of Lucknow and later defeated Tantia Topi on the plains of Jaora Alipur. In 1867 he was put in command of the Abyssinian expedition, and for his brilliant action at the storming of Magdala was created a peer. Subsequently he was appointed commander-in-chief of the forces in India (1870), governor of Gibraltar (1876-82), and constable of the Tower (1866). Appointed field marshal in 1883.

Napoleonic Wars The French revolutionary and Napoleonic wars took place between 1792 and 1815. Friction arose from the perceived threat to the established order posed by French revolutionary fervour and Napoleon's attempt to dominate Europe. The 'Decree of November the 19th' (1792) published by the French Convention, offered help 'to all those nations who desired to overthrow their kings'. The opening, contrary to treaty, of the navigation of the Scheldt by the French, and their threatened invasion of Holland, which was protected by a treaty with Britain, threatened British maritime security and European interests. The Duke of York conducted an abortive campaign in Flanders from the summer of 1793 until the British force, having escaped into Germany, was evacuated from Bremen in March 1795. Napoleon invaded Egypt in 1798 but was defeated by Nelson at the Battle of the Nile and, on 1 March 1801, by Sir Ralph Abercromby at Aboukir near Alexandria. Hostilities concluded with the Peace of Amiens in 1802. The second war with Napoleon (1805-15) was caused by Napoleon's annexation of the Parma, Placentia and Piedmont states in Italy and invasion of Switzerland, and the failure of Britain to meet its treaty obligation to leave Malta. Hostilities included the two campaigns in the Peninsula War (1808-09) and (1809-14) and the fall of Napoleon at Waterloo in 1815 which brought the wars to an end.

Narungombe First World War East Africa campaign battle honour marking an action in July 1917 in which a British force very nearly surrounded the German forces before Von Lettow slipped away across the Rufiji River. *See also: East Africa 1914-18; Kilimanjaro; Behobeho; Nyangao and Kamina.*

Narvik Second World War battle honour. On 13 April 1940 a British flotilla forced its way into Narvik Fjord and sank four German destroyers. A combined force of Norwegians, Poles, French and British made a strong attack on the German garrison at Narvik which was captured on 28 May, but on 10 June the Allied force was withdrawn. *See also: Norway 1940; Stien; Pothus; Vist; Kvam and Otta.*

National Army Museum Founded in 1960 and occupying purpose-built premises on the western side of the Royal Hospital (qv) in Royal Hospital Road, Chelsea. The museum houses a collection relating to the history and traditions of the British Army, the Militia, Yeomanry, Volunteers, Territorial Army, Territorial Army and Volunteer Reserve, the Army in India and the armies of the Honourable East India Company. The Museum's Department of Printed Books contains about 4,000 books: a full range of reference works, campaign histories, military biographies and drill books. The archives include the letters, journals and papers of many important military figures including Lord Roberts, Lord Raglan, the 1st Marquess of Anglesey and Lord Rawlinson. The Museum has an outstation at the Royal Military Academy Sandhurst (qv).

National Rifle Association Founded in 1860, and incorporated by Royal Charter in 1890, to encourage rifle shooting in the Queen's Dominions. From 1860-89 rifle meetings were held at Wimbledon, after which they were held at Bisley. The first shot at the first meeting at Wimbledon was fired by Queen Victoria from a Whitworth muzzle-loading rifle. The competitions at Bisley attract marksmen from all parts of the world. The Regular Army Skill at Arms Meeting is held annually at Bisley.

National Service *See: Conscription.*

Naval Crown Superscribed 12th April 1782 Battle honour awarded in 1909 to mark the service of the Welch Regiment in the ships of Admiral Rodney's Fleet when he defeated the French at the Battle of the Saintes.

Naval Crown Superscribed 1st June 1794 Battle honour awarded in 1909 to mark the service of the Queen's and Worcestershire Regiments in the ships of Admiral Howe's fleet when he defeated the French in the Battle of the Glorious First of June.

Naval Crown Superscribed 2nd April 1801 Battle honour awarded to 49th Foot and The Rifle Brigade in 1819 and 1821 respectively to mark their service with the fleet during the Battle of Copenhagen on that date.

Naval Gunfire Support In some instances it is possible to support operations ashore by fire from the guns of HM Ships. On such occasions it is usual for a representative party from the vessels providing support, or a naval gunfire support unit, to operate ashore with the forward troops.

Navy, Army and Air Force Institute (NAAFI) Originally, British army canteens were kept by civilians, but in 1857 they were put under control of the war office, and became a recognised Army institution. They were managed by a small committee of officers, and the goods were sold at practically cost price, any profit being spent for the benefit of the units served. The First World War revolutionised the system; the existing service was inadequate to the task and, in 1915, an Expeditionary Force Canteen (EFC) came into being to provide a canteen service overseas. After paying working expenses and repaying loans, all profits were devoted to the welfare of the troops at the discretion of the Army Council. In 1916 the Navy and Army Canteens Board (NACB) was formed, whose main business lay in the United Kingdom, but it also provided a canteen service overseas, the profits being disbursed in a manner similar to that of the EFC. The EFC, being a purely wartime measure, ceased to exist in 1919, and its stock etc., was taken over by the NACB. In 1920 an interdepartmental committee recommended that the NACB be enlarged and made permanent, and this found effect in the Navy, Army and Air Force Institute (NAAFI), which is under the control of a council of members of the three services. The surplus profits of the EFC and NACB were handed over to the United Services Fund after the dominion, colonial and US forces had been given an appropriate share. The operations of the NAAFI extend to every station at home and abroad, and a percentage of the profits in each locality is paid into unit funds. The NAAFI system, and its operational arm the Expeditionary Forces Institute (EFI) continue to meet the needs of the British army at home and abroad, in peace and at war. *See also: Canteen.*

***Ne Obliviscaris* (Do not forget)** Motto of 91st (Princess Louise's Argyllshire Highlanders) Regiment of Foot, and later of The Argyll and Sutherland Highlanders (Princess Louise's).

Nebi Samwil First World War Palestine campaign battle honour. Nebi Samwil Ridge dominates the western approach to Jerusalem and was captured by 75th Division after some weeks of fighting in early December 1917. The Turks then mounted a series of spirited counterattacks which were repulsed. *See also: Palestine 1917-18; Gaza; El Mughar; Jaffa; Jerusalem; Jericho; Tell Asur; Megiddo; Sharon; Nablus and Damascus.*

***Nec Aspera Terrent* (Nor do difficulties deter)** Motto of The Queen's Royal Hussars (Queen's Own and Royal Irish), The Queen's Own Hussars, 3rd The King's Own Hussars, The King's Own Scottish Borderers, The King's Regiment (Liverpool), The King's Regiment, The Prince of Wales's Own Regiment of Yorkshire, The West Yorkshire Regiment (The Prince of Wales's Own), 27th (Inniskilling) Regiment of Foot, The Royal Inniskilling Fusiliers, and The Royal Welch Fusiliers.

Nederijn Second World War battle honour marking the Second Army efforts to break through to Arnhem and relieve 1st Airborne Division 17-27 September 1944. *See also: North West Europe 1944-1945; Arnhem 1944; Nijmegen; Veghel and Best.*

Neerpelt Second World War battle honour marking the seizure, as darkness fell, of a vital bridge across the Meuse-Escaut canal on 10 September 1944 by 2nd Irish Guards. *See also: North West Europe 1944-1945; Antwerp; Gheel; Hechtel and Aart.*

***Nemo Me Impune Lacessit* (None shall provoke me with impunity)** Motto of The Royal Scots Dragoon Guards (Carabiniers and Greys), The Royal Scots Greys (2nd Dragoons), Scots Guards, The Royal Scots (The Royal Regiment) and The Black Watch (Royal Highland Regiment).

***Nemo Nos Impune Lacessit* (None shall provoke us with impunity)** Motto of The Royal Highland Fusiliers (Princess Margaret's Own Glasgow and Ayrshire Regiment).

Nerve Gas Any of the poisonous gases used in chemical warfare which affect the central nervous system.

Net Term applied to a communication network which links a number of stations. It is usual to identify the nature of the net e.g. command net, logistic net, battalion net.

Neutrality In international law the term neutrality describes the optional status established when one state chooses, expressly or by implication, not to participate in a war existing between third states, which choice is recognised by the belligerents. Neutrality imposes rights and duties upon both neutral and belligerents; essentially it requires the neutral state not to assist either belligerent and to ensure, by maintaining an impartial attitude, that neither belligerent obtains an advantage from the neutral state's behaviour. The rules of neutrality laid down in the 1907 Hague Convention on rights and duties of neutral powers and persons in war on land

(V) and at sea (XIII) are now accepted as general international law.

Neutralise To render an enemy's weapons temporarily ineffective, normally by the use of indirect fire.

Neuve Chapelle First World War battle honour marking the scene of the first British offensive of 1915, mounted on 10 March after a very heavy preparatory bombardment. Neuve Chapelle was captured and an advance of over a mile made across a two mile front. However, it proved impossible to exploit this success and capture the dominant Aubers Ridge. *See also: France and Flanders 1914-1918; Hill 60 and Ypres 1915.*

New Colonial Regimental quick march of the Military Provost Staff Corps.

New Zealand Battle honour marking service in the Maori Wars of 1846-47, 1860-61 and 1863-66, the latter war being particularly bloody due to the influence of the fanatical Hau Hau movement.

New Zealand Cross Gallantry award, unique to New Zealand and awarded only for services in the Maori Wars, instituted by an Order in Council made at Government House, Wellington, on 10 March 1869 'to be conferred on members of the Militia, Volunteers or Armed Constabulary, who may particularly distinguish themselves by their bravery in action, or devotion to their duty while on active service'.
Ribbon: Crimson, 1" wide, identical with that of the Victoria Cross.

New Zealand Medal 1845-1847 And 1860-1866 Authorised on 1 March 1869 to mark service in the campaign against the Maoris.
Ribbon: Dark blue, 1¼" wide, with a ⅜" wide red centre stripe.

Ngakyedauk Pass Second World War, Burma campaign battle honour marking the defeat of the Japanese thrust toward Chittagong during February and March 1944. *See also: Burma 1942-45; North Arakan; Defence of Sinzweya and Imphal.*

Niagara Battle honour marking the capture in December 1813 of Fort Niagara by a force mounted from Upper Canada during the campaign of 1812-14 in North America. *See also: Detroit; Miami; Queenstown and Bladensburg.*

Nickname A nickname is used as a form of easy reference to unclassified matters, and does not require formal approval from the chain of command. Recently nicknames have been much used to refer to major studies and trials such as the recent 'Lean Look' and 'Front Line First' studies. *See also: Codeword.*

Nieuport Battle honour marking the gallant defence, by 53rd Foot and elements of 42nd Foot, of Nieuport in October 1793 during a ten day siege by a force of 12,000 French. *See also: Lincelles; Villers-en-Couches; Beaumont; Willems; Tournay and Egmont-op-Zee.*

Nightingale Florence (1820-1910) Born in Florence; as a young person she did much philanthropic and social work in England, and in 1844 she visited many hospitals and reformatories in Europe. In 1851 she trained as a nurse at an institution of the Protestant Deaconesses at Kaiserwerth on the Rhine. On her return to England she devoted herself to the Governesses' Sanatorium in connection with the London Institute. At the beginning of the Crimean War (1854-55), appalled by the sufferings of the wounded, she volunteered her services and sailed in 1854 with a party of 38 nurses, including Sisters of Mercy from England and Ireland. She became known affectionately as 'the lady with the lamp'.

Nijmegen Second World War battle honour marking the clearing of the town and capture of a bridge over the Waal by British and US forces in late September 1944. *See also: North West Europe 1944-1945; Arnhem; Nederijn; Veghel and Best.*

Nijmegen Company A company formed from the officers and men of 2nd Battalion Grenadier Guards on 3 August 1994 when that battalion was placed in suspended animation. The role of the company is to act as an incremental company to battalions of Foot Guards when carrying out public duties in London. *See also: Grenadier Guards.*

Nil Sine Labore (Nothing without work) Motto of The Royal Corps of Transport.

Nile 1884-85 Battle honour marking the unsuccessful attempt to relieve General Gordon, who was besieged by Mahdists (qv) at Khartoum. *See also: Abu Klea; Kirbekan; Suakin 1885 and Tofrek.*

Ninth Army (Second World War) Formed in 1941 under the command of General Sir Henry Maitland Wilson, chiefly of British and Indian troops. It garrisoned Palestine, Syria and the Lebanon, sending reinforcements to 8th Army (qv) in the North Africa and Italy campaigns, and receiving 8th Army divisions for rest and refitting. It was commanded by Lieutenant General Sir W G Holmes from 3 August 1942 until 3 August 1945.

Nisi Dominus Frustra (Unless the Lord be with us all is in vain) One of the mottoes of The King's Own Scottish Borderers.

Nive Peninsula War (qv) battle honour marking the largely inconclusive encounter battle which took place between the British under Wellington and a strong French force under Soult at Nive 10-13 December 1813. However, the encounter proved to be Soult's last attempt to eject the British from France. *See also: Peninsula; Vittoria; Pyrenees; St Sebastian; Nivelle; Orthes and Toulouse.*

Nivelle Peninsula War (qv) battle honour marking Wellington's action on 10 November 1813 against French positions along the River Nivelle, centred on the Heights of Vera. *See also: Peninsula; Vittoria; Pyrenees; St Sebastian; Nive; Orthes and Toulouse.*

Noddy Suit Soldiers' slang for the nuclear, biological and chemical warfare protective oversuit issued to all ranks.

No Move Before The issue by a commander to his command of a 'no move before' date and time is used to give subordinate formations and units an indication of the time available to them for rest, regrouping and resupply before he intends to commit them to further operations.

Nofilia Second World War North Africa campaign battle honour marking the southern outflanking of the Nofilia position 13-17 December 1942 following the battle of El Alamein. *See also: North Africa 1940-43; El Alamein; El Agheila; Advance on Tripoli and Medinine.*

Noireau Crossing Second World War battle honour marking one of a number of actions which took place between the D-Day landing in Normandy in June 1944 and the crossing of the Seine 25-28 August 1944. *See also: North West Europe 1944-1945; Port-en-Bessin; Tourmauville Bridge; St Pierre La Veille; Estry; La Vie Crossing; La Touques Crossing; Risle Crossing and Foret de Bretonne.*

No Man's Land Term applied to the battle zone between opposing front line trenches in the First World War.

Non-Combatant Member of the army whose duties do not include fighting.

Non-Commissioned Officer A person who carries out the duties of a subordinate officer by virtue of appointment rather than warrant or commission.

Nonne Boschen First World War battle honour marking one of the actions in the First Battle of Ypres which began on 19 October 1914. It was against Nonne Boschen that the Germans made their final drive against Ypres on 11 November. *See also: France and Flanders 1914-1918; Ypres 1914; Langemarck 1914 and Gheluvelt.*

Nordenfelt Gun A hand-cranked three-barrel machine gun. Introduced in 1887 using 0.45" Martini-Henry ammunition. Although converted to 0.303" in 1890, the Nordenfelt was rapidly replaced by the Maxim (qv).

Norfolk Yeomanry (The King's Own Royal Regiment) A troop of cavalry and one of foot were raised in 1782 as The Norfolk Rangers, and accepted as Yeomanry Cavalry in 1794. By 1828 there were three regiments; 1st West, 2nd Mid and 3rd East Regiments of Yeomanry Cavalry. There followed a number of disbandments, changes of titles and reorganisations until, in 1901, a new regiment was raised at the express wish of the King and granted the suffix 'Royal' from its formation. In the First World War the regiment served at Gallipoli and in Egypt, Palestine and the Western Desert. The regiment converted to artillery in 1920, serving as such in the Second World War. In 1947 the Norfolk Yeomanry reformed as an anti-aircraft regiment, amalgamating again with the Suffolk Yeomanry in 1961. By 1967 the regiment formed 202 (Suffolk & Norfolk Yeomanry) Medium Battery of 100 (Eastern) Medium Regiment Royal Artillery (Volunteers), and its successors may now be found in 202 (Suffolk & Norfolk Yeomanry) Field Battery of 100 (Yeomanry) Field Regiment Royal Artillery (Volunteers).

Normandy Landing Second World War battle honour awarded to the units of 3rd, 50th, 6th Airborne and 3rd Canadian Divisions which successfully landed on the Normandy Coast, and on objectives inland, on 6 June 1944 in Operation OVERLORD. *See also: North West Europe 1944-1945; Pegasus Bridge and Merville Battery.*

North Africa 1940-43 Second World War battle honour marking the campaign waged in North Africa between 1940 and 1943. With the entry of Italy into the war in June 1940 the defence of Egypt against the large Italian force in Libya became a high priority. After some skirmishing on the Egyptian frontier in June 1940, the Italians invaded Egypt in September but got only as far as Sidi Barrani when, in December 1940, the British went on the offensive, driving the Italians back through Cyrenaica to

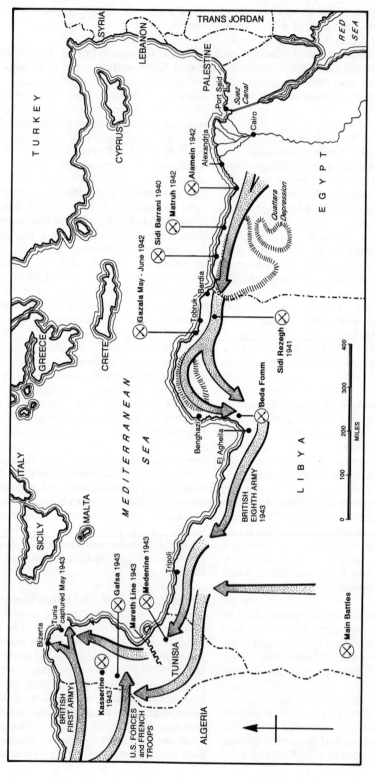

North Africa 1940-43

El Agheila. A number of troops were then detached from North Africa to Greece and Wavell had no longer the resources to exploit his initial success. In the meantime the hard core of the German Afrika Korps under General Rommel had landed in Tripoli, shaken out and, in March 1941, launched an offensive which drove the British back across the Egyptian frontier - although Tobruk was held. In the course of the summer of 1941 the British launched several unsuccessful attempts to expel the Germans until, in early December, following the battles around Sidi Rezegh, Tobruk was relieved and the Germans compelled to leave Cyrenaica. In January 1942 Rommel attacked again, forcing the British back to a defensive position at Gazala, from which the British were subsequently ousted by an Axis attack in May 1942 and driven back into Egypt with the loss of Tobruk. The Axis advance was finally halted by Auchinleck at the first battle of El Alamein which lasted throughout July 1942.

A period of relative inaction then ensued in which the new Eighth Army commander, General Montgomery, prepared to move to the offensive and Rommel, in August 1942, made an unsuccessful attempt to break through the Allied position in the area of Alam Halfa. In October 1942 Montgomery won a decisive victory at the second battle of El Alamein and the subsequent offensive drove the enemy out of Libya and into Tunisia. The Axis forces turned and made a stand at the Mareth Line, but were dislodged and subsequently eliminated in an Allied operation between Eighth Army and Anglo-American forces, including the British First Army which had advanced from Algeria.

North America 1763-64 Battle honour marking the campaign to subdue the Red Indian tribes who had rebelled under the leadership of Pontiac. The most significant action of the campaign was the relief of Fort Pitt (later Pittsburg) which defeated Pontiac's main force as it lay in ambush at Bushy Run.

North Arakan Second World War Burma campaign battle honour marking the 1944 offensive in to the Arakan. The Japanese fought with immense determination, but the British made slow and steady progress, supported by air resupply. *See also: Burma 1942-45; Buthidaung; Razibil; Kaladan; Mayu Tunnels; Alethangyaw; Maungdaw; Mowdok and Point 551.*

Northamptonshire Regiment (48th and 58th Foot) The 48th Foot was raised at Norwich in 1741 as Cholmondeley's Regiment of Foot, numbered 48th Foot in 1751 and titled 48th (Northamptonshire) Foot in 1782. The 58th Foot was raised in 1740, renumbered 47th Foot in 1748, became 60th Foot under the Colonelcy of Robert Anstruther in 1755 and was again renumbered 58th Foot in 1757. In 1782 the regiment was retitled 58th (Rutlandshire) Foot. In 1881 48th (Northamptonshire) Foot and 58th (Rutlandshire) Foot amalgamated to form The Northamptonshire Regiment (48th and 58th Foot). On 1 June 1960 The Royal Lincolnshire Regiment (10th Foot) and Northamptonshire Regiment (48th and 58th Foot) amalgamated to form 2nd East Anglian Regiment (Duchess of Gloucester's Own Royal Lincolnshire and Northamptonshire) Regiment. On 1 September 1964 the regiment amalgamated with 1st East Anglian Regiment (Norfolk and Suffolk) the 3rd East Anglian Regiment (16th/44th Foot) and The Royal Leicestershire Regiment (17th Foot) to form The Royal Anglian Regiment (9th, 10th, 12th, 16th, 17th, 44th, 48th, 56th and 58th Foot) (qv).
Headdress Badge: The castle and key superscribed 'GIBRALTAR'. Beneath, the battle honour 'TALAVERA'. All within a laurel wreath.
History: *History of The Northamptonshire Regiment 1742-1934* by R Gurney (1935); *History of The Northamptonshire Regiment 1934-1948* by W J Jervois (1953); and *The Northamptonshire Regiment* by M Barthrop (1974).

Northamptonshire Yeomanry A regiment of Yeomanry Cavalry was raised by Earl Spencer in 1794 and was in existence until 1828. In 1830 a number of independent troops was raised and all were disbanded by 1873. A new regiment was raised in 1902, serving in France and Italy during the First World War. In 1922 the regiment was reduced to squadron strength and became 25th (Northampton-shire Yeomanry) Armoured Car Company. At the outbreak of the Second World War this squadron expanded rapidly, ultimately forming two regiments, which landed in Normandy and served in North-West Europe. The second regiment was disbanded in August 1944 and the members drafted to other regiments. In 1947 the regiment re-formed as an armoured car regiment and joined the Inns of Court Regiment (qv) in 1961. Converted to Royal Engineers in 1963, the regiment was designated 250 (Northamptonshire Yeomanry) Field Squadron Royal Engineers; the unit was disbanded in 1967.

North Atlantic Treaty Organisation (NATO) The organisation has its origins in the years 1947-48, during which failure to come to terms with the Soviet Union and its satellites during a series of dramatic political events including direct threats to the sovereignty of Norway, Greece, Turkey and other European countries, the June 1948 coup in Czechoslovakia and the illegal blockade of Berlin which began in April 1948, forced the western countries to seek a common economic and security arrangement through the Brussels Treaty of March 1948. The following year, the North Atlantic Treaty was signed on 4 April 1949 in Washington by the USA, UK, Canada, France, Belgium, the Netherlands, Luxembourg, Norway, Denmark, Iceland, Italy and Portugal, under which the USA associated herself with the Western European countries in security arrangements for their common or mutual defence against possible aggression within Article 51 of the United Nations Charter. Greece and Turkey were admitted to the treaty in 1951 (effective 1952), the Federal Republic of Germany was admitted in 1954 and Spain in 1982.

The North Atlantic Treaty Organisation was organised in February 1952, its first secretary-general, Lord Ismay, being appointed in May and the headquarters being in Paris. The principal body of the organisation is the Council, on which members are usually represented by their foreign minister or defence minister and which meets once or twice a year at ministerial level, a permanent representative acting on the minister's behalf at other meetings. In 1950 the Council agreed to the establishment of a unified defence force, under a Supreme Allied Commander Europe (SACEUR), with a Supreme Headquarters Allied Powers Europe (SHAPE) near Paris. In 1966 France withdrew from the integrated military structure, forcing the withdrawal of all NATO troops from French territory and the movement of NATO headquarters to Brussels in October 1967 and the move of SHAPE to Casteau near Mons in March 1967.

The North Atlantic Alliance was thus founded on the basis of a treaty between member states entered into freely by each of them after public debate and due parliamentary process. The treaty upholds their individual rights as well as their international obligations in accordance with the charter of the United Nations. It commits each member country to sharing the risks and responsibilities as well as the benefits of collective security, and requires of each of them the undertaking not to enter into any other territorial commitment which might conflict with their treaty obligations. The fall of the Berlin Wall in November 1989, the unification of Germany in October 1990 and disintegration of the Soviet Union in December 1991 marked the end of the Cold War era, and decisions reached by the NATO Heads of State and Government at their summit meetings in London in July 1990 and in Rome in November 1991 have set NATO's approach to the new world order.

North Irish Brigade An administrative grouping in the infantry formed by Army Order 61 of 1948 comprising The Royal Inniskilling Fusiliers, The Royal Ulster Rifles and The Royal Irish Fusiliers (Princess Victoria's). The regiments of the brigade were amalgamated to form one regiment in July 1968 and that regiment,

The Royal Irish Rangers (27th (Inniskilling) 83rd and 87th) became part of the King's Division (qv).

North West Canada Medal 1858 The medal was authorised on 18 September 1885 for issue to all who had served in the suppression of Riel's rebellion.
Ribbon: blue-grey with two red stripes 2mm from each edge.
Clasp: Saskatchewan.
See also: Fenian Raids.

Northern Ireland Initially the British Army was committed to the support of the Royal Ulster Constabulary under the terms of Military Aid to the Civil Power (qv) in 1969 when severe rioting took place at a number of civil rights marches and demonstrations. Over the subsequent years all the major demands of the civil rights movement have been met, but the republican movement seized the opportunity offered by the widespread civil unrest to seek to further its demand for a united Ireland. As there was no majority interest in a united Ireland in the province, the republican movement, through the Irish Republican Army (IRA) and other republican paramilitary groups has sought to further its case by conducting a mindless and bloody terrorist campaign against the people of the province and the forces of law and order. The counter-terrorist campaign has developed in the British Army a high level of leadership, operational skills and equipment which places it at the very forefront of worldwide counter-terrorist expertise. At the time of going to press (September 1995), a ceasefire by the IRA and other paramilitaries had held for approximately a year, and small-scale reductions in the military presence in Northern Ireland had taken place.

Northern Malaya Second World War Malayan campaign battle honour marking the fighting 8-23 December 1941 during the early part of the Japanese invasion of Malaya which led ultimately to the fall of Singapore. *See also: Malaya 1941-42; Jitra; Grik Road; Central Malaya; Slim River; Ipoh; Kampar; Johore; Batu Pahat; Muar and Singapore Island.*

North Staffordshire Regiment (The Prince Of Wales's) (64th and 98th Foot) The 64th Foot originated in 1756 as 2nd Battalion 11th Foot. The regiment was augmented as a separate regiment under the command of Colonel The Hon John Barrington in April 1758 and ranked as 64th Foot. Designated 64th (2nd Staffordshire) Foot in 1782. The 98th Foot was raised in 1760 and disbanded in 1763, re-raised in 1779 and disbanded in 1784, re-raised as 98th (Highland) Regiment in 1793; and renumbered 91st Foot in 1802. Between 1803 and 1818 the regiment was renumbered and disbanded three times. Re-raised at Chichester in March 1824 under the Colonelcy of Henry Conran and ranked 98th Foot, becoming 98th (The Prince of Wales's) Foot in 1876. In May 1881 the 64th (2nd Staffordshire) Foot and 98th (The Prince of Wales's) Foot amalgamated to form The South Staffordshire Regiment (The Prince of Wales's) and was re-titled two months later as The North Staffordshire Regiment (The Prince of Wales's). On 31 January 1959 the regiment amalgamated with The South Staffordshire Regiment (38th and 80th Foot) to form The Staffordshire Regiment (The Prince of Wales's) (38th, 64th, 80th and 89th Foot) (qv).
Headdress Badge: The Staffordshire Knot ensigned with the Plume, Coronet and motto of the Prince of Wales. Below, a scroll inscribed 'NORTH STAFFORD'.
History: *History of The North Staffordshire Regiment* by H Cook (1970).

Northumberland Yeomanry (The Northumberland Hussars) A troop of yeomanry cavalry had been raised in Newcastle in 1797, but was disbanded in 1802. The Northumberland and Newcastle Regiment of Yeomanry Cavalry was raised in 1819. The regiment provided two companies for the 5th Battalion Imperial Yeomanry in the South Africa War (1899-1902). In the First World War the regiment served in Flanders and France. The 2nd/1st Northumberland Yeomanry served in England and Ireland until 1917 when it moved to France as a Corps Cavalry regiment before being amalgamated with 9th Battalion The Northumberland Fusiliers to form the 9th (Northumberland Hussars Yeomanry) Battalion. After the war the Northumberland Hussars was re-formed as a cavalry unit, but converted to artillery in 1940, serving in that role during the Second World War in the Middle East, Greece, Crete, North Africa and North-West Europe. Re-formed in 1947 the regiment was reduced to cadre strength in 1968 and the regiment is now represented in 'D' and 'HQ' (Northumberland Hussars) Squadrons of The Queen's Own Yeomanry.

North West Europe 1940 Second World War battle honour marking the fighting which took place between the arrival of the British Expeditionary Force in France in 1939 and the final evacuation through Dunkirk. *See also: Dyle; Withdrawal to Escaut; Defence of Escaut; Defence of Arras; Boulogne 1940; Calais 1940; St Omer-La Bassée; Wormhoudt; Cassel; Ypres-Comines Canal; Dunkirk 1940; Somme 1940; St Valery-en-Caux; Saar; Amiens 1940; Arras Counter Attack; French Frontier 1940; Forêt de Nieppe; Withdrawal to Seine and Withdrawal to Cherbourg.*

North West Europe 1942, '44-45 Second World War battle honour, awarded uniquely to the Parachute Regiment, to mark the successful raid by a party from 2nd Battalion The Parachute Regiment on a radio-locating station on the French coast at Bruneval on the night 27-28 February 1942. *See also: Bruneval.*

North West Europe 1944-45 Second World War battle honour marking the campaign in North-West Europe which began with the Allied landing in Normandy on 6 June 1940 and ended with the German surrender. Following the establishment of a 30 mile long allied bridgehead between the Rivers Vire and Orne there followed seven weeks' fierce fighting until the end of July when, the main German weight having been drawn to the British sector, the Americans broke out on the right and triggered an Allied advance which drove the Germans back across the Belgian frontier by the beginning of September 1944. German resistance hardened significantly as the Allies approached the German frontier and the advance to the Rhine involved fierce fighting; the difficulties being compounded by bad weather. The Rhine was eventually crossed in March 1945 the Allies then striking east and north-east until contact was made with the Red Army, the war in Europe ending officially on 8 May 1945. *See also: Normandy Landing; Pegasus Bridge; Merville Battery; Sully; Cambes; Putôt En Bessin; Bréville; Villers Bocage; Tilly Sur Seulles; Odon; Fontenay Le Pesnil; Cheux; Defence of Rauray; Caen; Bourgebous Ridge; Mont Pincon; Falaise; Dives Crossing; Lisieux, Seine 1944; Amiens 1944; Brussels; Antwerp; Neerpelt; Gheel; Hechtel; Aart; Le Havre; Boulogne 1944; Arnhem 1944; Nederrijn; Antwerp-Turnhout Canal; Scheldt; Aam; Venraij; Lower Maas; Meijel; Venlo Pocket; Geilenkirchen; Ourthe; Roer; Zetten; Rhineland; Rhine; Ibbenbüren; Leese; Aller; Brinkum; Bremen; Arnhem 1945 and Southern France.*

Norway 1940 Second World War battle honour marking the brief British campaign in Norway in 1940. On 9 April 1940 the Germans invaded Norway and a hastily mounted British expedition landed at Åndalsnes and Namsos in mid-April tasked to secure Trondheim and halt any German advance from the south. Neither mission was accomplished and the force was evacuated early in May, 15 Brigade fighting a gallant rearguard action to cover the withdrawal from Åndalsnes. Further troops had been sent in the meantime to Narvik in the north which had been seized by the Germans. The town was relieved, but the force had to be withdrawn following the German breakthrough in France. *See also: Stien; Pothus; Vist; Kvam and Otta.*

Norway 1941 Second World War battle honour awarded to the Commandos.

Notice to Move It is the practice in peace and war to hold formations, units and individuals at given degrees of notice to move. This ensures a level of readiness across the army which can be adjusted to meet changing circumstances.

(2nd Nottinghamshire) Regiment of Foot (59th Foot) *See: East Lancashire Regiment.*

Nottinghamshire - Sherwood Foresters Regiment of Foot (45th Foot) *See: The Sherwood Foresters (45th and 95th Foot).*

NOTTINGHAMSHIRE YEOMANRY
The Sherwood Rangers Yeomanry
Three troops were raised in 1794, one of which survived the 1802 disbandments. In 1828 the Sherwood Rangers Yeomanry was raised as a full regiment and provided a company for the 3rd Battalion Imperial Yeomanry during the South Africa War (1899-1902). In the First World War the regiment served as infantry in Gallipoli, Egypt, Salonika and Palestine. During the Second World War the regiment served as cavalry, lorried infantry, coastal artillery and, in 1941, converted to an armoured unit to fight in North Africa and North-West Europe. Reconstituted as an armoured regiment in 1947 the regiment has formed 'B' (Sherwood Rangers Yeomanry) Squadron of The Royal Yeomanry since 1967.

The South Nottinghamshire Hussars
A troop was raised as early as 1794, but it was not until 1826 that the troops were regimented as the South Nottinghamshire Regiment of Yeomanry Cavalry. During the First World war the regiment served at Gallipoli, in Egypt, Palestine and France. The regiment converted to artillery in 1920, serving as such in Palestine, North Africa, Sicily and North-West Europe during the Second World War. In 1947 the regiment re-formed as two artillery regiments, a Field Regiment and a Heavy Regiment. The Royal Horse Artillery title was restored and, in 1967, the regiment formed the South Notts Hussars Yeomanry (Royal Horse Artillery), Royal Artillery (Territorial). The successor sub-unit is 307 (South Notts Hussars Yeomanry RHA) Field Battery of 100 (Yeomanry) Field Regiment Royal Artillery (Volunteers).

Nowah Second Mahratta War (qv) battle honour marking the action on 21 January 1819 when the fort at Nowah was captured from a rebellious chief who had defied the power of the Hyderabad Nizam and the British Resident. *See also: Kirkee; Seetabuldee; Nagpore; Maheidpore; Corygaum; Bhurtpore; Hindoostan and India.*

Noyers Second World War battle honour marking one of the actions in the Battle of Caen 4-18 July 1944. The attack on the village of Noyers, which lies west of the River Odon, took place 15-18 July and, although it failed to capture the village, it did pin down German forces which might have been moved to reinforce the sector south of Caen. *See also: North West Europe 1944-1945; Caen; Hill 112; Orne and Esquay.*

Nullah A stream or drain. From Hindi.

Nulli Secundus (Second to none) Motto of the Coldstream Guards.

Number 1 Dress With the abolition of full dress in the British Army, the remaining orders of dress were numbered in sequence after the naval fashion. The nearest order to a ceremonial full dress was the Number 1 dress, the 'Blues' (or 'Greens' in the case of Light Infantry and Rifle regiments).

Nundy Droog Third Mysore War (qv) battle honour marking the storming on 19 October 1791 of what had been considered by the Mysoreans to be an impregnable stronghold, thus opening the way to the capture of Seringapatam. *See also: Seringapatam and Mysore.*

Nunshigum Second World War Burma campaign battle honour marking one of the actions during the Battle of Imphal from March to June 1944. The vital hill position of Nunshigum dominated the northern approaches to Imphal, and was the nearest point to Imphal that the Japanese managed to reach. During the fighting 5-13 April 1944 the Japanese seized the position, but it was retaken and held. *See also: Burma 1942-45; Imphal; Tuitum; Bishenpur; Kanglatongbi; Sakawng; Tamu Road; Shenam Pass and Litan.*

NW Frontier, India 1914-15, '16-17
First World War battle honour marking

actions on the North-West Frontier of India. It was feared that Turkish entry into the war would provoke a Muslim uprising in the Pathan tribes. Although no general or organised uprising took place trouble did occur in the Tochi area in 1914-15, operations were mounted against the Mohmands in 1916-17 and against the Mahsuds in 1917.

Nut Brown Maiden Pipe air of the Women's Royal Army Corps.

Nutcrackers Nickname for 3rd Foot, later The Buffs, (Royal East Kent Regiment), for their exploits against the French in the Peninsula War.

Nyangao First World War East Africa campaign battle honour marking an action fought at Nyangao in October 1917 which was the last major action to take place in German East Africa, the Germans inflicting heavy casualties on the British before escaping into Portuguese territory. *See also: East Africa 1914-18; Kilimanjaro; Behobeho; Narungombe and Kamina.*

Nyaungu Bridgehead Second World War Burma campaign battle honour marking one of the actions during the Meiktila operations in March 1945. The capture of Meiktila cut off the main Japanese forces from those to the south; Japanese attempts to recapture Meiktila were almost fanatical and cost them very significant numbers of casualties. *See also: Burma 1942-45; Meiktila; Capture of Meiktila; Defence of Meiktila and Taungtha.*

Oak Leaves The tradition of Prince Charles's (later Charles II) escape by hiding in the 'Boscobel Oak' is said to account for the oak leaves on the helmets and in the embroidery of the Household Cavalry. They also feature in the lace of field marshals and general officers.

Oath of Allegiance The Oath of Allegiance currently administered on attestation is: 'I . . . Swear by Almighty God that I will be faithful and bear true allegiance to Her Majesty Queen Elizabeth the Second, Her Heirs and Successors and that I will as in duty bound honestly and faithfully defend Her Majesty, Her Heirs and Successors, in Person, Crown and Dignity against all enemies and will observe and obey all orders of Her Majesty, Her Heirs and Successors and of the Generals and Officers set over me.'

Observation Post Vantage point, usually with some protection from enemy fire, from which enemy activity can be observed or fire directed. Observation posts may be covert or overt depending upon the operational situation.

Obstacle Natural or man-made obstruction, or combination of both, which will impede progress. Obstacles are described as being natural (rivers, slopes, trees etc.) or man-made (embankments, buildings etc.). When improvements are made to existing obstacles to enhance their delaying capability they are described as reinforced obstacles.

Obturation The sealing of the breech of a gun, or of a round within a barrel, to prevent the escape of gases following firing, thus increasing the velocity of the projectile.

Occupy Move into, and properly organise, an area to be used as a battle position.

Odon Second World War battle honour marking the British offensive 25 June - 2 July 1944 across the River Odon, aimed at encircling Caen from the south-west. Some progress was made, but attempts to exploit across the River Orne, and to capture the vital ground at Hill 112 were unsuccessful. *See also: North West Europe 1944-1945, Villers Bocage, Tilly sur Seulles, Fontenay le Pesnil; Cheux and Caen.*

Officer Person in the Army who holds a position of authority by virtue of a commission or warrant.

Officer Cadet School (OCS) *See: Royal Military Academy -Sandhurst.*

Officer Cadet Training Unit (OCTU) These units were established to meet the demands of a rapidly increasing officer training requirement brought about by the Second World War. Officer cadets wore white discs or patches behind the cap badge and white gorget patches. Most universities currently support an Officer Cadet Training Unit, but cadets are nevertheless required to undertake the full officer training programme at the Royal Military Academy, Sandhurst, before commissioning. *See also: Royal Military Academy - Sandhurst.*

Oft in the Stilly Night Regimental slow march of the Ulster Defence Regiment.

Old Bold Fifth Nickname for 5th Foot, later the Royal Northumberland Fusiliers.

Old Braggs Nickname for 28th Foot, later the Gloucestershire Regiment, from Lieutenant General Philip Bragg, Colonel of the Regiment 1734-59.

Old Contemptibles Nickname given to members of the British Expeditionary Force (qv) to France in 1914. So named from the Kaiser's alleged reference to them as a 'contemptible little army'.

Old Dozen Nickname for 12th Foot, later the Suffolk Regiment.

Old Fogs Nickname for 87th Foot, later the Royal Irish Rifles (Princess Victoria's), the name being taken from their war cry at Barrossa (1811), *'Faugh-a-Ballagh'* (Clear the Way).

Old Monmouthshire Regimental march (Military Band) of 7th Duke of Edinburgh's Own Gurkha Rifles.

Old Soldier An experienced soldier or veteran. The term is also applied to those seeking to avoid their duties by using well-tried excuses. hence, 'to come the old soldier' meaning to play upon the inexperience of another to one's own advantage.

Olivet Thread covered shapes or moulds worn instead of buttons.

Oman *See: Muscat and Oman 1957-59 and Dhofar 1970-76.*

Omars Second World War North Africa campaign battle honour marking one of the actions in the battle for Tobruk in 1941. Over the period 22 November - 2 December 1941 the enemy defensive positions on the frontier, known as the Omars, were eliminated. *See also: North Africa 1940-1943; Tobruk 1941; Gubi I; Sidi Rezegh 1941; Tobruk Sortie; Belhamed; Gabr Saleh; Taieb El Essem; Gubi II and Relief of Tobruk.*

Omdurman Regimental slow march of The Queen's Royal Lancers.

O'Meara, Barry Edward (1786-1836) Irish surgeon to Napoleon in St Helena. He entered the Army in 1804 as assistant-surgeon, served in Sicily and Calabria, and in 1807 went with General Fraser to Egypt, but was dismissed from the Army the same year for being second in a duel. After this he served as a naval surgeon, and was in *Bellerephon* when she conveyed Napoleon to St Helena. Here he remained for three years as surgeon to Napoleon, but being accused of intriguing with Napoleon, was recalled. In 1822 he published *Napoleon in Exile*, in which he attacked the treatment of Napoleon.

Omnia Audax **(In all things daring)** Motto of The Lancashire Fusiliers.

Omo Second World War Abyssinian campaign battle honour marking an action when the River Omo was crossed in October 1941 during the final stages of the campaign. *See also: Abyssinia 1940-41; Keren; Jebel Defeis; Jebel Shiba; Gogni; Agordat; Barentu; Karora-Marsa Taclai; Ad Teclesan; Mescelit Pass; Mt Engiahat; Massawa; Amb Alagi; Afodu; Gambela; El Wak; Moyale; Wal Garis; Juba; Bulo Erillo; Beles Gugani; Gelib; Alessandra; Goluin; Babile Gap; Bisidimo; Awash; Todenyang-Namaraputh; Soroppa; Giarso; Colito; Wadara; Marda Pass; Gondar; Ambazzo; Kulkaber; Fike and Lechemti.*

On Call Target A planned target on which fire is delivered when requested.

On Parade Regimental quick march of The Royal Logistic Corps.

One And All Motto of the County of Cornwall, 32nd (Cornwall) Light Infantry and later The Duke of Cornwall's Light Infantry.

One Up Term used to describe the number of units or sub-units in the vanguard of an advance, or nearest the enemy in a defensive position e.g. one up, two up etc.

Operation An action with a specified military objective.

Operational Concerned with operations. Alternatively, fit to engage in operations, or level of command between the strategic and tactical levels.

Operational Doctrine *See: Doctrine.*

Operations Officer An officer found at regimental and battalion level responsible to the commanding officer for operational staff matters.

Operator Any person operating equipment, but more usually used to denote a radio operator.

Opheusden Second World War battle honour marking one of a number of actions which took place in North-West Europe between the crossing of the River Seine in August 1944 and arrival on the Rhine in March 1945. *See also: North West Europe 1944-1945; Seine 1944; Brussels; Nederijn; Scheldt; Rhineland; Heppen and Asten.*

Opium War Name given to hostilities between Britain and China 1839-42, following the destruction of opium brought into China by British traders. The war resulted in the cession of Hong Kong and the opening of several ports to British trade. *See also: China - First China War.*

Opportunity Target An unexpected target engaged as it appears.

Oppy First World War battle honour marking the furthest point reached by the British Arras offensive of 9 April - 4 May 1917, during which the position held out against all assaults. However, it was captured in a local offensive action of 28 June 1917. *See also: France and Flanders 1914-1918; Arras 1917; Bullecourt; Hill 70 and Messines 1917.*

Optics Generic term for all vision enhancing equipment such as sights and night vision aids.

Or Glory Motto of 17th Lancers, 17th/21st Lancers and The Queen's Royal Lancers.

Orange Lilies Nickname for 35th Foot, later the Royal Sussex Regiment (qv). The regiment was raised in Belfast in 1701 by the Earl of Donegal, who chose orange facings in honour of William III. The 'lilies' comes from the white plumes which the regiment took from the French Regiment of Royal Roussillon, whom they defeated at Quebec in 1759.

Orders The instructions designed to co-ordinate the efforts of individuals and groups in such a manner as to achieve a desired objective. Such instructions may be given on a daily or routine basis, or for specific operations. The term is also used in some regiments to describe the routine parade at which commanding officers hear disciplinary cases and conduct interviews. *See also: Memorandum; Orderly Room and Levee.*

Order of Battle A listing of all the units and sub-units in a given formation or theatre. The order of battle will change from peace to war and from operation to operation.

Order of March The sequence in which vehicles or personnel are to move along a given route.

Order of the British Empire The medal of the Most Excellent Order of the British Empire was instituted by Letters Patent dated 4 June 1917 which were published in the London Gazette of 24 August 1917. The medal formed part of the Order of the British Empire to which persons, including foreigners, who had rendered important services to the Empire were to be admitted. The Medal of the Most Excellent Order of the British Empire was superseded on 29 December 1922 by the institution of the Medal of the Most Excellent Order of the British Empire for Gallantry (commonly known as the Empire Gallantry Medal), and the Medal of the Most Excellent Order of the British Empire, for Meritorious Service. The Military and Civil Medal of the Order was open to 'persons who perform acts of gallantry warranting such mark of Our Royal appreciation'. By an Additional Statute of 6 December 1957, notified in the London Gazette of 14 January 1958, it was announced that those receiving the medal in 'the Military or Civil Division, in recognition of gallantry, shall wear on the riband from which the badge or medal is suspended a silver Emblem of two oak leaves, and in the announcement of the conferment it shall be stated that the award has been made for gallantry'.

Ribbon: For the Civil Division this was purple and 1 and ¹⁄₁₆" wide; for the Military Division it was as for the Civil Division but with the addition of a vertical red stripe in the centre about ¹⁄₁₀" wide. On 30 July 1937, the Civil Division ribbon was changed to rose pink edged with pearl grey stripes and 1" wide; the ribbon of the Military Division was to be as for the Civil Division with the addition of a vertical pearl grey stripe in the centre about ¹⁄₁₆" wide.

Orderly A junior rank detailed to carry orders or to execute minor tasks in support of an officer. On operations he is usually also a runner, radio operator and/or driver. *See also: Batman and Soldier Servant.*

Orderly Officer The officer or warrant officer, usually detailed daily by the Adjutant, whose duty it is to take charge of the security of the unit's barracks or camp. Sometimes known as the officer of the day or picket officer.

Orderly Sergeant The senior non-commissioned officer, usually detailed daily by the Regimental Sergeant Major, who assists the Orderly Officer (q,v.) in the conduct of his duties.

Order of the Day The general directive of a commander-in-chief or the specific instructions of a commanding officer.

Orderly Room The room, or general area, in which individual and unit records are held, and in which the unit's clerks carry out their duties. The term orderly room is also used in some regiments to describe the routine parade at which a commanding officer hears disciplinary cases and conducts interviews. *See also: Levée; Memorandum and Orders.*

Ordnance Originally cannon or artillery; the term is now more generally applied to any weapons, ammunition and equipment.

Orientation The act of aligning the map with the ground and identifying the key features of the map on the ground.

Orne Second World War battle honour marking one of the actions during the Battle for Caen 4-18 July 1944. *See also: North West Europe 1944-1945; Caen; Hill 112; Noyers See and Esquay.*

Orsara Second World War Italian campaign battle honour marking one of the actions during the breaching of the Gothic Line in September 1944 and the launching of the final push into the Po Valley in April 1945. *See also: Italy 1943-1945; Montemello-Scorticato Ridge; Monte Reggiano; Savignano; San Martino Sogliano; Monte Farneto; Montilgallo; Carpineta; Monte Casalino; Casa Bettini; Pideura; Pergola Ridge; Senio Floodbank; Cesena; Conventello-Comacchio; Monte La Pieve; Monte Pianoereno; Monte Spaduro; Monte Cavallo; Tossignano and Catarelto Ridge.*

Orsogna Second World War Italian campaign battle honour marking one of the actions on the Eighth Army front in southern Italy in 1943. *See also: Italy 1943-1945; Landing at Porto San Venere; Taranto; San Salvo; Impossible Bridge and Caldari.*

Orthes Peninsula War (qv) battle honour marking the action fought by Wellington's army on 27 February 1814 with the intention of driving the French well clear of Bayonne. *See also: Peninsula; Nivelle; Nive and Toulouse.*

Otta Second World War Norwegian campaign battle honour marking one of the actions in Norway in 1940. *See also: Norway 1940; Stien; Pothus; Vist and Kvam.*

Oudenarde Battle honour marking Marlborough's great victory over the French under Vendôme on 30 June 1708 in Flanders during the War of the Spanish Succession (1702-13). After the battle Marlborough wanted to thrust deep into

France, but the allies would not agree and he was obliged to besiege Lille the 'key to Northern France'. *See also: Blenheim; Ramillies and Malplaquet.*

Oudna Second World War North Africa campaign battle honour marking the seizure on 30 November 1942 of Oudna airfield south of Tunis by 2nd Battalion The Parachute Regiment having been dropped some distance from their objective and 30 miles from the nearest British troops. Although surrounded the battalion was later successfully withdrawn. *See also: North Africa 1940-1943; Medjez El Bab; Tebourba Gap; Bou Arada; Robaa Valley and Kasserine.*

Oued Zarga Second World War North Africa campaign battle honour marking the advance of the British V Corps to occupy the line Touhabeur-Chaouach 7-15 April 1943. *See also: North Africa 1940-1943; Djebel Rmel; Mergeb Chaouach; Djebel Bel Mahdi; Djebel Bech Chekaoui and Djebel Ang.*

Ourthe Second World War battle honour marking operations along the River Ourthe, particularly around Bure, in support of the US counter-offensive in the Ardennes 3-14 January 1945. *See also: North West Europe 1944-1945; Roer and Zetten.*

Outer The outermost ring of a shooting target. *See also: Bullseye; Inner and Magpie.*

Outflank To go around the flank of an enemy, thus rendering his position untenable by appearing to his rear or forcing him to move. Also 'to get the better of'.

Outgun To surpass in fire-power. Also to surpass or excel generally.

Outlying Distant or remote from the main position or main body of the force.

Outmanoeuvre To secure a tactical or strategic advantage by skilful manoeuvre.

Outram, Sir James (1803-63) Entered the Indian Army in 1819, and soon acquired a reputation not only as a soldier but also as a political agent. He rendered valuable service in the First Sikh War (qv), and from 1847-51 was resident at Baroda, and from 1855 in Oudh. He went with Havelock to the relief of Lucknow, and commanded the garrison there during the siege. He was created baronet in 1858 and appointed military member of Lord Canning's council.

Outrank To be of higher rank than, or take priority over, another.

Outrider One who rides in front of or beside a vehicle, particularly a carriage, to clear a passage and provide security.

Outshoot To surpass or excel at shooting.

Overalls Originally intended to be worn over breeches and hose in action or on informal duties. When breeches and gaiters became obsolete in full dress in 1823, the term 'trousers' became common for infantry, but overalls continued in use in the cavalry and the term slowly became applied to the tight fitting trousers, often with a coloured vertical stripe or stripes along the outer seam, usually worn with ceremonial uniform or mess dress.

Overbear To be at a strength above the permitted establishment.

Overshoot To cause projectiles to land beyond the selected target.

Overt Operations Operations open to view and observable by an enemy or potential enemy.

Oxford Blues Nickname for The Royal Horse Guards and dating from 1690 when the Earl of Oxford was their commander; the 'Blues' is taken from their blue tunic which dates from 1661. The nickname was later shortened to 'The Blues' and was incorporated in the regiment's title as The Royal Horse Guards (The Blues). In March 1969 the regiment amalgamated with the Royal Dragoons (1st Dragoons) to form The Blues and Royals (Royal Horse Guards and 1st Dragoons) (qv).

Oxford Mixture A strong dark grey cloth used mainly for uniform trousers.

(Oxfordshire) Regiment of Foot (Light Infantry) (52nd Foot) *See: Oxfordshire and Buckinghamshire Light Infantry (43rd and 52nd Foot).*

Oxfordshire and Buckinghamshire Light Infantry (43rd and 52nd Foot) In 1748 the 54th Foot was renumbered 43rd Foot, and titled 43rd (Monmouthshire) Foot in 1782. In 1803 the regiment was redesignated 43rd (Monmouthshire Light Infantry) Regiment. In 1757 the 54th Foot, which had been raised in December 1755, was renumbered 52nd Foot. In 1782 the regiment was retitled 52nd (Oxfordshire) Foot and in 1803 52nd (Oxfordshire Light Infantry) Regiment. In 1881 43rd (Monmouthshire Light Infantry) Regiment amalgamated with 52nd (Oxfordshire Light Infantry) Regiment to form The Oxfordshire Light Infantry. In 1908 the title was changed to The Oxfordshire and Buckinghamshire Light Infantry (43rd and 52nd Foot). On 7 November 1958 the regiment was redesignated 1st Green Jackets (43rd and 52nd). On 1 January 1966 the regiment amalgamated with 2nd Green Jackets (The King's Royal Rifle Corps) and 3rd Green Jackets (The Rifle Brigade) to form The Royal Green Jackets (qv).

Headdress Badge: A stringed bugle-horn.

History: *Historical Records of The 43rd Regiment, Monmouthshire Light Infantry* by R Levinge (1868); *Historical Record of The 52nd Regiment, Oxfordshire Light Infantry* by R Bentley (1860); *The Oxfordshire and Buckinghamshire Light Infantry* by P Booth (1971); *History of 43rd and 52nd in The Great War* by J E H Neville (1938); *War Chronicles of The Oxfordshire and Buckinghamshire Light Infantry 1939-1945* (4 Vols) by J E H Neville (1949) and *An Outline History of The Oxfordshire and Buckinghamshire Light Infantry* by J M A Tillett (1990).

Oxfordshire Yeomanry (The Queen's Own Oxfordshire Hussars) The North Wooton troop was raised in 1798 and regimented in 1818 to for the North-West Regiment of Oxfordshire Yeomanry Cavalry, later the 1st Regiment. Other troops existed at different periods in the county, and the Oxfordshire Regiment of Yeomanry Cavalry was accepted for service in 1828, providing a company for 10th Battalion Imperial Yeomanry during the South Africa War (1899-1902). At the outbreak of the First World War the regiment went with the British Expeditionary Force (qv) to France, serving mounted in Flanders and France throughout the war. The regiment converted to artillery in 1920 serving in that role throughout the Second World War. Re-formed as a field artillery regiment after the war, the regiment amalgamated with the Buckinghamshire Yeomanry in 1950 to form 299 (Royal Bucks Yeomanry and Queen's Own Oxfordshire Hussars) Field Regiment Royal Artillery. Subsequently converted to signals, the successor sub-unit is 5 (Queen's Own Oxfordshire Hussars) Squadron, 39 (City of London) Signal Regiment (Special Communications) (Volunteers).

Paardeburg South Africa War battle honour marking an action during the war of 1899-1902. The Boer army under General Cronje had been surrounded in a bend of the Modder River at Paardeburg against which, on 18 February 1902, the British launched a series of ill-conceived, piecemeal attacks which were repulsed with huge casualties to the British. The Boer position was subjected to heavy artillery bombardment for some days and Cronje eventually surrendered on 27th February. *See also: South Africa 1899-1902; Modder River and Relief of Kimberley.*

Pack Container carried on the upper or lower back and forming part of a soldier's equipment.

Pack Drill Military punishment which entailed the offender being drilled in full equipment.

Pack Saddle Saddle designed for the carriage of loads on military pack animals.

Padang In Malaya, an open space used for parades, meetings and sports. *See also: Maidan.*

Padre A chaplain in the Army.

Pag Cloth tied over the head under the turban by Hindus.

Paget's Irregular Horse Nickname given to the 4th Hussars, now The Queen's Hussars (Queen's Own and Royal Irish). When the regiment returned to England in 1842 under Colonel Paget, it had lost almost 900 officers and men in its 20 years

in India. The replacements were not as well trained as the original men and the general standard fell, hence the nickname.

Pakchon Korean War battle honour marking a counter-attack by British and Australian battalions on 4-5 November 1950 which restored the US line after a North Korean penetration. *See also: Korea 1950-53; Naktong Bridgehead; Imjin; Kowang-San; The Hook 1952; The Hook 1953; Chongju; Chongchon II; Seoul; Chaum-Ni; Hill 327; Kapyong-Chon; Kapyong; Maryang-San and Hill 227 I.*

Palestine 1917-18 First World War battle honour commemorating the campaign in Palestine. Because of the evacuation of Gallipoli and the surrender of the British force under General Townshend at Kut (qv), British prestige in the Near East had declined. The success of operations in Palestine was a material factor in restoring confidence. British troops under Sir Archibald Murray began the offensive by advancing from northern Egypt and driving the Turks before them over the Sinai Desert. A halt then ensued to give time for the construction of a military railway from Kantara to Rafa on the south-west border of Palestine, from which the advance was resumed northward along the coast. But at this point the advancing force was held up by Turkish resistance at Gaza, the chief battle for the town being on 26 March 1917.

This check, however, marked the limit of Turkish success; General Murray was replaced by General, later Field Marshal, Allenby (qv) and the offensive was resumed in October. A considerable

Turkish force was occupied with operations against the Arabs of the Hedjaz East of the Dead Sea. Allenby took Beersheba in a surprise attack and then fought the Second Battle of Gaza on 6 November, the town falling on the following day. This success heralded the beginning of Allenby's victorious thrust through Palestine; Jerusalem was captured after the battles fought 7-9 December 1917, three weeks after the British had taken Jaffa, the latter town having fallen after the cutting of the Jerusalem-Jaffa railway at Ludd. Jerusalem was encircled, all the outer Turkish positions being taken by storm, and the city surrendered without standing a siege.

The following year Jericho was taken after fighting 19-21 February, and thereafter followed a long halt in operations during which the British hold on the country was consolidated. The culminating battle in the Palestine operations was that of Megiddo, 19-25 September 1918, which followed a brilliant outflanking move by the Desert Mounted Corps under the Australian cavalryman, Lieutenant General Sir H G Chauvel. The Arab effort, under T E Lawrence (qv) was of considerable value, and it was not the least of Allenby's achievements that he should have made the best of such volatile allies. *See also: Gaza; El Mughar; Nebi Samwil; Jaffa; Jerusalem; Jericho; Tell Asur; Jordan; Megiddo; Sharon; Nablus and Damascus.*

Palestine 1945-48 Campaign arising from the exercising by Britain of the 1917 League of Nations Mandate for Palestine and the associated Balfour Declaration of November 1917 to establish 'a National Homeland for the Jews'. In a White Paper of March 1939 the British government, responding to Arab concerns at the prospect of large-scale Jewish immigration, sought to restrict it to 75,000 over the next five years. The result was the disaffection of both Arab and Jew and a deep suspicion of Britain. With the exception of the notorious Stern gang, most Jews co-operated with Britain during the Second World War. Following the war Jewish paramilitary organisations such as Irgun, Lehi, and later the more moderate Haganah, waged a campaign of steadily escalating and increasingly bestial violence against the British, the problem being compounded by groups of armed and disaffected Palestinians. In November 1947 the United Nations decided on partition for Palestine, giving the Jews approximately half of Palestine although they only represented one third of the population. This provoked intense clashes between the Palestinian and Jewish communities. The plan of the British government was now to get out as quickly and painlessly as possible. The last British soldier left Palestine on 30 June 1948, the British Army having lost 223 killed and 478 wounded in the campaign.

Palisade Strong fence made of stakes driven into the ground to form a defensive perimeter.

Pallet A standard sized platform of box section open at two ends, to which loads may be secured, to permit the use of mechanical handling devices.

Palliasse A straw-filled mattress.

Palmyra Second World War Syrian campaign battle honour marking the capture of this desert airfield following offensive operations 21 June-1 July 1941. *See also: Syria 1941; Merjayun; Jebel Mazar and Deir Es Zor.*

Pals Battalions Battalions raised during the First World War as part of 'Kitchener's Army', and so called because it was guaranteed that recruits from a given locality would serve together. Although this was an attractive recruiting measure, it meant that some of the more severe battles wiped out a significant part of the male population of a relatively small area of the United Kingdom.

Panga Long, broad-bladed knife used in East Africa.

Pantaloons Close-fitting breeches reaching to the ankle, often coloured, originating in the 18th century. Although largely out of fashion by 1854, cloth pantaloons, of Berlin diagonal weave, were approved by

Queen Victoria for wear at evening functions and levées.

Parachute Regiment Formed under Army Order 128 of 1 August 1942, although a battalion of volunteer parachute troops had been formed, under Churchill's orders, at Ringway airport near Manchester, in June 1940 from No 2 Commando. The unit was renamed 11th Special Air Service Battalion in November 1940 and became 1st Parachute Battalion in September 1941. During 1941-42 three more battalions were formed, and the four were regimented as battalions of The Parachute Regiment on 1 August 1942. For administrative purposes the regiment was attached to the Army Air Corps (qv), but in 1949 it was transferred to the infantry of the line as a regiment in its own right. Until 1953 the regiment was manned by volunteers seconded from other units, but in that year direct enlistment was authorised for other ranks and, in 1958, a regular cadre of officers was approved, officers now being commissioned direct into the regiment.
Headdress Badge: Within a pair of wings an open parachute, ensigned with the royal crest.
Motto: *Utrinque Paratus* (Ready for anything).
Regimental marches:
Quick march: *Ride of the Valkyries.*
Slow march: *Pomp and Circumstance No 1.*
Regimental headquarters: Browning Barracks, Aldershot, Hampshire, GU11 2BU.
History: *The Red Devils* by G G Norton (1971); *The Story of The Parachute Regiment at War 1940-45* by H St G Sanders (1950) and *The Second World War 1939-45 - Airborne Forces* by T B H Otway (1991).

Parade An ordered military assembly or procession.

Parade Ground Large open space in camp or barracks used primarily for drill and parades.

Parapet A mound of earth around a trench giving protection from fire. Also, a breastwork of earth or timber.

Paratroops Troops trained and equipped to be dropped by parachute.

Parka Warm knee-length outer garment with hood for use in cold weather. The parka forms the outer layer of the combat kit range of field clothing.

Parole A military term from the French *parole d'honneur* (word of honour). This is a prisoner's promise that, if released, he will not attempt to escape or again take up arms in the conflict in which he has taken part. It is a rule of international law that prisoners of war may be set at liberty on parole only if the laws of their country authorise it. In such a case the prisoner must scrupulously observe the terms of his parole and cannot be forced by any government to undertake any service contrary to that parole. A prisoner of war cannot be forced to accept liberty on parole; similarly, a hostile government is not obliged to assent to a prisoner's request to be set at liberty on parole. The acceptance of liberty on parole is in direct conflict with the British Army's view that it is every serving man's duty to escape from captivity.

Partisan A staved weapon with a broad blade pointed at the top, and with a cutting edge on both sides. In the early 17th century partisans were carried by lieutenants and captains as a sign of rank. Withdrawn in 1684, partisans are still in use by Yeomen of the Guard. Alternatively, a guerrilla soldier in wartime.

Passage of Lines An operation in which one force moves through another force, either forward - to come into, or rearward - to come out of, contact with the enemy.

Passchendaele First World War battle honour marking the actions in the final phase of the Third Battle of Ypres 31 July - 10 November, fought largely in appalling weather conditions, which resulted in the capture of Passchendaele Ridge and the remains of the village. *See also: France and Flanders 1914-1918; Ypres 1917; Pilckem; Langemarck 1917; Menin Road; Polygon Wood; Broodseinde and Poelcappelle.*

Pass Out To satisfactorily complete a course of instruction. The event is sometimes marked by a 'passing out' parade.

Patchett *See: Sterling.*

Patrol A patrol is a formed unit of men and/or vehicles whose strength, weaponry and composition will be dictated by the task. There are three types of patrol: standing patrols, tasked to give early notice of enemy activity; reconnaissance patrols, tasked with gathering specific information; and fighting patrols, tasked with offensive operations.

Patrol Jacket The patrol jacket was worn increasingly from about 1867 instead of the blue frock coat. The jacket was of blue cloth, rounded in front and edged with black mohair braid all round and up the openings at the side. The front had four double drop-loops, netted olivets and pockets with flaps. The jacket was fastened by hooks and eyes at the front.

Patrol Master The officer responsible for the detailed organisation and co-ordination of patrols.

Patron Secure speech system linking district and higher headquarters within the United Kingdom. *See also: MENTOR.*

Paungde Second World War Burma campaign battle honour marking the offensive actions in the area from 28 to 30 March 1942 in an attempt to relieve Japanese pressure on the Chinese. *See also: Burma 1942-45; Sittang 1942; Pegu 1942; Taukyan; Yenangyaung 1942; Kyaukse 1942; Monywa 1942 and Donbaik.*

Paymaster Officer, formerly of the Royal Army Pay Corps and now of the Staff and Personnel Support Branch of the Adjutant General's Corps, held on the strength of a unit to handle all matters of pay and allowances, personnel records and occurrences, and to advise the commanding officer of accounting procedures. *See also: Royal Army Pay Corps.*

Paymaster-in-Chief Formerly the professional head of the Royal Army Pay Corps and now senior pay officer of the Staff and Personnel Support Branch of the Adjutant General's Corps. *See also: Royal Army Pay Corps.*

Peacekeeping Operations Those operations designed to prevent or contain outbreaks of fighting between hostile parties.

Peacemaking Operations Those operations designed to impose and maintain peace between warring parties.

Peebleshire Yeomanry A troop of cavalry was raised by Sir James Montgomery in 1803, and a further troop was raised, based on Eddleston, following the Radical disturbances of 1820. The Peebleshire Yeomanry Cavalry was disbanded in 1827.

Pegasus Bridge Second World War battle honour marking the capture and securing, in the early hours of 6 June 1944, of the two bridges over the Caen Canal and River Orne by a glider-borne force. *See also: North West Europe 1944-1945; Normandy Landing and Merville Battery.*

Pegu Second Burma War (1852-53) (qv) battle honour marking the annexation of the Province of Pegu, which included Rangoon, by an expedition under the command of General Godwin.

Pegu 1942 Second World War Burma campaign battle honour marking the rearguard action of 6-7 March 1942 covering the withdrawal from Rangoon. *See also: Burma 1942-45; Sittang 1942; Taukyan and Paungde.*

Pegu 1945 Second World War Burma campaign battle honour marking one of the actions in the final drive south to capture Rangoon, launched in conjunction with seaborne landings 1 April-6 May 1945. *See also: Burma 1942-45; Irrawaddy; Rangoon Road; Pyabwe and Toungoo.*

Peiwar Kotal Second Afghan War (1878-80) (qv) battle honour marking the defeat on 2 December 1878 of the Afghan forces by the Kurram Field Force under the command of Sir Frederick Roberts. *See also: Afghanistan 1878-80; Ali Masjid; Charasiah; Kabul 1879; Ahmad Khel and Kandahar 1880.*

Pekin 1860 Battle honour marking the capture of Pekin in October 1860 by a force under the command of Sir Hope Grant. *See also: China 1860-62 and Taku Forts.*

Pekin 1900 Battle honour marking the actions of British forces during the siege of the foreign legations in Pekin during the Boxer Rising (qv). The siege was lifted by an international force under the German Count Waldersee.

Pelisse A short jacket for wear as an outer garment in bad weather. When not worn closed it was usually carried slung over the left shoulder. It is claimed the original pelisse came from the wolfskin worn by Hungarian light cavalry in the 17th century.

Pembrokeshire Yeomanry (The Pembroke (Castlemartin) Yeomanry) The Castlemartin Yeomanry was raised in 1794 and, although not paid between 1828 and 1831, remained in being. During the period 1842-43 the regiment was on permanent duty in aid of the civil power for six months. The regiment found a company for 9th Battalion Imperial Yeomanry during the South Africa War (1899-1902). During the First World War the regiment served dismounted in Egypt and Palestine and in 1917 became 9th (Pembroke and Glamorgan Yeomanry) Battalion, The Welch Regiment, serving in France until the end of the war. In 1920 the regiment converted to artillery, serving in that role throughout the Second World War in Italy, North Africa and North-West Europe. In 1947 the regiment re-formed as 302 Field Regiment Royal Artillery but, from 1961, provided an armoured reconnaissance squadron for the Shropshire Yeomanry. By 1967 the regiment had been dismounted and found 'A' Company (Pembroke Yeomanry), 4th Battalion The Welch Regiment (Territorial). The successor sub-unit is 224 (Pembrokeshire Yeomanry) Squadron, 157 (Wales & Midlands) Transport Regiment (Volunteer) Royal Logistic Corps.

Penetration An offensive manoeuvre which breaks into an enemy's defensive positions.

Peninsula Campaign honour awarded to all the regiments which served under the Duke of Wellington from the date of his first landing at Figueras Bay in August 1808 to the Battle of Toulouse in April 1814. Regiments which served under Sir John Moore and were present at Corunna in January 1809, but were not fortunate enough to return to Spain, did not receive this honour. Gold medals and crosses were conferred on general and field officers during the campaign, but it was not until 1847 that the Duke of Richmond was able to persuade Queen Victoria to grant the few remaining survivors a silver medal with clasps for the Peninsula battles. *See also: Roliça; Vimiera; Sahagun; Corunna; Douro; Talavera; Busaco; Barrosa; Fuentes d'Onor; Albuhera; Arroyo Dos Molinos; Tarifa; Ciudad Rodrigo; Badajoz; Almaraz; Salamanca; Vittoria; Pyrenees; St Sebastian; Nivelle; Nive; Orthes and Toulouse.*

Peninsula War (1808-14) In 1806 Napoleon, knowing that Britain's strength lay in her commerce, issued the 'Berlin Decrees' which aimed to destroy Britain's foreign trade by declaring Britain to be in a state of blockade and forbade France or any of her allies to trade with Britain. The causes of the Peninsula War were the French invasion of Portugal, because of the latter's refusal to observe the 'Berlin Decrees', and Napoleon's conferral of the crown of Spain on his brother Joseph contrary to the wishes of the people of Spain, which led to an insurrection in favour of the rightful heir Ferdinand VII. In June 1808 Portugal appealed to Britain for help and an expedition under Sir Arthur Wellesley (qv) sailed for Corunna on 12 July 1808, and Joseph fled Madrid and retired to the River Ebro.

There were three broad areas of operations: the east, Portugal, and Andalusia. Wellesley's army, assisted by local insurgents, defeated Laborde at Roliça in August 1808 and Junot at Vimiera four days later, Junot being forced to sign the Convention of Cintra at Tôrres Vedras on 30 August, under which he evacuated Portugal and retired to France. Meanwhile, Napoleon had decided to lead the Grand Army into Spain in person. This he did, entering Madrid on 4 December 1808, but Spain was by no means subdued and there was extensive and bloody guerilla fighting. A force under Sir John Moore (qv), seeking to gain time for the Spaniards to rally, struck at the French line of communication in Spain, as Moore expected, and he was then forced to retreat - his conduct of the retreat being masterly, closely pursued by Napoleon and Soult. On 16 January 1809 Moore defeated the French at Corunna and, although he was killed, his army was able to embark safely. After the battle of Corunna Soult occupied Oporto and Northern Portugal, but Wellesley moved secretly across the River Douro and, having secured a foothold in Oporto, he forced Soult to evacuate the town and leave Portugal.

At the end of June 1809 Wellesley moved into Spain and linked up with a Spanish army under Cuesta. On 28 July 1809 they were attacked by a French force under Victor at Talavera, the full force of the French effort being directed at the British. The French were defeated and Wellesley was created Viscount Wellington for his victory but, due to the lack of Spanish support, he was obliged to retire to Portugal. During the winter 1809-10 he constructed on the heights of Tôrres Vedras, some distance north of Lisbon, three strong lines of fortified works, known as the 'lines of Tôrres Vedras', forming an invincible position extending some 50 miles in length from the River Tagus to the sea.

In 1810 the main French army under Masséna advanced into Portugal, and before Wellington withdrew behind the lines of Tôrres Vedras he inflicted a sharp defeat on Masséna at Busaco on 27 September 1810. Meantime Ney had captured Ciudad Rodrigo and Almeida. In Andalusia the French took Granada, Malaga and Seville and besieged Cadiz. In 1811 Masséna, isolated by 'scorched earth'

tactics and the impregnability of the Tôrres Vedras position, retreated from his winter quarters at Santarem to Salamanca, pursued by Wellington who, on 4 March 1811, defeated him at Barrosa and later, on 5 May 1811, at Fuentes d'Onor. Soult came to the assistance of Masséna and, although suffering a defeat at Albuhera on 16 May 1811, obliged the allies to raise the siege of Badajoz. On 28 October 1811 a division commanded by General, later Viscount, Rowland Hill, having marched from Portugal, defeated an isolated French division under Girard at Arroyo dos Molinos. For two weeks at the end of December 1811 and beginning of January 1812 the French besieged the allied base at Tarifa on the Spanish coast near Gibraltar.

In 1812 Wellington, having received reinforcements, captured Ciudad Rodrigo, the fortress covering the main northern route from Portugal into Spain, in January. Badajoz, which covered the main southern route into Spain, was captured by Wellington after a three week siege in 1812. In May 1812 a force under General Rowland Hill destroyed the bridge at Almaraz, thus preventing French troops south of the River Tagus from threatening the flank of Wellington's army as it advanced toward its great victory over Marmont's force at Salamanca on 22 July 1812, a victory which led to the occupation of Madrid, although Wellington had to retire into Portugal again after the unsuccessful siege of Burgos later in the year.

In 1813 Wellington again thrust into Spain, routing the French army under King Joseph at Vittoria on 21 June. After Vittoria Joseph fled into France but Soult, having returned from France to take command of the army again could not prevent Wellington from capturing San Sebastian on 31 August, crossing the Bidassoa into France on 7 October and taking Pamplona on 25 October. Wellington now struck inland at the French positions on the River Nivelle and drove them from their positions on 10 November 1813, crossed the River Nive and pushed on toward Bayonne. Soult then launched his counterattack, his final attempt to drive back the invaders, and an inconclusive encounter battle took place on 9 December 1813.

There followed fierce fighting in front of Bayonne culminating in the Battle of Orthes on 27 February 1814, after which Soult retreated to Toulouse.

On 10 April 1814 the final battle of the campaign took place at Toulouse, before it was known that a cessation of hostilities had already been agreed by the allied powers. It was Wellington's intention to crush Soult before he could be reinforced by Suchet's army which was withdrawing from Catalonia. As Napoleon himself admitted, the Peninsula War had been a constant drain on French resources and, perhaps more importantly, the victories achieved by Wellington demonstrated to the Europeans that Napoleon's armies were by no means the invincible weapon they had for so long seemed.

Pepper Potting Obsolete term for fire and manoeuvre, particularly at sub-unit level.

***Per Mare Per Terram* (By sea by land)** Motto of The Royal Marines.

Percussion Cap A small cap of paper or thin metal which fitted over the firing pin of the percussion lock. These caps were stored in a small pouch on the right side of the waist-belt, or in a small slit pocket in the tunic in a similar position.

Percussion Lock A gunlock in which the hammer strikes a percussion cap.

Pergola Ridge Second World War Italian campaign battle honour marking one of a number of actions which took place between the breaching of the Gothic Line in September 1944 and the launching of the final thrust into the valley of the River Po in April 1945. *See also: Italy 1943-1945; Montebello-Scorticata Ridge; Monte Reggiano; Savignano; San Martino Sogliano; Monte Farneto; Montilgallo; Carpineta; Monte Cavallo; Casa Bettini; Pideura; Senio Floodbank; Cesena; Conventello-Comacchio; Monte Casalino; Monte La Pieve; Monte Pianoereno; Monte Spaduro; Orsara; Tossignano and Catarelto Ridge.*

Periscope Up The positioning of an armoured vehicle behind cover in such a manner that the gunner can just see over a crest or embankment through his periscope, the vehicle being hidden from the enemy. *See also: Hull Down and Turret Down.*

Persia Battle honour awarded for service in the Anglo-Persian war 1856-57 which sought to bring about a Persian withdrawal from Herat in Afghanistan. An expeditionary force was launched from Bombay, its immediate objective being the capture of the port of Bushire on the Persian Gulf. *See also: Reshire; Bushire and Koosh-Ab.*

Persia 1915-19 First World War battle honour marking the actions which took place in Persia (Iran) following the deployment of British troops to protect the Abadan oilfields against Turkey and tribesmen incited by Turkey and Germany. Agreement was reached with Russia to establish joint control over the movement of dissident elements in eastern Persia. On the collapse of Russia British troops extended their efforts northward, entering Russia from both north-east and north-west Persia. *See also: Baku and Merv.*

Persian Gulf Battle honour marking service in 1819 under Sir W Grant Keir in the destruction of pirate strongholds in the Persian Gulf, where pirates had been seeking to interfere with the free passage of East India Squadron vessels. *See also: Beni Boo Ali.*

Perthshire Regiment (73rd Foot) *See: The Black Watch (Royal Highland Regiment) (42nd and 73rd Foot).*

Perthshire Volunteers - 90th Light Infantry Regiment *See: The Cameronians (Scottish Rifles) (26th and 90th Foot).*

Perthshire Yeomanry (The Scottish Horse) The Perthshire Yeomanry Cavalry was raised in June 1798, served until 1808, and was raised again in 1817 when it served as independent troops until disbandment in 1828. Two regiments of Scottish Horse saw service in the South Africa War (1899-1902): one recruited from Scots living in South Africa and one recruited from Scots from the homeland and Australia. After the South Africa War two new regiments of Scottish horse were raised and constituted as Yeomanry. On the outbreak of the First World War a third regiment was raised and the Scottish Horse became a brigade under Brigadier Lord Tullibardine - later Duke of Atholl. In 1939 the regiment converted to artillery, serving in that role in Sicily, Italy and North-West Europe. In 1956 the regiment was amalgamated with the Fife and Forfar Yeomanry and in 1969 became known as the Highland Yeomanry. The successor unit is 'C' (Fife and Forfar Yeomanry/Scottish Horse) Squadron, The Scottish Yeomanry.

Petard A device containing explosives used to breach walls, doors etc.

Peterloo Massacre Name given to the events of 16 August 1819 in Manchester. A large protest meeting in favour of parliamentary reform, under the leadership of Henry Hunt, had assembled at St Peter's Field (now the site of the Free Trade Hall). The magistrates ordered the meeting to be dispersed, calling out the military, including several troops of Yeomanry cavalry, as a result of which 11 lives were lost and some 500 people injured.

Peter's Corner Second World War North Africa campaign battle honour marking one of the actions during the Battle of Medjez Plain 23-30 April 1943. The battle was a preliminary to the final advance to Tunis. *See also: North Africa 1940-1943; Medjez Plain; Gueriat El Atach Ridge; Longstop Hill 1943; Djebel Bou Aoukaz 1943 I; Grich El Oued; Si Mediene; Si Abdallah; Gab Gab Gap and Sidi Ahmed.*

Petticoat Breeches Petticoat or 'Rhinegrave' breeches were worn in the mid-17th century and by elements of the army of Charles II.

Phase Line A line utilized for the control and co-ordination of military operations. It is usual for such lines to be selected so that they follow or link significant terrain features, and can thus readily be identified on the ground.

Phoenix Remotely piloted vehicle (RPV) intended, subject to reaching the required performance standards, to replace the obsolete Midge (qv). Phoenix should be capable of providing real-time target acquisition and surveillance information. A range of 70km and a field of view approximately 500m × 500m at a 1,000m slant range is anticipated.

Pian Di Castello Second World War Italian campaign battle honour marking one of the actions in the Battle of the Gothic Line 25 August-22 September 1944. *See also: Gothic Line; Tavoleto Coriano; Croce; Gemmano Ridge; Monte Gridolfo; Montegaudio; San Clemente and Poggio San Giovanni.*

Pian Di Maggio Second World War Italian campaign battle honour marking an action during the advance to the Gothic Line in July and August 1944. *See also: Italy 1943-45 and Citerna.*

Piave First World War Italian campaign battle honour. An Austrian offensive during October-November 1917 drove the Italians westward on to the line of the Piave River from the Central Alps to its mouth, and desultory fighting continued until the middle of June 1918, when the Austrians decided to turn the whole of the Italian front on the Piave by a breakthrough in the mountain area, supported by a frontal attack from Montello to the sea. The British contingent was stationed about Montello under General Plumer, who was succeeded in March 1918 by Lord Cavan. The Austrians had some initial success, but heavy floods broke down their bridges, disorganising the lines of communication, and a general withdrawal was ordered. On October 1918 General Diaz decided upon offensive action in this area, and the British forces took over an increased portion of the frontage for the operation. The offensive opened on the night of 26 October. On 27 October Lord Cavan crossed the Piave, and on the same day the Austrians made an offer of peace. On 3 November the Austrians accepted General Diaz's terms for an armistice. *See also: Italy 1917-18 and Vittorio Veneto.*

Pibroch A form of Scottish bagpipe music consisting of a theme and variations.

Pibroch O'Donuil Dubh Regimental quick march (Pipes and Drums) of the Queen's Own Highlanders (Seaforth and Cameron).

Pichon Second World War North Africa campaign battle honour marking one of the battles in the Fondouk operations of April 1943. *See also: North Africa 1940-1943; Fondouk; Kairouan; Bordj; Djebel El Rhorab; Fondouk Pass and Sidi Ali.*

Pickers Decorative pointed metal arrows worn on cavalry shoulder belts, originally used for clearing the touch-hole of a firearm.

Picket Military term used non-operationally to denote a body of troops who patrol or remain ready for an emergency, such as fire-fighting, upholding law and order or restoring discipline. On operations a picket is a body of troops used for protective purposes, such as at an outpost, hill feature or to guard a bridge. In some regiments the old spelling 'picquet' is still in use.

Pick Off To engage and destroy targets one by one.

Picton, Sir Thomas (1758-1815) Entered the Army in 1771, promoted to major in 1795 and took part in the capture of St Lucia in the following year. When Trinidad was taken from the Spanish in 1797 Picton was put in charge of the administration, his five years of office being characterised by arbitrary conduct but undoubted ability in maintaining order. He administered Trinidad so successfully that the inhabitants presented him with a golden sword when they petitioned against the retrocession of the island to Spain. He was present at the siege of Flushing (1809), and was appointed governor of the town. He served in the Peninsula War (qv) under Wellington, and distinguished himself at Badajoz and Vittoria. Picton commanded a division at Quatre Bras, and was shot dead while leading a charge at Waterloo.

Pideura Second World War Italian campaign battle honour marking one of a number of actions which took place between the breaching of the Gothic Line in September 1944 and the launching of the final thrust into the valley of the River Po in April 1945. *See also: Italy 1943-1945; Montebello-Scorticata Ridge; Monte Reggiano; Savignano; San Martino Sogliano; Monte Farneto; Montilgallo; Carpineta; Monte Cavallo; Casa Bettini; Pergola Ridge; Senio Floodbank; Cesena; Conventello-Comacchio; Monte Casalino; Monte La Pieve; Monte Pianoereno; Monte Spaduro; Orsara; Tossignano and Catarelto Ridge.*

Piedemonte Hill Second World War Italian campaign battle honour marking one of the actions during operations in the Liri Valley following the capture of Cassino in mid-May 1944. *See also: Italy 1943-1945; Liri Valley; Hitler Line; Monte Piccolo; Aquino and Melfa Crossing.*

Pig Soldiers' slang for the Humber 1-ton (qv), wheeled, armoured vehicle much used in Northern Ireland.

Pike A medieval weapon consisting of a spearhead joined to a long pole or pikestaff 14ft or 16ft in length. Replaced by the musket, they were still carried ceremonially as late as 1705.

Pikeman A soldier armed with a pike (qv).

Pilckem First World War battle honour marking the opening battle of the Third Battle of Ypres in July 1917. The Pilckem Ridge, which overlooks Ypres and was the main objective in the northern sector, was captured on 31 July. *See also: France and Flanders 1914-1918; Ypres 1917; Langemarck 1917; Menin Road; Polygon Wood; Broodseinde; Poelcappelle and Passchendaele.*

Pillbox A small fortified and enclosed emplacement, usually made of reinforced concrete.

Pinwe Second World War Burma campaign battle honour marking the clearing of the Japanese from the valley between

Mogaung and Indaw during the latter half of November 1944; a task which took 20 days of bitter fighting. *See also: Burma 1942-45; Mawlaik; Kalewa and Shwebo.*

Pioneer Soldier trained to undertake field engineering and light construction tasks. From the Spanish *peone* - a labourer. Qualified pioneers wear a badge depicting crossed hatchets or axes on the sleeve. *See also: Assault Pioneer.*

Pioneer Corps Regimental quick march of The Royal Pioneer Corps.

Pip Slang for the star worn by officers as part of their rank designation.

Pipe Major Warrant officer or non-commissioned officer responsible for the musical and military training of the pipers in a regiment. *See also: Bugle Major and Drum Major.*

Pipeclay A fine white pure clay once used for whitening leather and similar materials.

Piper Soldier qualified to play the bagpipes.

Piping The coloured edging on uniforms and Headdress.

Pistol A one-handed weapon for swift use in self-defence at short range. The precise origin of the word is unknown, but pistols have certainly existed since the late 14th century in Sweden, and the term covers single-shot pistols, revolvers and 'automatic' self-loading pistols. The development of the pistol followed the same progression as other firearms. Well known makes of pistol include Colt, Browning, Mauser, Luger, Walther and Beretta.

Pith Helmet An Indian topee or sun helmet made from the pith of spongewood trees. In 1861 this was also known as a cork helmet.

Piton A metal spike that may be driven into a crevice of rock or into ice and used to secure a rope when climbing.

Planters Order Term for an order of dress in plain clothes. No coat or jacket is required, but a tie is worn and the shirt-sleeves must be rolled down.

Plassey Battle honour marking the defeat of the army of Suraj-ud-Dowlah, the Nawab of Bengal on 23 June 1757 by a force under the command of Robert Clive. The victory at Plassey was the foundation stone of British supremacy in Bengal, as Arcot was in Madras. *See also: Arcot; Condore; Masulipatam; Badara; Buxar; Wandewash and Pondicherry.*

Plastic Bullet A solid PVC cylinder some 10cm long and 38mm in diameter used in riot dispersal. *See also: Baton Round.*

Plastron Broad piece of cloth worn on the chest of lancer and light cavalry jackets. From the Italian *'piastra'*, a breast plate.

Platoon A sub-unit of between 30 and 40 men, usually commanded by a subaltern. In the British Army an infantry company is normally divided into three platoons. In some other countries, and in arms other than the infantry, the organisation includes platoons. In most cases a platoon is divided into three sections of seven to ten men under a non-commissioned officer.

Plough Shaped plough-like blades fitted to the front of some armoured vehicles for mine clearance. The blades turn the soil, and with it any mines, away from the tracks.

Plumes Dressings of feather or hair worn on Headdress, and also under the throat of a horse.

Poelcappelle First World War battle honour marking the capture of the village of Poelcappelle, an intermediate objective in the securing of the high ground of Passchendaele Ridge, on 9 October 1917, during the Third Battle of Ypres in July 1917. *See also: France and Flanders 1914-1918; Ypres 1917; Langemarck 1917; Menin Road; Polygon Wood; Broodseinde; Pilckem and Passchendaele.*

Poggio Del Grillo Second World War Italian campaign battle honour marking the capture of the town on 8 August 1944 after five days of heavy fighting. *See also: Italy 1943-1945; Advance to Florence and Gothic Line.*

Poggio San Giovanni Second World War Italian campaign battle honour marking one of the actions in the Battle of the Gothic Line 25 August-22 September 1944. *See also: Italy 1943-1945; Gothic Line; Tavoleto; Coriano; Croce; Gemmano Ridge; Monte Gridolfo; Montegaudio; San Clemente and Pian di Castello.*

Point 93 Second World War North Africa campaign battle honour marking one of the actions during the first battle of El Alamein 1-27 July 1942. *See also: North Africa 1940-1943; Defence of Alamein Line; Ruweisat; Fuka Airfield; Deir El Shein and Ruweisat Ridge.*

Point 174 Second World War North Africa campaign battle honour marking one of the actions fought between the British withdrawal from Agedabia in 1941 and the occupation of the El Alamein line in July 1942. *See also: North Africa 1940-1943; Msus; Benghazi; Carmusa; Mersa Matruh; Minqar Qaim and Fuka.*

Point 201 (Arakan) Second World War Burma campaign battle honour marking an action during the 1943 Arakan offensive. *See also: Burma 1942-1945; Donbaik; Rathedaung and Htizwe.*

Point 201 (Roman Wall) Second World War North Africa campaign battle honour marking one of the actions in the Tebaga Gap operation 21-30 March 1943 which turned the Mareth Line. *See also: North Africa 1940-1943; Mareth Line; Tebaga Gap and El Hamma.*

Point 551 Second World War Burma campaign battle honour marking one of the actions in the North Arakan offensive 1 January-12 June 1944. *See also: Burma 1942-1945; North Arakan; Buthidaung; Razibil; Kaladan; Mayu Tunnels; Alethangyaw; Maungdaw and Mowdok.*

Point 1433 Second World War Burma campaign battle honour marking one of the actions in the Arakan during the latter part of 1944. *See also: Burma 1942-1945.*

Point Blank From the French *point blanc* (white spot); the centre of continental targets being marked with a white spot.

Pointsmen Men stationed at specific points on the periphery of a parade to indicate to those on parade where given actions have to take place. *See also: Markers.*

Polygon Wood First World War battle honour marking the capture of Polygon Wood and the village of Zonnebeke on 26 September 1917, the conclusion of a thrust launched on 20 September, and part of the Third Battle of Ypres. *See also: France and Flanders 1914-1918; Ypres 1917; Passchendaele; Langemarck 1917; Menin Road; Broodseinde; Poelcappelle and Pilckem.*

Pom-Pom Term used to describe an automatic, rapid firing, small calibre cannon, especially a type of anti-aircraft cannon, used during the Second World War.

Pomp and Circumstance No.1 Regimental slow march of The Parachute Regiment.

Pompadours Nickname given to 56th Foot, later The Essex Regiment. When the regiment was raised in 1755, the facings chosen were purple, the favourite colour of Madame de Pompadour, the mistress of Louis XV.

Poncho Rectangular waterproof sheet with a hole in the centre through which the head may be put. The poncho is used as a protective garment in wet weather or in the construction of a bivouac. It is usual for the poncho to have press studs along at least one side to permit two or more ponchos to be joined.

Pondicherry Battle honour marking the successful siege and subsequent capture of the principal French town in India in 1761. Having been defeated at Wandewash by Eyre Coote in 1761, Lally had withdrawn to Pondicherry, only to face Eyre Coote again. *See also: Arcot; Plassey; Condore; Masulipatam; Badara; Wandewash and Buxar.*

Pongo Slang term used by members of the Royal Navy and Royal Air Force to describe members of the Army.

Pontius Pilate's Bodyguard Nickname for 1st Foot, now The Royal Scots (The Royal Regiment). Tradition has it that when in French service as *Le Régiment de Douglas*, a dispute arose with the *Régiment de Picardie* as to seniority, and an officer of the latter declared his regiment was on duty on the night of the crucifixion, to which an officer of Douglas's regiment replied, 'Had we been on duty, we would not have slept at our post'.

Pontoon A watertight float or small boat-like hull used to provide the basis of a temporary bridge or ferry.

Poppy Day Informal name for Remembrance Day.

Pop-Up Characterised by, or having a mechanism that pops up. Notably pop-up targets.

Portcullis A strong grating of iron or timber, constructed to slide up and down in grooves cut in the sides of the gate tower, to repel assaults.

Port En Bessin Second World War battle honour marking one of the actions which took place between the Allied landing in Normandy on 6 June 1944 and the crossing of the River Seine in late August 1944. *See also: North West Europe 1944-1945; Tourmauville Bridge; St Pierre La Veille; Estry; Noireau Crossing; La Vie Crossing; La Touques Crossing and Risle Crossing.*

Posh Smart, elegant, genteel or associated with the upper class. The term is alleged to be an acronym of the phrase *'Port Out - Starboard Home'*, indicating the most desirable cabins on ships sailing to and from the east, being the north facing or shaded side.

Poshteen Indian native coat of sheepskin worn with the hair or fleece on the inside.

Position Selected area from which a unit intends to fight. There are three broad types of position: main, alternate and secondary.

Possible The maximum possible score, particularly in competition shooting.

Pot The simple metal helmet of rounded shape once worn by pikemen (qv) and regiments of horse.

Pothus Second World War battle honour marking one of the actions during the brief 1940 campaign in Norway. *See also: Norway 1940; Stien;Vist; Kvam and Otta.*

Potsdam Agreement Agreement arising from the Three-Power Conference held at Potsdam 17 July-1 August 1945 between Churchill and Atlee for Great Britain, Truman for the USA and Stalin for the USSR, to determine the future of Germany after the unconditional surrender of 7 May 1945. The agreement provided that: (1) a committee of foreign ministers of USA, USSR, Britain, France and China should be established to frame peace treaties with Germany's allies, to be submitted to the United Nations; (2) the commanders-in-chief of France, Britain, USA and USSR should exercise supreme authority in their respective zones of occupied Germany, on instructions from their governments, and also jointly, as members of the control council, in affairs concerning the whole of Germany; (3) the Allies should disarm and demilitarise Germany and prevent the future use of German industry for war purposes. Nazism should be entirely destroyed and the German people made aware of their defeat, and re-educated on democratic lines. For the time being no central German government should be established, but Germany should be one economic unit; (4) Königsberg should be transferred to the USSR, and special provisions made concerning reparations due to the USSR. The Oder-Neisse line was made the provisional Polish western frontier and (5) war criminals should be brought to trial, and any transfer of Germans from Poland, Hungary and Czechoslovakia should be humanely executed.

Pouch Small bag or container, usually suspended from the belt and used for carrying ammunition and other warlike stores.

Pouch-Belt The pouch-belt, as opposed to the bayonet-belt or cartridge-belt, became the mark of an officer. Often made of gold or silver lace on a leather backing or, in the case of rifle officers, plain black leather.

Powder Burn Superficial burn caused by exposure to an explosion.

Powder Flask Small flask or case formerly used to carry gunpowder.

Powder Horn Powder flask (qv) constructed from the horn of an animal.

Pozières First World War battle honour marking the fighting which took place to secure and hold positions on Pozières Ridge during the Battle of the Somme which took place between 1 July and 18 November 1916. *See also: France and Flanders 1914-1918; Somme 1916; Albert 1916; Bazentin; Delville Wood; Guillemont; Ginchy; Flers-Courcelette; Morval; Thiepval; Le Transloy; Ancre Heights and Ancre 1916.*

'PPR' The initials 'PPR' appeared on the uniform of the 'Paid Pensioner Recruiter' from 1924 to about 1933 when the title was changed to Army Recruiter and crossed flags were worn.

Pride of Lions Regimental quick march of the Adjutant General's Corps.

Primer Small charge used to detonate the main charge.

Primus In Indis (First in India) Motto of 39th (Dorsetshire) Regiment of Foot, The Dorset Regiment (39th and 54th Foot) and now The Devonshire and Dorset Regiment. The motto denotes the fact that 39th Foot was the first 'King's' regiment, as opposed to East India Company's, to

land in India in 1754, and was the only King's regiment to fight under Clive at the Battle of Plassey (1757).

Primasole Bridge Second World War Sicilian campaign battle honour marking the capture of the bridge over the River Lentini by airborne troops, their relief by a ground force, and subsequent consolidation of the position over the period 13-18 July 1943. *See also: Sicily 1943; Landing in Sicily and Sferro.*

Prince Consort's Library Established at Aldershot by Prince Albert at the cost to him personally of £4,183.3s.4d and opened in 1860. The library, which contain's the Prince Consort's personal collection of 2,000 military books, was originally intended as a reference library available only to officers in Aldershot. The library is now open to personnel of all Services and ranks and contains an unrivalled collection of some 60,000 military books and journals.

Prince of Wales's Leinster Regiment (Royal Canadians) (100th and 109th Foot) The 100th Foot was raised in 1761 as 100th (Highland) Regiment and disbanded in 1763. Re-raised in 1794 as 100th (Gordon Highlanders) Foot and redesignated 100th (Prince Regent's County of Dublin) Foot in 1805. In 1858 the regiment was redesignated 100th (Prince of Wales's Royal Canadian) Foot). The 109th was raised in 1761, disbanded in 1763 and re-raised in 1794 as 100th (Aberdeenshire) Foot and disbanded again in 1795. In 1861 the 109th (Bombay Infantry) Regiment, which had been raised in 1854 as 3rd (Bombay European) Regiment of the East India Company, was taken on the English establishment. In May 1881 the 100th (Prince of Wales's Royal Canadian) Foot amalgamated with 109th (Bombay Infantry) Regiment to form The Prince of Wales's Royal Canadian Regiment. The regiment was redesignated two months later as The Prince of Wales's Leinster Regiment (Royal Canadians). The regiment was disbanded in 1922, as were the other regiments which relied on recruits from the south of Ireland.

Headdress Badge: The Prince of Wales's plume, coronet and motto. Below, a scroll inscribed 'LEINSTER'.

History: *Prince of Wales's Leinster Regiment* (2 Parts) by F E Whitton.

Prince of Wales's Own Regiment of Yorkshire (14th and 15th Foot) Formed on 25 April 1958 through the amalgamation of The West Yorkshire Regiment (The Prince of Wales's Own) (14th Foot) and The East Yorkshire Regiment (Duke of York's Own) (15th Foot).

Headdress Badge: The White Horse of Hanover upon a wreath or ground.

Motto: *Nec Aspera Terrent* (Nor do difficulties deter).

Regimental marches:

Quick marches: *Ca Ira* and *The Yorkshire Lass.*

Slow marches: *God Bless The Prince of Wales,* and *March of XVth Regiment.*

Regimental headquarters: 3 Tower Street, York, YO1 1SB.

History: In production.

Prince of Wales's Division An administrative grouping in the infantry, created under Army Order 34 of 1968, comprising The Devonshire and Dorset Regiment, The Cheshire Regiment, The Royal Welch Fusiliers, The South Wales Borderers (until 1969), The Welch Regiment (until 1969), The Royal Regiment of Wales (from 1969), The Gloucestershire Regiment (until 1994), The Worcestershire Regiment (until 1970), The Sherwood Foresters (Nottinghamshire and Derbyshire Regiment) (until 1970), Worcestershire and Sherwood Foresters Regiment (from 1970), The Royal Hampshire Regiment (until 1992), The Staffordshire Regiment (The Prince of Wales's), The Duke of Edinburgh's Royal Regiment (Berkshire and Wiltshire) (1959-1994) and The Royal Gloucestershire, Berkshire and Wiltshire Regiment (from 27 April 1994).

Prince Regent's Allowance It was alleged in a statement to the House of Commons by Colonel Wood in 1834 that some officers who had no income but their pay were too poor to partake of the wine at the Mess. This was presented to the Prince Regent and it was decided that, rather than increase pay, a moderate allowance of wine would be given to enable such officers to drink two or three glasses of wine at dinner. This became know as the 'Prince Regent's Allowance' (Hansard Vol. XXI, p.1015).

Princess Charlotte of Wales's Regiment (49th Foot) *See: The Royal Berkshire Regiment (Princess Charlotte of Wales's) (49th and 66th Foot).*

Princess of Wales's Royal Regiment (Queen's And Royal Hampshires) (2nd, 3rd, 31st, 35th, 37th, 50th, 57th, 67th, 70th, 77th, 97th and 107th Foot) Formed on 9 September 1992 through the amalgamation of The Queen's Regiment (2nd, 3rd, 35th, 50th, 57th, 70th, 77th, 97th and 107th Foot) and The Royal Hampshire Regiment (37th and 67th Foot).

Headdress Badge: A dragon upon a mount with a double red rose fimbriated gold below within the Garter. Above the dragon and superimposed on the garter the plume of The Prince of Wales.

Regimental marches:

Quick march: *The Farmers Boy* leading to *The Soldiers of The Queen.*

Slow march: *The Minden Rose.*

Regimental headquarters: Howe Barracks, Canterbury, Kent, CT11 1JU.

Western headquarters: Searle's House, Southgate Street, Winchester, Hampshire, SO23 9EG.

Principles of War The ten principles of war, as applied in the British Army, are selection and maintenance of the aim, maintenance of morale, offensive action, surprise, concentration of force, economy of effort, security, flexibility, co-operation and administration.

Prisoner of War A serviceman captured by an enemy in time of war.

***Pristinae Virtutis Memores* (Mindful of former valour)** Motto of 8th King's Royal Irish Hussars and The Queen's Royal Irish Hussars, The Queen's Royal Regiment (West Surrey).

Private From 'Private Gentleman', the lowest rank of trained soldier. The name given the equivalent rank varies between regiments and corps: Trooper, Gunner, Sapper, Signalman, Guardsman, Fusilier, Rifleman, Kingsman, Queensman, Ranger, Craftsman, Driver etc. *See also: Rank.*

Pro Rege Et Patria (For King and Country) Motto of The Queen's Bays (2nd Dragoon Guards) and 1st The Queen's Dragoon Guards.

Pro Rege, Pro Lege, Pro Patria Conamur (For King, for laws, for country we strive) Motto of 18th Hussars (Queen Mary's Own) and 13th/18th Royal Hussars (Queen Mary's Own).

Proasteion Second World War battle honour marking the rearguard action fought on 13 April 1941 during the withdrawal to the Aliakmon position during the campaign in Greece. *See also: Greece 1941; Veve and Corinth Canal.*

Projecter Infantry Anti-Tank (PIAT) Second World War single shot spigot discharger projecting a 3lb hollow charge projectile.

Promote To raise in rank. Promotion may be local, acting or substantive.

Provost Court A military court for trying people charged with minor offences in an occupied area.

Provost Marshal Senior Army officer on the staff of the Ministry of Defence (Army Department). He has Assistant and Deputy Provost Marshals at the headquarters of most static and field headquarters. These officers control the members of the Provost Branch of the Adjutant General's Corps and are responsible for enforcing orders and military discipline outside the areas of unit responsibility. The Provost Marshal and his subordinates are also responsible for traffic control during military operations and on certain ceremonial occasions.

Provost Sergeant The non-commissioned officer in charge of the regimental police in a regiment or battalion.

Proximity Fuse A device which detonates a warhead at a preset distance from the target. The most common types are radar proximity and infra-red proximity fuses.

Proxy The use by terrorists of innocents or third parties to unwillingly commit or assist in acts of terrorism.

Prussian Collar A stand-up collar which fastened the whole way up, as opposed to just at the bottom. This type of collar came into use in about 1820 and was said to improve the posture.

Ptarmigan Primary trunk radio relay communication system which replaced the obsolete Bruin (qv) system. Ptarmigan offers a mobile, secure and reliable battlefield communications system.

Puggree, Puggaree Indian word for a turban. A scarf, usually pleated, worn around the crown of hats or helmets.

Pukka Properly or correctly done. From Hindi *Pakka* meaning firm.

Pullthrough Cord, weighted at one end, and with two or more loops at the other, used for cleaning the barrel of rifles and other small arms.

Pump Gun A repeating gun operated by a slide action mechanism forward of the trigger which ejects spent cartridges and reloads from a magazine.

Punjab Frontier Battle honour marking the campaign of 1897-98 which suppressed the general rising of Pathan tribes on the North-West Frontier.

Punjab Campaign Medal 1848-49 Medal authorised by a General Order dated 2 April 1849 to mark the actions against the Sikhs between 7 September 1848 and 14 March 1849.
Ribbon: Dark blue with yellow edges.

Clasps: Mooltan; Chilianwala and Goojerat.

Punjaub Battle honour marking the actions in the Second Sikh War (1849), which resulted in the annexation of the Punjaub. *See also: Mooltan; Chillianwallah and Goojerat.*

Punniar Battle honour marking one of the battles which took place on 29 December 1843 in a very short and successful campaign to persuade the military oligarchy in the Mahratta state of Gwalior to disband their army, which was a standing menace to the peace of the North-West Frontier. *See also: Maharajpore.*

Pursuit Operation in which a defeated or withdrawing enemy is pursued; the opportunity being seized to inflict further casualties on an already demoralised and probably disorganised force.

Pursuit to Messina Second World War Sicilian campaign battle honour marking one of the actions toward the end of the campaign. *See also: Sicily 1943; Monte Rivoglia and Malleto.*

Pursuit to Mons First World War battle honour marking the final advance of October and November 1918. *See also: France and Flanders 1914-1918;Valenciennes and Sambre.*

Putôt En Bessin Second World War battle honour marking the recapture on 9 June 1944 of Putôt En Bessin, which lies on the Caen-Bayeux road. *See also: North West Europe 1944-1945; Normandy Landing; Sully; Cambes and Bréville.*

Puttee A strip of cloth, originally cotton but later made of wool, bound around the ankle (short puttee) or from ankle to just below the knee (long puttee). From the Hindi *patti* meaning cloth.

Pyabwe Second World War Burma campaign battle honour marking one of the actions in the final drive south to capture Rangoon, launched in conjunction with seaborne landings 1 April-6 May 1945. *See also: Burma 1942-1945; Irrawaddy; Rangoon Road; Pegu 1945 and Toungoo.*

Pyrenees Peninsula War (qv) battle honour marking the series of actions which took place in the Pyrenees to counter Soult's efforts to relieve Pamplona and San Sebastian where the French had left garrisons on withdrawing from Spain. The decisive action took place at Sorauren followed by a pursuit of the retreating French. *See also: Peninsula; Vittoria; St Sebastian; Nivelle; Nive; Orthes and Toulouse.*

Pyrotechnics Term used to describe training explosives and illuminants.

Quarry Hill Second World War battle honour marking one of the actions in the British offensive launched south-westwards from the Caumont area on 30 July 1944 which culminated in the capture of Mont Pincon on 6 August. Quarry Hill was an important objective in the opening phase of the operation. *See also: North West Europe 1944-1945; Mont Pincon; Souleuvre; Catheolles; Le Perier Ridge; Brieux Bridgehead; Jurques and La Varinière.*

Quarter Guard Guard tasked with the security of the quarters or accommodation of the unit.

Quartermaster Officer, usually holding a late entry or quartermaster commission, responsible to the commanding officer for all logistic aspects of a battalion or regiment.

Quartermaster General Third Military Member of the Army Board. Responsible for all aspects of the logistic support of the Army in peace and war. The appointment was founded in 1686.

Quartermaster General's Department The following directors, individuals and staffs fall within the Quartermaster General's Department: Chief of Staff Headquarters Quartermaster General; Director Logistic Operations (Army); Director Logistic Information Systems (Army); Director General of Logistic Support (Army); Director Logistic Support Policy; Director Transport and Movement (Army); Director Base Depots; Director Material Supply and Distribution (Army); Director Clothing and Textiles; Director Catering (Army); Directorate of Land Service Ammunition; Logistic Support (Finance and Secretariat); Assistant Under Secretary of State (Quartermaster); Head of Quartermaster General Secretariat; Director General Equipment Support (Army); Director Equipment Support; Director General Command and Information Systems (Army); Director Command and Information Systems (Army) and Director Communication Staff (Army).

Quartermaster Sergeant In 1802 four chevrons were introduced to indicate the rank of quartermaster sergeant. These were worn point down on the upper right sleeve. The positioning was altered in 1869 to point down on the lower sleeve, below waist level and, in 1881 this was altered to point upward. Until the First World War a regimental quartermaster sergeant wore, in addition, an eight-pointed star. During the First World War the grades of senior non-commissioned officers were reorganised and the regimental quartermaster sergeant received warrant officer rank and the appropriate crown within a wreath badge. The squadron, battery or company quartermaster sergeant rank was indicated by a crown surmounting three, pointdown, chevrons.

Quatre-Bras Village in the Belgian province of Brabant, situated some 10 miles south of Waterloo. It was the scene of a battle on 16 June 1815 between the British under Wellington and the French under Ney, when the latter was repulsed. Simultaneously Napoleon was attacking Blúcher at Ligny as part of the plan to separate and destroy in detail the British and Prussian forces. *See also:Waterloo.*

Quebec 1759 Battle honour marking General Wolfe's capture of Quebec, the capital of Canada, following nearly three months of operations and finally achieved through a night approach march part of which included the scaling of the 'Heights of Abraham' (qv).

Queen Alexandra's Imperial Military Nursing Service Following the valued service of Florence Nightingale (qv) and her nurses during the Crimean War (qv), serious thought was given to the nursing of sick and wounded soldiers. A purpose-built military hospital was opened at Netley, near Southampton, by Queen Victoria in 1856. In 1866 Queen Victoria approved the appointment of civilian nurses to military hospitals, and these nurses were incorporated into the Army Nursing Service on its formation in 1881. In keeping with the objectives of the Cardwell reforms (qv) a Nursing Reserve was established in 1897. Both the Army Nursing Service and the Nursing Reserve were reorganised after the South Africa War (1899-1902) and, under the patronage of Queen Alexandra, designated Queen Alexandra's Imperial Military Nursing Service in March 1902. This remained on an auxiliary basis until it was redesignated Queen Alexandra's Royal Army Nursing Corps (qv), and taken on the regular establishment under Army Order 5 of 1949.

Queen Alexandra's Royal Army Nursing Corps Formed on the regular establishment under Army Order 5 of 1949 drawing on the experience of Queen Alexandra's Imperial Military Nursing Service (qv).
Headdress Badge: The cypher of HM the late Queen Alexandra upon the Dannebrog, the whole within a laurel wreath inscribed with the corps motto *'Sub Cruce Candida'* (Under the White Cross). All ensigned with the crown. On the lower portion of the wreath a scroll inscribed 'QARANC'.
Corps quick march: *Grey and Scarlet.*
Corps headquarters: QARANC Training Centre, The Royal Pavilion, Farnborough

Road, Aldershot, Hampshire, GU11 1PZ.
History: *Queen Alexandra's Royal Army Nursing Corps* by Juliet Piggott (1990).

Queen Charlotte, The Regimental slow march of 16th/5th The Queen's Royal Lancers.

Queen Elizabeth's Own Regimental quick march (Pipes) of 6th Queen Elizabeth's Own Gurkha Rifles.

Queen Mary's Army Auxiliary Corps *See:Women's Royal Army Corps.*

Queen's Bays Nickname for 2nd Dragoon Guards. From 1767 the regiment was mounted on bays, while other cavalry regiments (except the Greys) had black horses. In 1870 the name became official, the regiment being titled 2nd Dragoon Guards (Queen's Bays).

Queen's Body Guard for Scotland Royal Company of Archers The precise origins of this body are obscure. However, it is widely recorded that it originated in 1676 and was re-constituted in 1703. Certainly in 1676 the citizens of Edinburgh formed themselves into a 'particular society and company for Archery and Shutting with Bowes and Arrowes to be called His Majesty's Company of Archers in time comeing'. A letter to Queen Anne in 1703 requests Her Majesty to grant a new establishment of the Royal Company of Archers, which was granted in the following year. The present uniform of 'Border-green' cloth and black with red velvet facings dates from about 1831. The field dress bonnet for Gentlemen of the Body Guard is green trimmed with black braid and has a crimson tuft or 'toorie'; a single eagle's feather indicating a gentleman, two feathers an officer and three feathers the Captain-General. The Company consists of a Captain-General and Gold Stick for Scotland, captains, lieutenants, ensigns and brigadiers. The Company attends the sovereign on all state occasions in Scotland.

Queen's Body Guard of the Yeomen of the Guard Instituted by Henry VII in

1485 as part of the sovereign's retinue and employed on state occasions. The body guard consists of six officers (a captain, a lieutenant, an ensign, a clerk of the cheque and two exons) and 80 men, all selected for long and distinguished service in the regular Army, Royal Marines or Royal Air Force. There has been little change in the body guard's uniform since Tudor times, but the officers' uniform was changed by command of William IV from a Tudor style to that of their present uniform, that of a field officer of the Waterloo period.

Queen's Division An administrative grouping in the infantry, created under Army Order 34 of 1968, comprising The Queen's Regiment (1966-1992), The Royal Regiment of Fusiliers, The Royal Anglian Regiment and The Princess of Wales's Royal Regiment (Queen's and Royal Hampshires) (from 1992).

Queen's Dragoon Guards *See: Dragoon Guards.*

Queens Gallantry Medal Instituted in 1974, and open to all ranks of all Services for 'Exemplary acts of bravery' of a slightly lower degree than the George Cross. The award of the Order of the British Empire for acts of gallantry was discontinued, the Queens Gallantry Medal being deemed more appropriate.
Ribbon: Dark blue 1" wide, with a central vertical stripe of pearl grey and a narrow vertical stripe of rose pink at the centre.

Queen's Gurkha Engineers *See: Gurkhas.*

Queen's Gurkha Signals *See: Gurkhas.*

Queen's Mediterranean Medal 1899-1902 Awarded to garrisons in the Mediterranean during the South Africa War, including St Helena, an important Boer prisoner of war camp.
Ribbon: A broad vertical band at the centre, flanked on either side by a blue vertical stripe and broader vertical red stripe.

Queen's Lancashire Regiment (30th, 40th, 47th, 59th, 81st and 82nd Foot) Formed on 25 March 1970 through the amalgamation of The Lancashire Regiment (Prince of Wales's Volunteers) (30th, 40th, 59th and 82nd Foot) and The Loyal Regiment (North Lancashire) (47th and 81st Foot).
Headdress Badge: Within an oval inscribed 'THE QUEEN'S LANCASHIRE REGIMENT' the rose of Lancaster ensigned with the crown. Below, a scroll inscribed 'LOYALLY I SERVE'.
Motto: Loyally I Serve.
Regimental marches:
Quick march: *L'Attaque - The Red Rose.*
Slow march: *Long Live Elizabeth* (from Selection No. 2 Merrie England).
Regimental headquarters: Fulwood Barracks, Preston, PR2 4AA, Lancashire.
History: *Loyally They Served* by B S Mackenzie (1979).

Queen's Own Buffs The Royal West Kent Regiment (3rd, 50th and 97th Foot) Formed on 1 March 1961 through the amalgamation of The Buffs (Royal East Kent Regiment) (3rd Foot) and The Queen's Own Royal West Kent Regiment (50th and 97th Foot). On 31 December 1966 the regiment amalgamated with The Queen's Royal Surrey Regiment (2nd, 31st and 70th Foot), The Royal Sussex Regiment (35th and 107th Foot) and The Middlesex Regiment (Duke of Cambridge's Own) (57th and 77th Foot) to form The Queen's Regiment. On 9 September 1992 The Queen's Regiment amalgamated with The Royal Hampshire Regiment to form The Princess of Wales's Royal Regiment (Queen's and Royal Hampshires) (qv).
Headdress Badge: Upon a scroll inscribed 'INVICTA' in Old English lettering the White Horse of Kent.
History: *History of The Queen's Own Buffs 1961-66* by G Blaxland (1974).

Queen's Own Cameron Highlanders (79th Foot) Raised mainly in Lochaber and North Argyll in 1793 and designated 79th Regiment of Foot (Cameronian Volunteers) in that year. Redesignated 79th Foot (Cameronian Highlanders) in 1804 and 79th Foot or Cameron Highlanders in 1806. In 1873 the regiment was retitled 79th Regiment, The Queen's Own Cameron Highlanders and subsequently became The Queen's Own Cameron Highlanders in 1881, a second battalion of the regiment being raised in 1897. On 7 February 1961 the regiment amalgamated with the Seaforth Highlanders (Ross-shire Buffs, The Duke of Albany's) (72nd and 78th Foot) to form the Queen's Own Highlanders (Seaforth and Camerons) (72nd, 78th and 79th Foot) (qv).

Headdress Badge: Saint Andrew and his cross within a wreath of thistles. Below, a scroll inscribed 'CAMERON'.

History: *Historical Records of The Cameron Highlanders* (7 Vols) (Published between 1909 and 1962).

Queen's Own Gurkha Transport Regiment *See: Gurkhas.*

Queen's Own Highlanders (Seaforth And Camerons) (72nd, 78th and 79th Foot) Formed on 7 February 1961 through the amalgamation of the Seaforth Highlanders (Ross-shire Buffs, The Duke of Albany's) (72nd and 78th Foot) and the Queen's Own Cameron Highlanders (79th Foot). On 17 September 1994 the regiment amalgamated with The Gordon Highlanders (75th and 92nd Foot) to form The Highlanders (Seaforth, Gordons, and Camerons) (72nd, 75th, 78th, 79th, and 92nd Foot (qv).

Headdress Badge: A stag's head caboshed, between the attires the thistle ensigned with the crown. Below, a scroll inscribed 'CUIDICH'N RIGH' (Help to the King). The whole ensigned with the crown.

Motto: *Cuidich'n Righ* (Help to the King).

Regimental marches:

Quick marches: *Pibroch of Donuil Dubh* (Pipes and Drums) and *Regimental March of Queen's Own Highlanders* (An arrangement of *Scotland for Ever* and *The March of the Cameron Men*) (Regimental Band).

Slow march: *The Garb of Old Gaul* (Pipes and Drums and Regimental Band).

Regimental headquarters: Cameron Barracks, Inverness, Scotland, IV2 3XD.

History: *'Cuidich'n Righ' - A History of The Queen's Own Highlanders, Seaforth and Camerons* by A A Fairrie (1983).

Queen's Own Hussars *See: Hussars.*

Queen's Own Mercian Yeomanry Yeomanry cavalry regiment on the Territorial Army order of battle until 1 November 1992 when the regiment amalgamated with The Duke of Lancashire's Own Yeomanry (qv) to form The Royal Mercian and Lancastrian Yeomanry (qv).

Headdress Badge: Within a circle inscribed 'QUEEN'S OWN MERCIAN YEOMANRY' a double-headed eagle ensigned with Saxon crown, the whole surmounted by St Edward's crown.

Regimental marches:

Quick march: *The Light of Foot.*

Slow march: *Scipio.*

Queen's Own Regiment (50th Foot) *See: The Queen's Own Royal West Kent Regiment (50th and 97th Foot).*

Queen's Own Royal West Kent Regiment (50th and 97th Foot) The 50th Foot was raised in January 1756 under the colonelcy of James Abercromby as 52nd Foot and renumbered 50th Foot in the December of that year. The regiment was designated 50th (West Kent) Foot in 1782 and redesignated 50th (Duke of Clarence's) Foot in 1827. In 1831 the regiment was retitled 50th (The Queen's Own) Regiment of Foot. The 97th was raised in 1759 and disbanded in 1763, re-raised in 1779 and again disbanded in 1783, re-raised as 97th (Strathspey Highlanders) Regiment in 1794 and disbanded a year later. The regiment was re-raised in 1798 as 97th (Queen's Germans), renumbered 98th Foot in 1804 and disbanded in 1818 as 97th Foot. Re-raised in March 1824 as 97th (Earl of Ulster's) Foot, the regiment amalgamated with 50th (The Queen's Own) Regiment of Foot in May 1881 to form The Royal West Kent Regiment (The Queen's Own), and was retitled two months later as The Queen's Own (Royal West Kent Regiment). On 1 March 1961 the regiment amalgamated with The Buffs (Royal East Kent Regiment) (3rd Foot) to form The Queen's Own Buffs, The Royal Kent Regiment (3rd, 50th and 97th Foot). On 31 December 1966 The Queen's Own Buffs, The Royal Kent Regiment amalgamated with The Queen's Royal Surrey Regiment (2nd, 31st and 70th Foot), The Royal Sussex Regiment (35th and 107th Foot) and The Middlesex Regiment (Duke of Cambridge's Own) (57th and 77th Foot) to form The Queen's Regiment (qv). On 9 September 1992 The Queen's Regiment amalgamated with The Royal Hampshire Regiment to form The Princess of Wales's Royal Regiment (Queen's and Royal Hampshires) (qv).

Headdress Badge: Upon a scroll 'INVICTA' in Old English lettering the White Horse of Kent. Below, a scroll inscribed 'ROYAL WEST KENT'.

History: *The History of the 50th (The Queen's Own) Regiment* by A E Fyler; *The 97th or Earl of Ulster's Regiment 1824-1881* by H D Chaplin; *The Queen's Own Royal West Kent Regiment 1881-1914* by H D Chaplin; *'INVICTA' With the 1st Battalion The Queen's Own Royal West Kent Regiment in The Great War* by C V Molony; *The Queen's Own Royal West Kent Regiment 1914-1919,* by C T Atkinson; *The Queen's Own Royal West Kent Regiment 1920-1950* by H D Chaplin and *From Kent to Kohima, being the History of the 4th Battalion The Queen's Own Royal West Kent Regiment (TA) 1939-1947* by E B Stanley Clarke and A T Tillot.

Queen's Own Yeomanry Formed as a Territorial Army medium reconnaissance regiment on 1 April 1971 from squadrons drawn from The Queen's Own Yorkshire Yeomanry, The Ayrshire Yeomanry, The Cheshire Yeomanry and the Northumberland Hussars. The regiment was given a reconnaissance role in support of the British Army of the Rhine. Following a reorganisation in 1992, the Ayrshire Yeomanry squadron was replaced by a squadron from the Sherwood Rangers Yeomanry. The regiment's current role is in support of the Allied Command Europe Rapid Reaction Corps. As at April 1994 the regiment comprised 'Y' (Yorkshire Yeomanry) Squadron, 'B' (Sherwood Rangers Yeomanry) Squadron, 'C' (The Cheshire (Earl of Chester's) Yeomanry) Squadron, 'D' (Northumberland Hussars), 'RHQ' and 'HQ' (Northumberland Hussars) Squadron.

Badge: A fox. Below, a scroll inscribed 'QUEEN'S OWN YEOMANRY'. However, squadrons wear their own regimental cap badges.

Regimental quick march: *D'ye ken John Peel.*

Queen's Regiment (8th Foot) *See: The King's Regiment (8th, 63rd and 96th Foot).*

Queen's Regiment (2nd, 3rd, 31st, 35th, 50th, 57th, 70th, 77th, 97th and 107th Foot) Formed on 31 December 1966 through the amalgamation of The Queen's Royal Surrey Regiment (2nd, 31st and 70th Foot), The Queen's Own Buffs, The Royal Kent Regiment (3rd, 50th and 97th Foot), The Royal Sussex Regiment (35th and 107th Foot), and The Middlesex Regiment (Duke of Cambridge's Own) (57th and 77th Foot). On 9 September 1992 the regiment amalgamated with The Royal Hampshire Regiment (37th and 67th Foot) to form The Princess of Wales's Royal Regiment (Queen's and Royal Hampshires (qv).

Headdress Badge: Within the garter the dragon. Above, the plume and coronet of The Prince of Wales. Below, upon a scroll, the title 'QUEEN'S'.

History: *Soldiers of the Queen, The History of The Queen's Regiment 1966-1992* by J P Riley (1993).

Queen's Regulations More properly, Queen's Regulations for the Army 1975. A set of general regulations for the good government of the Army, which are periodically reviewed, and may be supplemented by other instructions issued by the Ministry of Defence from time to time. *See also: Military Law.*

Queen's Royal Irish Hussars *See: Hussars.*

Queen's Royal Lancers *See: Lancers.*

Queen's Royal Surrey Regiment (2nd, 31st and 70th Foot) Formed on 14 October 1959 through the amalgamation of The Queen's Royal Regiment (West Surrey) (2nd Foot) and The East Surrey Regiment (31st and 70th Foot). On 31

December 1966 The Queen's Royal Surrey Regiment amalgamated with The Queen's Own Buffs, The Royal Kent Regiment (3rd, 50th and 97th Foot), The Royal Sussex Regiment (35th and 107th Foot), and The Middlesex Regiment (Duke of Cambridge's Own) (57th and 77th Foot), to form The Queen's Regiment (qv). On 9 September 1992 The Queen's Regiment amalgamated with The Royal Hampshire Regiment to form The Princess of Wales's Royal Regiment (Queen's and Royal Hampshires) (qv).

Headdress Badge: Upon an eight-pointed star the Paschal Lamb and flag, ensigned with the crown.

History: *History of The Queen's Royal Surrey Regiment* by J P Riley.

Queen's Royal Regiment (West Surrey) (2nd Foot) Raised in September 1661 by Henry Mordaunt, Earl of Peterborough, as part of the Tangier garrison and styled The Tangier Regiment. Retitled The Queen's Regiment in 1684, The Queen Dowager's Regiment in 1686, The Queen's Royal Regiment in 1703, The Princess of Wales's Own Regiment of Foot in 1727, The Royal West Surrey Regiment (The Queen's) in May 1881, and, two months later, The Queen's (Royal West Surrey Regiment). In 1921 the regiment was retitled The Queen's Royal Regiment (West Surrey). On 14 October 1959 the regiment amalgamated with The East Surrey Regiment (31st and 70th Foot) to form The Queen's Royal Surrey Regiment (2nd, 31st and 70th Foot). On 31 December 1966 The Queen's Royal Surrey Regiment amalgamated with The Queen's Own Buffs, The Royal Kent Regiment (3rd, 50th and 97th Foot), The Royal Sussex Regiment (35th and 107th Foot), and The Middlesex Regiment (Duke of Cambridge's Own) (57th and 77th Foot), to form The Queen's Regiment (qv). On 9 September 1992 The Queen's Regiment amalgamated with The Royal Hampshire Regiment to form The Princess of Wales's Royal Regiment (Queen's and Royal Hampshires) (qv).

Headdress Badge: On a ground the Paschal Lamb and flag.

History: *History of The Queen's Royal Regiment* (9 Vols), (Vol 9 - 1948-59) by Foster (1961) and *History of The Queen's Royal Regiment* by J Haswell.

Queen's Shilling *See: King's Shilling.*

Queen's South Africa Medal 1899-1902 Issued to mark service in the South African or Boer Wars.

Ribbon: A broad vertical orange band at the centre is flanked on either side by a blue vertical stripe and a wider vertical red stripe.

Clasps: Cape Colony; Natal; Rhodesia; Relief of Mafeking; Defence of Kimberley; Talana; Elands-Laagte; Defence of Ladysmith; Belmont; Modder River; Tugela Heights; Relief of Kimberley; Paaderberg; Orange Free State; Relief of Ladysmith; Driefontein; Wepener; Defence of Mafeking; Transvaal; Johannesburg; Laing's Nek; Diamond Hill; Wittebergen; Belfast; South Africa 1901 and South Africa 1902.

Queens' Sudan Medal 1896-97 Awarded in 1899 to those who served in the reconquest of the Sudan.

Ribbon: Half yellow, half black, with a thin vertical red stripe in the centre.

Queenstown Battle honour marking the defeat of the main American invasion in October 1812 by General Brock in command of a mainly Canadian force. The battle is sometimes known as the battle of Queenstown Heights. *See also: Detroit; Miami; Niagara and Bladensburg.*

Queue The hair of a soldier bound back and secured into a pigtail. *See also: Flash.*

Quick Attack The quick attack is one in which preparation time is deliberately traded for speed in order to exploit an opportunity.

Quick March The regulation rates of the march in quick time are: foot guards - 116 paces to the minute; light infantry and rifle regiments - 140 paces to the minute; highland regiments - 110 paces to the minute and infantry of the line and other dismounted regiments -120 paces to the minute.

Quick Reaction Force (QRF) A formed unit or sub-unit, usually held at immediate or very short notice to move, to assist or support operations by other individuals, units or sub-units. The strength, equipment and weaponry of a quick reaction force will reflect likely tasks.

Quillons Cross bars or side pieces on the hilt of a sword to prevent the hand sliding down to the blade.

Quis Separabit **(Who shall separate?)** Motto of 4th Royal Irish Dragoon Guards, 4th/7th Royal Dragoon Guards, 5th Royal Irish Lancers, Irish Guards, The Royal Ulster Rifles and 86th (Royal County Down) Regiment of Foot.

Quo Fas Et Gloria Ducunt **(Whither Right and Glory Lead)** Motto of the Royal Regiment of Artillery, the Corps of Royal Engineers, The Queen's Own Royal West Kent Regiment and 97th (Earl of Ulster's) Regiment of Foot.

Quo Fata Vocant **(Whither the Fates lead)** Motto of 7th Dragoon Guards (Princess Royal's) and The Royal Northumberland Fusiliers.

Racoon Initially it was usual for grenadiers and fusiliers to wear bearskin caps but, in the 1870s, black racoon-skin caps 9" high were authorised for fusilier regiments. Dress regulations of 1900 allowed either bearskin or racoon skin.

Radetsky March and ***Rusty Buckles*** An arrangement of these two tunes forms the regimental quick march of 1st The Queen's Dragoon Guards. *Radetsky March* is taken from 1st King's Dragoon Guards and *Rusty Buckles* from The Queen's Bay's (2nd Dragoon Guards).

Radfan *See: South Arabia 1964-1967.*

Radio Appointment Titles Titles used in operational communications to describe specific appointments or specialists at any level of command. It is not clear when such titles were first used; there is an early reference to the use of 'Sunray' (commander) in a training manual on switchboard procedures dated 1942, and the first reference to the complete list of titles appears in a Signals Training Manual of 1943.

Radio Silence A condition under which, for operational reasons, all or selected radio equipments are kept inoperative in order to reduce or eliminate radiation.

Rafah First World War Egyptian campaign battle honour marking the capture of this town on the Palestine border in early 1917 as a preliminary to the British advance against the Turks in Palestine in March 1917. *See also: Egypt 1915-17; Palestine 1917-18; Suez Canal; Agagiya; Rumani and Gaza.*

Rag Nickname for the Army and Navy Club at 36 Pall Mall, London. The club was founded on 31 August 1837 at a meeting of the Board of Officers. The nickname is derived from a tavern where gambling took place, called the 'Rag and Famish', in Cranborne Alley. On return to the club one evening Captain William (Billy) Duff and his colleagues demanded supper. The supper offered was so meagre that Captain Duff declared it to be a 'Rag and Famish' affair. The nickname, at first derogatory, is now one of affection and much used.

Raggie A single-breasted undress garment which could be worn as a pelisse adopted by some mounted men in the early 19th century.

Raglan, Lord Fitzroy James Henry Somerset, first Baron (1788-1855) Entered the Army in 1804 and went to Portugal in 1808 as aide-de-camp to Wellington. As a result of a wound received at Waterloo, his right arm was amputated. Military Secretary at the Horse Guards from 1827 until 1852 when he was appointed Master General of the Ordnance and raised to the peerage. In 1854 he was appointed to command the British troops sent against Russia in the Crimean War, but died of dysentery before Sevastopol.

Ragoubet Souissi Second World War North Africa campaign battle honour marking one of the engagements in the breakthrough to and capture of Tunis on 7 May 1943. *See also: North Africa 1940-1943; Tunis; Hammam Lif; Djebel Bou Aoukaz 1943 II; Creteville Pass; Gromballa; and Bou Ficha.*

Raj The British government in India before 1947.

Rajput, Rajpoot A Hindu military caste claiming descent from the *Kshatriya*, the original warrior caste.

Rake to direct gunfire along the length of a target.

Ramillies Battle honour marking Marlborough's great victory over the French under Villleroi on 12 May 1706. *See also: Blenheim; Oudenarde and Malplaquet.*

Ramree Second World War Burma campaign battle honour marking one of the actions during the final operations in the Arakan, January to April 1945, which brought the campaign to an end. *See also: Burma 1942-1945; Arakan Beaches; Dalet; Tamandu; Taungup; Myebon and Kangaw.*

Ramrod A rod for cleaning the barrel of a rifle or other small arms. Also, a rod used for ramming in the charge or projectile from either muzzle or breech end of the barrel.

Range The effective distance a projectile can be fired from a weapon. The distance from firer to target. An area set aside for the live firing of weapons. The distance a vehicle can go without refuelling, and over which electro-magnetic signals can be transmitted.

Rangefinder Instrument for establishing the distance from observer to target. Formerly optical instruments, now largely laser.

Ranger A private soldier (qv) in the Royal Irish Rangers.

Ranger Mine An anti-personnel mine which is launched from a projector mounted on the roof of an AFV432. The projector can carry 72 tubes, each tube capable of holding 18 mines, each mine containing a 10g charge of high explosive. The mine casing is of plastic-type material and difficult to detect. *See also: Vehicle Launched Scatterable Mine System.*

Rangoon Road Second World War Burma campaign battle honour marking the advance Southward to capture Rangoon 1 April-6 May 1945. *See also: Burma 1942-1945; Pyabwe; Toungoo and Pegu 1945.*

Rank The use of titles denoting military rank with their present meaning is relatively modern; only captain having been used in late medieval times to denote the commander of a company, which was the largest permanently organised body of professional soldiers that existed up to Elizabethan times. The captain's deputy was called lieutenant, like any other deputy, and for a long time had to be particularised as lieutenant-captain. Below the lieutenant ranked the ensign or ancient, vulgarly known as the 'rag carrier', which adequately explains his duties in action. The equivalent rank in the cavalry up to about 1872 was cornet; now obsolete. Sergeant in its military sense also dates from the Middle Ages, originally denoting one whose feudal tenure of land obliged him to follow armed to the field the tenant-in-chief. Over the years it acquired the meaning of one deputed to enforce discipline. As the unit of trained soldiers became larger the chief sergeant of a group of companies or regiment was called sergeant-major, and at the time of the Civil War, this officer ranked above captain and fulfilled the duties of a modern adjutant. Then the word was taken to mean the disciplinary chief of a company, the corresponding officer of a regiment being called simply major. The whole force at this time was administered by the sergeant-major-general, now abbreviated to major-general, under the command of the captain-general, now simply general, whose deputy was a lieutenant-general. Colonel originally meant the commander of a column of companies, and in the 17th century his primary function was to recruit and pay a regiment which would bear his name. As the colonel might at the same time be a general, actual command of the regiment or its battalions, if there were more than one, was exercised by a lieutenant colonel. This is the origin of the modern system of appointing honorary colonels of regiments. A relic of the *condottieri* (mercenaries, usually English or German, in the service of the Italian city-states) is found in the title corporal, an officer of the lowest rank commanding a small body (or *Corpo*) of men. The prefix lance (from the Italian for veteran) meant a senior soldier or lance corporal acting in the place of a corporal; or lance sergeant, a senior corporal carrying out the duties of a sergeant. In the Household Cavalry (qv) sergeants are known as corporals of horse and warrant officers as corporals-major. The name given to the rank of private soldiers will vary in accordance with their regiment, arm or service; such as trooper, gunner, sapper, signalman, guardsman, fusilier, rifleman, driver, craftsman etc.

Rank and File Term used to describe the Army excluding the commissioned officers.

Ranker Term, now obsolete, for a person commissioned from the ranks.

Rapier Area low level air defence missile system with semi-automatic to line of sight guidance, firing a missile of 13.3cm diameter with high explosive warhead at a speed in excess of Mach 2. For planning purposes it has a minimum range of 900m, and a maximum range of 5,000m. Produced in both tracked and wheel-mounted versions.

Rathedaung Second World War Burma campaign battle honour marking one of the actions during the British offensive into the Arakan, directed at Akyab, in early 1943 which was repulsed by the Japanese. *See also: Burma 1942-1945; Donbaik; Htizwe and Point 201 (Arakan).*

Rattan A light cane used in India to form the insides of sun helmets.

Rawlinson of Trent, Sir Henry Seymour Rawlinson, 1st Baron and 2nd Baronet (1864-1925) Educated Eton and Sandhurst and commissioned into the King's Royal Rifle Corps in 1884. Served on Kitchener's staff in the Sudan 1898, and in the South African War. In 1914 he led the 7th Division to Ypres and was appointed to command the new Fourth

Army in 1915. He organised the principal Somme offensive of 1916. After a period on the Versailles Council he returned to command the reorganised Fourth Army in the final offensives of the First World War. In 1919 he executed the evacuation of Murmansk and Archangel, for which he received a Barony. From November 1920 he was Commander-in-Chief India.

Razibil Second World War Burma campaign battle honour marking fighting which took place between January and March 1944 in the North Arakan offensive. Razibil was taken by the British in mid-March after earlier attacks had been repulsed. *See also: Burma 1942-1945; North Arakan; Buthidaung; Kaladan; Mayu Tunnels; Alethangyaw; Maungdaw; Mowdok and Point 551.*

Razor Wire Development of barbed wire. Sharp-edged projections are formed at regular intervals on a sharp-edged metal ribbon.

Rearguard A force tasked to protect the rear of a moving formation.

Rear Sight The sight nearest the firer's eye, usually consisting of an aperture or V-shape through which the foresight and target are viewed.

Recce Flight Regimental quick march of the Army Air Corps.

Recognition The ability to identify, and differentiate between, by observation, or another detection method, friendly and hostile vehicles, equipment and personnel.

Recoil The rearward force when a weapon is fired.

Recoilless Term used to denote a weapon in which the back blast caused by the weapon firing is vented or dissipated to reduce recoil.

RECONNAISSANCE
The obtaining by visual observation, or another detection method, of information

about the activities and resources of an enemy or potential enemy. The term may also be applied to the obtaining of meteorological, hydrographic or geographic information. There are four broad types of reconnaissance:

Combat Reconnaissance This is carried out by the combat arms while observing or engaging the enemy in close combat.

Close Reconnaissance This is carried out by reconnaissance patrols which may be air or vehicle-mounted or on foot, to provide information of interest to a battle group commander.

Medium Reconnaissance This is carried out by reconnaissance and aviation regiments to acquire information, preferably by stealth, for a formation commander.

Long Range Reconnaissance This is the deep reconnaissance of enemy rear areas carried out by special forces, satellites, aircraft, drones and remotely-piloted vehicles to identify enemy installations, dumps, routes, parachute dropping zones and helicopter landing sites.

Reconnaissance Patrol A small patrol tasked to gain information, preferably by stealth, about an enemy. *See also: Patrol.*

Reconstitution In the British Army the term reconstitution is used in an operational sense to mean the ability to restore units that have suffered attrition to a level of combat effectiveness commensurate with their anticipated future tasks by reinforcement and the provision of the necessary weapon, equipment, ammunition and combat resources. *See also: Regeneration.*

Record Office More usually known as a Manning and Record Office. The place where all unit personal records, less those of officers, are held.

Recruit To enlist individuals into the Army. A newly joined and as yet untrained member of the Army.

Redan A defensive work consisting of two parapets at a salient angle.

Redcap Nickname for a member of the Royal Corps of Military Police, derived from the red covers to their caps.

Redcoat The British soldier.

Red Cross Distinctive emblem of the medical services of the Army and armed Services. Protection may be claimed under the First Geneva Convention (1864) for medical personnel, buildings, equipment and transport when operating as part of those medical services.

Red Devils Nickname for The Parachute Regiment bestowed on them by the Germans following their stubborn fight at the battle of Tamera 5-15 March 1943 during the campaign in North Africa.

Red Feathers Nickname given to 46th Foot, later The Duke of Cornwall's Light Infantry. During the American War of Independence the 46th Foot surprised and put to the bayonet an American force at Brandywine (1777). The Americans swore revenge and the 46th Foot dyed their cap feathers red to make themselves identifiable to the avenging Americans.

Redoubt An outwork or detached earthwork defending a pass or hilltop. A temporary defensive earthwork constructed within a fortified area as a position of final defence.

Redress of Grievance The procedure under which a member of the Army may seek the setting right of a wrong.

Re-Enlistment A person who rejoins the Army having previously been discharged.

Reference Point Prominent landscape feature, natural or man-made, with reference to which directions can be given to assist an observer identify other objects or targets.

Regalbuto Second World War Sicilian campaign battle honour marking the fighting 29 July - 3 August 1943 which led to the capture of Regalbuto. *See also: Sicily 1943; Primosole Bridge; Sferro; Centuripe and Adrano.*

Regeneration In the British Army the term regeneration is applied to the ability to bring units from their current establishment to full war establishment. This may be applied to particular units and formations or to the Army as a whole, when it would include at least some of the mobilisation measures. *See also: Reconstitution.*

Regency Shako Pattern of shako worn during the regency of Prince George, later George IV (1820-1830). *See also: Shako.*

Regiment The largest permanently established unit of the Royal Armoured Corps, Royal Artillery, Royal Engineers, Royal Signals, Infantry and Army Air Corps; usually commanded by a lieutenant colonel. An infantry regiment may comprise a number of battalions, each commanded by a lieutenant colonel, and further divided into companies usually commanded by majors. Non-infantry regiments are composed of a number of squadrons or, in the case of the Royal Artillery, batteries, which broadly equate in size to infantry companies and are also commanded by majors.

Regimental Quartermaster Sergeant A warrant officer class 2, senior warrant officer in either the orderly room or the quartermasters department of a regiment or battalion. The titles regimental quartermaster-corporal and orderly room corporal of horse are used in the Household Cavalry.

Regimental Sergeant-Major A warrant officer class 1 and the senior warrant officer in a regiment or battalion. He is responsible to the commanding officer through the adjutant for all aspects of duty and discipline of the warrant officers, non-commissioned officers and men. The titles regimental corporal major or farrier corporal major are used in the Household Cavalry.

Regrouping The adjustment of the constitution (task organisation) of a force before an operation to better suit it for its given mission in the light of the overall resources available.

Regular A volunteer, full-time, professional member of the Army.

Regular Commission A regular commission provides a full pensionable career for officers, normally to the age of 55 years.

Regular Commissions Board The board is now responsible for examining all candidates for commissions in the Army. The board is required to make a recommendation as to their suitability. Assessment is carried out through a programme of interviews and tests lasting three and a half days. The board is located at Leighton House, Westbury, Wiltshire.

Reichswald Second World War battle honour marking one of the actions during the Allied advance from the River Roer to the Rhine in early 1945. This wooded area was cleared following a preparatory artillery bombardment of great intensity by mid-February. *See also: North West Europe 1944-1945; Rhineland; Cleve; Goch; Weeze; Schaddenhof; Hochwald; Waal Flats; Moyland; Moyland Wood and Xanten.*

Relief Authorised replacement at a task or duty. It is usual for such relief to be supervised so that the individual assuming the duty or task is properly prepared.

Relief in Place The operation in which, at the direction of higher authority, all or part of a force or unit is replaced in a given area by an incoming force or unit which normally assumes the mission of the relieved force or unit.

Relief of Kimberley South Africa War battle honour marking the relief of Kimberley, which had been besieged by the Boers from 14 October 1899 to 15 February 1900 during the second South Africa or Boer War. *See also: South Africa 1899-1902; Defence of Ladysmith; Relief of Ladysmith; Defence of Kimberley; Modder River and Paardeburg.*

Relief of Kohima Second World War Burma campaign battle honour marking the relief of Kohima in June 1944 following repeated attempts by the Japanese to capture the town which lies astride the route to the Assam Valley. *See also: Burma 1942-1945; Kohima; Defence of Kohima; Aradura; Naga Village and Mao Songsang.*

Relief of Ladysmith South Africa War battle honour marking the relief of Ladysmith which had been besieged from 29 October 1899 to 28 February 1900 during the second South Africa or Boer War. *See also: South Africa 1899-1902; Defence of Ladysmith; Defence of Kimberley; Relief of Kimberley; Modder River and Paardeburg.*

Relief of Tobruk Second World War North Africa campaign battle honour marking the successful conclusion of Operation CRUSADER in November and December 1941 after a period of confused and inconclusive fighting. Tobruk was relieved and the enemy forced to withdraw from most of Cyrenaica, having held temporarily on the Gazala position. *See also: North Africa 1940-1943; Tobruk 1941; Gubi I; Sidi Rezegh 1941; Tobruk Sortie; Omars; Belhamed Gabr Saleh; Taieb El Essem and Gubi II.*

Remote Term given to the facility (and the equipment) which permits an individual to operate an equipment from a position at some distance from the equipment.

Rendezvous A pre-arranged meeting at an agreed time and location.

Renfrewshire Yeomanry Evidence exists of there having been a corps of yeomanry in Renfrewshire from 1795 until 1802. In 1813 three troops are recorded, and evidence of service until 1839 has been found.

Report Line A line at right angles to the axis, linking or following easily recognizable features, which is used to monitor and control progress. Moving units are required to report their arrival at report lines, such lines usually being given nicknames.

Research Department Explosive A white crystalline insoluble explosive prepared by the action of nitric acid on hexamethylenetrinitramine. Also known as Cyclonite or RDX.

Reserve Army The reserve army consists of two broad categories: the 'Regular Reserves' comprising ex-service men and women with a reserve liability, and the 'Volunteer Reserves', consisting of Volunteer units and individuals. A draft Reserve Forces Act is currently under discussion which seeks to introduce: a new power of call-out for peacekeeping, humanitarian and disaster relief operations; opportunities for reservists to undertake tasks other than training in peacetime; two new categories of reserve, and improved conditions and terms of service for both reservists and employers.

Reserves Reserves may be quantities of stocks held against emergency, unforseen fluctuations and expenditure, delays in production or transit. Reserves may also be personnel, units or formations earmarked for future use on mobilization or against an operational requirement, or withheld from action at the beginning of an engagement. During operations it is usual for reserves to be held at all levels but, due to the scarcity of resources, it is unusual for such reserves to be held uncommitted to any role.

Reshire Battle honour marking an action in the Anglo-Persian War 1856-57, in which a British expeditionary force from Bombay captured the Dutch fort at Reshire on 7 December 1856, which lay on its route to Bushire on the Persian Gulf. *See also: Persia; Bushire and Koosh-Ab.*

Residence The official home of a senior officer, which he occupies by virtue of his appointment.

Residency The term is now obsolete, but was formerly used to describe the official house of the governor-general at the court of a native ruler in India.

Respirator Equipment which covers the eyes, nose and mouth of the soldier and provides him with filtered air, thus preventing the inhalation of biological or chemical agents.

Rest and Recuperation The term used for a recreational break from operations or arduous training, known widely as 'R and R'.

Restriction of Privileges An authorised form of punishment in the Army, usually awarded for minor offences. The privileges most usually restricted are the wearing of plain clothes and permission to leave barracks after duty.

Retimo Second World War Crete campaign battle honour marking an action during the German airborne attack on Crete on 20 May 1941. *See also: Crete; Canea; Heraklion and Withdrawal to Sphakia.*

Retirement The movement away from the enemy of a force which is not at the time in contact with the enemy. This is usually for administrative or logistic reasons. *See also: Withdrawal.*

Retma Second World War North Africa campaign battle honour marking one of the actions during the German assault on the Gazala Line 26 May - 21 June 1942. On 27 May the Germans launched an attack on an isolated brigade at Retma which, after a night withdrawal from the position, re-established itself at El Gubi. *See also: North Africa 1940-1943; Gazala; Bir El Aslagh; Bir Hacheim; Cauldron; Knightsbridge; Tobruk 1942; Bir El Igela; Hagiag Er Raml; Gabr El Fachri; Via Balbia; Zt El Mrasses and Sidi Rezegh 1942.*

Retreat A planned, controlled and co-ordinated operation of war, either forced or strategical, by which a force retires before an enemy. Also the playing, beating or sounding of 'Retreat' by a military band, drums, pipes or bugles at sunset, or at some other time which may be laid down in regulations. *See also: Beating Retreat and Sounding Retreat.*

Retreat from Mons First World War battle honour marking the retreat of the British Expeditionary Force from Mons following its first contact with the advancing German army on 23 August 1914. The British force in Mons, inspite of inflicting a very heavy toll on the Germans, was clearly going to be overwhelmed and a 240 mile retreat, often punctuated by sharp rearguard actions, was conducted over a 16 day period. *See also: France and Flanders 1914-1918; Mons; Le Cateau and Marne 1914.*

Reveille Signal given by bugle, drum or bagpipe to rouse soldiers from sleep.

Reverse Slope Any slope which descends away from an enemy. A reverse slope position is one that is not exposed to direct fire or observation. *See also: Forward Slope.*

Review Formal inspection and ceremonial parade of one or more units by the Sovereign, a senior officer or other dignitary.

Revolver A pistol having a revolving multi-chambered cylinder which rotates exposing a new chamber at each firing, thus aligning a fresh cartridge with the firing mechanism.

Rhine Second World War battle honour marking the assault river crossing of the River Rhine on 23 March 1945 and subsequent build up in the bridgehead. *See also: North West Europe 1944-1945 and Rhineland.*

Rhineland Second World War battle honour marking the advance from the River Roer to the Rhine which took place between 8 February and 10 March 1945. *See also: North West Europe 1944-1945; Reichswald; Cleve; Goch; Weeze; Schaddenhof; Hochwald; Waal Flats; Moyland; Moyland Wood and Xanten.*

Ricochet To rebound from a surface or surfaces, usually with a characteristic whining sound. A bullet which ricochets.

Ride of the Valkyries Regimental quick march of the Parachute Regiment.

Rienzi Regimental slow march of 17th/21st Lancers.

Rifle A small arm having a long barrel with a spirally grooved interior (the rifling) which imparts a spinning motion to the projectile giving it greater accuracy over a longer range. Sights may be open (iron), aperture or telescopic. Also, the process of cutting or moulding grooves inside the barrel of a gun. Although some authorities consider that rifling of an early type was first used as early as 1498, the first issue of rifles in any quantity in the British Army was made to the 'Experimental Corps of Riflemen' (later the Rifle Brigade) in 1800 and used by them in the Peninsula War. Many different models of rifle have featured in the history of the British Army, but the most significant and most widely issued were the Baker, Minié, Enfield, Martini-Henry, Lee-Metford, Short Magazine Lee Enfield, Lee Enfield Number 4, Self-Loading Rifle L1A1 and SA80.

Rifle-Bird or Rifleman Bird Bird of paradise (*Ptiloris paradisea*) which occurs in Australia and New Guinea. It is alleged to have been given the name by early settlers in Australia from the resemblance of its plumage to the uniform of the Rifle Brigade.

Rifle Brigade (Prince Consort's Own) (95th Foot) Raised in 1800 from selected detachments from other regiments, as The Experimental Corps of Riflemen, commanded by Colonel Coote Manningham, and designated 95th (Rifle) Regiment in 1803. In 1816 the regiment was removed from the numbered regiments of the line and titled The Rifle Brigade. In 1862 the regiment was retitled The Prince Consort's Own Rifle Brigade, and in May 1881 Rifle Brigade (The Prince Consort's Own), only to be redesignated The Prince Consort's Own (Rifle Brigade) two months later. In 1920 the regiment reverted to the style of May 1881 as The Rifle Brigade (Prince Consort's Own). On 7 November 1958 the regiment was redesignated 3rd Green Jackets (The Rifle Brigade) and, on 1 January 1966, amalgamated with 1st Green Jackets (43rd and 52nd), and 2nd Green Jackets (The King's Royal Rifle Corps) to form The Royal Green Jackets (qv).

Headdress Badge: A maltese cross bearing a circle enclosing a stringed bugle-horn, all within a laurel wreath. On the arms of the cross 16 battle honours. Below, a naval crown superscribed 'COPENHAGEN, 2 APRIL, 1801'. Above, 'WATERLOO' upon a tablet, ensigned with the guelphic crown.

History: *The History of the Rifle Brigade* by W H Cope (1877); *History and Campaigns of the Rifle Brigade* (2 Parts) by W Verner (1912 and 1919); *The Rifle Brigade 1914-18* (2 Vols.) by R Berkeley (1927) and W Seymour (1936); *The Rifle Brigade 1939-45* by Hastings (1950); *Jackets of Green* by Arthur Bryant (1972) and *The Rifle Brigade* by B Harvey (1975).

Rifle Green Dark green as used in the uniforms of rifle and light infantry regiments.

Rifle Grenade Grenade discharged from a rifle.

Rifleman A private soldier (qv) in a rifle regiment. The term is also in general use to describe a soldier, of any of any arm, who is armed with a rifle.

Right of the Line When on parade the order of precedence runs from right to left flank, the senior regiment being on the right flank. However, it is usual for rifle regiments to forego their place in the order of precedence and parade on the extreme left flank of the parade.

Rim Projecting edge around the base of a cartridge which provides a point of attachment for the ejection mechanism. *See also: Rim-less.*

Rim-Fire A cartridge having the primer in the rim of the base. *See also: Centre-fire.*

Rimini Line Second World War Italian campaign battle honour marking the penetration of the German defences in the Rimini area by the Eighth Army in September 1944. *See also: Italy 1943-1945; Ceriano Ridge; Monte Colombo; Casa Fabri Ridge; Montescudo; Frisoni and San Marino.*

Rim-Less A cartridge which has no projecting rim around the base. In such cases it is usual for there to be groove around the base of the cartridge which is engaged by the ejection mechanism.

Riot Act A statute of 1715 which provided that if riotous assemblies of 12 or more persons did not disperse after the reading of a proclamation by a local government officer - more usually a magistrate - ordering them, in the name of the Sovereign, to do so, they would be guilty of a felony punishable by death. The so-called 'reading of the riot act' was a precursor to the ordering of troops to disperse rioters.

Riot Gun Large calibre hand gun used to fire baton (qv) rounds, tear gas cartridges or, very occasionally, shot.

Riot Shield Large transparent shield, usually proof against low velocity bullets, used in riot situations to protect soldiers from missiles thrown by the rioters.

Ripa Ridge Second World War Italian campaign battle honour marking one of the actions during the advance following the fall of Rome in June 1944 and first contact with the German Gothic Line defensive positions which stretched from Pisa to Rimini, in August 1944. *See also: Italy 1943-1945; Advance to Florence; Monte Rotondo; Monte Gabbione; Gabbiano and Arezzo.*

Rising of the Lark Regimental quick march of the Welsh Guards.

Risle Crossing Second World War battle honour marking one of the actions which took place between the Allied landings in Normandy in June 1944 and the crossing of the River Seine in August 1944. *See also: North West Europe 1944-1945; Port-en-Bessin; Tourmauville Bridge; St Pierre La Veille; Estry; Noireau Crossing; La Vie Crossing; La Touques Crossing and Foret de Bretonne.*

Roadblock Barriers set up across a road, usually in the form of a chicane, in order to stop and inspect vehicles.

Road to the Isles Regimental double march of The Royal Green Jackets.

Robaa Valley Second World War North Africa campaign battle honour marking a hard fought and successful defensive action by British troops on 31 January 1943 during the German offensive against British, French and American positions. *See also: North Africa 1940-1943; Bou Arada and Kasserine.*

Roccheta E Croce Second World War Italian campaign battle honour marking one of the actions which took place between the United States Fifth Army, including the British X Corps, landing at Salerno on 9 September 1943 and its contact with the Gustav Line in October 1943. *See also: Italy 1943-1945; Capture of Naples; Cappezano; Monte Stella; Cava di Tirreni; Scafati Bridge; Cardito; Volturno Crossing; Monte Maro and Colle Cedro.*

Rocket Self-propelling device, usually cylindrical in shape, which may be the vehicle for the delivery of a high explosive warhead or for illuminating or distress flares.

Roer Second World War battle honour marking the fighting which took place in the move to close on the line of the River Roer 16-31 January 1945. *See also: North West Europe 1944-1945; Scheldt; Ourthe and Rhineland.*

Rohilcand 1774 Battle honour marking the First Rohilla War campaign by a Bengal army force commanded by Colonel Champion in support of the Nawab of Oudh, a British ally, against the Rohillas. The key engagement of the campaign was at Kutra near Bareilly on 23 April, resulting in the capture of significant booty.

Rohilcand 1794 Battle honour marking operations in the Second Rohilla War by a force led by Lord Cornwallis against the rebel state of Rampur. As in the First Rohilla War, the key action took place near Bareilly, this time at Bithaura.

Rohilla Wars *See: Rohilcand 1774 (First*

Rohilla War) and Rohilcand 1794 (Second Rohilla War).

Roliça Peninsula War battle honour marking the first major action of the war on 17 August 1808 when a British force recently landed in Portugal, under Sir Arthur Wellesley, defeated a French division under Laborde. *See also: Peninsula; Vimiera; Sahagun; Corunna and Douro.*

Rolling Attack Two or more successive attacks on the same enemy by armed helicopters.

Romagnoli Second World War Italian campaign battle honour marking an action in the battle of the Sangro, 19 November to 3 December 1943. *See also: Italy 1943-1945; Sangro; Mozzagrogna and Fossacesia.*

Roman Helmet Official designation of an all-metal helmet worn by heavy cavalry from 1817 until it was replaced by the Albert Helmet (qv) in about 1842.

Rome Second World War Italian campaign battle honour marking the actions covering before and during the capture of Rome 22 May-4 June 1944. *See also: Italy 1943-1945 and Advance to Tiber.*

Rorke's Drift Small settlement on the Tugela River, 28 miles from Dundee, Natal, South Africa at which a detachment of 24th Foot (The South Wales Borderers) made a successful stand against a Zulu army on 22 January 1879. *See also: South Africa 1879.*

Rose And Laurel Regimental quick march of the Intelligence Corps.

Rosières First World War battle honour marking the stand by Fifth Army, and particularly that by 61st Brigade on 26 March 1918, during the German Somme offensive of 21 March - 5 April 1918. *See also: France and Flanders 1914-1918; Somme 1918; St Quentin; Bapaume 1918; Arras 1918; Avre and Ancre 1918.*

Ross-Shire Buffs *See: Seaforth Highlanders.*

Round A single cartridge or charge. More properly, the projectile.

Rover A unit or sub-unit commander's vehicle, fitted with the appropriate communications. From 'Land Rover', the vehicle most frequently used for such purpose.

Rover Group Term applied to the team which travels with, and supports, a commanding officer in his 'Rover'. It is customary for the Rover Group to include an escort vehicle and crew.

Roxburghshire Yeomanry (The Roxburghshire Yeomanry Light Dragoons) The Western and Eastern troops of Roxburghshire Yeomanry Cavalry were raised in 1797. The Corps became known as the Roxburghshire Yeomanry Light Dragoons. In 1828 the regiment was disbanded. In 1872 the 1st Roxburghshire (The Border) Mounted Rifle Volunteer Corps was formed, but was disbanded in 1892.

Royal Anglian Regiment (9th, 10th, 12th, 16th, 17th, 44th, 48th, 56th and 58th Foot) Formed on 1 September 1964 through the amalgamation of 1st East Anglian Regiment (Royal Norfolk and Suffolk) (9th and 12th Foot), 2nd East Anglian Regiment (Duchess of Gloucester's Own Royal Lincolnshire and Northamptonshire) (10th, 48th and 58th Foot), 3rd East Anglian Regiment (16th, 44th and 56th Foot) and The Royal Leicestershire Regiment (17th Foot).
Headdress Badge: The castle and key of Gibraltar upon an eight-pointed star.
Motto: *Montis Insignia Calpe* (Sign of the Rock of Gibraltar).
Regimental marches:
Quick marches: *Rule Britannia* and *Speed the Plough.*
Slow march: *Slow March of The Northamptonshire Regiment.*
Regimental headquarters: The Keep, Gibraltar Barracks, Bury St Edmunds, Suffolk, IP33 3RN.
History: *Crater to Creggan 1964-74* by M Barthorp.

Royal Armoured Corps Formed under Army Order 58 of 1939 to embrace The

Royal Tank Corps and such line cavalry regiments as had then been mechanised. Subsequently the remaining cavalry regiments (except the Household Cavalry), some Yeomanry regiments, and the mechanised regiments raised during the Second World War were added to the corps. Since the end of the Second World War The Royal Armoured Corps has largely reverted to its pre-war status and become an administrative, doctrinal and training grouping which co-ordinates the activities of the individual regiments of cavalry and The Royal Tank Regiment.

Headdress Badge: In front of two concentric circles, barbed, a gauntlet clenched, with a billet inscribed 'RAC', all ensigned with the crown.

History: *History of the Royal Armoured Corps and its Predecessors 1914-1975* by K Macksey (1983).

Royal Army Chaplains' Department

Until the late 1700s chaplains were recruited on a regimental basis, but a Royal Warrant of 23 September 1796 directed that chaplains be appointed centrally in the proportion of roughly one to each brigade, or to every three or four regiments. Initially only Church of England chaplains could be appointed, but Presbyterians were recognised in 1827, Roman Catholics in 1836, Wesleyans in 1881 and Jewish in 1892. The title 'Royal' was conferred on the department in February 1919.

Headdress Badge: Upon a wreath of laurel and oak a maltese cross. In the centre a quatrefoil voided with a circle inscribed with the motto 'In this Sign Conquer'. The whole ensigned with the crown.

Jewish Chaplains: Upon a wreath of laurel and oak a Star of David. In the centre of the star, a circle containing a quatrefoil voided. The whole ensigned with the crown.

Motto: In this Sign Conquer.

Regimental marches:

Quick march: *Trumpet Voluntary*.

Slow march: *Trumpet Voluntary*.

Regimental headquarters: Bagshot Park, Bagshot, Surrey, GU19 5PL.

History: *In This Sign Conquer* by J Smyth (1968).

Royal Army Dental Corps

The Corps was formed under Army Order 4 of 1921, the 'Royal' title being conferred in 1946. Prior to 1921 dental officers were held on the establishment of all medical units.

Headdress Badge: Within a laurel wreath a dragon's head; beneath, a scroll bearing the motto 'Ex dentibus ensis'.

Motto: *Ex dentibus ensis* (From the teeth a sword).

Regimental quick march: *Green Facings*.

Corps headquarters: Headquarters and Central Group RADC, Evelyn Woods Road, Aldershot, Hampshire, GU11 2LS.

History: *History of The Royal Army Dental Corps* Ed. L J Godden (1971).

Royal Army Educational Corps

On 2 July 1846 a Corps of Army Schoolmasters was formed and a Director-General of Military Education was appointed in 1870. Army Order 231 of 1920 disbanded The Corps of Army Schoolmasters and formed The Army Educational Corps. The 'Royal' title was conferred in 1946. On 6 April 1992 the Royal Army Education Corps became the Educational and Training Services Branch of The Adjutant General's Corps (qv).

Headdress Badge: A fluted flambeau of five flames, thereon a crown and below a scroll inscribed 'RAEC'.

History: *The Story of Army Education 1643-1963* by A C T White (1963).

Royal Army Medical Corps

Until the mid-19th century medical services were organised on a private, strictly regimental basis. A Medical Staff Corps, composed of other rank medical orderlies, was established by Royal Warrant in June 1855; this was subsequently replaced by the Army Hospital Corps in August 1857. In March 1873 the Army Medical Department, composed of medical officers, was established and, in September 1884, this Department and the Medical Staff Corps were linked. Finally, in June 1898, the Royal Army Medical Corps was formed.

Headdress Badge: The rod of Aesculapius the serpent within a wreath of laurel, thereunder a scroll inscribed 'In Arduis Fidelis', the whole ensigned with the crown.

Motto: *In arduis Fidelis* (Faithful in adversity).
Regimental marches:
Quick march: *Here's a Health unto His Majesty.*
Slow march: *Her Bright Smile Haunts Me Still.*
Regimental headquarters: Keogh Barracks, Ash Vale, Aldershot, Hampshire, GU12 5RQ.
History: *The Royal Army Medical Corps* by R McLaughlin (1972).

Royal Army Ordnance Corps The Corps has its origins in the Office of Ordnance of 1414 and the Board of Ordnance of 1683, but its more recent development has roots in the much needed reorganisation of the Army which followed the Crimean War. In 1858 a Corps of Armourer-Sergeants was formed, followed shortly by a Military Stores Department, composed of officers, in 1861 and a Military Store Staff Corps, composed of other ranks, in 1865. In 1870 the officers of the Military Stores Department were transferred to the newly established Control Department, the other rank members of the Military Store Staff Corps being absorbed into the newly raised Army Service Corps. In 1875 the Control Department was abolished and the duties and responsibilities split between Ordnance Store Department (officers), formed in 1875, and the Ordnance Store Branch (other ranks) formed in 1877. In 1881 the Ordnance Store Corps was formed and assumed the duties of the Ordnance Store Branch. In 1896 the Army Ordnance Department (officers) and Army Ordnance Corps (other ranks) superseded the Ordnance Store Department and Army Ordnance Corps respectively. In 1918 the Army Ordnance Department and Army Ordnance Corps merged to form the Royal Army Ordnance Corps. On 5 April 1993 the Corps amalgamated with the Royal Corps of Transport, the Army Catering Corps and Royal Pioneer Corps to form the Royal Logistic Corps (qv).
Headdress Badge: The arms of the Board of Ordnance within the garter and surmounted by the crown. Beneath, the motto 'Sua tela tonanti'.

Motto: *Sua Tela Tonanti* (Literally 'His Missiles Thundering' (of Jupiter). By common usage 'To the Warrior his Arms').
History: *A History of the Army Ordnance Services* (3 Vols) by A Forbes; *A History of the Royal Army Ordnance Corps (1920-1945)* by A H Fernyhough; *A Short History of the RAOC* by A H Fernyhough (1980) and *A History of The Royal Army Ordnance Corps (1945-82)* by L T H Phelps (1991).

Royal Army Pay Corps Until the late 19th century paymasters were employed on a regimental basis. A pay sub-department was established within the newly formed Control Board in 1870. In 1877 the Army Pay Department (officers) was established by Royal Warrant and an Army Pay Corps (other ranks) in 1893. In 1905 the Army Pay Department was redesignated the Army Accounts Department, but it was abolished in 1909 and reconstructed as the Army Pay Department. The title 'Royal' was conferred on the Army Pay Department and Army Pay Corps in 1920 and, in the same year, the Department and the Corps were merged to form the Royal Army Pay Corps. On 6 April 1992 the Corps became part of the Staff and Personnel Support Branch of the Adjutant General's Corps (qv).
Headdress Badge: The royal crest, thereunder a scroll inscribed 'FIDE ET FIDUCIA'.
Motto: *Fide et Fiducia* (In Faith and Trust).
History: *Trust and be Trusted* by L G Hinchcliffe (1983).

Royal Army Service Corps The Corps has its roots in the supply and transport service under the Commissary General and Board of Ordnance. In 1794 a Corps of Waggoners was formed to support operations on the continent under the commander-in-chief, the Duke of York. In 1796 this corps was reorganized as the Royal Wagon Train. Thereafter the supply and transport organisation developed in a somewhat haphazard way to meet the demands of operations at the time. As with other logistic services officer and other rank elements developed in parallel but separate organisations. In 1853 the Purveyors' Department, composed of officers, was formed, and there followed the Land Transport Corps in 1855, the Military Train in 1856 and the Commissariat Department in 1858. A Commissariat Staff Corps, composed of other ranks, was raised in 1859. The establishment of the Control Department in 1870 the other ranks of the Military Train, the Commissariat Staff Corps, the Military Store Staff Corps and the Barrack Department were absorbed in the Army Service Corps. On the abolition of the Control Department in 1875 the supply and transport functions were separated, the transport function becoming the responsibility of the Commissariat and Transport Department. There followed the Commissariat and Transport Branch in 1877, the Commissariat and Transport Staff in 1880 and the Commissariat and Transport Corps in 1881. Under Army Order 3 of 1889 the Commissariat Staff and the Commissariat and Transport Corps were merged into the Army Service Corps, the prefix 'Royal' being granted in 1918. In July 1965 the remaining transport and movement control functions of the Corps of Royal Engineers were absorbed in the redesignated Royal Corps of Transport (qv). On 5 April 1993 the Royal Corps of Transport amalgamated with the Royal Army Ordnance Corps, the Army Catering Corps and Royal Pioneer Corps to form the Royal Logistic Corps (qv).

Headdress Badge: An eight-pointed star ensigned with the crown. Upon the star a wreath with scroll inscribed 'ROYAL ARMY SERVICE CORPS', and within it the garter, motto, and the royal cypher.

History: *The Royal Army Service Corps, The History of Supply and Transport in the British Army (early times-1902)* by J Fortescue (1930); *The Royal Army Service Corps, The History of Supply and Transport in the British Army (1902-18)* by R H Beadon (1931); *The Turn of the Wheel (1919-39)* by P Turpin (1988); *The Story of The Royal Army Service Corps 1939-45* author unknown (1955); *The Story of The Royal Army Service Corps and Royal Corps of Transport 1945-82* (1983); *The Royal Army Service Corps* by G Crew (1970) and *Wait for The Wagon 1794-1993* (1995).

Royal Army Veterinary Corps Until the mid-19th century the care of service horses was the responsibility of farriers. In July 1859 the Veterinary Medical Department was formed, composed of commissioned veterinary surgeons, and all regimental appointments, other than those in the Household Cavalry, were abolished. The veterinary officers gained corporate identity as members of the Army Veterinary Department when it was formed in April 1881. In 1903 an Army Veterinary Corps, composed of other ranks, was formed and the corps and department were merged later that year as the Army Veterinary Corps, the prefix 'Royal' being conferred in 1918.

Headdress Badge: The figure of Chiron the centaur within a laurel wreath and ensigned with the crown.

Regimental marches:

Quick march: An arrangement of *Drink Puppy Drink* and *A Hunting We Will Go*.

Slow march: *Golden Spurs*.

Regimental headquarters: The Defence Animal Centre, Melton Mowbray, Leicestershire, LE13 0SL.

History: *A History of The RAVC 1796-1919* by Sir Frederick Smith (1927 and 1983) and *A History of The RAVC 1919-1963* by J Clabby (1963).

Royal Berkshire Regiment (Princess Charlotte Of Wales's) (49th and 66th Foot) The 49th Foot was raised in 1742 as Cotterell's Marines and disbanded in 1743. Re-raised in Jamaica in December 1743 by Colonel Edward Trelawny, the Governor of Jamaica, as 63rd or Trelawney's Foot, renumbered 49th Foot in 1748. In 1782 the regiment was redesignated 49th (Hertfordshire) Foot and it became 49th (Princess of Wales's) Hertfordshire Foot in 1816. The 66th Foot was raised in 1755 as 2nd Battalion of 19th Foot augmented as a separate regiment under the colonelcy of Edward Sandford, numbered 66th Foot in 1758 and re-designated 66th (Berkshire) Foot in 1782. In May 1881 the 49th (Princess of Wales's) Hertfordshire Foot and 66th (Berkshire) Foot amalgamated to form The Berkshire Regiment (Princess Charlotte of Wales's), the title being reversed two months later to

Princess Charlotte of Wales's (Berkshire Regiment). In 1885 the regiment was redesignated Princess Charlotte of Wales's (Royal Berkshire Regiment), the title being reversed in 1921 to The Royal Berkshire Regiment (Princess Charlotte of Wales's). On 9 June 1959 the regiment amalgamated with The Wiltshire Regiment (Duke of Edinburgh's) (62nd and 99th Foot) to form The Duke of Edinburgh's Royal Regiment (Berkshire and Wiltshire). On 27 April 1994 the Duke of Edinburgh's Royal Regiment amalgamated with the Gloucestershire Regiment (28th and 61st Foot) to form The Royal Gloucestershire, Berkshire and Wiltshire Regiment (qv).

Headdress Badge: Upon a ground the China dragon. The officers' badge was the dragon upon a coil of naval rope. Beneath, a scroll inscribed 'ROYAL BERKSHIRE'.
History: *The Royal Berkshire Regiment (Princess Charlotte of Wales's)* (2 Vols) by F Loraine Petre; *The History of the Royal Berkshire Regiment 1920-47* by G Blight; and *The Royal Berkshire Regiment* by F Myatt.

Royal British Legion An organisation of British ex-servicemen founded as the British Legion in 1921 by the amalgamation of four ex-service societies to form one national organisation under the leadership of Field Marshal Earl Haig, its first president. A Royal Charter of incorporation was granted in April 1925. The Royal British Legion is democratic, non-political and non-sectarian, and membership is open to all British (or naturalised) men and women who have served in the forces. The aim of the legion is to assist all ex-servicemen and women, their widows and dependents in pension matters, the relief of distress, training for civilian employment, finding civilian employment, housing, convalescence and many other welfare matters. These benefits and services are equally available to members and non-members. Revenue is largely derived from the Poppy Day appeal in November each year. The Royal British Legion is a registered charity and Her Majesty The Queen is patron. The headquarters of the Royal British Legion is at 48 Pall Mall, London SW1Y 5JY.

Royal Corps of Signals The corps has its roots in the Royal Engineers Signal Service, which had been made responsible for all Army communications in 1908. The rapid growth of Army communications during the First World War prompted formation of the Royal Corps of Signals in 1920 the corps being granted precedence immediately after the Royal Engineers.
Headdress Badge: The figure of Mercury holding a caduceus or winged staff in the left hand the right hand aloft poised with the left foot on a globe. Above the globe a scroll inscribed '*Certa Cito*'. The whole ensigned with the crown.
Motto: *Certa Cito* (Swift and Sure).
Regimental marches:
Quick march: *Begone dull care.*
Slow march: *HRH The Princess Royal.*
Corps headquarters: 56 Regency Street, London, SW1P 4AD.
History: *The Royal Corps of Signals* by R F H Nalder (1956) and *The Vital Link* by P Warner (1989).

Royal Corps of Transport Formed in 1965 from the Royal Army Service Corps (qv) when it assumed the transport and movement control responsibilities of the Corps of Royal Engineers. On 5 April 1993 the corps amalgamated with the Royal Army Ordnance Corps, the Army Catering Corps and Royal Pioneer Corps to form the Royal Logistic Corps (qv).
Headdress Badge: An eight-pointed star ensigned with the crown. Upon the star a wreath with scroll inscribed 'ROYAL CORPS OF TRANSPORT'. Within the wreath, the garter motto and royal cypher.
History: *The Story of the Royal Army Service Corps and Royal Corps of Transport 1945-82* (1983) and *Wait for The Wagon 1794-1993* (1995).

Royal Dragoon Guards *See: Dragoons.*

Royal Dublin Fusiliers (102nd and 103rd Foot) The regiment has its origins in two East India Company regiments. The Madras European Regiment was raised in 1648 and became The East India Company's European Regiment in 1702, the East India Company's Madras (European) Regiment in 1830, 1st Madras

(European) Regiment in 1839, 1st Madras (European) Fusiliers in 1843, 1st Madras Fusiliers in 1858 and 102nd Royal Madras Fusiliers in 1861. The Bombay regiment was raised in 1661 and became the East India Company's Bombay (European) Regiment in 1668, the East India Company's 1st Bombay (European) Regiment in 1839, the East India Company's 1st Bombay (European) Fusiliers in 1844, 1st Bombay Fusiliers in 1858 and 103rd Royal Bombay Fusiliers in 1861. In 1881 102nd Royal Madras Fusiliers and 103rd Royal Bombay Fusiliers amalgamated to form The Royal Dublin Fusiliers (102nd and 103rd Foot). The regiment was disbanded at the inception of the Irish Free State in 1922.

Headdress Badge: A grenade fired proper with, on the base, the elephant and the royal tiger. Below, a scroll inscribed 'ROYAL DUBLIN FUSILIERS'.

History: *Neill's 'Blue Caps'* (3 Vols) by H C Wylly.

Royal Flying Corps Formed on 13 May 1912. The Royal Flying Corps developed out of the Air Battalion of the Royal Engineers which had been established on 1 April 1911 and was based upon a two-company structure, one dealing with airships and one with aeroplanes. The Royal Flying Corps was divided into a naval wing and a military wing, the former being detached to form the Royal Naval Air Service in July 1914. On 1 April 1918 the Royal Flying Corps and elements of the Royal Naval Air Service were merged into the new Royal Air Force. Among the army officers seconded to the Royal Flying Corps on its formation was Major Hugh Trenchard, of the Royal Scots Fusiliers (later Marshal of the Royal Air Force and Chief of the Air Staff), generally regarded as 'Father' of the Royal Air Force.

Headdress Badge: The letters 'RFC' within a wreath and ensigned with the crown.

History: *The Royal Flying Corps* by G Norris (1965) and *The Royal Flying Corps* by Sir Robert Thompson (1968)

Royal Fusiliers (City of London Regiment) (7th Foot) Raised at the Tower of London by James II in June 1685 as Our Royal Regiment of Fuziliers or Our Ordnance Regiment, as escort for the artillery train quartered at the Tower, the first colonel being George Legge, 1st Lord Dartmouth, who was also Master General of the Ordnance. Designated 7th Regiment of Foot (Royal Fusiliers) in 1688. In May 1881 the regiment was redesignated The City of London Regiment (Royal Fusiliers), this being reversed two months later to The Royal Fusiliers (City of London Regiment). On 23 April 1968 the regiment amalgamated with The Royal Northumberland Fusiliers (5th Foot), The Royal Warwickshire Fusiliers (6th Foot) and The Lancashire Fusiliers (20th Foot) to form The Royal Regiment of Fusiliers (qv).

Headdress Badge: A grenade fired proper with, on the base, a rose within the garter and motto *'Honi Soit Qui Mal y Pense'* (Evil to him who evil thinks).

History: *Historical Records of the 7th (or Royal Regiment of Fusiliers)* by P Groves (1903); *The Royal Fusiliers in the Great War* by H C O'Neill (1922) and *Always A Fusilier* by C Northcote Parkinson (1949).

Royal Gloucestershire, Berkshire and Wiltshire Regiment (28th, 49th, 61st, 62nd, 66th and 99th Foot) Formed on 27 April 1994 through the amalgamation of The Gloucestershire Regiment (28th and 61st Foot), and The Duke of Edinburgh's Royal Regiment (Berkshire and Wiltshire (49th, 62nd, 66th and 99th Foot).

Headdress Badge: On a square of crimson a cross pattee, charged with a sphinx couchant upon a pedestal inscribed 'EGYPT'.

Regimental marches:
Quick march: *The Sphinx and Dragon.*
Slow march: *Scipio.*
Regimental headquarters: The Custom House, Commercial Road, Gloucester, GL1 2HE.

Royal Green Jackets (43rd, 52nd, 60th and 95th Foot) Formed on 1 January 1966 through the amalgamation of 1st Green Jackets (43rd and 52nd) 2nd Green Jackets (The King's Royal Rifle Corps) and 3rd Green Jackets (The Rifle Brigade).

Headdress Badge: A maltese cross

inscribed with selected battle honours thereon a bugle-horn stringed and encircled with the title of the regiment all within a wreath of laurel ensigned with the crown resting upon a plinth inscribed 'PENINSULA' across the tie a naval crown superscribed 'COPENHAGEN 2 APRIL 1801'.

Regimental marches:

Quick march: An arrangement of *Huntsman's Chorus* and *Italian Song*.

Double March: *The Road to the Isles*.

Regimental headquarters: Peninsula Barracks, Romsey Road, Winchester, Hampshire, SO23 8TS.

History: *Royal Green Jackets Chronicles* (Vols 1-27).

Royal Gurkha Rifles *See: Gurkhas.*

Royal Hampshire Regiment (37th and 67th Foot) The 37th Foot was raised in Ireland by Colonel Thomas Meredith in February 1702 as Meredith's Regiment of Foot and was numbered 37th Foot in 1751. In 1782 the regiment became 37th (North Hampshire) Foot. The 67th Foot was raised in 1756 as 2nd Battalion, 10th Foot and augmented as a separate regiment in April 1758. Re-designated 67th (South Hampshire) Foot in 1782. In 1881 the 37th (North Hampshire) Foot and 67th (South Hampshire) Foot amalgamated to form The Hampshire Regiment, becoming the Royal Hampshire Regiment in 1946. On 9 September 1992 the regiment amalgamated with The Queen's Regiment (2nd, 3rd, 35th, 50th, 57th, 70th, 77th, 97th and 107th Foot) to form The Princess of Wales's Royal Regiment (Queen's and Royal Hampshires) (qv).

Headdress Badge: Within a laurel wreath the Hampshire rose and above the royal tiger. Below a scroll inscribed 'ROYAL HAMPSHIRE'. All ensigned with the crown.

History: *Regimental History The Royal Hampshire Regiment (1702-1914)* by C T Atkinson (1950); *Regimental History The Royal Hampshire Regiment (1914-1918)* by C T Atkinson (1952) and *Regimental History The Royal Hampshire Regiment (1918-1954)* by D Scott Daniell (1955).

Royal Highland Fusiliers (Princess Margaret's Own Glasgow and Ayrshire Regiment) (21st, 71st and 74th Foot) Formed on 20 January 1959 through the amalgamation of The Royal Scots Fusiliers (21st Foot) and The Highland Light Infantry (City of Glasgow Regiment) (71st and 74th Foot).

Headdress Badge: A grenade fired proper with, on the base, the monogram 'HLI' surmounted by the crown.

Motto: *Nemo Nos Impune Lacessit* (None shall provoke us with impunity).

Regimental marches:

Quick marches: *Hielan' Laddie* and *Blue Bonnets are over the Border* (Pipes and Drums) and *British Grenadiers* and *Whistle o'er the Lave o't* (Regimental Band).

Slow marches: *My Home* (Pipes and Drums), *Garb of Old Gaul* and *March of 21st Regiment* (Regimental Band).

Regimental headquarters: 518 Sauchiehall Street, Glasgow, G2 3LW.

History: *A Soldier's History* (1987).

Royal Horse Artillery Two troops of Royal Horse Artillery were raised in February 1793 for the support of cavalry. In 1899 the Royal Artillery was reorganised into two broad groups: The Royal Horse Artillery and Royal Field Artillery in one, and the Royal Garrison Artillery in the other. In 1924 the groups were merged into a single regiment, the Royal Regiment of Artillery, although the Royal Horse Artillery retained its title and distinctive badge. In 1945 King George VI directed that a mounted troop of the Royal Horse Artillery be raised for ceremonial duties, and this formed in 1946. In October 1947 the King visited the 'Riding Troop' and bestowed on it the title 'King's Troop'. In addition to the ceremonial King's Troop there are currently three 'field' regiments bearing the title Royal Horse Artillery in the Royal Artillery order of battle.

Headdress Badge: The royal Cypher within the garter with motto, ensigned with the crown. Below, a scroll inscribed 'ROYAL HORSE ARTILLERY'.

History: See: *Royal Regiment of Artillery.*

Royal Horse Guards (The Blues) Raised by Charles II in January 1661 from

Colonel Unton Crook's Regiment of Horse of the disbanded Parliamentary Army. Command of the regiment was given to Aubrey, Earl of Oxford and the regiment became The Earl of Oxford's Regiment of Horse and took the Earl's blue livery. Between 1661 and 1750 the regiment was at various times called The King's Regiment of Horse Guards, The Royal Regiment of Horse Guards and The Oxford Blues. In 1750 the regiment was designated The Royal Horse Guards (Blue) and, in 1819, this was extended to The Royal Horse Guards (The Blues). On 29 March 1969 the regiment amalgamated with The Royal Dragoons (1st Dragoons) to form The Blues and Royals (Royal Horse Guards and 1st Dragoons) (qv).

Headdress Badge: The royal cypher within a circle bearing the regiment's title, ensigned with the crown.

History: *The Story of the Household Cavalry* (3 Vols) by G Arthur; *The Second Household Cavalry Regiment* by R Orde and *The Story of The Blues and Royals - Royal Horse Guards and 1st Dragoons* by J N P Watson.

Royal Hospital Founded at Chelsea by King Charles II in 1682 as a retreat for veterans of the regular Army, re-established 21 years earlier, who had become unfit for duty, either after 20 years' service or as a result of wounds. Charles II received no support for this project, clearly inspired by the Hôtel des Invalides founded in Paris by Louis XIV in 1670, from the Treasury Commissioners, with the notable exception of Sir Stephen Fox, a former Paymaster-General who surrendered his commission of fourpence in the pound deducted from army pay, which had been granted him in recognition of his services raising money for the Army. This and other deductions from army pay and pensions was the main source of income until 1847, when the government assumed responsibility for funding the hospital from parliamentary votes, which are supplemented by a small income from its own property and bequests.

Since its foundation the hospital has been governed by a Board of Commissioners and, although the composition of the board has varied, the Paymaster-General has always been the chairman. Built to a design of Sir Christopher Wren between 1682 and 1692 of brick with stone quoins, cornices, door and window dressings, the grounds are extensive and include the old Ranelagh Gardens. Some alterations, mainly to the interior of officers' apartments, were made by Robert Adam who served as clerk of works from 1765 to 1792. Sir John Soane, clerk of works from 1807 to 1837, was responsible for most of the buildings now standing on the outer sides of the east and west roads and for a new infirmary in the north-western corner of the grounds which was destroyed by enemy bombing in 1941. A new infirmary of modern design was opened by Her Majesty Queen Elizabeth the Queen Mother in 1961, and a social centre, the Prince of Wales Hall, was opened in 1985.

The pensioners, as intended by Charles II, have always been organised on military lines, originally in eight companies formed from the foot and dragoons, and a ninth from the horse, each with its proper complement of officers, non-commissioned officers and drummers. In the early days the burden of guard duties was onerous, but parades are now limited to those for church and pay. The scarlet coats and tricorn hats of the in-pensioners are a modernised version of the service dress of Marlborough's time. The original intention that the hospital should accommodate all the soldiers entitled to pension was overtaken by the growth of the standing army and James II established a regular system of money pensions for the overflow, who became known as out-pensioners, to distinguish them from the in-pensioners accommodated in the building. The Commissioners remain responsible for the management of the Hospital. The Hospital accommodates about 400 in-pensioners drawn from out-pensioners of good character and not normally less than 65 years of age. A younger man may be admitted if he is certified as unfit to earn his living and his disability is attributable to his army service. Some 120 in-pensioners are employed, on a voluntary basis, within the hospital, and each company has a company sergeant-major and a complement of non-commissioned officers drawn from the in-pensioners to assist in the routine administration of the company. The chapel, great hall and museum are open to the public on weekdays and visitors are welcomed at the chapel services on Sundays.

History: *The Royal Hospital Chelsea* by C G T Dean (1950) and *A Village in Chelsea* by D Ascoli (1974).

Royal Inniskilling Fusiliers (27th and 108th Foot) The 27th Foot was raised in 1689 by Colonel Zachariah Tiffinas Tiffin's Regiment of Foot, but not taken on the regular establishment until January 1690. Redesignated 27th (Inniskilling) Foot in 1751. The 108th was raised by the East India Company in 1854 as the Company's 3rd (Madras Infantry) Regiment, and was redesignated 3rd (Madras) Regiment in 1858 and 108th (Madras Infantry) Regiment in 1861. In 1881 the 27th (Inniskilling) Foot and 108th (Madras Infantry) Regiment amalgamated to form The Royal Inniskilling Fusiliers (27th and 108th Foot). On 1 July 1968 the regiment amalgamated with The Royal Ulster Rifles (83rd and 86th Foot) and The Royal Irish Fusiliers (Princess Victoria's) (87th and 89th Foot) to form The Royal Irish Rangers (27th (Inniskilling), 83rd and 87th). In 1992 The Royal Irish Rangers merged with the Ulster Defence Regiment to form The Royal Irish Regiment (27th (Inniskilling), 83rd, 87th and The Ulster Defence Regiment) (qv).

Headdress Badge: A grenade fired proper with, on the base, the Castle of Enniskillen.

History: *The Royal Inniskilling Fusiliers December 1688 to July 1914* a compilation of historical records (1928); *The Royal Inniskilling Fusiliers in the First World War* by F Fox (1928); *The Royal Inniskilling Fusiliers in the Second World War* by F Fox (1951) and *The Royal Inniskilling Fusiliers 1945-1968* by J Filmer-Bennett.

Royal Irish Artillery The Royal Irish Artillery was raised in 1755 and comprised two battalions. After the Union of Ireland with Great Britain in 1800 it was amalgamated with the Royal Regiment of Artillery, ten companies forming the 7th Battalion, the remainder being reduced.

Royal Irish Fusiliers (Princess Victoria's) (87th and 89th Foot) The 87th (The Prince of Wales's Irish) Foot was raised in Ireland in September 1793 by Colonel John Doyle, being redesignated 87th (The Prince of Wales's Own Irish) Foot in 1811 and 87th (The Royal Irish Fusiliers) in 1827. The 89th Foot was raised in December 1793 by Colonel William Crosbie. In 1866 the regiment was redesignated 89th (Princess Victoria's) Regiment of Foot. In May 1881 the 87th (The Royal Irish Fusiliers) and the 89th (Princess Victoria's) Foot amalgamated to form The Royal Irish Fusiliers (Princess Victoria's). The title was reversed in July 1881 to Princess Victoria's (The Royal Irish Fusiliers), but returned to the May 1881 title in 1920. On 1 July 1968 the regiment amalgamated with The Royal Inniskilling Fusiliers (27th and 108th Foot) and The Royal Ulster Rifles (83rd and 86th Foot) to form The Royal Irish Rangers (27th (Inniskilling), 83rd and 87th). In 1992 The Royal Irish Rangers merged with the Ulster Defence Regiment to form The Royal Irish Regiment (27th (Inniskilling), 83rd, 87th and The Ulster Defence Regiment) (qv).

Headdress Badge: A grenade fired proper with, on the base, the angel harp and Prince of Wales's plume, all surmounted by the coronet of Princess Victoria.

Motto: *Faugh-a-Ballagh* (Clear the way).

History: *The Royal Irish Fusiliers 1793-1968* by M Cunliffe (1970).

Royal Irish Rangers (27th (Inniskilling) 83rd and 87th) Formed on 1 July 1968 through the amalgamation of The Royal Inniskilling Fusiliers (27th and 108th Foot), The Royal Ulster Rifles (83rd and 86th Foot) and The Royal Irish Fusiliers (Princess Victoria's) (87th and 89th Foot). On 1 July 1992 The Royal Irish Rangers merged with the Ulster Defence Regiment to form The Royal Irish Regiment (27th (Inniskilling), 83rd, 87th and The Ulster Defence Regiment) (qv).

Headdress Badge: The angel harp ensigned with the crown. Below, a scroll inscribed 'ROYAL IRISH RANGERS'.

Motto: *Faugh-a-Ballagh* (Clear the way).
History: *The Outline History of The Royal Irish Rangers (27th Inniskilling) 83rd and 87th (1689-1979)* by M J P M Corbally (1979) and *The Royal Irish Rangers 1969-1992* (1992).

Royal Irish Regiment (18th Foot) Raised in 1684 as The Earl of Granard's Regiment of Foot, and titled The Royal Regiment of Ireland in 1695. In 1751 the regiment was redesignated 18th (The Royal Irish) Foot, becoming the Royal Irish Regiment in 1881. In 1922 the regiment was disbanded on the formation of the Irish Free State.
Headdress Badge: The Erin harp ensigned with the crown.
Motto: *Virtutis Namurcensis Praemium* (The Reward for Virtue at Namur)
History: *Campaigns and History of The Royal Irish Regiment* (2 Vols) by G Le M Gretton (1911); and S Georghegan (1927).

Royal Irish Regiment (27th (Inniskilling) 83rd, 87th Foot and the Ulster Defence Regiment) Formed on 1 July 1992 by the merger of The Royal Irish Rangers (27th (Inniskilling) 83rd and 87th Foot) with the Ulster Defence Regiment.
Headdress Badge: An Irish harp and crown surrounded by a wreath of shamrock with the regimental title inscribed.
Regimental quick march: *Killaloe*.
Regimental headquarters: St Patrick's Barracks, British Forces Post Office 808.

Royal Irish Rifles (83rd and 86th) The 83rd Foot was raised in Dublin in September 1793 as Fitch's Corps, numbered 83rd Foot in 1794 and designated 83rd (County of Dublin) Foot in 1859. The 86th Foot was raised at Shrewsbury in October 1793 by Major General Sir Cornelius Cuyler and known as Cuyler's Shropshire Volunteers. The regiment was numbered 86th Foot in 1794, designated 86th (The Leinster) Foot in 1809 and 86th (Royal County Down) Foot in 1812. In 1881 the 83rd (County of Dublin) Foot and the 86th (Royal County Down) Foot amalgamated to form The Royal Irish Rifles (83rd and 86th Foot). In anticipa-

tion of the formation of the Irish Free State the regiment's title was changed to The Royal Ulster Rifles in 1921.
Headdress Badge: The angel harp with motto 'Quis Separabit?' above a stringed bugle-horn, all ensigned with the crown.
Motto: *Quis Separabit?* (Who shall separate?)
History: *History of The Royal Irish Rifles* by G B Laurie (1914) and *History of the First Seven Battalions The Royal Irish Rifles (Now The Royal Ulster Rifles) in the Great War* by C Falls (1925).
See also: Royal Ulster Rifles.

Royal Leicestershire Regiment (17th Foot) Raised at London in September 1688 by Colonel Solomon Richards and known as Richard's Regiment of Foot. Numbered 17th Foot in 1751 and designated 17th (Leicestershire) Foot in 1782, The Leicestershire Regiment in 1881 and The Royal Leicestershire Regiment in 1946. On 1 September 1964 the regiment amalgamated with 1st East Anglian Regiment (Royal Norfolk and Suffolk), 2nd East Anglian Regiment (Duchess of Gloucester's Own Royal Lincolnshire and Northamptonshire) and 3rd East Anglian Regiment (16th and 44th Foot) to form The Royal Anglian Regiment (qv).
Headdress Badge: On a ground the royal tiger superscribed 'HINDOOSTAN'. Below, a scroll inscribed 'ROYAL LEICESTERSHIRE'.
History: *A History of the Services of The 17th (The Leicestershire) Regiment* by E A H Webb (1912) and *The Royal Leicestershire Regiment 1928-1956* by W E Underhill (1957).

Royal Lincolnshire Regiment (10th Foot) Raised at Plymouth in June 1685 from independent companies commanded by Colonel John Granville, 1st Earl of Bath, and known as Granville's Regiment of Foot. Numbered 10th Foot in 1685, and designated 10th (North Lincolnshire) Foot in 1782, The Lincolnshire Regiment in 1881 and The Royal Lincolnshire Regiment in 1946. On 1 June 1960 the regiment amalgamated with The Northamptonshire Regiment (48th and 58th Foot) to form the 2nd East Anglian

Regiment (Duchess of Gloucester's Own Royal Lincolnshire and Northamptonshire). On 1 September 1964 the regiment amalgamated with 1st East Anglian Regiment (Royal Norfolk and Suffolk), 3rd East Anglian Regiment (16th and 44th Foot) and The Royal Leicestershire Regiment (17th Foot) to form The Royal Anglian Regiment (qv).

Headdress Badge: The sphinx upon a tablet inscribed 'EGYPT'. Below, a scroll inscribed 'ROYAL LINCOLNSHIRE REGIMENT'.

History: *A History of the Tenth Foot (The Lincolnshire Regiment)* (2 Vols) by A Lee (1911); *The History of The Lincolnshire Regiment 1914-18* by C R Simpson (1931); *The History of the Tenth Foot 1919-1950* by L C Gates (1953) and *The Last Decade, The Tenth Foot Royal Lincolnshire Regiment 1950-1960* by G Moore.

Royal Logistic Corps Formed on 3 April 1993 through the amalgamation of the Royal Corps of Transport, Royal Army Ordnance Corps, Royal Pioneer Corps and Army Catering Corps.

Headdress Badge: On a star of eight greater and 40 lesser points a laurel wreath surmounted by two axes in saltire superimposed thereon a roundel encircled by the garter ensigned by the royal crown and charged with a shield of arms being that of the Board of Ordnance on a scroll the motto 'We Sustain'.

Motto: We Sustain.

Regimental quick march: *On Parade*.

Corps headquarters: Dettingen House, The Princess Royal Barracks, Blackdown, Deepcut, Camberley, Surrey, GU16 6RW.

Royal Marines The Royal Marines fall on the establishment of the Royal Navy. However, no less than 32 regiments of infantry of the line have, at some time, served as marines, and many hold a naval distinction on their colours. When on parade with the Army the Royal Marines take precedence after The Black Watch (Royal Highland Regiment)(42nd and 73rd Foot).

Headdress Badge: The globe (eastern hemisphere displayed) within a laurel wreath surmounted by the royal crest.

Royal Mercian and Lancastrian Yeomanry Yeomanry cavalry regiment on the Territorial Army order of battle formed on 1 November 1992 through the amalgamation of The Queen's Own Mercian Yeomanry and The Duke of Lancaster's Own Yeomanry. As at April 1994 the regiment comprised 'A' (Queen's Own Warwickshire & Worcestershire Yeomanry) Squadron, 'B' (Staffordshire Yeomanry) Squadron, 'D' (Duke of Lancaster's Own Yeomanry) Squadron and 'RHQ' and 'HQ' (Shropshire Yeomanry) Squadron.

Badge: A Mercian eagle topped by a Saxon crown superimposed upon a Lancastrian rose below the Duke of Lancaster's coronet. However, squadrons wear their own regimental cap badges.

Regimental marches:

Quick march: *Light of Foot*.

Slow march: *Scipio*.

Royal Military Academy Band Corps The exact formation date of this corps is not known: the earliest record of the band's existence at the Royal Military College dates from 1815. The corps was disbanded in 1985.

Headdress Badge: The royal cypher within a circlet bearing the words 'ROYAL MILITARY ACADEMY SANDHURST' surmounted by a crown. Below the circlet a scroll inscribed 'SERVE TO LEAD'.

Royal Military Academy - Sandhurst Formed on 7 November 1946 as the training centre for all future regular officers in the Army, and combining the pre-war functions of the Royal Military Academy at Woolwich (qv) and the Royal Military College (qv) at Sandhurst. The Academy could not however meet the demand for junior officers during the period of National Service. As in the war, conscripts awarded National Service commissions were trained at two of the wartime Officer Cadet Training Units (OCTUs), one at Mons Barracks, Aldershot and the other at Eaton Hall in Chester. With the ending of National Service in 1960 the two OCTUs merged to become Mons Officer Cadet School, offering a six-month course for those seeking short service commissions. In

1972 Mons Officer Cadet School moved to Sandhurst to become Mons College, and thereafter all officer cadets, whether for regular or short service commissions, were trained together. The Royal Military Academy Sandhurst is now the centre for all officer cadet training in the Army.

History: *Sandhurst - The Royal Military Academy Sandhurst and its Predecessors* by A Shepherd (1980) and *Sandhurst - The Royal Military Academy* by A Shepperd (1980).

See also: Royal Military Academy - Woolwich; Royal Military College and Staff College.

Royal Military Academy - Woolwich

The Royal Military Academy was established inside the Woolwich Arsenal, partly on a piece of land known as the 'Warren' and including 'a great Mansion or Manor House called Tower Place' and a number of warehouses and workshops, in 1741. The then Master General of the Ordnance, the Duke of Montagu, obtained a Royal Charter to establish: 'an Academy or School...for instructing the people belonging to the Military Branch of the Ordnance in the several parts of Mathematics necessary to qualify them for the service of the Artillery and the business of the Engineers'. These specialists were the responsibility of the Master General of the Ordnance from whom officers of the artillery and engineers received their commissions. The close association which developed between the Academy and the adjacent workshops is widely held to be the reason the Royal Military Academy at Woolwich became known as 'The Shop'. Originally open to all officers, cadets and soldiers based at Woolwich and carrying out a function similar to those now performed at the Royal School of Artillery at Larkhill, and the Royal School of Military Engineering at Chatham, it became a college of gentlemen cadets in 1744 following the concentration for instruction of gentlemen cadets from the seven marching companies of the Royal Regiment of Artillery. The course was divided between military subjects, taught by serving officers, and relevant academic subjects taught by civilian masters and professors. The syllabus of 1744 included mathematics, ballistics, fortifications. '...the several pieces of ordnance...the composition of metal of which ordnance is made; the composition of gunpowder; and several sorts of fireworks'. Between 1741 and 1820 there was no fixed course length, attendance varying with the age and progress of the cadets and the demands of the Service. This system continued from 1820 to 1854, but experiences in the Crimean War prompted major organisational changes to the Ordnance Branch. The system was also much affected by the increased demand for officers for service in the Crimea (1854-56), the Indian Mutiny (1857-58) and to meet the threat of a French invasion (1859-60). The abolition of the East India Company's Military Seminary and of the local Indian Artillery and Engineers in 1861 compounded these problems, and these pressures brought about a gradual reduction in course length. The course was reduced to 12 months during the South Africa War (1899-1902) and fluctuated between six months and a year during the First World War. The academy continued to provide the Army with professional officers of artillery and engineers until 1946, when it merged with the Royal Military College (qv) in 1946. *See also: Royal Military College; Royal Military Academy - Sandhurst and Staff College.*

Royal Military College

A school for the education of officers in the non-technical arms was first established at High Wycombe in May 1798. There had been proposals for such an establishment earlier in the 18th century, but not until December 1798 was permission given by the Adjutant General for a course of lectures to be given by General Jarry, an officer of French extraction who had held a senior appointment at the Prussian Military Academy in Berlin, to officers desirous of employment on the Army Staff. In parallel Colonel John Gaspard Le Marchant proposed to King George III the creation of a military college, consisting of three departments: one department to offer a general education to boys intending to join the Army as officers; the second department would give a purely military education to cadets graduating from the first; the third department would be an expansion of General Jarry's school, and there would be a 'Legion' for the education of the sons of non-commissioned officers and soldiers, which would act as 'demonstration battalion for the other two departments'. The concept of a 'Legion' had to be abandoned, but was eventually introduced in the form of the Duke of York's School, established at Chelsea in June 1801.

General Jarry's establishment at High Wycombe was recognised as the Royal Military College by a Royal Warrant of 24 June 1801, filling the role allotted to the third division of Le Marchant's original plan. The planned first and second divisions were combined and, by a Royal Warrant of 4 May 1802, established at Great Marlow. The two divisions remained part of the Royal Military College, sharing the same Governor and many of the same staff, sometimes located together and sometimes separated, until 1858, when the senior division was renamed the Staff College (qv) and became a separate organisation. Fees were assessed on the ability of parents to pay and ranged between £122.10s. and £400 annually. It had been clear for some time that the High Wycombe and Great Marlow sites were inadequate and, at great cost and considerable public indignation, the Royal Military College was established in 1813 at a new site in the parish of Sandhurst on the London to Exeter road near the bridge-point and village of Blackwater. The accommodation of the Royal Military College developed over the years, but in 1911 new buildings were completed to provide for 600 gentleman cadets.

Before the First World War instruction was on a military basis, except for English and a foreign language, but later the curriculum came to include a wider range of subjects. The fees were regulated to the resources of parents or guardians and ranged from £122.10s. to £400 annually. During the First World War the Staff College (qv) was taken over for officer cadet training, and some 4,000 cadets who had passed through the college lost their lives. Immediately war was declared in September 1939, all the Gentlemen Cadets were sworn in as members of their local units of the Territorial Army (qv). The seniors were commissioned at once; the juniors underwent a few weeks further training at specially formed Officer Cadet Training Units (OCTUs), before being granted regular commissions, the last officers to receive them for the duration of hostilities. Parents' fees were returned; the Gentlemen Cadets were redesignated Officer Cadets and joined the first intake of potential officers selected from men called up for war service. At Sandhurst the future infantry officers among the juniors were formed into 161 Infantry OCTU, those for the other arms and services being posted out to the appropriate OCTU elsewhere. The Sandhurst OCTU was joined by 101 Royal Armoured Corps (RAC) OCTU, formed from the Inns of Court Yeomanry Regiment, and the two OCTUs remained there until July 1942, when the infantry unit, still retaining the title Royal Military College, moved to Mons Barracks, Aldershot.

In January 1946, 161 Infantry OCTU, still wearing the college cap badge, returned to Sandhurst to be disbanded on 6 November 1946. On 7 November 1946, the Royal Military Academy Sandhurst (qv) was formed, combining the functions of the pre-war cadet colleges of the Royal Military Academy (qv) at Woolwich, and the Royal Military College, Sandhurst. *See also: Royal Military Academy Woolwich and Staff College.*

Royal Military College of Science The early days of military science are firmly rooted in the history of the Royal Artillery. In 1716 Albert Borgard, the Colonel of Artillery, organised for the first time the systematic construction and proving of guns and other artillery equipment. In 1771 two young artillery officers, Williams and Jardine, founded the Military Society at Woolwich for the scientific study of gunnery which was to remain in existence for eight years. In 1839 two artillery officers, Eardley-Wilmot and Lefroy, proposed the establishment of an institution for the study of science and modern languages and, in the following year, the Royal Artillery Institution at Woolwich was founded, the first Director of Studies being appointed in 1850, and relations were developed with the Royal Arsenal and the Ordnance Select Committee. This indefinite arrangement led, in 1864, to the establishment of a two-year course of organised instruction known as the Advanced Class, which continued until 1940. Instruction of the Advanced Class took place in the Institution until 1885 when the Royal Artillery College was established at Woolwich. In 1889 it became the Ordnance College; it was renamed the Artillery College after the First World War and was renamed the Military College of Science in 1927 and awarded the honour 'Royal' in 1953.

The College dispersed from Woolwich during the Second World War and was re-established at Shrivenham, near Swindon in Wiltshire, in 1946, the Advanced Class being replaced by the Technical Staff Course, open to officers from all arms and Commonwealth land forces. In 1953 a short course was introduced for officers selected for staff training at the Staff College at Camberley; this became the ten-week General Staff Science Course in 1962. In 1965 the new Army Staff Course system, based on the concept of one staff, was introduced, replacing the Technical Staff Course and the General Staff Science Course. The period 1965-84 saw the introduction of a wide range of specialist courses open to officers from all Services and the Civil Service. Courses available included First Degrees in Applied Science and Engineering (from 1968) and Council of National Academic Awards Higher Degrees (from 1971). In August 1984 the academic teaching responsibilities were placed on contract with the Cranfield Institute of Technology (CIT) (Cranfield University since 1993) and in 1985 degrees were awarded for the first time under the auspices of CIT. In 1983 the Frodsham Report recommended that RAF officers reading for in-service degrees should do so at the Royal Military College of Science, and the first RAF undergraduates arrived in 1984.

Royal Military School of Music The School was formed in 1857 at the direction

of Field Marshal HRH The Duke of Cambridge, at that time commander-in-chief of the Army. It was established at Kneller Hall, Twickenham, which had been built by Sir Christopher Wren between 1709 and 1711 as a country house for Sir Godfrey Kneller, the celebrated court painter of the time. The house was burned down and rebuilt in the 1840s. The School trains all Army bandsmen; the two main courses being a one-year foundation course for recruit bandsmen, and a three-year bandmasters' course for experienced military musicians who have been recommended as future bandmasters. The team of civilian and military instructors also instruct on a number of other courses such as band sergeants, band sergeant majors and potential directors of music. All Army musicians are also trained for operational tasks such as medical assistant, which they can be called upon to perform in support of operations. During the 1991 Gulf War 34 British Army bands were deployed on active service as medical assistants.

Royal Monmouthshire Royal Engineers (Militia) Senior regiment of the Territorial Army and the only surviving representative of the historic Militia (qv) force. Originally an infantry regiment, it became an engineer unit in 1877. The regiment was one of four county Militia regiments which maintained a separate existence when the Militia was absorbed in the Special Reserve in 1908. When the rest of the Special Reserve was discontinued after 1921 it survived as a Supplementary Reserve unit and, although incorporated in the Territorial Army in 1953, was allowed to keep the word 'Militia' in its title.
Headdress Badge: The Prince of Wales's coronet, plumes and motto surmounted by a crown. On either side of the plume the letters R and E. Below, a scroll inscribed 'ROYAL MONMOUTHSHIRE'.
History: *The History of The Royal Monmouthshire Royal Engineers (Militia)* by C Low and H M Everett (1969).

Royal Munster Fusiliers (101st and 104th Foot) The 101st Foot was founded in 1759 as the East India Company's

Bengal (European) Regiment and was redesignated 1st Bengal (European) regiment in 1840, 1st (Bengal European) Light Infantry in 1841, 1st (Bengal European) Fusiliers in 1846, 1st Bengal Fusiliers in 1858 and 101st (Royal Bengal Fusiliers) in 1861. The 104th Foot was founded in 1839 as the East India Company's 2nd Bengal (European) Regiment and redesignated 2nd (Bengal European) Fusiliers in 1850, 2nd Bengal Fusiliers in 1858 and 104th Bengal Fusiliers in 1861. In 1881 101st (Royal Bengal Fusiliers) and 104th Bengal Fusiliers amalgamated to form The Royal Munster Fusiliers. The regiment was disbanded in 1922 on the formation of the Irish Free State.

Headdress Badge: A grenade fired proper, on the base, the royal tiger.

History: *History of The Royal Munster Fusiliers* (2 Vols.) by S McCance (1927).

Royal Norfolk Regiment (9th Foot) Raised in June 1685 as Colonel Henry Cornwell's Regiment of Foot; numbered 9th Foot in 1751 and designated 9th (East Norfolk) Foot in 1782, The Norfolk Regiment in 1881 and The Royal Norfolk Regiment in 1935. On 29 August 1959 the regiment amalgamated with The Suffolk Regiment (12th Foot) to form The 1st East Anglian Regiment (Royal Norfolk and Suffolk). On 1 September 1964 The 1st East Anglian Regiment (Royal Norfolk and Suffolk) amalgamated with The 2nd East Anglian Regiment (Duchess of Gloucester's Own Royal Lincolnshire and Northamptonshire) (10th, 48th and 58th Foot), The 3rd East Anglian Regiment (16th and 44th Foot) and The Royal Leicestershire Regiment (17th Foot) to form The Royal Anglian Regiment (qv).

Headdress Badge: The figure of Britannia seated, awarded by Queen Anne in 1707.

History: *History of The Norfolk Regiment 1685-1918* (2 Vols) by F Loraine Petre; *History of The Royal Norfolk Regiment 1919-51* by P K Kemp; *History of The Royal Norfolk Regiment 1951-69* by F A Godfrey and *The Royal Norfolk Regiment* by T Carew (1967).

Royal Northumberland Fusiliers (5th Foot) Raised in August 1674 for service in the Netherlands with Prince William of Orange, the Colonel being Daniel O'Brien, 3rd Viscount Clare. The regiment returned to England in 1685 at the direction of James II, but returned to the low countries in 1686. In 1688 the regiment accompanied Prince William to England and, on his accession, was taken on the regular establishment as Colonel Tollemache's Regiment of Foot. Numbered 5th Foot in 1751; designated 5th or Northumberland Foot in 1782, 5th or Northumberland Fusiliers in 1836, The Northumberland Fusiliers in 1881 and The Royal Northumberland Fusiliers in 1935. On 23 April 1968 the regiment amalgamated with The Royal Warwickshire Fusiliers (6th Foot), The Royal Fusiliers (City of London Regiment) (7th Foot) and The Lancashire Fusiliers (20th Foot) to form The Royal Regiment of Fusiliers (qv).

Headdress Badge: A grenade fired proper with, on the base, St George and Dragon within a circle bearing the motto '*Quo fata vocant*'.

Motto: *Quo fata vocant*, (Wherever fate calls).

History: *The 5th Foot The Northumberland Fusiliers* by W W Wood (1901); *A History of the Northumberland Fusiliers 1614-1902* by H M Walker (1901); *The Fifth in the Great War, A History of 1st and 2nd Northumberland Fusiliers 1914-1918* by H R Sandilands (1938) and *The History of the Royal Northumberland Fusiliers in the Second World War* by C N Barclay.

Royal Ordnance Factory Name given to British government factories for the production of war material. During the two World Wars these factories came under the direction of the Ministry of Supply and were greatly expanded. Since 1945 defence material has increasingly been developed and manufactured by the public sector. The Royal Ordnance Factories have steadily reduced in number, the most famous, that at Woolwich, closed in March 1967.

Royal Pioneer Corps Raised in 1762 and disbanded in 1763. In 1917, during the First World War, a non-combatant Labour Corps was raised, and disbanded in 1919.

Under Army Order 200 of 1939 a combatant Auxiliary Military Pioneer Corps was formed, and redesignated Pioneer Corps in 1940. The title 'Royal' was conferred in 1946. In 1950 the corps ceased to be an auxiliary force and was transferred to the regular establishment. On 5 April 1993 the corps amalgamated with The Royal Corps of Transport, The Royal Army Ordnance Corps and the Army Catering Corps; to form the Royal Logistic Corps (qv).

Headdress Badge: A rifle, a shovel and a pick 'piled'. On them a laurel wreath, all ensigned with a crown. Beneath, a scroll inscribed 'Labor Omnia Vincit'.

Motto: *Labor Omnia vincit* (Work conquers all).

History: *A War History of the Royal Pioneer Corps 1939-45* by E H Rhodes-Wood; and *Royal Pioneers 1945-93* by E R Elliott (1993).

Royal Red Cross Decoration for nurses instituted by Queen Victoria in 1883. It consists of a crimson enamel cross, gilt-edged, fastened by a bow of dark blue, red-edged, ribbon. Conferred on nurses or other persons, either British or foreign, recommended by the Secretary of State for Defence in recognition of services in nursing and providing for sick and wounded soldiers and sailors.

Royal Regiment of Artillery Traditionally artillery 'Traynes' had been raised by Royal Warrant and organised for specific campaigns and subsequently disbanded. By Royal Warrant of George I dated 26 May 1716 two regular companies (batteries) of field artillery were raised at Woolwich. On 1 April 1722 these 'companies' were grouped with independent 'trains' at Gibraltar and Minorca to form a regiment -The Royal Regiment of Artillery. During the 18th century the regiment expanded rapidly, the 'companies' (batteries) being formed into 'battalions' (later called 'brigades'), and two troops of Royal Horse Artillery were raised in February 1793 to provide fire support for the cavalry. Like the Corps of Royal Engineers the Royal Regiment of Artillery was under the control of the Board of Ordnance and, when the Board was abolished in 1855,

came under the control of the Commander-in-Chief and War Office. The Royal Irish Artillery and the East India Company's Horse Artillery were absorbed in to the Royal Regiment of Artillery in 1801 and in the 1860s respectively. In 1861 the artillery units of the East India Company were transferred to the British establishment. In 1899 the Royal Regiment of Artillery was reorganised into two groups: The Royal Horse Artillery and Royal Field Artillery in one group and the Coast Defence, Mountain and Heavy batteries in the second group, designated The Royal Garrison Artillery. In 1924 the two groups were merged into the present Royal Regiment of Artillery, although the Royal Horse Artillery have retained a separate identity.

Headdress Badge: A gun between two scrolls, that above inscribed 'UBIQUE', that beneath inscribed 'QUO FAS ET GLORIA DUCUNT'. The whole ensigned with the crown.

Mottoes: *Ubique* (Everywhere) and *Quo fas et gloria ducunt* (Where Right and Glory lead).

Regimental marches:
Quick march: *The Royal Artillery Quick March*.
Slow march: *The Royal Artillery Slow March*.

Regimental headquarters: Government House, Woolwich New Road, London SE18 6XR.

History: *History of The Royal Regiment of Artillery* (2 Vols, to 1815) by F Duncan (1872 and 1879); *History of The Royal Regiment of Artillery 1815-1853* by H W L Hime (1908); *The History of The Royal Artillery* (Crimean Period) by J R J Jocelyn (1911); *The History of The Royal and Indian Artillery in the Mutiny of 1857* by J R J Jocelyn (1915); *The History of the Royal Artillery from the Indian Mutiny to the Great War* (3 Vols) by C Caldwell and J Headlam (1931-40); *The History of Coast Artillery in the British Army* by K W Maurice-Jones (1959) and *History of The Royal Regiment of Artillery* (New Series): *Western Front 1914-18* by M Farndale (1986); *The Forgotten Fronts and The Home Base 1914-18* by M Farndale (1988); *Between The Wars 1919-39* by B P Hughes (1992); *Anti-Aircraft*

Artillery 1914-55 by N W Routledge (1994) and further volumes in production.
See also: Royal Horse Artillery.

Royal Regiment of Fusiliers (5th, 6th, 7th and 20th Foot) Formed on 23 April 1968 through the amalgamation of The Royal Northumberland Fusiliers (5th Foot), The Royal Warwickshire Fusiliers (6th Foot), The Royal Fusiliers (City of London Regiment) (7th Foot) and The Lancashire Fusiliers (20th Foot).

Headdress Badge: A grenade fired proper with, on the base, St George and Dragon within a wreath and ensigned with the crown.

Motto: *Honi Soit Qui Mal Y Pense,* (Evil to him who evil thinks).

Regimental marches:

Quick march: *The British Grenadiers.*

Slow marches: *Rule Britannia* and *De Normandie.* Also: *St George* (Northumberland), *Macbean's Slow March* (Warwickshire), *De Normandie* (London), and the former *Lancashire Fusiliers Slow March.*

Regimental headquarters: HM Tower of London, Tower Hill, London EC3N 4AB.

Royal Regiment of Wales (24th and 41st Foot) Formed on 11 June 1969 through the amalgamation of The South Wales Borderers (24th Foot) and The Welch Regiment (41st and 69th Foot).

Headdress Badge: The plume, coronet and motto of the Prince of Wales.

Motto: *Gwell angau na Chywilydd* (Better death than dishonour).

Regimental marches:

Quick march: *Men of Harlech.*

Slow march: *Scipio.*

Regimental headquarters: The Barracks, Cardiff, CF4 3YE.

History: *A History of The Royal Regiment of Wales (24th/41st Foot) 1689-1989* by J M Brereton (1989) and *A Short History of The Royal Regiment of Wales (24th/41st Foot)* by J Margesson (Ed.) (1993).

Royal School for Daughters of Officers of the Army Founded at Bath in 1864 for daughters or grand-daughters of officers who have held permanent regular commissions in the Army, Royal Marines or as Chaplains. The children of non-Service parents are now admitted.

Royal Scots (The Royal Regiment) (1st Foot) Raised in 1633 when Charles I warranted Colonel Sir John Hepburn to raise a Scottish regiment for service in France, and this was later augmented by Scots who had earlier been serving under Gustavus Adolphus and Louis XIII. The regiment served abroad as Le Régiment d'Hébron (Hepburn) from 1633-1637 and Le Régiment de Douglas 1637-1678. The regiment was brought onto the British establishment in 1661 but did not return to England until 1678 when it was designated The Earl of Dumbarton's Regiment (1st Foot). Redesignated The Royal Regiment of Foot in 1684, 1st or Royal Regiment of Foot in 1751, 1st Regiment of Foot or Royal Scots in 1812, 1st or The Royal Regiment of Foot in 1821, 1st or The Royal Scots Regiment in 1871, The Lothian Regiment (Royal Scots) in May 1881, The Royal Scots (The Lothian Regiment) in July 1881 and The Royal Scots (The Royal Regiment) (1st Foot) in 1920.

Headdress Badge: The star of the Order of the Thistle. In the centre St Andrew and cross.

Motto: *Nemo Me Impune Lacessit* (No one provokes me with impunity).

Regimental marches:

Quick marches: *Dumbarton's Drums* (Pipes and Drums and Regimental Band).

Slow marches: *The Garb of Old Gaul* (Pipers and Drums and Regimental Band).

Regimental headquarters: The Castle, Edinburgh, EH1 2YT.

History: *The Regimental Records of the Royal Scots* by J C Leask and H M McCance (1915); *The Story of The Royal Scots* by L Weaver (1915); *The Royal Scots 1914-19* (2 Vols.) by J Ewing (1925); *The First of Foot* by A Muir (1961); *The Royal Scots* by A M Brander (1976); *A Regiment at War, The Royal Scots 1939-45* by S W McBain (1988) and *Royal Scots in The Gulf, Operation Granby 1990-91* by L Milner (1994).

Royal Scots Fusiliers (21st Foot) Raised in September 1678 by Colonel Charles

Erskine, 5th Earl of Mar, as the Earl of Mar's Regiment of Foot. Designated The Scots Fusiliers Regiment of Foot in 1686, The Royal North British Fusiliers in 1712, 21st (Royal North British) Fusiliers in 1751, 21st (Royal Scots Fusiliers) in 1877 and The Royal Scots Fusiliers in 1881. On 20 January 1959 the regiment amalgamated with The Highland Light Infantry (City of Glasgow Regiment) (71st and 74th Foot) to form The Royal Highland Fusiliers (Princess Margaret's Own Glasgow and Ayrshire Regiment) (qv).

Headdress Badge: A grenade fired proper with, on the base, the royal coat of arms.

History: *The History of The Royal Scots Fusiliers 1678-1918* by J Buchan (1925) and *The History of The Royal Scots Fusiliers 1919-1959* by J C Kemp (1963).

Royal Sussex Regimental quick march of 14th/20th King's Hussars.

Royal Sussex Regiment (35th and 107th Foot) The 35th Foot was raised at Belfast in June 1701 by Colonel Arthur Chichester, 3rd Earl of Donegal, and known as The Earl of Donegal's Regiment of Foot, locally as the 'Belfast Regiment'. Numbered 35th Foot in 1751 and designated 35th (Dorsetshire) Foot in 1782, 35th (Sussex) Foot in 1805 and 35th (Royal Sussex) Foot in 1832. The 107th was raised as the East India Company's 3rd (Bengal European Light Infantry) Regiment, redesignated 3rd (Bengal Light Infantry) Regiment in 1858 and 107th Bengal Infantry Regiment in 1861. In 1881 35th (Royal Sussex) Foot amalgamated with 107th Bengal Infantry Regiment to form The Royal Sussex Regiment (35th and 107th Foot). On 31 December 1966 the regiment amalgamated with The Queen's Royal Surrey Regiment (2nd, 31st and 70th Foot), The Queen's Own Buffs, The Royal Kent Regiment (3rd, 50th and 97th Foot) and The Middlesex Regiment (Duke of Cambridge's Own) (57th and 77th Foot) to form The Queen's Regiment (qv).

Headdress Badge: The star and motto of the Order of the Garter, upon the Roussillon plume. Below, a scroll inscribed 'THE ROYAL SUSSEX REGT'.

History: *History of the Royal Sussex Regiment* by Martineau; *The Shiny Ninth* by Murray Gillings; *History of 1st Battalion The Royal Sussex Regiment* by Skinner; *A Short Record of The Royal Sussex Regiment 1801-1905* and *The Royal Sussex Regiment 'The Last Twenty Years' 1948-1967* by J F Ainsworth.

Royal Tank Corps In 1916 six companies of The Armoured Car Section Motor Machine Gun Corps were formed; retitled Heavy Section Machine Gun Corps in February 1916 and Heavy Branch Machine Gun Corps in November 1916. On 27 July 1917 the title Tank Corps was granted by Royal Warrant, the 'Royal' prefix being conferred on 18 October 1923.

History: *The Tanks* by B H Liddell-Hart (1959).

See also: *Royal Tank Regiment.*

Royal Tank Regiment On 4 April 1939 the Royal Tank Corps was redesignated The Royal Tank Regiment and formed part of the Royal Armoured Corps, ranking in precedence after the cavalry of the line.

Headdress Badge: Within a laurel wreath, a tank facing to the right and ensigned with the crown. Below, the motto 'FEAR NAUGHT'.

Motto: Fear Naught.

Regimental Marches:

Quick march: *My Boy Willie.*

Slow march: *Royal Tank Regiment Slow March.*

Regimental headquarters: Bovington Camp, Nr Wareham, Dorset, BH20 6JB.

History: *The Tanks* by B H Liddell-Hart (1959); *The Tanks - The History of The Royal Tank Regiment 1945-75* by K Macksey (1979) and *A Pictorial History of The Royal Tank Regiment* by G Forty (1988).

Royal Ulster Rifles (83rd and 86th Foot) The Royal Irish Rifles (83rd and 86th Foot) (qv) was redesignated The Royal Ulster Rifles (83rd and 86th Foot) in 1921 on the formation of the Irish Free State. On 1 July 1968 the regiment amalgamated with The Royal Inniskilling Fusiliers (27th and 108th Foot) and The Royal Irish Fusiliers (Princess Victoria's) (87th and 89th Foot) to form The Royal

Irish Rangers (27th (Inniskilling) 83rd and 87th). In 1992 the Royal Irish Rangers merged with the Ulster Defence Regiment to form The Royal Irish Regiment (27th (Inniskilling) 83rd, 87th and The Ulster Defence Regiment) (qv).

Headdress Badge: The badge of the former Royal Irish Rifles (restyled in 1920). The angel harp with motto 'Quis Separabit?' above a stringed bugle-horn, all ensigned with the crown.

Motto: *Quis Separabit?* (Who shall separate us?).

History: *History of The Royal Irish Rifles* by G B Laurie (1914); *History of the First Seven Battalions The Royal Irish Rifles (Now The Royal Ulster Rifles) in The Great War* by C Falls (1925); *The Royal Ulster Rifles* by C Graves (1950) and *The Royal Ulster Rifles 1793-1960* by M J P M Corbally.

See also: Royal Irish Rifles.

Royal United Service Institute For Defence Studies Founded in 1831 by William IV as the Naval and Military Library and Museum and originally housed in Vanbrugh House, Whitehall Yard. It moved to its present home adjoining the Banqueting House in 1896. In 1962 the government decided to make wider use of the Banqueting House and the museum was closed and the collection dispersed largely to other Service museums. However, the Institute was to carry out its work as before and, besides possessing one of the finest military libraries, it holds lectures and seminars and publishes important studies on defence matters.

Royal Warwickshire Regiment (6th Foot) Raised in 1674 from British companies fighting in the Dutch service under the command of Sir Walter Vane, the first Colonel being Luke Lillington. The regiment was taken on the English establishment in 1685 and numbered 6th Foot in 1751. Designated 6th (1st Warwickshire) Foot in 1782, 6th (Royal Warwickshire) Foot in 1832, The Royal Warwickshire Regiment in 1881 and The Royal Warwickshire Fusiliers in 1963. On 23 April 1968 the regiment amalgamated with The Royal Northumberland Fusiliers (5th Foot), The Royal Fusiliers (City of London Regiment) (7th Foot) and The Lancashire Fusiliers (20th Foot) to form The Royal Regiment of Fusiliers (qv).

Headdress Badge: Upon a ground the antelope with coronet and chain. Below, a scroll inscribed 'ROYAL WARWICK-SHIRE'.

Motto: *Honi Soit Qui Mal y Pense* (Evil to him who evil thinks).

History: *The Story of the Royal Warwickshire Regiment 1674-1919* by C L Kingford (1921); *The History of the Royal Warwickshire Regiment 1919-1955* by M Cunliffe (1956) and *Royal Warwickshire 1955-1968* by Illing (1984).

Royal Welch Fusiliers (23rd Foot) Raised at Ludlow in March 1689 by Colonel Henry Herbert, 4th Lord Herbert, as Lord Herbert of Cherbury's Regiment of Foot. Designated Welsh Regiment of Fuzileers in 1702, The Royal Regiment of Welsh Fuzileers in 1713, The Prince of Wales's Own Royal Regiment of Welsh Fuzileers in 1714, The Royal Welch Fuzileers in 1727, 23rd (Royal Welch Fusiliers) Regiment of Foot in 1751, The Royal Welsh Fusiliers in 1881 and The Royal Welch Fusiliers in 1920.

Headdress Badge: A grenade flamed proper with, on the base, within a circle inscribed 'ROYAL WELCH FUSILIERS' the plume, motto and coronet of the Prince of Wales.

Regimental marches:
Quick march: *The British Grenadiers.*
Slow marches: *The War Song of the Men of Glamorgan* and *Forth to the Battle.*

Regimental headquarters: Hightown Barracks, Wrexham, Clwyd, LL13 8RD.

History: *Regimental Records of The Royal Welch Fusiliers (late the 23rd Foot) (4 Vols.):* Vol I 1689-1815 *and* Vol II 1816-1914 *by A D L Cary and S McCance (1921 and 1923);* Vol III 1914-1918 France and Flanders *by C H Dudley Ward (1928);* Vol IV 1915-1918 Turkey, Bulgaria and Austria *by C H Dudley Ward (1929);* The Red Dragon, The Story of The Royal Welch Fusiliers 1919-1945 *by P K Kemp and J Graves (1960) and* The Astonishing Infantry *by M Glover (1989).*

Royal Wessex Yeomanry The regiment was formed as a Territorial Army infantry

battalion on 1 April 1971 from squadrons of The Royal Gloucestershire Hussars, The Royal Wiltshire Yeomanry and the Royal Devon Yeomanry. The 'Royal' prefix was granted on 8 June 1979 and, in 1983, the regiment was re-roled to a medium reconnaissance role. A reorganisation in 1992 disbanded one of the two Royal Gloucestershire Hussars squadrons. As at April 1994 the regiment comprised 'A' (Royal Gloucestershire Hussars) Squadron, 'B' (Royal Wiltshire Yeomanry) Squadron, 'D' (Royal Devon Yeomanry), 'RHQ' (Royal Gloucestershire Hussars) and the regimental band of The Royal Gloucestershire Hussars.
Badge: squadrons wear their own regimental cap badges.
Regimental march: the marches of the several regiments from which squadrons are drawn.

Royal Windsor* and *Young May Moon
An arrangement of these two tunes forms the regimental quick march of the Worcestershire and Sherwood Foresters Regiment. *Royal Windsor* (Princess Augusta) is from 29th (Worcestershire) Regiment of Foot and *Young May Moon* comes from The Sherwood Foresters (Nottinghamshire and Derbyshire Regiment) and 45th (Nottinghamshire-Sherwood Foresters) Regiment of Foot.

Royal Yeomanry The regiment was formed as a Territorial Army armoured medium reconnaissance regiment on 1 April 1967 from squadrons of five old county yeomanry regiments. The regiment's original squadrons were drawn from The Royal Wiltshire Yeomanry, the Sherwood Rangers, The Kent Sharpshooters and Yeomanry, The North Irish Horse and, as Headquarters Squadron, The Westminster Dragoons. The band was drawn from The Inns of Court and City Yeomanry. A reorganisation in 1992 transferred the Sherwood Rangers squadron and made the North Irish Horse squadron an independent squadron in Northern Ireland. A newly-formed squadron of the Leicestershire & Derbyshire Yeomanry was transferred in to the regiment. As at April 1994 the regiment

comprised 'A' (Royal Wiltshire Yeomanry) Squadron, 'B' (Leicestershire & Derbyshire Yeomanry) Squadron, 'C' (Kent and Sharpshooters Yeomanry) Squadron, 'HQ' (Westminster Dragoons) Squadron and a band (Inns of Court and City Yeomanry).
Badge: The letters RY surmounted by a crown. However, squadrons wear their own regimental cap badges.
Regimental march: *The Farmers Boy.*

Rucksack Large bag-like container fitted to a frame and designed for carriage on the back, the weight being borne by the shoulders. Used for carrying heavy loads. From the German *Rücken* (back) and *Sack* (bag).

Ruffle A low continuous drumbeat. To beat a drum with a low repetitive beat.

Rule Britannia Regimental slow march of the Royal Regiment of Fusiliers, the Royal Norfolk Regiment and one of the regimental quick marches of the Royal Anglian Regiment.

Rumani First World War Egyptian campaign battle honour marking an action in which a Turkish attempt to advance to the Suez Canal in October 1916 was roundly repulsed by the British at Rumani in Sinai. *See also: Egypt 1915-17; Suez Canal; Agagiya and Rafah.*

Rumanian Front (First World War) From the outset of the First World War (qv) Rumanian sympathy was with the Entente, but German successes on almost every front, and more especially within easy reach of the Rumanian frontier, introduced an element of caution. However, on 27 August 1916 Rumania declared war on Austria-Hungary and her troops crossed the Carpathian Alps. The Bulgarians were preparing for an assault on Rumania, and on 3 September crossed the Danube and captured some 21,000 Rumanians, triggering a Rumanian withdrawal on all fronts. For the Rumanian army in Transylvania there was further trouble: a German army had been rapidly concentrated against them and, on 28 September the Rumanian force was routed at Hermannstadt (Sibiu). remnants of the Rumanian army withdrew hurriedly over the Carpathians and were again defeated by the Germans covering Bucharest. For all practical purposes the Rumanian Army had ceased to exist by early 1917. After the final Allied victory in 1918 Rumania annexed territory which more than doubled its size.

Russia Braid Narrow braid of double weave in metal or thread used in tracing, embroidery and trimming on jackets and tunics.

Russian Front (First World War) The German main effort being against France, only a weak force, the Eighth German Army (one cavalry and eight infantry divisions) under General von Prittwitz, had been left to secure East Prussia. To assist the hard-pressed French the Russians mounted an offensive before their mobilisation was complete, and an initial Russian success at Gumbinnen caused von Prittwitz to retire behind the River Vistula. Unhappy about this withdrawal, the German High Command replaced von Prittwitz with General von Hindenburg, with von Ludendorff as his chief-of-staff, and the Germans took the offensive, winning a great victory against the Russian Second Army at Tannenberg 27-30 August 1914, bringing about the total destruction of that army and the suicide of its commander, General Samsonov. The Germans, now reinforced by 2 Corps from France, turned their efforts against General Rennenkampf's First Russian Army in the north. At the battle of the Masurian Lakes 8/9 September 1914 the Germans defeated the Russians but failed to inflict significant losses.

The southern element of the Russian forces had moved against the Austrians and Russky and Brusilov defeated them decisively in August 1914 on the line of the River Bug. By the end of August Brusilov had entered Galicia at Tarnopol, invested Przemysl at the end of September and then made for the passes across the Carpathians. The Germans mounted a counter-offensive across Poland in October 1914, causing the Russian southern forces to withdraw beyond Przemysl. The Russians, having regrouped and received some reinforcement, attacked Austro-German forces east of the River San, driving them beyond the river. The Russians the moved against Cracow in the first week of December 1914, but were held and subsequently withdrew behind the River Dunajec.

In the opening part of 1915 a battle for the Carpathian passes took place, but the Austrians could make no significant headway. By August Hindenburg had managed to clear the Russians from Warsaw and, farther to the north, the Germans were largely successful in their advance to Riga.

In 1916 the Russians defeated the Austrians around Czernowitz and made some ground between Dubno and Kovel during the summer, and unsuccessful efforts were made toward the end of the year to link up with the Rumanians. The Russian revolution broke out in March 1917 and, although the Russian army remained in the field for some months, few significant operations took place.

Rutlandshire Regiment (58th Foot) *See: Northamptonshire Regiment 48th and 58th Foot).*

Rutlandshire Yeomanry It is thought that the first Yeomanry corps to be accepted for service under the Act of 1794 was the Rutland Light Dragoons raised by the Earl of Winchilsea in April 1794. The regiment appears to have been later absorbed into the Rutland Legion, which itself disappeared in 1825.

Ruweisat Second World War North Africa campaign battle honour marking one of the actions in the defence of the Alamein Line 1-27 July 1942 when Auchinleck (qv) put a stop to the Axis advance into Egypt. *See also: North Africa 1940-1943; Defence of Alamein Line; Ruweisat Ridge; Point 93; Deir El Shein; Fuka Airfield and Alam El Halfa.*

Ruweisat Ridge Second World War North Africa campaign battle honour marking one of the actions in the defence of the Alamein Line 1-27 July 1942 when Auchinleck (qv) put a stop to the Axis advance into Egypt. *See also: North Africa 1940-1943; Defence of Alamein Line; Ruweisat; Point 93; Deir El Shein; Fuka Airfield and Alam El Halfa.*

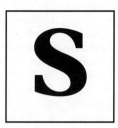

SA80 Current British assault rifle brought into service during the late 1980s to replace the Self Loading Rifle, and also known as L85A1. This 5.56mm calibre weapon fed from a 30-round magazine is a development of the earlier 4.85mm calibre infantry weapon which was not taken into service. The SA80 is fitted with a x4 magnification optical sight and has an effective range of about 400m. *See also: Self Loading Rifle and Rifle.*

Saar Second World War battle honour awarded to British units then serving under French command and marking the repulse of a German attack on 13 May 1940 during the so-called 'phoney war'. *See also: North West Europe 1940.*

Sabotage The deliberate and usually covert destruction, disruption or damaging of equipment or utilities with a view to obstructing or delaying enemy war plans or associated industrial production.

Sabre Tracked reconnaissance vehicle developed by Alvis to replace the Scorpion (qv) in the mid-1990s. Sabre consists of the Scorpion chassis fitted with the turret of a Fox armoured car mounting a 30mm cannon and a 7.62mm chain gun. It is anticipated that 140 Scorpions will be converted to the Sabre configuration. *See also: Scorpion; Striker; Spartan; Samaritan; Sultan; Samson and Scimitar.*

Sabre Single-edged cutting weapon with a curved blade used by the cavalry and now only carried on ceremonial occasions.

Sabre Squadron Battle fighting sub-unit of a cavalry regiment, as opposed to the headquarters or administrative sub-units.

Sabretache Leather case, usually with a decorated front, suspended from a cavalryman's belt by long straps to hang close to the sword or sabre.

Sackville, Lord George (1716-85) Served in the Army at Dettingen (1743) and Fontenoy (1745). At the battle of Minden (1759) Sackville commanded the British forces under Prince Ferdinand of Brunswick. Having failed to execute the Prince's order for the cavalry to charge, he was court martialled and adjudged incapable of serving thereafter in any military capacity. Thereafter he followed a political career.

Saddle Cloth Light cloth, usually decorated, put under a horse's saddle to prevent rubbing.

Saddler A badge depicting a horse's bit was worn on the sleeve of both saddlers and collar makers.

Safa Indian cavalry headdress made of a long piece of cloth.

Safe Conduct A document giving official permission to travel through a region, especially in time of military operations or deployment.

Safety Catch Small lever or catch applied to prevent the accidental operation of a firearm or weapon system.

Safety Pin Metal pin which, whilst in

place, prevents a grenade or shell becoming armed.

Sagaing Second World War Burma campaign battle honour marking the fighting which took place in January and February 1945 in the Sagaing area, clearing pockets of Japanese resistance remaining west of the Irrawaddy River. *See also: Burma 1942-1945; Ukhrul; Monywa 1945; Kyaukmyaung Bridgehead and Mandalay.*

Sahagun Peninsula War battle honour marking an action on 21 December 1808 between a British force under Sir John Moore and French forces. The British cavalry, under Lord Henry Paget, routed a greatly superior number of French horse. *See also: Peninsula and Corunna.*

Saint Andrew's Cross Regimental slow march (Pipes and Drums) of the Gordon Highlanders.

Saint George One of the regimental slow marches of the Royal Regiment of Fusiliers.

Saint Patrick's Day Regimental quick march of 4th Royal Irish Dragoon Guards, 4th/7th Royal Dragoon Guards, 8th King's Royal Irish Hussars, Queen's Royal Irish Hussars, 5th Royal Irish Lancers and the Irish Guards.

St Helena An unusual battle honour granted to two Militia battalions for their service on the island, where a number of Boer prisoners were held during the South Africa War of 1899-1902. *See also: Mediterranean.*

St Julien First World War battle honour marking a number of British counterattacks, centred on the village of St Julien, launched to recover ground lost in the opening phase of the Second Battle of Ypres in April 1915. *See also: France and Flanders 1914-1918; Ypres 1915; Gravenstafel; Frezenberg and Bellewaarde.*

St Lucia Second World War Italian campaign battle honour marking one of the actions following the Allied landing at Salerno on 9 September 1943. *See also: Italy 1943-1945; Salerno; Vietri Pass; Salerno Hills and Battipaglia.*

St Lucia 1778 Battle honour marking the capture of this island from the French on 28 December 1778 during the American War of Independence.

St Lucia 1796 The island, which had been taken from the French in 1778, was subsequently lost in 1794 and re-taken from the French on 15 May 1796.

St Lucia 1803 The island was returned to France under the Treaty of Amiens (1802) and had to be re-taken by a small force when war with the French broke out again.

St Nazaire Second World War battle honour awarded to the Commandos to mark the raid mounted to destroy the submarine base at St Nazaire on 28 March 1942. HM destroyer *Campbeltown* (formerly USS *Buchanan*) was brought alongside the lock gate leading to the submarine base and blown up. Commando troops landed and lively fighting took place between light naval forces on both sides.

St Omer - La Bassée Second World War battle honour marking the action of the British Expeditionary Force in May 1940. A defensive line was established along the canals and rivers between St Omer and La Bassée to meet the threat posed from the south and cover the withdrawal through Dunkirk. *See also: North West Europe 1940; Somme 1940 and Dunkirk 1940.*

St Pierre La Veille Second World War battle honour marking one of the actions between the Normandy landings in June 1944 and the crossing of the River Seine 25-28 August 1944. *See also: North West Europe 1944-1945; Port-En-Bessin; Tourmauville Bridge; Estry; Noireau Crossing; La Vie Crossing; La Touques Crossing; Risle Crossing and Foret de Bretonne.*

St Quentin First World War battle honour marking an action in the First Battle of the Somme and covers the opening phase of the German offensive on 21 March 1918 and its break through the Fifth Army front. Many British forward battalions were overrun and virtually annihilated, fighting to the last round against a greatly superior number of Germans. *See also: France and Flanders 1914-1918; Somme 1918; Bapaume 1918; Arras 1918; Avre and Ancre 1918.*

St Quentin Canal First World War battle honour marking one of the actions in the Battle of the Hindenburg Line 12 September-6 October 1918. The main German defensive positions lay along the St Quentin Canal and were attacked on 29 September. *See also: France and Flanders 1914-1918; Hindenburg Line; Havrincourt; Canal du Nord; Beaurevoir and Cambrai 1918.*

St Sebastian Peninsula War battle honour. The fortress of San Sebastian on the north coast of Spain dominated the main road into France. After an unsuccessful attempt on 25 July the fortress was eventually carried on 8 September 1813. *See also: Peninsula; Vittoria; Pyrenees; Nivelle; Nive; Orthes and Toulouse.*

St Valery En Caux Second World War battle honour marking the gallant fight at St Valery en Caux by surrounded elements of the British Expeditionary Force in June 1940. *See also: North West Europe 1940 and Somme 1940.*

St Vincent 1797 Battle honour marking service in the ships of Admiral Jervis' fleet in his defeat of the Spanish off Cape St Vincent on 14 February.

Sakawng Second World War Burma campaign battle honour marking one of the actions in the battle of Imphal March - June 1944, which contained and defeated the Japanese offensive against Imphal. *See also: Burma 1942-1945; Imphal; Tuitum; Nungshigum; Bishenpur; Kanglatongbi; Tamu Road; Shenam Pass and Litan.*

Saladin Six-wheeled armoured car manufactured by Alvis and developed as a successor to the Second World War Daimler armoured car. Designed in the late 1940s, the vehicle did not enter service

until 1958. By 1972 some 1,100 Saladins had been delivered. Now obsolete.

Salamanca Peninsula War battle honour marking the defeat of a French force under Marmont by a force under Wellington on 22 July 1812. Salamanca was an outstanding piece of generalship by Wellington who 'beat 40,000 Frenchmen in 40 minutes', but the British suffered heavy casualties in the exploitation phase. *See also: Peninsula; Badajoz; Almaraz; Vittoria and Pyrenees.*

Salerno Second World War Italian campaign battle honour marking the landing on 9 September 1943 by the United States Fifth Army, which included British X Corps, from which the 46th and 56th Divisions were in the assault. *See also: Italy 1943-1945; St Lucia; Vietri Pass; Salerno Hills and Battipaglia.*

Salerno Hills Second World War Italian campaign battle honour marking one of the actions following the Allied landing at Salerno on 9 September 1943. *See also: Italy 1943-1945; Salerno; St Lucia; Vietri Pass and Battipaglia.*

Salso Crossing Second World War Sicilian campaign battle honour marking one of the actions during the Allied advance through Sicily July - September 1943. *See also: Sicily 1943; Landing in Sicily; Primosole Bridge; Sferro; Regalbuto and Centuripe.*

Salute Formal military gesture of greeting. The nature of the salute may vary from a simple greeting between men at arms to a formal salute accompanied by the appropriate military music.

Salvo A ceremonial discharge from weapons in unison, or the concentrated fire of a number of weapons. *See also: Feu de joie.*

Samana Battle honour marking the defence of Fort Gulistan on the Samana Ridge against the Orakzais 12-14 September 1897. This was one of a number of actions fought on the North-West Frontier in the period 1895-97. *See also: Defence of Chitral; Chitral; Malakand; Punjab Frontier and Tirah.*

Samaritan Ambulance version (Fighting Vehicle 104) of the Scorpion (qv) tracked light reconnaissance vehicle. Can be fitted with five stretchers. *See also: Striker; Scorpion; Sabre; Spartan; Sultan; Samson and Scimitar.*

Sambre First World War battle honour marking one of the closing actions of the war. On 4 November 1918 a three-army offensive was launched against German defensive positions astride the Sambre River. *See also: France and Flanders 1914-1918; Hindenburg Line; Ypres 1918 and Pursuit to Mons.*

Sam Browne Belt and cross-strap, usually of leather, to which items of equipment may be attached for ease of carriage. Named after its inventor, the one-armed General Sir Samuel Browne (1824-1901). The Army discarded the belt for field service after 1939, but it is still worn by officers and some warrant officers on formal occasions.

Samson Repair and recovery version (Fighting Vehicle 106) of the Scorpion (qv) tracked light reconnaissance vehicle. Fitted with a 12-ton winch and light crane. *See also: Striker; Scorpion; Sabre; Spartan; Sultan; Samaritan and Scimitar.*

San Clemente Second World War Italian campaign battle honour marking one of the actions in the Battle of the Gothic Line 25 August-22 September 1944. *See also: Italy 1943-1945; Gothic Line; Tavoleto; Coriano; Croce; Gemmano Ridge; Monte Gridolfo; Montegaudio; Poggio San Giovanni and Pian di Castello.*

Sandbag Hessian bag filled with earth or sand and used to construct field defences offering some protection against blast and projectiles.

Sandhurst *See: Royal Military Academy - Sandhurst.*

Sand Table Flat surface covered with sand. The sand is modelled to represent real or imaginary terrain features and, usually with the addition of model military equipments, is used to support operational briefings or tactical instruction.

Sanfatuchio Second World War Italian campaign battle honour marking the capture of a key position in the battle to break through the Trasimene Line 20-30 June 1944. *See also: Italy 1943-1945 and Trasimene Line.*

Sangar A small defensive structure of sandbags, rocks, sods or other material used when the ground is too hard to dig trenches or when trenches would be unsuitable. The term is taken from the Pashto.

Sangro Second World War Italian campaign battle honour marking the forcing of the River Sangro by the Eighth Army 19 November - 3 December 1943. *See also: Italy 1943-1945; Mozzagrogna; Fossacesia and Romagnoli.*

Sankey's Horse Nickname given 39th Foot, later The Devonshire and Dorset Regiment. Sankey was colonel of the regiment when in Spain (1708-1711), and tradition has it that he mounted the men on mules to deploy them rapidly to the site of a battle.

San Marino Second World War Italian campaign battle honour marking one of the actions during the operation to break through the German defences in the area of Rimini 14-21 September 1944. *See also: Italy 1943-1945; Rimini Line; Ceriano Ridge; Monte Colombo; Casa Fabri Ridge; Montescudo and Frisoni.*

San Martino Sogliano Second World War Italian campaign battle honour marking one of the actions which took place between the breaching of the Gothic Line in September 1944 and the thrust to the Po valley in April 1945. *See also: Italy 1943-1945; Montebello-Scorticata Ridge; Monte Reggiano; Savignano; San Martino Sogliano; Monte Farneto; Montilgallo; Carpineta; Monte Cavallo; Casa Bettini; Pideura; Pergola Ridge; Senio Floodbank; Cesena; Conventello-Comacchio; Monte Casalino; Monte La Pieve; Monte Pianoereno; Monte Spaduro; Orsara; Tossignano and Catarelto Ridge.*

San Nicolo Canal Second World War Italian campaign battle honour marking one of the actions in the Battle of the Argenta Gap 13-21 April 1945. *See also: Italy 1943-1945; Argenta Gap and Fossa Cambalina.*

San Salvo Second World War Italian campaign battle honour marking one of the actions during the Eighth Army advance in 1943. *See also: Italy 1943-1945; Landing at Porto San Venere; Taranto; Orsogna; Impossible Bridge and Caldari.*

Sans Peur **(Fearless)** Motto of 93rd (Sutherland Highlanders) Regiment of Foot and later of The Argyll and Sutherland Highlanders (Princess Louise's).

Santarcangelo Second World War Italian campaign battle honour marking the capture, after stiff fighting between 20 and 24 September 1944, of this village during the advance from the Gothic Line. *See also: Italy 1943-1945; Gothic Line; Monte Chicco and Capture of Forli.*

Santerno Crossing Second World War Italian campaign battle honour marking the crossing of the Rivers Senio and Santerno in early April 1945. *See also: Italy 1943-45 and Senio.*

Sap A deep and narrow trench used to approach or undermine an enemy position.

Saphead The end of a sap (qv) nearest the enemy.

Sapper The lowest rank in the Corps of Royal Engineers and equivalent to private (qv). The term sapper is also loosely used to describe any member of the Corps of Royal Engineers.

Saracen Six-wheeled armoured personnel carrier based on the Saladin (qv) chassis, Saracen (Fighting Vehicle 603) was designed and produced by Alvis; had a crew of two, mounted a 0.30" machine gun and could carry a fully equipped section of ten men. Introduced in 1952, they were withdrawn from service in the 1970s, although some continued in service as troop carriers in Northern Ireland.

Sardar Title used before the name of Sikh men. A leader. *See also: Sirdar.*

Sari Bair First World War Gallipoli campaign battle honour marking the series of attacks mounted against the Sari Bair Ridge from 6 August onward out of the Anzac beachhead. *See also: Gallipoli 1915-1916; Suvla; Landing at Suvla and Scimitar Hill.*

Sash Originally made of silk, which is both light and strong, and used for the removal of wounded officers from the field. Sashes had necessarily to be full enough to enclose the whole body, and were worn either round the waist or over the shoulder. A clothing regulation of 1747 directed that officers of infantry wear the sash over the right shoulder, and those of cavalry over the left, and that non-commissioned officers of both arms wear it round the waist. As the field utility of the sash diminished, and its value as a rank distinction increased, there were, between 1768 and 1845 a number of further directions concerning the colour, quality and wearing of sashes, but by 1912 all officers wore their sashes round the waist and knotted on the left, warrant officers and sergeants wearing theirs over the right shoulder and knotted at the left hip. However, following a Somerset Light Infantry (Prince Albert's) tradition, the origin of which is uncertain, the Light Infantry wear their sashes over the left shoulder, the sash being knotted on the right for officers, warrant officers and sergeants.

Saucy Greens Nickname used for 51st Regiment of Foot (The King's Own Yorkshire Light Infantry) in a recruiting poster of the late 18th century.

Saucy Seventh Nickname given 7th Queen's Own Hussars, now The Queen's Royal Hussars (The Queen's Own and Royal Irish). A regimental recruiting poster of c.1809 uses this name, an allusion to the regiment's smart appearance.

Saucy Sixth Nickname given 6th Foot, later The Royal Warwickshire Regiment (qv). In 1795 the regiment returned from the West Indies and recruited in Warwickshire, but the required standard was so high that few recruits were found, and the name was coined.

Saunnu Second World War North Africa campaign battle honour marking a rear-guard action during the withdrawal to the Gazala position in early January 1942. *See also: North Africa 1940-1943; Tobruk 1941 and Gazala.*

Savignano Second World War Italian campaign battle honour marking one of the actions which took place between the breaching of the Gothic Line in September 1944 and the thrust to the Po valley in April 1945. *See also: Italy 1943-1945; Montebello-Scorticata Ridge; Monte Reggiano; San Martino Sogliano; San Martino Sogliano; Monte Farneto; Montigallo; Carpineta; Monte Cavallo; Casa Bettini; Pideura; Pergola Ridge; Senio Floodbank; Cesena; Conventello-Comacchio; Monte Casalino; Monte La Pieve; Monte Pianoereno; Monte Spaduro; Orsara; Tossignano and Catarelto Ridge.*

Savio Bridgehead Second World War Italian campaign battle honour marking the crossing of the River Savio 20-23 October 1944. *See also: Italy 1943-1945; Rimini Line; Capture of Ravenna and Marradi.*

Saxon Four-wheeled armoured personnel carrier, developed as AT105 by GKN in the 1970s as a private venture, and taken into service as a section vehicle in mechanised infantry battalions from the mid-1980s. Saxon has a crew of two, is fitted with a 7.62mm machine gun and can carry a fully equipped infantry section of ten men. Command, recovery and ambulance variants of the vehicle are also in service.

Sbiba Second World War North Africa campaign battle honour marking an action during defensive operations to check a German thrust through the Kasserine Pass in late February 1943. *See also: North Africa 1940-1943; Kasserine and Thala.*

Scabbard Holder or sheath for a bladed weapon such as a sabre, sword or bayonet. Usually attached to the belt by frog or sling.

Scafati Bridge Second World War Italian campaign battle honour marking one of a number of actions which took place on the Fifth Army front during the advance to the Gustav Line in late 1943. *See also: Italy 1943-1945; Monte Camino; Capture of Naples; Cappezano; Monte Stella; Cava di Tirreni; Cardito; Volturno Crossing; Monte Maro; Roccheta e Croce and Colle Cedro.*

Scale-Loop Series of metal 'scales' forming a loop on a cocked hat.

Scales of Justice Regimental quick march of the Army Legal Corps and Army Legal Services Branch of the Adjutant General's Corps.

Scarf Worn by drum majors of the Foot Guards when in state clothing. Formerly worn by officers in the 17th century.

Scarlet Scarlet has been a distinguishing feature of British Army uniform since the 16th century. The royal soldiers of Charles II's reign all wore red coats, even the artillerymen.

Scarlet and Green Regimental quick march of 16th/5th The Queen's Royal Lancers.

Scarpe 1917 First World War battle honour marking one of the actions in the 1917 Battle of Arras 23 April-4 May, the British advancing from Arras along the Scarpe valley. *See also: France and Flanders 1914-1918; Bapaume 1917; Arras 1917; Vimy 1917 and Arleux.*

Scarpe 1918 First World War battle honour marking the opening phase of the Arras offensive launched on 26 August 1918. *See also: France and Flanders 1914-1918; Amiens; Albert 1918; Drocourt-Quéant and Hindenburg Line.*

Schadendorf Second World War battle honour marking one of the actions during the advance from the River Roer to the River Rhine 8 February-10 March 1945. *See also: North West Europe 1944-1945; Rhineland; Reichswald; Cleve; Goch; Weeze; Hochwald; Waal Flats; Moyland; Moyland Wood and Xanten.*

Scheldt Second World War battle honour marking operations to clear the Scheldt (French: Escaut) estuary, Beveland, the Breskens pocket and the capture of Walcheren Island 24-29 September 1944. *See also: North West Europe 1944-1945; Nederrijn; Antwerp-Turnhout Canal; Walcheren Causeway; Flushing; Westkapelle and South Beveland.*

Scherpenberg First World War battle honour marking the final phase of the Battle of the Lys 9-29 April 1918. A German attempt to capture the high ground of the Scherpenberg was contained and repulsed. *See also: France and Flanders 1914-1918; Lys; Estaires; Messines 1918; Hazebrouck; Bailleul; Kemmel and Béthune.*

Scimitar Reconnaissance version (Fighting Vehicle 107) of the Scorpion (qv) light tracked reconnaissance vehicle, with a crew of three, and mounting a 30mm Rarden cannon and 7.62mm machine gun. *See also: Striker; Scorpion; Sabre; Spartan; Samaritan; Sultan and Samson.*

Scimitar A combat net communications system with a frequency-hopping capability for use where the electronic counter measures (ECM) threat is high. Alternatively, an oriental sword with a curved blade broadening toward the point.

Scimitar Hill First World War Gallipoli campaign battle honour marking one of the Suvla operations to capture Scimitar Hill and Sari Bair thus linking with the advance from Anzac. *See also: Gallipoli 1915-1916; Anzac; Landing at Anzac; Defence of Anzac; Suvla; Sari Bair and Landing at Suvla.*

Scinde Battle honour marking the Sind War of 1843. The reverses suffered by the British Army during the First Afghan War

had encouraged the Amirs of Scinde to violate their treaty. Following a Baluchi attack on the residency at Hyderabad a small force led by Sir Charles Napier defeated the Baluchis at Meeanee, a few miles from the city. A second successful action at Hyderabad resulted in the annexation of Scinde. There is no evidence to suggest that the story that, at the conclusion of the campaign, Napier telegraphed to London *'Peccavi'* (I have sinned), is anything other than apocryphal. *See also: Meeanee and Hyderabad.*

Scinde Campaign Medals 1843 There are three strikings of this medal commemorating the campaign against the Emirs of Scinde 6 January - 24 March 1843: MEANEE 1842; HYDERABAD 1842; and MEANEE HYDERABAD 1843.
Ribbon: Rainbow pattern watered red, white, yellow, white and blue. 1" wide.

Scipio One of the regimental slow marches of the Grenadier Guards; and regimental slow march of The Queen's Own Mercian Yeomanry and The Royal Mercian and Lancastrian Yeomanry.

Scorpion Tracked light reconnaissance vehicle (Fighting Vehicle 101). Lead member of the 'Fighting Vehicle 100' family of light armoured vehicles developed by Alvis from the early 1960s to meet an Army requirement for an airportable tracked reconnaissance vehicle. The prototype was produced in 1969 and the first production vehicles appeared in 1972. Scorpion has a crew of three, and mounts a 76mm L23 gun and a 7.62mm machine gun. *See also: Scorpion; Sabre; Striker; Spartan; Samaritan; Sultan; Samson and Scimitar.*

Scotland the Brave Regimental quick march of the Queen's Gurkha Signals and 52nd Lowland Volunteers.

Scots Guards The regiment has its origins in the 'Royal Regiment' of Scotsmen raised for Charles I in March 1642, under the command of the 1st Marquis of Argyll, for service in the Irish rebellion. More usually the regiment's origins are associated with the company of guards raised by

Charles II at Edinburgh in October 1660, and shortly thereafter at Dumbarton. On 1 May 1662 a Royal Warrant directed that these companies of guards be augmented by four additional companies and all six regimented as the 'New Regiment of Foot Guards'. Between 1662 and 1686 the regiment underwent a number of title changes including: Our Regiment of Guards, His Majesties Regiment of Guards, The King's Regiment, The King's Foot Guards, The King's Lyfe Guards of Foot and Scotch Guards (or Scots Guards). Numbered 3rd regiment of Foot Guards in 1712 and redesignated The Scots Fusilier Guards in 1831, the regiment became the Scots Guards in 1877.

Headdress Badge: The tar of the Order of the Thistle with otto.

Motto: *Nemo Me Impune Lacessit* (No one provokes me with impunity).

Regimental marches:
Quick march: *Hielan' Laddie* (Pipes and Drums and Regimental Band).
Slow march: *The Garb of Old Gaul* (Pipes and Drums and Regimental band).

Regimental headquarters: Wellington Barracks, Birdcage Walk, London, SW1E 6HQ.

History: *The History of the Scots Guards* (1642-1914 in 2 Vols) by F Maurice (1934) and *The Scots Guards 1919-1955* by D Erskine (1956).

Scottish Division An administrative grouping in the infantry, created under Army Order 34 of 1986, comprising The Royal Scots (The Royal Regiment), The Royal Highland Fusiliers (Princess Margaret's Own Glasgow and Ayrshire Regiment) (1959), The King's Own Scottish Borderers, The Cameronians (Scottish Rifles) (disbanded 1968), Black Watch (Royal Highland Regiment), Queen's Own Highlanders (Seaforth and Camerons) (1961-1994), The Gordon Highlanders (until 1994), The Argyll and Sutherland Highlanders (Princess Louise's) and The Highlanders (Seaforth, Gordons and Camerons) (from 17 September 1994).

Scottish Yeomanry Formed as a Yeomanry reconnaissance regiment in the Territorial Army order of battle on 1 November 1992. As at April 1994 the regiment comprised 'A' (Ayrshire(Earl of Carrick's Own) Yeomanry) Squadron, 'B' (Lanarkshire amd Queen's Own Royal Glasgow Yeomanry) Squadron, 'C' (Fife and Forfar Yeomanry/Scottish Horse) Squadron and 'HQ' (Lothians and Border Horse) Squadron.

Badge: A scottish lion rampant against lances crossed in saltire. Below, a scroll inscribed 'THE SCOTTISH YEOMANRY'. The whole ensigned with the crown. However, squadrons wear their own regimental cap badges.

Regimental marches:
Quick march: *Holyrood*
Slow march: *Garb of Old Gaul*

Scout General purpose light helicopter developed and produced by Saunders Roe/Westland Aircraft Ltd, in service with the Army since 1961 in the reconnaissance, training, casualty evacuation and anti-tank roles, but now obsolescent. Provision exists for the fitting of four SS11 anti-tank wire-guided missiles and machine guns. Capable of carrying three passengers, four stretcher cases or 700kg of freight at a cruising speed of 150kt over a range of 272 miles.

Scrape Shallow depression scraped in the ground to provide a minimum level of protection when the situation offers neither the time nor the opportunity to dig trenches.

Screen A small security force, placed forward or to the flank of the main force, tasked to observe, identify and report. A screen fights only in self-protection. *See also: Covering Force and Guard.*

Seaforth Highlanders (Ross-Shire Buffs, The Duke of Albany's) (72nd and 78th Foot) The 72nd regiment was raised mainly in Ross-shire and Lewis in May 1778 by Lieutenant Colonel Kenneth MacKenzie, Earl of Seaforth, and known as 78th Highland Regiment (Seaforth's Highlanders). Redesignated 72nd (Highland) Regiment in 1786 and 72nd or The Duke of Albany's Own Highlanders in

1823. The 78th was raised in July 1793 by Lieutenant Colonel Francis Humbertson Mackenzie (later Lord Seaforth, Baron Mackenzie of Kintail) as 78th (Highland) Regiment or The Ross-shire Buffs. In 1881 72nd or Duke of Albany's Own Highlanders amalgamated with 78th (Highland) Regiment or Ross-shire Buffs to form The Seaforth Highlanders (Ross-shire Buffs, The Duke of Albany's). On 7 February 1961 the regiment amalgamated with The Queen's Own Cameron Highlanders (79th Foot) to form The Queen's Own Highlanders (Seaforth and Camerons) (qv).

Headdress Badge: A stag's head. Below, a scroll inscribed 'CUIDICH'N RIGH'.

Motto: *Cuidich'n Righ* (Help The King).

History: *A Short History of the Seaforth Highlanders* by Dingwick (1928).

Sealed Pattern An article approved by the Board of Ordnance and sealed with wax, thus becoming the definitive pattern for that item.

Sealskin Used in the full dress caps of riflemen, light infantry buglers and bandsmen.

Searchlight Equipment consisting of a light source and a reflecting surface which projects a powerful beam of light in a selected direction. Primarily used for the illumination of air and maritime intruders so that they can be engaged with fire and destroyed. In the Second World War searchlights were used in the 'movement light' role: a large number of searchlights were projected onto low cloud producing so-called 'artificial moonlight' which gave sufficient light for night attacks, the movement of troops or logistic movement. Special 'flickering' searchlights were mounted on tanks which were used for 'blinding' the enemy at defended obstacles such as river crossings.

Sebket En Noual Second World War North Africa campaign battle honour marking one of a number of actions which took place between the occupation of the Alamein Line in June 1942 and the end of the campaign in North Africa in May 1943. *See also: North Africa 1940-1943; Deir El Munassib; Capture of Halfaya Pass; Matmata Hills; Chebket En Nouiges; Djebel El Telil and Djebel Tebaga.*

Second Army (Second World War) Formed in Britain in 1941 under the command of Lieutenant General Miles Dempsey; landed in Normandy 6 June 1944. With 1st Canadian Army it formed 21st Army Group. Fought in France, Belgium, Holland and Germany on the left flank of 6th and 12th Army Groups, aiding United States armies to counter the Ardennes offensive in December 1944. Disbanded in June 1945.

Second China War Medal 1857-1860 Authorised in a General Order dated 6 March 1861 and awarded to all Services involved in the campaign.

Ribbon: Originally multi-coloured with five equally spaced stripes of blue, yellow, red, white and green. Subsequently changed to crimson with yellow edges.

Clasps: China 1842; Fatshan 1857; Taku Forts 1858; Canton 1857; Taku Forts 1860 and Pekin 1860.

Second Lieutenant An officer holding the lowest of the commissioned ranks in the Army. The rank is denoted by one star on each epaulette. *See also: Lieutenant; Subaltern and Rank.*

Second World War The Second World War began on 1 September 1939 with Germany's invasion of Poland, and Britain declared war on Germany, as did France, on 3 September to honour the guarantee they had given Poland on 31 March 1939. Germany had signed a treaty of military assistance with Italy on 23 May 1939, and a non-aggression pact with Russia on 21 August 1939. Poland was subjected to attack by Germany from the west and, from 17 September by Russia seeking to recover territory lost at Brest-Litovsk in December 1917, from the east. For similar reasons the Russians invaded Finland on 30 November, and embarked upon a conflict with the Finns which was to last until 13 March 1940 when the Finns capitulated.

Meanwhile France had entered the period known as the 'phoney war' during which the British Expeditionary Force (qv) under Gort (qv) moved to the continent and took over a section of the Franco-Belgian frontier with its headquarters at Arras, and spent the winter of 1939 fortifying a position north of the Maginot Line defences. On 10 May 1940 Germany launched an offensive into the Low Countries and France, driving the British and French forces rapidly back; the British force being eventually evacuated through Dunkirk (qv), and the French capitulating on 17 June 1940. On 9 April 1940 Hitler launched a rapid thrust into Denmark and Norway (qv) which fell following a brief and unsatisfactory allied campaign in Norway. By the summer of 1940 Hitler controlled the European coast from northern Norway to the Atlantic coast of France, but by the end of the 'Battle of Britain' in mid-September 1940, his opportunity to invade Britain had passed.

On 27 September 1940 Germany, Italy and Japan signed the Ten-Year Mutual Assistance Pact, securing the Berlin-Rome-Tokio axis. Mussolini, confident that the Axis had all but won the war declared war on both Britain and France, and opened campaigns in Abyssinia (qv) and Greece (qv) in October 1940 and North Africa (qv) in December 1940. These three campaigns were all to prove beyond the capacity of the Italians and the Germans were eventually drawn in to support their ally

In the spring of 1941 Hitler directed his attention away from the west, striking southward against Yugoslavia and Greece to assist the embattled Italians and then, on 22 June 1941, against Russia. Although the Germans had also intervened in North Africa it was the Russian front that preoccupied them throughout the latter part of 1941.

On 7 December 1941 the Japanese attacked the US Pacific Fleet at Pearl Harbor, drawing the United States into the war. Hong Kong (qv) fell to the Japanese in December 1941 and, in the same month the Japanese invaded Malaya(qv), thrust down through the Malay peninsula, largely outflanking British forces in the area, and

Singapore Island (qv) fell to them in February 1942. In January 1942 the Japanese invaded Burma (qv), forcing the British to retire across the River Chindwin into India.

During early 1942 Britain suffered a number of reverses; not only the Japanese successes in the Far East, but also in North Africa where Rommel defeated the Eighth Army and seemed close to driving the British out of the Middle East. But, by the latter part of 1942 the tide had turned. United States forces were having increasing success in the Pacific. On 23 October 1942 Montgomery opened the Second Battle of El Alamein, defeated Rommel and began to advance to Tripoli and a rendezvous with the Anglo-United States force which landed in November 1942 in Operation TORCH. On 19 November 1942 the Russians launched a massive counter-attack which was to lead to the surrounding and surrender of the German Sixth Army at Stalingrad. In May 1943 the Allies landed in Sicily (qv) and from there, on 3 September 1943, to Italy (qv) driving Axis forces before them. The German homeland was also being subjected to heavy bombing.

On 6 June 1944 - 'D-Day' - a substantial allied invasion force landed in Normandy, further Allied landings being made on 15 August in southern France. After fierce fighting in Normandy the Allies broke out in August 1944 and drove hard toward the Low Countries and the Rhine. In an attempt to turn the German line, and thus shorten the war, an allied parachute force was dropped in September 1944 to seize the bridges over the Maas, Waal and lower Rhine. Ground forces successfully linked up with the two western airborne divisions, but were delayed at Nijmegen (qv) and arrived too late at Arnhem where the British airborne forces, fighting like tigers against overwhelming German forces, suffered severe casualties. By the end of November 1944, the allies were very extended and the Germans had reorganized and, on 16 December 1944, von Rundstedt launched an offensive, which was contained by the Allies, in the Ardennes.

With the turn of the year, the Russians

swept along a massive front to the plains of Poland, Prussia and Austria. From the Baltic to Budapest their armies. which had already liberated Warsaw, Radom, Lodz and Cracow were tearing great gaps in the German eastern front in a grand final offensive on three main fronts: in the north under Rokossovsky; the centre under Zhukov; and the south under Konev. On the western front between February and April 1945 stubborn fighting took place across the Dutch waterways and for the great Roer dams. The Roer was forced and its chief strongholds, Jülich and Düren were captured on 24 and 25 February. In the north the allied armies closed on the Rhine crossings (qv) at Xanten, Wesel and Rheinberg and on 7 March captured Cologne. On the same day United States troops crossed the Rhine at Remagen and pressed forward at speed into central and southern Germany; Mainz fell on 20 March and Frankfurt on 26 March. The British Second Army advanced through Osnabrück and on to Hamburg and Lüneburg Heath.

When the western Allies reached the line of the River Elbe they were ordered to halt, evidently in order not to encroach on a sphere already earmarked for the Russians. Hitler's death was announced on 1 May 1945, Berlin surrendered to the Russians on 2 May and, on 5 May all German forces in north-west Germany, Holland and Denmark surrendered to Field Marshal Montgomery. The final capitulation took place on 7 May at Rheims, effective from midnight 8-9 May; formal ratification taking place in Berlin on 9 May 1945.

By this time the British Fourteenth Army, the so-called 'Forgotten Army' in Burma, was having significant success against the .Japanese, and United States forces were well advanced in the clearance of the Pacific islands. However, matters with Japan were brought to a head when, on 6 August and 9 August the United States dropped atomic bombs on Hiroshima and Nagasaki respectively, and the Japanese sued for peace on 10 August 1945. The official surrender in South-East Asia took place on 12 September 1945 at Singapore.

The Second World War was remarkable for its global nature and the totality of its nature; the entire resources of the participants being developed to the utmost and bent toward military success. Remarkable too was the setting aside of any idea of the 'Rules of War', air power making irrelevant the distinction between combatant and civilian. *See also: Norway 1940; North West Europe 1940; North West Europe 1942; North West Europe 1944-1945; North Africa 1940-1943; Sicily 1943; Italy 1943-1945; Burma 1942-1945; Abyssinia 1940-1941; Iraq 1941; Syria 1941; Greece 1941; Greece 1944-1945; Middle East; Crete; Madagascar; Leros; Cos; Adriatic; Malta 1940-1942 and Malaya 1941-1942.*

SECOND WORLD WAR MEDALS

1939-1945 Star This award covers the period 3 September 1939-15 August 1945 - the latter date reflecting the day on which active operations against Japan ceased. For Army personnel to qualify it was necessary to have completed at least six months' service in an operational command, but only one day in the case of Dunkirk, Norway and certain specified commando raids or, for airborne forces, to have taken part in an airborne operation.
Ribbon: Three equal vertical stripes of dark blue, red and light blue.

Africa Star The qualifying period for this award was one or more days' service in North Africa, Abyssinia, Italian Somaliland, Sudan, Eritrea or Malta between 10 June 1940 and 12 May 1942.
Ribbon: Pale buff with a wide red vertical stripe at the centre. Equidistant between the edges and the central red stripe are a thin vertical dark blue stripe on the left and a similar pale blue stripe on the right.
Clasps: 8TH ARMY; 1ST ARMY and NORTH AFRICA 1942-43.

Atlantic Star The qualification for this award is six months' service afloat in the Atlantic, home waters, convoys to Russia or certain parts of the South Atlantic during the period 3 September 1939 to May 1945. Army personnel serving in Merchant Navy or Royal Navy vessels were eligible.
Ribbon: Shaded and watered blue, white and sea green.

Burma Star The Army qualification

requirement for this medal was service in Burma between 11 December 1941 and 2 September 1945; in Bengal and Assam between 1 May 1942 and 2 September 1945 or in Malaya and China between 16 February 1942 and 2 September 1945.

Ribbon: A broad red central vertical stripe flanked on either side by a vertical blue stripe of similar width, in the centre of each blue stripe a narrow orange stripe.

Defence Medal Awarded for three years' service in Great Britain until 8 May 1945, or six months' service overseas in territories subjected to, or threatened by, enemy attacks over the period 3 September 1939 to 15 August 1945.

Ribbon: Flame coloured with green edges, down the centre of each edge a narrow black vertical stripe.

France and Germany Star Awarded for operational service in France, Belgium, Holland and Germany between 6 June 1944 and 8 May 1945.

Ribbon: Equal vertical stripes of blue, white, red, white and blue.

Clasp: Atlantic.

Italy Star Awarded for active service in Italy, Sicily, Greece, Yugoslavia, Corsica, Sardinia, Elba and the Aegean and Dodecanese between 11 June 1943 and 8 May 1945. However, service in Sicily after 17 August 1943, Sardinia after 19 September 1943 and in Corsica after 4 October 1943 did not count.

Ribbon: Five vertical bands of equal width, red, white, green, white and red.

War Medal Awarded to all full time Army personnel who completed 28 days' service in the period 3 September 1939 to 2 September 1945. Service terminated by death, wounds or capture also qualified.

Ribbon: Vertical stripes of equal width in red, blue, white, blue and red, with a thin vertical red stripe down the centre of the white stripe.

Secondary Position A new position, normally at least part-prepared, but certainly reconnoitred, to which a unit or sub-unit will move once its primary position has become untenable or when its primary position has, through the flow of battle, become ineffective.

Secretary of State for Defence The Secretary of State for Defence is chairman of the Defence Council and of the Army Board of the Defence Council.

Secrète An iron skull cap or similar protection worn by cavalrymen under their hats as a safeguard against sword-cuts in the 18th century after the iron helmet went out of fashion.

Secure To take possession of a position or terrain feature and to deploy thereon such a force as will prevent, as far as possible, its destruction or loss by enemy action.

Sedgemoor Area of wetland between Bridgwater and King's Weston in Somerset where the royal forces defeated Monmouth in 1685.

Sedjenane I Second World War North Africa campaign battle honour marking one of a number of actions which took place between the Kasserine and Fondouk operations February-April 1943. *See also: North Africa 1940-1943; El Hadjeba; Djebel Djaffa; Sidi Nsir; Fort McGregor; Stuka Farm; Steamroller Farm; Montagne Farm; Kef Ouiba Pass; Djebel Guerba; Maknassy; Djebel Dahra; Kef El Debna and Djebel Choucha.*

Seedaseer Fourth Mysore War battle honour marking the action near Coorg on 6 March 1799 in which the advance guard of a Bombay column of three brigades under Major General Stuart contained an attack by Tippoo Sahib's main forces for six hours until the main body of the column arrived to drive them off. *See also: Fourth Mysore War and Seringapatam.*

Seetabuldee Second Maratha War battle honour marking an action on 26 November 1817 in which a small force some 1,300 strong contained and eventually repelled an attack by an 18,000 strong army of the Raja of Nagpore. *See also: Second Maratha War; Kirkee; Nagpore; Maheidpore and Corygaum.*

Seikpyu Second World War Burma campaign battle honour marking an action which took place following the advance to the Irrawaddy River in early 1945. *See also: Burma 1942-1945; Irrawaddy; Letse and Kyaukse 1945.*

Seine 1944 Second World War battle honour marking the crossing of the River Seine, mainly in the Vernon and Elbeuf areas, 25-28 August 1944. *See also: North West Europe 1944-1945; Dives Crossing; Lisieux and Amiens 1944.*

Self-Loading Rifle L1A1 This 7.62mm calibre rifle fed by a 20-round magazine was based on a design by Fabrique Nationale of Belgium and made under license in Britain. It replaced the Lee Enfield Number 4 rifle (qv) as the British Army service rifle in 1957 and was itself replaced in the late 1980s by SA80 (qv). *See also: Rifle.*

Self-Propelled An equipment, more usually a gun, provided with its own source of tractive power rather than an external prime mover.

Selkirkshire Yeomanry (The Selkirkshire Yeomanry Light Dragoons) The Selkirkshire Corps of Yeomanry Cavalry was formed in January 1798 and, having given notice of their willingness to serve after the Peace of Amiens, became known as the Selkirkshire Yeomanry Light Dragoons. The regiment disbanded in 1828, although an unsuccessful attempt was made in 1859 to form the 'Volunteer Ettrick Forest Carabiniers' or 'Ettrick Forest Mounted Rifles'.

Selle First World War battle honour marking the fighting on the River Selle, centred on Le Cateau, during the period 17-25 October 1918. *See also: France and Flanders 1914-1918; Ypres 1918; Courtrai; Valenciennes; Sambre and Pursuit to Mons.*

Semper Fidelis (Ever faithful) Motto of The Devonshire Regiment and later The Devonshire and Dorset Regiment.

Senio Second World War Italian campaign battle honour marking the operations to effect an assault crossing of the Senio and Santerno Rivers 9-12 April 1945. *See also: Italy 1943-1945 and Santerno Crossing.*

Senio Floodbank Second World War Italian campaign battle honour marking one of the actions which took place between the breaching of the Gothic Line in September 1944 and the thrust to the Po valley in April 1945. *See also: Italy 1943-1945; Montebello-Scorticata Ridge; Monte Reggiano; San Martino Sogliano; San Martino Sogliano; Monte Farneto; Montigallo; Carpineta; Monte Cavallo; Casa Bettini; Pideura; Pergola Ridge; Savignano, Cesena, Conventello-Comacchio; Monte Casalino; Monte La Pieve; Monte Pianoereno; Monte Spaduro; Orsara; Tossignano and Catarelto Ridge.*

Senio Pocket Second World War Italian campaign battle honour marking the clearance and securing of an area east of the River Senio on 4 and 5 January 1945; a prerequisite to any further advance. *See also: Italy 1943-1945; Senio and Senio Floodbank.*

Sentinel Obsolete term for a person, such as a sentry, assigned to keep guard.

Sentry A person who guards or prevents unauthorised access to a place, or keeps watch to provide early warning.

Sentry Box Small shelter with an open front in which a sentry may stand to be sheltered from foul weather.

Seoul Korean War battle honour. *See also: Korea 1951-53; Naktong Bridgehead; Pakchon; Imjin; Kowang-San; The Hook 1952; The Hook 1953; Chongchon II; Chaum-Ni; Hill 327; Kapyong-Chon; Kapyong; Maryang San and Hill 227 I.*

Sepoy An Indian soldier of the old, pre-1947, Indian Army. The term was used loosely for men of all Indian units. More correctly it was applied to distinguish the infantry soldier from the cavalry trooper or sowar.

Septemur Agendo (Let us be judged by our deeds) Motto of The Royal Dragoons

(1st Dragoons), the East Lancashire Regiment; and 30th (1st Cambridgeshire) Regiment of Foot.

Sergeant Non-commissioned officer ranking above corporal and below staff sergeant or colour sergeant. Identified by the wearing of three chevrons on the upper arm. The title corporal of horse is used in the Household Cavalry.

Sergeant Major Abbreviated title for squadron, battery, or company sergeant major. The warrant officer second class appointed as senior warrant officer to a squadron, battery or company. In the Foot Guards the title sergeant major is used for the regimental sergeant major (qv). The title squadron corporal major is used in the Household Cavalry.

Seringapatam Fourth Mysore War battle honour marking the storming, following a siege of three weeks, of Tippoo Sahib's capital by a Bombay column of three brigades under Major General Stuart 4 May 1799 in which Tippoo Sahib was killed. This victory brought the Fourth Mysore War to an end and secured British supremacy in southern India. *See also: Fourth Mysore War and Seedaseer.*

Serjeant Early spelling of sergeant still used in some regiments.

Serve To Lead Motto of the Royal Military Academy Sandhurst and of the Royal Military Academy Sandhurst Band Corps.

Service Dress Order of dress originally worn in service conditions, rather than full or ceremonial dress. Khaki or service drab was introduced in 1902 for field service uniform. Although khaki service or 'Number 2' dress is still worn by officers and men on formal occasions, it has been replaced by the range of disrupted pattern combat clothing for use in the field.

Set Piece Term applied to a military operation or manoeuvre which has been carefully planned and even perhaps rehearsed.

Sevastopol Crimean War battle honour marking the siege and a number of unsuccessful attempts to capture the Russian fortress of Sevastopol which took place between September 1854 and the Russian surrender in October 1855. *See also: Alma; Balaklava and Inkerman.*

Seven Years War (1756-63) Also known as the Third Silesian War, fought in Europe by Frederick The Great of Prussia, aided by subsidies and troops from Britain against a coalition of Austria, Russia, France, Sweden and Saxony. In parallel, Britain fought France and Spain at sea and on land, mainly in North America and India. Frederick's campaign laid the foundations of the German state, and Britain's campaign can be identified with the foundation of British naval supremacy, the Indian empire and the reduction of French influence in North America. At the close of the war the Peace of Paris (1763) left Britain as practically the sole colonising power and mastery of the high seas. The Peace of Hubertusburg in the same year, established Prussia in Pomerania and Silesia, and recognised her as the equal of Austria. *See also: Minden; Emsdorf; Warburg; Belle Isle and Wilhelmstahl.*

Sferro Second World War Sicily campaign battle honour marking operations 15-20 July 1943 which resulted in the capture of Sferro. *See also: Sicily 1943, Landing in Sicily; Primosole Bridge; Regalbuto and Centuripe.*

Sferro Hills Second World War Sicily campaign battle honour marking one of a number of actions which took place during the Allied campaign of July and August 1943 to secure the island. *See also: Sicily 1943; Solarino; Vizzini; Augusta; Francofonte; Lentini; Simeto Bridgehead; Gerbini; Agira; Adrano; Salso Crossing; Simeto Crossing; Monte Rivoglia; Malleto and Pursuit to Messina.*

Sgian-Dhu *See: Skean-dhu.*

Shabraque The cloth or skin worn on a horse under the saddle. These were usually embroidered in the corners with regimental or rank devices. In the British Army the cavalry ceased using shabraques at the end of Queen Victoria's reign.

Shaiba First World War Mesopotamia campaign battle honour marking the defeat, after three days of fighting, of the Turkish offensive of April 1915, the aim of which was to eject the British from the Persian Gulf area. *See also: Mesopotamia 1914-1918; Basra; Kut Al Amara 1915; Ctesiphon; Defence of Kut Al Amara; Tigris 1916; Kut Al Amara 1917; Baghdad; Khan Baghdadi and Sharqat.*

Shake Out To adopt an advance or attack formation after a period at rest, or after moving through a defile or close country.

Shako Peaked cap issued under General Order of 23 February 1800 to the British infantry and known as the 'stovepipe'. Subsequently worn in a number of shapes such as Waterloo, Regency, Bell-topped, Albert, French and Quilted, by the infantry and some cavalry and artillery units, until the introduction of the helmet in about 1878.

Shalloon A cloth originally used for lining uniforms. From *châlon* in France.

Shamrock Pattern of lace approved for wear by Irish regiments. British Army orders permit all Irish soldiers to wear shamrock on Saint Patrick's Day in honour of the gallantry of their countrymen in the South Africa War (1899-1902).

Shaped Charge Also known as a hollow charge; a directional explosive charge which exploits the 'Monroe effect' to penetrate armour and concrete.

Sharon First World War Palestine campaign battle honour marking one of the actions in the Battle of Megiddo in September 1918. *See also: Palestine 1917-1918; Gaza; El Mughar; Nebi Samwil; Jaffa; Jerusalem; Jericho; Tell Asur; Jordan; Megiddo; Nablus and Damascus.*

Sharpshooter A skilled marksman, especially with a rifle. A sniper.

Sharqat First World War Mesopotamia campaign battle honour marking the defeat of the main Turkish force on the River Tigris during the final British advance to Mosul in October 1918. *See also: Mesopotamia 1914-1918; Basra; Kut Al Amara 1915; Ctesiphon; Defence of Kut Al Amara; Tigris 1916; Kut Al Amara 1917; Baghdad; Khan Baghdadi and Shaiba.*

Shawl Worn over the shoulder by Irish pipers.

Sheepskin Or lambskin, worn by some mounted officers over saddlery.

***Sheitan Ke Bacchi* (Children of Satan).** Nickname given by the Sikhs to 3rd Light Dragoons(qv) who, having defeated the Sikh horse at Moodkee (qv), charged along the rear of the position inflicting heavy losses on the Sikhs, during the First Sikh War (qv).

Shell A hollow artillery projectile filled with high explosive primed to explode either during flight, on impact or after penetration. Also, an obsolete lightweight garment, usually without sleeves.

Shell Dressing Sterile dressing prepared for the initial treatment of large wounds in the field. *See also: Field dressing.*

Shell Jacket Short, waist length jacket without tails for undress wear introduced into the British infantry in 1830. This red jacket replaced the white waistcoat as a fatigue dress. The white shell or drill jacket continued in wear by the Highlanders and Foot Guards. The shell jacket later evolved into the mess dress (qv) jacket.

Shenam Pass Second World War Burma campaign battle honour marking one of the actions in the Battle of Imphal March to June 1944, which contained and defeated the Japanese offensive against Imphal. *See also: Burma 1942-1945; Imphal; Tuitum; Nungshigum; Bishenpur; Kanglatongbi; Tamu Road; Shenam Pass and Litan.*

Sheriff County or city officer. The appointment of sheriff is rooted in the

Norman judicial and financial administrative system. In early times the office of sheriff was open to grave abuses. Although the sheriff was the means of exerting the royal authority, he could impede it, especially if he was a powerful baron. Henry I abolished the baron-sheriffs and substituted officials of the royal household, holding office for one year only; this tenure of office was confirmed in the Provisions of Oxford (1258). In 1557 Lords Lieutenants (qv) were first appointed to act as the chief military officer of the County, and the chief military duty of the sheriff, as defined in the Sheriffs Act 1887, is now to suppress riots, having the power in that connection to call out the '*posse comitatus*' (the strength (manpower) of the county). *See also: High Sheriff.*

Sherwood Foresters (Nottinghamshire and Derbyshire Regiment) (45th and 95th Foot) The 45th Foot was raised in January 1741 by Colonel David Houghton as 56th Regiment of Foot and renumbered 45th Foot in 1748. Redesignated 45th (1st Nottinghamshire) Foot in 1782 and 45th (Nottinghamshire Regiment) Sherwood Foresters in 1866. The 95th Foot was raised in December 1823 by Colonel Sir Colin Halkett and designated 95th or Derbyshire Foot in 1825. In 1881 45th (Nottinghamshire Regiment) Sherwood Foresters amalgamated with 95th or Derbyshire Foot to form The Derbyshire Regiment (Sherwood Foresters), redesignated The Sherwood Foresters (Derbyshire Regiment) in July 1881. In 1902 the regiment was redesignated The Sherwood Foresters (Nottinghamshire and Derbyshire Regiment). On 28 February 1970 the regiment amalgamated with The Worcestershire Regiment (29th and 36th Foot) (qv) to form The Worcestershire and Sherwood Foresters Regiment (29th and 45th Foot) (qv).
Headdress Badge: A maltese cross. Within an oak wreath a white hart, left and right the title 'SHERWOOD FORESTERS'. Below, a scroll inscribed 'NOTTS AND DERBY'. All ensigned with the crown.
History: *1st and 2nd Battalions The Sherwood Foresters Nottinghamshire and Derbyshire Regiment 1740-1914* (2 Vols) by Wylly (1929); *History of the 45th Regiment of Foot* by Dalbiac (1902) and *History of The Sherwood Foresters (Nottinghamshire and Derbyshire Regiment) 1919-1957* by Barclay (1959).

Shirtsleeve Order Warm weather order of dress in uniform. No tie is worn and the shirtsleeves are rolled up to the elbow.

Shock Troops Soldiers specially trained and equipped to carry out an assault or raid.

Sholinghur Second Mysore War battle honour marking the battle fought near Arcot in the Carnatic on 27 September 1781 between Sir Eyre Coote's forces and those of Hyder Ali. *See also: Second Mysore War and Mangalore.*

Shorts The concept of shortened trousers is attributed to the Askaris in Kumassi in 1873. The wearing of shorts spread through Africa and, by 1904, khaki shorts were being worn in India. Shorts were declared obsolete in the late 1960s following a change in medical opinion.

Short Magazine Lee Enfield Rifle Produced as a result of experiences in the South Africa War the Mark II version of this 0.303", 10-round magazine, weapon appeared in 1907 and was used throughout the First World War. A Mark V version with improved sights was produced in the 1920s and, although due to be replaced by the Lee Enfield Number 4 Rifle, these weapons were still in use by Allied soldiers in the Second World war. *See also: Rifle.*

Shotgun A firearm, usually fired from the shoulder, with an unrifled bore and designed for the discharge of shot of varying sizes at short range.

Shoulder Belt Belts worn over the shoulder include those needed to carry a pouch, carbine, sword or bayonet. Shoulder or 'cross' belts are now worn for ornamental reasons.

Shoulder Chain Piece of chain mail worn on the shoulders to protect the wearer against blows from edged weapons. Now purely decorative.

Shoulder Cords Gold cords worn by officers after 1800 to carry rank badges. Also, narrow cords worn on the shoulders by cavalrymen to keep belts in position. Shoulder straps of flat pieces of cloth served the same purpose.

Shoulder Knot Worn in the early 18th century to keep the sword belt in place.

Shoulder Scales Groups of tapering metal scales worn over the shoulders as protection against blows by edged weapons.

Shrapnel Type of ammunition, consisting, in the original, of a spherical iron shell containing a large number of bullets, sufficient powder being mixed with the bullets to burst the shell when the fuse ignited the charge. It was initially called spherical case shot, and was designed to attain a longer range than grape shot or common case shot. The bursting charge was of just sufficient strength to blow open the case and enable the bullets to be propelled forward in a cone-shaped shower over a large area. The later kind of shrapnel had its bursting charge in a cylinder in the middle of the elongated projectile used with rifled guns. It was invented in 1784 by Henry Shrapnel (1761-1842), an officer in the Royal Artillery, and adopted by the Army in 1803, but not employed until 1808. Shrapnel ammunition was increasingly used and, in the First World War, provoked the invention of the 'shrapnel helmet'. Early anti-aircraft guns used shrapnel almost exclusively, but by 1939 the fragmentation effect of high explosive ammunition had so far improved as to render shrapnel obsolescent and, though the term was still loosely used to describe splinters from high explosive shells, the use of shrapnel proper was largely confined to anti-personnel mines.

Shropshire Yeomanry In 1795 troops were raised at Wellington and Market Drayton and, in the early years, there were 11 corps in the county including the Wrekin Company, Hales Owen Cavalry, Pimhill Light Horse and Oswestry Rangers. The Brimstree Loyal Legion served for some years, but was disbanded in 1802. In 1824 the existing corps were regimented to form three regiments: the South Shropshire, Shrewsbury and North Shropshire Yeomanry Cavalry Regiments. The first two amalgamated in 1828 to form the South Salopian Yeomanry Cavalry, and the North Shropshire regiment changed its name to North Salopian Yeomanry Cavalry. The two regiments amalgamated in 1872. During the South Africa War (1899-1902) the regiment found a company for the 5th Battalion Imperial Yeomanry.

In the First World War the regiment served dismounted in Egypt from March 1916 and a year later amalgamated with the Cheshire Yeomanry to form 10th (Shropshire and Cheshire Yeomanry) Battalion, The King's Shropshire Light Infantry, fighting in Palestine, France and Belgium. Although restored to the mounted role in 1920 the regiment converted to artillery in 1940, serving in that role in the Middle East and Italy. In 1947 the regiment converted to armour as a divisional regiment of the Royal Armoured Corps. The Pembrokeshire Yeomanry and Shropshire Royal Horse Artillery were incorporated in the regiment in 1967. Reduced to a cadre and a signal squadron in 1969, a squadron was formed from the cadre in 1971, serving in the infantry role with the Queen's Own Mercian Yeomanry. The successor sub-units are 'HQ' (Shropshire Yeomanry) Squadron of The Royal Mercian and Lancastrian Yeomanry and 95 (Shropshire Yeomanry) Signal Squadron, 35 (South Midlands) Signal Regiment (Volunteers).

Shwebo Second World War Burma campaign battle honour marking the capture on 9 January 1945 of Shwebo, which lay on the railway north from Mandalay. *See also: Burma 1942-1945.*

Shwegyin Second World War Burma campaign battle honour marking one of the actions during the British withdrawal from Burma in 1942. *See also: Burma 1942-1945 and Monywa 1942.*

Shweli Second World War Burma campaign battle honour marking the crossing of the River Irrawaddy and advance along the River Shweli during January and February 1945. *See also: Burma 1942-1945. Ukhrul, Kyaukmyaung Bridgehead and Sagaing.*

Si Abdallah Second World War North Africa campaign battle honour marking one of the actions in the battle of Medjez Plain 23-30 April 1943. *See also: North Africa 1940-1943; Medjez Plain; Gueriat El Atach Ridge; Longstop Hill 1943; Djebel Bou Aoukaz 1943; Grich El Oued; Peter's Corner; Si Mediene; Gab Gab Gap and Sidi Ahmed.*

Siberia 1918-19 First World War battle honour marking the action of British troops, originally tasked to safeguard Allied stores at Vladivostock, and later drawn into co-operation with the White Armies in the Russian civil war. British troops marched westwards along the Trans-Siberian railway to link up with the Czech Legion. *See also: Archangel 1918-19; Troitsa; Murmansk 1918-19 and Dukhovskaya.*

Sicily 1943 Second World War battle honour marking the campaign to eject Axis forces from Sicily. On 10 July 1943 an Allied force mounted in North Africa landed in the south-east corner of Sicily, the British Eighth Army on the right and advancing in an anti-clockwise direction to seize Syracuse and the Catania airfields and the United States Seventh Army on the left advancing clockwise around the island. Strong German resistance was encountered in the area North of the River Simeto and around Mount Etna. The Allies entered Messina on 17 August 1943 and all resistance collapsed. *See also: Landing in Sicily; Primosole Bridge; Sferro; Regalbuto; Centuripe; Solarino; Vizzini; Augusta; Francofonte; Lentini; Simeto Bridgehead; Gerbini; Agira; Adrano; Sferro Hills; Salso Crossing; Simeto Crossing; Monte Rivoglia; Malleto and Pursuit to Messina.*

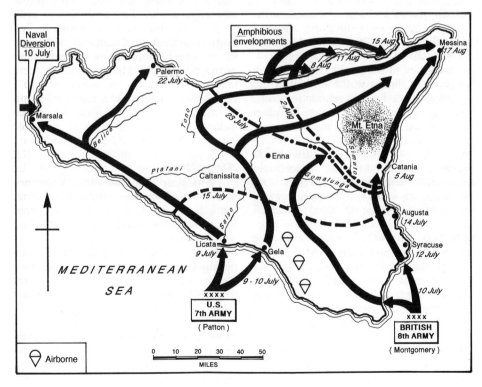

Sicily 1943

Sidi Ahmad Second World War North Africa campaign battle honour marking one of the actions in the battle of Medjez Plain 23-30 April 1943 which preceded the advance into Tunis. *See also: North Africa 1940-1943; Medjez Plain; Gueriat El Atach Ridge; Longstop Hill 1943; Djebel Bou Aoukaz 1943; Grich El Oued; Peter's Corner; Si Mediene and Gab Gab Gap.*

Sidi Ali Second World War North Africa campaign battle honour marking one of the actions in the Fondouk operations of early April 1943 in which Anglo-United States forces sought to break through the Fondouk pass towards Kairouan. *See also: North Africa 1940-1943; Fondouk; Kairouan; Bordj; Pichon; Djebel El Rhorab and Fondouk Pass.*

Sidi Barrani Second World War North Africa campaign battle honour marking the decisive British victory over the Italians in December 1940. After a two-night advance across the desert, five Italian divisions were neutralised and 39,000 prisoners taken at the cost of only 600 British casualties. *See also: North Africa 1940-1943; Egyptian Frontier 1940; Buq Buq; Capture of Tobruk and Beda Fomm.*

Sidi Nsir Second World War North Africa campaign battle honour marking one of a number of actions which took place between the Kasserine and Fondouk operations February-April 1943. *See also: North Africa 1940-1943; El Hadjeba; Djebel Djaffa; Sedjenane I; Fort McGregor; Stuka Farm; Steamroller Farm; Montagne Farm; Kef Ouiba Pass; Djebel Guerba; Maknassy; Djebel Dahra; Kef El Debna and Djebel Choucha.*

Sidi Rezegh 1941 Second World War North Africa campaign battle honour marking the heavy fighting around the Sidi Rezegh feature in the Battle of Tobruk in November and December 1941. *See also: North Africa 1940-1943; Tobruk 1941; Gubi I; Tobruk Sortie; Omars; Belhamed; Gabr Saleh; Taieb El Essem; Gubi II and Relief of Tobruk.*

Sidi Rezegh 1942 Second World War North Africa campaign battle honour marking one of the actions in the Battle of the Gazala Line in May and June 1942. *See also: North Africa 1940-1943; Gazala; Retma; Bir El Aslagh; Bir Hacheim; Cauldron; Knightsbridge; Tobruk 1942; Bir El Igela; Hagiag Er Raml; Gabr El Fachri; Via Balbia and Zt El Mrasses.*

Sidi Suleiman Second World War North Africa campaign battle honour marking the unsuccessful British offensive known as Operation BATTLEAXE 15-17 June 1941. British armour was subjected, for the first time, to the devastating effect of the German 88mm anti-aircraft gun employed in the anti-tank role. *See also: North Africa 1940-1943; Mersa El Brega; Agedabia; Derna Aerodrome and Halfaya 1941.*

Sierra Leone 1898 Battle honour marking operations in the colony of Sierra Leone between 1898 and 1899. Following an attempt to raise house tax, some of the chiefs rebelled and about 100 British subjects, African and European, were murdered. Operations were mounted to restore order.

Signal An electro-magnetic emission. Communication over a distance by hand gesture or any other means.

Signalman The most junior rank in the Royal Corps of Signals, equivalent to private (qv).

SIKH WARS

First Sikh War (1845-46) British frontiers in north-west India had been extended to those of the Sikh monarchy, but after the death of Ranjit Singh the Sikh army crossed the boundary on the River Sutlej, considered as an act of war. The first action of the war was at Moodkee on 18 December 1845, where the Ludhiana and Umballa divisions under Sir Hugh Gough defeated the Sikhs. Three days later at Ferozeshah, severe casualties were taken by both sides and the Sikhs withdrew over the frontier. In January 1846, the Sikhs again crossed the Sutlej but were routed at Aliwal. The final action of the war was at Sobraon, the British suffering significant casualties. *See also: Moodkee; Ferozeshah; Aliwal and Sobraon.*

Second Sikh War (1848-49) Also known as the Punjab War. Although the administration of the Sikh kingdom had been entrusted to a council of regency by the peace treaty drawn up after the Battle of Sobraon, unrest continued and the British prepared to conquer the Punjab. Under orders from the Governor-General, Lord Gough attacked the strongly entrenched position of Chillianwallah on 13 January 1849. The Sikhs fell back during the night, but Gough's army had suffered significant casualties. The siege of Mooltan had begun in September 1848, but the Sikh commander surrendered on 22 January 1849 before the final assault was launched. The final battle took place at Goojerat on 21 February 1849, bringing a successful campaign by Gough to an end. *See also: Mooltan; Chillianwallah; Goojerat and Punjaub.*

Silencer Tubular device fitted to the muzzle of small arms to reduce the sound of firing.

Silent Attack An offensive operation for which there is no preparatory bombardment or other activity which would indicate to the enemy that an attack has been launched. It is usual for the attack to become 'noisy' when the attacking force comes under enemy fire. Given modern surveillance devices it is unlikely that an attacking force will reach its objective without an exchange of fire.

Sillaro Crossing Second World War Italian campaign battle honour marking one of the actions during the assault on German positions in the Bologna area 14-21 April 1945, the final Fifth Army offensive of the campaign. *See also: Italy 1943-1945; Medicina; Gaiana Crossing and Idice Bridgehead.*

Silver War Badge A silver war badge was approved in 1916 for issue to officers and men of the British, Indian and Overseas forces who had served at home since 4 August 1914, and who, on account of age or from physical infirmity arising from

wounds or sickness caused by military service, had, in the case of officers, retired or resigned their commissions, or, in the case of men, been discharged from the Army. In view of the provisions of the Military Service (Review of Exceptions) Act 1917, the conditions of the granting of this medal were modified and various terms used in the original grant defined. A similar device was instituted for the Second World War, named The King's Badge and issued by the Ministry of Pensions.

Si Mediene Second World War North Africa campaign battle honour marking one of the actions in the Battle of Medjez Plain 23-30 April 1943. *See also: North Africa 1940-1943; Medjez Plain; Gueriat El Atach Ridge; Longstop Hill 1943; Djebel Bou Aoukaz 1943; Grich El Oued; Peter's Corner; Si Abdallah; Gab Gab Gap and Sidi Ahmed.*

Simeto Bridgehead Second World War Sicilian campaign battle honour marking one of a number of actions which took place during the Allied campaign of July and August 1943 to secure the island. *See also: Sicily 1943; Solarino; Vizzini; Augusta; Francofonte; Lentini; Sferro Hills; Gerbini; Agira; Adrano; Salso Crossing; Simeto Crossing; Monte Rivoglia; Malleto and Pursuit to Messina.*

Simeto Crossing Second World War Sicilian campaign battle honour marking one of a number of actions which took place during the Allied campaign of July and August 1943 to secure the island. *See also: Sicily 1943; Solarino; Vizzini; Augusta; Francofonte; Lentini; Sferro Hills; Gerbini; Agira; Adrano; Salso Crossing; Simeto Bridgehead; Monte Rivoglia; Malleto and Pursuit to Messina.*

SIMRAD Lightweight laser range finder with a range of 6,000m used by artillery forward observation parties to locate targets and bring fire to bear on them more rapidly.

Simulation The safe representation of battle effects to enhance the value and realism of training.

Simulator A device or equipment designed to reproduce, as safely and realistically as possible, the effects of battlefield weapons, and thus enhance the value and realism of training.

Singapore Island Second World War Malayan campaign battle honour marking the defensive operations on Singapore Island 8-15 February 1942. *See also: Malaya 1941-1942; Northern Malaya; Central Malaya; Johore; Batu Pahat and Muar.*

Single Action A firearm which requires the hammer to be cocked by hand before each firing.

Single File A line of soldiers or vehicles, ranged one behind the other, either stationary or on the move.

Sioux Light utility helicopter developed and produced by Augusta Bell/Westland Aircraft Ltd, in service with the Army since 1964 and now obsolete. Provision existed for the fitting of a door-mounted machine gun. Capable of carrying two passengers at a maximum speed of 105mph over a range of 215 miles.

Sirdar A general or military leader in Pakistan and India. The title of the British commander-in-chief of the Egyptian army. From Hindi *Sardar*.

Sittang 1942 Second World War Burma campaign battle honour marking the attempts by 17th Indian Division to hold the Japanese on the line of the Rivers Bilin and Sittang in early 1942. In this action the bridge over the Sittang was prematurely demolished, leaving two brigades of the division caught between the enemy and the river. *See also: Burma 1942-1945; Pegu 1942; Taukyan; Paungde; Yenangyaung 1942; Kyaukse 1942 and Monywa 1942.*

Sittang 1945 Second World War Burma campaign battle honour marking the successful operations 10 May-15 August to prevent the Japanese Twenty-Eighth Army breaking out of the Pegu Yomas intact to cross the River Sittang, and the defeat of the Thirty-Third Army. *See also: Burma 1942-1945 and Arakan Beaches.*

Sit to Attention Compliment or form of salute in which individuals remain seated, but the upper body and head are erect and the arms held to the sides.

Skean Dhu A small dirk carried in the stocking by officers in highland regiments. From the Gaelic meaning 'black knife'.

Skeeter Light utility helicopter developed and produced by Saunders-Roe Ltd, in service with the Army from 1957 as a reconnaissance, liaison and training aircraft but now obsolete. Maximum speed 104mph, range 213 miles.

Skirmish A small scale military engagement. To employ the tactic of fire and manoeuvre.

Skirt Flaps Ornamental shape on the back of tunics somewhat resembling the obsolete pocket-flap.

Skye Boat Song Regimental slow march (Pipes and Drums) of the Argyll and Sutherland Highlanders (Princess Louise's).

Slashers, The Nickname given to 28th Foot, later The Gloucestershire Regiment. When the regiment was stationed in Canada in 1764, a magistrate harassed the soldiers and their families. A party of heavily disguised soldiers broke into the magistrate's house at night, and during the ensuing scuffle the magistrate's ear was cut off. Officially, the identity of the culprits was never discovered, but after the incident the 28th rapidly acquired the nickname.

Slim, 1st Viscount of Yarralumba and Bishopston, William Joseph (1891-1970) Having been an elementary school teacher in Birmingham, Slim joined the Army at the outbreak of the First World War, was commissioned, and served in Gallipoli and Mesopotamia. After the war he joined the Indian Army. He commanded the First Burma Corps in 1942, and directed the fighting withdrawal to India. He returned to Burma to direct the

15th Indian Corps at Arakan in October 1943 and became commander of the Fourteenth Army (qv), whose operations during 1944 marked the turning point of the Burma campaign (qv) and he was knighted in 1944. His leadership and ability were of such quality that he inspired the men of his 'forgotten army' with renewed confidence. In September 1945 Slim was appointed commander of the Allied land forces in South-East Asia. Becoming commandant of the Imperial Defence College, he was appointed chairman of the Railway Executive in 1948, but relinquished this post on being appointed Field Marshal and Chief of the Imperial General Staff in succession to Montgomery. He was Governor General and Commander-in-Chief of Australia 1953-60 and was created Viscount in 1960.

Slim River Second World War Malayan campaign battle honour marking the action which preceded the fall of Kuala Lumpur during the campaign in central Malaya 26 December 1941 to 10 January 1942. *See also: Malaya 1941-1942; Northern Malaya; Central Malaya; Ipoh and Kampar.*

Sling Strap of leather, webbing or other material attached at two or more points to small arms, particularly rifles and light machine guns, to facilitate aiming and carriage.

Slit Trench A narrow trench dug to protect individuals from small arms and artillery fire.

Slouch Hat Broad-brimmed colonial hat worn by the Australians in Queen Victoria's reign and subsequently adopted for wear in the South Africa War (1899-1902). Wearing of the slouch hat gradually lapsed, but it came back into favour in the Far East and parts of Africa during the Second World War.

Slow March A march in slow time, 60 paces per minute, used on ceremonial and solemn occasions.

Small Arms Light, portable weapons of small calibre such as pistols, rifles, light machine guns and sub-machine guns. The origin of the term is unclear, but a 'Keeper of Our Small Arms' was appointed in 1683.

Small Arms School Corps The origins of this small Corps can be traced to the School of Musketry established at Hythe, Kent in 1854. In 1919 the School of Musketry was redesignated Small Arms School and a Machine Gun School was formed at Seaford, Sussex, later moving to Netheravon in Wiltshire. In 1923 the instructional staff of both schools were given corps status with the title Corps of Small Arms and Machine Gun Schools, retaining their separate identities and locations. In 1929 the Machine Gun School was absorbed into the Small Arms School at Hythe and the two elements of the Corps amalgamated under the present title.
Headdress Badge: A Vickers Machine Gun, thereon a pair of crossed rifles with bayonets fixed, a crown within the angle formed by the rifles above the machine gun; the whole within a laurel wreath inscribed 'SMALL ARMS SCHOOL'.
Regimental quick march: *March of the Bowmen.*
Corps headquarters: Tactics and Small Arms Wing, School of Infantry, Warminster, Wiltshire, BA12 0DJ.
History: *A Brief History of The Small Arms School Corps and Small Arms Wing School of Infantry, Hythe* by A J Parsons (1953) and *History of The Small Arms School Corps* by F Myatt (1972).

Smoker Informal social gathering, more usually held at sub-unit level, e.g. company smoker.

Smoothbore Firearm having a smooth, unrifled, bore.

Smuts, Jan Christian (1870-1950) South African soldier and statesman. Read law at Cambridge and graduated from Christ's College in 1894, and began to practice at the Cape Town Bar in 1895. The Jameson Raid of 1896 persuaded him to the Republican view and in 1898 he became State Attorney under President

Kruger. In 1899 he published a statement of the Boer case against Britain, entitled *A Century of Wrong*. In 1901 he was given supreme command of the Boer forces in Cape Colony and proved a daring and able commando leader. Under British rule he became Colonial Secretary of the Transvaal in 1907, and was subsequently Minister of Mines 1910-12, Defence 1910-20 and Finance 1912-13. He commanded British troops in British East Africa 1917-18. Throughout the First World War he was instrumental in quelling pro-German separatist groups within the Union, and continued to work for Anglo-Boer co-operation. At the outbreak of the Second World War Smuts advocated co-operation between South Africa and the Allies and was able to prevail against those favouring neutrality led by Hertzog and Malan. Smuts became supreme commander of the Union defence forces in 1940 and was appointed field marshal, the first dominion soldier to be so appointed, in 1941. Smuts helped draft the UN Charter in 1945 and was leader of the South African delegation to the UN Assembly in New York. Defeated by Malan in the election of 1948, Smuts became leader of the Anglo-Afrikaner opposition, protesting vehemently against the government's policy of racial segregation.

Snake Hook The 'S' shaped hook fastening on the early 19th century waist-belt. Still worn by some rifle regiments.

Snaphaunce Firing mechanism, of Dutch origin, which lies midway between the wheel-lock (qv) and the flintlock in terms of firearms development. *See also: Flintlock; Matchlock; Musket and Rifle.*

Snappers, The Nickname given 15th Foot, later The Prince of Wales's Own Regiment of Yorkshire. During the Battle of Brandywine (1777), with ammunition exhausted, the men 'snapped' their muskets to give the impression that they were firing; this simulation was sufficiently realistic to convince the Americans to retire.

Sniper Formerly called sharpshooters.

Now found in every infantry battalion and usually deployed in pairs. Men with very highly developed marksmanship and fieldcraft skills, tasked to engage high value targets, slow enemy movement or dominate open areas with single shot small arms fire. The term can also be applied to tanks individually sited, usually forward of the main position, tasked with early attrition of enemy armour.

Sniper Rifle Specially accurised weapon, fitted with a telescopic sight for use by snipers. The two most recent sniper rifles in service with the British Army are a 7.62mm calibre version (L42 Sniper) of the Lee Enfield Number 4 Rifle (qv) and the 7.62mm calibre L96A1 Sniper which replaced the L42 Sniper in 1986.

Sobraon First Sikh War battle honour marking General Gough's decisive victory over the main Sikh army on 10 February 1846. *See also: First Sikh War; Moodkee; Ferozeshah and Aliwal.*

Soissonais-Ourcq First World War battle honour marking the attack launched toward Soissons on 23 July 1918 as part of the 1918 Battle of the Marne. *See also: France and Flanders 1914-1918; Marne 1918 and Tardenois.*

Solarino Second World War Sicilian campaign battle honour marking one of a number of actions which took place during the Allied campaign of July and August 1943 to secure the island. *See also: Sicily 1943; Simeto Crossing; Vizzini; Augusta; Francofonte; Lentini; Sferro Hills; Gerbini; Agira; Adrano; Salso Crossing; Simeto Bridgehead; Monte Rivoglia; Malleto and Pursuit to Messina.*

Soldier A person who serves or has served in the Army.

Soldiers Chorus This chorus from Gounod's *Faust* is the regimental slow march of 5th Dragoon Guards (Princess Charlotte of Wales's) and 5th Royal Inniskilling Dragoon Guards.

Soldier of Fortune A mercenary.

Soldiers of the Queen Regimental quick march of The Queen's Regiment and part of the regimental quick march of The Princess of Wales's Royal Regiment (Queen's and Royal Hampshires).

Soldier On To persist in one's efforts in spite of the difficulties.

Soldiers' Sailors' and Airmen's Families Asscociation (SSAFA) A nationwide voluntary organisation established in 1885 to assist servicemen, ex-servicemen and their families and provide relief when they are in distress. There are many branches within the United Kingdom and in garrisons and stations overseas, manned by voluntary workers and maintained almost entirely by voluntary subscriptions.

Soldier Settlement Term denoting the crown land in Australia allocated to ex-servicemen for farming.

Soldier Servant Term used in some regiments for the junior rank appointed to carry out minor tasks in support of an officer. On operations he is usually also a runner, radio operator and/or driver. *See also: Batman and Orderly.*

Soleuvre Second World War battle honour marking the crossing of the River Souleuvre as part of the Mount Pincon operations 30 July-6 August 1944 aimed at thrusting south-westwards from the Caumont area in conjunction with the break out of United States forces near St Lô. *See also: North West Europe 1944-1945; Mount Pincon; Quarry Hill; Catheolles; Le Perier Ridge; Brieux Bridgehead; Jurques and La Varinière.*

Somaliland 1901-1904 Battle honour marking the early campaigns against the 'Mad Mullah' who emerged at the turn of the century in this arid semi-desert pastoral area as the fanatical leader of raiding Dervish bands. The first British campaign against him was in 1900-01; there was another in 1903 and others were called for repeatedly until the Mullah's death in 1921.

Somerset Light Infantry (Prince Albert's) (13th Foot) Raised in June 1685 by Theophilus, Earl of Huntingdon and mustered at Buckingham as The Earl of Huntingdon's Regiment of Foot. Designated 13th Foot in 1751, 13th (1st Somersetshire)) Foot in 1782, 13th (1st Somerset Light Infantry) in 1822, 13th (1st Somersetshire) (Prince Albert's Light Infantry) in 1842, The Somersetshire Regiment (Prince Albert's Light Infantry) in May 1881, Prince Albert's Light Infantry (Somersetshire Regiment) in July 1881 and The Somerset Light Infantry (Prince Albert's) in 1921. On 6 October 1959 the regiment amalgamated with The Duke of Cornwall's Light Infantry (32nd and 46th Foot) to form The Somerset and Cornwall Light Infantry (13th, 32nd and 46th Foot). On 10 July 1968 the Somerset and Cornwall Light Infantry amalgamated with The King's Own Yorkshire Light Infantry (51st and 105th Foot), The King's Shropshire Light Infantry (53rd and 85th Foot) and The Durham Light Infantry (68th and 106th Foot) to form The Light Infantry (qv).

Headdress Badge: Within the strings of a bugle-horn the initials 'P.A.' (Prince Albert's) and, above, a mural.

History: *The Somerset Light Infantry 1685-1914* by H Everett (1934); *The Somerset Light Infantry 1914-1919* by E Wyrall (1927); *The Somerset Light Infantry 1919-1945* by G Molesworth (1951); *The Somerset Light Infantry 1946-1960* by K Whitehead and *The Somerset Light Infantry* by H Popham (1968).

Somerset and Cornwall Light Infantry (13th, 32nd and 46th Foot) Formed on 6 October 1959 through the amalgamation of The Somerset Light Infantry (Prince Albert's) (13th Foot) and The Duke of Cornwall's Light Infantry (32nd and 46th Foot) to form The Somerset and Cornwall Light Infantry (13th, 32nd and 46th Foot). On 10 July 1968 the Somerset and Cornwall Light Infantry amalgamated with The King's Own Yorkshire Light Infantry (51st and 105th Foot), The King's Shropshire Light Infantry (53rd and 85th Foot) and The Durham Light Infantry (68th and 106th Foot) to form The Light Infantry (qv).

Headddress Badge: A stringed bugle-horn with, above, a mural crown upon a red cloth backing.

SOMERSET YEOMANRY

The North Somerset Yeomanry A troop was raised in Frome in 1798 and, with the troops from Bath, Wells, Rode and Wolverton and Beckington, disbanded in 1802. In 1804 the Frome troop was re-raised and formed the East Mendip Corps, The Frome and East Mendip Regiment of Yeomanry Cavalry - renamed the North Somerset Yeomanry in 1814. In the South Africa War (1899-1902) the regiment found a company of 7th Battalion Imperial Yeomanry. During the First World War the regiment served on the Western front. Having started the Second World War in the mounted role in the Middle East the regiment converted to signals in 1942, serving in Sicily, Italy and North-West Europe. In 1956 the regiment amalgamated with 44th Royal Tank Regiment and was redesignated the North Somerset and Bristol Yeomanry. In 1947 the regiment was absorbed into the infantry and the successor unit is 6th Battalion The (Somerset and Cornwall) Light Infantry (Volunteers).

The West Somerset Yeomanry A troop was raised in Bridgwater in 1794, and the regiment in 1798, serving without pay from 1828 to 1831. Members of the regiment served in 7th Battalion Imperial Yeomanry during the South Africa War (1899-1902). In the First World War the regiment went to Gallipoli in October 1915, was subsequently converted to infantry as 12th (West Somerset Yeomanry) Battalion, The Somerset Light Infantry, serving in Palestine and France. In 1920 the regiment converted to artillery following amalgamation with the Dorset Yeomanry and Somerset Royal Horse Artillery, and served in the artillery role throughout the Second World War at home and in North-West Europe. The successor unit is 6th Battalion The (Somerset and Cornwall) Light Infantry (Volunteers).

East Somerset Yeomanry Cavalry A troop was raised in Castle Cary in 1794 and later formed the nucleus of the East Somerset Yeomanry Cavalry Regiment. In 1828 the regiment was disbanded except for the Taunton troop which lingered on until 1843. There is evidence of the existence of a troop at Ilminster between 1831 and 1847.

Somme 1916 First World War battle honour marking the great British offensive of 1916 launched on 1 July across a 15 mile front. Fighting lasted some six months, the weather being particularly bad in October, and about six and a half miles were gained, without a breakthrough being achieved, at a cost of some 410,000 British casualties. German casualties, including those lost to a parallel French assault, amounted to about 650,000. *See also: France and Flanders 1914-1918; Albert 1916; Bazentin; Delville Wood; Pozières; Guillemont; Ginchy; Flers-Courcelette; Morval; Thiepval; Le Transloy; Ancre Heights and Ancre 1916.*

Somme 1918 First World War battle honour covering two distinct battles. The first, a German assault launched against the Fifth Army and right flank of the Third Army launched on 21 March. Although the German thrust covered nearly 40 miles, it was halted on 5 April still some eight miles short of Amiens. The second battle was the second phase of the British offensive launched on 21 August which halted on 3 September having gained some 15 miles. *See also: France and Flanders 1914-1918; St Quentin; Bapaume 1918; Rosières; Arras 1918; Avre and Ancre 1918.*

Somme 1940 Second World War battle honour marking the operations of troops cut off from the British Expeditionary Force by the German breakthrough to the sea 24 May-5 June, during which they were under French command and tasked to secure crossings across the River Somme, along which the French army made an attempt to stand. *See also: North West Europe 1940 and St Valery-En-Caux.*

Sopwith The Sopwith 1½ Strutter, manufactured by the Sopwith Aviation Co, was flown as a fighter and reconnaissance aircraft by the Royal Flying Corps from about 1916-18.

Soroppa Second World War Abyssinian campaign battle honour marking operations during a subsidiary thrust into Abyssinia from Kenya east and west of Lake Rudolf. *See also: Abyssinia 1940-41; Keren; Jebel Defeis; Jebel Shiba; Gogni; Agordat; Barentu; Karora-Marsa Taclai; Ad Teclesan; Mescelit Pass; Mt Engiahat; Massawa; Amb Alagi; Afodu; Gambela; El Wak; Moyale; Wal Garis; Juba; Bulo Erillo; Beles Gugani; Gelib; Alessandra; Goluin; Babile Gap; Bisidimo; Awash; Todenyang-Namaraputh; Marda Pass; Giarso; Colito; Wadara; Omo; Gondar; Ambazzo; Kulkaber; Fike and Lechemti.*

Soudia Second World War North Africa campaign battle honour marking one of a number of actions preceding the Kasserine operation of mid-February 1943. *See also: North Africa 1940-1943; Kasserine; Djebel Abiod; Tebourba; Djedeida; Djebel Azzag 1942; Longstop Hill 1942; Djebel Azzag 1943; Two Tree Hill and Djebel Aliliga.*

Sound To play a trumpet or bugle call.

Sound Ranging Technique used to locate artillery and mortar positions by using bearings obtained through a network of microphones to fix the point of origin of selected sounds.

Sounding Retreat Term used in rifle and light infantry regiments to denote the formal ceremony to mark the end of the day, known in other regiments as beating retreat.

South Africa 1835 Battle honour marking the Sixth Kaffir War, when the Xhosa tribes crossed the Keiskamma River and invaded the settled areas of the Eastern Cape Colony. The rising was quelled by a detachment from Cape Colony commanded by Colonel Sir Harry Smith. *See also: South Africa 1846-7 and South Africa 1851-52-53.*

South Africa 1846-47 Battle honour marking the Seventh Kaffir War, also

known as 'the war of the axe'. The Xhosa tribes again crossed the Keiskamma River and met with a sharp defeat at the hands of a small force from Cape Colony. *See also: South Africa 1835; South Africa 1851-52-53 and South Africa 1877-78-79.*

South Africa 1851-52-53 Battle honour marking the Eighth Kaffir War, occasioned by a series of simultaneous attacks across the frontier and massacre of a number of white settlers by Kaffir tribes led by Sandili. The restoration of peace proved a protracted business even though some of the British troops were armed with improved rifles. *See also: South Africa 1835; South Africa 1846-47 and South Africa 1877-78-79.*

South Africa 1877-78-79 Battle honour marking the Ninth Kaffir War against the Gaikwas, operations against Chief Sekukuni in Swaziland and the Zulu War of 1879. The Zulu War is mainly remembered for the annihilation of 1st/24th Foot (later The South Wales Borderers) at Isandhlwana, and the gallant stand by a detachment of 2nd/24th at Rorke's Drift. A final decisive victory over the Zulus at Ulundi brought the war to an end. *See also: South Africa 1835; South Africa 1846-47 and South Africa 1851-52-53.*

South Africa 1899-1902 Battle honour marking the South Africa or Boer War (qv), against the Boer republics of the Transvaal and Orange Free State. *See also: Defence of Ladysmith; Relief of Ladysmith; Defence of Kimberley; Modder River; Relief of Kimberley and Paardeburg.*

South African Campaigns Medal 1813-1853 Authorised on 22 November 1854 for service in the Kaffir Wars (qv).
Ribbon: Watered orange with two wide and two narrow dark blue stripes.

South Arabia 1964-67 The opening phase of this campaign took place against Egyptian- and Yemeni-backed National Liberation Front guerilla forces in the Radfan area in January 1964. By 8 June 1964 the rebels had been brought to battle and rendered largely ineffective.

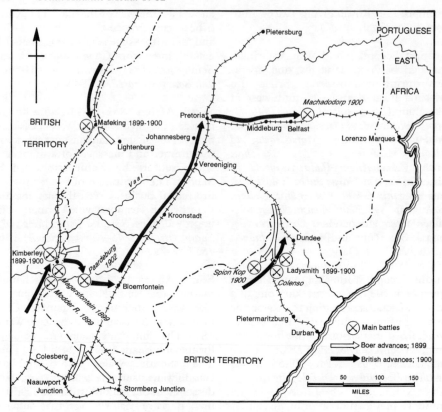

South Africa 1899-1902

Meanwhile the second phase of the campaign was taking place in Aden where the internal security situation had deteriorated rapidly. A power struggle was taking place between nationalist groups hoping to take power when Britain granted independence to South Arabia, as declared in the Defence White Paper of July 1964, some time before 1968. There were three main nationalist groups: the South Arabian League (SAL), the National Liberation Front (NLF) and the Front for the Liberation of Occupied South Yemen (FLOSY). These groups not only fought the British but also fought between themselves; but it was the NLF who prevailed and, when the last British troops left Aden on the afternoon of 29th November 1967, it was the NLF who formed the government of the independent state of the People's Republic of South Yemen on 30 November 1967. British Army casual-

ties in the campaign were 90 killed and 510 wounded.

South Atlantic Medal 1982 Awarded for the recapture of the Falkland Islands. There are two broad qualifying groups. 1. With rosette: one or more days in the Falkland Islands, their dependencies or the South Atlantic south of 35° south and north of 60° south between 2 April and 14 June 1982. 2. Without rosette: service of 30 days or more in the South Atlantic south of 7° south and north of 35° south between 2 April and 14 June 1982.
Ribbon: Five vertical stripes of equal width, shaded and watered, in empire blue, white, sea green, white and empire blue.

South Beveland Second World War battle honour marking an action during the Scheldt operations of October and

November 1944. *See also: North West Europe 1944-45; Scheldt; Walcheren Causeway; Flushing and Westkapelle.*

South East Asia 1941 Second World War battle honour marking the fighting against the Japanese in Hong Kong in December 1941 and in British North Borneo. *See also: Malaya 1941-42 and Hong Kong.*

South Lancashire Regiment (The Prince of Wales's Volunteers) (40th and 82nd Foot) The 40th Foot was raised on 25 August 1717 by Colonel Richard Phillips from independent companies of foot in Nova Scotia and known as Phillip's Regiment of Foot. Designated 40th Foot in 1751 and 40th (2nd Somersetshire) Foot in 1782. The 82nd Foot was raised on 27 September 1793 by Colonel Charles Leigh and known as 82nd Regiment of Foot or Prince of Wales's Volunteers. In 1881 the 40th (2nd Somersetshire) Foot and 82nd Regiment of Foot or Prince of Wales's amalgamated to form The South Lancashire Regiment (The Prince of Wales's Volunteers). On 1 July 1958 the regiment amalgamated with The East Lancashire Regiment (30th and 59th Foot) to form The Lancashire Regiment (Prince of Wales's Volunteers). On 25 March 1970 The Lancashire Regiment (Prince of Wales's Volunteers) amalgamated with The Loyal Regiment (North Lancashire) (47th and 81st Foot) to form The Queen's Lancashire Regiment (qv).
Headdress Badge: The plume, coronet and motto of the Prince of Wales above the sphinx upon a tablet 'EGYPT', all within a laurel wreath.
History: *The South Lancashire Regiment, The Prince of Wales's Volunteers* by B R Mullaly; *'Ich Dien' The Prince of Wales's Volunteers (South Lancashire) 1914-34* by H Whalley-Kelly and *The Autobiography of Sergeant William Lawrence 40th (2nd Somersetshire) Regiment of Foot.*

South Staffordshire Regiment (38th and 80th Foot) The 38th Foot was raised at Lichfield in March 1705 by Colonel Luke Lillingston and known initially as Lillingston's Regiment of Foot. The regiment was numbered 38th Foot in 1751 and designated 38th (1st Staffordshire) Regiment of Foot in 1782. The 80th Foot was raised as 80th (Light Armed) Foot in 1758 and disbanded in 1764, re-raised as 80th (Royal Edinburgh Volunteers) Foot in 1778 and disbanded again in 1784. Re-raised at Chatham in September 1793, largely recruited from the Staffordshire Militia, by Lieutenant Colonel Henry Lord Paget and designated 80th (Staffordshire Volunteers) Foot. In May 1881 38th (1st Staffordshire) Regiment of Foot and 80th (Staffordshire Volunteers) Regiment of Foot amalgamated to form The North Staffordshire (The Prince of Wales's) Regiment, the title being changed in July 1881 to The South Staffordshire Regiment (38th and 80th Foot). On 31 January 1959 The South Staffordshire Regiment amalgamated with The North Staffordshire Regiment (The Prince of Wales's) (64th and 98th Foot) to form The Staffordshire Regiment (The Prince of Wales's) (qv).
Headdress Badge: The Staffordshire knot ensigned with the crown upon a scroll inscribed 'SOUTH STAFFORDSHIRE'.
History: *History of the South Staffordshire Regiment* by W L Vale (1969) and *History of The South Staffordshire Regiment* by J P Jones (1923).

South Wales Borderers (24th Foot) Raised at Kent in March 1689 as Sir Edward Dering's Regiment of Foot and numbered 24th Foot in 1751. Designated 24th (2nd Warwickshire) Foot in 1782 and The South Wales Borderers in 1881. On 11 June 1969 The South Wales Borderers (24th Foot) amalgamated with The Welch Regiment (41st and 69th Foot) to form The Royal Regiment of Wales (24th and 41st Foot) (qv).
Headdress Badge: Within a wreath of Immortelles the sphinx upon a tablet 'EGYPT' and, below, the initials 'SWB'.
History: *Historical Records of The 24th Regiment from its Formation in 1689* by G Paton, F Glennie, W P Symons and H B Moffat (1892); *The South Wales Borderers, 24th Foot, 1689-1937* by C T Atkinson (1937); *The History of The South Wales Borderers 1914-1918* by C T Atkinson

(1931) and *History of The South Wales Borderers and Monmouthshire Regiment 1937-1952* (5 Parts) by G A Brett and others (1953-6).

Southern France Second World War battle honour marking an invasion of southern France by United States forces in August 1944, in which British airborne troops took part. See also: *North West Europe 1944-45.*

Sowar An Indian cavalry trooper of the old, pre-1947, Indian Army.

Soyer Stove Improved field cooker devised for the British Army by Alexis Benoît Soyer (1809-1858). Soyer was a well known French chef who worked at the Reform Club, London. He visited the Crimean War to advise on nutrition for the British Army.

Spartan Troop carrying version (Fighting Vehicle 103) of the Scorpion (qv) light tracked reconnaissance vehicle. Capable of carrying up to eight men, and mounting a 7.62mm machine gun. *See also: Striker; Sabre; Samaritan; Sultan; Scorpion; Samson and Scimitar.*

Spear A weapon consisting of a long shaft with a sharp pointed end or spearhead, which may be thrown or thrust at an enemy.

Special Air Service Regiment Army commando units had been created by Winston Churchill in 1940, but the Special Air Service Regiment owes its origins to the small force raised by Colonel David Stirling in July 1941 and titled 'L' Detachment Special Air Service Brigade (a brigade which was in fact only 66 men strong!). By July 1943 the much expanded force was designated 1st Special Air Service Regiment. In 1944 the regiment was added, as a third component, to The Army Air Corps and subsequently disbanded in 1946. Reconstituted as 22nd Special Air Service Regiment in 1947, independent status for the regiment was authorised under Army Order 66 of 1950, taking precedence after the infantry of the line.

Headdress Badge: A pair of wings issuing from below the hilt of a dagger. Below, a scroll inscribed 'WHO DARES WINS'.
Motto: Who Dares Wins.
Regimental quick march: *Marche du Régiment Parachutiste Belge.*
Regimental headquarters: Centre Block, Duke of York's Headquarters, London SW3 4RY.
History: *A History of the SAS* by J Strawson (1984).

Special Investigation Branch Branch of the Royal Corps of Military Police tasked with the investigation of serious crime.

Special List The 'Special List' exists for the purpose of ensuring the promotion chances from major to lieutenant colonel remain constant as required by the regular officer career structure and promotion policy. Substantive (qv) lieutenant colonels for whom there is no prospect of further promotion may, on reaching the age for appointment, be transferred to the 'Special List'; alternatively, they may elect to retire voluntarily at the same age. The age for appointment to the 'Special List' may be varied from time to time for structural reasons. Officers electing to transfer to the 'Special List' may continue to serve to the normal retirement age of 55. The 'Special List' is restricted to lieutenant colonels in the following corps: Household Cavalry, Royal Armoured Corps, Royal Artillery, Royal Engineers, Royal Signals, Infantry, Army Air Corps, Intelligence Corps, Royal Logistic Corps, Royal Electrical and Mechanical Engineers and the Adjutant General's Corps (excluding the Army Legal Service). *See: General List.*

Special Regular Commission (SRC) Appointment to a Special Regular Commission will initially be granted for a minimum period of service of 10 years, or such longer periods as may be necessary to complete 16 years reckonable service for officer's retired pay. Promotion, except for medical and dental officers, is limited to the rank of major.

Special Service Brigade First formed in 1940 as a parent organisation for

commandos. Subsequently operational Special Service Brigades were formed and disbanded as follows:
1 Brigade (1943-46);
2 Brigade (1943-46) formed in Italy;
3 Brigade (1943-46) later transferred to Royal Marines;
4 Brigade (1943-44).

Special Service Group Formed in October 1943 to administer the commandos until they became the responsibility of the Royal Marines in 1946.

Speed The Plough Part of the regimental quick march of The Royal Anglian Regiment and regimental quick march of The Suffolk Regiment.

Spectemur Agendo **(Let us be judged by our deeds *or* By our deeds we are known)** Motto of The Royal Dragoons (1st Dragoons) and The East Lancashire Regiment.

Sphinx Superscribed Egypt Battle honour commemorating the successful campaign of 1801 under Sir Ralph Abercromby (qv) tasked to eject the French from Egypt, which they had conquered under Napoleon in 1798. *See also: Aboukir Bay.*

Spike To render a gun or cannon useless by blocking the vent with a spike.

Spine Pad These were first worn to protect the backbone from excessive heat in Sierra Leone in about 1908. Introduced officially two years later, the spine pad quickly went out of favour, although some were still in use in India as late as 1942.

Spion Kop Hill in Natal, South Africa on the Tugela River some 18 miles south-west of Ladysmith. During the siege of Ladysmith in the South Africa War, Spion Kop was the scene of a battle on 24-25 January 1900 in which British troops captured the hill, but subsequently abandoned the position as untenable.

Spit and Polish Punctilious attention to cleanliness and turnout. The term is derived from the mixture of spit and polish used to bring leather-work to a high polish.

Splinter Metal fragment from an exploding shell, bomb or mine.

Spontoon A long staved weapon with a metal spike head carried by officers up to about 1775. The sergeant's halberd was replaced in 1791 by a spontoon and carried until 1830.

Sporran A purse suspended round the waist by chains or straps and worn by kilted regiments.

Sprig of Shillelagh One of the regimental quick marches of The Ulster Defence Regiment.

Springers, The Nickname given 62nd Foot, later The Duke of Edinburgh's Royal Regiment (Berkshire and Wiltshire). In 1775-1776 during the American War of Independence (qv) the 62nd Foot was used as Light Infantry and the nickname commemorates their alertness and speed in that role.

Sprocket Wheel The toothed driving wheels on tracked vehicles.

Spur Box The metal lined cavity in the heel of a boot which is fitted to take the spur and thus hold it in place.

Spurs Pointed device or sharp rowel worn at the heel of mounted personnel to enable them to goad their mount. Spurs are also worn by dismounted personnel in some orders of dress. In the days of chivalry the use of the spur was limited to knights, and it was among the emblems of knighthood, and still forms part of British regalia.

Squad Term used to describe a small formation of men, particularly a drill formation.

Squadron Term used to denote a Royal Armoured Corps, Royal Engineer, Royal Corps of Signals or Army Air Corps sub-unit. Usually between 50 and 100 men strong and divided into a number of troops, sections or flights.

Squadron and Company Group The grouping of a complete armoured squadron and complete infantry company, operating under command of either the squadron leader or the company commander.

Squadron Group An armoured squadron or part of a squadron, including the squadron headquarters, with attachments to its normal establishment.

Squadron Leader The commander of a cavalry or armoured squadron.

Square Formation adopted to meet a cavalry or multi-directional assault in which ranks of armed men face outward on four sides of a square with the colours at the centre of the square, the size of the square being reduced as casualties are taken. Also the large open space, usually at the centre of a barracks or camp, used for drill parades and other assemblies.

Square Bashing Soldier's slang for drill.

Stable Belt Originally essentially a working belt, the stable belt has become increasingly decorative, usually in regimental or corps colours, and sometimes sporting a decorative metal plate at the front.

Stable Jacket Regimental quick march of The Queen's Royal Lancers.

Staff The staff exists to assist commanders at all levels in the execution of their duties, and to transmit their orders to their command. At each headquarters the activities of the staff are co-ordinated by a senior staff officer, usually called the chief of staff. In the .Ministry of Defence (Army Department) the staff is divided into a number of directorates, which act as staff to the appropriate Army Board member. The staff is divided into three broad groups: the General Staff, dealing with operational, intelligence and collective training; the administrative staff, responsible for personnel matters, discipline and terms and conditions of service and the logistic staff, responsible, as the name implies, for all logistic aspects of the Army.

In recent years the British Army has moved to the NATO staff classification system as follows:
G1. Personnel matters.
G2. Intelligence/Security.
G3. Operations and training.
G4. Logistics/Quartering.
G5. Civil Affairs.

Staff Captain Formerly a 'Grade 3' staff officer in an administrative or logistic staff appointment.

Staff College The Staff College is charged with the provision of command and staff courses to suit candidates destined for appointments on the staff of the Ministry of Defence, static or field headquarters. The first course opened in April 1858, in buildings of the Royal Military College (qv), and the Staff College moved to its present fine building at Camberley in 1862. In July 1905 a Staff College was opened at Quetta in India (now in Pakistan) for officers of the Indian and British armies serving in India.

Staffordshire Regiment (The Prince Of Wales's) (38th, 64th, 80th and 98th Foot) Formed on 31 January 1959 through the amalgamation of The South Staffordshire Regiment (38th and 80th Foot) and The North Staffordshire Regiment (The Prince of Wales's) (45th and 95th Foot) (qv).
Headdress Badge: The Staffordshire knot ensigned with the plume, coronet and motto of the Prince of Wales.
Regimental marches:
Quick march: An arrangement of *Come Lassies and Lads* and *The Days We Went a-Gipsying*.
Slow march: *God Bless The Prince of Wales*.
Regimental headquarters: Whittington Barracks, Lichfield, Staffordshire, WS14 9PY.
History: *Rats Tales* by N Benson (1993).

Staffordshire Yeomanry (The Staffordshire Yeomanry (Queen's Own Royal Regiment)) The Regiment of Staffordshire Yeomanry Cavalry was commissioned in 1794 and the royal title conferred in 1838. During the South Africa

War (1899-1902) the regiment found two companies for 4th Battalion Imperial Yeomanry. In the First World War the regiment served in 22 Mounted Brigade in Egypt and Palestine. In 1941 the regiment converted to armour, fighting in North Africa and North-West Europe. The regiment re-formed as an armoured regiment in 1947, converted to armoured cars in 1958 and reduced to cadre strength in 1967. In 1971 the cadre expanded to squadron strength and may now be found in 'B' (Staffordshire Yeomanry) Squadron The Royal Mercian and Lancastrian Yeomanry.

Staff Sergeant Non-commissioned officer ranking above sergeant but below warrant officer 2nd class. Rank is denoted by the wearing of a crown above three chevrons on the upper sleeve. Also known as a staff corporal in the Household Cavalry and colour sergeant in the infantry.

Stag Soldiers' slang for a period of sentry duty. The term is derived from the practice of overlapping or staggering the tours so that one of a pair of sentries changed every hour.

Stages of Defence Term given to the three progressive and co-ordinated stages in the preparation and improvement of a defensive position.

Staging Area Area used as a checkpoint or resupply and regrouping area for military formations in transit.

Staging Post Selected point at which a journey is broken, particularly on long deployments by air.

Standard The distinguishing flag of heavy cavalry such as Household Cavalry or Dragoon Guards. Rectangular and fringed. *See also: Colours and Guidons.*

Stand of Colours Both colours of a regiment.

Stand By To bring to, or maintain at, a state of readiness.

Stand Down To revert to normal alert state after a period of 'stand to' (qv).

Stand Easy A period of relaxation or, a word of command authorising the relaxation of the upper body when on parade.

Stand To A high state of alertness. It is usual when in the field to 'stand to' for an hour either side of dawn and dusk, or in a period of increased threat.

Standing Army An army of paid soldiers permanently maintained in being by authority of the government.

Standing Operating Procedure (SOP) Instructions covering those features of operations which lend themselves to a definite or standardised procedure without loss of effectiveness. The existence of such procedures avoids constant repetition and gives all individuals a clear understanding of their responsibilities.

Standing Order An order of long term validity which remains in effect until formally rescinded.

Standing Patrol A patrol of a strength decided by the commander allotting the task. Its role may be reconnaissance, listening, fighting or a combination of these. It differs from a reconnaissance, fighting or listening patrol in that, having taken up its allotted position, it is not free to manoeuvre without permission in performance of its task. *See also: Patrols.*

Star The star forms part of the rank badges of most commissioned ranks. The design of the star is drawn from one of the orders of knighthood and will vary from regiment to regiment. Such stars are incorrectly called 'pips' in some circles.

Star Plate Plates affixed to the front and rear of a vehicle carrying a general officer to denote his rank. Such plates will display the appropriate number of silver stars upon a scarlet background. *See also: Star rank.*

Star Rank Term denoting rank differences in the general ranks: one star - a brigadier (formerly brigadier general); two star - a major general; three star - lieutenant general; four star - a general and five star - a field marshal.

Starstreak Close air defence weapon produced by Short Brothers of Belfast which can be shoulder-launched using the lightweight multiple launcher or launched from an eight-round launcher mounted on the Alvis Stormer armoured personnel carrier. Starstreak is a high velocity missile with a high explosive warhead, a minimum range of 1,000m and a maximum range of about 5,000m.

State Colour A colour presented to the Scots Guards by Queen Victoria in 1899. This colour is only carried by guards of honour mounted on state occasions at which the Sovereign is present. It is made of crimson silk heavily encrusted with gold and measures six feet by five feet. In the centre is the star of the Order of the Thistle within the collar of the order, encircled by a wreath of roses, thistles and shamrocks and surmounted by the imperial crown. The colour also bears the silver sphinx below the word 'Egypt' and 12 selected battle honours.

Static Line A line attaching the pack of a parachute to a point in the delivering aircraft, so that the parachute is opened when it has fallen clear of the aircraft.

Steamroller Farm Second World War North Africa campaign battle honour marking one of a number of actions which took place between the Kasserine and Fondouk operations February-April 1943. *See also: North Africa 1940-1943; El Hadjeba; Djebel Djaffa; Sedjenane I; Fort McGregor; Stuka Farm; Sidi Nsir; Montagne Farm; Kef Ouiba Pass; Djebel Guerba; Maknassy; Djebel Dahra; Kef El Debna and Djebel Choucha.*

Steel Helmet Although iron or steel helmets had been worn for many years, it was not until the First World War that a bulletproof helmet was designed, being worn in action for the first time in March 1916.

Sten Gun Sub-machine gun developed in Britain from a design by Major Shepherd

and Mr Turpin in early 1941 and brought into service in the British Army as the Sten (named after Shepherd, Turpin and Enfield) in June of that year. There were six different marks of the weapon including the Mark VI (Silenced). Made mainly of stamped steel parts suitable for mass production, and with a magazine of 32 rounds, it had a simple 'blow-back' open bolt action, and was of a calibre which permitted it to fire the standard 9mm German ammunition. Thousands of these weapons were dropped to partisans in occupied Europe. The Sten Gun was replaced in the British Army by the Sterling sub-machine gun in 1953. *See also: Sub-machine gun.*

Sterling Sub-machine gun, originally known as the Patchett, a handful of these weapons were issued in the Second World War. In 1953 the weapon, based on the Sten gun but with a curved magazine holding 32 9mm rounds and a folding stock, was brought into service as the Sterling L2A3 to replace the Sten gun. There is also a silenced version of the Sterling. *See also: Sub-machine gun.*

Stern Gang *See: Palestine 1945-48.*

Stick An aircraft load for parachute operations. *See also: Chalk.*

Stien Second World War Norway campaign battle honour. *See also: Norway 1940; Pothus; Vist; Kvam and Otta.*

Stirlingshire Yeomanry The Stirlingshire Yeomanry Cavalry was formed in 1798 and there are records of its existence up to the late 1830s.

Stock In about 1786 the stock was made of leather, although in the West Indies black cloth was preferred. In 1845 a more supple stock was worn, but later again stiffened. In 1862 the stock was finally replaced by a small leather tab which covered the opening of the collar.

Stonk Slang: to bombard with artillery.

Stormer Armoured personnel carrier produced by Alvis based on the Scorpion

(Fighting Vehicle 101) (qv) design. As an armoured personnel carrier it can carry a fully equipped infantry section of 10 men. In the British Army it is in service as the carrier for the Starstreak (qv) High Velocity Missile (HVM) and the Vehicle Launched Scatterable Mine System (VLSMS) (qv).

Stovepipe Pattern of shako (qv) worn in the 19th century.

Striker Anti-tank version (Fighting Vehicle 102) of the Scorpion (qv) tracked light reconnaissance vehicle. Introduced in 1978 and mounting five Swingfire anti-tank guided missile launchers, a further five missiles being carried in the vehicle. Striker has a crew of three, and mounts a 7.62mm machine gun. *See also: Scorpion; Sabre; Spartan; Samaritan; Sultan; Samson and Scimitar.*

Strip To break a weapon down into its component parts for cleaning or training purposes.

Struma First World War Macedonian campaign battle honour marking the operations in the Struma Valley in September and October 1916 aimed at containing the Bulgars in this area while Allied attacks were launched elsewhere. *See also: Macedonia 1915-1918; Kosturino; Doiran 1917 and Doiran 1918.*

Stuka Farm Second World War North Africa campaign battle honour marking one of a number of actions which took place between the Kasserine and Fondouk operations February-April 1943. *See also: North Africa 1940-1943; El Hadjeba; Djebel Djaffa; Sedjenane I; Fort McGregor; Steamroller Farm; Sidi Nsir; Montagne Farm; Kef Ouiba Pass; Djebel Guerba; Maknassy; Djebel Dahra; Kef El Debna and Djebel Choucha.*

Stop Line A line selected on tactically significant terrain, on which the guard element of a covering force (qv) will halt the enemy and attempt to force him into a deliberate attack.

Strategy A science, an art or a plan for the

co-ordination and application of the political, economic, psychological and military resources of a nation or group of nations in such a manner that the policies and interests of that nation or group of nations will prevail.

Strategic That which pertains to strategy; the highest levels of national interest and decision making. The highest level of command (strategic, operational and tactical). Frequently used as a synonym for long-range, as in 'strategic' transport, and to describe weapons, particularly nuclear weapons, or attacks directed at the homeland of an enemy.

Stripes Term in general usage to describe the chevrons used to denote rank.

Strongpoint A key point in a defensive position, usually pivotal to the successful defence of the area and heavily defended, around which other positions are grouped for its protection.

***Sua Tela Tonanti* (Literally: 'His missiles thundering' (of Jupiter) but common usage is: 'To the warrior his arms')** Motto of The Royal Army Ordnance Corps.

Suakin 1885 Battle honour marking the operations mounted out of Suakin on the Red Sea to divert Mahdist (qv) attention from Lord Wolseley's unsuccessful Nile expedition of 1884-85 to relieve General Gordon. *See also Nile 1884-5; Abu Klea; Kirbekan and Tofrek.*

***Suaviter In Modo, Fortiter In Re* (Gentle in manner, resolute in deed)** Motto of the Women's Royal Army Corps.

Subadar or Subahdar The chief native officer of a company of Indian soldiers in the British service.

Subaltern Commissioned officer below the rank of captain. *See also: Rank.*

***Sub Cruce Candida* (Under the white cross)** Motto of Queen Alexandra's Royal Army Nursing Corps.

Sub-Machine Gun A hand-held automatic weapon firing small calibre rounds. The concept probably originated with the light machine gun designed by the German Theodor Bergmann in 1916 and known as the 'Bergmann Musquete'; the Bergmann *Maschinenpistole 18* being the first true sub-machine gun. The Thompson, Lanchester, Sten, De Lisle Carbine and Sterling sub-machine guns have all seen service with the British Army at some time. In 1949 BSA developed a 9mm sub-machine gun which was however not taken into service. Special forces have drawn on a wider selection of sub-machine guns.

Substantive Rank Confirmed permanent and fully paid rank. *See also: Rank; Acting Rank; Local Rank and Temporary Rank.*

Sudan Medal 1910 Authorised by the Khedive in 1911 to replace the Khedive's Sudan Medal of 1897 (qv).
Ribbon: 1.3" wide; black watered centre flanked on each side by a thin green vertical stripe and a 5mm wide red stripe.
Clasps: Atwot (February-April 1910); S.Kordofan 1910; Sudan 1912; Zeraf 1913-14; Mandal; Miri; Mongalla 1915-16; Darfur 1916; Fasher; Lau Nuer; Nyima 1917-18; Atwot (January-May 1918); Garjak Nuer; Aliab Dinka; Nyala and Darfur.

Suez 1956 Under Article 8 of the Anglo-Egyptian Treaty of 1936 the defence of the Suez Canal Zone was maintained by British troops; this responsibility was passed to Egypt in November 1955 and the last British combatant troops left on 31 March 1956. Following the sudden withdrawal in July 1956 by the UK and USA of undertakings to finance the building of the Aswan High Dam, President Nasser of Egypt responded by seizing the Suez Canal Company's fixed property and nationalising all its assets - including the Suez canal itself. Tension rose rapidly and unsuccessful attempts were made by the UN to mediate in the dispute. In October 1956, with French connivance, Israel attacked Egypt. Britain and France issued a 12-hour ultimatum to both sides to cease fire; Egypt rejected this and, on 31 October, British

and French aircraft struck Egyptian targets. This Anglo-French action was widely condemned, particularly by the USA, and even in Britain opinion was sharply divided. The UN General Assembly called for a ceasefire. On 5-6 November Anglo-French forces invaded Egypt, but a ceasefire was agreed and the UN established an international force to police the area. On 3 December the immediate withdrawal of Anglo-French forces from Egypt was announced, and this was completed by 22 December 1956.

Suez Canal First World War Egyptian campaign battle honour marking the repulse of the Turkish attack on the Suez Canal in February 1915. *See also: Egypt 1915-17; Agagiya; Rumani and Rafah.*

Suffolk Regiment (12th Foot) The regiment has its origin in an independent company of foot raised in 1660 as garrison for Windsor Castle, and commanded by Henry Howard, 7th Duke of Norfolk. In June 1685 the company was augmented and taken on establishment as the Duke of Norfolk's Regiment of Foot. Numbered 12th Foot in 1751 and designated 12th (East Suffolk) Foot in 1782 and The Suffolk Regiment in 1881. On 29 August 1959 the regiment amalgamated with The Royal Norfolk Regiment (9th Foot) to form The 1st East Anglian Regiment (Royal Norfolk and Suffolk). On 1 September 1964 1st East Anglian Regiment (Royal Norfolk and Suffolk) amalgamated with 2nd East Anglian Regiment (Duchess of Gloucester's Own Royal Lincolnshire and Northamptonshire) and 3rd East Anglian Regiment (16th/44th Foot) to form The Royal Anglian Regiment (qv).
Headdress Badge: The castle and key of Gibraltar within a circle inscribed 'MONTIS INSIGNIA CALPE', all within a wreath and ensigned with the crown.
Motto: *Montis Insignia Calpe* (from the Arms of Gibraltar).
History: *History of the 12th (The Suffolk) Regiment 1685-1913* by E A H Webb (1914); *History of The Suffolk Regiment 1914-27* by C C R Murphy; *The Suffolk Regiment 1928-46* by W N Nicholson; *The*

Suffolk Regiment 1946-59 by F A Godfrey (1988) and *The Suffolk Regiment* by G Moir (1969).

Suffolk Yeomanry (The Duke of York's Own Loyal Suffolk Hussars) A number of troops, raised in Suffolk in 1793, were regimented to form 1st Regiment of Loyal Suffolk Yeomanry Cavalry in 1814. The regiment was disbanded in 1827 and re-raised in 1831, amalgamating with the Long Melford troop in 1868 to form the West Suffolk Regiment of Yeomanry Cavalry. The regiment was retitled Loyal Suffolk Hussars in 1875 and added Duke of York's in 1894 when the Duke of York assumed the colonelcy. During the South Africa War (1899-1902) the regiment found two companies for 12th Battalion Imperial Yeomanry. During the First World War the regiment served at Gallipoli and in Egypt, finishing the war as 15th Battalion The Suffolk Regiment in France. The regiment converted to artillery in 1920, serving as such throughout the Second World War. The regiment re-formed in 1947 as 308 (Suffolk Yeomanry) Anti-Tank Regiment Royal Artillery. Amalgamation with the Norfolk Yeomanry in 1967 created 202 (Suffolk & Norfolk Yeomanry) Medium Battery, 100 (Eastern) Medium Regiment Royal Artillery (Volunteers). The successor sub-unit is 202 (Suffolk & Norfolk Yeomanry) Field Battery, 100 (Yeomanry) Field Regiment (Royal Artillery) (Volunteers).

Sugar and Spice Regimental quick march of the Army Catering Corps.

Sully Second World War battle honour marking the clearance on 9 June 1944 of a German strongpoint which had held up movement inland from the Normandy beaches for two days. *See also: North West Europe 1944-1945; Normandy Landing; Cambes; Putôt En Bessin; Bréville and Villers Bocage.*

Sultan Command post version (Fighting Vehicle 105) of the Scorpion (qv) tracked light reconnaissance vehicle. Sultan can accommodate a crew of six, and mounts a 7.62mm machine gun. *See also: Striker;* *Scorpion; Sabre; Spartan; Samaritan; Samson and Scimitar.*

Sunken Top From 1812 for cavalry and 1816 for infantry, the shako (qv) had a sunken leather top.

Suppressive Fire Fire directed at an enemy to destroy or temporarily degrade his capability. More usually employed to cover the critical movement of friendly forces, particularly in the approach to an assault.

Surinam After the Treaty of Amiens (1802) hostilities were resumed against the Dutch. This battle honour marks the operations by a British naval and military expedition from Barbados which arrived off the mouth of the River Surinam on 25 April 1804. After the refusal of the Dutch commander to surrender, three regiments and a naval brigade were landed and the colony was captured, with only light British casualties, after three days.

Surrey Yeomanry (The Surrey Yeomanry (Queen Mary's Regiment)) Raised in 1794, six troops were regimented, and a further 12 troops remained independent. Disbanded in 1828, re-raised in 1831 and again disbanded in 1848. The Surrey Imperial Yeomanry was raised in 1901 and granted the title Prince of Wales's, later altered to Queen Mary's on the accession of George V. During the First World War elements of the regiment served in Egypt, Salonika, Macedonia and France, C Squadron finishing the war as 10th Battalion Royal West Surrey Regiment. In 1922 the regiment re-formed as artillery, serving as such throughout the Second World War. In 1947 the regiment re-formed as what was to become Surrey Yeomanry (Queen Mary's Regiment), Royal Artillery (Territorial). The successor sub-unit is 'A' (Salerno) Company, 6th/7th (Volunteer) Battalion The Princess of Wales's Royal Regiment (Queen's and Royal Hampshire).

Surveillance and Target Acquisition (STA) The systematic observation by visual, electronic, aural, photographic or other means of air and ground to detect identify and locate targets in sufficient detail to permit the effective engagement of these targets in a given priority. A commander is required to co-ordinate the surveillance and target acquisition resources at his disposal as part of his plan.

Sussex Yeomanry Troops of Yeomanry Cavalry were raised in the county in 1794, but disbanded in 1828. Some troops were re-raised in 1831 but had all disbanded by August 1848, although a Brighton troop was serving with the Middlesex Hussars in the 1880s. In 1901 The Sussex Imperial Yeomanry was formed, a company having already been raised to serve with the Imperial Yeomanry in South Africa in 1900. During the First World War the regiment served in Gallipoli, Palestine and Egypt, finishing the war in France as 16th Battalion (Sussex Yeomanry) The Royal Sussex Regiment. In 1922 the regiment was amalgamated with the Surrey Yeomanry, having earlier converted to artillery. The regiment served throughout the Second World War in the artillery role, seeing action in the Sudan, Egypt, Libya, Iraq, Persia, Palestine, North Africa, Italy and North-West Europe. In 1947 the regiment re-formed as a light anti-aircraft and searchlight regiment. By 1967 the regiment had been reduced to one battery - 200 (Sussex Yeomanry) Field Battery Royal Artillery (Volunteers). The successor subunit is 127 (Sussex Yeomanry) Field Squadron Royal Engineers, 78 (Fortress) Engineer Regiment (Volunteers).

Sutlej Campaign Medal 1845-1846 Marking the campaign against the Sikhs in the Sikh Wars 18 December 1845 to 22 February 1846. There were four different exergues: MOODKEE 1845; FEROZE-SHUHUR 1845; ALIWAL 1846 and SOBRAON 1846, clasps being awarded for the battles which did not feature on the exergue.
Ribbon: Dark blue with crimson edges.
Clasps: Moodkee 1845; Ferozeshuhur 1845; Aliwal 1846 and Sobraon 1846.

Suvla First World War Gallipoli campaign battle honour marking operations in the Suvla sector, the main object of which was to secure, in conjunction with a thrust from the Anzac beachhead, the Sari Bair Ridge, thus cutting the lines of communication of the Turks on the Helles front. The operations were unsuccessful. *See also: Gallipoli 1915-16; Helles; Landing at Helles; Krithia; Anzac; Sari Bair; Landing at Suvla and Scimitar Hill.*

Swan's Feathers Swan's feathers were worn on the headdress of general officers, gentlemen-at-arms, lancers and, periodically, by drum-majors of the Royal Scots Greys and Royal Artillery.

SW Africa 1914 First World War battle honour marking the operations by South African and Northern Rhodesian forces in 1914 which resulted in the capture of German South-West Africa.

Swingfire Wire guided command-to-line-of-sight anti-tank missile with a high explosive anti-tank hollow charge warhead. Range approximately 4,000m. Mounted on an Armoured Fighting Vehicle 438 or 102 (Striker) (qv). There is also a separated sight capability which allows the operator to control the flight of the missile from a position up to 100m from the launch vehicle.

Sword Straight, single-edged cutting weapon now only worn on ceremonial occasions.

Sword Belt Belt, usually hidden beneath sash or the jacket, from which a sword is suspended by a sling (qv).

Sword Frog Attachment for securing the scabbard of a sword to the Sam Browne (qv) or other belt.

Sword Knot A loop attached to the hilt of a sword by which it could be attached to the wrist. Now purely decorative.

Sword Sling Two adjustable straps, one shorter than the other, for attaching the scabbard of a sword to the sword belt.

Sycamore Obsolete light helicopter developed and produced by Bristol Aeroplane

Co Ltd and evaluated by the Army in the early 1950s but never taken into service.

Syce, Sice or Saice Formerly an Indian servant employed to drive and look after horses and carriages.

Synergy Much misused term meaning joint working, co-ordination of resources and co-operation. Increased effectiveness, achievement etc., produced as a result of combined and synchronised action or co-operation.

Syria 1941 Battle honour marking the invasion of Syria on 7 June mounted from Palestine with the object of capturing Damascus and thus stopping the Vichy authorities supporting German operations. Damascus fell on 21 June, and the Vichy forces sued for an armistice on 12 July 1941. *See also: Merjayun; Palmyra; Jebel Mazar and Deir Es Zor.*

Taieb El Essem Second World War North Africa campaign battle honour marking one of the actions in the 1941 Battle of Tobruk. *See also: North Africa 1940-1943; Tobruk 1941; Gubi I; Sidi Rezegh 1941; Tobruk Sortie; Omars; Belhamed; Gabr Saleh; Gubi II and Relief of Tobruk.*

Tactical Area of Operational Responsibility (TAOR) The area over which a given commander exercises sole responsibility for tactical operations.

Tactical Doctrine See: Doctrine.

Tactical Exercise Without Troops (TEWT) Form of training in which commanders examine a number of tactical problems within the framework of a hypothetical operation, set against a pre-selected area of country. Such exercises usually follow a pattern in which selected incidents are studied after the participants have walked the ground or viewed the area from a selected viewpoint. Exercises without troops offer valuable opportunities to develop tactics and understanding of battle procedure without disrupting unit training or causing damage.

Tactical Pertaining to tactics. The lowest level of command (strategic, operational and tactical). An adjective used to describe shorter-range weapons and low-yield nuclear weapons (under 100KT) intended for battlefield use.

Tactics The art and science of the detailed direction and control of movement or manoeuvre of forces in battle to achieve a given aim.

Tadjira Khir Second World War North Africa campaign battle honour marking one of the actions in the Battle of Medinine in March 1945. *See also: North Africa 1940-1943; Medinine and Zemlet El Lebene.*

Tails The long portions of a coat or coatee at the back.

Takrouna Second World War North Africa campaign battle honour marking an action during the Enfidaville operations 19-29 April 1943. *See also: North Africa 1940-1943; Enfidaville and Djebel Garci.*

Taku Forts Second China War battle honour marking the capture of these forts, at the mouth of the Peiho River by an Anglo-French force under Sir Hope Grant on 12 August 1860. *See also: China 1858-9; China 1860-62 and Pekin.*

Talavera Peninsula War battle honour marking the defeat of the French under Victor by a British force at Talavera under Wellesley on 28 July 1809. The French were beaten but, lacking Spanish support, Wellesley, created Viscount Wellington for the victory, was obliged thereafter to retire into Portugal. *See also: Peninsula; Corunna; Douro; and Busaco.*

Tam-o-Shanter Broad topped Scottish bonnet with toorie.

Tamandu Second World War Burma campaign battle honour marking one of the captures of this town in the final Arakan operations of 12 January - 29 April 1945. *See also: Burma 1942-1945; Arakan Beaches; Dalet; Taungup; Myebon; Ramree and Kangaw.*

Tamera Second World War North Africa campaign battle honour marking the fighting of 5-15 March 1943 in which the Germans forced the 139th and 1st Parachute Brigades off the Tamera position. *See also: North Africa 1940-1943.*

Tamu Road Second World War Burma campaign battle honour marking one of the actions in the Battle of Imphal in March 1944. *See also: Burma 1942-1945; Imphal; Tuitum; Nungshigum; Bishenpur; Kanglatongbi; Sakawng; Shenam Pass and Litan.*

Tangerines, The Nickname given to 2nd Foot, later The Queen's Royal Regiment (West Surrey). The regiment was raised in 1661 for service in Tangier, which had become a British possession as part of the dowry of Catherine of Braganza, Queen of Charles II.

Tangier 1662-80 The earliest British battle honour. Tangier was ceded to England as part of the dowry of Catherine of Braganza on her marriage to King Charles II, and was garrisoned by Britain from 1662. The garrison was subject to continuous harassment by the Moors and, given that the garrison was largely confined within walls with only drink and women to console it, morale was surprisingly buoyant. In 1680 the garrison was reinforced and thus able to conduct operations beyond the garrison. Tangier was finally evacuated in 1684.

Tank Although the concept is quite ancient, it was not until 1915 that the Admiralty, at the instigation of Winston Churchill, developed a mobile fort capable of introducing an element of mobility to the war in the trenches. The term 'tank' was used during development for security reasons, the rhomboidal hulls being shipped to France as 'water tanks'. Early models were produced in both 'male' and 'female' versions; the 'male' carrying two six-pounder guns, and the 'female' four Vickers machine guns. The tanks were first used on the Somme on 15 September 1916, but it was not until the Battle of Cambrai in 1917 that they were used in strength and with devastating effect on

German morale. The earliest model known as 'Little Willie' was produced in 1915 and followed a year later by 'Big Willie' or 'Mother', a much improved version which became the prototype for all the British tanks produced during the First World War. The first of a series of medium tanks, intended for more mobile roles, was introduced in 1918. However, after the armistice all tank production was stopped, except for the completion of a few medium tanks.

It was hoped that the medium tank, and a lighter vehicle known as the light infantry tank, would meet the needs of the Army in the post-war years. However, the designs proved unsatisfactory, and it was the Vickers Light Tank Mark I (later known as Medium Mark I) which was eventually accepted for service and the Vickers Medium Tank, Marks I-III (1923-28), of which 160 were delivered to the Army, which were to prove the backbone of the Royal Tank Corps during the inter-war years; indeed, some of these tanks remained in service at the outbreak of the Second World War.

By the 1930s the tank had more or less acquired its present configuration, the main armament having been moved from side-mounted sponsons into a rotating armoured turret mounted on top of the hull, giving the tank an all-round engagement capability, and a driver positioned forward. Between the wars tank design improved. It was felt that small cheap tanks in large numbers to support the infantry were a better proposition than a few relatively expensive medium tanks, and some one- and two-man tanks were produced by Messrs Carden and Loyd. These 'tankettes' were not used for the close support of infantry, but for reconnaissance, and led to the development of the Light Tank Mark I, based on the Carden-Loyd tankettes in 1929. In this period the operational requirement as perceived in Britain, France and the Soviet Union had crystallised into three broad types of tank: light for reconnaissance, medium or cruiser ('C' tanks) to engage enemy armour, and heavy or infantry ('I' tanks), to accompany infantry in the attack. At the outbreak of the Second World War the main types of tank in service, or just coming into service, were the Light Tank Mark VI; Infantry Tanks Marks I and II and Cruiser Tanks Mark III-IV.

The Germans, prohibited by the Treaty of Versailles from producing tanks, recognized that the tank offered the prospect of a new way of operating. The product of German study and experimentation was a tank which combined the virtues of speed, reasonable protection and good firepower rather than distinct 'I' or 'C' types. Cruiser or 'C' tanks became the decisive arm in the Western Desert, and it became rapidly clear that the German tanks could outrun and outshoot the British Matilda and Valentine 'I' tanks and the Covenanter and Crusader 'C' tanks. The British developed the Churchill and Comet tanks, but these were no match for the German 44-ton Panther and 56-ton Tiger, the latter mounting the celebrated 88mm gun, which appeared in 1943. From 1942 onwards the British largely employed the American Grant and Sherman cruisers as 'I' tanks, also Canadian Rams.

Special vehicles were also developed using tank hulls, such as the Armoured Vehicle Royal Engineers (AVRE), based on the Churchill hull mounting a heavy demolition mortar or petard; flamethrowers or 'Crocodiles', and 'Crabs' mounting mine clearing flails. The Centurion was introduced into the British Army shortly after the end of the Second World War, being replaced by Chieftain with its powerful 120mm gun in the 1960s. (Conqueror, the first British tank to mount a 120mm gun, had served alongside the Centurion for several years in the long-range tank destroyer role.) The 63-ton Challenger is now the main battle tank in the British Army. *See also: Light Tanks, Infantry Tanks and Cruiser Tanks.*

Tank Trap Obstacles, such as concrete pyramids, designed to hinder or stop tracked vehicles.

Taranto Second World War Italian campaign battle honour marking an action on the Eight Army front in 1943. *See also: Italy 1943-1945; Landing at Porto San Venere; San Salvo; Orsogna; Impossible Bridge and Caldari.*

Tardenois First World War battle honour marking operations in the valley of the River Ardre during the Battle of the Marne in July 1918 in which Ville-en-Tardenois was captured. *See also: France and Flanders 1914-1918; Marne 1918 and Soissonais-Ourcq.*

Target Object or area at which fire is directed. Targets for small arms competition shooting usually consist of a series of concentric circles with the bullseye at the centre, an inner ring, a magpie ring and an outer ring. Also, the name given to the shape of lace on the front of the shako after Waterloo.

Tarifa Peninsula War battle honour marking the defence of the allied base on the coast not far from Gibraltar against a two-week French offensive in December 1811 and January 1812. *See also: Peninsula; Barrosa; Fuentes d'Onor; Albuhera; Arroyo dos Molinos; Ciudad Rodrigo and Badajoz.*

Tarleton Name given to the helmet of leather with a bearskin crest made popular by Banastre Tarleton (1754-1833) of the British Legion in the American War of Independence. Worn by light dragoons and light infantry.

Task Force A temporary grouping of formations, units or sub-units formed to undertake a specific mission.

Task Organisation *See: Task Force.*

Tassels Ornaments used on the cords of headdress and on sporrans.

Tattoo From the Dutch tap toe, literally tap shut, the closing of public houses. This was customarily signalled by drum-beat or bugle and indicated that soldiers should return to their quarters for the night, and was followed by 'lights out'. Over the years this has developed into a spectacular event with military bands conducting an extensive programme of music and complicated evolutions, usually accompanied by a number of non-musical military displays.

Tavoleto Second World War Italian campaign battle honour marking the repulse of enemy counter-attacks 1-4 September 1944 during the Battle of the Gothic Line. *See also: Italy 1943-1945; Gothic Line; Coriano; Croce; Gemmano Ridge; Monte Gridolfo; Montegaudio; San Clemente; Poggio San Giovanni and Pian di Castello.*

Taukyan Second World War Burma campaign battle honour marking a successful rearguard action 7-8 March 1942 during the withdrawal through Burma. *See also:Burma 1942-1945; Sittang 1942; Pegu 1942; Paungde;Yenangyaung 1942; Kyaukse 1942 and Monywa 1942.*

Taungtha Second World War Burma campaign battle honour marking one of the actions during the advance down the Myittka Valley, crossing of the Irrawaddy and thrust to Meiktila in early 1945. *See also: Burma 1942-1945; Meiktila; Nyaungu Bridgehead; Capture of Meiktila; Defence of Meiktila and Irrawaddy.*

Taungup Second World War Burma campaign battle honour marking the capture of the town and subsequent local operations 3-29 April 1945 during the final Arakan operations. *See also: Burma 1942-1945; Arakan Beaches; Dalet; Tamandu; Myebon; Ramree and Kangaw.*

Teano Second World War Italian campaign battle honour marking the capture of Teano, an important communication centre, following fighting in the area 28-31 October 1943. *See also: Italy 1943-1945; Salerno and Monte Camino.*

Tear Gas A lachrymatory irritant used as a riot control agent.

Tebaga Gap Second World War North Africa campaign battle honour marking the flanking movement which turned the flank of the Mareth Line, and the pursuit to Gabes 21-30 March 1945. *See also: North Africa 1940-1943; Mareth; El Hamma and Point 201 (Roman Wall).*

Tebourba Second World War North Africa campaign battle honour marking one of a number of actions which took place prior to the Kasserine operations of February

and March 1943. *See also: North Africa 1940-1943; Kasserine; Djebel Abiod; Soudia; Djedeida; Djebel Azzag 1942; Longstop Hill 1942; Djebel Azzag 1943; Two Tree Hill and Djebel Aliliga.*

Tebourba Gap Second World War North Africa campaign battle honour marking the repulse of the German attack on Tebourba in early December 1942. *See also: North Africa 1940-1943; Medjez El Bab; Oudna; Bou Arada and Robaa Valley.*

Teeth Arms The fighting arms: armour, artillery, engineer, infantry and army air.

Tegnoupal Second World War Burma campaign battle honour marking the ejection of the Japanese from the Shenam Pass in late July 1944. *See also: Burma 1942-1945; Kohima; Kennedy Peak and Mawlaik.*

Tel-El-Kebir Battle honour marking Wolseley's decisive victory over Arabi Pasha on 12 September 1882 during the Egypt campaign of 1882. *See also: Egypt 1882.*

Telescopic Sight Optical sight fitted to a weapon to offer magnification of the target and enhance accuracy. Such sights are a feature of sniper rifles.

Tell Asur First World War Palestine campaign battle honour marking the operations carried out in March 1918 to improve the British defensive positions north of Jerusalem. *See also: Palestine 1917-18; Gaza; El Mughar; Nebi Samwil; Jaffa; Jerusalem; Jordan; Megiddo; Nablus and Damascus.*

Templer, Sir Gerald (Walter Robert) (1898-1979) Educated at Wellington and the Royal Military College. Commissioned into the Royal Irish Fusiliers in 1916 and served in France and Belgium. Between the wars he served in Persia, Iraq and Palestine. During the Second World War he commanded 1st and 56th Divisions and 6th Armoured Division. After the war he was General Officer Commanding Eastern Command when the need arose for a 'strong man' in Malaya, where a campaign by communist terrorists was causing serious concern. Sent to Malaya as High Commissioner with extensive military powers, his vigorous and original measures were very successful. Templer was Chief of the Imperial General Staff from 1955-58, during which he was appointed field marshal.

Temporary Rank Rank granted for a period of short duration, usually for the duration of a specific task.

Tent Pegging Formerly a training exercise, now a sport. Wooden tent pegs driven at intervals into the ground are lifted on the point of a lance by a mounted soldier armed with a lance and approaching at the gallop.

Tenth Army (Second World War) Formed in 1942 under the command of Lieutenant General E P Quinan. Principally Indian Army with some British units in its divisions, it operated in Persia and Iraq, guarding the allied supply route to Russia. The army became part of Persia-Iraq Command, Lieutenant General Sir Henry Pownall assuming command in March 1943.

Termoli Second World War Italian campaign battle honour marking the capture of this town on the Adriatic coast in early October 1943. *See also: Italy 1943-1945; Trigno and Sangro.*

Ternate Battle honour marking the capture of Ternate, one of the Molucca Islands, from the Dutch by an expeditionary force from India in 1801, and its re-capture in 1810. *See also: Amboyna and Banda.*

Terriers Nickname for members of the Territorial Army, a force noted for its courage and terrier-like tenacity.

Territorial Army (TA) Under Lord Cardwell's (qv) reform of 1881 the British infantry was territorialised, and the Yeomanry and Volunteer Rifle Corps were linked with regular and militia units to form the regimental district. Thus most territorial force infantry units came to bear the title of a line regiment with a battalion number of four or above. However, there were exceptions: 'expatriate' units such as London Scottish; battalions from counties such as Monmouthshire which did not support a regular regiment; numerous London Light Infantry units with roots in the 1819 Volunteer (qv) movement such as the Artist's Rifles, Queen's Westminsters etc., and the Honourable Artillery Company, which predates the line regiments. Notwithstanding its origins, every territorial unit was affiliated to some regular unit, even though it did not share the same name.

Viscount Haldane was appointed Secretary of State for War in late 1905 and dedicated his considerable intellect to the improvement of the Army. Haldane proposed the reorganisation of the auxiliary forces in Great Britain into two groups: the Territorial Force (TF) consisting of the Yeomanry (qv) and the Volunteers (qv) and the Militia (qv) which would become the Special Reserve (SR) capable, in time of emergency, of supplying drafts to regular units and conducting home defence and lines of communication tasks. In Ireland the reorganisation took a different direction: the Militia became part of the Special Reserve but the Yeomanry became part of the Cavalry Special Reserve and did not form part of the Territorial Force. The Territorial and Reserve Forces Act of 1907, and more particularly Lord Haldane's implementation of it, put in place the new structure under the county Territorial Forces Associations which raised and administered (but did not command) the new Territorial Force. On 1 January 1908 the post of Director of Auxiliary Forces was redesignated Director General of the Territorial Force. The Territorial Force was intended originally for home service only, provision being made for individuals to serve overseas. However, in 1914 so many members of the force volunteered that war units were mobilised in their entirety and brigaded in the 15 Territorial (and Yeomanry) Divisions which took part in the First World War.

In 1920 the Territorial Force was reconstituted as the Territorial Army (TA) altering the pre-1914 order of Special Reserve (Militia) being at second line and the Territorial Force (Yeomanry and Volunteers) at third line; and effectively put the Territorial Army at second line, with an obligation on all members to serve overseas. The Special Reserve reverted to its old name of Militia, but in practice no Militia was raised until 1939. A new establishment for the TA was written and largely implemented in 1935 and, for the first time, a number of old promises were kept: some divisions and brigades being commanded by TA officers, and a TA officer was appointed as Deputy Director General. Just before the outbreak of the Second World War the Militia returned as six-month full-time conscription for men; the TA was embodied and, before the first Militia conscript intake was released, the Armed Forces Act made all auxiliary forces full-time and part of the regular forces; with home defence battalions of regiments and Auxiliary Military Pioneer Corps formed for older men. The TA ceased to exist as a separate force, and recruiting for it ceased.

On 1 January 1947 the TA was re-established and National Servicemen, having completed their regular service, were obliged to undertake a further 3 1/2 years TA service. On 31 March 1967 the TA was disbanded and, on 1 April 1968, the Territorial and Army Volunteer Reserve (TAVR) was formed. The Army Emergency Reserve (AER) also disappeared and its units became an integral part of the TAVR. The TAVR was divided into four categories. TAVR I, the 'Ever Readies', consisted of units and individuals who had volunteered for a call-out liability to reinforce the regular army when so required for a period up to six months. TAVR II, mostly logistic units, were liable for call-out in support of the regular army in NATO (qv) when warlike operations were in progress or preparation. TAVR III, consisting of 87 infantry-type units, was funded by the Home Office for home service only, mainly in aid of the civil authority. TAVR IV was made up of a number of other units such as Officer Training Corps, bands and units with no role in the other categories.

The TAVR is administered by 14 Territorial Army and Volunteer Reserve Associations (TAVRAs), successors to the old TA Associations, but regionally rather than county based, each established under its own scheme as outlined by act of parliament. These TAVRAs are tasked with the provision of essential administrative support for the TA, the provision of accommodation for independent TA units, for Royal Naval Reserve, Royal Marines Reserve, Royal Auxiliary Air Force, Combined Cadet Force, Army Cadet Force and Air Training Corps units. They also give advice to the Sea Cadet Corps in matters of common interest to cadet forces. Associations are responsible for building and maintaining the accommodation which they provide. They also have a recruiting, public relations and welfare role. In 1968 it was announced that TAVR III was to be disbanded. For nine months men in these units carried on without pay or allowances. On 1 January 1969 the 87 infantry-type units were reduced to cadre form, each with an establishment of three officers and five soldiers. Their main role was custodial, to carry the name, traditions and property of their regiment against the possibility of any future expansion.

In 1970 plans were announced for an expansion of the TAVR, and on 1 April 1971 one additional armoured car regiment and 20 infantry-type units made up of 77 sub-units, most of which were based on the cadres, were formed. The new units were given the same overseas liability as the old units, but were initially earmarked for home defence. All category numbers were discarded and the TAVR became one force. The AER units which had become part of the TAVR on its formation became 'Sponsored Units', administered by a Central Volunteer Headquarters on a scale of one for each corps. In 1981 a further expansion of the TA establishment, from 70,000 to 86,000, was announced, and accompanied by an increase in the permitted man training days. A pilot scheme for a Home Service Force (qv), a lower liability TA home defence force, was begun in 1982 and, in 1986, a further expansion of the TA, this time to 90,000 by 1992, was announced. However, the collapse of the

Soviet Union and the Warsaw Pact, and the pressure for a 'peace dividend' brought reductions in the TA establishment under the 'Options for Change' programme. The Home Service Force was disbanded in 1993 and the TA establishment reduced to 68,195 in 1993, 65,000 in 1994 and to 59,000 by 1995-96. Legislation adjusting the call-out liability of elements of the TA, to make them more readily available, is expected shortly. *See also: Militia; Volunteers and Yeomanry.*

Tetrarch Light tank Mark VII produced by Metropolitan-Cammell Carriage and Wagon Co. Ltd. between 1940 and 1942. Only about 300 Tetrarchs were produced and were used primarily for airborne operations. Tetrarch had a crew of three, weighed 7.5 tons, and mounted a 2pdr gun and Besa machine gun. *See also: Tank and Light Tanks.*

Thala Second World War North Africa campaign battle honour marking the fighting which took place 20-22 February 1943 and halted the German advance during the Kasserine operations. *See also: North Africa 1940-1943; Kasserine; and Sbiba.*

Theatre A geographically distinct region within which military operations can interact, even when not subject to close coordination.

The Hook 1952 Korean War battle honour marking the defence of the Hook feature against Chinese attacks on 18-19 November 1952. *See also: Korea 1951-1953; Naktong Bridgehead; Pakchon; Imjin; Kowang-San; The Hook 1953; Chongju; Chongchon II; Seoul; Chaum-Ni; Hill 327; Kapyong-Chon; Kapyong; Maryang San and Hill 227 I.*

The Hook 1953 Korean War battle honour marking the defence of the Hook feature against Chinese attacks on 28-29 May 1953. *See also: Korea 1951-1953; Naktong Bridgehead; Pakchon; Imjin; Kowang-San; The Hook 1952; Chongju; Chongchon II; Seoul; Chaum-Ni; Hill 327; Kapyong-Chon; Kapyong; Maryang San and Hill 227 I.*

Thermal Imaging Equipment which produces an image of the target from infra-red emissions transmitted by the target.

Thiepval First World War battle honour marking the capture of Thiepval above the valley of the Ancre by Fifth Army during the Battle of the Somme July-November 1916. *See also: France and Flanders 1914-1918; Somme 1916; Albert 1916; Bazentin; Delville Wood; Pozières; Guillemont; Ginchy; Flers-Courcelette; Morval; Le Transloy; Ancre Heights and Ancre 1916.*

Thin Red Line Regimental quick march (Regimental Band) of The Argyll and Sutherland Highlanders (Princess Louise's) from 93rd (Sutherland Highlanders) Regiment of Foot.

Third China War Medal 1900 Issued to those serving in the Boxer Rebellion.
Ribbon: Crimson with yellow edges 6mm wide.
Clasps: Taku Forts; Defence of Legations; and Relief of Pekin.

Thirty Years War (1618-48) The war was broadly the product of the German Reformation and the Counter-Reformation, and began in 1618 when the crown of Bohemia was offered to the Lutheran Prince, the Elector of the Palatinate, son-in-law of James I of England and father of the Princes Rupert and Maurice. The Treaty of Westphalia was signed in October 1648 bringing the war to an end. The territorial gains of France and Sweden, and the independence of the German Princes, were recognised. The attempted revival of the power of Catholicism by the sword had failed, and the imperial power became nominal except in Austria. The independence of Switzerland and the United Provinces (Holland) was also recognised under the treaty.

Thistle Pattern of lace authorised for Scottish regiments.

Thompson American sub-machine gun, of 0.45" calibre. Issued to the British Army in 1939, and widely known as the 'Tommy' gun, it was replaced by the Sten gun from 1940. The M1928 weapon was developed during the First World War by Colonel J T Thompson of the US Army. The first magazine was a 50-round drum, although a 20-round box magazine was available. The M1A1 version was simplified for wartime mass production for the US Army. *See also: Sub-machine gun.*

Three DGs Regimental quick march (Military Band) of The Royal Scots Dragoon Guards (Carabiniers and Greys) and 3rd Carabiniers (Prince of Wales's Dragoon Guards).

Throat Microphone A microphone secured around the neck which is operated by voice vibrations. Such microphones leave the operator's hands free to operate weapons or other equipment.

Throat Plume A hair plume, usually in regimental or corps colours, hung underneath a horses neck.

Thunderbox Soldiers' slang for the portable box-like lavatory seat that can be placed over a hole in the ground for use as a lavatory in the field.

Thunderflash Explosive pyrotechnic used in training to simulate grenades.

Tibet Medal 1903-1904 Authorised in 1905 for issue to members of the Tibet Mission between 13 December 1903 and 23 September 1904.
Ribbon: Maroon centre flanked by a white vertical stripe on each side and 6mm wide green stripes on each edge.
Clasp: Gyantse.

Ticking A striped cotton or linen material formerly used for lining of trousers in warm climates.

Tiger Moth The De Havilland Tiger Moth DH82A bi-plane was used for flying training during the Second World War until replaced by the Chipmunk (qv).

Tigris 1916 First World War Mesopotamia campaign battle honour marking the

abortive attempts to relieve Kut in 1916. The Turkish positions at Sheikh Saad and Hanna were carried, but Sannaiyat proved too strong. *See also: Mesopotamia 1914-18; Basra; Shaiba; Kut Al Amara 1915; Ctesiphon; Defence of Kut Al Amara; Kut Al Amara 1917; Baghdad; Khan Baghdadi and Sharqat.*

Tilly sur Seulles Second World War battle honour marking the defeat of german counter-attacks in the Tilly sector, the capture of Tilly and subsequent thrust toward Hottot 14-19 June 1944 following the Allied landings in Normandy in June 1944. *See also: North West Europe 1944-45; Normandy landing; Sully; Cambes; Putôt En Bessin; Bréville; Villers Bocage; Odon; Fontenay Le Pesnil; Cheux; Defence of Rauray and Caen.*

Time-Beater Name applied to the coloured men formerly attached to military bands. They were not military drummers.

Tin Hat A steel helmet.

Tinma Second World War Burma campaign battle honour marking fighting in the Arakan in the latter part of 1944. *See also: Burma 1942-1945; Point 1433 and Mayu Valley.*

Tirah Battle honour marking the hard-fought campaign in the mountains west of Peshawar on the Indian North-West Frontier against the Afridis and Orakzais 1897-98 under the command of Sir William Lockhart. The storming of the Dargai Heights in October 1897 was a remarkable achievement.

Tobias Seismic intrusion alarm system with wire data link-up.

Tobruk 1941 Second World War North Africa campaign battle honour marking the British offensive, known as Operation CRUSADER launched on 18 November 1941 which concluded with the relief of Tobruk and withdrawal of the enemy, first to the Gazala position, and then from most of Cyrenaica. *See also: North Africa 1940-1943; Gubi I; Sidi Rezegh 1941; Tobruk*

Sortie; Omars; Belhamed; Gabr Saleh; Taieb El Essem; Gubi II and Relief of Tobruk.

Tobruk 1942 Second World War North Africa campaign battle honour marking the fierce fighting in June 1942 which preceded the German capture of Tobruk and surrender of the garrison. *See also: North Africa 1940-1943; Gazala; Retma; Bir El Aslagh; Bir Hacheim; Cauldron; Knightsbridge; Bir El Igela; Hagiag Er Raml; Gabr El Fachri; Via Balbia; Zt El Mrasses and Sidi Rezegh 1942.*

Tobruk Sortie Second World War North Africa campaign battle honour marking an attempt by the garrison to link-up with relieving forces over the period 21-23 November 1941. *See also: North Africa 1940-1943; Tobruk 1941; Gubi I; Sidi Rezegh 1941; Omars; Belhamed; Gabr Saleh; Taieb El Essem; Gubi II and Relief of Tobruk.*

Toc H Movement for world-wide interdenominational Christian fellowship. The name Toc H comes from the Army signallers' designation of the initials T H, which stood for Talbot House, opened in December 1915 at Poperinghe in Flanders as a chapel and club for soldiers. It was a memorial to Gilbert Talbot, who was killed in July 1915, and was founded by his brother, Neville Talbot, later Bishop of Pretoria, and the Reverend P B (Tubby) Clayton. In 1920 Clayton formed a small Toc H group in London, and in 1922 Toc H was incorporated by Royal Charter.

Todenyang-Namaraputh Second World War Abyssinian campaign battle honour marking operations during a subsidiary advance from Kenya into Abyssinia east and west round Lake Rudolf. *See also: Abyssinia 1940-41; Keren; Juba; Marda Pass; Babile Gap and Gondar.*

Tofrek Battle honour marking the main action of the Suakin operations of 1885 during the Nile campaign of 1884-85. A British column was surprised by Mahdists (qv), but after a stiff action the attack was driven off. *See also: Nile 1884-85; Abu Klea; Kirbekan and Suakin 1885.*

Toggle Rope Short length of rope with a loop at one end and a wooden toggle at the other. A number of such toggle ropes could be joined by passing the toggles through the loops to form a length of rope.

Tommy Atkins *See: Atkins.*

Tommy Gun Nickname for the Thompson sub-machine gun. *See: Thompson and Sub-Machine Gun.*

Toms Nickname for the men of the Parachute Regiment.

Toorie The short ends, or bobble, on the top of a Scottish bonnet.

Topi/Topee Pith helmet worn in the tropics.

Tortoise *See: Heavy Assault Tank (A.39).*

Tossignano Second World War Italian campaign battle honour marking one of the actions which took place between the breaching of the Gothic Line in September 1944 and the thrust to the Po valley in April 1945. *See also: Italy 1943-1945; Montebello-Scorticata Ridge; Monte Reggiano; San Martino Sogliano; San Martino Sogliano; Monte Farneto; Montigallo; Carpineta; Monte Cavallo; Casa Bettini; Pideura; Pergola Ridge; Senio Floodbank; Cesena; Conventello-Comacchio; Monte Casalino; Monte La Pieve; Monte Pianoereno; Monte Spaduro; Orsara; Savignano and Catarelto Ridge.*

Toulouse Peninsula War battle honour marking the final action of the war. Toulouse was carried on 10 April 1814, Wellington's object being to defeat Soult before he could be reinforced by Suchet's army. *See also: Peninsula; Nive and Orthes.*

Toungoo Second World War Burma campaign battle honour marking one of the actions during the final drive south to capture Rangoon 1 April-6 May 1945. *See also: Burma 1942-1945; Rangoon Road; Pyabwe and Pegu 1945.*

Tour Term used to describe a period of duty in a particular appointment or location.

Tourmauville Bridge Second World War battle honour marking one of the actions which took place between the Allied landing in Normandy in June 1944 and the crossing of the River Seine 25-28 August 1944. *See also: North West Europe 1944-1945; Port-En-Bessin; St Pierre La Veille; Estry; Noireau Crossing; La Vie Crossing; La Touques Crossing; Risle Crossing and Foret de Bretonne.*

Tournay Flanders campaign battle honour marking the successful action of the allied against the French under Pichegru on 22 May 1794. *See also: Nieuport; Villers-En-Cauchies; Beaumont and Willems.*

TOW Abbreviation for Tube launched, Optically tracked, Wire-guided anti-tank missile. This US missile has a hollow charge warhead, and a maximum range of 3,750m, and is fitted to the Lynx (qv) helicopter.

Traghetto Second World War Italian campaign battle honour marking the final action of the campaign. The German army in Italy surrendered on 29 April 1945. *See also: Italy 1943-1945 and Bologna.*

Trained Bands Also 'train' or 'trayn' bands and the élite of the General Levy of the Tudor period, provided by the larger towns, and better trained because they could be assembled more regularly and for longer periods. Provincial train bands all appear to have been modelled on those of London, who appear to have owed their efficiency to the leaven of the Honourable Artillery Company (qv). In 1539 Henry VIII reviewed the City of London militia, and in 1585 the first line of London train bands, some 4,000 musketeers, exercised at Mile End Field and were reviewed at Greenwich. In 1614 James I organised the London train bands in companies and, in 1616 into four regiments. In 1661 Charles II abolished all train bands except those in London. The London train bands continued until 1794 when the four regiments were reorganised as two regiments of militia.

Training The preparation of formations, units, sub-units and individuals for their role in war. The training of formations, units and sub-units is collective training, as opposed to individual training.

Trajectory The path described by a projectile following firing.

Transfer To change from one regiment or corps to another.

Transit Camp A camp in which units and individuals are accommodated temporarily before moving to other destinations.

Transport Medal 1899-1902 Although not strictly a campaign medal this medal was sanctioned on 8 November 1903 for issue to senior officers of troop transports to the South Africa War and Boxer Rebellion. Ribbon: Red with a blue 5mm wide vertical stripe inset 3mm from each edge. Clasps: South Africa 1899-1902; and China 1900.

Trasimine Line Second World War Italian campaign battle honour marking the fighting leading to the break through the German defences in the area of Lake Trasimene 20-30 June 1944. *See also: Italy 1943-1945; Monte Malbe and Sanfatucchio.*

Travel Warrant Document authorising travel at government expense, exchanged for a ticket at the point of departure.

Traverse To turn in a horizontal plane.

Trelawny Regimental slow march of The King's Own Royal Border Regiment and The King's Own Royal Regiment (Lancaster).

Trench A narrow ditch dug as a fortification or defensive position, the excavated earth forming a parapet around the trench.

Trench Coat Double-breasted waterproof coat of gaberdine, usually cut in a military style with epaulettes and belt.

Trenches A system of inter-connecting excavations incorporating rest areas with overhead cover, command posts and fire trenches.

Trench Fever An acute infectious disease characterised by fever and muscular aches and pains, caused by the micro-organism Rickettsia quintana and transmitted by the bite of a body louse.

Trench Foot A form of frostbite affecting the feet of persons standing for long periods in cold water or mud.

Trench Knife A double edged fighting knife, so called because such knives were carried in the trenches during the First World War for hand-to-hand combat.

Trench Mortar Portable mortar used in trench warfare to shoot projectiles at a high trajectory over short ranges, thus making it possible to drop bombs into the opposing trenches.

Trench Mouth A bacterial ulcerative disease characterised by inflammation of the tonsils and gum, etc., so called because of its prevalence in the trenches during the First World War.

Trench Warfare A type of warfare, prevalent in the First World War, in which opposing forces face each other in entrenched positions. The introduction of armour has brought with it a return to more mobile operations.

Treu und Fest **(Staunch and Steadfast)** Motto of 11th Hussars (Prince Albert's Own).

Trews Scottish name for trousers. Usually of tartan and often cut on the bias.

Tricorne Hat In the early days of the Army normal Headdress was the civilian broad-brimmed hat. Passing fashion brought about the turning up of one, two (bicorne) or three (tricorne) sides of the brim, and these 'cocked' sides were often fastened with a loop, rosette or later a plume. The bicorne hat had the brim formed or 'cocked' into two points and is worn today by some officers as the 'cocked hat'. The tricorne hat is 'cocked ' on three sides.

TRIGAT Third generation anti-tank missiles being produced as a European collaborative project. The long-range version (TRIGAT LR) should replace Swingfire (qv) in the British Army, and the medium range version (TRIGAT MR), with a range of 2,000m, is designed to replace Milan (qv).

Trigno Second World War Italian campaign battle honour marking the establishment of a bridgehead over the River Trigno following fierce fighting 22 October-5 November 1943. The capture of San Salvo Ridge, which dominates the area north of the river, was an important ingredient in the success of the operation. *See also: Italy 1943-1945 and Sangro.*

Tripod Three legged rest used for the mounting of machine guns and other weapons.

Troarn Second World War battle honour marking one of the actions during Operation GOODWOOD, between 18-21 July 1944, the aim of which was to exploit the success at Caen and secure the Bourgebous Ridge south-east of the city. The German 88mm anti-aircraft guns inflicted heavy casualties on the British armour and the offensive was repulsed. *See also: North West Europe 1944-1945; Bourgebous Ridge; Maltot and Cagny.*

Troitsa First World War battle honour marking the fighting around the village of Troitsa during the British advance from Archangel along the River Dvina 9 July - 10 August 1919. *See also: Archangel 1918-19; Murman 1918-19; Siberia 1918-19 and Dukhovskaya.*

Troop Sub-unit of a cavalry squadron or artillery battery, broadly equivalent to an infantry platoon. To ceremonially parade the ensign, guidon or colours of a regiment.

Trooper Lowest rank in the Royal Armoured Corps and Army Air Corps. Equivalent in rank to a private soldier in the infantry. The term is also applied to aircraft or ships used to transport military personnel.

Trophy Originally the spoils of war. Later, an embroidered design including military equipment such as flags, weapons and musical instruments, sometimes appearing on the caps of grenadiers or horse furniture.

Trumpeter Soldier trained and qualified to play the military trumpet.

Trumpet Tune Regimental slow march of the Intelligence Corps.

Trumpet Voluntary Regimental quick and slow marches of the Royal Army Chaplains' Department.

Tsingtao First World War battle honour marking the reduction of this German-owned port in northern China by a Japanese force containing a small British presence on 7 November 1914.

Tuft Term applied to the decorative ball on a Headdress, the thick fringe on shoulder straps and the rosettes of gorget ribbons.

Tug Argan Second World War battle honour marking the fighting of 11-15 August 1940 during the British campaign in British Somaliland. *See also: British Somaliland 1940 and Barkasan.*

Tuitum Second World War Burma campaign battle honour marking the capture and subsequent defence of Tuitum Ridge 16-24 March 1944 during the operations around Imphal. *See also: Burma 1942-1945; Nungshigum; Bishenpur; Kanglatongbi; Sakawng; Tamu Road; Shenam Pass and Litan.*

Tumbledown Mountain Falkland Islands campaign battle honour marking the capture of this feature by the Scots Guards during the Falkland Islands campaign of 1982. *See also: Falkland Islands 1982; Goose Green; Mount Longdon and Wireless Ridge.*

Tunic Jacket with skirts all round, which replaced tailed coatee in 1855. Now used to describe the jackets worn by the Household Cavalry and Foot Guards on ceremonial occasions.

Tunis Second World War North Africa campaign battle honour marking the capture of Tunis and exploitation towards the Cape Bon Peninsula in May 1943 which resulted in the surrender of Axis forces in North Africa. *See also: North Africa 1940-1943; Hammam Lif; Djebel Bou Aoukaz 1943 II; Montarnaud; Ragoubet Souissi; Creteville Pass; Gromballa and Bou Ficha.*

Tuori Second World War Italian campaign battle honour marking the capture and subsequent defence of a German position on 5 July 1944. *See also: Italy 1943-1945 and Arezzo.*

Turn-Backs The front skirts of the coat or the front opening at the neck and chest.

Turret A traversing structure fitted to the top of armoured vehicle hulls which usually contains the commander and gunner. A small tower that projects from the wall of a castle. A tall wooden tower on wheels formerly used by besiegers to scale the walls of a castle or fortress.

Turret Down Siting of an armoured vehicle so that the vehicle is wholly hidden from enemy view by a ground feature, but the commander can still just observe the enemy from his turret. *See also: Hull Down and Periscope Up.*

Twelfth Army (Second World War) Formed in June 1945 under the command of Lieutenant General Sir Montagu Stopford and based at Rangoon with a strength of three divisions including British, Gurkha, Indian, West and East African and Burmese troops. With 14th Army (qv) it formed part of Allied Land Forces South-East Asia and took part in the final operations in Burma. Disbanded on 1 January 1946 when Burma Command was formed.

Twente Canal Second World War battle honour marking one of the actions which took place between the crossing of the Rhine on 23 March 1945 and the end of the campaign. *See also: North West Europe 1944-1945; Uelzen; Lingen; Bentheim; Dreirwalde and Artlenberg.*

Two Tree Hill Second World War North Africa campaign battle honour marking one of a number of actions which took place prior to the Kasserine operations of February and March 1943. *See also: North Africa 1940-1943; Kasserine; Djebel Abiod; Soudia; Djedeida; Djebel Azzag 1942; Longstop Hill 1942; Djebel Azzag 1943; Tebourba and Djebel Aliliga.*

Ubique (**Everywhere**) Motto of the Royal Regiment of Artillery and Corps of Royal Engineers.

Uelzen Second World War battle honour marking one of the actions which took place between the crossing of the Rhine on 23 March 1945 and the end of the campaign. *See also: North West Europe 1944-45; Twente Canal; Lingen; Bentheim; Dreirwalde and Artlenberg.*

Ukhrul Second World War Burma campaign battle honour marking an action during the advance to the River Irrawaddy in November and December 1944. *See also: Burma 1942-1945 and Monywa 1945.*

Ulster Defence Regiment (UDR) Formed on 1 April 1970 for service in Northern Ireland, and comprising part-time volunteers with a small core of regular personnel. On 1 July 1992 the regiment merged with The Royal Irish Rangers (27th (Inniskilling), 83rd and 87th Foot) to form The Royal Irish Regiment (27th (Inniskilling), 83rd, 87th Foot and The Ulster Defence Regiment) (qv).
Headdress Badge: A harp ensigned with crown in gold.
Regimental marches:
Quck marches: *Sprig of Shillelagh* and *Garryowen.*
Slow march: *Oft in the Stilly Night.*
History: In preparation.

Ulster Defence Regiment Medal Instituted in 1982 for award to officers and men of the Ulster Defence Regiment, now part of the Royal Irish Regiment, for 12 years' continuous service since 1 April

1970. A bar for each additional five year period of service is also awarded.
Ribbon: Dark green, with a vertical band of orange, edged in red, at the centre.

Unaccompanied Tour A tour of duty undertaken without families or dependents. It is usual for such tours to be of about six to nine months and to include a short period of rest and recuperation.

Unconditional Surrender A total surrender, made without limit or conditions.

Unconquered I Serve Motto of The Queen's Regiment.

Under Officer A rank, with several grades of seniority, given to officer cadets in the British Army.

Undress A relaxed form of any order of uniform of a lesser degree than (full) dress. Clothing for non-ceremonial occasions, in barracks or walking out.

Uniform Military uniforms were first introduced into England by the Tudor kings, whose first political act on attaining the throne was the abolition of the feudal armies which had fought the Wars of the Roses. These retainers of great lords were distinguished not so much by their dress as by the badges of their employers. The legislation of Henry VII restricted the wearing of livery to domestic servants, and specifically forbade the wearing of badges. It was Henry VII who formed the Yeomen of the Guard in 1485, whose uniform is the oldest extant in England.

By the end of the 17th century the Army

was clothed either as household troops, whose uniform was usually wholly or partly red, or as line regiments raised by officers under royal licence. The line regiments were both clothed and paid by the officer who raised the regiment, and thus clothing was usually uniform across the regiment, but there was no uniformity between regiments. At the outbreak of the Civil War neither side had uniformity of dress, and this led to considerable confusion in the earlier engagements. When the Parliamentary forces were reorganised in the New Model Army in 1645 all regiments composing it were clothed in red. This colour was subsequently adopted for the Commonwealth forces as a whole, and continued in use after the Restoration.

During the later Stuart and early Hanoverian reigns an attempt was made to reduce the diversity of clothing details to a system, and by 1751 there was a generic type of uniform common to all units of an army: all infantry were dressed alike, while regiments differed by facings and lace. Regional costume has played a part in the design of uniforms, particularly the Scottish and Irish regiments. Similarly items of foreign uniform were adopted to mirror the prestige of particular foreign units: the full-dress of lancers and hussars is of Polish and Hungarian origin respectively, and the 'rifle green' of the British rifle and light infantry regiments was copied from the *Jäger* regiments of various German principalities. The beret, which by 1945 had become widely used in the British Army, was borrowed from the French *chasseur alpin*, and the forage cap which preceded it was widely used on the continent, being ultimately of German origin. Although the foot guards had worn the greatcoat before the First World War, there was, in 1949, the tentative introduction into more of the British Army of an active service dress which included a greatcoat of distinctly German cut and a variety of the German *Einheitsmütze*, a peaked cap, originally worn by the Austrian *Kaiserjäger*, then by German *Gebirgsjäger*, the Afrika Korps and subsequently by the entire German infantry.

Since 1899, when protective colouring was adopted on a large scale as a result of experience in the South Africa War, considerations of utility have predominated. The field service or Number 2 dress has now become the parade and 'walking-out' uniform for most of the Army. The Number 1 dress of blue or green is no longer on issue to individuals, but may be drawn from dwindling stocks for ceremonial occasions. However, the Household Cavalry, Foot Guards and King's Troop Royal Horse Artillery still continue to receive a full personal scale of ceremonial uniform. Disrupted pattern combat uniform, based upon a number of layers of clothing, is now the recognised dress for operations and training.

Union Flag The national flag of the United Kingdom of Great Britain and Northern Ireland. *See also: Flag stations.*

United Kingdom Support Command (Germany) Established on 28 October 1994 on the demise of the British Army of the Rhine. Tasked with the support of the remaining British forces in Germany, the bulk of whom are committed to the Allied Command Europe Rapid Reaction Corps.

United Nations (UN) Members of the British Armed Forces have served, or are still serving, in a number of United Nations 'peacekeeping' operations. United Nations service in this context is specifically defined as service 'under command' of the UN Secretary-General which interalia is recognised by the award of a UN peacekeeping medal. National operations 'in support' of the UN are not strictly regarded as UN operations. In addition to UN 'peacekeeping' operations there have been UN mandated conventional operations, such as Korea and the Gulf War, in which UK servicemen have been involved. United Nations 'peacekeeping' operations in which members of the British Armed Forces have been or are still involved are: UN Operations in Congo, 1960-64 (ONUC); UN Peacekeeping Force in Cyprus, 1964- (UNFICYP); UN Transition Assistance Group in Namibia, 1989-90 (UNTAG); UN Iran-Kuwait Observer Mission, 1991- (UNIKOM); UN Mission for the Referendum in Western

Sahara, 1991- (MINURSO); UN Advance Mission in Cambodia, 1991-92(UNAMIC); UN Protection Force in the Former Yugoslavia, 1992- (UNPRO-FOR); UN Transitional Authority in Cambodia, 1992-93 (UNTAC); UN Observer Mission in Georgia, 1993- (UNOMIG) and UN Assistance Mission for Rwanda, 1993- (UNAMIR).

Unknown Soldier or Warrior The body of an unidentified British soldier of World War I brought home from one of the battlefields on the Western Front and 'buried among the kings' in Westminster Abbey on 11 November 1920. Part of the inscription on the gravestone reads: 'Thus are commemorated the many multitudes who during the Great War of 1914-1918 gave the most that man can give, life itself...'.

Unlimber To disengage a gun from its limber.

Unload To remove the ammunition from a weapon.

***Utrinque Paratus* (Ready for anything)** Motto of The Parachute Regiment.

Vaagso Second World War battle honour awarded to the Commandos marking a commando raid on the islands of Vaagso and Maaloy on 27 December 1941. The aim of the raids was the destruction of oil stores, wireless stations and industrial plant.

Valenciennes First World War battle honour marking the British offensive along the River Scheldt toward Valenciennes, which fell on 2 November 1918.

Valentine Second World War Infantry Mark III tank. Produced as a private initiative by Vickers-Armstrong, some 8,275 being produced between 1940 and early 1944. The name is derived from the fact that Vickers submitted the design proposal to the War Office on St Valentine's Day 1938. Although designed as an infantry tank, a shortage of cruiser tanks in 1940-41 made it necessary to use Valentines to equip the newly formed armoured divisions. Later marks of Valentine had a crew of three, weighed 17 tons, and mounted a 75mm gun and a Besa machine gun. *See also: Tank and Infantry tank.*

Valiant Second World War infantry tank (A.38) developed by Ruston & Hornsby Ltd. Based upon an upgrading of the Valentine (qv), the prototype Valiant was not completed until 1944, by which time it had been outclassed, and never went into quantity production. The Valiant had a crew of five, weighed 50 tons and mounted a 17pdr gun and two Besa machine guns. *See also: Tank and Infantry tank.*

Valise Infantryman's pack of the late 18th and 19th centuries. Originally worn on the hip, it was raised to the centre of the back by 1882.

Valise Ornament Distinctive badge worn on the valise. The Worcestershire Regiment wore a distinctive star plate.

Valli Di Comacchio Second World War Italy campaign battle honour marking one of the preliminary operations for the crossing of the River Senio 3-8 April 1945. *See also: Italy 1943-45 and Senio.*

Veghel Second World War battle honour marking an action in the unsuccessful attempts by Second Army to break through to Arnhem 17-27 September 1944. *See also: North West Europe 1944-45, Arnhem, Nederrijn, Nijmegen and Best.*

Vehicle Check Point Temporary (called 'snap'), or permanent, check point much used in internal security operations to permit the searching of vehicles and their occupants. It is usual for such check points to include a chicane and caltrops to prevent vehicles rushing through the check point.

Vehicle Launched Scatterable Mine System (VLSMS) Six integrated mine launchers, each of 20 tubes, each tube containing five mines, mounted on a Stormer (qv) chassis. Due in service in 1996, VLSMS is expected to be capable of scattering mines out to 300m. *See also: Ranger Mine.*

Vein Openers, The Nickname given to 29th Foot, later The Worcestershire Regiment (qv). In 1770 the regiment was in Boston during a period of marked American discontent with the British colonial administration. A detachment of the regiment which was guarding the Custom House was pelted by the mob. During the ensuing scuffle a soldier mistook a shout from the crowd for the order to fire. Other soldiers then opened fire and four rioters were killed and several wounded. The name was given to the regiment by the Americans for their part in what the Americans chose to call the 'Boston Massacre'.

***Vel Exuviae Triumphant* (Even in defeat triumphant)** Motto of The Queen's Royal Regiment (West Surrey); also translated as 'Even in defeat there can be triumph'.

***Veni Et Vici* (I came and I conquered)** Motto of The Royal Leicestershire Regiment between 1841 and 1845.

Venlo Pocket Second World War battle honour marking the operation of 14 November-3 December 1944 to clear Germans from their last positions west of the Maas. *See also: North West Europe 1944-45; Venraij; Lower Maas; Meijel; Geilenkirchen; Ourthe and Roer.*

Venraij Second World War battle honour marking operations conducted between 12 and 18 October 1944 as a preliminary to the Venlo Pocket operations. *See also: North West Europe 1944-45; Venlo Pocket; Lower Maas; Geilenkirchen; Ourthe and Roer.*

Vest Sleeveless garment worn under the mess jacket.

***Vestigia Nulla Retrorsum* (We do not retreat)** Motto of 5th Royal Inniskilling Dragoon Guards, 5th Dragoon Guards (Princess Charlotte of Wales's).

***Veteri Frondescit Honore* (Ever green with ancient honour)** Motto of The Buffs (Royal East Kent Regiment).

Veve Second World War battle honour marking fighting from 10-12 April 1941 which contained the German thrust from

the Monastir Gap during the 1941 campaign in Greece. *See also: Greece 1941; Proasteion and Corinth Canal.*

Via Balbi Second World War North Africa campaign battle honour marking one of the actions in the Battle of the Gazala Line in May and June 1942. *See also: North Africa 1940-43; Gazala; Retma; Bir El Aslagh; Bir Hacheim; Cauldron; Knightsbridge; Tobruk 1942; Bir El Igela; Hagiag Er Raml; Gabr El Fachri; Sidi Rezegh 1942 and Zt El Mrasses.*

Viceroy Governor of a country, province or colony who acts for, and rules in the name of, the Sovereign or government.

Vickers Machine Gun An updated and improved water-cooled version of the Maxim (qv). Fed by canvas belt and firing a 0.303" round, the Vickers was brought into service in the British Army in 1912 and was to remain in use until the mid-1960s. Variants included vehicle and aircraft mounted weapons.

Vickers-Berthier Light machine gun designed by Lieutenant André Berthier of the French Army, the rights being bought by Vickers in 1925. The gun, firing the 0.303" round from a 30-round magazine, was considered for British Army service but rejected in favour of the Bren (qv). However, the weapon was used very successfully by the Indian Army throughout the Second World War.

Victoria Cross Highest British decoration for 'conspicuous bravery or devotion to the country in the presence of the enemy' and open to officers and men alike. Instituted in a Royal Warrant dated 29 January 1856 towards the conclusion of the Crimean War (1856), the crosses being cast from the metal of Russian guns taken at Sevastopol. It consists of a maltese cross made of bronze, bearing in the centre the royal crown surmounted by a lion upon a scroll inscribed 'For Valour'. The winning of the Victoria Cross brings with it a small tax-free annuity.
Ribbon: Crimson (described as 'red' in the Warrants), 1" wide. Originally the ribbon was dark blue for the Royal Navy and

crimson for the Army but, following the formation of the Royal Air Force in 1918, the crimson ribbon was adopted for all recipients.

Victory Medal *See: First World War Medals.*

Vietri Pass Second World War Italian campaign battle honour marking one of the actions following the Allied landing at Salerno on 9 September 1943. *See also: Italy 1943-45; Salerno; St Lucia; Salerno Hills and Battipaglia.*

Villa Grande Second World War Italian campaign battle honour marking a series of actions which took place between 22 and 28 December 1943 to support the capture of Ortona by the Canadians. *See also: Italy 1943-45.*

Village Blacksmith Regimental quick march of the Royal Army Ordnance Corps.

Villers Bocage Second World War battle honour marking the attempts to capture the Villers Bocage Ridge and subsequent fighting in the Tilly sur Selles area between 8 and 13 June 1944 following the Allied landings on 6 June 1944. *See also: North West Europe 1944-45; Normandy Landing; Sully; Cambes; Putôt En Bessin; Bréville; Tilly Sur Selles; Odon; Fontenay Le Pesnil; Cheux; Defence of Rauray and Caen.*

Villers Bretonneaux First World War battle honour marking the German attack made towards Amiens on 24 April 1918 against the high ground at Villers Bretonneaux. This was the first ever tank versus tank encounter. The Germans captured the town, but it was almost immediately recaptured by a bold Australian counter-attack.

Villers En Cauchies Battle honour marking an action during the Flanders campaign of 1794. The British and Austrian cavalry routed a French force on 24 April 1794. *See also: Nieuport; Beaumont; Willems and Tournay.*

Vimiera Peninsula War battle honour marking Wellesley's defeat of the French under Junot on 21 August 1808. *See also: Peninsula; Roliça; Sahagun; Corunna; Douro and Talavera.*

Vimy 1917 First World War battle honour marking the opening phase of the 1917 Battle of Arras 23 April-4 May 1917. The dominating Vimy Ridge, which the Germans had held since 1914, was captured. *See also: France and Flanders 1914-1918; Arras 1917; Scarpe 1917 and Arleux.*

***Viret In Aeternum* (It flourishes for ever)** Motto of 13th/18th Royal Hussars (Queen Mary's Own), 13th Hussars.

Virgin Mary's Bodyguard Nickname given 7th Royal Dragoons, later 4th/7th Royal Dragoon Guards. During the reign of George II the regiment was sent to assist the Archduchess Maria Theresa of Austria.

***Virtutis Fortuna Comes* (Fortune is the companion of valour)** Motto of 33rd (Duke of Wellington's Regiment) and later of The Duke of Wellington's Regiment (West Riding).

Visor Formerly a piece of armour fixed or hinged to the helmet to protect the eyes. Now the name given to a transparent, splinter-proof shield fitted to the steel helmet to protect the eyes in riot situations. The modern visor is resistant to low-velocity small arms rounds.

Vist Second World War Norwegian campaign battle honour. *See also: Norway 1940; Stien; Pothus; Kvam and Otta.*

Vital Ground Terrain of such importance that it must be controlled for the success of the mission.

Vittoria Peninsula War battle honour marking Wellington's rout of the French army under King Joseph, on 21 June 1813. The spoils of war included the personal belongings of King Joseph including his silver chamber-pot, captured by 14th Light Dragoons and bringing with it the nickname 'Emperor's Chambermaids'. *See also: Peninsula; Badajoz; Almaraz; Salamanca; Pyrenees and St Sebastian.*

Vittorio Veneto First World War Italian campaign battle honour marking the final allied offensive in Italy which started on 26 October 1918 with the crossing of the River Piave and resulted in the Austrians asking for an armistice. *See also: Italy 1917-18 and Piave.*

VIXEN Automatic system for processing electronic intelligence.

Vizzini Second World War, Italian campaign battle honour marking one of the actions during the Allied advance through Sicily July-September 1943. *See also: Sicily 1943; Landing in Sicily; Primosole Bridge; Sferro; Regalbuto and Centuripe.*

Volturno Crossing Second World War Italian campaign battle honour marking one of a number of actions which took place on the Fifth Army front during the advance to the Gustav Line in late 1943. *See also: Italy 1943-45; Monte Camino; Capture of Naples; Cappezano; Monte Stella; Cava di Tirreni; Cardito; Scafati Bridge; Monte Maro; Roccheta e Croce and Colle Cedro.*

Volunteers Although there is evidence of a voluntary military movement developing as early as 1537, it is the case that the Volunteers are, in historical terms, junior to the Militia. Volunteers in British armies were usually individuals serving of their own will, sometimes to gain military experience before seeking a commission.

In the second half of the 18th century the Militia (qv) was embodied for long periods at a time; many who would have been exempt from military ballot or could have become so on payment of a fine chose instead to serve as Volunteers and formed Volunteer companies within the county Militia regiments. The first Volunteer Act of 1782 provided that if such companies served away from their own town or county the rank and file would be paid, lodged and rationed as regulars. Similar Acts in1794, 1798 and 1802 confirmed this arrangement and bound Volunteer and Yeomanry (qv) to act in support of the civil power. The formation of such units had the effect of drawing off the more dependable elements of the Militia, and legislation from 1804 onward was designed to discourage the enlistment of Volunteers as such and to pressure them, largely through attractive scales of pay and allowances, toward joining the local Militia. In some cases complete Volunteer units transferred bodily to the Militia.

By 1816 all Volunteer units had been disbanded. But between 1848 and 1859 distrust of France as the dominant continental power, and Wellington's warnings about the weakness of the regular army, gave rise to a popular Volunteer movement amongst the prosperous middle class, who formed a number of 'Rifle Volunteer Corps', most of which were grudgingly recognised by the government. From 1859 to 1863 the War Office deigned to take an interest in these corps which, for administrative convenience, were formed into battalions, many of which survive today as Territorial units. The military value of these corps cannot be judged as they were never in action, but some of them found companies which were attached to line regiments during the South African War, and a new City of London Imperial Volunteer regiment was formed.

In 1908 the Volunteer force was merged with the Yeomanry in the new territorial force, later the Territorial Army (qv). The title Volunteer was revived during the First World War, when a home defence force of older men was raised. In the Second World War the Home Guard was initially known as Local Defence Volunteers. *See also: Militia; Yeomanry and Territorial Army.*

Vulnerable Point A facility which is vital to the operational function of a Key Point (qv).

Waal Flats Second World War battle honour marking one of the actions which took place during the advance from the River Roer to the River Rhine 8 February to 10 March 1945. *See also: North West Europe 1944-1945; Rhineland; Reichswald; Cleve; Goch; Weeze; Schaddenhof; Hochwald; Moyland; Moyland Wood and Xanten.*

Wadara Second World War Abyssinian campaign battle honour marking the fighting 6 April-10 May 1941 during the advance from Negheli. *See also: Abyssinia 1940-1941; Keren; Juba; Marda Pass; Babile Gap and Gondar.*

Wadi A dry watercourse.

Wadi Akarit East Second World War North Africa campaign battle honour marking one of the actions during the defeat of Axis forces attempting to make a stand on the line of the Wadi Akarit 6 and 7 April 1943. *See also: North Africa 1940-1943; Akarit; Djebel El Meida and Djebel Roumana.*

Wadi Al Batin Battle honour awarded for the successful 1st Armoured Division operations in Operation DESERT STORM 24-28 February 1991 in which Iraq was defeated and Kuwait liberated. *See also: Gulf 1991 and Western Iraq.*

Wadi Zeuss East Second World War North Africa campaign battle honour marking one of the actions during the breaching of the Mareth Line 16-23 March 1943. *See also: North Africa 1940-1943; Mareth and Wadi Zigzau.*

Wadi Zigzau Second World War North Africa campaign battle honour marking one of the actions during the breaching of the Mareth Line 16-23 March 1943. *See also: North Africa 1940-43; Mareth; and Wadi Zeuss East.*

Waist-Belt Belt worn around the waist originally to carry the sword or occasionally a pouch. Now part of field equipment.

Waistcoat Garment worn under a coat, shaped to the waist with flaps continuing below. In the 18th century it was issued as a fatigue or undress item, sometimes with sleeves, and later to become a type of jacket. In a mess dress the waistcoat is known as a 'vest'.

Wait for the Wagon Regimental quick march of The Royal Corps of Transport and the Gurkha Transport Regiment.

Walcheren Causeway Second World War battle honour marking the clearing of the approaches to Walcheren during the Scheldt estuary operations of late October and early November 1944. *See also: North West Europe 1944-1945; Scheldt; Flushing; Westkapelle and South Beveland.*

Wal Garis Second World War Abyssinian campaign battle honour marking an action during the capture of an Italian post at El Wak on the Kenya border in mid-December 1940. *See also: Abyssinia 1940-1941; Keren; El Wak; Moyale; Marda Pass; Babile Gap and Gondar.*

Wales Yeomanry (The Welsh Horse) This regiment, the last Yeomanry regiment to be raised, was raised in South Africa in August 1914 as a Yeomanry regiment, sent to Gallipoli in September 1915, and moved to Egypt at the end of 1915. In 1916 the regiment amalgamated to form the 25th (Montgomeryshire and Welsh Horse Yeomanry) Battalion, The Royal Welch Fusiliers, which fought in Palestine and France. The regiment was disbanded in 1919.

Wandewash Battle honour marking the defeat of the army of Hyder Ali with its French allies led by Lally, by British and Indian troops commanded by Eyre Coote on 22 January 1760. The battle marked the beginning of the end of French power in India. Pondicherry subsequently surrendered after four months' siege. *See also: Pondicherry.*

War Crime A crime committed in wartime in violation of the accepted rules and customs of war or Geneva conventions, such as genocide, ill-treatment of prisoners of war, etc.

War Establishment The full unit wartime complement of men, vehicles and equipment.

Warfare The act, process, or an instance of waging war.

War Game An exercise, usually conducted indoors, using maps or models to train commanders at any given level in addressing tactical problems, without the deployment of any military units in the field.

Warhead That part of a missile or projectile which contains explosives.

War Horse Formerly a horse ridden in battle. Now a term applied to a veteran soldier.

War Medals *See: First World War Medals and Second World War Medals.*

War Office Until 1 April 1964 the War Office was the government department responsible for Army administration and operations. The War Office developed out of the Council of War, first recorded in 1620, and was formally established in 1785. The office of 'Secretary at War', which had emerged during the reign of Charles II evolving from that of 'Clerk to the General', declined after the creation in 1794 of the 'Secretary of State for War', being abolished in 1863. Between 1801 and 1854 the Secretary of State for War was also responsible for the colonies. The status of the War Office was greatly enhanced when, as a result of the findings of the Esher Committee, the appointment of Commander-in-Chief was abolished and his duties assumed by the Army Council at the War Office. Since 1 April 1964 the War Office has been known as the Ministry of Defence (Army Department).

War Service Stripes In January 1918 chevrons were authorised for service overseas, one red if earned before 31 December 1914, and one blue for each subsequent year. These were worn point upward on the lower right sleeve. The practice was discontinued in 1922 but reinstated in February 1944 until the end of the Second World War.

War Song of the Men of Glamorgan One of the regimental slow marches of The Royal Welch Fusiliers.

Warburg Seven Years' War battle honour marking the victory of the allied, and largely Prussian, army under the Duke of Brunswick over a French force seeking to invade Hanover on 31 July 1760. The British cavalry under the Marquis of Granby was eager to wipe out the slur generated by their inactivity at Minden (1759), and drove the French cavalry from the field. *See also: Minden; Emsdorf; Belle Isle and Wilhelmstahl.*

Warrant Officer There are at present two classes of warrant officer, holding their rank by virtue of a warrant from the Secretary of State. Warrant officer class I, the higher grade, is denoted by the royal arms worn on the lower sleeve. A warrant officer class II is denoted by a crown within a wreath, also worn on the lower sleeve. For a short time up to 1941 there were also warrant officers class III, who commanded platoon or equivalent sub-units as platoon or troop sergeant-major. Warrant officers rank above non-commissioned officers and below commissioned officers.

Warrior (MCV 80) The current mechanised infantry combat vehicle, which replaced the FV432 in armoured infantry companies in the early 1990s. Warrior has a crew of two and is capable of carrying eight fully equipped infantrymen. Mounting a 30mm Rarden cannon in the turret and a co-axial EX-34 7.62mm Hughes helicopter chain gun, the vehicle is NBC proof, and has a full range of night vision equipment.

Warwickshire Yeomanry The earliest troops were raised in July 1794, and were regimented in 1797. The regiment found a company of 2nd Battalion Imperial Yeomanry for the South African War (1899-1902). In August 1915 the regiment was sent, dismounted, to Gallipoli and later served in Palestine as part of the Desert Mounted Corps. In the final months of the First World war the regiment amalgamated with the South Notts Hussars and formed 100th Battalion The Machine Gun Corps. At the start of the Second World War the regiment returned to Palestine, converted to lorried infantry and finally fought as a tank regiment in North Africa and Italy. In 1947 the regiment re-formed as an armoured regiment, amalgamated with the Worcestershire Yeomanry to form the Queen's Own Warwickshire & Worcestershire Yeomanry (Territorial) in 1956, and was reduced to cadre strength in 1969. The regiment's successor sub-units are 'A' (Queen's Own Warwickshire & Worcestershire Yeomanry) Squadron, Royal Mercian & Lancastrian Yeomanry and 67 (Queen's Own Warwickshire & Worcestershire Yeomanry) Signal Squadron, 37 (Wessex & Welsh) Signal Regiment (Volunteers).

Wastage Reduction in the strength of the Army or units caused by retirement, resignation or discharge.

Watchtower Regimental quick march of the Corps of Royal Military Police and the Provost Branch of the Adjutant General's Corps.

Water Bag A bag made of animal skin, canvas or other material for holding, carrying, and keeping water.

Water Bottle Container for drinking water carried on the man as part of his personal equipment. During the mid-1600s the old leather water bottle was slowly replaced by one of ironstone pottery. From the mid-1700s a tin water bottle, fundamentally of German design, was used until that too was replaced in the early 1800s by a wooden bottle of cylindrical design. Many types of water bottle were in use during the South Africa War (1899-1902), but the introduction of new equipment in 1903 brought with it a standardised metal bottle.

Water Cannon Vehicle mounted apparatus for pumping water through a nozzle at high pressure, used in riot dispersal.

Watering Cap Term used for an undress cap worn when watering horses; but used on other occasions as well.

Waterloo The great battle of 18 June 1815 which concluded the Napoleonic War and Napoleon's 'Hundred Days'. The victory of Wellington and Blücher was remarkable: Wellington's army was only about one third British and many of his experienced Peninsula regiments had already been sent to America and the reliability of some of the allied troops was open to doubt. The battle falls into three broad phases: an attack by the French infantry; a succession of French cavalry charges which failed to break the British squares and finally, as Blücher arrived and pressure developed on the French flank, an attack by the Imperial Guard, the repulse of which marked the turn of the battle. Throughout the battle the Flank Companies of the Guards had defended the farmhouse of Hougomont, forward of the allied right flank, against the best efforts of two French divisions. A number of army traditions and sayings have their origin in this victory.

Waterloo Medal Instituted by an order dated 10 March 1816. Ribbon: Crimson, 1½" wide, with ¼" dark blue edges.

Waterloo Shako Pattern of shako, retrospectively named, worn between 1812 and 1816.

Wavell A battlefield automatic data processing computer system, designed to accept information from all battlefield sources, and produce the information in collated form on demand, in hard copy or on a visual display unit.

Waziristan 1895 Battle honour marking the operations by 4th Gurkha Rifles against tribesmen in this area.

Weapon System A weapon and the additional components necessary to its proper function, such as sights, mountings and power sources.

Webbing Strong fabric adopted after the South Africa War (1899-1902) and used for the belts, packs, braces and pouches which form part of the soldier's personal equipment. Now a generic term for the fighting equipment worn on the person.

We Sustain Motto of the Army Catering Corps and Royal Logistic Corps.

Wee Highland Laddie Regimental quick march (Pipes and Drums and Military Band) of The Highlanders (Seaforth, Gordon and Cameron).

Weeze Second World War battle honour marking the advance to and capture of Weeze 24 February-2 March 1945 during the advance from the River Roer to the River Rhine. *See also: North West Europe 1944-45; Rhineland; Reichswald; Cleve; Goch; Schaddenhof; Hochwald; Waal Flats; Moyland; Moyland Wood and Xanten.*

Welch Regiment (41st and 69th Foot) The 41st Foot was raised in March 1719 by Colonel Edmund Fielding as independent companies of invalids and was designated The Royal Invalids (41st Regiment of Foot) in 1747. Redesignated 41st Foot in 1787 and 41st (The Welsh) Foot in 1822. The 69th Foot was raised in August 1756 as 2nd Battalion 24th Foot, not becoming 69th Regiment of Foot until 1758. In 1782 the regiment was redesignated 6th (South Lincolnshire) Foot. In 1881 41st (The Welsh) Foot amalgamated with 69th (South Lincolnshire) Foot to form The Welsh Regiment, redesignated The Welch Regiment in 1920. On 11 June 1969 The Welch Regiment amalgamated with The South Wales Borderers (24th Foot) to form The Royal Regiment of Wales (24th and 41st Foot) (qv).

Headdress Badge: The plume, coronet and motto of the Prince of Wales upon a scroll inscribed 'THE WELCH'.

Motto: *Gwell Angau Na Chywilydd* (Better death than dishonour).

History: *A History of the Services of The 41st (The Welch) Regiment (Now 1st Battalion The Welch Regiment) from its Formation in 1719 to 1895* by D A N Lomax (1899); *A Narrative of Historical Events Connected with The Sixty-Ninth Regiment* by W F Butler (1870); *The History of The Welch Regiment* (2 Parts) by T O Marden (1932) and *The History of The Welch Regiment 1919-1951* by C E N Lomax (1952).

Wellesley Regimental quick march of The Duke of Wellington's Regiment and 33rd (Duke of Wellington's Regiment).

Wellesley, Arthur *See: Wellington, Arthur Wellesley, 1st Duke of (1769-1852).*

Wellington, Arthur Wellesley, 1st Duke of (1769-1852) Educated at Eton and Pignerol's Military Academy at Angers. Commissioned into the 73rd regiment in 1787, and then for a few years sat as member of parliament for Trim. He commanded a brigade in Holland in 1794, but it was in India as a colonel that he first showed conspicuous military talent. In 1803 he was appointed chief political and military agent in the Deccan and Southern Mahratta states and, on the fresh outbreak of trouble with the native chiefs, of Sindhia and Holkar as well. He greatly enhanced his reputation by inflicting a crushing defeat on a much larger force at Assaye (qv).

He received the thanks of parliament and was knighted for his services, but he resigned his command and appointment in the early part of 1805 and shortly thereafter sailed for England. In 1806 he became member of parliament for Rye, and a year later chief secretary for Ireland and a privy councillor, but on the threat of French invasion was again on active service.

After a short campaign in Denmark, which ended in the rout of the Danes, he was sent to Spain. He landed at Corunna in July 1808, but was almost immediately involved in difficulties with incompetent rivals like Dalrymple and Burrard. In 1809 he returned to England and resigned, but was sent out again, this time in sole command. From his return to Spain he embarked upon a series of remarkable victories which resulted in the ejection of France from Portugal and Spain, proving that Napoleon's army was by no means invincible. In 1815, loaded with honours, Wellington was ambassador to the restored Bourbon court and British representative at the congress of European powers in Vienna, when news came of Napoleon's escape from Elba. There followed his best known campaign, culminating in the great victory at Waterloo (qv). He returned to England and was granted £200,000 for the purchase of the house and estate at Stratfield Saye.

In 1818 as a staunch Tory he again took up his political career and became Prime Minister in 1828, carrying through the Roman Catholic emancipation, but he resigned in 1830, refusing to agree to electoral reform. He was Foreign Secretary under Peel (1834-35) and minister without portfolio (1841-46), supporting Peel's repeal of the Corn Laws. He died at Walmer Castle, and was buried in St Paul's Cathedral beside Nelson. *See also: Peninsula campaign.*

Wellington Boot Formerly a leather boot, named after the Duke of Wellington, covering the front of the knee, but cut away at the back to permit the knee to bend. The term is now applied to a lightweight leather boot, usually with spur box in the heel, reaching about half way up the calf worn with mess kit.

Welsh Brigade An administrative grouping in the infantry formed by Army Order 61 of 1948 comprising The South Wales Borderers (until 1969), The Welch Regiment (until 1969), The Royal Regiment of Wales (from 1969) and The Royal Welch Fusiliers. The regiments of the brigade were absorbed into the Prince of Wales's Division (qv) in 1968.

Welsh Guards Raised on 26 February 1915 by Royal Warrant of King George V. Headdress Badge: The leek.
Motto: *Cymru Am Byth* (Wales for ever).
Regimental marches:
Quick march: *Rising of the Lark*.
Slow march: *Men of Harlech*.
Regimental headquarters: Wellington Barracks, Birdcage Walk, London, SW1E 6HQ.
History: *History of The Welsh Guards* by C H Dudley-Ward (1920 and 1988); *Welsh Guards at War* by L F Ellis (1946 and 1988); *The Welsh Guards* by J Retallack (1981) and *Anatomy of a Regiment* by T Royle (1990).

Wessex Brigade An administrative grouping in the infantry formed by Army Order 61 of 1948 comprising The Devonshire Regiment (until 1958), The Dorset Regiment (until 1958), The Devonshire and Dorset Regiment (from 1958), The Gloucestershire Regiment, The Royal Hampshire Regiment, The Royal Berkshire Regiment (Princess Charlotte of Wales's) (until 1959), The Wiltshire Regiment (Duke of Edinburgh's) (until 1959) and The Duke of Edinburgh's Royal Regiment (Berkshire and Wiltshire) (from 1959)). The regiments of the brigade were subsequently absorbed into The Prince of Wales's Division (qv) in 1968.

West Africa 1887 Battle honour marking operations against the Yonnie tribe in Nigeria.

West Africa 1892-93-94 Battle honour marking operations in Nigeria and the Gambia.

Western Iraq Battle honour marking Special Air Service Regiment operations in western Iraq in support of Operation DESERT STORM 20 January - 28 February 1991. The regiment was able to make a significant contribution to the successful outcome of coalition operations by successfully disrupting Iraqi communications, and locating and destroying Iraqi 'Scud' missile launchers. *See also: Gulf 1991 and Wadi Al Batin.*

Westkapelle Second World War battle honour marking the capture of a German artillery battery by amphibious assault on 3 November 1944 during operations to clear the Scheldt estuary. *See also: North West Europe 1944-45; Scheldt; Walcheren Causeway; Flushing and South Beveland.*

Westmorland Yeomanry (The Westmorland and Cumberland Yeomanry) The Westmorland Yeomanry Cavalry was raised in October 1819. In 1843 the regiment was retitled the Westmorland and Cumberland Yeomanry Cavalry. The regiment provided a company for 8th Battalion Imperial Yeomanry in the South Africa War (1899-1902). In the First World War the regiment was initially dispersed by squadrons, but re-formed in 1917 to fight as 7th (Westmorland and Cumberland Yeomanry) Battalion, The Border Regiment. Converted to artillery in 1920, the regiment fought as such in Norway and Burma during the Second World War. Although the regiment was re-formed in 1947, the title was to disappear in 1967.

West Point Second World War North Africa campaign battle honour marking a diversionary attack made on 1 September 1942 in the Battle of Alam El Halfa. *See also: North Africa 1940-1943 and Alam El Halfa.*

West Yorkshire Regiment (Prince of Wales's Own) (14th Foot) Raised at Canterbury in June 1685 by Colonel Sir Edward Hales and known as Hales's Regiment of Foot. Numbered 14th Foot in 1751 and designated 14th (Bedfordshire) Foot in 1782, 14th (Buckinghamshire) Foot in 1809, 14th (Buckinghamshire - The Prince of Wales's Own) Foot in 1876, The West Yorkshire Regiment (Prince of Wales's Own) in May 1881, The Prince of Wales's Own (West Yorkshire Regiment) in July 1881 and The West Yorkshire Regiment (The Prince of Wales's Own) in 1920. On 25 April 1958 the regiment amalgamated with The East Yorkshire Regiment (Duke of York's Own) (15th Foot) to form The Prince of Wales's Own Regiment of Yorkshire (14th and 15th Foot) (qv).

Badge: On a ground the White Horse of Hanover. Below, a scroll inscribed 'WEST YORKSHIRE'.

Motto: *Nec Aspera Terrent* (Nor do difficulties deter).

History: *Historical Records of the 14th Regiment 1685 to 1892* Ed. H O'Donnell; *The West Yorkshire Regiment in the War 1914-1918* (2 Vols.) by E Wyrall; *From Pyramid to Pagoda, The Story of the West Yorkshire Regiment in the War 1939-45* by E W C Sandes and *The West Yorkshire Regiment* by A J Barker.

We've Lived and Loved Together This tune forms part of the regimental quick march of The Devonshire and Dorset Regiment, and was one of the regimental quick marches of The Devonshire Regiment.

Wha Wadna Fecht for Charlie Regimental quick march of The Cheshire Regiment.

What's A' the Steer Kimmer? One of the regimental quick marches of 2nd King Edward VII's Own Gurkha Rifles (The Sirmoor Rifles).

Wheel-Lock Type of gun lock. Before the development of the wheel-lock the only method of firing a gun was by means of a length of burning quick-match, which made it inconvenient to carry. The wheel-lock enabled a person to cock the weapon and conceal it on his person, carrying it in this condition until it became necessary to draw the weapon and fire. *See also: Matchlock; Flintlock; Snaphaunce; Musket and Rifle.*

Whistle o'er the Lave o't One of the regimental quick marches (Regimental Band) of The Royal Highland Fusiliers (Princess Margaret's Own Glasgow and Ayrshire Regiment); and of The Highland Light Infantry (City of Glasgow Regiment).

White Lancer *Regimental* quick march of 17th/21st Lancers and of 17th Lancers (Duke of Cambridge's Own).

White Metal Term used to describe silver or any other silver-coloured metal. *See also: Yellow metal.*

Who Dares Wins Motto of The Special Air Service Regiment.

Wicker Helmet Sun helmets made in India in about 1858 had a framework of wicker or rattan, with a covering of felt or other cloth. The wicker helmet was replaced by the lighter and more comfortable pith helmet.

Widdows Men Early 18th century practice under which fictitious soldiers were borne on the strength of a regiment. Their pay was drawn and saved so that it could be used to make payments to the widows of men of the regiment.

Widecombe Fair This tune forms part of the regimental quick march of The Devonshire and Dorset Regiment and The Devonshire Regiment.

Wigtownshire Yeomanry There is evidence of a troop being raised in Wigtown in 1797 which remained in service until the 1820s. Troops appear to have been re-raised in Wigtown and Stranraer in 1831.

Wilco Obsolete signal jargon indicating that a message has been received and will be complied with.

Wilhelmstahl Seven Years' War battle honour marking the battle fought near Kassel in Germany on 24 June 1762 in which eight British battalions launched a successful attack on a French rearguard. *See also: Minden; Emsdorf; Warburg and Belle Isle.*

Willems Battle honour marking the defeat by British cavalry of a French force which

was advancing against the allied army near Tournai on 10 May 1794 during the campaign in Flanders. *See also: Villers-en-Cauchies; Beaumont and Tournay.*

Wiltshire Regiment (Duke of Edinburgh's) (62nd and 99th Foot) The 62nd Foot has its roots in 2nd Battalion, 4th King's Own Regiment raised in 1756, and numbered 62nd Foot in 1758. The regiment was designated 62nd (Wiltshire) Regiment of Foot in 1782. A 99th Foot was raised and disbanded several times between 1760 and 1818, but it was re-raised in March 1824 as 99th (Lanarkshire) Regiment of Foot. The regiment was redesignated 99th (The Duke of Edinburgh's) Regiment of Foot in 1874. In 1881 62nd (Wiltshire) and 99th (The Duke of Edinburgh's) regiments amalgamated to form The Wiltshire Regiment (Duke of Edinburgh's) (62nd and 99th Foot). On 9 June 1959 The Wiltshire Regiment (Duke of Edinburgh's) amalgamated with The Royal Berkshire Regiment (Princess Charlotte of Wales's) (49th and 66th Foot) to form The Duke of Edinburgh's Royal Regiment (Berkshire and Wiltshire). On 27 April 1994 The Duke of Edinburgh's Royal Regiment amalgamated with The Gloucestershire Regiment (28th and 61st Foot) to form The Royal Gloucestershire, Berkshire and Wiltshire Regiment (28th, 49th, 61st, 62nd, 66th and 99th Foot) (qv).

Headdress Badge: A cross pattée. Upon it reversed and intertwined the cypher of Prince Philip, Duke of Edinburgh, ensigned with a Prince Consort's coronet. Below, a scroll inscribed 'THE WILTSHIRE REGIMENT'.

History: *The Story of The Wiltshire Regiment (Duke of Edinburgh's) 1756-59* by N C E Kenrick and *The Wiltshire Regiment* by T Gibson.

Wiltshire Yeomanry (The Royal Wiltshire Yeomanry (Prince of Wales's Own)) A number of troops were raised in 1794 and regimented in 1797. The prefix 'Royal' was granted in 1831 and the title 'Prince of Wales's Own' in 1863. The regiment found two companies for 1st Battalion Imperial Yeomanry in the South

Africa War (1899-1902). During the first year of the First World War the regiment served as dispersed squadrons, was re-formed in 1916 and became 6th (Wiltshire Yeomanry) Battalion, The Wiltshire Regiment. In the Second World War the regiment was sent to the Middle East in the mounted role in 1940; and later served as lorried infantry in Iraq, Syria and Persia. The regiment later converted to armour and served in North Africa and Italy. In 1947 the regiment re-formed, was reduced to one squadron in 1967, and raised to two squadrons in 1971. The successor sub-units are 'A' (Royal Wiltshire Yeomanry) Squadron, Royal Yeomanry and 'B' (Royal Wiltshire Yeomanry) Squadron, Royal Wessex Yeomanry.

Wings One of the regimental quick marches of the Corps of Royal Engineers; and the regimental quick march (Military Band) of The Queen's Gurkha Engineers.

Wings Badge denoting a qualified parachutist or Army Air Corps pilot. Also applied to the attachments to the shoulder seams, usually of cloth with the addition of tape or lace, originally worn by grenadiers and light infantry, and now worn by bandsmen.

Winter Quarters Quarters occupied by a military force during the winter months. In earlier warfare it was customary to withdraw to winter quarters at the end of the campaigning season.

Wireless Ridge Falkland Islands campaign battle honour marking the capture of this feature by the Parachute Regiment. *See also: Falkland Islands 1982; Tumbledown Mountain; Goose Green and Mount Longdon.*

Withdrawal A planned operation in which a force in contact with the enemy is disengaged. *See also: Retirement.*

Withdrawal to Cherbourg Second World War battle honour marking one of the actions during operations by the British Expeditionary Force in 1940. *See also: North West Europe 1940; Boulogne 1940; Calais 1940 and Dunkirk 1940.*

Withdrawal to Escaut Second World War battle honour marking the withdrawal of elements of the British Expeditionary Force from the Dyle positions to the River Escaut (Scheldt) 17-19 May 1940. *See also: North West Europe 1940; Dyle; Defence of Escaut and Dunkirk.*

Withdrawal to Matruh Second World War North Africa campaign battle honour marking one of the actions during the opening phase of the campaign in North Africa in April 1941. *See also: North Africa 1940-1943; Sidi Barrani; Capture of Tobruk; Beda Fomm; Bir Enba and Bardia 1941.*

Withdrawal to Seine Second World War battle honour marking an action by elements of the British Expeditionary Force in 1940. *See also: North West Europe 1940; Arras Counter Attack; Amiens 1940; French Frontier 1940; Forêt de Nieppe and Withdrawal to Cherbourg.*

Withdrawal to Sphakia Second World War Crete campaign battle honour marking the withdrawal of troops from Canea and Suda Bay over the mountains to the south coast following the German airborne invasion of Crete on 20 May 1941. *See also: Crete; Canea; Heraklion and Retimo.*

Wolfe, James (1727-59) Joined the Army in 1741, he and his brother Edward taking part in the battle of Dettingen (1743). In 1745 Wolfe, now a lieutenant, was sent to Scotland to join Cumberland's force crushing the rebellion in support of the Young Pretender. During the Seven Years' War (qv) Wolfe had charge of Britain's operations in America under Amherst. In 1758 Wolfe was tasked to take Louisburg, which he did in July, and was given command of the expedition against Quebec in 1759. A 12-week siege of Quebec began on 26 June, but the first assault, on 31 July, failed. Later, by distracting the French with surprise attacks in other quarters, and by using an unguarded path, Wolfe in a night assault succeeded in placing an army on the heights called the Plains of Abraham (qv). The French commander, the Marquis de Montcalm, immediately gave battle. The

British were victorious, but Wolfe, thrice wounded, died in the hour of victory.

Wolfe's Own Nickname given to 47th Foot, later The Queen's Lancashire Regiment. So called for their distinguished service under General Wolfe (qv) at Quebec (1759).

Wolseley Helmet A khaki, cork sun helmet approved in September 1899, and worn by the West Africa and Chinese regiments. By 1904 it was the authorised headwear for service at all stations abroad, with many regiments and corps adding authorised embellishments such as plumes and hackles over the years. In January 1939 the pith helmet was authorised in India and Burma and, in 1948, the tropical helmet was abolished.

Wombat Obsolescent recoilless anti-tank gun of 120mm calibre and fitted with a 0.5" spotting rifle. The Wombat fires a high explosive squash head round out to about 1,000m.

Women's Royal Army Corps The Corps has its origins in the Women's Army Auxiliary Corps, formed in 1917 for non-combatant duties in France. Renamed Queen Mary's Army Auxiliary Corps in 1918, it was disbanded a year later. In anticipation of the Second World War a women's service was again raised, and titled Auxiliary Training Service (ATS) (qv). The Women's Royal Army Corps was formed on 1 February 1949 (Army Order 6 of 1949), incorporating the remaining cadre of the ATS, and taken on the regular establishment. On 6 April 1992 the corps was disbanded and its members dispersed among the regiments and corps of the Army.
Headdress Badge: a laurel wreath surmounted by the crown. Within the wreath a lioness rampant.
Motto: *Suaviter in Modo, Fortiter in Re* (Gentle in manner, resolute in deed).
History: *A Short History of Queen Mary's Army Auxiliary Corps* by J M Cowper (1967); *The Auxiliary Territorial Service 1939-45* by J M Cowper (1949); *The Women's Royal Army Corps* by S Bidwell

(1977) and *The Women's Royal Army Corps 1949-92* by D Ryder and V C Robertson (1992).

Wood, Sir (Henry) Evelyn (1838-1919) First served in the Royal Navy, which he entered in 1852, and was with the Naval Brigade in the Crimea. Transferring his services to the Army, he gained the Victoria Cross during the Indian Mutiny, and served through the Ashanti War in the rank of lieutenant colonel. He commanded in the Boer War of 1881. In 1883 he raised the Egyptian Army, becoming its Commander-in-Chief, and served in the Nile expedition of 1894-95. He was appointed field marshal in 1903.

Worcestershire Regiment (29th and 36th Foot) The 29th Foot was raised in February 1694 by Colonel Thomas Farrington, reduced and put on half pay in 1698, and re-formed under the same colonel in February 1702. Numbered 29th Foot in 1751 and designated 29th (Worcestershire) regiment of Foot in 1782. The 36th Foot was raised in Ireland in June 1701 by Colonel William Caulfield, Viscount Charlemont, and known as Charlemont's Regiment of Foot. Numbered 36th Foot in 1751 and designated 36th (Herefordshire) Regiment of Foot in 1782. In 1881 29th (Worcestershire) and 36th (Herefordshire) regiments of Foot amalgamated to form The Worcestershire Regiment (29th and 36th Foot). On 28 February 1970 the regiment amalgamated with The Sherwood Foresters (Nottinghamshire and Derbyshire Regiment) (45th and 95th Foot) to form The Worcestershire and Sherwood Foresters Regiment (29th and 45th Foot) (qv).
Badge: The star of the Order of the Garter. Within the garter, the lion of the royal crest upon a tablet 'FIRM'.
Motto: Firm.
History: *History of 29th (or Worcestershire) Regiment of Foot* by H Everard (1891); *Historical Record of 36th Foot* (2 Parts) by R Cannon (1853 and 1883); *The Worcestershire Regiment in the Great War* by H Fitz M Stacke (1928); *The Worcestershire Regiment 1922-1950* by Lord Birdwood

(1952) and *The Worcestershire Regiment* by R Gale (1970)

Worcestershire and Sherwood Foresters Regiment (29th and 45th Foot) Formed on 28 February 1970 through the amalgamation of The Worcestershire Regiment (29th and 36th Foot) and The Sherwood Foresters (Nottinghamshire and Derbyshire Regiment) (45th and 95th Foot).
Headdress Badge: A maltese cross pommettee charged with the garter encircling a stag lodged on water thereunder a plinth inscribed 'FIRM', the whole upon an elongated star of eight points.
Motto: Firm.
Regimental marches:
Quick march: An arrangement of *Young May Moon* and *Royal Windsor*.
Slow march: *Duchess of Kent*.
Regimental headquarters: Norton Barracks, Worcester, WR5 2PA.

Worcestershire Yeomanry (The Queen's Own Worcestershire Hussars)
Raised in 1794, disbanded in 1827 and re-raised in 1831. The regiment found a company for 5th Battalion Imperial Yeomanry in the South Africa War (1899-1902). During the First World War the regiment served in Gallipoli, Egypt and Palestine. The regiment converted to artillery in 1920, serving as such in the Second World War in North-West Europe.

In 1950 the regiment was transferred to the Royal Armoured Corps as The Queen's Own Worcestershire Hussars and was amalgamated with the Warwickshire Yeomanry to form the Queen's Own Warwickshire & Worcestershire Yeomanry (Territorial) in 1956. The successor sub-units are 'A' (Queen's Own Warwickshire & Worcestershire Yeomanry) Squadron, Royal Mercian & Lancastrian Yeomanry and 67 (Queen's Own Warwickshire & Worcestershire Yeomanry) Signal Squadron, 37 (Wessex & Welsh) Signal Regiment (Volunteers).

Wormhoudt Second World War battle honour marking the repulse of a German thrust which had broken through the St Omer-La Bassée line on 26 May 1940 during operations by the British Expeditionary Force. *See also: North West Europe 1940; Defence of Escaut; Defence of Arras; St Omer-La Bassée; Ypres-Comines Canal and Dunkirk.*

Wound Stripe A system of wound stripes to indicate wounds gained on active service was introduced in August 1916. One gold stripe of narrow braid 1" long was worn upright on the left sleeve to indicate each wound. Wounds for previous wars were to be marked by red rayon braid. The practice became obsolete in 1922 but was reinstated in February 1944, only to lapse again after the Second World War.

XYZ

Xanten Second World War battle honour marking one of the actions which took place during the advance from the River Roer to the River Rhine 8 February to 10 March 1945. *See also: North West Europe 1944-1945; Rhineland; Reichswald; Cleve; Goch; Weeze; Schaddenhof; Hochwald; Moyland; Moyland Wood and Waal Flats.*

'X' Factor The introduction of the 'military salary' in the late 1960s meant that the level of Service pay was in future to be arrived at through a process of comparison with similar occupations in the civilian market. Recognising that few civilian occupations matched service life for turbulence, separation, danger and frequent and sustained periods of readiness, an 'X' Factor, putting a monetary value on these peculiar conditions, was added to the pay rates.

Y Ddraig Goch **(The Red Dragon)** Motto of The Royal Welch Fusiliers.

Yellow Metal Term applied to dress items and accoutrements of gold or any other yellow-coloured metal.

Yenangyaung 1942 Second World War Burma campaign battle honour marking operations in mid-April 1942 to cover the destruction of the Yenangyaung oilfields. *See also: Burma 1942-1945; Sittang 1942; Pegu 1942; Taukyan; Paungde; Kyaukse 1942 and Monywa.*

Yenangyaung 1945 Second World War Burma campaign battle honour marking an action during operations astride the River Irrawaddy 29 March - 30 May 1945, aimed at destroying the Japanese Twenty-Eighth Army. *See also: Burma 1942-1945; Irrawaddy; Mt Popa; Magwe and Kama.*

Yeoman of Signals The yeomen of signals are the senior non-commissioned signal traffic managers of the Royal Corps of Signals and are selected from the telecommunications operators (radio), (data) and (telegraph) trades. Yeomen are responsible for managing and supervising message processing, the operation of signals equipments, and for advice on the use of communications facilities, procedures and signal security. The first yeoman of signals appeared in the Royal Corps of Signals in May 1962.

Yeoman Warders Guardians of the Tower of London and probably in existence as a body since 1078, when William the Conqueror began the building of the White Tower. They were not appointed members of the yeomen of the guard (extraordinary) until 1552, when Edward VI also granted their existing state dress. They do not wear the cross-belt of the yeomen of the guard. Their blue undress uniform was granted by Queen Victoria in 1858.

Yeomanry Bodies of volunteer horse were raised during the reign of William III and at the time of the 1745 rising. On 24 March 1794, fearing a French invasion and spread of French revolutionary fervour to Britain, the government passed a bill which invited Lord Lieutenants to raise volunteer troops of cavalry to be composed of gentlemen and Yeomanry, the latter being one who farmed land as a freeholder or tenant farmer. The Lord Lieutenants were tasked with; 'encouraging and disciplining such Corps and companies of men, as shall voluntarily enrol themselves for the defence of their counties, towns or coasts, or for the general defence of the kingdom, during the present war'. The first units of any permanence being the London and Westminster Light Horse Volunteers and the Norfolk Rangers (1779) which were incorporated into the Yeomanry of 1794. By May 1794 32 corps were in being; the first was the Rutland Corps (qv) with three troops, followed by Kent and Surrey with seven and six troops respectively. A troop had anything between 40 and 80 effectives. By 1798 every county and several large towns had raised yeomanry to a total for the whole country of 163 troops, each nominally 150 strong, although there were probably no more than 16,000 effectives in all. Regulations for the raising and maintenance of such troops were in general the same as for Volunteers (qv), the government providing only ammunition except on actual service. The Yeomanry were bound to act as mounted police in case of riot or disturbance; Lord Lieutenants or High Sheriffs could call out the Volunteers and, once embodied, they made ready to defend their counties.

After 1816 the Yeomanry was reduced but not, like the infantry volunteers, disbanded, and for many years, until the establishment of county police forces, played an important part in the maintenance of law and order. Between 1899 and 1918 15 new Yeomanry regiments were raised, of which two, The Lovat Scouts (qv) and The Scottish Horse (qv), served as regiments in the South Africa War (1899-1902). The rest provided companies for battalions of the Imperial Yeomanry.

In 1914 there were 53 regiments of Yeomanry; some served dismounted on the Western Front and one cavalry division of the Egyptian Expeditionary Force consisted entirely of Yeomanry. When the Territorial Force was constituted in 1908 the Yeomanry was merged with the Volunteers, and when it was revived in 1921 as the Territorial Army it included 55 Yeomanry regiments, a number of which were converted to other arms and services, mostly artillery, and served as such in the Second World War. The revival of the Territorial Army in 1947 began a series of reorganisations of the Yeomanry which culminated in the major reductions of 1967 which reduced the Royal Armoured Corps Yeomanry regiments to one, named The Royal Yeomanry. Each of the Royal Yeomanry squadrons bore the title of its former regiment, and this practice continues. Only five Yeomanry regiments now exist in the cavalry role: The Royal Yeomanry; The Royal Wessex Yeomanry; The Royal Mercian and Lancastrian Yeomanry; The Queen's Own Yeomanry and The Scottish Yeomanry. *See also: Militia; Volunteers and Territorial Army.*

York and Lancaster Regiment (65th and 84th Foot) The 65th Foot was originally 2nd Battalion 12th Foot (The Suffolk Regiment) raised in 1756. In April 1758 the regiment was numbered 65th Regiment of Foot under the Colonelcy of Major General Robert Armiger. In 1782 the regiment was redesignated 65th (2nd Yorkshire, North Riding) Regiment of Foot. The 84th Foot was raised in March 1794 by Lieutenant Colonel George Bernard and designated 84th (York and Lancaster) regiment of Foot in 1809. In 1881 65th (2nd Yorkshire, North Riding) and 84th (York and Lancaster) Regiments of Foot amalgamated to form The York and Lancaster Regiment (65th and 84th Foot). The regiment favoured disbandment to further amalgamation and was disbanded on 14 December 1968.
Badge: The royal tiger. Above it the union rose surmounted by a ducal coronet within a laurel wreath.

Yorkshire and Northumberland Brigade Renamed the Yorkshire Brigade in 1957. An administrative grouping in the infantry formed by Army Order 61 of 1948 comprising: The Royal Northumberland Fusiliers (to the Fusilier Brigade in 1950), The West Yorkshire Regiment and East Yorkshire Regiment (amalgamated to form The Prince of Wales's Own Regiment of Yorkshire in 1958), The Green Howards, The Duke of Wellington's Regiment (West Riding) and The York and Lancaster Regiment (disbanded in 1968). With the exception of the Royal Northumberland Fusiliers, which went to the Queen's Division (qv), the regiments of the brigade were absorbed into the King's Division (qv) in 1968.

Yorkshire Lass Part of the regimental quick march of The Prince of Wales's Own Regiment of Yorkshire (qv) and the regimental quick march of The East Yorkshire Regiment (The Duke of York's Own).

YORKSHIRE YEOMANRY

The Yorkshire Hussars (Alexandra, Princess of Wales's Own) Raised in 1794 as 2nd or Northern Regiment of West Riding Yeomanry Cavalry and re-numbered 1st, and taking the title 'Hussars' in 1802. The regiment found a company for 3rd Battalion Imperial Yeomanry in the South Africa War (1899-1902). For the first three years of the First World War the regiment served as cavalry and subsequently became infantry as 9th (Yorkshire Hussars Yeomanry) Battalion, The West Yorkshire Regiment. From 1940-42 the regiment served in Palestine, was then converted to armour, and fought in North Africa until it returned home in 1943. In 1947 the regiment re-formed as an armoured regiment, and was reduced to one squadron strength as part of The Queen's Own Yorkshire Yeomanry (Territorial). After further reduction to cadre strength in 1967, the Yorkshire Squadron of the Queen's Own Yeomanry was formed in 1971. The successor subunit is 'Y' (Yorkshire Yeomanry) Squadron, The Queen's Own Yeomanry.

The Yorkshire Dragoons (The Queen's Own) Raised as 1st or Southern Regiment of West Riding Yeomanry Cavalry in August 1794 and disbanded in 1802. A number of title changes took place and, in 1897, the regiment became The Queen's Own Yorkshire Yeomanry Dragoons. The regiment found in excess of one company for the Imperial Yeomanry in the South Africa War (1899-1902). Between 1914 and 1916 the regiment served in France, but in 1916 the regiment was dismounted and became a cyclist battalion for the rest of the war. In the Second

World War the regiment served in Palestine and Syria and, having fought as a motor battalion at El Alamein, became 9th Battalion, The King's Own Yorkshire Light Infantry in 1942 and served in the campaign in Italy. Re-formed as an armoured regiment in 1947 and amalgamated with the Yorkshire Hussars and East Riding Yeomanry to form The Queen's Own Yorkshire Yeomanry in 1956. The successor unit is 'Y' (Yorkshire Yeomanry) Squadron, The Queen's Own Yeomanry.

The Prince of Wales's Own 2nd West Yorkshire Yeomanry Cavalry Raised in 1798 and disbanded in 1802. Re-raised in 1803 as the West Yorkshire Yeomanry Cavalry but disbanded again in 1900. Re-raised in 1817 and 1843, the regiment was finally disbanded in 1894.

The East Riding Yeomanry Raised in 1794 and disbanded in 1814. After the South African War (1899-1902) a new regiment was raised called The East Riding of Yorkshire Imperial Yeomanry, later known as Lord Wenlock's Horse. In the First World War the regiment served in Palestine and, in 1918, was dismounted and amalgamated to become 102nd (Lincolnshire and East Riding Yeomanry) Battalion, The Machine Gun Corps. In 1939 two regiments were formed, the 1st fighting in Normandy and the 2nd converting to infantry (initially as 10th Battalion The Green Howards, later 12th Battalion The Parachute Regiment) and fighting in North-West Europe. In 1956 the regiment amalgamated with the Yorkshire Dragoons and Yorkshire Hussars to form the Queen's Own Yorkshire Yeomanry. The successor unit is Y (Yorkshire) Squadron, The Queen's Own Yeomanry.

North Riding Four troops of Yeomanry Cavalry were raised in the North Riding in 1794 and served until 1802. In 1818 four troops, of six raised in 1803, were regimented as The Richmond Foresters, becoming The York North Riding Yeomanry Cavalry in 1831. The regiment was disbanded in 1838.

King's Own Yorkshire Light Reconnaissance Regiment This is a new light reconnaissance regiment of Yeomanry created by re-roling the 8th Battalion The (Yorkshire) Light Infantry

(Volunteers). The regiment is to form in 1996 and little detail is available at this stage. The need to re-role infantry to Royal Armoured Corps (Yeomanry) arose from the 1994 review of the role, organisation and structure of the Territorial Army.

Young May Moon This tune forms part of the regimental quick march of the Worcestershire and Sherwood Foresters Regiment and was one of the regimental quick marches of The Sherwood Foresters (Nottinghamshire and Derbyshire Regiment). It is also the regimental quick march (Regimental Band) of 6th Queen Elizabeth's Own Gurkha Rifles.

Ypres 1914 First World War battle honour marking the first Battle of Ypres in October and November 1914. A contact between the newly landed 7th Division and the advancing Germans at Gheluvelt developed, after British reinforcement, into a months' defensive battle around Ypres. The battle resulted in the Ypres salient which was to remain in British hands until the final advance of 1981. *Seealso: France and Flanders 1914-1918; Langemarck 1914; Gheluvelt and Nonne Boschen.*

Ypres 1915 First World War battle honour marking the Second Battle of Ypres which opened on 27 April with a German offensive to capture Ypres. Fighting lasted about four weeks and, although the Germans made some advances, they failed to achieve their objective. *See also: France and Flanders 1914-1918; Gravenstafel; St Julien; Frezenberg and Bellewaarde.*

Ypres 1917 First World War battle honour marking the British offensive called the Third Battle of Ypres, or 'Passchendaele', which lasted from 31 July until 10 November. The offensive was conducted in atrocious weather and consisted of a broad thrust astride the Menin road. By the end of the battle, in which the Germans employed mustard gas for the first time, some five miles had been gained at the cost of some 300,000 casualties. *See also: France and Flanders 1914-1918; Pilckem; Langemarck 1917; Menin Road; Polygon Wood; Broodseinde; Poelcappelle and Passchendaele.*

Ypres 1918 First World War battle honour marking the British offensive launched on 20 September which recaptured all the territory lost in the Battle of Lys earlier in the year. The offensive closed on 2 October. *See also: France and Flanders 1914-1918; Hindenburg Line; Courtrai; Selle and Valenciennes.*

Ypres-Comines Canal Second World War battle honour marking the fighting by elements of the British Expeditionary Force on the hastily prepared defensive line on the Ypres-Comines Canal 26-28 May 1940. *See also: North West Europe 1940; Dyle; Defence of Escaut; Defence of Arras; Calais 1940; St Omer-La Bassée; Wormhoudt; Cassel and Dunkirk 1940.*

Yu Second World War Burma campaign battle honour marking an attack on a Japanese strongpoint on the River Yu, a tributary of the Chindwin, in January 1944. *See also: Burma 1942-1945; Donbaik; Rathedaung; Htizwe; Point 201 (Arakan) and North Arakan.*

ZB 298 Obsolete surveillance radar, formerly in service with armoured and artillery units. Man-packed or vehicle-borne, ZB 298 is able to detect men and vehicles out to a range of 10,000m. It was replaced by MSTARS (qv).

Zemlet El Lebene Second World War North Africa campaign battle honour marking an action during the Medinine battle of 6 March 1943. The Germans launched an attack, which was repulsed, on the Eighth Army as it was preparing to assault the German Mareth Line positions. *See also: North Africa 1940-1943; Medinine; Tadjira Khir and Mareth.*

Zetten Second World War battle honour marking the defeat of German attempts to recapture the town in January 1945. *See also: North West Europe 1944-1945; Ourthe; Roer and Rhineland.*

Zt El Mrasses Second World War North Africa campaign battle honour marking one of the actions in 1942. *See also: North Africa 1940-1943; Tobruk 1942; Bir El Igela;*

Hagiag Er Raml; Gabr El Fachri; Via Balbia and Sidi Rezegh 1942.

Zulu Muster The location at which armoured personnel carriers not involved in giving fire support are held once fighting troops have dismounted from them.

Zulu War The war (1879) arose out of Zulu-Boer disputes over the possession of lands on the Transvaal border. When the Transvaal was annexed Cetewayo, the Zulu king, believed the British would be just, but Shepstone, Administrator of the Transvaal, decided that the Zulu claim was unfounded, and Sir Bartle Frere, the High Commissioner, was led to agree. Frere then sent an ultimatum to Cetewayo calling on him to disband his army, and justified his demand on grounds of the oppressive rule of the Zulus. Cetewayo refused and the British crossed into Zululand in five columns under Lord Chelmsford. One of these columns was promptly cut up at Isandhlwana. This defeat was followed by the heroic stand of a detachment of the 2nd/24th Foot (later The South Wales Borderers) at Rorke's Drift in which eight Victoria Crosses were won. Louis Napoleon, Prince Imperial of France, who was serving with the British forces, was killed whilst on patrol. The Zulus were finally crushed at Ulundi in 1879; Cetewayo fled, but was later captured. *See also: South Africa 1879.*

Zulu and Basuto War Medal 1877-1879 Authorised in 1880. Although it was possible to be awarded the medal without any bar (for service in Natal between 11 January and 1 September 1879) it was usually issued with one of five dated clasps: 1877-78 for actions against the Galekas; 1878 for operations against the Griquas; 1879 for the Zulu War (qv) or operations against Chiefs Sekukini or Moirosi, or 1878-79 or 1877-8-9 for men engaged in more than one campaign.
Ribbon: Watered orange with two wide and two narrow dark blue stripes.

Zulu Rebellion Medal 1906 Granted by the Natal Government in 1906.
Ribbon: Crimson with black edges.

BIBLIOGRAPHY

BIBLIOGRAPHY

(In alphabetical order by title within each section)

BATTLE HONOURS

Battle Honours of the British and Commonwealth Armies
By Anthony Baker, Ian Allan Ltd (1986).
ISBN 0 7110 1600 3

The Battle Honours of the British and Indian Armies 1662-1982
By H C B Cook, Leo Cooper (1987) in association with William Heinemann Ltd,
Limited Edn. 750 copies.
ISBN 0 85052 0827

Battle Honours of the British and Indian Armies 1695-1965
By N B Leslie, Leo Cooper Ltd (1970).
ISBN 0 85052 004 5

Battle Honours of the British Army
By C B Norman, John Murray, London (1911)
Reprinted by David and Charles (Publishers) Ltd (1971).
ISBN 0 153 5398 5

DRESS

Badges and Insignia of the British Armed Services
By W Y Carman and others, A & C Black (1978).
ISBN 0 7136 1344 0

British Army Uniforms and Insignia of World War II
By B L Davis, Arms and Armour Press (2nd Edn 1992)
ISBN 1 85409 159 X

British Military Uniforms 1768-96, The Dress of the British Army From Official Sources
By H Strachan, Arms and Armour Press (1975).
ISBN 085368 349 2

A Dictionary of Military Uniform
By W Y Carman, Batsford (1977).
ISBN 0 7134 0191 5

Military Fashion
By J Mollo, Barrie & Jenkins (1972).
ISBN 0 214 653498

HISTORICAL

Britain and Her Army 1590-1970
By Correlli Barnett, Allen Lane, The Penguin Press (1970).
ISBN 07139 0112 8

The British Army of the Eighteenth Century
By Col H C B Rogers, George Allen and Unwin Ltd (1977).
ISBN 004 355011 8

Brush Fire Wars - Campaigns of the British Army Since 1945
By M Dewar, Robert Hale Ltd (1984).
ISBN 0 312 10674 2

The Chiefs - The Story of the United Kingdom Chiefs of Staff
By B Jackson and D Bramall, Brassey's (UK) Ltd (1992).
ISBN 0 08 040370 0

Commandos and Rangers of World War II
By J Ladd, David & Charles (1989).
ISBN 0 7153 9449 5

A Companion to the British Army 1660-1983
By David Ascoli, Harrap (1983).
ISBN 0 245 53960 3

The Development of the British Army 1899-1914
By J K Dunlop, Methuen (1938).

English Historical Documents (Volumes VIII-XII)
Edited by D C Douglas et al, Eyre and Spottiswoode.

The Guinness History of the British Army
By J Pimlott, Guinness Publishing Ltd (1993).
ISBN 0 85112 7118

Haldane: An Army Reformer
By Edward Spiers, Edinburgh University Press (1980).
ISBN 085224 3707

A History of the British Army (13 Volumes)
By Sir John Fortescue, MacMillan (1930).

The History of British Military Bands, Volume 1
By G Turner and A Turner, Spellmount Publishers (1994).

History of the British Standing Army 1660-1700
By Clifford Walton, Harrison and Sons (1894).

Lord Cardwell at the War Office
By Sir Robert Biddulph, John Murray (1904).

The Oxford Illustrated History of the British Army
Edited by D Chandler and I Beckett, OUP (1994).
ISBN 0 19 869178 5

Sandhurst: A Documentary
By M Yardley, Harrap (1987).
ISBN 0 245544925

Sandhurst - The Royal Military Academy Sandhurst and its Predecessors
By Alan Shepherd, Country Life Books (1980).
ISBN 0 600 38251 6

Sandhurst: The Royal Military Academy Woolwich, The Royal Military College Sandhurst and The Royal Military Academy Sandhurst 1741-1961
By Sir John Smyth, Weidenfeld & Nicolson (1961).

The Second Great War - A Standard History (8 Volumes)
Edited by Sir John Hammerton and Sir Charles Gwynn,
The Amalgamated Press Ltd (1946).

The Second World War 1939-1945, Airborne Forces
By Lt Col T B H Otway, Imperial War Museum Department of Printed Books (1990).
ISBN 0 901627 57 7

Storm Command - A Personal Account of the Gulf War
By General Sir Peter de la Billière, Harper Collins (1992).
ISBN 0 00 255138 1

Victorian Military Campaigns
Edited by Brian Bond, Hutchinson & Co (1967)
Reprinted in 1994.
ISBN 1 871085 21 7

Who's Who in Military History from 1453 to the Present Day
By John Keegan and Andrew Wheatcroft, Hutchinson (1987).
ISBN 0 09 170520 7

REGIMENTAL AND CORPS HISTORIES

A Bibliography of Regimental Histories of the British Army
By A S White, London Stamp Exchange (1988).
ISBN 0 948130 61 X

Encyclopaedia of Modern British Army Regiments
By D Griffin, Patrick Stephens Ltd (Thompson Publishing Group).
ISBN 0 85059 708 0

Encyclopedia of the Modern Territorial Army
By B Peedle, Patrick Stephens Ltd (1990).
ISBN 0 85059 938 5

Forward Everywhere: Her Majesty's Territorials
By S S Baldwin, Brassey's (UK) Ltd (1994).
ISBN 0 08 040716 1

A Guide to the Regiments and Corps of the British Army on the Regular Establishment
By J M Brereton, Bodley Head (1985).
ISBN 0 370 30578 7

The Handbook of British Regiments
By C Chant, Routledge (1988).
ISBN 0 415 00241 9

Lineage Book of the British Army Mounted Corps and Infantry 1660-1968
By J B M Frederick, Hope Farm Press (1969).

Regiments and Corps of the British Army
By I S Hallows, Arms and Armour (Cassell) (1991).
ISBN 0 85368 998 9

Reserve Forces and the British Territorial Army
By W E Walker, Tri-Service Press (1990).
ISBN 1 85488 065 9

The Royal Engineers
By T J Gander,   Ian Allan Ltd (1985).
ISBN 0 7110 15171

Sons of the Brave - The Story of Boy Soldiers
By A W Cockerill, Leo Cooper in association with Secker and Warburg (1984).
ISBN 0 436 10294 3

Year of the Yeomanry
By The Army Museums Ogilby Trust (1994).
ISBN 0 951571486

The Yeomanry Regiments - A Pictorial History
By P J R Mileham, Spellmount Ltd (1985).
ISBN 0 946771 96 0

ORDERS, DECORATIONS AND MEDALS

British Battles and Medals
By L L Gordon, Spink & Son (5th Edn 1979).

British Campaign Medals - Waterloo to the Gulf
By R W Gould, Arms and Armour Press (1994).
ISBN 1 85409 224 3

British Gallantry Awards
By P E Abbott and J M A Tamplin, Nimrod Dix & Co (1981).
ISBN 0 902639 74 0

British Orders, Decorations and Medals
By Donald Hall, Balfour Publications (Photo Precision Ltd) (1973).

WEAPONS, VEHICLES AND EQUIPMENT

British Service Helicopters
By R E Gardner and R Longstaff, Robert Hale (1985).
ISBN 0 7090 2127 5

British Tanks and Fighting Vehicles 1914-1945
By B T White, Ian Allan (1970).
ISBN 07110 0123 5

Encyclopedia of Tanks
By D Crow and R J Icks, Barnie and Jenkins (1975).
ISBN 0 214 20080 9

The Fighting Tanks 1916-1933
By James, Rarey and Icks, WE Inc. (1933)

Military Small Arms
Edited by Graham Smith, Salamander Books Limited (1994).
ISBN 0 86101 688 2

Military Transport of World War 1
By C Ellis and D Bishop, Blandford Press (1970).
ISBN 07137 0701 1

Modern British Armoured Fighting Vehicles
By T Gander, Patrick Stephens Ltd (1986).
ISBN 0 85059 836 2

The Penguin Encyclopedia of Weapons and Military Technology from Prehistory to the Present Day
By K Macksey, Viking-Penguin Group (1993).

Tank - A History of the Armoured Fighting Vehicle
By K Macksey and J H Batchelor, MacDonald and Jane's (1970).
ISBN 0 356 03461 5

GENERAL

The Dictionary of Modern War
By Edward Luttwak and Stuart L Koehl, Harper Collins (1991).
ISBN 0 06 270021 9

Guinness Book of Military Anecdotes
By G Regan, Guinness Publishing Ltd (1992).
ISBN 0 85112 519 0

Hobson-Jobson
By H Yule and A C Burnell, Edited by W Crooke, Rupa and Co (1990).

Military Customs
By T J Edwards, Gale and Polden (1954).

Military Origins
By L L Gordon, Kaye and Ward (1971).
ISBN 0 7182 0876 5

Oxford Book of Military Anecdotes
Edited by M Hastings, OUP (1985).
ISBN 0 19 214107 4

The Penguin Encyclopedia of Modern Warfare - 1850 to the Present Day
By K Macksey and W Woodhouse, Viking (1991).
Published by Penguin Books (1993).
ISBN 0 14 051301 9

US Department of Defence Dictionary of Military Terms
By The Joint Chiefs of Staff, Greenhill (Also by Bath Press) (1987).

MISCELLANEOUS PUBLICATIONS

A. Journals of the Royal United Services Institute for Defence Studies

B. Journals of the Society for Army Historical Research

C. Army Quarterly and Defence Journal

D. British Army Review

E. The Army List (Part 1)

F. Regimental histories and other regimental publications